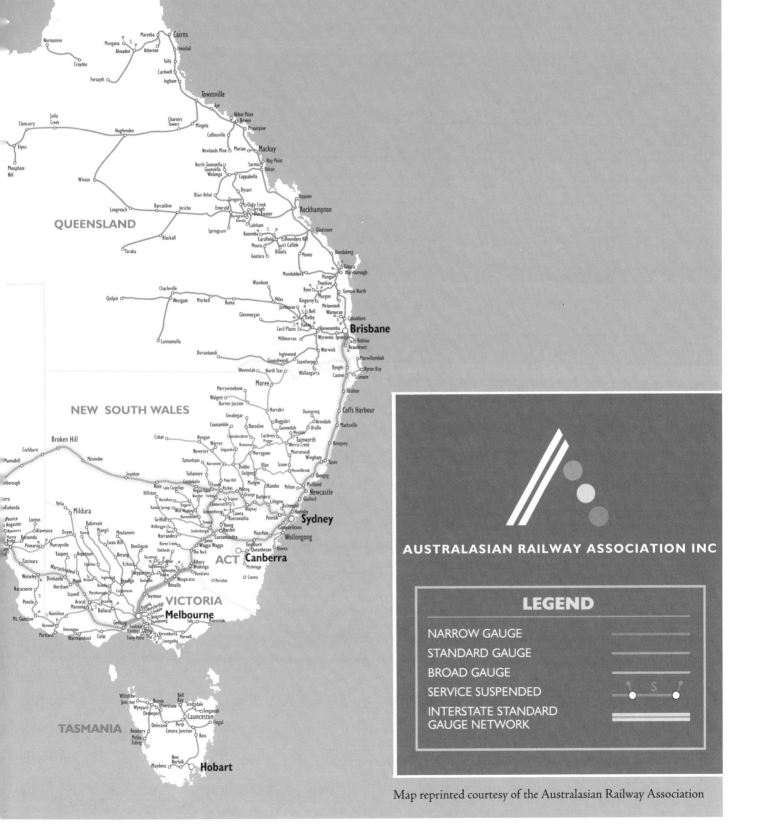

QUEENSLAND

Andoom
Weipa
Normanton
Mungana S
Croydon
Almaden
Atherton
Mareeba
Cairns
Innisfail
Tully
Cardwell
Forsayth
Ingham
Townsville
Ayr
Charters Towers
Mingela
Abbot Point
Bowen
Proserpine
Cloncurry
Julia Creek
Hughenden
Collinsville
Newlands Mine
Marian
Mackay
Hay Point
Flynn
Phosphate Hill
Winton
North Goonyella
Goonyella
Wotonga
Sarina
Jilalan
Coppabella
Blair Athol
Dysart
Longreach
Barcaldine
Jericho
Emerald
Gregory
Oaky Creek
Curragh
Blackwater
Burngrove
Kinrola
Yeppoon
Rockhampton
Blackall
Yaraka
Springsure
Laleham S
Koomba
Earlsfield
Moura
Boundary Hill
Callide
Biloela
Gladstone
Monto
Bundaberg
Goolara
Takura
Maryborough
Mundubbera
Mungar S
Wandoan
Theebine
Charleville
Quilpie
Westgate
Mitchell
Roma
Miles
Byee S
Kingaroy
Murgon
Gympie North
Glenmorgan
Jandowae
Bell
Wamuran
Melawondi
Dalby S
Oakey
Wyreema
Toowoomba
Ipswich
Caboolture
Cecil Plains
Millmerran
Brisbane
Connamulla
Robina
Dirranbandi
Inglewood
Goondiwindi
Stanthorpe
Warwick
Beaudesert
Murwillumbah
Weemelah
North Star
Wallangarra
Kyogle
Byron Bay
Casino
Lismore

NEW SOUTH WALES

Moree
Merrywinebone
Walgett
Burren Junction
Grafton
Narrabri
Dumaresq
Coffs Harbour
Coonamble
Baradine
Boggabri
Gunnedah
Armidale
Uralla
Macksville
Gwabegar
Curlewis
Cobar
Nyngan
Coonabarabran
Premer
Tamworth
Werris Creek
Kempsey
Warren
Gilgandra
Binnaway
Merrygoen
Murrurundi
Wingham
Broken Hill
Nevertire
Narromine
Ulan
Scone
Taree
Cockburn
Menindee
Tottenham
Dubbo
Gulgong
Muswellbrook
Ivanhoe
Tullamore
Condobolin
Peak Hill
Mudgee
Dungog
Roto
Lake Cargelligo
Trundle
Kandos
Pelton
Maitland
Rankin Springs
Bogan Gate
Parkes
Molong
Orange
Lithgow
Newcastle
Hillston
Naradhan
Burcher
Cowra
Blayney
Bathurst
Richmond
Gosford
Ungarie
West Wyalong
Grenfell
Koorawatha
Penrith
Hornsby
Griffith
Condowindra S
Young
Harden
Sydney
Wilbriggie
Barmedman
Temora
Stockinbingal
Cootamundra
Narrandera
Junee
Moss Vale
Boree Creek
Wagga Wagga
Campbelltown
Oaklands
The Rock
Goulburn
Queanbeyan
Wollongong
Nowra
Tocumwal
ACT
Canberra
Michelago

VICTORIA

Yelta
Mildura
Robinvale
Loxton
Alawoona
Ouyen
Euston
Piangil
Moulamein
Pinnaroo
Murrayville
Swan Hill
Deniliquin
Tintinara
Warracknabeal
Kerang
Echuca
Tarrawingee
Albury
Wodonga
Wangaratta
Benalla
Perisher
Wolseley
Dimboola
Hopetoun
Charlton
Shepparton
Tocumwal
Toolamba
Bandiana
Naracoorte
Horsham
Maryborough
Seymour
Penola
Stawell
Ararat
Maroona
Castlemaine
VICTORIA
Mt. Gambier S Hamilton
Ballarat
Bendigo
Bacchus Marsh
Ballan
Epping
Horsebridge
Clydale S
Cooma
Heywood
Dennington
Perth
Geelong
Belgrave
Melbourne
Portland
Warrnambool
Colac
Hastings
Frankston
Dandenong
Korumburra
Morwell
Stony Point
Leongatha
Sale
Bairnsdale

TASMANIA

Wiltshire Junction
Burnie
Bell Bay
Wynyard
Ulverstone
Scottsdale
Devonport
Tonganah
Launceston
Fingal
Rosebery
Deloraine
Melba Siding
Conara Junction
Ross
New Norfolk
Maydena
Hobart

AUSTRALASIAN RAILWAY ASSOCIATION INC

LEGEND

NARROW GAUGE
STANDARD GAUGE
BROAD GAUGE
SERVICE SUSPENDED — S
INTERSTATE STANDARD GAUGE NETWORK

Map reprinted courtesy of the Australasian Railway Association

LOCOMOTIVES
of Australia
1854 to 2010

The distinctive 'bullnose' cover for the third cylinder's valve mechanism is shown to advantage as NSWGR D58-class 4-8-2, No. 5805, eases into Leura with an Up goods in 1957, just weeks before Blue Mountains electrification and the resultant withdrawal of this short-lived class of 13 locomotives. (Late Ron Preston)

LOCOMOTIVES
of Australia
1854 to 2010

Leon Oberg

One of the most exciting periods of recent railway interest occurred from October 1988 to December 1989 when the famous English London North Eastern Railway Pacific locomotive, 4472 *Flying Scotsman*, visited as part of Australia's Bicentennial programme. The remarkable 3-cylinder Gresley A3 locomotive visited all mainland states and established several steam records into the bargain. This photograph shows 4472 staging a special run into Goulburn (NSW) station with the ARHS ACT Division's diminutive British-built Beyer, Peacock 4-4-0, 1210, on 21 May 1989. Locomotive 1210 was itself rebuilt as a Bicentenary project and has since seen regular service, including a starring role in the September 2005 NSW Railways' 150th anniversary celebrations. (Leon Oberg)

ROSENBERG

Dedication

This book is dedicated to all those friends and acquaintances
who regularly help make up the on-going editions a reality.

Other books by Leon Oberg
Diesel Locomotives of Australia
TRAINS
Motive Power
Australian Rail at Work

This 5th edition first published in Australia in 2010
by Rosenberg Publishing Pty Ltd
PO Box 6125, Dural Delivery Centre NSW 2158
Phone: 61 2 9654 1502 Fax: 61 2 9654 1338
Email: rosenbergpub@smartchat.net.au
Web: www.rosenbergpub.com.au
Reprinted 2011 with light updates

National Library of Australia Cataloguing-in-Publication data:
      Oberg, Leon.
      Locomotives of Australia, 1850s-2010.

      5th ed.
      Bibliography.
      Includes index.
      ISBN 9781921719011 (hbk.).

      1. Locomotives - Australia - History. I. Title.

      625.260994

Set in 12 on 14 point Adobe Jenson Pro
Printed in China by Everbest Printing Co Limited

Front of jacket: The C-class, ten of which were built in South Australia during 1977-1978 for Victorian Railways' heavy freight haulage, have in recent years attracted something of a cult following. Now in the hands of several private operators where most have not only been electrically and mechanically updated, several have since seen some service in most mainland states, the design's aggressive cab/nose styling and distinctive guttural exhaust beat makes them firm favorites with many modern-day rail enthusiasts. This image, which shows the C-class' rugged styling to maximum advantage, depicts CFLA's C508 (leading an Alco powered 8037) as they haul a Canberra line ballast train near Joppa Junction on 21 May, 2010. (Leon Oberg)

Contents

Two of eight Tasmanian Government Railways H-class 4-8-2 Mountain-type freight locomotives undergo their pre-delivery steam tests outside the Vulcan Foundry's Newton-le-Willows UK plant in 1951. All eight members of this class arrived in Tasmania aboard the one ship in October 1951. They were basically similar to locomotives supplied by the manufacturer for use in Ghana, North Africa, prior to World War II. (Roydon Burk collection)

Preface

Railways have fascinated generations of people since the appearance in England of the first 'fare-paying' passenger line in 1807. Commercially, conventional trains have been part of the Australian scene since the Melbourne & Hobson's Bay Railway Company launched its first passenger service between Melbourne's Flinders Street station and the shipping port of Hobson's Bay, on 12 September 1854.

While railways mean different things to different people, most are intrigued how slender steel wheels and a few millimetres of flange can guide a train, sometimes of up to 240 vehicles and weighing 33 500 tonnes, along seemingly endless ribbons of rails.

Railways are enjoying a major comeback in Australia following several decades of falling fortunes brought about by improved roads and less than equal cost sharing. Throughout the 1990s, a number of railway administrations, including privateers, have channelled many millions of dollars into improving trains, stations and the railway routes as well in a bid to make rail travel more comfortable and to improve the haulage and efficiency of freight.

Private and public companies, armed with new rail access documents, joined this rail renaissance, which has already seen the introduction of several dedicated freight trains sweeping across the nation. Add to this the mass carve-ups of traditional government-owned rail systems to a growing list of joint ventures which include US and British railway entrepreneurs, banks and locomotive manufacturers, and the rail scene already is totally different to the one that flourished in this country for more than four generations.

Already the emphasis is on speed, with some heavy 1800 metre-long freight trains covering the 3490 km journey from Melbourne to Perth in just 69 hours. Compare this impressive performance with the best across-country freight movement of less than ten years ago when Melbourne to Perth goods vehicles were required to undergo bogie (gauge) changes in Adelaide. This extended travelling time to almost a week—longer for some classes of traffic.

Much of the rail resurgence followed the early 1990s launch of the National Rail Corporation (NRC). While this body initially acquired the total sum of interstate rail freight (influencing the standardisation of the afore-mentioned Melbourne to Adelaide route), rail access laws enacted since that time dealt a severe body blow to this company which was established as a partnership by the NSW Government's FreightCorp, Victoria's V/Line Freight, and the Commonwealth Government's Australian National Rail. As a result of these access agreements, the NRC saw much of its business whittled away following the introduction of 'private company trains' which made an art form of servicing the lucrative Melbourne–Adelaide–Perth corridor.

Until the NRC was eventually purchased in 2002 by two substantial transport and freight handling firms, thus forming Pacific National, it must be remembered that while private operators are good for the Australian rail scene, it is important for the industry as a whole to concentrate on encouraging new on-rail business, not simply taking each other's cargos through cheaper non-sustainable pricing.

One of the earliest players going out on a limb to establish new rail freight was the small Junee-based company, the former Australian Traction Company (now Austrac), which in 1998 successfully sought to haul export pine logs to Port Kembla. Another larger government rail system attempted to wrest some of this business away, only to see its unsuitable wagons destroyed after just one trip.

Some government railway administrators foolishly allowed wagon-load commodities to slip through their hands over many years. Most wanted to cart only the bulk freight consignments such as coal, limestone and wheat. Many simply drove away smaller goods shipments like wool, livestock, fuel oils, superphosphate, milk and hosts of other wares by either scrapping the dedicated wagons or closing rural branch lines.

As a result of those branch-line closures, many main routes came under threat, for without a free flow of trains, those lines and their intermediate stations became uneconomical to keep open too. The more those misinformed administrators and extreme economic rationalists cut services and branch lines, the greater the overall losses became, for instead of having a brace of maintenance, yard, station and signal staff on duty to handle hitherto large volumes of daily trains, a decade later most were still required to be on hand to maintain perhaps no more than a handful of services.

Sadly, most of the politicians, the public servants and civic figures who aided and abetted those decisions are long gone from the scene, the result being that many in the community, particularly in country areas, will tragically spend decades or more picking up the pieces of basically flawed decision making.

That said, altered rail access laws and ensuring the privatisation of rail transport tasks have seen some key branch lines reopen and a vibrant brace of focused public companies armed with hard-won haulage contracts (including some goods previously lost to rail) tackle their rundown ex-government locomotive and rolling-stock fleets.

This movement has been almost Australia-wide and, apart from the construction of the $1.4 billion 1420 km Alice Springs to Darwin railway, which was aimed not only at wresting considerable tonnages from international shipping but also from road haulage, it has already started to win contracts from mining companies along the route. Most of those promised operations have only really become viable due to the rail link.

For the future, others are confident that proposals to build Very High Speed Trains for the Sydney–Melbourne route and commuter routes between the Greater Sydney, Newcastle and perhaps Wollongong areas, using magnetic levitation, will eventually bear fruit and add yet another fillip to the modern Australian commercial railway scene.

From a locomotive point of view, few countries can lay claim to a greater diversity of types—steam, diesel and, to a smaller extent, electric, than those which have operated in Australia over the past 152 years.

In the three decades since the humble first edition of this book appeared, Australia has seen a massive technological change in locomotive development. Sophisticated computer/radar-linked wheel-creep equipment has enabled breathtaking advances in train starting capabilities. Improved fuel efficiencies across the board have enabled the newest locomotives to perform the higher haulage tasks even more economically. And tell someone a few years ago that railway operators might be operating automated trains controlled from an office some 1300 kilometers away, many people may have laughed. But in the Western Australian Pilbara region, driverless trains running over 1200 kilometers of track connecting a clutch of far-flung mines with ports, eliminating the need for hands-on operators, has already been mooted—and to some extent trialled—by one global mining company!

As I mentioned in the previous edition, when compared with the largest steam locomotives, today's diesel-electrics are awe-inspiring performers. For instance, a single 60-class Beyer-Garratt could haul coal trains of up to 1050 tonnes in the Hunter Valley. Today, three 2862 kW PN 90-class EMD diesel-electrics are hauling single trains that would require almost eight 60-class locomotives.

Our latest generation diesel locomotives types also boast sophisticated equipment such as on-board computer fault diagnostic capabilities linked to the engine management and electrical systems. The theory is that, should a locomotive develop a fault in a remote location, or in the midst of a heavily trafficked metropolitan area where train delays can mean calamity and costly retrieval, an on-board computer is able to 'speak' by satellite to a linked terminal within the a central servicing depot and a technician will probably be able to correct the fault from his own keyboard within minutes. Some locomotives also have remote-control secondary position equipment which allows a crew member to remove the driving controls and operate the unit from outside the cab at loading and unloading points or yards.

Leon Oberg
Goulburn, NSW July 2010

Introduction

Except for heavy haul industrial railways in West Australia's Pilbara region, at Comalco's Weipa (North Queensland) bauxite mines, the then BHP's three steel mills and the huge multi-mill Queensland sugar cane belt, the bulk of Australia's railways were until recent years in the hands of the State and Commonwealth governments.

The bubble burst in September 1991 when the NSW, Victorian and Commonwealth governments announced the establishment of the National Rail Corporation employing a key selection of those operators' best locomotives and rolling stock. About this time, the NSW State Rail Authority established it own freight-carrying entity, FreightCorp, while the remaining Victorian intrastate operations were conducted as V/Line Freight.

At the same time, the federal government continued to operate its freight railway, Australian National—all of which added to the casual onlooker's confusion, not to mention corporate losses—for, in short, the best business had largely been taken away from those three operators by the new entity.

On 8 November 1997, AN was sold to a US consortium led by Genesee & Wyoming, initially forming Australian Southern Railroad. After this firm obtained Westrail from the West Australian Government on 2 December 2000, the operation became known as the Australian Railroad Group, and was administered from Perth. This company also provided the locomotives and rolling stock for the FreightLink Darwin route. However, ARG was sold to emerging Queensland Rail National in a $1.3 billion deal announced on 14 February 2006 and eventually cemented on 1 June that year. But Genesee & Wyoming did not sever its Australian rail interests, retaining its South Australian intrastate business, basically the business it originally bought in 1997 when forming ASR. In addition, the deal sees it maintain its prestigious FreightLink (Darwin line) interests.

Meanwhile, V/Line Freight was acquired in February 1999 by US-based short line parent, Rail America, which initially called the business Freight Victoria.

After it won contracts to operate trains into Western Australia and New South Wales, the company started trading as Freight Australia. The V/Line passenger business was sold to British-led National Express Group PLC four months later. However, this company went into receivership in January 2003, the passenger operations returning to the State government. The business has been re-offered for sale.

Proving nothing stands still in this fast-moving Australian railway world, the NSW FreightCorp and multi-owned National Rail Corporation were finally sold as one complete package to a private transport consortium on 21 February 2002, forming Pacific National, whose trains or locomotives today operate into every mainland state. The company has also ordered new locomotives to use in Queensland and NSW intermodal and mineral service, the first entering service in 2005.

While the Tasmanian Government's Tasrail system was bought by a consortium headed by US interests and trading as Australian Transport Network Tasrail, it too was on-sold early in 2004 to mainland operator Pacific National. This purchase also saw rival standard gauge east coast grain haulage specialist, Australian Transport Network Access, absorbed by Pacific National along with its brace of three ex-Westrail L-class Co-Co locomotives and three ex-Australian National 830-class branch line Alco units.

The strength of Pacific National's business saw it welcome its rival Freight Australia to the fold on 1 September 2004, further complicating matters for the casual observer.

Although some smaller rail operators have been conducting business, generally employing overhauled discarded locomotives and rolling stock from the former government systems, Queensland Rail managed to acquire a substantial standard gauge foothold in 2001 when it bought the Casino, NSW-based short line and tourist operator, Northern Rivers Railroad, initially forming a new business entity, Interail. This business, which slowly extended its operations by hauling NSW Hunter

Valley coal trains and North Coast ballast, started running intermodal trains into Melbourne from early 2004 under the Queensland Rail National banner. As mentioned above, Queensland really put the National into national when it bought the 'above rail' portion of the Australian Railroad Group's business from joint venturers, Genesee & Wyoming and Wesfarmers, in June 2006.

QR has not been sleeping in Queensland either, for it has added new rolling stock and hosts of new and upgraded diesel and electric locomotives, leading then State Premier Peter Beattie to announce on 4 May 2005 that QR's entire home state freight business would also be re-badged Queensland National.

The business expects to be annually carting some 235 million tonnes of coal in Queensland alone by 2010. (This is a huge growth when considering its coal haulage task in 2004/2005 was around 150 million tonnes, while a decade earlier it was 'just' 79 million tonnes.)

Another player of particular note is US-parented Chicago Freight Car Leasing Australia, which surged onto the scene with the purchase on 13 November 1998 of 12 GE-powered former Australian National EL-class locomotives. Apart from working its own stock, the firm also financed acquisitions for smaller organisations and operators in several states. This company now owns some 65 locomotives, examples of which (together with more than 1100 company-owned freight wagons) can be seen on long-term lease or spot hire virtually across the nation in tasks ranging from ballast to heavy intermodal.

Southern & Silverton Railway Pty Ltd became another strong player. It was created in February 2006 with the sale of Silverton Rail locomotives and rolling stock to Allco Finance. That company had already made arrangements with the experienced Midland (WA)-based operator South Spur Rail Services, and engineering company Rail Technical Support Group (RTS), to acquire relevant portions of Silverton Rail, a company whose roots dated back to 1886. RTS, a division of the longstanding engineering, logistics and manufacturing firm, Coote Industrial, officially took over South Spur on 1 July 2007. Coote had been undertaking locomotive engineering work for South Spur and its extensive collection of 79 locomotives were soon in daily use across both the standard and 1067 mm gauges specifically working infrastructure, coal and ore trains. However, in a $16 million deal announced in March 2010, P&O

Trans Australia acquired the complete South Spur business including a pre-payment for maintenance work which Coote will provide.

Other companies forging names for themselves are Independent Railways of Australia, which from 16 December 2006 acquired the assets of Lachlan Valley Rail Freight; and Southern Shorthaul Railroad, a firm which today owns eight locomotives, all meticulously refurbished (or being rebuilt) ex VR B, G, S and T-classes.

But the big game continues to be played out in the WA Pilbara where, according to Western Australian Ministry of Planning and Infrastructure, the projected growth of iron ore exports through the three key Pilbara ports is expected to reach 650 million tonnes by 2015 as new mines from several existing and new companies come on stream. One of these new players, the Fortescue Metals Group, whose $3.7 billion Christmas Creek and Cloud Break project started production in April 2008, is already paying dividends despite a savage 2008/2009 fiscal global downturn, with plans unveiled in November 2009 to spend a further $3.6 billion creating a third mine to be known as the Solomon Iron Ore Project.

In 2010, several new schemes are on the drawing board, but none as ambitious as the planned 3300 km railway linking Queensland and Western Australia. The $20 billion "Iron Boomerang" railway calls for a new standard gauge line across Australia to connect iron ore mines in the Western Australian Pilbara with the rich coal deposits of Queensland's Bowen Basin. The project includes the building of six industrial smelter park precincts at each end of the railway to manufacture pig iron and steel billets for export to second-stage rolling mills located within geographical mass market-consuming countries.

And mining magnate Clive Palmer announced this year that he had secured Australia's 'biggest export deal', a $70b agreement to sell coal to China. The Resourcehouse chairman said the company's proposed China First coalmine and infrastructure project in central Queensland had reached a 20-year agreement with one of China's largest power companies to supply 30 million tonnes of coal a year for more than 20 years. The coal will be mined in the Galilee Basin region near Alpha. A private 495 km rail line will be built and new jetties and ports erected at Abbott Point, near Bowen. A generous brace of new locomotives will form part of this project.

Acknowledgments

A book of this type would be impossible to produce without the dedicated assistance and goodwill provided by a host of friends and associates, railway staff, locomotive manufacturers and private railway operators.

Special thanks must go to the public relations and locomotive/mechanical departments of the former Australian National Railways Commission; the State Rail Authority of NSW; Queensland Railways (particularly Andrew McLennan, information officer, Corporate Relations); the former Westrail; State Transport Authority, Victoria; the former South Australian and Tasmanian Railways; Hamersley Iron; the Broken Hill Proprietary Co Ltd (steel and iron ore divisions); the Clyde Engineering Co (now part of EDI); the former Commonwealth Engineering Co; United Group Rail (formerly A. Goninan & Co); the former State Electricity Commission of Victoria; the former Australian Paper Manufacturers; and Walkers Limited (now part of EDI).

Thanks go to the Australasian Railway Association also for graciously allowing use of their map of the Australian rail scene.

I would like to offer particular thanks to historians John Browning, Michael Dix, Noel Inglis, Christopher Malone, Richard Montgomery and Chris Walters for graciously checking (enlarging and sometimes offering advice on) extensive portions of text.

Individually I also want to acknowledge the valuable assistance and goodwill over the life of this publication of Peter Allwork; Kim Andronicus; John Armstrong; Brian Andrews; Peter Attenborough; Robert Ashworth; Jeff Austin; Philip D. Avard; David G. Bailey; Willem Bekker (ISCOR, Pretoria); Barry Blair; Tom Bowling (Hydro Electric Commission, Tasmania); Stephen Buck; Tony Burgess; Roydon Burk; David Butters; Bruce Belbin; Jim Bisdee; Wayne Carman; Brian Chamberlain; James Chuang; Trevor Christensen (of Australian Paper Manufacturers); Peter Clark; John Cleverdon; Graham Cotterall; Ken Cowen; Ian Crellin; Melanie Dennis; Ron Drummond; the late Don Drysdale; Bill Dunn; John Dunn; the late Gifford Eardley (for permission to use portions of his early published locomotive research); Ray Ellis; R.P. Evetts (former manager, Emu Bay Railway); Jason Ferguson; E.J. (Ted) Flint; Bob Gioia; Eric Girdler; John H. Godfrey; Philip G. Graham; David Griffiths; Phillip Harrison; Jenni Holgate; Winnie Hong (Kowloon Canton Railway); Andy Hourigan; G.J. Hunt; Noel Hutchinson; Geoffrey Higham; Andy Inserra; Michael James; David Jehan; Michael Lee; the late Tony Maston; Rob Mewett; R.F. Moag; David Mewes; Bruce Macdonald; Paul Moore; Roy Mullard; Eric Nicolle; Peter Neve; David Parsons; David Phillips; Lou Rae; Peter Rowledge; R. Ruggiero (F.R. Tulk & Co); Bruce Russell; Bob Sampson; Matt Sexton (UK); Ben Scanlon; Barry Scharenberg, the late Paul Smith; Tony Smithson; Les Standen; Michael Stigwood; Chris Stratton; Lucas van Vuuren; John Whatham, John Watkins; Peter Watts; Tony Wells; David Werrier; A.G. Willox; Craig Wilson; Gordon Wilson; Ken Winney and E. Woodland.

My thanks also go to the many unnamed railwaymen working for government and privately owned systems in all states for their assistance with all things railway. The photographs have been acknowledged in the appropriate places and copyright is invested in the individual contributors' works.

Notes on 2010 Edition

Conceptional work on this book started in 1969 in an effort to place between two covers an account of Australia's more popular and interesting locomotive types. While the first edition appeared in 1975, the author's thirst for further research has since seen this book grow in size and matter, with completely revised and enlarged editions appearing in 1984 and 1996 and 2007.

This edition takes the opportunity to revise the many fleet movements since 2007 and to include some of the new locomotive types introduced during the past four years. These include two types of mainline diesel-electric locomotive being marketed by rival companies that have already cemented themselves as "universal' designs. Both types make provision for in-line fuelling, a feature that will gain increasingly more importance as we continue to move into a world sure to see fuel become more expensive. One of its benefits is that fuel can be bought at capital city prices. Time-consuming stops to refuel en route can also be eliminated.

While *Locomotives of Australia* illustrates an amazing variety and volume of locomotive types used by government and private operators in this country, the author has never pretended that those appearing under this title represent all makes and models. However, with readers' continuing help, both in respect to snippets of research, information and old photographs, the task might be completed one day.

Locomotives of Australia has been compiled from official sources (records held by the various railway systems, private railway operators and manufacturers), from select enthusiast-held records, publications, personal testimony from men in railway service and from the author's own library, gathered over a 45-year period.

The locomotives discussed generally appear in chronological order and are listed under the name of the original customer. In following this order, where a number of examples of the same type or design have been operated by different owners, they have, where prudent, been listed under the original purchaser. For instance, the popular Alco model DL-531 which was acquired by NSWGR, SAR and the Silverton Tramway, appear together under the model's initial purchaser, NSWGR (see 48-class of 1959). This logic has since been vindicated, for with the recent massive railway carve-ups and subsequent privatisation, many owners now operate examples of the DL-531 (and other collective locomotive types) that were originally used on rival systems.

Values used in the specifications throughout this book are expressed in both imperial and metric to enable a satisfactory comparison to be made between locomotives of a bygone era and those of today. Within the body text itself, values have been generally expressed in metric to allow free-flowing prose. Locomotive power outputs have been standardised to reveal the respective engine's rating at the rail rather than its maximum flywheel output.

It must be remembered that a certain amount of diesel engine power is shed driving accessories such as the cooling equipment and electrical systems, including air-conditioning. For example, an Alco/MLW turbo-charged 251CE 12-cylinder engine as used by Comeng in the manufacture of the NSW State Rail Authority's 80-class exerts 1604 kW (or 2150 horsepower in imperial terms) but only 1491 kW (2000 hp) is available for traction purposes. But the power available will vary depending upon how many of the locomotive's auxiliaries are working at any given time and at what altitude above mean sea level it is operating.

All tractive effort figures provided can only be regarded as theoretical and used for comparison purposes. To be totally meaningful, speed, gearing and an adhesion factor should also be expressed. As space limitations dictate against that extra information, one can say that most starting tractive effort figures are given at approximately 30 per cent adhesion. All steam locomotive tractive effort figures have been recalculated using the world standard 1911 equation. To obtain a tractive effort figure, the square of the cylinder diameter is multiplied by the stroke then by the given maximum boiler pressure. That figure is then divided by the driving wheel diameter. The final step is dictated by whether the locomotive is fitted with a saturated or superheated boiler. The accepted method is to represent 80 per cent of the boiler pressure for a saturated type and 85 per cent for a superheated version.

For example, the equation for a former Commonwealth Railways C-class 4-6-0 express locomotive, which bears cylinders of 23 in diameter and 26 in stroke, a 180 psi superheated boiler pressure and coupled wheels of 69 in diameter reads:

$$\frac{23 \times 23 \times 26 \times 180 \times 85}{69 \times 100} = 30\,498 \text{ lb}$$

To obtain the tractive effort in kilonewtons the final figure should be multiplied by 0.00445. To convert kilowatts (1000 watts) to horsepower, one kW equals 1.341 hp. One kilometre (1000 metres) equals 0.6214 of a mile and one metric tonne (1000 kg) equals 0.9842 of an imperial ton. Thus the metric equation for the above C-class example would read:

$$\frac{0.5842 \times 0.5842 \times 66.04 \times 1241 \times 85}{175.26 \times 100} = 135.7 \text{ kN}$$

Abbreviations

Alco	American Locomotive Company
AN	Australian National Railway Commission
ATN	Australian Transport Network Access
AI&S	Australian Iron and Steel Pty Ltd
ARHS	Australian Railway Historical Society
ARG	Australian Railroad Group
ASG	Australian Standard Garratt
BHP	Broken Hill Proprietary Co Ltd (The)
CFCLA	Chicago Freight Car Leasing (Australia)
CME	Chief mechanical engineer
CR	Commonwealth Railways
EMD	Electro Motive Division of the General Motors Corporation
MKA	Morrison Knudsen Australia
MLW	Montreal Locomotive Works (The)
NSWGR	New South Wales Government Railways, which became the NSW Public Transport Commission in 1972, NSW State Rail Authority in 1980, and is now RailCorp.
NSWRTM	New South Wales Rail Transport Museum
NSWSRA	New South Wales State Rail Authority (now part of RailCorp)
PN	Pacific National
PWD	Public Works Department (various states)
QR	Queensland Railways
QRN	Queensland Railways National (the freight arm of QR)
QRN-W	Queensland Railways National–West (the former ARG business)
ROD	British Railway Operating Division
SAR	South Australian Railways
SMR	South Maitland Railways
SSR	Southern Shorthaul Railroad
TML	Tasmanian Main Line Company
TGR	Tasmanian Government Railways
V/Line	State Transport Authority, Victoria (formerly VR)
VR	Victorian Railways (now V/Line)
WAGR	Western Australian Government Railways, later Westrail

Bibliography

A Measure of Greatness, E.M. Johnston-Liik, George Liik and R.G. Ward, Melbourne University Press.

Australian Model Railway Magazine, SCR Publications (various).

Australian Rail at Work, Leon Oberg, Kangaroo Press, Sydney, 1995.

Australian Steam Locomotives 1855–1895, Jim Turner, Kangaroo Press, Sydney, 1998.

Australian Sugar Industry Locomotives, John Browning and David Mewes, Australia Narrow Gauge Railway Museum Society, Queensland.

Bulletin, journal of the ARHS and its associated supplements.

BHP Tramways Centenary History, David Griffiths, Mile End Railway Museum, Adelaide, 1985.

Catchpoint, National Railway Museum (Port Adelaide) journal (various).

A Century Plus of Locomotives, ARHS NSW Division, Sydney, 1965.

Comeng, a 1980s in-house publication by the Rollingstock Division of the ANI Corporation.

Diesel Locomotives of the LMS, Peter Rowledge, Oakwood Press, Dorset UK, 1975.

Joadja Creek, Leonie Knapman, Hale & Iremonger, Sydney, 1988.

Loco Profile—ROD 2-8-0, Profile Publications, Berkshire, UK.

Locomotive Journal, AFULE magazine (various copies).

Locomotive Profile 1981, an in-house unpublished work by The Clyde Engineering Company.

Man of Steam, David Burke, Iron Horse Press, 1986.

Motive Power, Leon Oberg, Kangaroo Press, Sydney, 1995.

Motive Power, magazine (various).

Statement of Corporate Intent, National Rail Corporation (and sundry published documents from that body).

Network, Australasian Railway Association (various).

Newsrail, divisional publication by the ARHS Victorian Division (various).

Rail Australia, Bowenia Publications (various).

Railway Digest, monthly journal of the ARHS NSW Division (various).

Railway Museum, ARHS Victorian division.

Railway Transportation, Shennan Publishing (various).

Railways of Australia, C.C. Singleton & David Burke, Angus & Robertson, Sydney, 1963.

Railways of the South Maitland Coalfields, Gifford Eardley, ARHS NSW Division, Sydney 1969.

Railways of J. & A. Brown (The), Gifford Eardley, ARHS NSW Division, Sydney, 1972.

Redbank Railway Museum, ARHS Queensland division.

Steam Locomotive Data, State Rail Authority of New South Wales.

Steam and Rails in Newcastle, Keith McDonald, Light Railway Research Society.

The A7 Era, Peter Bermingham, Horsepower Histories, Victoria, 1995.

The Great Steam Trek, C.P. Lewis and A.A. Jorgensen, C. Struik Publishers, Capetown SA, 1978.

The Last of the Hudswells, Ian Stocks, Australian Narrow Gauge Railway Museum Society.

The Mile End Railway Museum, ARHS South Australian Division, 1970.

The Locomotives of the SAR, ARHS South Australian Division, 1972.

The Locomotives of Commonwealth Railways, ARHS South Australian Division.

The Locomotives of the Pilbara, J. Joyce and A. Tilley.

The Puffing Billy Story, Puffing Billy Preservation Society.

The Second Diesel Locomotive Spotters Book, Jerry A. Pinkepank, Kalmbach Books, Milwaukee, 1973.

This is Clyde Motive Power, The Clyde Engineering Co. [n.d.]

Track and Signal Magazine (various).

WAGR Locomotives 1940–1968, ARHS Western Australian Division, 1968.

Working Timetables, General Orders and *Weekly Notices*, as published by the Australian railway systems (various).

38, John Thompson, Eveleigh Press, Sydney, 1992.

48: Backbone of the Railways, Ron Preston, Eveleigh Press, Sydney, 2005.

Standards in Steam, the 50 Class, Ron Preston, Eveleigh Press, Sydney 1992.

500, ARHS South Australian Division, 1969.

600, ARHS South Australian Division, 1971.

700, ARHS South Australian Division, undated, *c.* 1972.

2-2-2WT

Australia's first steam railway, the Melbourne & Hobsons Bay Railway Co's private 4.5 kilometre link between Melbourne (Flinders Street) and Port Melbourne (then Sandridge), was officially opened on 12 September 1854. But it was not without its problems.

Work had begun only the year before and orders had been placed with British firm Robert Stephenson & Co for four 2-4-0 locomotives to be delivered in May 1854. As work on the line progressed, it became clear that the locomotives would not be delivered in time, so a local firm, Robertson, Martin & Smith, was asked to provide a makeshift locomotive for the contractor which could be used to haul a construction train including ballast wagons.

Using a 2.98 kW pile-driving engine, this heavy engineering firm utilised a 4-wheel ballast truck and produced the engine, which was tested successfully on 30 May 1854. Soon afterwards, directors of the railway company were taken for a ride, sitting behind the locomotive in ballast trucks. On this run a speed of 29 km/h was reached, to the astonishment of all.

Soon afterwards, the directors were informed that the English-built 2-4-0s would be further delayed, and as the line was practically ready for traffic, an order was placed on about 1 July for one small conventional locomotive to tide the company over. The project was again entrusted to Robertson, Martin & Smith, and their creation became the first conventional steam locomotive building project in Australia. As the builder's engineer had some experience with locomotives in England, he prepared the drawings for a 2-2-2WT which was subsequently capable of developing around 22.4 kW. The Port Phillip firm, Langlands, constructed its boiler.

The locomotive was available for traffic in just ten weeks and had its trial run on 9 September 1854. Records indicate that the locomotive became derailed on points in Flinders Street yard during that trial.

Fitted with 20 cm diameter cylinders, a contemporary report said the tiny locomotive was able to reach a speed of 40 km/h and haul up to 130 tonnes.

With driver William Pattison at the controls, the opening day's first official train consisted of a first

A delightful S.T. Gill period illustration showing the Melbourne & Hobsons Bay Railway Co's opening day train at Sandridge using the interim locomotive constructed upon a ballast wagon chassis. It employed parts from a pile driver. (Author's collection)

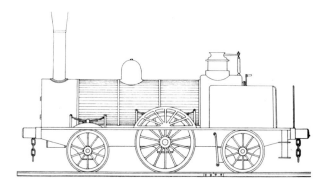

An imaginative sketch prepared for VR's centenary celebrations in 1954 depicting Australia's very first orthodox railway locomotive. It was built for the Melbourne & Hobsons Bay Railway Co by the Port Melbourne firm, Langlands. (V/Line archives, author's collection)

class car for the viceregal party and the directors, two second class cars for the guests and an open third class vehicle to convey the band. Three more trips were later made to convey the guests to an elaborate banquet within the locomotive shed at Sandridge. All went well until, on the return journey, the little 2-2-2's cranks found dead centre (due to the employment of a single cylinder) and it simply refused to budge. Finally the train was emptied and the police were able to push it to release the cranks, thus allowing the viceregal party and guests to resume their journey.

Services continued successfully for six days until the 2-2-2 fractured a crank axle. To maintain timetables, the original ballast engine was used until the locomotive was repaired. The blame for the fracture was levelled at the unequal stress imposed by the unfavourable conditions of having to start on the sharp curve at Flinders Street station. This curvature was eased and the platform adjusted accordingly.

On 9 October, the 2-2-2 again fractured its crank and was out of traffic for two days. Repair work was done but on 1 December, the troublesome crank 'smashed into a thousand atoms', and as a result the company ceased all services 'until further notice'.

In the meantime, the first two Stephenson-built locomotives had arrived at Hobsons Bay (on 23 November 1854) aboard the ship *Jane Francis* after 127 days at sea. Entering service on Christmas Day 1854, the first engine—*Melbourne*—provided a trouble-free service for patrons, and very soon the two locomotives were alternating on a daily service.

The two remaining engines reached Hobsons Bay on 23 January 1855, and by April that year all four were in service, each bearing a name. In order of arrival they were *Melbourne*, *Sandridge*, *Yarra* and *Victoria*. A fifth locomotive, *St Kilda*, was added to

this fleet in July 1857.

All gave outstanding service until sales reduced their ranks. In 1859, *Victoria* was sold to the Suburban Railway Co (another early Melbourne railway company), and in February 1861 *Melbourne* became the property of the Brighton Suburban Private Co. *Sandridge* followed soon afterwards. However, they were all destined to be reunited, for in June 1865 these private lines were amalgamated to form the Melbourne & Hobsons Bay United Railway Co.

The first recorded withdrawal was *Yarra* which, after lying idle for a time, was scrapped in 1873. *Sandridge* was withdrawn the following year and scrapped. Unfortunately no other details appear to be available as to the fate of the remaining locomotives, except that the *Argus* of 6 September 1861 reported that the original conventional 2-2-2 of the Melbourne & Hobsons Bay line was used on the construction of Victoria's Geelong–Ballarat line.

1855 Sydney Railway Company

1-Class 0-4-2

Robert Stephenson & Co, Newcastle on Tyne was contracted by the Sydney Railway Co to construct four 0-4-2 locomotives engines to work the original Sydney to Parramatta line. The Sydney Railway Co, which had its roots firmly established as far back as 1846 following meetings of politicians, businessmen and pastoralists in both Sydney and Goulburn, ordered the locomotives, which were built to the designs of Mr J.E. McConnell of the Southern Division of England's London & North Western Railway. McConnell was the consulting engineer for the Sydney Railway Co.

Introduced as the 1-class, the design was basically similar to that of the Stephenson-built 0-4-2 heavy goods locomotives then in service on the LNWR, although the NSW engines were intended for both goods and passenger service.

On 29 March 1855, No. 1 began running trials between Sydney and Newtown, using water purchased from a Redfern milkman at 15 cents a cartload. Fourteen days before the opening of the Parramatta line, the State took over the company's assets, effectively creating the NSW Government Railways.

On 26 September 1855, No. 2 worked the first official train between Sydney and Parramatta, but the engines were subsequently found to be too heavy for the Barlow type rails in situ at the time. Lighter engines were ordered for passenger service. Upon their arrival, the 1-class engines were confined to slower goods service until the rail link was rebuilt years later to accommodate the gradually increasing train weights.

Throughout their lives these four locomotives were captive to the greater Sydney area, eventually working out as far out as Penrith and Liverpool following ongoing railway corridor extensions.

The first to be withdrawn was No. 1, on 15 March 1877, due to an accident that bent its main frame. Finally all four were retired, with No. 2 being the last in traffic, its last reported role being a regular passenger-car shunter in the Sydney yard until December 1879.

Fortunately this locomotive was saved, eventually receiving the boiler, chimney, works plates and other key components off the damaged No. 1, which at that time still sat derelict at the Eveleigh Railway Workshops minus its tender. In May 1884, this engine became the property of the Museum of Arts and Sciences and today takes pride of place within the (now) Powerhouse Museum at Ultimo. Together with a clutch of period coaches, it underwent major conservation just prior to RailCorp's September 2005 150th anniversary celebrations of the NSW railway system.

Continuing the theme

Three basically similar 0-4-2s were delivered in March 1857 by the UK firm, William Fairbairn & Sons. They had been ordered by the promoters of the isolated Newcastle–Maitland Railway, the Hunter River Railway Co. In company with the early Sydney Railway Co, this company was also taken over by the state (on 30 July 1855), and upon the locomotives' arrival they were numbered 1N to 3N, the N denoting the northern district allocation.

Although of basically similar proportions to the Sydney 1-class, the Fairbairn steeds were 1 tonne lighter.

The opening of the Hawkesbury River railway bridge in 1889 brought the two systems together and, as a result, all northern engines were renumbered into the one common group. Thus the lNs were given the 388–390 number series. However, they did not last

long as their boilers were now in poor condition and two were withdrawn the following year. The survivor, 389, battled on for a further year before it too was stopped.

According to RailCorp records, all were quickly broken up. It is interesting to note that they managed to travel in excess of 800 000 km during their careers.

The need for further locomotives saw four more built to the same basic proportions as the early 1-class. Unlike those before them, these were constructed locally, becoming the (M) 36-class, eight of which were built for Sydney-area goods and passenger service between September 1870 and December 1877.

This class was the very first built in New South Wales and as a result the first, No. 36, was exhibited at the International Exhibition in Sydney before it entered railway service.

One could say that these locomotives were also an improved, 'technologically advanced' version of the 1-class, for their boilers were pressed an extra 34.5 kPa, they possessed larger grates and were slightly longer between tubeplates. The 36-class was equipped with standard domes instead of the earlier 1 and 1N-classes' ornate and polished McConnell-type domes. In addition, they were the first on the system to be provided with left-hand driving controls.

Built in two batches, the first four came from Mort & Company's Sydney works, the final four being built by the Railway's own workshops at Redfern. These latter engines, whose driving position reverted to the right-hand side, were actually built on frames originally intended as replacements for the 1-class and as such received the old locomotives' tenders. (One of those tenders fortunately survived to be

The No. 1 locomotive was sporting a later M36-class tender when pictured in 1905 with a representative opening day train of first, second and third class carriages. A decade afterwards, it was re-equipped with an original pattern 1-class tender which had been in service behind an M78-

Locomotive No. 1 as it appeared in Sydney's Powerhouse Museum on 26 September 2005, the day it helped celebrate the NSW railway system's gala 150th birthday. The locomotive and the attached first, second and third class cars had been completely revamped earlier that year in readiness for the occasion. (Leon Oberg)

The surviving brass maker's plate as attached to locomotive No. 1, showing the elegant script of the era. (Leon Oberg)

reunited with the Museum No. 1 locomotive during the early 1900s.)

All had been removed from the register by late 1892. However, 78 must have been born beneath a lucky star, for it was sold to a railway construction firm in September 1896 for work on the Bogan Gate–Condobolin route. It was returned to the NSWGR two years later, only to be transferred to the NSW Public Works Department as PWD 13 when that authority took over state railway construction.

In 1917, the veteran returned to NSWGR ownership and was placed upon a plinth at Enfield locomotive depot. It can be seen today, preserved at the Thirlmere Railway Museum.

SPECIFICATIONS

	1 AND 1N-CLASSES	M36-CLASS
	IMPERIAL (METRIC)	IMPERIAL (METRIC)
CYLINDERS:	16 X 24 IN (41 X 61 CM)	16 X 24 IN (41 X 61 CM)
BOILER PRESSURE:	120 PSI (827 KPA)	125 PSI (862 KPA)
COUPLED WHEELS:	5 FT 6 IN (168 CM)	5 FT 6 IN (168 CM)
TRACTIVE EFFORT:	8937 LB (39.8 KN)	9309 LB (41.4 KN)
GRATE AREA:	13.8 SQ FT (1.282 M²)	15 SQ FT (1.394 M²)
TOTAL WEIGHT:	46.5 TONS (47.4 T)	52 TONS (53 T)
GAUGE:	1435 MM	1435 MM
ROAD NUMBERS:	1-CLASS: 1—4	36—39, 77—78
	1N-CLASS: 1N—3N	
	(THEY BECAME 388—390 IN 1889)	

No. 1 *Adelaide* after it was converted into a tender engine. (SA archives)

1856 South Australian Railways

2-4-0WT

Authority regulating the construction of railways in South Australia was passed in March 1847. This set the scene for the private consortium known as the Adelaide City & Port Railway Co to start planning a standard gauge link between the expanding city of Adelaide and its port, located about 8 kilometres to the north-west.

However, dealings with the government eventually met with complications so in October 1851, the Governor and Legislative Council decided to provide the funding to build a state-owned railway. As work advanced, the government, which by now had decided on the 5 ft 3 in (1600 mm) gauge that had initially been adopted in New South Wales, ordered three 2-4-0 well-tank locomotives from Messrs William Fairbairn of Manchester, England. They were shipped to Port Adelaide and unloaded in mid-January 1856.

Numbered 1, 2 and 3, the little engines were resplendent in green livery relieved by much polished brass work. With work on the state's first public railway linking Adelaide with Port Adelaide almost complete, the locomotives were soon steam-tested in preparation for the 8 February 1856 opening day.

No. 1 worked the first official train, successfully hauling 12 period vehicles over the route. However, trouble surfaced for the locomotives because a short section of track had been laid with broad-flanged Barlow rails without sleepers. The weight of the passing locomotives put such downward pressure on

the rails that derailments became common and the section had to be replaced by conventional materials.

The three locomotives, which were named *Adelaide, Victoria* and *Albert*, continued to trundle over the relatively flat Port line hauling mixed-type trains until overhauls and rebuilding became necessary 13 years later. While in the workshops, all three locomotives were provided with tenders and thus emerged as 2-4-0s, but they were not destined to last long. In spite of their use over the new Port Adelaide–Dry Creek extension, No. 1 was withdrawn in 1871 and Nos 2 and 3 during 1874.

They were all dismantled and No. 3's motion and cylinders were used to drive the shafting in the Railway Department's sawmill at the Islington Railway Workshops. The driving wheels of the other two found further useful service beneath a special crocodile wagon built to transport narrow gauge Departmental vehicles over the state's extensive broad gauge system. It was finally written off during the early 1980s, one pair of wheels being acquired by the National Railway Museum, Port Adelaide. The other pair was acquired by an enthusiast society.

SPECIFICATIONS

	Imperial (Metric)
Cylinders:	15 x 24 in (38 x 61 cm)
Boiler pressure:	80 psi (551 kPa)
Coupled wheels:	5 ft 3 in (160 cm)
Tractive effort:	5486 lb (24.4 kN)
Total weight:	[about] 37 tons (38t)
Gauge:	1600 mm
Road numbers/names:	1 Adelaide, 2 Victoria and 3 Albert

No. 4, pictured in 1875, after its conversion from a tender-type engine to a well-tank type. (former SAR)

1856 SOUTH AUSTRALIAN RAILWAYS

B-class 2-4-0

Due to the impending opening of a railway linking Adelaide and the beachside suburb of Gawler in 1856, the South Australian government railway administration contracted Robert Stephenson & Co in England to build two 2-4-0 tender locomotives for mixed traffic purposes. The first engine, No. 4, arrived in November 1856 and the second, No. 7, in March 1858.

Described as 'beasts' by the crews of the day, both engines were reported to have given 'considerable trouble'. Nonetheless, the railway administration persevered and the locomotives continued to work the relatively level Gawler route and in addition were reported operating over the pioneer Adelaide to Port Adelaide link.

In an effort to improve the two locomotives, both were shopped in the late winter of 1875 and rebuilt as 2-4-0 well-tank locomotives. No. 4 was the first to emerge in November of that year, followed three months later by No. 7.

Boasting more comfortable enclosed cabs which gave some protection for the crews, the B-class was finally deemed to be 'more successful' and both remained in constant service over the Port Adelaide line until further heavy maintenance became necessary

in 1887. No. 7 was the first to be shopped but by then, with more-powerful passenger locomotives available and heavier trains to contend with, the need for lighter types of engines had all but vanished. Thus No. 7 emerged as a crane locomotive and was employed at the Islington Railway Workshops. During its rebuild, the well tanks beneath the coal bunker were removed and side tanks were substituted. This crane was available for lifts up to 3 tonnes.

No. 4 remained in its well-tank form, save for the fitting of Westinghouse brake equipment, until condemned in 1891. However, it must have been built under a guiding star, for two years later it emerged from the Islington Railway Workshops rebuilt with a crane in the same way as its sister engine.

Both locomotives were finally withdrawn from service, No. 7 being condemned in July 1935 and No. 4 in April 1938. Both were subsequently scrapped.

SPECIFICATIONS

IMPERIAL (METRIC)

CYLINDERS:	14 x 20 IN (36 x 51 CM)
BOILER PRESSURE:	130 PSI (896 KPA)
COUPLED WHEELS:	5 FT 6 IN (168 CM)
GRATE AREA	11 SQ FT (1.068 M²)
TRACTIVE EFFORT:	6177 LB (27.5 KN)
TOTAL WEIGHT:	33 TONS (33.7 T)
GAUGE:	1600 MM
ROAD NUMBERS:	4 AND 7

Ex 'Pier Donkey' No. 5, while working under the ownership of rail construction contractors Rawdon & Baxter during the building of South Australia's Outer Harbour project at Port Adelaide circa 1905. (V/Line archives, Len Whalley collection)

1858 MELBOURNE & HOBSONS BAY RAILWAY

'Pier Donkeys' 0-4-0WT

Small in every respect and bearing an old-fashioned look, even at that time, the Melbourne & Hobsons Bay Railway Co's 'Pier Donkeys' were true champions of the sailing ship era.

With huge quantities of cargo passing through the Port of Melbourne, fuelled by the state's gold rush, the fledgling railway company seized upon this business potential by building a railway to link its company-owned port with Flinders Street station in Melbourne.

Rail traffic had expanded to such an extent that by the second half of the 1850s the need arose for a purpose-built locomotive to handle what was on offer. Accordingly, the company engaged Robert Stephenson & Co in England to construct one little 0-4-0WT shunting locomotive, which entered traffic in September 1858.

With its two mini 21 x 36 cm cylinders slanted at a seemingly crazy angle behind the leading driving wheel, one of the shortest connecting rods ever seen in Australian locomotive practice was provided. This drove the trailing coupled axle. An external steam pipe fed each cylinder.

Built on a US-style bar frame, absolutely no shelter was provided for the crew against the squalls that often blew in over Hobsons Bay. However, one design prerequisite was that the locomotive had to have sufficient clearance beneath its axles and firebox to clear the many cast iron rolling-stock traversers which were located at intervals along the wharf.

Expanding business prompted the purchase of a second, slightly larger locomotive from the same manufacturer in 1875. While similar in appearance, this locomotive was equipped with a more conventional steam dome and cylinder feed and exerted about half as much power again. It was numbered 24.

Both locomotives passed into Victorian Railways' ownership on 1 July 1879, the original delivery being re-boilered the following year. Both were eventually withdrawn from active service during the late to mid-1890s and placed in store at Newport Workshops. Whereas 24 was eventually scrapped in 1904, the class-leader was snapped up that year by construction company Rawdon & Baxter in connection with the building of the Outer Harbour at Port Adelaide, South Australia, and nicknamed 'Casey's Dream'. Enough pressure must have been placed on the new owner by its locomotive crew that a photograph taken in 1907 shows the engine operating with an enclosed home-made cab.

The locomotive was scrapped circa 1910.

	No. 5	No. 24
	IMPERIAL (METRIC)	IMPERIAL (METRIC)
CYLINDERS:	8 x 14 IN (21 x 36 CM)	9 x 15 IN (23 x 36 CM)
BOILER PRESSURE:	130 PSI (896 KPA)	130 PSI (896 KPA)
COUPLED WHEELS:	3 FT 9 IN (114 CM)	3 FT 9 IN (114 CM)
TRACTIVE EFFORT:	2070 LB (12.2 KN)	2808 LB (13.1 KN)
GRATE AREA:	5.25 SQ FT (0.4871 M²)	5.42 SQ FT (1.005 M²)
TOTAL WEIGHT:	10 TONS 11 CWT (13.4 T)	13 TONS 3 CWT (13.5 T)
GAUGE:	1600 MM	1600 MM

1858 Victorian Railways

No. 1 2-2-2

With the commencement of Victoria's government-owned railways in 1856, following the takeover of the private Murray River Railway Co, the new Department quickly set about reorganising contracts for railway construction, locomotives and rolling stock.

The first order placed with the Melbourne agency, Messrs de Pass Bros, was for four 0-6-0 goods and one 2-2-2 passenger locomotives. Their construction was carried out by the London firm, George England & Co.

All four locomotives arrived in Melbourne during September 1858, and the 2-2-2 was honoured by becoming No. 1 on the roster. This locomotive made its trial run from Williamstown to Maribyrnong River on 16 September 1858. Four months later, the line linking Melbourne and Sunbury (38 km) was opened and No. 1 had the distinction of hauling the first viceregal train.

The success of this little 2-2-2 led to the addition of another five engines, which arrived in May 1860. A policy of numbering passenger locomotives with even numbers and goods engines with odd numbers had just been introduced, and the new 2-2-2s became Nos. 2 to 10 (evens) while the original No. 1 became the railway's No. 12.

During 1871, No. 12 was converted to a 2-4-0 as heavier trains were becoming out of range for single-wheeled engines. It was then used for many years on the Echuca line, working out of Bendigo.

In May 1890, No. 12 was sold to the Yarrawonga Shire for use over the Katamatite Tramway near Shepparton. Continuous losses resulted in that line's closure two years later and the engine was returned to the VR. Another, newer engine had been numbered 12 in the meantime, so the old 2-4-0 now became 528.

As the VR decided to take over the Katamatite Tramway, the 2-4-0 continued to be used there until 1904, when it was sold to a contracting firm engaged in building the Outer Harbour near Adelaide. When this work was completed in 1908, the veteran was taken over by the South Australian Harbour Board but, since it was worn out, was broken up around 1910.

SPECIFICATIONS

	IMPERIAL (METRIC)
CYLINDERS:	14 x 22 IN (36 x 56 CM)
BOILER PRESSURE:	100 PSI (689 KPA)
COUPLED WHEELS:	6 FT 0 IN (183 CM)
GRATE AREA:	16.4 SQ FT (1.52 M²)
TRACTIVE EFFORT:	4791 LB (21.3 KN)
GAUGE:	1600 MM
ROAD NUMBERS:	1, 2–10 EVEN NUMBERS (NO. 1 BECAME NO. 12 IN 1860 AND NO. 528 IN 1892)

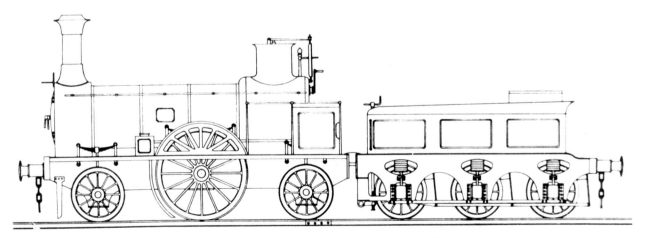

An impression of Victorian Railways' No. 1 locomotive in its original form. (V/Line archives, author's collection)

D-class 4-4-0

To meet SAR requirements for light mixed-traffic locomotives for use over the lightly laid (18 kg) Gawler–Kapunda line, leading British builder Robert Stephenson & Co personally recommended the 4-4-0 wheel arrangement.

The firm received a contract for two locomotives, which arrived at Port Adelaide in August 1859. The design was found to be sound, and popular with the rail crews, leading to six more being constructed for SAR between 1862 and 1867.

These 48-tonne locomotives found ready employment, working both copper and wheat traffic.

Described as 'my best and strongest engines' by the Railways' Chief Engineer, these locomotives were obviously worked to the limit because by 1875 four were in dire need of heavy overhaul. However, repairs did not take place until 1881, when progressively each engine was rebuilt with a new boiler and improved cab, and transferred to the northern area of the state for further wheat and general traffic haulage.

As the pioneer-type light lines were gradually rebuilt with heavier rails capable of carrying stronger and heavier locomotives, the D-class became redundant, so in February 1896 No. 11 was condemned, followed by No. 17 in 1900, with two more withdrawn in December 1904. With the construction of the Tailem Bend–Pinnaroo line in the state's north-east, the remaining four enjoyed a reprieve when pressed into railway construction duties over that route. Locomotive No. 18 even found a short career under private ownership after it was sold to a contractor engaged on that railway.

By November 1906 No. 18 had been returned to the Department and all four 4-4-0s found employment on the Pinnaroo line until their replacement by more powerful engines in the early 1920s. All were then transferred to the Mile End depot for a period of light shunting until No. 10 was withdrawn early in 1928. The class-leader, No. 8, was the longest lived, surviving until November 1932.

SPECIFICATIONS

	IMPERIAL (METRIC)
CYLINDERS:	15½ x 22 IN (39 x 56 CM)
BOILER PRESSURE:	130 PSI (896 KPA)
COUPLED WHEELS:	5 FT 4 IN (163 CM)
TRACTIVE EFFORT:	8589 LB (38.2 KN)
GRATE AREA:	14.7 SQ FT (1.366 M²)
TOTAL WEIGHT:	47 TONS (48 T)
GAUGE:	1600 MM
ROAD NUMBERS:	8, 9, 11, 12, 15–18

SAR No. 18's crew have their well-proportioned 4-4-0 locomotive in pristine condition for its next assignment. (former SAR archives)

These two 2-4-0STs, 22 and 18, had just arrived when pictured in 1860 being prepared for commissioning. Note how one engine had received its cab while the other was yet to be so fitted. (V/Line archives, Len Whalley collection)

1860 Victorian Railways

L-class 2-4-0ST

This class, which eventually numbered ten, was destined to be the only saddle tank-type locomotive on the Victorian Railways. Delivered during the latter half of 1860, the initial batch of seven came from the London (UK) workshops of George England & Co. They were bestowed the road numbers 14 to 26 (even numbers only, as was then the practice for passenger engines).

An additional three locomotives numbered 28, 30 and 32 were delivered virtually simultaneously, this time from the British firm Slaughter, Grunning, whose heavy workshop was located at Bristol.

While most of the engines were commissioned almost immediately, several were found to have been damaged on the sea voyage to Melbourne, necessitating heavy repairs, and the fleet did not become fully operational until the winter of 1861.

Although ordered for passenger service, particularly in and around the Melbourne metropolitan area, some found early, albeit temporary glory in 1862 on the newly opened North Geelong to Ballarat link due to a delay in the delivery of heavier 2-4-0 B-class tender passenger engines.

In 1886, the ten until now un-classed locomotives became the L-class. By that time they were generally captive to the busy Williamstown line.

By the turn of the century, with more powerful locomotive types on hand (and on the drawing boards), class members were taken out of commercial service as heavy repairs fell due. While 28 spent many years from 1900 working as a stationary boiler at Newport Workshops, and 16 was forwarded to the department's Matheson's Siding metal quarry (near Kilmore East) two years later and used as a stationary engine, the rest had been scrapped by 1906, except for 32, which was sold to the Sanderson family of Forrest to generate steam for their timber mill.

SPECIFICATIONS

	IMPERIAL (METRIC)
CYLINDERS:	16 x 22 IN (41 x 56 CM)
BOILER PRESSURE:	130 PSI (896 KPA)
COUPLED WHEELS:	5 FT 0 IN (152 CM)
TRACTIVE EFFORT:	9380 LB (41.7 KN)
GRATE AREA:	APPROX 11.25 SQ FT (1.045 M²)
TOTAL WEIGHT:	36 TONS (36.7 T)
GAUGE:	1600 MM
ROAD NUMBERS:	14—32 (EVEN NUMBERS ONLY)

An early view of B-class 110. Note the wood fuel stacked in the tender, the reason behind several members of the class being equipped with spark-arresting funnels early in their careers. (Len Whalley collection)

1861 Victorian Railways

B-class 2-4-0

With the Geelong–Ballarat and Melbourne–Sand-hurst (Bendigo) lines both well under construction in 1860, the opportunity was taken to order thirteen main line 2-4-0 passenger locomotives from Beyer, Peacock & Co of Manchester, England, and six 0-6-0 freight engines from Slaughter, Grunning of Bristol, England.

As all the VR locomotives to date had been rather on the light side and were unsuitable for operation over the new, heavily graded routes, these acquisitions were regarded as the first main line locomotives on the system.

They all entered service in 1861 and 1862, along with an additional thirteen 2-4-0s from R.W. Hawthorn & Co. Both kinds of locomotive boasted the unusual Cudworth-type firebox and midfeather, a novel design introduced in England early in the 1850s. This design had a divided firebox with two firehole doors and was experimentally received in Victoria in an effort to gain maximum heat from the wood fuels of the day.

The 2-4-0s featured external frames with coupled wheels driven through outside bearings and they quickly received the understandable nickname of 'The Overarmers'. (The goods engines were of similar construction.) They were favourably regarded as free steamers and fast runners and an additional six were ordered from Beyer, Peacock & Co. These were received between May and July 1862. The local firm, Phoenix Foundry of Ballarat, delivered an additional two in October 1880 and May 1881, although these were built with conventional fireboxes.

With the opening of the Albury line on 20 August 1883, No. 88 had the honour of working the first official train.

The 2-4-0s were superseded from 1887 due to the arrival of more-powerful D and (Old) A-class locomotives, and relegated to secondary services until they were rebuilt during the 1880s with 2.5 cm larger cylinders. This increased their tractive effort by 1.7 kN. Shortly afterwards, 16 were further rebuilt with 44.5 cm diameter cylinders which, combined with an increased 70 kPa boiler pressure, produced an extra 6.3 kN of tractive effort.

In VR's 1889 reclassification scheme, the remaining 2-4-0s became the system's B-class. By then, accidents had started to deplete their ranks. On 2 April 1884, locos 82 and 92 collided violently at picturesque Little River (between Melbourne and Geelong). Both were write-offs. Four months later, 72's boiler burst at Warrenheip (above Ballarat). All three locomotives were set aside, their useful parts gradually going to sister engines.

From 1904, class members were starting to feel their age, and poor boiler condition and general deterioration dictated withdrawals. The last two in service were 56 and 76, which were used as carriage shunters at North Melbourne sheds and Spencer Street station until May and June 1917.

	Imperial (Metric)
CYLINDERS:	16 x 24 IN (41 x 61 CM)
BOILER PRESSURE:	130 PSI (896 KPA)
COUPLED WHEELS:	6 FT 0 IN (183 CM)
TRACTIVE EFFORT:	8875 LB (39.5 KN)
GRATE AREA:	5.27 SQ FT (1.419 M²)
TOTAL WEIGHT:	35.3 TONS (36 T)
GAUGE:	1600 MM
ROAD NUMBERS:	46–96, 102–112, 186 AND 188 (EVEN NUMBERS ONLY)

1862 VICTORIAN RAILWAYS

O-class 0-6-0

For such a numerically small class, the Victorian Railways' O-class freight engines featured in more misadventures than perhaps any other Australian type. They suffered a number of boiler explosions, and were frequently involved in accidents. Like the earlier B-class passenger 2-4-0 locomotives, this class was designed with outside framing.

Introduced in 1862 for main line working between Geelong–Ballarat and Melbourne–Sandhurst, the first six were built by Slaughter, Grunning of Bristol, England. Later that year, a further 12 were delivered by Robert Stephenson & Co. The class was regarded as the first main line goods engine on the VR. When traffic increased, a further eight were constructed by Beyer, Peacock & Co and delivered in two batches between 1866 and 1871.

With the gradual extension of the state's broad gauge railway network, the Yorkshire Engine Co of Sheffield added six more to the class in 1872, despite the fact that more modern locomotive types were then being introduced. The reason for this, claim some historians, was that the elderly 0-6-0s were considered free steamers and sound, reliable engines. As a result, even more were ordered but this time they were made locally. The VR's Williamstown Workshops released two in 1879 and 1881 while the Phoenix Foundry of Ballarat boosted the tally by an additional seven.

Not to be outdone, Beyer, Peacock & Co supplied a final three, and the last of the class had been delivered by July 1879. All 44 became the O-class in the 1889 reclassification system.

These locomotives, like many of the era, were equipped with Salter safety valves, which the enginemen could adjust by hanging weights on levers to increase or decrease boiler working pressure. Over-enthusiasm in carrying out the procedure meant they suffered a total of four boiler explosions.

A proud crew with engine 23 in the late 1860s. (V/Line archives, Len Whalley collection)

(In fact, engine 51 exploded twice.) Altogether, these O-class engines featured in no less than 20 incidents involving explosions or accidents.

All engines in the class were progressively rebuilt in later years with 45 cm diameter cylinders which increased their tractive effort by 3.2 kN.

The first of the class to vanish appears to have been loco 47, in August 1904. Others were sold, and key parts of 57 were used to drive a Murray River steamboat. The last engine in government service was 79, withdrawn in April 1921. All were scrapped.

SPECIFICATIONS

	IMPERIAL (METRIC)
CYLINDERS:	17 x 24 IN (43 x 61 CM)
BOILER PRESSURE	:130 PSI (896 KPA)
COUPLED WHEELS:	5 FT 0 IN (152 CM)
TRACTIVE EFFORT:	12 022 LB (53.5 KN)
GRATE AREA:	17.8 SQ FT (1.654 M²)
TOTAL WEIGHT:	64 TONS (65.3 T)
GAUGE:	1600 MM
ROAD NUMBERS:	19—69, 127—149 (ODD NUMBERS ONLY)

B (A10) class 0-4-2

Queensland Railways, which today operates some 9639 route km of 1067 mm gauge railways, commenced operations humbly on 31 July 1865 with the running of a train from Ipswich to Grandchester, when it was known as the Southern & Western Railway.

The early railways of Queensland were originally isolated systems but as the widely scattered population increased, railway construction continued poking inland, and along the vast coastline, until most lines finally met to form today's impressive network.

To work trains over that very first Grandchester line, four little 23-tonne 2-4-0 tender locomotives were acquired from the British firm Avonside Engine Co, eventually becoming the system's A-class.

Soon afterwards, a second locomotive type was introduced, but of the 0-4-2 wheel arrangement. Boasting leading dimensions virtually identical to the earlier A-class, the newer locomotives, numbering four, were built by Neilson & Co, and later became the B-class. Considered very capable machines, an additional eight were ordered, again from Neilson, all of which were in service by late 1866.

With railway construction forging onwards with gusto, QR sold one of its original B-class to a contractor during the latter half of 1865. After coming into the hands of a second rail-building contractor, that engine eventually found its way back

Diminutive but nicely balanced, A10 No. 6 after its rescue by QR for preservation almost half a century ago. (QR)

into QR stock during 1876. Another contracting firm, Peto Brassey & Betts, had purchased a similar 0-4-2 new; after operating it as PBB No. 1, they eventually sold it to QR, giving QR a total of 13 B-class locomotives.

Between November 1887 and May 1890, four of the locos entered shops for rebuild and emerged as 2-4-4 tank locomotives (classified 4D10-class in the state's 1889 general re-classification initiative) for local passenger working. But they did not last long in government ownership, being sold soon afterwards. No. 10, after spending some 18 years hauling timber on Fraser Island, remained in service at Fairymead Sugar Mill, Bundaberg, until the end of the 1955 sugar season. Another was sold to a railway-building contractor while others saw service on the Fraser Island timber tramways.

Meanwhile, the remaining tender engines had been reclassified A10-class in 1889 and, as lines were being upgraded to carry heavier locomotives, the small 0-4-2s quickly became obsolete. No. 13 was the first to be written off, in 1895, and five more followed seven years later.

In 1887, No. 6 was sold to yet another railway contracting firm and, after a brief return to QR from 1895, was again sold, this time to the Bingera Sugar Mill, Bundaberg. Receiving a new 1206 kPa (175 psi) boiler in 1958, this locomotive, known as No. 2 *Nelson* at the mill, remained in traffic there until 1965 when mill management offered the relic to QR for its centenary celebrations. After working a pioneer train from Ipswich to Grandchester, the mill offered No. 6 for preservation. It took pride of place at the former Redbank Museum until 1989, after which the little relic was out-shopped by QR in 1991 for use with state sponsored rail tour programmes. It became the oldest working steam locomotive in Australia and is housed today at The Workshops Rail Museum at North Ipswich.

Another engine with an interesting history is No. 3 which, after working along Bowen wharf for 12 years, was taken into store at Ipswich in 1914 where it lay decaying for a further 22 years before being shopped for overhaul to enable it to work trains during QR's 1936 special celebrations. No. 3 was then displayed at Brisbane's Roma Street station until track alterations in 1959 forced its removal. The locomotive has now been preserved in Queen's Park, Ipswich.

All other A10 locomotives have been scrapped.

SPECIFICATIONS

	Imperial (Metric)
Cylinders:	10 x 18 in (25 x 46 cm)
Boiler pressure:	120 psi (827 kPa)
Coupled wheels:	3 ft 0 in (91 cm)
Tractive effort:	4800 lb (21.4 kN)
Grate area:	7.1 sq ft (0.659 m²)
Total weight:	22.5 tons (23 t)
Gauge:	1067 mm
Road numbers:	2–14 (Nos. 7, 9–11 being converted to 4D10-class)

1865 Railways of New South Wales

(E) 17-class 0-6-0

In New South Wales, construction of the Goulburn and Bathurst lines was well under way by the early 1860s. Because grades as torrid as 1 in 30 existed over both routes, it was obvious a powerful goods locomotive type would be necessary. As a result, Robert Stephenson & Co was asked to deliver six 0-6-0s, the first of which arrived in May 1865.

Their exceptional performance and generally trouble-free operation soon led to additional orders being placed with that builder, and with the Sydney firm of Vale & Lacy (whose works stood in Druitt Street). With railway construction forging nearer to Goulburn and Bathurst, many of these new locomotives were on hand when those lines eventually opened later that decade.

By July 1879, a total of 23 engines had been built, seven of them for the then-isolated Newcastle district rail network. All were used on the state's main line freight services until withdrawals commenced on the Newcastle section with 11N in 1889. Others were sold about this time to coal-mining interests while four were transferred to another government authority, the Public Works Department, where they saw extensive use in rail construction projects. Two of these returned to the NSWGR fold when all rail construction duties were placed into railway hands, making them the last of their breed in government service, receiving miscellaneous stock numbers in 1924.

Of the last two PWD locomotives, the authority sold 40 to BHP in 1914 where it became that company's No. 1. It was initially used in steel plant construction duties. The veteran locomotive was

Vale & Lacy-built E17-class 0-6-0, No. 41X, just prior to its in January 1900 sale to the NSWPWD for railway construction duties. In that service it carried the PWD number 14. The engine returned to the NSWGR again in 1917 when that body assumed control of all railway building work. It was withdrawn in June 1921 and scrapped in March 1927 as 1003, a number believed not to have been physically applied to the engine. (NSWGR)

later converted into an 0-6-0ST to enable it to more easily negotiate the works' tight curvature. BHP transport department staff affectionately dubbed the engine 'Old Lizzie', a name that stuck right up until its scrapping in 1960.

However, one coal industry locomotive lasted a little longer. No. 18, which had been acquired by the Southern Coal Co at Corrimal in 1897, continued in regular service until 1963, when it was dismantled for repairs. While this work was going on, the Australian Iron and Steel Co bought the colliery and the repairs were never completed. The relic was presented to the NSW Rail Transport Museum the following year and it is on exhibition in the Thirlmere Railway

Museum.

Another long-lived engine was Vale & Lacy engine 42, which was acquired by the Caledonian Coal Co at West Wallsend, Newcastle in February 1903. Two years later it was bought by Mt Kembla Colliery near Wollongong. Australian Iron & Steel took over the mine and locomotive in 1946 and, despite a major railway upgrade and the introduction of Bo-Bo diesels in 1950, the engine continued shunting Mt Kembla coal until it was withdrawn in June 1958 due to poor boiler condition. No. 42 was immediately transferred to the company's Cringila Workshops and by April 1959 had been scrapped.

These 51.5-tonne locomotives paved the way for

Still carrying its original NSWGR number '42', more than half a century after its sale to industry, Australian Iron & Steel's Mt Kembla Colliery is the setting for this rare image of the locomotive working out its last years. The engine was eventually withdrawn in June 1958. (Late Colin Oakley)

a long line of successful, slightly heavier long-boiler 0-6-0s on the NSWGR, one of which remained in commercial service until 1972.

SPECIFICATIONS

	IMPERIAL (METRIC)
CYLINDERS:	18 x 24 IN (46 x 61 CM)
BOILER PRESSURE:	120 PSI (827 KPA)
COUPLED WHEELS:	4 FT 0 IN (122 CM)
TRACTIVE EFFORT:	15 522 LB (69 KN)
GRATE AREA:	17.9 SQ FT (1.663 M²)
TOTAL WEIGHT:	50.5 TONS (51.5 T)
GAUGE:	1435 MM
ROAD NUMBERS:	17–22, 40–47, 11N–13N, 18N, 19N, 21N, 22N, 2ND 52 AND 2ND 103

1865 RAILWAYS OF NEW SOUTH WALES

(G) 23-class 2-4-0

By 1865, the NSW railway network had reached Picton in the south and Penrith and Richmond in the west, while the isolated northern section now served all points between Newcastle and Singleton. With work underway to further expand these lines to Goulburn, Murrurundi and Bathurst (over the Blue Mountains), orders were placed with Beyer, Peacock & Co for four 2-4-0 express passenger locomotives and with Robert Stephenson & Co for nine 0-6-0 freight engines (see (E) 17-class).

Entering service between September and October 1865, the passenger engines became the 23-class on the Southern section and the 14N-class on the then isolated Northern section. Subsequent ordering found a total of 13 of these dainty 2-4-0s in traffic by December 1870.

The design was based on the successful London Metropolitan underground tank locomotives then in service in England, a type regarded as 'free steaming and mechanically trouble free'.

However, operating problems arose in New South Wales when it became apparent the steep 1 in 30 grades between Picton and Mittagong were too taxing for the locomotives' 175 cm coupled wheels. Because of this, the final four of the class were fitted with smaller 168 cm wheels which increased their tractive effort by some 2.23 kN. To ease the problem on the earlier engines, about 2 tonnes of adhesion weights were fitted.

The arrival of larger 79-class 4-4-0 Beyer, Peacock-built passenger engines from 1877 found the old 2-4-0s relegated to the less hilly portions of the network until finally, in the 1890s, they were

No. 15N as running the then isolated Northern Division in the early 1870s. (RailCorp archives)

This wonderful study of 2-2-2 No. 15, looking every bit the sleek racehorse, was taken at Redfern paddocks circa 1871. (RailCorp archives)

withdrawn altogether as major overhauls became due. Interestingly, all were kept in store for over ten years until a need for branch line locomotives arose, when they were shopped and emerged as 4-4-0s (being equipped with leading Bissell bogies similar to the C79-class) and new 965 kPa (140 psi) Belpaire boilers. This increased their tractive effort by almost a fifth and their weight by 9 tonnes.

These revamped old ladies were then transferred to south-western and far-western depots where there were few grades.

Reclassified Z14-class under the 1924 renumbering system, the class-leader, 1401, was withdrawn from traffic in December 1921, followed by three more in 1929. Despite the proliferation of higher-powered 4-6-0s on the branch lines from 1928, overhauls on some engines continued through the 1930s–40s with one, 1405, surviving until boiler renewals became necessary early in 1952. It was scrapped in June of that year after an 86- year lifetime and 1 866 880 km of service. None of this class remains.

SPECIFICATIONS

	IMPERIAL (METRIC)
CYLINDERS:	18 x 24 IN (46 x 61 CM)
BOILER PRESSURE:	120 PSI (827 KPA)
COUPLED WHEELS:	5 FT 9 IN (175 CM)
TRACTIVE EFFORT:	10 818 LB (48.1 KN)
GRATE AREA:	14.75 SQ FT (1.37 M²)
TOTAL WEIGHT:	52.75 TONS (53.8 T)
GAUGE:	1435 MM
ROAD NUMBERS:	(ORIGINAL) 14N–16N, 23–28, 32–35
	(1924) 1401–1413

(T) 14-class 2-2-2

The three delightful single driving-axled express passenger locomotives that constituted this class were the last singles acquired by the Railways of NSW. This design was a popular one for express working, particularly in England and in some Australian states.

All three engines were built by Beyer, Peacock & Co and delivered unassembled during the winter of 1865. They were imported for high-speed passenger running over the easily graded Picton and Penrith routes and one of them (No. 15, pictured) rose to fame when it became legendary driver John Heron's original *Fish* locomotive, operating the daily business train between Parramatta Junction and Penrith.

The *Fish*, of course, has since become world famous and in subsequent years, when the express began working into the Blue Mountains destinations, it was the fastest timetabled mountain train in the world.

No. 15 also made the headlines when, on Boxing Day 1879 it collided with a train in Parramatta station while working a race special. Although badly damaged, the engine was rebuilt and continued working the Penrith line.

During the mid-1880s, the 14-class was relieved of its main line duties due to increasingly heavy trains and, by 1887, was working mail trains between Dubbo and Nyngan, with at least one transferred to Junee for Narrandera-line mail train working.

In the NSW reclassification system of 1889, they all became the T-14 class. However, they were not destined to remain in service for long and were soon withdrawn due to deteriorating boiler and mechanical condition. The first to go was 15 in 1890; the other two went in 1892. The following year the boilers of all three were removed and the locomotives' remains cut up.

SPECIFICATIONS

	IMPERIAL (METRIC)
CYLINDERS:	16 × 20 IN (41 × 51 CM)
BOILER PRESSURE:	125 PSI (861 KPA)
COUPLED WHEELS:	6 FT 0 IN (183 CM)
TRACTIVE EFFORT:	7111 LB (31.6 KN)
GRATE AREA:	(ABOUT) 11 SQ FT (1.022 M²)
TOTAL WEIGHT:	45.6 TONS (46.6 T)
GAUGE:	1435 MM
ROAD NUMBERS:	14, 15 AND 16

1867 QUEENSLAND RAILWAYS

Double Fairlies
0-4-4-0 / 0-6-6-0

These ungainly QR locomotives were possibly the most unsuccessful locomotives ever to see service in Australia. For a time, the government system operated two distinct types of Double Fairlie locomotives, an 0-6-6-0 type and an 0-4-4-0 type. The first to arrive were the 0-6-6-0s, ordered from the firm of James Cross in St Helens, England. Three were delivered late in 1867 in unassembled form.

By December of that year, one had been assembled.

It ran a short trial at Ipswich where it was found that steam was difficult to maintain. In addition, the locomotive spread the rails through some curves. (It was subsequently learnt that the engine was 6 tonnes above the specified 30 tonnes.)

The locomotive ran another trial the following month, this time on the main line through the Little Liverpool Range, where again the engine lost steam, ran out of water, threw numerous curves out of true and finally derailed after covering 38 km. As a result it was shipped back to its maker, along with the two unassembled engines.

These Double Fairlie articulated locomotives were the first of this unique design to come to Australia. Patented by Robert Fairlie, the arrangement allowed for a flexible form of 'double' engine which in theory would provide more power over steep and winding terrain. It was powered by two boilers which were fed by one common firebox. In fact, it was the firebox arrangement which the QR engineers believed to be the cause of the lack of steaming qualities. They claimed the firebox should have boasted a midfeather (a divider).

The three locomotives were subsequently rebuilt to standard gauge by their maker, and the one which had run trials over Queensland metals (Builder's No. 29) later went to Burry Port and Gwendraeth Railway in Wales. The other two (Builder's Nos 28 and 30) saw service with the Central Uruguay Railway in South America.

One would assume that QR would have had enough of Double Fairlies. But in 1876, a demonstration model 0-4-4-0, built by the Vulcan Foundry, arrived and started trials on the difficult

One of the few known pictures of QR's 0-4-4-0 Double Fairlie, *Governor Cairns*. (QR archives)

Kitson 0-6-0ST No. 4 after it was saved for preservation. (Leon Oberg)

Toowoomba Range route. Being a little more successful, the engine was purchased and named *Governor Cairns*. But three years later it was set aside following flexible steam pipe fractures caused by the sharp curves of the area through which it operated. In 1880, the locomotive was repaired and forwarded to Brisbane, where it worked metal trains over the more level Ipswich portion of the route. In 1882, this previously unnumbered engine was listed as 41 and in 1889 became the sole member of the 8D11-class.

It continued to give trouble and, as boiler repairs were necessary, was written off in 1902.

SPECIFICATIONS

	0-6-6-0	0-4-4-0
	IMPERIAL (METRIC)	IMPERIAL (METRIC)
CYLINDERS:	(4) 11 x 8 IN (28 x 46 CM)	(4) 11 x 18 IN (28 x 46 CM)
BOILER PRESSURE:	110 PSI (758 KPA)	110 PSI (758 KPA)
COUPLED WHEELS:	3 FT 0 IN (91 CM)	3 FT 3 IN (99 CM)
TRACTIVE EFFORT:	10 648 LB (47.4 KN)	9 829 LB (43.7 KN)
TOTAL WEIGHT:	36 TONS (36.7 T)	34.6 TONS (35.3 T)
GAUGE:	1067 MM	1067 MM
ROAD NUMBER:	NIL	41 GOVERNOR CAIRNS

1870 MR J. B. WATT

Kitson 0-6-0ST

Built in a period when several locomotive firms were producing light industrial engines, this small 0-6-0ST, delivered by Kitson of Leeds in 1870, was ideal for northern New South Wales line railway construction contractor, Mr J.B. Watt.

The NSW Government purchased the engine in June 1872 when Watt had no more contracts to honour. The Railways of NSW promptly numbered the engine 20N in its isolated Northern Division system and it was put to work hauling short-distance coal trains, particularly between Newcastle Harbour and Hexham. It was while running in this capacity that Hexham coal magnate, John Brown, developed an admiration for the tiny loco and on numerous occasions offered to buy it for his Richmond Vale colliery railway. On each occasion his request failed. In 1889 the engine was renumbered 403.

Thinking he would never be able to purchase the engine, Brown contacted the builders and ordered a similar one. This arrived in 1878 and was numbered '3', being virtually identical to No. 20N/403 except for the provision of sliding side cab windows.

Early in 1891, No. 403 was withdrawn and John Brown swooped, this time successfully arranging

4-4-0WT No. 262 in Victorian Railways ownership. (V/Line archives, author's collection)

purchase. He took delivery in May 1891 and promptly numbered it '4' on his roster. He put the engine to work alongside his No. 3, hauling workers' passenger trains over the flat and swampy Hexham to Minmi route. No. 4 continued in traffic until it needed a major overhaul about 1902, when it received larger capacity side tanks.

When the Minmi link was closed early last century, the 0-6-0s were employed as shunters on Hexham jetty, remaining in service until 1967. Both were then abandoned until tenders were called for their purchase in 1973. Enthusiast groups eagerly sought the engines and the NSW Rail Transport Museum obtained No. 4 and after many years on exhibit at the NSWRTM Thirlmere Museum, it was forwarded to East Greta on 16 February 2010 for cosmetic restoration to original condition and renumbering back to '20N'. Its first public display was Maitland Steam Fest two months later. It is now an exhibit at Newcastle Regional Museum (Honeysuckle).

Meanwhile, No. 3 resides at the Dorrigo Steam Railway & Museum.

SPECIFICATIONS

	IMPERIAL (METRIC)
CYLINDERS:	16 x 24 IN (41 x 61 CM)
BOILER PRESSURE:	120 PSI (827 KPA)
COUPLED WHEELS:	4 FT 0 IN (122 CM)
TRACTIVE EFFORT:	12 288 LB (54.7 KN)
GRATE AREA:	13.7 SQ FT (1.273 M²)
TOTAL WEIGHT:	35 TONS (35.7 T)
GAUGE:	1435 MM
ROAD NUMBERS:	(ORIGINAL) 20N, BECOME 403 IN 1889, THEN (J. & A. BROWN) NO. 4; NO. 3 BOUGHT NEW.

1871 MELBOURNE & HOBSONS BAY UNITED RAILWAY

4-4-0WT

Robert Stephenson & Co constructed six small 4-4-0 well-tank locomotives early in 1871 for the Melbourne-based Melbourne & Hobson's Bay United Railway Co, for passenger and mixed train service. All were operational by 1878.

When the State government acquired the assets of this private company in 1878, the 4-4-0s continued working over their home route as the relatively flat Hobson's Bay line suited such locomotives with large coupled wheels.

These 4-4-0s were so successful in the administration's eyes that Robinson Bros of Melbourne began delivering an additional eight from July 1880. Another 12 were ordered from the Phoenix Foundry, Ballarat, for good measure. They were all running by mid-October 1883. In 1889, all 26 locomotives became VR's C-class.

Virtually their entire lives were spent over the original line, although they were also noted on the Outer Circle and Glen Iris lines following the construction of a viaduct between Flinders Street and Spencer Street stations around 1890. With this link, more powerful locomotives were able to operate through services, thus saving on engine power. Subsequently, the C-class became redundant and by late 1890 no less than 16 were in store. The remaining ten were based at Port Melbourne.

Engines 272, 282, 296 and 306 were modified with the fitting of extra handrails, cowcatchers and

An artist's impression of *Ballaarat* as delivered. (former Westrail archives)

stepboards for motor running over light branch lines such as the Rupanyup and Castlemaine–Maldon lines. Some of these and other C-class engines also assigned to these duties were fitted with larger 41 cm cylinders.

Scrappings commenced on 23 March 1904 with 296. Twelve more followed in the same year. By 1910, only four remained. One of these had been working as a boiler washout engine at North Melbourne since 1906, where it remained for many more years. The last engine in regular service was 294, which remained operational until 19 February 1916. All were eventually scrapped.

SPECIFICATIONS

	IMPERIAL (METRIC)
CYLINDERS:	15 x 22 IN (38 x 56 CM)
BOILER PRESSURE:	130 PSI (896 KPA)
COUPLED WHEELS:	5 FT 0 IN (152 CM)
TRACTIVE EFFORT:	8580 LB (38.6 KN)
GRATE AREA:	10.5 SQ FT (0.975 M²)
TOTAL WEIGHT:	37.85 TONS (38.6 T)
GAUGE:	1600 MM
ROAD NUMBERS:	(MELBOURNE & HOBSONS BAY) 20–23, 25 AND 26
	(VR) 42, 262–310 (EVEN NUMBERS ONLY)

1871 WESTERN AUSTRALIAN TIMBER CO

Ballaarat 0-4-0WT

With the vast timber resources of Western Australia becoming more apparent, it was only a matter of time before businessmen began to exploit them. Before

long, saw mills sprang up and markets as far afield as India were arranged.

The main demand was for sleepers and piles for railway construction. To transport the lumber, the timber interests began looking to tramways. The first to employ such means was the Western Australian Timber Co. Financed by a group of Victorian businessmen, the line linking Lockville with the giant jarrah forests 19 km inland at Yokonup, opened on 23 December 1871.

Laid to the 1067 mm gauge, it is of little surprise that the first engine was constructed in the directors' home state by the Victoria Foundry at Ballarat. Named *Ballaarat* (the original spelling of the township's name), this small 0-4-0 well-tank engine became the first locomotive to work in Western Australia and commenced its service in about May 1871. The line was described as 'easy going', as were the grades because, with the exception of one heavy pinch near Yokonup, it traversed mostly flat country.

Although the locomotive was renamed *Governor Weld* in December 1871, after a visit by the governor of the state, the old name *Ballaarat* remained.

It is known that about 1916–17 a visiting Western Australian Railways station master found the old locomotive lying in a dry creek bed just out of Busselton. He immediately interested a number of fellow enthusiasts in preserving the relic. Today, the spartan remains are to be seen in a children's park at Busselton. Although it is now under cover, locomotive historians believe such an historic artefact deserves better than this.

Locomotive 100 following its 1902 major rebuild at Newport Workshops. An enclosed steel cab and improved funnel were among a number of upgrades made during that overhaul. (V/Line archives, Len Whalley collection)

SPECIFICATIONS

	IMPERIAL (METRIC)
CYLINDERS:	7 x 14 IN (18 x 36 CM)
BOILER PRESSURE:	80–90 PSI (551–620 KPA)
COUPLED WHEELS:	3 FT 0 IN (91 CM)
TRACTIVE EFFORT:	(APPROX) 1372 LB (61 KN)
GRATE AREA:	5 SQ FT (0.465 M²)
TOTAL WEIGHT:	8 TONS (8.2 T)
GAUGE:	1067 MM

1872 VICTORIAN RAILWAYS

No. 100 2-4-0

Although quite a number of locomotives had been built in Victoria up until 1872, No. 100 marked a milestone for Victorian Railways in that it was the first locomotive designed and built for a specific use.

Designed under the direction of the railway's General Overseer of Locomotives and Workshops, Bill Meikle, this small 2-4-0 was to rise to prominence in that it was destined to become a regular 'Commissioner's Train' engine for over 30 years. It was built in the department's old Williamstown Workshops and issued to traffic during the latter part of 1872.

Although the cab was fitted with a front spectacle plate and a small roof, little other protection existed for the crew. But, unlike many other locomotives of the era which sported Salter safety valves, No. 100 was an up-to-date machine indeed with its less-tamperable Ramsbottom type safety valves.

Used for main line mixed traffic, No. 100 briefly became an E-class in a new state-wide reclassification scheme. When a new design 2-4-2 tank type became

the E-class three years later, No. 100, being a one-off, officially became unclassified and remained so for the rest of its life.

By 1902, No. 100 was due for a general overhaul and the opportunity was taken to bring its design in line with existing VR practice. Accordingly, the unique locomotive emerged from Newport Workshops with a 140 psi boiler in lieu of its original 130 psi one, increasing the tractive effort to 10 513 lb (46.6 kN). A new smokebox was built and a standard VR funnel provided as a replacement for the original, rather bland stovepipe type. Although the locomotive had earlier been provided with an improved cab in consideration of the crew, a further improved all-steel facility was provided during its rebuild.

The now much more handsome No. 100 re-entered service sporting the system's new Canadian-red paint job. In this grander form, the locomotive continued to serve on 'Commissioner's Train' duty but age, along with the proliferation of more modern power, overcame the veteran and after a short time lying in store at Newport Workshops it was unceremoniously scrapped in June 1916.

SPECIFICATIONS

	IMPERIAL (METRIC)
CYLINDERS:	16 x 22 IN (41 x 56 CM)
BOILER PRESSURE:	130 PSI (896 KPA)
COUPLED WHEELS:	5 FT 0 IN (152 CM)
TRACTIVE EFFORT:	9386 LB (41.8 KN)
GRATE AREA:	14.30 SQ FT (1.33 M²)
TOTAL WEIGHT:	58 TONS 12 CWT (59 T)
GAUGE:	1600 MM
ROAD NUMBER:	100

Q-class 0-6-0 No. 89 in a later form. (V/Line archives)

1873 VICTORIAN RAILWAYS

Q-class 0-6-0

In the 1870s Victoria's country rail route expansion was exceeding the overseas capacity to deliver locomotives, and the obvious answer was to build locomotives locally.

The head of VR's locomotive department, Bill Meikle, prepared two sets of drawings; one for No. 100, the 2-4-0 engine built in 1873 at Williamstown Railway Workshops (the subject of the previous story) and the other for what eventually became the railway's Q-class.

This was an 0-6-0 goods type, ten of which were built by the emerging Phoenix Foundry of Ballarat. All were delivered between April 1873 and February 1874, at a total contract price of £30,710.

The Q-class locomotives soon became entangled in controversy when the chief civil engineer of the day claimed they were causing serious track damage. This controversy culminated in a top-level government inquiry which, after exhaustive tests, found the Q-class locomotives to be good, solid engines and showed that the original trackwork had been inferior.

The Q-class originally boasted one handbrake, fitted to the tender, but steam brakes were subsequently provided to the fleet. Between 1896 and 1897, all engines received more reliable and new Westinghouse air equipment. Other modifications made during their lifetime included the provision of cab windows replacing their former cutaway cabs, and the raising of the tender sides to increase fuel capacity and thus extend their effective range.

Early duties for the class included turns over the Seymour, Bendigo and Wodonga main lines, the latter opening early in 1874. In fact, it has been

reported that a Q-class featured in the breaking-up of the notorious Ned Kelly gang at Glenrowan by working a special police train.

In February 1905, engines 85 and 93 were scrapped; the remaining engines quickly followed, with the exception of 95 and 97, which finished as stationary steam plants, and 99, which was sold to a private coal company. By October 1907, all had vanished from the VR engine register.

SPECIFICATIONS

	IMPERIAL (METRIC)
CYLINDERS:	16 x 24 IN (41 x 61 CM)
BOILER PRESSURE:	130 PSI (896 KPA)
COUPLED WHEELS:	4 FT 6 IN (137 CM)
GRATE AREA:	14.75 SQ FT (1.37 M²)
TRACTIVE EFFORT:	11 833 LB (52.7 KN)
TOTAL WEIGHT:	55 TONS (56.1 T)
GAUGE:	1600 MM
ROAD NUMBERS:	83–101 (ODD NUMBERS ONLY)

1874 VICTORIAN RAILWAYS

T-class 0-6-0

This class was introduced in June 1874, designed for VR main line goods and mixed traffic, and eventually totalled 23 locomotives.

Beyer, Peacock & Co delivered class-leader No. 125 and, upon its success, 18 more were ordered locally from the Phoenix Foundry of Ballarat, being delivered between September 1884 and February 1885. Although the original locomotive arrived with a 4-wheel tender, the local engines were fitted with 6-wheel vehicles to provide an extended fuel range.

Following their delivery, six of the class were based at the

The last locomotive of the T-class, 283, pictured outside Casterton engine shed in June 1910. (V/Line archives, author's collection)

Benalla and Ararat depots and a further four operated out of Stawell. The remainder were based at Ballarat, Seymour and Maryborough. In the 1889 renumbering system, these locomotives became the T-class.

Meanwhile, the privately built Deniliquin & Moama Railway of southern New South Wales, also built to the 1600 mm gauge, was opened in July 1876. The operators admired the VR 0-6-0s, and selected the T-class design for its own motive power needs. Beyer, Peacock & Co delivered two engines just before opening day, and another two shortly afterwards. Numbered 1 to 4, they were taken over by the VR along with the railway in December 1923. As all the engines were in very poor condition, three were scrapped during May 1925 and No. 3 was absorbed into the T-class numbering to become 96 on the VR system.

Reductions were also under way with the original T-class, following the sale of 279 to a South Australian rail-laying contractor in March 1915. Two more were scrapped the following year and although others followed, loco 267 was spared when it was sold to the northern Victorian shire council-owned Kerang & Koondrook Tramway in 1922. This locomotive, given the affectionate nickname 'Bucking Kate', was still in service when the line was taken over by the government in 1952.

Scrappings continued during the 1920s and by September 1927 only two remained in service (92 and 94, which had been renumbered in 1923). Their final years were spent pottering around the Newport powerhouse and they were both officially withdrawn in 1951. No. 94 was spared the scrapper's torch and placed in the ARHS's Newport Railway Museum.

SPECIFICATIONS

	IMPERIAL (METRIC)
CYLINDERS:	16½ × 20 IN (42 × 51 CM)
BOILER PRESSURE:	160 PSI (1102 KPA)
COUPLED WHEELS:	4 FT 3 IN (130 CM)
TRACTIVE EFFORT:	13 666 LB (60.8 KN)
GRATE AREA:	16 SQ FT (1.486 M²)
TOTAL WEIGHT:	55.7 TONS (56.8 T)
GAUGE:	1600 MM
ROAD NUMBERS:	(ORIGINAL) 125, 249–283 (ODD NUMBERS ONLY)
	(1923 NUMBERING) 90–92, 94 (LARGE GAPS DUE TO DISPOSALS)
	(DENILIQUIN & MOAMA ENGINES IN GOVERNMENT SERVICE) T1, T2 96 AND T4

1874 TASMANIAN MAIN LINE RAILWAY CO

Hunslet 4-6-0T

The Tasmanian Main Line Railway Co was formed in 1870 and became the second public railway in Tasmania, operating between Launceston and Hobart, a distance of 217 km. The line, which was laid to 1067 mm gauge, was opened for traffic in November 1876.

A wide-angle study of locomotive E+3 taken at Zeehan during the 1870s. (former Tasrail archives)

Although two construction locomotives had arrived from Fox Walker & Co at Bristol in 1872, additional and more powerful engines were required to work the regular services. In 1873 an order was placed with the Hunslet Engine Co, England, for eight mixed-traffic 4-6-0 tank locomotives and two passenger-type 4-4-0 tank engines.

The first three 4-6-0Ts arrived in July 1874 and were immediately placed into ballasting duties. But it was not long before problems arose due to their weight. As a result their side tanks were removed and they carried their water supply in three 1816 litre wooden tanks lashed to an open wagon hauled behind each locomotive as a tender. Only five such tenders were provided and the solid fuel continued to be carried in each locomotive's bunker.

Before all of the 4-6-0s were delivered, the sixth was withdrawn from the Tasmanian allotment by the railway's London-based promoters and re-directed in June 1874 to their Rio Tinto Railway project in Spain where it became that railway's No. 1. The Tasmanian 4-6-0Ts had all arrived by late November 1874.

Further trouble was found with these locomotives, with derailments a regular occurrence on the company's inadequately light 18 kg/m track. By 1875 they were converted to 4-4-0s by removing the original leading flangeless driving wheels. (One now has to wonder how the light trackwork stood up to the added axle load.)

In 1887, rebuilding commenced when No. 5 received a new boiler and enlarged 36 x 51 cm cylinders. Their weight was increased to 41.3 tonnes. Two years later, the ranks of the class were thinned when No. 3 was sold to the contractors of

the Devonport–Ulverstone line. Meanwhile, No. 6 entered construction work and was used on the Mole Creek branch.

In 1890, No. 2 was sold to the contractor engaged in the building of the Strahan–Zeehan line, leaving only four locomotives in actual service. On 1 October 1890, the Tasmanian government took over the assets of the Tasmanian Main Line Railway Co (as a means of connecting its then isolated branch lines) and the Hunslet locomotives were classified E+-class.

With the repurchase of No. 2 from the Zeehan line contractor in 1897, all numbers were subjected to a complicated reshuffle due to gaps resulting from earlier sales. In 1907, E+1 was transferred to the state's Public Works Department, followed by E+2 during 1910. Gradually, others followed and the last in service on the TGR was E+3, at Zeehan, which was sold for scrap in 1929 after it had been lying out of service for eight years.

The PWD engines saw further construction work, finally wearing themselves out and being sold for scrap in 1929. It has been reported that they were sold for £7 10s each.

SPECIFICATIONS

	IMPERIAL (METRIC)
CYLINDERS:	14 x 18 IN (36 x 46 CM)
BOILER PRESSURE:	140 PSI (965 KPA)
COUPLED WHEELS:	3 FT 6 IN (107 CM)
TRACTIVE EFFORT:	9408 LB (41.9 KN)
GRATE AREA:	11.25 SQ FT (1.045 M²)
TOTAL WEIGHT:	33 TONS (33.7 T)
GAUGE:	1067 MM
ROAD NUMBERS:	(TMLR CO) 1–7
	(TGR) E+1 TO E+5 (SOME SOLD PRIOR)

The J-class leader, No. 32, early in its 54-year career. (former SAR archives)

1875 SOUTH AUSTRALIAN RAILWAYS

J-class 0-6-0

Unlike most major Australian railways, the South Australian Railways employed only one 0-6-0 locomotive type. This design was introduced in England and used extensively in Australia and in other parts of the world. The NSWGR and VR staked virtually everything on 0-6-0s for a time and used them for both passenger and freight traffic.

It was only by chance that South Australia used this design. After Beyer, Peacock & Co had constructed a number of 0-6-0s for an Irish railway which could not accept delivery, the SAR purchased two of them. They arrived in April 1875.

At first they became the I-class but were reclassified shortly afterwards as J-class. The engines entered service over the Port Adelaide–Kapunda route, working both copper and wheat trains and sporting all the polished brass and copper of the period.

The Kapunda line had many stiff 1 in 62 grades, and the rather large 154 cm coupled wheels of the class were more akin to those of passenger engines. This meant that the locomotives' maximum load over this line was a rather uneconomical 200 tonnes.

Later, both locomotives were employed hauling heavy goods trains over the fairly level Adelaide–Port Adelaide route; when heavier rails were provided over the Terowie line, this further extended their range.

By 1888, both were in dire need of major overhauls and, while they were waiting to be shopped, were relegated to shunting duties only. The first engine was treated in September 1890 and the other some 14 months later. They were originally fitted with raised fireboxes, but while in the workshops were given flush top boiler/fireboxes. They continued in their original role until yet another rebuild became necessary in 1919 when, among a number of modifications, they received larger cabs.

Their last days were spent working cattle trains between Dry Creek and Terowie in addition to turns at shunting at Mile End yards. The first engine to be withdrawn was class-leader 32 in April 1929. No. 33 followed in October 1934.

SPECIFICATIONS

	IMPERIAL (METRIC)
CYLINDERS:	17 x 24 IN (43 x 61 CM)
BOILER PRESSURE:	130 PSI (896 KPA)
COUPLED WHEELS:	5 FT 0.5 IN (154 CM)
TRACTIVE EFFORT:	11 923 LB (53 KN)
GRATE AREA:	15 SQ FT (1.394 M²)
TOTAL WEIGHT:	48.2 TONS (49.2 T)
GAUGE:	1600 MM
ROAD NUMBERS:	32 AND 33

Beyer, Peacock-built 90 in original condition. This locomotive was converted to a 4-4-2 tank type in June 1897, remaining in service until August 1924, long enough to receive its final road number, 1305. (RailCorp archives)

1877 RAILWAYS OF NEW SOUTH WALES

(C) 79-class 4-4-0

This class finally totalled 68 engines and was the mainstay of the NSWGR's express and passenger operations for nearly 20 years. Designed by Beyer, Peacock & Co, it was largely an improved, heavier and more powerful (G)23-class 2-4-0 of 1865. A 4-wheel Bissell bogie was provided while an increased boiler pressure and smaller diameter coupled wheels provided 20 per cent greater tractive effort.

An initial order for 30 engines was placed, all entering traffic between 1877 and 1879. Dubs & Co constructed an additional 26, while in 1881 Beyer, Peacock & Co delivered a further four. With an ever-expanding network, the need for even more engines arose and the Sydney company Atlas Engineering hastily provided a further eight in 1882.

These locomotives were regarded as fast, efficient and trouble free, and trains as important as theSydney–Albury section of the *Melbourne Express* were regularly worked by them. During the early 1890s, however, the class was gradually displaced by larger Baldwin-built O-class 4-6-0s and Beyer, Peacock & Co P-class 4-6-0s. Many of these elderly 4-4-0s were then transferred onto pioneer-type branch lines.

Meanwhile, metropolitan passenger traffic was growing faster than new locomotives could be afford-ed and 20 of these (C)79-class 4-4-0s were converted into 4-4-2 tank locomotives between 1896 and 1902 at the Eveleigh Railway Workshops. With the arrival of 145 powerful purpose-built 4-6-4T S-class engines from 1903 onwards, the converted tank engines were again swept aside and transferred to

short tramway sections including Yass, Morpeth and Warren, while others found work over the Picton–Mittagong loop, the Border Loop school train and the Carlingford line.

In August 1907, locos 82 and 83 were sold to the East Greta Railway (later to become South Maitland Railway) for passenger service. They were both scrapped in 1935 after a fire destroyed all of that company's passenger vehicles.

In 1914 it was decided to convert all CC-class 4-4-2Ts back to tender engines for more useful branch line service. In February of that year loco 149 was sent to Eveleigh Workshops for conversion. It was stripped and its frame put under shears. At this time, five new C-class frames were being manufactured nearby and plans were formulated to shop other engines. However, the outbreak of World War I thwarted the idea so 149 and several other CC-class were stored until scrapped in the 1920s, the first to go being the stripped 149, on 5 January 1921.

Ashtonfields colliery at Thornton also had faith in the big-wheeled 4-4-2s and in 1922 purchased engine 87 for coal haulage. The company's faith was misplaced, however, because the veteran was too light on its feet and it was scrapped soon afterwards.

In the NSWGR's renumbering system of 1924, the 4-4-0 tender engines became the system's Z12-class and the remaining 4-4-2 tankers the Z13-class. Up until then the tender engines had been giving fine service in their branch line role but, with the electrification of Sydney suburban services from 1928, 77 S-class 4-6-4Ts became surplus and were gradually converted to tender C30T-class for branch line service. Time was now running out for the ageing 4-4-0s and withdrawals commenced in June 1930 with 1242. By 1938, no less than 23 tender engines

Then almost 75 years old, 4-4-0 No. 1210 looked in immaculate condition following yet another general overhaul and boiler change-out at Eveleigh Workshops in 1951. By then the old engine had long gained electric lighting for branch line use and a higher capacity 6-wheel tender discarded from an original P6 (C32)-class locomotive. This relic of the rails is today a prized active exhibit at the ARHS ACT Division museum in Canberra. (RailCorp archives)

had been cut up for scrap.

With the need to keep a handful of both classes for light mail and tramway service, further overhauls took place, and ten Z12s and eight Z13s managed to remain operational up until the mid-1950s and dieselisation.

Today, 1210 is preserved operational by the ACT Division of the ARHS. This locomotive had sat on a plinth outside Canberra railway station for a quarter of a century until re-steamed in 1988 as a Commonwealth Bicentennial project. No. 1219, the last engine actually in revenue service, is on display at Thirlmere Railway Museum. No. 1243, which was retained in pristine condition by the NSW Railways well into full dieselisation, saw many years of service with special Vintage Train services and is today exhibited at Sydney's Powerhouse Museum.

Of the Z13 class, 1307 remained in service shunting wagons at the Clyde Railway Workshop until June 1972. No. 1301, which saw many years of Vintage Train service, today languishes in the Thirlmere Railway Museum with its rather derelict

sister engine 1308. After spending several decades at that museum also, 1307 was transferred to the Yass Station railway museum on 2 December 1999 for exhibition. This loco had spent many years running the Yass Town branch.

SPECIFICATIONS

	IMPERIAL (METRIC)
CYLINDERS:	18 x 24 IN (46 x 61 CM)
BOILER PRESSURE:	140 PSI (965 KPA)
COUPLED WHEELS:	5 FT 6 IN (168 CM)
TRACTIVE EFFORT:	13 196 LB (58.7 KN)
GRATE AREA:	14.75 SQ FT (1.37 M²)
TOTAL WEIGHT:	Z12-CLASS 59.5 TONS (60.7 T)
	Z13-CLASS 52 TONS (53 T)
GAUGE:	1435 MM
ROAD NUMBERS:	(ORIGINAL) 79–92, 118–126, 143–157, 165–182, 27N, 30N, 37N–39N, 47N–51N
	(1924 TENDER ENGINES) 1201–1248
	(1924 TANK ENGINES) 1301–1316

One of Australia's oldest working locomotives, the fastidiously maintained and nurtured 4-4-0 No. 1210, gallops away from Joppa Junction with a Bicentennial year tourist train. (Leon Oberg)

Class-leader C79 at Yass Town soon after its December 1896 conversion as a CC79-class 2-4-2 tank engine. In the 1924 renumbering system it became 1301. (Author's collection)

1877 Victorian Railways

H-class 4-4-0

These eight nimble-looking 4-4-0s, built by the Phoenix Foundry at Ballarat to a classic British-inspired design, entered service between September 1877 and June 1878. Intended for main line passenger service, this locomotive type was the last on the Victorian Railways to receive 4-wheel tenders.

They were shopped for rebuilding between June 1885 and March 1891, at which time they were given new boilers. All eight became the H-class under the VR's 1889 renumbering system.

Displaced from main line passenger service by the ever increasing D and A classes, the H-class found further employment working less important short-distance commuter services. Some also worked branch line trains for a time.

Although two locomotives were further rebuilt early in 1904, no more were shopped due to the resounding success of the new DD-class 4-6-0 pattern engine 560 and the subsequent introduction of many of this type. Scrapping of the H-class commenced in March 1905 with 154, followed five months later by two sister engines.

All of the class had vanished by July 1911 with the exception of 150, which was sold in May 1909 to the Trawalla & Waterloo Tramway. This engine later came under the ownership of a South Australian railway contractor and was noted lying in poor repair at Mile End Railway Workshops as late as 1922, possibly waiting cutting up.

SPECIFICATIONS

IMPERIAL (METRIC)

CYLINDERS:	15 x 22 IN (38 x 56 CM)
BOILER PRESSURE:	130 PSI (896 KPA)
COUPLED WHEELS:	5 FT 0 IN (152 CM)
TRACTIVE EFFORT:	8580 LB (38.6 KN)
TOTAL WEIGHT:	48 TONS (49T)
GAUGE:	1600 MM
ROAD NUMBERS:	146–160 (EVEN NUMBERS ONLY)

The dainty lines of the VR's H-class are evident in this period portrait of a new class member. (V/Line archives, author's collection)

A rather shabby W221 standing outside Bendigo workshops. As an historic aside, this was the first of the class to be fitted with Westinghouse air braking in April 1889. (J.C. Rolland, Whalley collection)

1877 VICTORIAN RAILWAYS

W and S classes 4-6-0

While Australian government railway operators based their initial operations on British steam locomotive practice, most also experimented with US products. They were largely lured by cost and often simplicity, albeit in a lighter chassis construction but one able to softly tread the sometimes indifferent tracks in the colonies.

Victorian Railways started its association with US products in 1877 when it imported two classic 4-4-0 engines for passenger service from the Rogers Locomotive Works of Patterson, New Jersey. Boasting bar frames and 5 ft 0 in (152 cm) coupled wheels and weighing 58 tons (59.1 tonnes), the duo became the system's D-class. Proving rather too light for the job, they were relegated to the unclassed listings in 1888 and eventually scrapped in 1907.

VR again turned to North America when needing powerful freight locomotives, taking delivery of 12 long-boilered 4-6-0 locomotives from the Baldwin Locomotive Works during 1879–83. Weighing just 1 tonne more than the earlier D-class, but much more useful with 130 cm coupled wheels, these locomotives became the railway's W-class. A novel feature was the unusual 6-wheel tenders which employed a leading fixed axle and a trailing bogie arrangement.

Working to the basic W-class plans, another US-styled locomotive type soon followed, this one built locally in the productive Ballarat-based Phoenix Foundry's workshops from 1883. Boasting slightly smaller cylinders, extended smokeboxes (a feature soon afterwards given to the W-class) and 122 cm driving wheels, these ten locomotives, which were also equipped with the above locomotives' tender type, became known as the S-class.

Of particular interest was the last locomotive in the S-class, S197, which in 1908 was rebuilt as a W-class, lasting in that form until scrapped in 1926. Its S-class brethren were scrapped between 1904 and 1908 after

S207 stands in Boort station with a mixed train very early in its career. (V/Line archives, Len Whalley collection)

working principally in the Maryborough district.

The W-class, with their unflanged leading coupled wheels, was flexible enough to work the far-flung branch lines, in particular the Mildura, Warburton and Orbost lines. Others were to be found working Korumburra coal trains.

The first W-class scrapped was 253 in June 1924, while three lingered on until June 1926.

SPECIFICATIONS

	W-CLASS	S-CLASS
	IMPERIAL (METRIC)	IMPERIAL (METRIC)
CYLINDERS:	16 x 24 IN (38 x 61 CM)	15 x 24 IN (38 x 61 CM)
BOILER PRESSURE:	130 PSI (896 KPA)*	130 PSI (896 KPA)
COUPLED WHEELS:	4 FT 3 IN (122 CM)	4 FT 0IN (122 CM)
TRACTIVE EFFORT:	12 400 LB (55.3 KN)	11 700 LB (52.6 KN)
GRATE AREA:	18.26 SQ FT (1.701 M²)	18.26 SQ FT (1.701 M²)
TOTAL WEIGHT:	58 TONS (58.8 T)	56 TONS (56.5 T)
GAUGE:	1600 MM	1600 MM
ROAD NUMBERS:	153, 155, 217–235	197–215 (ODD NUMBERS) 197
	ODD NUMBERS, AND 197	CONVERTED TO W-CLASSODD

* PRESSURES RAISED TO 140 PSI (965 KPA) FROM 1907

1877 RAILWAYS OF NEW SOUTH WALES

(A) 93-class 0-6-0

These classic locomotives became one of the longest-living types on the Australian railway scene, one being out-shopped as late as December 1970 after an extensive overhaul. Introduced as the 93-class, the initial order consisted of 18 engines which were a basic improvement of the 1865-vintage 17-class 0-6-0s built by Robert Stephenson & Co.

All were ordered for freight service and, as the railway network was growing at an unprecedented rate at that time with the Albury, Hay and Jerilderie routes under construction in the south, Mudgee and Bourke in the west and Narrabri and Glen Innes in the north, further orders and purchases from contractors found 78 in service by January 1890.

Builders included Beyer, Peacock & Co (59), Henry Vale of Sydney (18) and Robert Stephenson & Co (2). One of these, No. 103, had been written off following a violent collision near Emu Plains in January 1878. Robert Stephenson & Co built a new engine to replace it.

In the state-wide renumbering scheme of 1889, these locomotives became the A93-class.

Until 1891, all engines had open cabs but in that year a start was made on fitting new steel cabs, which was a welcome relief to crews working over the blustery New England and Southern Highlands routes. Seven years later the entire class began entering workshops for new Belpaire boilers of 70 kPa increased pressure.

From 1896 the arrival of heavier 2-8-0 T-class freight engines for main line goods service saw the elderly 0-6-0s reduced to secondary roles and to coal service in the Newcastle area. Fourteen redundant locomotives were converted into 2-6-4 tank engines for coal and mineral haulage. These were rebuilt at the Eveleigh Railway Workshops between April 1902 and February 1910, where they joined 12 similar engines constructed new in 1890–91 by Beyer, Peacock & Co.

These and a further seven built new at the Eveleigh Railway Workshops in 1911 became the Z20-class in 1924, while the original tender engines became the Z19-class.

Battling on in their coal traffic role, the tender

A rare recent find is this image showing an A-class with ex-Baldwin bogie tender engaged in the construction of the Dorrigo line in 1924. (John Dymock family collection)

Sporting a cutaway steel cab and bogie tender for use over the Oberon line, 1942 filled in time shunting in Bathurst on 6 July 1962. (Leon Oberg)

Bent and bruised after a lifetime of hard work, 2029 was one of seven 2-6-4Ts built new at Eveleigh to the basic 'AE' design. This one was seeing out its final days shunting the Liverpool area. (Graham Cotterall)

version was replaced by the T-class from the 1920s. Withdrawals followed with no fewer than 18 retired during 1929–31. This grew to 24 engines by 1933 and, with the earlier sale of two, only 36 tender engines remained in service.

Despite the subsequent arrival of more modern power, the 19-class was considered powerful enough for shunting and light enough for coal stage and dock area work. Overhauls therefore continued and a number were even fitted with bogie Baldwin tenders for the working of the abnormally steep and curvy Batlow and Oberon lines. In fact, no other class of locomotive was permitted over these routes until dieselisation came in 1962 and 1963.

In the meantime, the Z20-class tank engines had been relegated to light Newcastle and Sydney suburban service and worked into Morpeth,

Carlingford, Camden and Kurrajong. In addition, others were put to work shunting the Port Kembla network.

Although seven of the converted engines were sold to industry during the 1930s, withdrawals had commenced as early as 1930. The last tank convert in service was 2010, which retired in February 1965. Loco 2029, one of the later Eveleigh batch built from new materials, survives today in the NSWRTM's Thirlmere Railway Museum collection.

Scrapping of the tender engines started again in 1962, their last duties being shunters at the Darling Harbour and Newcastle district yards. The last engines, 1904 and 1923, remained operational at Port Waratah up until August 1972 and both have been conserved at the Dorrigo Steam Railway and Museum. No. 1919 is preserved operational at

Believe it or not, this bulky-looking saddle-tank locomotive was once A-class 0-6-0 tender engine 99. Sold to BHP Newcastle works in 1915, it became that company's No. 6 engine, remaining in service until 1961. (BHP)

the neighbouring Glenreagh Mountain Railway while 1905 is exhibited at the Thirlmere Railway Museum.

SPECIFICATIONS

	ORIGINAL 93-CLASS	Z20-CLASS
	IMPERIAL (METRIC)	IMPERIAL (METRIC)
CYLINDERS:	18 x 24 IN (46 x 61 CM)	18 x 24 IN (46 x 61 CM)
BOILER PRESSURE:	140 PSI (965 KPA)	150 PSI (1034 KPA)
COUPLED WHEELS:	4 FT 0 IN (122 CM)	4 FT 0 IN (122 CM)
TRACTIVE EFFORT:	18 144 LB (80.7 KN)	19 440 LB (86.5 KN)
GRATE AREA:	17.9 SQ FT (1.663 M²)	17.9 SQ FT (1.663 M²)
TOTAL WEIGHT:	56.6 TONS (57.7 T)	57.4 TONS (58.6 T)
GAUGE: 1435 MM	1435 MM	
ROAD NUMBERS:	(ORIGINAL 32N, 35N, 40N, 42N–44N. 46N, 1–6, 93 97, 99–104, 106, 107, 109–117, 142, 164, 183, 184, 187–190, 192–196, 198–204, 291, 369–372, 385–387 (1924 TENDER ENGINES) 1901–1960 (1924 TANK ENGINES), 2001–2026 (2027–2033 BUILT NEW)	

1878 SOUTH AUSTRALIAN RAILWAYS

W-class 2-6-0

Just as diesel locomotive builders today can offer a basic design to suit a particular railway's need, so Beyer, Peacock & Co had developed a highly successful inclined-cylinder 2-6-0 steam type for pioneer and light railway service in the nineteenth century.

These simple engines entered service in a number of places around the world, and were introduced to Australian conditions by the SAR in February 1878 as its W-class. Two, ordered for the 1067 mm gauge Port Pirie to Jamestown line, constituted the initial order and were an immediate success. Further orders were placed and by December 1883 a total of 35 had been listed on the SAR's books although, because sales of some to rail-laying contractors had begun, not all were available for service at any one time. The SAR later repurchased some of them.

The WAGR administration had been watching the W-class with interest and subsequently ordered nine for the Fremantle–Perth line then under construction. Deliveries started in 1880, one of them working the first passenger train over the route in March 1881.

The WAGR locomotives became the A-class and saw service over much of the state's expanding rail system. An additional three 2-6-0s came under WAGR's ownership, two of which were Beyer, Peacock & Co engines called *Day Dawn* and *Mt Magnet*. The former had started its career as W43 on the SAR but had been sold to the rail-laying contractors, Baxter & Saddler, for the construction of the WAGR Mullewa–Cue line. In 1886, it was stored at Geraldton before coming into government service.

Mt Magnet had been operated by the contractors Baxter & Prince and was later sold to the Western Australian PWD, coming under railway ownership in 1898.

The two named engines were never given road numbers and both were sold in 1900 to the Goldfields Firewood Supply Co, operators of a lengthy light railway near Kalgoorlie.

The third 2-6-0 built to this general design was erected by Dubs & Co for a Western Australian rail construction firm. The WAGR bought it in October 1892 and this swelled class numbers to twelve.

The introduction of larger locomotives saw the A-class generally relegated to the light branch lines, jetty and general shunting duties. No. 15 was fitted with a new boiler early in 1921 but no further reboilering was carried out until September 1948, when both 10 and 11 were so fitted during a heavy overhaul.

However, their ranks were beginning to thin with further sales to timber milling interests. No. 4 went to Buckingham Bros in April 1920. The Australian Lumber Co bought No. 3 two years later (but sold it back to WAGR in March 1925). Eleven years later it was again sold, this time to Whittaker Bros.

Dubs-built WAGR A-class 31, in its later form. (former Westrail archives)

The first engine actually to be written off in Western Australia was 16, in December 1939. No more were withdrawn until 10 and 11 were stopped in January 1955. No. 11 was subsequently saved from the scrapper's torch and placed on display at South Perth Zoo. Thirty years later it was removed to the ARHS's Bassendean Rail Transport Museum.

The last engine in service in Western Australia was 21, written off as late as May 1958. It must also be recorded that 15, last used as a jetty shunter at Bunbury, has been preserved at that location.

Back in South Australia, all W-class engines had become due for reboilering by the early 1900s and, although four were scrapped and some rebuilt to their original specifications, 16 were given higher power 999 kPa boilers between 1903 and 1912. These became the Wx-class.

Other unrebuilt engines were sold to contractors all over the country. They helped to build sections of the North Australia and Central Australia railways as well as South Australian government lines. While

some were repurchased, others were sold to Western Australian interests (as already mentioned) and in 1911 three were taken over by the Commonwealth Railways to work the North Australia Railway. These became that owner's Nf-class. Four more followed in 1916–17, from which three locomotives were made serviceable.

While Nf6 was blown into Darwin harbour during the first Japanese air raid on 19 February 1942 (and never salvaged), all Commonwealth-owned engines had been withdrawn by the close of World War II. Today, an engine bearing the number plates Nf2 (believed to be actually Nf5) has been restored to operating condition by the Pine Creek Community Government Council's tourist railway project (being part of a mining, Aboriginal and Chinese culture museum). Prior to that it was a museum piece in Darwin.

While most of the South Australian locomotives were condemned during the 1920s, four remained in traffic until the 1950s, the last engine, Wx18, being replaced by diesels over the Naracoorte–Kingston

An early glass-plate image of a WAGR A-class with tiny 4-wheel tender, a spark-arrester chimney and Salter-type safety valves. (former Westrail archives)

line in 1959. After lying in 'preservation' at Naracoorte for some decades, the relic was still undergoing full working restoration by the Quorn-based Pichi Richi Railway when this book closed for press.

SPECIFICATIONS

SAR W-CLASS/CR NF-CLASS

IMPERIAL (METRIC)

CYLINDERS:	12 x 20 IN (30 x 51 CM)
BOILER PRESSURE:	130 PSI (896 KPA)
COUPLED WHEELS:	3 FT 3 IN (99 CM)
TRACTIVE EFFORT:	7680 LB (34.2 KN)
GRATE AREA:	9.7 SQ FT (0.901 M²)
TOTAL WEIGHT:	29.18 TONS (29.8 T)
GAUGE:	1067 MM
ROAD NUMBERS:	(SAR) 13–43, 53–56 (NO. 22 CARRIED TWICE) (CR) 2–7

SAR WX-CLASS

IMPERIAL (METRIC)

CYLINDERS:	12 x 20 IN (30 x 51 CM)
BOILER PRESSURE:	145 PSI (999 KPA)
COUPLED WHEELS:	3 FT 3 IN (99 CM)
TRACTIVE EFFORT:	8566 LB (38.1 KN)
GRATE AREA:	9.7 SQ FT (0.901 M²)
TOTAL WEIGHT:	31.5 TONS (32.1 T)
GAUGE:	1067 MM
ROAD NUMBERS:	15, 17–20, 25, 26, 28, 29, 31, 33, 34, 37, 39, 40 AND 56

WAGR A-CLASS

IMPERIAL (METRIC)

CYLINDERS:	12 x 20 IN (30 x 51 CM)
BOILER PRESSURE:	120 PSI (827 KPA)
COUPLED WHEELS:	3 FT 3 IN (99 CM)
TRACTIVE EFFORT:	7089 LB (31.6 KN)
GRATE AREA:	9.7 SQ FT (0.901 M²)
TOTAL WEIGHT:	29.5 TONS (30.1 T)
GAUGE:	1067 MM
ROAD NUMBERS:	35, 7, 10, 11, 15, 16, 21, 31, DAY DAWN AND MT MAGNET

E-class 2-4-4-2T Double Fairlie

Western Australia's railway history started with the construction of a light private timber line extending from Lockville into nearby forests, opened in 1871.

The following year another timber line opened between Rockingham and Jarrahdale but it was not until 26 July 1879 that the people of Western Australia saw the first government line opened, after nearly five years of construction. This line, some 53 km long, ran between Geraldton and Northampton and was built to assist the lead and copper mining industries of the area.

Using lightweight 17 kg/m wrought iron rails, the railway traversed unusually hilly country and, not surprisingly, boasted many tight curves. To work the traffic over this line, two Double Fairlie 2-4-4-2T locomotives were ordered from the Avonside Engineering Co in England. They arrived early in 1879 carrying the E-class numbers 1 and 2.

A feature of their design was the special radial movement of each 2-wheeled pony axlebox. To all intents and purposes, they were a semi-articulated design, a necessity for the terrain that they had to negotiate.

Although not favourites with their crews, these locomotives remained on the Northampton line until 1885 when E.2 was transferred to Fremantle in poor condition. Soon afterwards, it was sold to Mr M.C. Davis of Karridale.

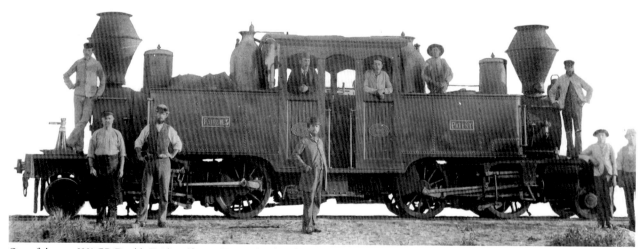

One of the two WAGR Double Fairlies. (former Westrail archives)

E.1 was also wearing out and in 1892 it too was transferred to Fremantle and, with the exception of its twin boilers and some other parts, was cut up. One boiler of this engine, one engine unit and pony axle were used in the construction of a New F-class 2-4-2 tank locomotive in 1893. It was not a success but was sold to the Public Works Department in 1901. The remaining boiler from E.1 was utilised to drive overhead shafting at the Fremantle Railway Workshops.

Fairlie locomotives were never a success in this country. In general, wherever they operated they were withdrawn after only a few years in service.

SPECIFICATIONS

	IMPERIAL (METRIC)
CYLINDERS:	(4) 10 x 18 IN (25 x 46 CM)
BOILER PRESSURE:	120 PSI (827 KPA)
COUPLED WHEELS:	3 FT 3 IN (99 CM)
TRACTIVE EFFORT:	8861 LB (39.4 KN)
GRATE AREA:	13 SQ FT (1.208 M²)
TOTAL WEIGHT:	33.9 TONS (34.6 T)
GAUGE:	1067 MM
ROAD NUMBERS:	E.I AND E.2 (LATER RENUMBERED 20 AND 7 RESPECTIVELY)

R-class 0-6-0

The VR ordered an 0-6-0 from Beyer, Peacock & Co as a pattern 'all lines' mixed-traffic engine, which was delivered in May 1879. After it had run successful trials, 55 additional engines were ordered from the local firm, the Phoenix Foundry. They were delivered between 1881 and 1886. The local locomotives differed from the pattern engine in that they were equipped with timber cabs instead of the former's open type cab.

Highly regarded among the crews, the class soon received the affectionate nickname 'Bulldogs', a name they carried to the end because of their ruggedness and reliability.

All became the VR's R-class in the late 1880s renumbering system, but in official circles they were known as the 'Old R-class' following the delivery of five similar Belgian-built 0-6-0s which were also classified 'R'.

Three additional 'Old R-class' were progressively absorbed into VR stock in 1888, 1893 and 1894. These locos, imported from Beyer, Peacock & Co by rail-building contractors, featured the English cutaway cab seen on the original pattern engine. They were numbered with the original class, becoming Nos. 11, 13 and 443.

This class of engine excelled and was used in all types of service, from branch line mixed to main line freight traffic, from shunting duty and even medium

An early view of 'Old R-class' engine 151 showing its cutaway cab. (V/Line archives, Len Whalley collection)

passenger haulage. As such they could be seen over the entire system at one time or another.

No. 161 received an Austin's patent spark arrestor and then an extended smokebox early in its career, while three were equipped for wood fuel burning. From March 1907, almost all were reboilered with high pressure E-class boilers which increased their tractive effort by about 13.4 kN.

Scrapping commenced in 1915 and by 1919 eleven had vanished. A further 33 were cut up during the 1920s and the last engine, 317, was scrapped in September 1944 after many years of shunting at the Newport powerhouse.

SPECIFICATIONS

	ORIGINAL	REBUILT FORM
	IMPERIAL (METRIC)	IMPERIAL (METRIC)
CYLINDERS:	17 x 24 IN (43 x 61 CM)	17½ x 24 IN (45 x 61 CM)
BOILER PRESSURE:	130 PSI (896 kPA)	150 PSI (1034 kPA)
COUPLED WHEELS:	4 FT 6 IN (132 CM)	4 FT 6 IN (132 CM)
TRACTIVE EFFORT:	13 358 LB (59.4 kN)	16 333 LB (72.7 kN)
GRATE AREA:	16.5 SQ FT (1.533 M²)	16.5 SQ FT (1.533 M²)
TOTAL WEIGHT:	57.25 TONS (58.4 T)	61.17 TONS (62.4 T)
GAUGE:	1600 MM 1600 MM	
ROAD NUMBERS:	(ORIGINAL) 11, 13, 151, 157–195, 285–351, 443 (ODD NUMBERS ONLY)	
	(1923 NUMBERING) ALL REMAINING ENGINES NUMBERED BELOW 300 WERE THEN RENUMBERED ABOVE 300—EVEN NUMBERS ONLY.	

1879 AUSTRALIAN KEROSENE OIL & MINERAL CO

Barclay 0-4-0 / 0-6-0ST

During the latter part of the nineteenth century, an isolated valley in the NSW Southern Highlands flourished on the shale oil, coal and fruit it produced. The catalyst in this enterprise was the Scottish-inspired Australian Kerosene Oil & Mineral Co, incorporated in 1878. The company introduced large-scale production techniques to its operation deep inside the Joadja Valley. Its kerosene, candles and other products supplied the Australian marketplace with goods that, until then, had to be imported.

A town sprang up inside the remote valley to cater for the company's eventual 2000-strong workforce. Until a railway and 600 ft (183 m) incline was built, everything had to be brought in (and out) by horse or bullock team.

Initially, the company could only obtain the

right to construct a 1067 mm gauge railway as far as the Wombeyan Caves road, a distance of about 10 kilometres. (Property owners were reluctant to allow locomotives, with their showers of sparks, access to their land.) The skips laden with shale and coal were drawn to this point by horse and then had to be unloaded into wagons which were hauled the remainder of the distance to the government rail head at Mittagong.

The passing of the Joadja Creek Railway Act late in 1878 allowed the company to construct a railway over private land and in November 1880 the valley was linked directly to Mittagong with a 27 km line.

Allied to the cross-country haul railway, the company constructed about 16 route kilometres of railway inside the valley, linking the mining activity with the retorts, an orchard and other industry.

In June 1879, the first of an eventual four steam locomotives arrived from the Scottish firm Andrew Barclay & Co of Kilmarnock. While this one and the third to arrive were of 0-6-0ST configuration, they varied slightly in appointments, cab profile and leading dimensions. The second and fourth locos were built as 0-4-0ST and were generally confined to the valley network. Again, these two varied in leading dimensions—for instance, the first possessed 18 x 38 cm cylinders whereas the last one was provided with 25 x 46 cm cylinders, identical to later 0-6-0ST deliveries.

Although the trains were nominally freight carriers, a passenger carriage was provided each Tuesday and Friday. On other days, anyone making the trip had to ride on the engine or freight vehicles.

Industrial problems through much of the 1890s marked the beginning of the end for the company. Although from 1899 mining did not justify the maintenance of the railway, the company battled on until it was forced to close on 3 October 1903, following the collapse of the Australian oil market due to cheap imports from the USA. The fate of the enterprise was sealed two years afterwards when a serious bushfire destroyed many buildings and the company's records. Within a few years, most saleable items, including the railway, locomotives and wagons, were taken to Mittagong and auctioned.

All were acquired by northern NSW timber companies. No. 1 went to the Coffs Harbour Timber Co and given a home-made tender; No. 2 was acquired by H.E. Day of Bonville, converted into an 0-4-0 and also provided with a tender; No. 3 saw service at the British Australian Timber Co at Boambe and No. 4

The first of the four 0-6-0ST locomotives with a train poised to depart the top of the Joadja incline for Mittagong. Passengers often braved the sometimes raw Southern Highlands elements and rode on the loaded trucks. (Leonie Knapman collection)

was snapped up by Allan Taylor for his Mayer's Point (Port Stephens) mill and in fact was the last of the type to see service, being withdrawn in 1948. Some parts still remain in the undergrowth there.

SPECIFICATIONS

(THE MOST COMMON 0-6-0ST)

	IMPERIAL (METRIC)
CYLINDERS:	10 x 18 IN (25 x 46 CM)
BOILER PRESSURE:	140 PSI (965 KPA)
COUPLED WHEELS:	3 FT 0 IN (91 CM)
TRACTIVE EFFORT:	5600 LB (50.5 KN)
TOTAL WEIGHT:	APPROX. 18 TONS (18.3 T)
GAUGE:	1067 MM
ROAD NUMBERS:	1–4

1880 RAILWAYS & TRAMWAYS OF
NEW SOUTH WALES

(Q) 158-class 4-4-0T

With the expansion of Sydney suburban rail services in the late 1870s, extra engines were needed and an order was placed with Beyer, Peacock & Co in England for six 4-4-0 tank locomotives. These small engines,

which entered traffic between July and September 1880, were reported to have been intended for the Isle of Wight Railway but were unsuitable for that line due to their heavy coupled-wheel axle loads.

Similar problems arose in New South Wales and the chief mechanical engineer of the day, William Thow, recommended in 1889 that they all be converted to 4-4-0 tender engines. Meanwhile, newer F and R class tank locomotives had arrived for suburban work, releasing some of the old 4-4-0Ts for the Newcastle and Wollongong suburban services.

Despite Thow's thoughts on the unsuitability of the Q-class, no changes were made. However, a serious suburban train derailment at Sydenham in 1901, for which an F-class engine was blamed, saw all of those steeds banned from suburban working.

The progressive arrival of larger 4-6-4T S-class locomotives from 1903 once more saw the elderly Q-class returned to both Newcastle and Wollongong workings. Shortly afterwards, loco 163 disgraced itself at Thornton when its boiler exploded.

As loads expanded beyond the Q-class's capabilities, Mr Thow's conversion idea finally became a reality, although by then the system's rails were heavier and axle loadings were not a real issue. In February 1910, No. 162 emerged from Eveleigh Railway Workshops as a tender engine. Within

158-class No. 159 as originally delivered. (RailCorp archives)

a matter of months, all six of this class had been similarly treated. However, they were not destined to last long, for in October 1912 four were sold to the newly created Commonwealth Railways to act as railway construction engines. The remaining two followed three months later.

Under Commonwealth ownership, the locomotives became D-class but retained their NSWGR road numbers. Life as tender engines was short for some; in 1921, No. 159 was withdrawn, followed by another four in 1926. The last engine in service was 162, which was finally withdrawn at Port Augusta in July 1943 after years of shunting service. It joined its rust-streaked associates (and other withdrawn CR steam locomotives) at Port Augusta's locomotives graveyard, where they were all scrapped during the early 1950s, their boilers blown apart by dynamite.

SPECIFICATIONS

	IMPERIAL (METRIC)
CYLINDERS:	16 x 24 IN (41 x 61 CM)
BOILER PRESSURE:	140 PSI (965 KPA)
COUPLED WHEELS:	5 FT 0 IN (152 CM)
TRACTIVE EFFORT:	11 469 LB (51 KN)
GRATE AREA:	14.75 SQ FT (1.37 M²)
TOTAL WEIGHT:	40 TONS (40.7 T)
TENDER TYPE:	59 TONS (60.2 T)
GAUGE:	1435 MM
ROAD NUMBERS:	(BOTH SYSTEMS) 158–163

1881 SOUTH AUSTRALIAN RAILWAYS

X-class 2-6-0

South Australian Railways ordered eight lightweight 2-6-0 locomotives in 1880 from US builder, The Baldwin Locomotive Works, for use over several of its northern-area narrow gauge lines. It was a type identical to locomotives running on the Denver South Park & Pacific Railroad in the USA.

The first engine, 44, was issued to traffic over the Port Wakefield Division on 21 April 1881. This section of track had been built to serve the district's early wheat farmers. No. 48 was made operational two months later and sent to the Port Augusta Division, where it was used through the formidable Flinders Ranges, running as far north as Farina (then Government Gums).

Gradually the rest were assembled and the last to be commissioned was 50, on 17 June 1882. At that stage, two were working over the Port Wakefield route, two were attached to the Port Pirie Division and the remaining four were at Port Augusta.

Some were used later that decade in the construction of the Cockburn line, a route over which the emerging Broken Hill Proprietary Company was to transport its rich ore to the Port Pirie smelters. After the line was commissioned, linking up with the 56 km Silverton Tramway, some X-class locomotives were assigned to Petersburg (now Peterborough) to work trains. Contemporary accounts even mention how the little Baldwin locomotives actually border-hopped, working trains in and out of Broken Hill.

Class members remained virtually as built, although 48 was experimentally fitted with an extended smokebox for test-burning of Leigh Creek coal. This coal had always been unsuitable for locomotives because of its extremely high ash content. Renowned locomotive historian, the late Gifford Eardley, reported that on one test there were some anxious moments when it was noticed that several wagons had been set alight by the stream of sparks emitted from the loco's chimney.

The first recorded withdrawal was on 29 December 1896, when 49 was sold to West Australian timber millers Millar Bros. This company soon dispensed with the locomotive's US-style balloon chimney stack, substituting a flared stovepipe variety. Now named *Grafter*, its appearance was further altered with the fabrication of a new steel cab and a 'plough' type cowcatcher. This locomotive was withdrawn during the 1930s and eventually scrapped in 1942.

The remaining SAR engines were condemned during the 1900s, five going in December 1904 and the last in April 1907. Several of their bogie tenders were retained for some decades as water carriers.

SPECIFICATIONS

	IMPERIAL (METRIC)
CYLINDERS:	14½ x 18 IN (37 x 46 CM)
BOILER PRESSURE:	130 PSI (896 KPA)
COUPLED WHEELS:	3 FT 2 IN (97 CM)
TRACTIVE EFFORT:	10 358 LB (46.1 KN)
GRATE AREA:	14.57 SQ FT (1.354 M²)
TOTAL WEIGHT:	39 TONS 9 CWT (40 T)
GAUGE:	1067 MM
ROAD NUMBERS:	44–51 (NO. 49 BECAME GRAFTER AT MILLARS)

(B) 205-class 2-6-0

Although large numbers of British-built A93-class and American-type freight locomotives had been placed in service, the need for additional freight power continued as NSWGR rail construction projects continued at an ever-increasing pace.

Accordingly, an order was placed with Beyer, Peacock & Co in 1880 for 20 Mogul 2-6-0 freight locomotives. They arrived between January and May 1882.

These engines were quickly seen to be free steamers and powerful for their day, and no fewer than 77 were finally acquired. Their lumbering gait was felt in almost every corner of the state. One of their main stamping grounds was the rugged 1 in 33 Blue Mountains railway. They were gradually superseded over that route from 1896 with the arrival of the larger and heavier T-class 2-8-0 type locomotives.

Originally equipped with round-top fireboxes and open cabs, all were gradually rebuilt from 1902 with raised Belpaire boilers. Some were even provided with enclosed wooden cabs and square side windows. Others received steel cabs with cutaway side look-outs.

With the aforementioned arrival of the T-class 2-8-0s, the B-class found useful employment over the further flung portions of the state's main lines, eventually moving onto lighter branch lines and Newcastle coal traffic as additional classes of new goods power arrived.

In the NSWGR's 1924 renumbering scheme, this locomotive type became the Z25-class.

Apart from boilers and cabs, very few modific-

An official Baldwin Locomotive Works photograph of B-class 2-6-0 No. 45. (Author's collection)

One of the later Beyer, Peacock deliveries displaying a refined steel-sided cutaway cab. No. 328 was renumbered 2565 in NSWGR's 1924 renumbering system, the engine lasting in service until May 1932. (Ron Drummond collection)

ations were made to these engines during their lifetime. Some received electric lighting, many received repositioned injector feed valves, and they were all fitted with Westinghouse air equipment when it became available. In 1923, two engines (2531 and 2534) were experimentally fitted with superheaters and the necessary extended smokeboxes for operation out of Cowra depot. Although no further engines were treated in this way, at least two others (2501 and 2540) were given extended smokeboxes to relieve lower tube blockages.

Superheating gave locomotive departments greater economy for it was discovered that the expansion property of steam was greater the hotter (drier) it became. Accordingly, drier steam could perform more work than 'cooler' (wet) steam. The superheater consisted of small tubes which were encased inside specially designed, larger than normal fire tubes high inside the boilers. Although remaining at its correct pressure, the superheated steam was able to reach the cylinders devoid of most of its water content at temperatures of 650° F, or 3.27 cubic feet per pound, instead of the 'saturated' temperature of about 365° F.

Owing to this increased volume of steam and the elimination of cylinder condensation, railways found water and coal savings of up to 35 and 25 per cent respectively could be obtained with superheated locomotives.

During the Depression years many of the 25-class fell into derelict condition after becoming due for overhaul. While some of these were used on the testing of the Sydney Harbour Bridge in 1932, no less than 58 were scrapped during the 1930s. However, some were saved and repaired and saw

The 25-class in its final form with electric headlight, square-windowed timber cab, Belpaire boiler and increased capacity tender. The last one in government service, 2532, stands in Harden station with a Boorowa-bound train on 1 April 1962. (Leon Oberg)

The class-leader of the six-member 255-class, shown in original condition. All were rebuilt in 1901–02 with more efficient square-topped Belpaire boilers. In 1924, this locomotive was renumbered 1501, remaining in service until November 1929. (Ron Drummond collection)

many more years useful service by private industrial and colliery operators.

By 1947, only nine remained on NSWGR, most of which were at country locations for branch line and shunting work. Slowly they were withdrawn and the last in service was 2532, stopped after working an enthusiast tour train to Boorowa in April 1962. No. 2535, which had been in store at Narrabri West since 1959, was sold to Corrimal colliery. It remained in service there and later at Bulli colliery until mid-1971 when it was preserved by its owners, AI&S, at the Port Kembla Steel Works visitors centre. It has since been obtained by Dorrigo Steam Railway and Museum for more serious preservation. No. 2510 is preserved at the Thirlmere Railway Museum.

Footnote: Beyer Peacock built another two in 1895 and 1897 for the British Midland & South Western Junction Railway. Numbered 14 and 16, they worked between Cheltenham and Southampton Docks. While No. 14 was sold in 1914 (ending its days with the Cramlington Coal Co in 1943), No. 16 *Galloping Alice* made it into Great Western Railway ownership and underwent a rebuild, was renumbered 24, and worked goods trains between Swindon and Stoke Gifford yard until withdrawn in 1930. Astonishingly the Swindon & Cricklade Railway Trust today plans building an operating replica of No. 16 and is inviting Australian input!

SPECIFICATIONS

	ORIGINAL	SUPERHEATED
	IMPERIAL (METRIC)	IMPERIAL (METRIC)
CYLINDERS:	18 x 26 IN (46 x 66 CM)	18 x 26 IN (46 x 66 CM)
BOILER PRESSURE:	140 PSI (965 KPA)	140 PSI (965 KPA)
COUPLED WHEELS:	4 FT 0 IN (122 CM)	4 FT 0 IN (122 CM)
TRACTIVE EFFORT:	19 656 LB (87.5 KN)	21 830 LB (97.2 KN)
GRATE AREA:	21 SQ FT (1.951 M²)	21 SQ FT (1.951 M²)
TOTAL WEIGHT:	66.14 TONS (67.5 T)	73.10 TONS (74.7 T)
GAUGE:	1435 MM	1435 MM
ROAD NUMBERS:	(ORIGINAL) 205–254, 314–333	
	(1924) 2501–2570	

(D) 255/261/334-classes 4-4-0

Due to the slow average speed of the NSW Railways 79-class 4-4-0s, and with the projected opening of the easily-graded Albury extension (subsequently commissioned in February 1881), the railway administration of the day expressed a desire to employ faster locomotives.

Accordingly, specifications were prepared by the locomotive branch for six heavier and larger-wheeled 4-4-0 tender engines. After design adjustments by their British builders, Beyer, Peacock & Co, they became the system's (D) 255-class.

Boasting 183 cm diameter driving wheels, higher boiler pressure and a 79-class pattern Bissell leading bogie, all were freighted to Sydney on the one sailing ship and, after assembly, entered traffic between November 1882 and January 1883.

During early tests it became obvious the new engines lacked the power of the older 79-class, the combinations of lengthy 1 in 40 grades and large driving wheels being the main problem.

By then, another 24 similar engines had been ordered from Dubs & Co, but hurried cables expressing the Railway's desire to fit smaller 152 cm driving wheels (for greater power) and a longer wheelbase leading bogie (for increased stability) apparently arrived too late. However, while their power was slightly increased with the fitting of 46 cm diameter cylinders (in lieu of the earlier 43 cm), strangely their boilers were down-rated by 69 kPa.

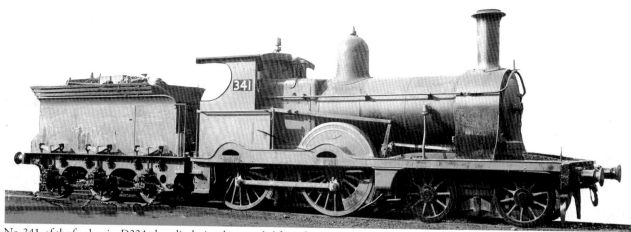

No. 341, of the final series D334-class displaying the extended front framing provided to accommodate the more stable Adams leading bogie. In August 1924 this locomotive was renumbered 1629, lasting in traffic until January 1929. (Rev. Bob Richardson)

Because of these alterations, the new locomotives became the (D) 261-class and were commissioned over a 6-month period starting in October 1883.

As main lines continued to pincer the state's hinterland, another 17 engines were ordered from Dubs later in 1884. They were built with an improved 183 cm wheelbase Adams-type bogie, and all came equipped with the Joy valve gear in lieu of the earlier engines' inside Stephenson's link motion. These locomotives were distinguished from the other two look-alike types as the D334-class.

Originally, all three types were built with round-top firebox boilers, but when reboilering became necessary between 1901 and 1909 they were equipped with new Belpaire (square-top) fireboxes. In addition, the original 255-class's coupled wheels were increased by 13 mm while those of the 261 and 334 classes were increased by 25 mm. Except for three 261-class engines (262, 272 and 283) which had received larger 46.4 cm cylinders in 1894 for *Melbourne Express* working between Junee and Albury, no other engines were so equipped during the rebuild and, because their boiler pressure remained at original specifications, the engines became less powerful.

The three types were used on Southern and Northern line passenger and mail services until well after the turn of the century when, beginning to be displaced by the sheer volume of new P-class 4-6-0 deliveries, they were put to work on the regular Sydney to Katoomba, Moss Vale and Wollongong passenger services.

With P-class deliveries extending into the 1910s, the D-classes were sent further afield. Most of them spent their final years assisting the more powerful types on the Northern District mail and express rosters. Others trod some of the state's lighter branch lines for a short period.

Despite the three classes being renumbered in 1924 and reclassified into two, they were not destined to remain in service for long, for their boilers were again giving out. For the record, the early Beyer, Peacock & Co 255-class became the Z15-class while the two Dubs types became the Z16-class.

First withdrawn was 1606 (an early Dubs engine) in October 1926. Most were out of service by 1930. Lying in workshop and depot yards, most were finally scrapped by November 1937, one survivor being 1623, which was retained at Chullora Locomotive Workshops for steam and hot water generation purposes until condemned in March 1941. Nos 1625 and 1630 were sold to the outer Sydney Nepean Sand & Gravel Co, one of them continuing to operate well into the 1950s. Although efforts were made to secure the relic for preservation, it is believed that a flood finally washed the engine into the Nepean River. Thus none remain.

During their lives these locomotives ran some extraordinary distances. Each of the 15-class exceeded 1.5 million km while all the Dubs types ran well over 1 million km each.

SPECIFICATIONS

	D255-CLASS	AS REBUILT
	IMPERIAL (METRIC)	IMPERIAL (METRIC)
CYLINDERS:	17 x 26 IN (43 x 66 CM)	17 x 26 IN (43 x 66 CM)
BOILER PRESSURE:	150 PSI (1034 KPA)	150 PSI (1034 KPA)
COUPLED WHEELS:	6 FT 0 IN (183 CM)	6 FT .05 IN (184 CM)
TRACTIVE EFFORT:	12 523 LB (55.7 KN)	12 437 LB (55.3 KN)
GRATE AREA:	16.75 SQ FT (1.556 M²)	16.90 SQ FT (1.570 M²)
TOTAL WEIGHT:	63.18 TONS (64.4 T)	66.11 TONS (67.4 T)
GAUGE:	1435 MM	1435 MM

	D261-CLASS	AS REBUILT
	IMPERIAL (METRIC)	IMPERIAL (METRIC)
CYLINDERS:	18 x 26 IN (46 x 66 CM)	18 x 26 IN (46 x 66 CM)
BOILER PRESSURE:	140 PSI (965 KPa)	140 PSI (965 KPa)
COUPLED WHEELS:	6 FT 0 IN (183 CM)	6 FT 1 IN (185 CM)
TRACTIVE EFFORT:	13 104 LB (58.3 KN)	12 924 LB (57.5 KN)
GRATE AREA:	16.75 SQ FT (1.556 M²)	16.75 SQ FT (1.556 M²)
TOTAL WEIGHT:	64.1 TONS (65.4 T)	65.8 TONS (67.1 T)
GAUGE:	1435 MM	1435 MM
ROAD NUMBERS:	(ORIGINAL) 261–284	
	(1924) 1601–1624	

	D334-CLASS	AS REBUILT
	IMPERIAL (METRIC)	IMPERIAL (METRIC)
CYLINDERS:	18 x 26 IN (46 x 66 CM)	18 x 26 IN (46 x 66 CM)
BOILER PRESSURE:	140 PSI (965 KPa)	140 PSI (965 KPa)
COUPLED WHEELS:	6 FT 0 IN (183 CM)	6 FT 1 IN (185 CM)
TRACTIVE EFFORT:	13 104 LB (58.3 KN)	12 924 LB (57.5 KN)
GRATE AREA:	16.75 SQ FT (1.556 M²)	16.75 SQ FT (1.556 M²)
TOTAL WEIGHT:	65.4 TONS (66.7 T)	66.4 TONS (67.5 T)
GAUGE:	1435 MM	1435 MM
ROAD NUMBERS:	(ORIGINAL) 334–350	
	(1924) 1625–1641	

ROAD NUMBERS: (ORIGINAL) 255–260
(1924) 1501–1506

Fowler 0-4-2T

This unique, small jackshaft-drive locomotive is thought to be the only engine of its type remaining in the world. Originally built for the Mourilyan Sugar Mill near Innisfail, Queensland, by John Fowler & Co of Leeds, the engine (maker's number 4668) arrived in 1883 and found employment working construction trains over the mill's 610 mm gauge tramway linking the port of Mourilyan and the mill site. It was among the pioneers of narrow gauge canefield railways in Australia.

Becoming No. 1 on the mill's roster, the locomotive remained in mill service until around 1913, the year it was advertised for sale in the *Australian Sugar Journal*. Recent research indicates the locomotive was eventually acquired by Melbourne firm Cameron & Sutherland, after which it was noted in the employ of a South Australian contracting firm in 1919.

A South Melbourne machinery merchant finally acquired the relic in 1924 and, after overhauling it, again offered it for sale. This firm was unsuccessful in finding a buyer and the locomotive lay beneath a tarpaulin inside the merchant's premises, totally

In September 1976, the little Fowler raised steam at the Goulburn Steam Museum for the first time in perhaps 60 years. After successfully running tourist train trips at the museum, it was sent to the Australian Sugar Industry Museum at Mourilyan early the following year. (Leon Oberg)

forgotten by most of the outside world. It saw the light of day just twice in the following half century, once for exhibition at a show and again in 1961 when paraded through Melbourne's streets on the back of a lorry during the city's annual Moomba Festival.

One enthusiast who knew of the locomotive's existence was Bruce Macdonald, then curator of Goulburn's Steam Museum. In fact, he had been attempting to acquire the relic for some decades. Following prolonged negotiations, he finally took delivery on 9 September 1976.

After restoring the engine to its original condition and altering its paint scheme from green to red, Mr Macdonald paraded it (in steam) down Goulburn's main street on the back of a lorry, as part of that city's annual Lilac City Festival in October 1976.

Local enthusiasts and museum visitors were then treated to tourist train haulage by the 'little red engine', as it was affectionately dubbed by the local press. But the veteran did not remain in this role for long, for it was returned to its Queensland home early in 1977 for preservation within the Australian Sugar Industry Museum at Mourilyan.

SPECIFICATIONS

	IMPERIAL (METRIC)
CYLINDERS:	6 x 9 IN (15 x 23 CM)
BOILER PRESSURE:	180 PSI (1240 KPA)
COUPLED WHEELS:	1 FT 8 IN (51 CM)
TRACTIVE EFFORT:	2333 LB (10.4 KN)
GRATE AREA:	4 SQ FT (0.36 M²)
TOTAL WEIGHT:	8.5 TONS (8.7 T)
GAUGE:	610MM
ROAD NUMBER:	1

1883 QUEENSLAND RAILWAYS

F (B13) class 4-6-0

Described as the workhorse of the QR, particularly during the late 1800s and early 1900s, this class, which finally totalled 112 locomotives, was considered the most powerful on the system at the time it was introduced.

The first batch of 19 arrived from Dubs and Co in June 1883 for service over the isolated sections of the QR including the Great Northern, Central, Southern and Western and Maryborough lines.

Rated an immediate success, further orders were placed with Dubs & Co (52), Kitson of Leeds (26)

and the Phoenix Foundry of Ipswich (15). These popular little 4-6-0s were working to virtually all corners of the state by 1892. With the gradual link-up of the various far-flung isolated systems, they were all reclassified B13-class in 1889.

Although a number had been built to burn wood fuel, featuring 'Wild West' diamond stacks into the bargain, numerous modifications were carried out to the engines, even during construction. For instance, deeper fireboxes arrived in 1885 and in the following year extended smokeboxes were provided, which later became standard on all examples.

While the B13s were technically freight engines, their sphere of work involved the operation of numerous mixed passenger services as well.

Rebuilding commenced around the turn of the century when most, if not all, were progressively fitted with higher-pressure boilers and wider fireboxes, thus increasing their tractive effort from 37 kN to 46.3 kN. Improved cab accommodation was also introduced.

About that time, the class was gradually displaced from main line running with the delivery of higher powered PB15-class engines. Six were sold between 1913 and 1919 to the Commonwealth Railways, where they became that system's Ng-class. These locomotives, 44, 51, 128, 159, 226 and 165, were renumbered 9 to 14 respectively. The first withdrawn was No. 9 in January 1933. The last three operated until April 1944. Shunting narrow gauge rolling stock for loading exchange onto CR standard gauge trains, at both Kalgoorlie and Port Augusta, was among the last tasks for this class.

Back in Queensland, scrappings commenced during the 1920s but some were sold to private enterprise, mainly sugar interests, the first such unit being 52, which went to the Beaudesert Shire Council in 1921. It was withdrawn in 1939 and replaced by 185. After the Council closed down its rail interests, 185 was sold to the Isis Central Sugar Mill.

In 1935, the Bingera Sugar Mill took delivery of 49, followed by 48 in 1944 and N79 in 1951. No. 175 was also purchased about this time for spare parts to keep the other three locomotives operational. Millaquin Mill also operated two of the class, purchasing its first, 81, in the late 1930s. That engine lasted until 1963.

The last B13 in service on the QR, 130, was sold to Millaquin Sugar Mill in September 1951, twelve months after it had been withdrawn. No. 48 was donated to the QR for preservation in 1967. This engine, which today resides at the Ipswich Railway

B13 No. 48, shown operating at Bundaberg on 2 December 1966, has been retained for preservation. (David G. Bailey)

Workshops Museum, had been fitted with a 1240 kPa boiler in 1958.

SPECIFICATIONS

	ORIGINAL	AS REBUILT
	IMPERIAL (METRIC)	IMPERIAL (METRIC)
CYLINDERS:	13 x 20 IN (33 x 51 CM)	13 x 20 IN (33 x 51 CM)
BOILER PRESSURE:	120 PSI (827 KPA)	150 PSI (1034 KPA)
COUPLED WHEELS:	3 FT 3 IN (99 CM)	3 FT 3 IN (99 CM)
TRACTIVE EFFORT:	8 320 LB (37 KN)	10 400 LB (46.3 KN)
GRATE AREA:	11.25 SQ FT (1.045 M²)	18.75 SQ FT (1.742 M²)
TOTAL WEIGHT:	49.5 TONS (50.5 T)	50.25 TONS (51.3 T)
GAUGE:	1067 MM	1067 MM
ROAD NUMBERS:	(ORIGINALLY CARRIED NUMBERS FROM 1 WHILE ON ISOLATED SYSTEMS.) AFTER GROUPING, NUMBERS WERE AS FOLLOWS: (QR): 44–61, 78–94, 100–102, 119–128, 129, 130, 145–166, 173–175, 180–201, 220–234 (CR): 9–14	

1884 RAILWAYS & TRAMWAYS OF NEW SOUTH WALES

(R) 285-class 0-6-0T

Originally ordered in February 1882 as a 2-4-0T type for Sydney metropolitan suburban service, the English builder, the Vulcan Foundry, was asked five months later to alter the contract and instead supply six 0-6-0T locomotives to the manufacturer's design.

Weighing 33 tons 2 cwt, the engines were delivered in a single shipload as the 285-class and placed in traffic between 1 April and 31 May 1884. Boasting domeless boilers, a regulator system activated within the upper reaches of the smokebox and Joy valve gear, their diminutive size with specifications to match quickly found the engines wanting—lacking the power needed for the service required because of their small 4 ft 0 in (122 cm) driving wheels, a type more at home on freight engines.

Although these engines were known for their even ride, the 285-class 'experiment' was not perpetuated as traffic density grew, and orders for additional suburban tank engines of the earlier 2-4-0T design were quickly placed. These heavier engines, which became the 351-class, employed larger 5 ft 1 in (155 cm) coupled wheels and a boiler offering a greater firebox heating service.

By 1892, when sufficient deliveries of these, and a fleet of 15 heavier M40-class 4-4-0T locomotives were running, the little 0-6-0Ts were (except for dire engine shortages) largely relegated to passenger carriage shunting duties in Sydney yard.

Beginning in 1907, the class was progressively rebuilt with slightly larger domed boilers. While no improvement in output followed, the extra weight added 3 tons 4 cwt to the design, increasing their factor of adhesion from 6.61 to 7.74. Delivered new with a screw reverse, intriguingly, the engines were provided with power reverse gear during the rebuilds, beating by 22 years this equipment—albeit more sophisticated—being provided standard on many newer main line locomotive types. However, it was later replaced with an archaic Johnson bar lever

285-class No. 1803, which operated in government service for 78 years, spent its last years shunting in Port Kembla. It was pictured in 1957 at Reid's Hill, where the district's shunting fleet was serviced. (Late Ron Preston)

reverse system, which remained with the locomotives to their end.

Becoming the Z18-class in 1924, most had found employment in locomotive depots from the 1920s, with three of the fleet equipped with coal grabs the following decade. Others found industrial shunting work in expanding Port Kembla until nudged out by 70-class diesels during the early 1960s. One of those was 1802, which had been sold to the PWD as 75 in October 1927. Other sales saw 1801 and 1806 go to J. & A. Brown Collieries in November 1957, where they enjoyed eight more years hauling coal trains at pretty Catherine Hill Bay Colliery south of Newcastle.

Two 0-6-0Ts have been preserved, 1803 at the Thirlmere Railway Museum and 1804 at Goulburn Rail Heritage Centre where it carries the number 1076 due to its many years working as a 'miscellaneous' asset.

SPECIFICATIONS

	IMPERIAL (METRIC)
CYLINDERS:	15 x 22 IN (38 x 56 CM)
BOILER PRESSURE:	140 PSI (964KPA)
COUPLED WHEELS:	4 FT 0 IN (122 CM)
TRACTIVE EFFORT:	11 500 LB (51.15 KN)
GRATE AREA:	13.13 SQ FT (1.20 M²)
TOTAL WEIGHT:	33.19 TONS (34.5 T)
GAUGE:	1435 MM
ROAD NUMBERS:	285–290; (1801–1806)
NOTE:	1801 RAN FOR A TIME AS 1078; 1803 AS 1077 AND 1804 AS 1076.

Baldwin 0-4-0ST

Few locomotives in the country have had as diverse careers as this family of eight little 0-4-0 saddle tanks.

Built by the US-based Baldwin Locomotive Works between 1884 and 1891, the first four were introduced to Australia by the Melbourne import firm Newell & Co, which ordered them on behalf of the Victorian Government's Melbourne Harbour Trust. The Trust needed the locomotives to carry dredged material from an expansion and deepening of the Yarra River. This spoil was then used to help reclaim swampland at a location known as Fishermen's Bend at Port Melbourne.

The first two (Builder's Nos 7108 and 7111) were steam-tested on 2 July 1884. While the third one (B/No. 7556 of 1885) worked at the site too, it technically remained the property of the importer who, it seems, acquired it and a fourth engine (in 1886) on speculation of acquiring a buyer. That fourth locomotive (B/No. 7860) was on-sold to railway building contracting firm C. & E. Millar and forwarded to Darwin in the Northern Territory. Given the nickname 'Sandfly', the diminutive locomotive, the first used in the territory, was employed on Darwin wharf shunting materials trains connected with the construction of the Darwin to Pine Creek railway. When that line was completed in October 1899, 'Sandfly' was sold to the South Australian Railways, becoming 107 on the operator's roster four months later.

The railway was acquired by the Commonwealth in 1911, when the little engine was classified and renumbered NA1. It continued to be used in the Darwin harbour, yards and workshops until 1944 when it was transferred to Katherine. Withdrawn from service in 1950, NA1 fortunately survived another decade of storage when it was mounted on Port Augusta platform. It remained there until 1982 when it was fully restored and today holds pride of place at Keswick (Adelaide) station.

Newell and Co's fifth engine (B/No. 8130) went directly to the Jarrah Wood & Saw Mills Co of Lockeville, Western Australia, in 1886, where it operated from Wonnerup to Jarrahwood. When that line become part of an expanded Millars (WA) Pty Ltd operation in 1902, the locomotive was named *Yarloop* on the Millars roster. After operating at several company establishments, including its Perth yard, the engine, now fitted with a fresh boiler, was noted out of service for a time, having been acquired by Smith & Timms in 1912 for rail construction projects in South Australia, notably the Willunga line. Records indicate this locomotive also saw service under the ownership of the Engineering & Water Supply Department of South Australia in the construction of weirs and locks along the Murray River during the 1920s.

The sixth (B/No. 9086) and the eighth (B/No. 12007) were imported in 1888 and 1891 respectively by the Sorrento Tramway Co, which operated on Victoria's Mornington Peninsula. Both later found work in Victorian timber mills.

The seventh (B/No. 10770) was built for Millars' Elleker to Denmark Railway and named *Denmark*. Its diverse life included stints in the ownership of Western Australian Firewood Supply Ltd for use on the Eastern Goldfields Railway between Coolgardie and Kalgoorlie. In 1905 it was sold to Bunning Brothers at Mt Helena. In 1920 it was sold to C. Plavin & Co but four years later was noted in the employ of the Australian Timber Co, which went into liquidation in 1927. *Denmark*'s remains were discovered in the 1990s basking on a Darling Ranges rural property. They were taken to the shire's depot in 1999 and after four years, forwarded to the Denmark tip.

While the fate of the first locomotive is unknown to this author, B/No. 7111 was acquired by the Jarrah Wood & Sawmills Co for work outside Busselton. It was also absorbed into the Millars register in 1902, and employed at Waroona. The next 60 years saw the engine operating at several Millars locations including Carnarvon, Perth and Bunbury, carrying the name *Kia Ora*. In 1962 it was handed over to the ARHS for preservation at Bassendean.

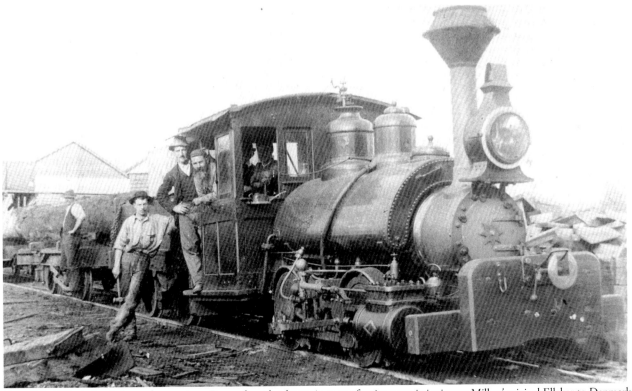

One of the WA timber industry locomotives, *Denmark*, with a log train soon after its commissioning on Millars' original Elleker to Denmark railway in 1890. (Noel Inglis collection)

SPECIFICATIONS

	IMPERIAL (METRIC)
CYLINDERS:	8 x 12 IN (41 x 30 CM)
BOILER PRESSURE:	150 PSI (1034 KPA)*
COUPLED WHEELS:	2 FT 4 IN (145 CM)
TRACTIVE EFFORT:	3400 LB (15.1 KN)
GRATE AREA:	4.6 SQ FT (0.442 M²)
TOTAL WEIGHT:	7.1 TO 9 TONS (7.1 TO 9.2 T)
GAUGE:	1067 MM

* BOILER PRESSURES VARIED, SOME HAVING WORKED AT 155 PSI (1033 KPA) AND 140 PSI (965 KPA) AT TIMES.

1884 VICTORIAN RAILWAYS

A-class 4-4-0

As new railway routes forged their way into country Victoria to cater for burgeoning population expansion and pastoral activity, the existing lightweight 'big-wheeled' passenger-type locomotives were hard pressed to haul the greater loads asked of them.

By 1883, the main line network had spread to Dimboola and Albury. Clearly, new locomotives were needed, particularly to haul expresses to Albury (which had been reached two years earlier by the NSWGR), and Beyer, Peacock & Co was contracted to supply ten 4-4-0 express locomotives. Their design, including tenders, was loosely a broad gauge version of the NSWGR (D)255-class, right down to the provision of a Bissell bogie truck and 183 cm coupled wheels. The six (D)255s were by then in use over the Sydney to Albury line.

Numbered 190 to 208 (even numbers only), the first engine into service was loco 194 on 20 August 1884. All

had been commissioned by 10 November that year.

While no more were built, they did pave the way for a slightly heavier Kitson-designed locally-built 4-4-0 express locomotive type which, when delivered from 1889, became the 'New' A-class. To avoid confusion, the Beyer, Peacock machines became known as the 'Old' A-class.

Over the years, many tests were carried out on the locomotives. One in 1885 involved the provision of a Victorian-designed Woods hydraulic brake to locomotive 202. This was eventually removed in favour of the standard Westinghouse air system three years later. During that time, three other engines, 204, 206 and 208, were fitted with vacuum brake equipment for comparative trials. This too was removed in 1888.

No. 208 was experimentally fitted with a Knone's feed water heater in 1895 and, in an effort to further improve the locomotives, the same engine temporarily received a Morris superheater in 1896.

Beginning with loco 196, all 'Old' A's were gradually rebuilt between March 1900 and June 1903 with larger 175 psi 'New' A-class pattern boilers, which increased their tractive effort from 13 100 lb to 16 380 lb. This, along with a slight increase in tender water capacity, increased the weight of these locomotives from their original 70 tons to 73 tons 17 cwt.

The rebuilt 'Old' A's were generally pooled with the 'New' A's, but records indicate most of the former spent their remaining years working over the North East line with examples based at Melbourne, Seymour and Benalla. Their later years were spent as assistant engines on trains with heavy loadings. The first class-member removed from the register was 194 in April 1919 and the last running, 206 (a Royal

A198 as originally built. (V/Line archives, Len Whalley collection)

Exhibiting its rebuilt form, 'Old' A-class 192 stands in Melbourne's Spencer Street station with an Up Albury-bound passenger service, circa 1903. (V/Line archives, Len Whalley collection)

A highly decorated A206 prepares for Royal Train duty. (V/Line archives, Len Whalley collection)

Train engine), was finally withdrawn in 1924. One locomotive's boiler was salvaged in 1920 and for many years supplied steam for Newport Workshops.

SPECIFICATIONS

	IMPERIAL (METRIC)
CYLINDERS:	18 x 26 IN (46 x 66 CM)
COUPLED WHEELS:	6 FT 0 IN (183 CM)
BOILER PRESSURE:	140 PSI (965 KPA)
TRACTIVE EFFORT:	13 100 LB (59.1 KN)
GRATE AREA:	18.24 SQ FT (1.700 M²)
TOTAL WEIGHT:	64 TONS 19 CWT (66.2 T)
GAUGE:	1600 MM
ROAD NUMBERS:	190–208 (EVEN NUMBERS)

884 SOUTH AUSTRALIAN RAILWAYS

P-class 2-4-0T

The demand for additional engine power to deal with the ever-increasing worker and shopping traffic over the Adelaide–Port Adelaide line led to the commissioning of six Beyer, Peacock & Co 2-4-0 tank locomotives between 29 August 1884 and the end of the following month.

Deemed an immediate success, a further 14 of these little locomotives were ordered, this time from local firm James Martin, which had established a highly productive engineering works at nearby Gawler. These entered traffic between May and December 1893, bringing to 20 the number of engines now available.

On 9 February 1927, engine 72 was condemned and lay derelict for more than a decade. For reasons not fathomable, it was shopped for a complete overhaul early in 1939 and re-entered service the following July where it remained in traffic until June 1957, becoming one of the last of the class in actual service.

Nos. 22 and 74 were also condemned in 1929 but, like 72 earlier mentioned, 74 had its condemnation eventually cancelled.

As larger main line locomotives became available, the remaining locomotives were relegated to broad gauge secondary duties such as shunting yards, workshops and depots until they were finally withdrawn during 1956–57. Fortunately, one was destined to be saved for, subsequent to its condemnation in December 1956, loco 117 was handed over to the Australian Transport Museum and was stored at the Kilburn works of Stewart Lloyds (Australia) Pty Ltd. Today it is an exhibit in

P-class No. 75 trundling through Gillman yard in Adelaide's port district on 30 May 1952. (D.A. Colquhoun)

the National Railway Museum, Port Adelaide.

SPECIFICATIONS

	IMPERIAL (METRIC)
CYLINDERS:	16 x 20 IN (41 x 51 CM)
BOILER PRESSURE:	130 PSI (896 KPA)
COUPLED WHEELS:	5 FT 0 IN (152 CM)
TRACTIVE EFFORT:	8875 LB (39.5 KN)
GRATE AREA:	14.7 SQ FT (1.366 M²)
TOTAL WEIGHT:	33.7 TONS (34.4 T)
GAUGE:	1600 MM
ROAD NUMBERS:	21, 22, 70–75, 115–126

1885 TASMANIAN GOVERNMENT RAILWAYS

C-class 2-6-0

With the start of construction of new branch lines and an extension of the Western line, the Tasmanian Government Railways started looking for suitable motive power to run the services and selected two locomotive types from the Beyer, Peacock & Co catalogue. One was a 4-4-0 passenger design which became the B-class (see page 72) and the other was a 2-6-0 freight version which became the TGR C-class.

Although it could not have been foreseen at the time, this trouble-free and simple 2-6-0 design was destined to see service in almost all Australian states under both government and private ownership.

The original 19 C-class locomotives arrived between 1885 and 1892 and soon won themselves a name for their workmanship and trouble-free characteristics. Because of their success, coupled with a sharp increase in traffic at the turn of the century, Beyer, Peacock & Co was asked to supply an additional eight.

Not long afterwards, the rebuilding of earlier deliveries became necessary. Following the success of the Belpaire boilers which had been introduced in Tasmania on the 4-6-0 E-class in 1907, six C-class received Belpaire boilers with slightly larger grates and smokeboxes from 1912 and were reclassified CC. Those locomotives modified were 16–19, 26 and 27.

Further conversions were carried out in 1924 when four more received similar boilers as well as Walschaerts valve gear. These locomotives, 21, 23, 24 and 25, were reclassified CCS.

As the TGR system developed, these locomotives saw operation throughout the state; withdrawals did not start until 1936, when four were set aside at Launceston. In later years, the remaining engines were generally utilised in shunting roles.

Meanwhile, the Emu Bay Railway, operator of an ore-carrying line on Tasmania's West Coast, turned to this rugged 2-6-0 design in December 1897, and bought one James Martin-built engine for the construction of the Zeehan extension. Numbered 4 on the company's roster, its purchase was followed by a similar engine, No. 5, a few months later. As traffic increased, a third, No. 9, arrived from James Martin in 1906. (The Martin locomotives were almost a metre shorter and 4 tonnes lighter than the Beyer, Peacock & Co equivalent.) An order for a fourth engine had been placed with Beyer, Peacock & Co in 1908 but this did not carry its road number 10 for long, as it was later sold to the Tasmanian PWD for railway construction work. It came under TGR ownership in 1937, where it became C28.

Today, two CCS engines (23 and 25) are held by the Don River Railway at Devonport; C1 is exhibited at the West Coast Pioneers Memorial Museum at Zeehan; and C22 is under restoration at the Tasmanian Transport Museum, Glenorchy.

Mainland adopts design

Meanwhile, South Australian Railways had been taking delivery of many examples of this little 2-6-0 design. Between October 1885 and November 1898 no less than 129 entered service, some of which were sourced second-hand. These locomotives became the backbone of that state's narrow gauge system for many decades and worked virtually all types of train.

At this time, the Silverton Tramway, operators of a 58 km ore-carrying line linking Broken Hill in New South Wales with the SAR's system at Cockburn, looked to this dainty 2-6-0 for its chief motive power too. Between 1888 and 1907, 21 locomotives were delivered and classified in a similar way to the SAR locomotives (as Y-class). Many remained in service for nearly 40 years, a few being provided with side tanks for additional water capacity.

Five were subsequently rebuilt with 180 lb boilers, vastly improving their efficiency, particularly when lead weights were attached to the running boards to provide added adhesion. Three Y-class were also equipped with superheaters.

Apparently the Silverton Tramway over-ordered, because its third and fourth locomotives were sold new to the SAR. All these locomotives had been built by Beyer, Peacock & Co, but in 1892 the

Silverton Tramway took delivery of a replacement engine for No. 3, which was acquired second-hand from the Tarrawingee Tramway, a 40 mile (64 km) line built in 1891 northwards from Broken Hill to serve mining enterprises. This engine had been built in South Australia by James Martin & Co. The second Tarrawingee 2-6-0 (also from Martin) was sold at that time to a rail-building contractor who eventually resold it to SAR as its No. 195. The Silverton Tramway then provided all motive power for the Tarrawingee railway until it closed on 31 December 1929.

Dieselisation of the Silverton Tramway in 1961 saw the withdrawal of the remaining seven Y-class locomotives, their last days having been spent in shunting service. While most were scrapped, class-leader Y1 was retained for preservation in Broken Hill, being given pride of place outside the city's once proud Sulphide Street railway station; Y11 is in a tourist park at Silverton and Y12 at the National Railway Museum, Port Adelaide.

In South Australia, rebuilding started in 1904 when no less than 58 Y-class engines were fitted with higher-pressure boilers which produced a bonus 15.4 kN of tractive effort. These became the Yx-class; the last one was rebuilt in April 1924. From this time onwards it becomes difficult to trace all the locomotives as several were sold, loaned, borrowed or scrounged by South Australian rail-construction contractors and Western Australian timber millers. It is known that three went to the Victorian Construction Co and that BHP purchased Y61 in 1926. After the depression years, others were lost to the scrapyards.

With the outbreak of World War II, the Commonwealth Railways narrow gauge Central Australian and Northern Australian railways urgently needed motive power to shift increasing numbers of troop and equipment trains. Between September 1941 and January 1945, CR purchased eighteen 2-6-0s from the SAR and classified them Nfb. These were numbered 43–49, 51 and 88–97 and initially placed in service on the North Australia Railway. Three were transferred to the Central Australian system following hostilities in the far North, and seven were sold to TGR where they became that system's F-class. Because some of the seven were in poor condition, only four were actually absorbed into the active TGR traffic roster. The remaining three were utilised for spare parts. The operational Tasmanian locomotives were all withdrawn by 1957, the last engine in traffic being F.3, which had been shunting at Hobart.

To further confuse the issue, F.1 was sold to the Emu Bay Railway in 1956 where it was numbered 19. This was the last 2-6-0 to operate on that railway, being withdrawn on 23 July 1963, a month prior to the arrival of 10-class diesel-hydraulic locomotives.

The CR actually purchased some of the remaining 'borrowed' Nfb-class after the war for continued use on the NAR and converted five to burn fuel oil. They were gradually withdrawn and stored from 1949. Three were still in existence as late as 1964, when tenders were called for their purchase. Nfb88 survived the scrappers and today resides at Katherine's former railway station, where it forms part of a railway and military history museum.

Of the 129 locomotives that at one time belonged to the SAR, 50 were built by Beyer, Peacock & Co, two were built at the SAR's Islington Workshops and the remainder were constructed by James Martin & Co of Gawler. The class carried road numbers as follows: 22, 38, 43, 49, 57–106, 108–142, 147–179 and 195. Two sets of engines carried the numbers 153–159—the first batch was sold to WAGR shortly after they arrived.

The last Y-class in service in South Australia was Y97, which was condemned in May 1970. It is now preserved at the National Railway Museum, Port Adelaide. Y82 and Yx141 have also been preserved, and are at Peterborough and the Quorn-based Pichi Richi Railway respectively.

Western Australian interest

WAGR took delivery of seven of the class too. In fact, the type had been introduced for mixed traffic as early as 1889 as that system's G-class. These Beyer, Peacock-built locomotives were quickly followed by a further 28 from James Martin & Co. In addition, Neilson & Co delivered a further twelve during 1895 and 1896. Some were Y-class acquired from the SAR.

Thus by 1899, forty-seven 2-6-0s were available for traffic on the WAGR; they carried the road numbers: 17, 32, 33, 42–49, 51–61, 64–68, 109–112, 126–132, 156–161 and 233–235.

Tracing the Western Australian examples is also difficult, as a number of those locomotives were sold to rail-laying contractors and timber interests. Others were sold, or exchanged for other locomotive types with the state's PWD. During World War II, 13 were sent to the CR (as with the SAR Y-class)

TGR C12 preparing to depart Smithton with the Marrawah Tramway's Redpa goods in February 1950. (Ken Winney)

Tasmanian Railways' CCS23 at Western Junction on 4 August 1973. (*Launceston Examiner*, Roydon Burk collection)

An outstanding study of WAGR's 2-6-0, G233, shunting at Bunbury jetty on 3 March 1971. (Bob Grant)

A James Martin-constructed 2-6-0, Yx118, at Terowie in 1951. (Bruce Macdonald)

Nfb49, one of 18 SAR Yx-class 2-6-0s taken over by Commonwealth Railways during World War II. It was pictured at Port Augusta in 1951. (Bruce Macdonald)

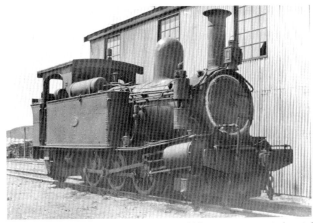

BHP Whyalla steel plant's No. 3A, which was assembled from the Silverton Tramway Nos 2 and 4 parts for use over the Iron Knob tramway hauling iron ore. It was scrapped in 1958 with the coming of EMD Bo-Bo diesels. (BHP archives)

One of Whyalla steel plant's three 2-6-2T locomotives, an industrial adaptation of the popular 2-6-0 tender design. No. 2A was pictured at the Whyalla works during the 1940s. (BHP archives)

A 4-6-0 version of the WAGR G-class, No. 123 stands side by side with the conventional 2-6-0 type represented by G233, pictured on shed at Collie on 27 February 1971. (Bob Grant)

One of five Silverton Tramway 2-6-0s rebuilt with 180 lb boilers and lead adhesion weights (above the coupled wheel splashers). No. Y11 is preserved in Penrose Park, Silverton (Leon Oberg)

An April 1912 photograph showing a 2-6-0 G-class No. 3 on a train loading Kalgoorlie-bound vegetable produce at Hartin's Siding. The guard, Alan Wansborough, later became MLA for Albany. (Noel Inglis collection)

SPECIFICATIONS

TGR C-CLASS/SAR Y-CLASS

Imperial (Metric)

Cylinders:	14½ x 20 in (37 x 51 cm)
Boiler pressure:	140 psi (965 kPa)
Coupled wheels:	3 ft 3 in (99 cm)
Tractive effort:	12 507 lb (55.7 kN)
Grate area:	13.3 sq ft (1.213 m²)
Total weight:	42–47 tons (42.8–47.9 t)
Gauge:	1067 mm

SAR Yx-CLASS

Imperial (Metric)

14½ x 20 in (37 x 51 cm)
185 psi (1275 kPa)
3 ft 3 in (99 cm)
15 957 lb (71 kN)
14.6 sq ft (1.356 m²)
50 tons (51 t)
1067 mm

TGR CCS-CLASS

Imperial (Metric)

Cylinders:	15 x 20 cm (38 x 51 cm)
Boiler pressure:	175 psi (1206 kPa)
Coupled wheels:	3 ft 3 in (99 cm)
Tractive effort:	13 661 lb (60.8 kN)
Grate area:	15.75 sq ft (1.450 m²)
Total weight:	56 tons (57.1 t)
Gauge:	1067 mm 1067 mm

WAGR G-CLASS 2-6-0

Imperial (Metric)

14½ x 20 in (37 x 51 cm)
160 psi (1102 kPa)
3 ft 3.5 in (100 cm)
13 626 lb (60.6 kN)
4.6 sq ft (1.356 m²)
42 tons (42.8 t)

WAGR G-CLASS 4-6-0

Imperial (Metric)

14½ x 20 in (37 x 51 cm)
135 psi (910 kPa)
3 ft 3.5 in (100 cm)
11 497 lb (51.2 kN)
14.6 sq ft (1.356 m²)
43.5 tons (44.4 t)
1067 mm

for use on the North Australia Railway. Classified Nfc-class and numbered 66 to 78, four were returned to the WAGR while another six were subsequently disposed of equally to State Sawmills of WA and the Goldfields Firewood Co. Two of the Nfc units were not repatriated because they were totally worn out, and were scrapped in the Northern Territory.

CR's records indicate the last Nfc had been withdrawn by 1948.

A further five WAGR G-class were sold to private saw-milling interests.

WAGR greatly altered this basic 2-6-0 design when, between 1895 and 1897, the administration introduced an additional 21 G-class with a 4-6-0 wheel arrangement. One of these, G50, was built by Beyer, Peacock & Co and the rest, G107, G108, G113, G125 and G133–137, were constructed by Dubs & Co. All bore lower-pressure 930 kPa boilers but were used in conjunction with their 2-6-0 prototype.

Thirteen of these 4-6-0s were obtained by CR between October 1940 and May 1943 for use over the North Australia Railway, becoming the Nga-class. They were numbered 39–42 and 79–87. They were not destined to last long, however, for withdrawals started in September 1947. Two returned to the WAGR, two others were snapped up by the WA PWD in 1947, and another pair was acquired by Western Australian State Sawmills in 1948.

Sales of both 2-6-0 and 4-6-0 locomotives continued in Western Australia and many saw useful, lengthy service in the timber industry, with at least one remaining in traffic as late as 1972.

Queensland had entered the equation too, for five WAGR G-class 2-6-0s were sold to the Chillagoe Railway in the north of the state. Two of these were taken over by the QR in 1919 as its AY and BY classes. One Chillagoe 2-6-0, which saw service both on the railway and at the smelters, actually returned to Western Australia in 1950, after its purchase by Bunning Bros timber millers.

Several G-class locomotives remain operational in Western Australia. They include G233, a 2-6-0 named *Leschenault Lady*, which works the Golden Mile Tourist Railway at Kalgoorlie/Boulder, and G118, a 4-6-0 called *Koombama Queen*, which is on semi-permanent loan to the Hotham Valley Railway.

A further variation on the theme was this rather ungainly looking 2-6-0ST built in 1914 for the Zinc Corporation in Broken Hill. It was sold to BHP in 1941 and operated at Whyalla as 1A until withdrawn and scrapped in 1962. It was basically similar to a locomotive built for BHP by Beyer, Peacock in 1905 which ran as No. 1 *Big Ben*. (BHP archives)

Others, largely obtained from saw-milling companies, can be found in many parts of the state.

In South Australia, four Y, one Yx and a former Silverton Tramway Y-class remain, with representatives being exhibited at the National Railway Museum, Port Adelaide, Peterborough and Port Lincoln.

Tank versions too

Beyer, Peacock & Co had also offered the world's railways a 2-6-2 tank engine version of its popular 2-6-0 design. The first to appear in Australia had maker's number 3170, dated 1890, and was imported by the Silverton Tramway as Y5. Eight years later it passed into the ownership of the Sulphide Corporation in Broken Hill, finally being transferred to BHP Whyalla in 1940 as that company's No. 2A. It was eventually withdrawn in 1962.

The second 2-6-2T to come to Australia was Beyer, Peacock maker's number 3357 of 1891. This locomotive was purchased by BHP for use in Broken Hill. After a brief period on loan to the SAR and Silverton Tramway, the little engine, now numbered 2 by BHP, was forwarded to Hummock Hill (Whyalla) in 1901 for early iron-ore train haulage over the Iron Knob tramway. Displaced from that working by larger locomotives, it finally found service hauling Whyalla ironworks ladle vehicles until a new steel mill, along with standard gauge rails, replaced the old 1067 mm gauge network in 1963. The locomotive was then preserved beside Spencer Gulf by BHP and Whyalla's civic authorities.

A third 2-6-2T appeared in 1908. It was built for Broken Hill South Mine and carried Beyer, Peacock's maker's number 5125. It was acquired by BHP in 1940 for use in Whyalla as the company's second No. 3. With gauge standardisation within the plant in 1963, the engine was preserved in a children's playground in Whyalla.

Two 2-6-0 saddle-tank versions also appeared, the first in 1905 for BHP Whyalla where it ran as No. 1 *Big Ben*, and another delivered in 1914 to the Sulphide Corporation in Broken Hill. This locomotive was sold to BHP in 1941 for use at its Whyalla ironworks, running beside the earlier 2-6-0ST as No. 1A. The latter remained operational until 1962. While based on the standard 2-6-0 described above, the 2-6-0ST engines owe their parentage to locomotives built in 1885 for the Taltal Railway in Chile.

A TGR B-class locomotive as running in later years. (former TGR)

1885 Tasmanian Government Railways

B-class 4-4-0

Following the takeover of the Launceston & Western Railway Co by the Tasmanian government in 1872, plans were made to transform operations from the 1600 mm gauge to the more easily financed 1067 mm gauge. Although the government operated the broad gauge for a number of years, locomotives and rolling-stock were becoming run down generally. On conversion of the line to narrow gauge, four of the original five locomotives were sold and the fifth was converted to 1067 mm gauge.

Meanwhile, railway officials had been looking for suitable new motive power to work on the expanding system and two of Beyer, Peacock & Co's basic tried and tested locomotives were selected. These became the B-class 4-4-0 passenger class and the C-class 2-6-0 freight or mixed-traffic type. (The original Launceston & Western Railway Co's converted locomotive became the A-class.) All the new locomotives arrived between 1885 and 1892.

A total of 15 B-class entered traffic and worked over most of the rapidly expanding railway system.

Following the 1890 takeover of the Tasmanian Main Line Railway Co (which had been operating services between Launceston and Hobart since 1876), the B and C classes were hard pressed to maintain services because of the run-down nature of the Tasmanian Main Line Railway Co's engines. Thus additional 4-4-0s of an improved and heavier design were ordered. These arrived as the (new-series) A-class from 1892 (see page 95).

Withdrawals began with five B-class in the 1930s following the arrival of heavy Q-class 4-8-2s. The remaining ten continued working, but mainly over the lighter branch lines or in a shunting capacity at Hobart and Launceston. They also appeared occasionally on Hobart suburban freight services.

The arrival of new Bo-Bo X-class diesels from 1950 spelt the end for the B-class, and all had been withdrawn from active service by 1952 although for some their steaming days were not quite over. B3 became the Launceston shed steam cleaner until replaced some years later by B4. This locomotive was eventually cut up circa 1959.

Specifications

	Imperial (Metric)
Cylinders:	14½ x 20 in (37 x 51 cm)
Boiler pressure:	140 psi (965 kPa)
Coupled wheels:	4 ft 0 in (122 cm)
Tractive effort:	9811 lb (39.7 kN)
Grate area:	14.33 sq ft (1.332 m²)
Total weight:	46 tons (46.7 t)
Gauge:	1067 mm
Road numbers:	1–15

The surviving (F) 351-class 2-4-0T locomotives saw out their last decades in steam generation and/or light shunting duties in railway workshops and depots. Engine 1033 was coupled to a pipe and used to supply steam to test boilers at Sydney's Eveleigh Workshops, moving only when its coal supply required replenishing. This picture was taken in the mid-1950s. (Late Ron Preston)

1885 Railways and Tramways of
New South Wales

(F) 351-class 2-4-0T

Built to the basic design of engines delivered to the Isle of Wight railway from 1864, these 18 tank locomotives were purchased for Sydney suburban service, appearing from 6 November 1885. Beyer, Peacock & Co built the first 12 while the Sydney firm Henry Vale provided the other six. All were running by July 1887, being classified firstly 351-class, then (F) 351-class from 1889.

Contemporary reports described them as 'efficient, trouble-free engines', and they did sterling work with the Sydney services until a serious accident at Sydenham in 1901, involving 363, saw the entire class confined to shunting duties at yards, locomotive depots and workshops.

Starting in 1905, the ranks of the class began to thin as no less than ten were sold to private railway operators such as coal, quarry, sand and gravel concerns. One of these locomotives was seen at Bulli colliery as late as 1956. Of the remaining government engines, 363 (the aforementioned accident victim) was withdrawn immediately and finally cut up in May 1912.

Those remaining by the time the NSWGR reclassified its entire motive power fleet in 1924 became the rather nondescript Z10-class. After more years of service in workshop and depot roles, withdrawals began again and, by 1940, only three remained—1033, eventually withdrawn from the Eveleigh Railway Workshops in November 1967 and now residing at the NSWRTM's Thirlmere Railway Museum; 1036, retired from the Junee Depot in January 1966; and 1042, which pottered around the Cardiff Railway Workshops until February 1973. This locomotive received its last overhaul as recently as 1970 and it has been preserved at Maitland 'steamshed', a feature being developed on the north eastern side of the town's railway station to honour the area's steam heritage.

SPECIFICATIONS

Imperial (Metric)

Cylinders:	15 x 22 in (38 x 56 cm)
Boiler pressure:	140 psi (965 kPa)
Coupled wheels:	5 ft 1 in (155 cm)
Tractive effort:	9089 lb (40.5 kN)
Grate area:	14 sq ft (1.301 m²)
Total weight:	38.5 tons (39.3 t)
Gauge:	1435 mm
Road numbers:	(original) 351–368
	(1924) 1031–1033, 1035–1037, 1039–1043

The last of the (L) 304-class in active service, 2109, in steam at Inverell in 1924. (RailCorp archives)

1885 Railways and Tramways of New South Wales

(L) 304-class 2-6-0

To relieve an acute passenger-locomotive shortage in New South Wales during the early 1880s, brought about by a record amount of railway construction, ten 2-6-0 tender engines were ordered from the Baldwin Locomotive Works. They entered service between March and September 1885.

All were fitted with the somewhat unconventional domeless boiler. Nevertheless, when placed on the steeply-graded Blue Mountains route where grades of up to 1 in 33 were the order of the day, the new locomotives returned faster schedules than could be achieved by the older 79-class English-built 4-4-0s, then the mainstay of the state's passenger service.

In the early 1890s, the L304s were displaced from the mountains run by 4-6-0 P-class and transferred further west for Orange and Dubbo district working.

By 1902–03, all of the (L) 304-class fell due for reboilering and were reissued to traffic, principally in the state's north-west and lower southern regions. Here they worked until further reboilering was necessary around 1920, when most received domed boilers.

This locomotive type became the Z21-class in the 1924 renumbering system. However, they were not destined to last long, for already (in 1919) Dubbo engine 2106 had been set aside; with the availability of more productive converted S-class tank engines for branch-line service, further boiler renewals were suspended. The old 2-6-0s began to be withdrawn in large numbers from 1929 onwards.

The last of them to go was 2109, which was retired in December 1939. They had all been scrapped by early 1941.

SPECIFICATIONS

	Imperial (Metric)
Cylinders:	18 x 26 in (46 x 66 cm)
Boiler pressure:	140 psi (965 kPa)
Coupled wheels:	5 ft 1 in (155 cm)
Tractive effort:	15 467 lb (68.8 kN)
Grate area:	16.9 sq ft (1.57 m²)
Total weight:	69.3 tons (70.7 t)
Gauge:	1435 mm
Road numbers:	(original) 304–313
	(1924) 2101–2110

1886 South Australian Railways

R-class 4-6-0

The locomotives of this class, which became the backbone of the SAR for decades, were introduced in 1886 to haul mixed traffic over the state's broad-gauge system. The first six were built by Dubs & Co, then the local firm James Martin of Gawler was contracted to construct an additional 24. All had been delivered by November 1895.

By this time the earlier engines were becoming due for general overhauls and from 1899 each was systematically rebuilt with higher-pressure Belpaire boilers, and reclassified Rx. The success of these revamped locomotives led to additional orders being placed for a total 54 new Rx-class. They were built at the SAR's Islington Railway Workshops (14), the North British Co, England (15) and Walkers Ltd, Queensland (25). They were all running by May 1916.

Preserved Rx-class 207 with an Adelaide–Angaston excursion train on 15 May 1972. (Graham Cotterall)

Although intended for mixed-traffic duties, these locomotives were often seen at the head of the state's top link expresses, including the Melbourne–Adelaide service. Enthusiasts of the era reported up to three Rx-class locomotives at a time hauling (and pushing) that express though the predominantly 1 in 45 Adelaide Hills during times of peak holiday loadings.

To produce additional power, 16 of the class were fitted with superheaters between 1925 and 1946, which increased their tractive effort by a nominal 5.61 kN.

The arrival of the 227-tonne 500-class super-power engines in mid-1926 displaced the Rx-class from main line express duties and they were transferred to gentler far-flung main lines as well as branch lines, including those in the Murray and Mallee country.

The first to be scrapped was 196 in June 1928. From 1935–38, scrapping started in earnest with the disposal of some 19 engines. The surviving examples were further overhauled and remained in traffic until 1957 when, due to dieselisation, scrapping started in earnest once more.

Their later years were spent shunting a number of metropolitan and country yards. The last depot with active Rx locomotives was Tailem Bend; the operation of Rx214 on 1 December 1967 at that location drew the curtain on SAR broad-gauge steam as far as regular revenue operations were concerned. Today, two remain available for enthusiast passenger service while Rx93 is on exhibit at the National Railway Museum, Port Adelaide. Seven more are displayed in country locations: Kadina, Kapunda, Loxton, Murray Bridge, Nuriootpa, Tailem Bend and Victor Harbor.

SPECIFICATIONS

	ORIGINAL	REBUILT AS RX
	IMPERIAL (METRIC)	IMPERIAL (METRIC)
CYLINDERS:	18 X 24 IN (46 X 61 CM)	18 X 24 IN (46 X 61 CM)
BOILER PRESSURE:	145 PSI (999 KPA)	175 PSI (1206 KPA)
COUPLED WHEELS:	4 FT 6 IN (137 CM)	4 FT 6 IN (137 CM)
TRACTIVE EFFORT:	16 704 LB (74.3 KN)	20 160 LB (87.9 KN)
GRATE AREA:	20.3 SQ FT (1.88 M²)	20.3 SQ FT (1.88 M²)
TOTAL WEIGHT:	64 TONS (65.9 T)	88.12 TONS (89.3 T)
GAUGE:	1600 MM	1600 MM
ROAD NUMBERS:	5, 9, 10, 15, 20, 25, 48, 55, 56, 91–96, 102–107, 138–153, 155, 158, 160, 190–203, 206–235	

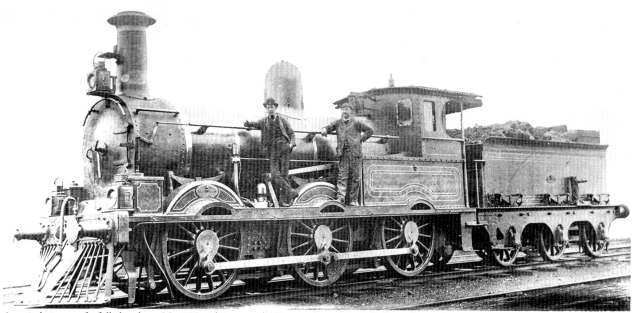

A period picture of a fully lined-out No. 359 with its crew. (V/Line archives, Len Whalley collection)

1886 Victorian Railways

X-class 0-6-0

These 15 locomotives were basically an enlarged version of the R-class 'Bulldogs' introduced in 1879.

Built in Ballarat by the Phoenix Foundry, they entered service in 1886 and 1887, each resplendent in fully lined green paintwork and finished off with brass domes and copper chimney caps. Nicknamed 'Jumbos' because of their great size, they were 10 tonnes heavier than the old 'Bulldogs' and about 12 per cent more powerful. Though intended for freight traffic, on many occasions these engines were called upon to work special excursion and race trains. Some reports claimed that they occasionally worked express passenger services when a passenger-type engine had failed.

All were reboilered during the 1900s; in 1915 some received rebored cylinders which increased their tractive effort by 12 kPa.

One interesting fact about this class is that out of just 15 locomotives, no fewer than eight were involved in accidents. In fact, three of them were involved in two accidents each while engine 365 managed to feature in three, bringing the total number of accidents involving the class to fifteen.

By January 1917, their general mechanical and boiler condition had deteriorated and, as a number of more modern locomotives were available, plans to further overhaul the X-class were suspended. Thus withdrawals began that month with 367.

No. 373 was the last in service, remaining until November 1920.

SPECIFICATIONS

	ORIGINAL	AS REBUILT
	IMPERIAL (METRIC)	IMPERIAL (METRIC)
CYLINDERS:	18 x 26 IN (46 x 66 CM)	18½ x 26 IN (47 x 66 CM)
BOILER PRESSURE:	140 PSI (965 KPA)	155 PSI (1068 KPA)
COUPLED WHEELS:	5 FT 0 IN (152 CM)	5 FT 0 IN (152 CM)
TRACTIVE EFFORT:	15 725 LB (70 KN)	18 390 LB (81.8 KN)
GRATE AREA:	21.7 SQ FT (2.016 M²)	21.7 SQ FT (2.016 M²)
TOTAL WEIGHT:	67 TONS (68.3 T)	67 TONS (68.3 T)
GAUGE:	1600 MM	1600 MM
ROAD NUMBERS:	353–381 (ODD NUMBERS ONLY)	

1887 Railways and Tramways of New South Wales

(H) 373-class 4-4-0

Even though the 12 express passenger locomotives of this class were not initially regarded as a 'really successful' locomotive type, the H373-class eventually proved to be good solid workhorses.

All were constructed by the Vulcan Foundry for operation on the Sydney–Newcastle and Illawarra line passenger services. They entered service between May and September 1887.

With the introduction and constant delivery of heavier P6-class 4-6-0s during the 1890s, the H-class was relegated to assistant duties or sent to country

No. 1710 was 67 years of age when withdrawn from steam generation duties at Chullora Workshops in May 1954. The by then battered veteran was pictured during its last months of service. (Bruce Macdonald)

depots such as Cootamundra, Parkes and Wellington for branch-line or 'outer main line' working.

Regarded as rough riders and heavy on tracks due to their high axle load, all were rebuilt from 1905 with new Belpaire boilers and snub-nose smokeboxes, and treated to 25 mm smaller diameter cylinders. These modifications provided the basis for a successful engine.

The locomotives were returned to the branch lines following their rebuilds and became the Z17-class in the state-wide 1924 renumbering system.

Withdrawals started in January 1934, as further reboilering became necessary. No. 1712 was the first to go, followed by another three over the next two years. By mid-1948, only four were in traffic.

Their last duties included steam generation at Enfield depot and workshop shunting at Chullora. No. 1709 was later overhauled for the state's Vintage Train, until withdrawn in 1974 for exhibition at the NSWRTM's Thirlmere Railway Museum. But it was reactivated in September 2005 to work a special NSW rail system 150th anniversary Vice Regal train from Sydney to Parramatta.

SPECIFICATIONS

	ORIGINAL	AS REBUILT
	IMPERIAL (METRIC)	IMPERIAL (METRIC)
CYLINDERS:	19 x 26 IN (48 x 66 CM)	18 x 26 IN (46 x 66 CM)
BOILER PRESSURE:	140 PSI (965 KPA)	140 PSI (965 KPA)
COUPLED WHEELS:	5 FT 6 IN (168 CM)	5 FT 6 IN (168 CM)
TRACTIVE EFFORT:	15 928 LB (70.9 KN)	14 295 LB (63.6 KN)
GRATE AREA:	20 SQ FT (1.858 M²)	20 SQ FT (1.858 M²)
TOTAL WEIGHT:	75.4 TONS (76.9 T)	74.25 TONS (75.7 T)
GAUGE:	1435 MM	1435 MM
ROAD NUMBERS:	(ORIGINAL) 373–384	(1924) 1701–1712

1888 INDUSTRIAL AND AGRICULTURE
LOCOMOTIVES

Krauss 0-4-0T / 0-6-0T / 0-6-2T

Lokomotivfabrik Krauss & Co, a firm of locomotive builders which opened its first plant in Munich, Germany, in 1866, manufactured a large number of small 0-4-0, 0-6-0 and 0-6-2 tank engines for delivery to various Australian industrial and construction authorities. In all, a total of 49 Krauss locomotives operated in this country. It is believed the first one, which arrived in 1888, was for the Melbourne Exposition.

That little locomotive is believed to have been a 600 mm gauge 0-4-0T that eventually found its way to several Western Australian owners including the Kalgoorlie and Boulder Firewood Co. It was scrapped during the later stages of World War II.

Because of that 1888 exposition, eleven additional locomotives were sold within four years, but all of 610 mm gauge. The first commercial customer was a Mr J. Robb, contractor for the Victorian government's Happy Valley Reservoir construction project. He took delivery of six 0-4-0T 5.6-tonne locomotives. Following completion of this project in 1896, the locomotives were sold hither and yon. Since Mr Robb owned the Cudgen Sugar Mill in northern New South Wales, one went there. In 1912, Cudgen Mill was sold to the Colonial Sugar Refining Co, which operated the nearby Condong Sugar Mill at Murwillumbah. The Cudgen trackage

Archie, one of four 0-4-0T locomotives delivered in 1908 to the NSW Water Conservation & Irrigation Commission to haul construction materials trains between Goondah station and Burrinjuck Dam in southern New South Wales. The photograph was taken near the dam site. (Author's collection)

and the Krauss then served the Condong Mill, the locomotive eventually being scrapped about 1941.

Another of these locomotives was sold to Tasmanian Railways in 1896, where it became that system's H-class No. 1. Two more 0-4-0Ts of similar design were acquired for shunting the smelters and hauling light local traffic on the other TGR tramways in the Zeehan area. These locomotives, numbered H2 and H3, were acquired second-hand in 1898 and 1899 respectively.

A fourth H-class of basically similar design was purchased new and added to the fleet in 1899. While both it and H1 were retained by the railway for several more decades, H2 and H3 were sold to the Victorian PWD in 1906. Two years later, H2 was sold to the Corrimal Colliery in New South Wales, where it operated the company's narrow-gauge escarpment tramway until 1933, when it was simply abandoned and left to rot beside the line.

No. H3 was sold in 1911 to the Rubicon Timber & Tramway Co of Victoria, remaining in service until 1935 and being scrapped about 1951. While H1 was partially dismantled about 1930, H4 continued under TGR ownership until it was sold to Tasmania's Catamaran Colliery in 1926. By then the engine was in poor order, for early in 1930 it and another Krauss, which was also in service at the colliery, were united to form one serviceable engine. This hybrid remained operational until scrapped in 1938.

The NSW Water Conservation & Irrigation Commission purchased four 0-4-0T Krauss locomotives new in 1908 for construction of the Burrinjuck Dam. These were slightly larger 7.8-tonne machines. All four were later sold to private operators, including the State Metal Quarries of New South Wales and various Queensland sugar plantations. Three remain, *Archie* at Burrinjuck Dam, *Jack* at the Lake Macquarie Light Railway, Edgeworth (NSW), and *Dulce* held privately at Burpengary (Q).

Eleven similar 0-4-0T locomotives were acquired by Tasmania's Mt Lyell Mining & Railway Co. Several of these were preserved too, one at the West Coast Pioneers Memorial Museum, others at Tullah and the Queen Victoria Museum & Art Gallery, Launceston.

Basically, the Australian-operated Krauss locomotives were of two types. The 4-coupled type was between 4 and 7.8 tonnes in weight, while the 6-coupled type was of either the 8 or 10 tonne variety. The smaller locomotives did not have side tanks so the water supply was carried in a small tank on one side of the cab and in well tanks between the frames. The larger locomotives had side tanks and more elaborate fixtures. Several of these also had well tanks.

The larger 6-coupled locomotives found ready employment within the sugar industry, one of the largest being the second last example to arrive in Australia, an 0-6-2T built new in 1914 for the 762 mm

Another of the four NSW Water Conservation & Irrigation Commission 0-4-0T locomotives, *Archie* erroneously carrying the nameplate *Jack*, when employed in tourist service at Goulburn on 31 January 1975. This locomotive was recently cosmetically restored for exhibition at Burrinjuck Dam. (Leon Oberg)

gauge Maroochy Shire Tramway in Queensland. In 1935, the locomotive was forwarded to Walkers Ltd in Maryborough for conversion to 610 mm gauge, in which form it worked until 1962 at Bingera Sugar Mill.

The last Krauss imported new into Australia was maker's number 6927 of 1914, built for the Balgownie & Corrimal Coal Co, New South Wales. This locomotive's arrival in Australia coincided with the outbreak of World War I in which the British Empire was in conflict with Germany. It immediately became unfashionable in Australia to buy German-built locomotives despite their workmanship and operational flexibility. No. 6927 had a 30-year working life, however, being eventually withdrawn in 1944 to lie derelict for 27 years. Its remains are today stored at the Illawarra Light Railway Museum Society at Albion Park.

Krauss locomotives had been built for every conceivable gauge, from 381 mm to 1677 mm. They were fine, solid, trouble-free locomotives which had a good reputation wherever they operated. While most that came to Australia have now been scrapped, about nine have been given places in various museums.

Perhaps the most unusual of them all is the locomotive in use at the Illawarra Light Railway

Museum Society, which uses 0-4-0T Krauss No. 2179's frame and wheels. It was one of the initial six imported in 1889 by building contractor John Robb for the Victoria Dock construction. After passing through several owners' hands, this locomotive was operated by the NSWGR until it was sold in 1936 to Newbolds General Refactory Co to haul clay at Pattimore quarry, Milton. Within two years, the locomotive was working the company's Thirroul works but during World War II, with the Allies again fighting Germany, boiler parts were allegedly unobtainable. So company engineers stripped the locomotive to its chassis and rebuilt the remains using a 1920s Leyland bus petrol engine and mechanical transmission.

In 1945, the locomotive was transferred to the company's operations at Home Rule (in central-western NSW) where it saw limited service before facing withdrawal about 1947, when it was stored. It was subsequently donated to the Illawarra Light Railway in 1973, eventually arriving at Albion Park two years later. Following a full overhaul, named *Newbold*, the unit went into museum railway service in June 1976.

A similar 0-4-0WT, No. 2181, built specifically to the order of John Robb, made its way to the

The Leyland-engined 0-4-0 locomotive which started life as Krauss steam locomotive, maker's number 2179, in action at the Illawarra Light Railway and Museum at Albion Park, NSW. (Leon Oberg)

East Murchison United Gold Mines Pty Ltd in Western Australia around 1919 following further construction project employment in Victoria and South Australia. One of only three Krauss products to work in Western Australia, the little 4.2 tonne engine sat in a Kalgoorlie machinery dealer's yard until rescued by a Perth collector for preservation in 1963. It was last reported in the possession of the Western Australian Light Railway Preservation Association at Whiteman Park.

SPECIFICATIONS

(AN EXAMPLE ONLY OF THE PROLIFIC 0-4-0T)

IMPERIAL (METRIC)

CYLINDERS:	7 x 12 IN (18 x 30 CM)
BOILER PRESSURE:	175 PSI (1206 KPA)
COUPLED WHEELS:	2 FT 0 IN (61 CM)
TRACTIVE EFFORT:	3430 LB (15.3 KN)
GRATE AREA:	3.23 SQ FT (0.3 M²)
TOTAL WEIGHT:	5.5 TONS (5.6 T)
GAUGE:	610 MM
BUILDER'S NUMBERS:	AS MOST OF THESE LOCOMOTIVES WERE UNNUMBERED, THE FOLLOWING IS A LIST OF THE OFFICIAL WORKS NUMBERS OF THOSE KRAUSS COMPANY AUSTRALIAN LOCOMOTIVES: 1824, 2178–2181, 2195, 2196, 2437, 2459, 2549, 2589, 2591, 2640, 3263, 3266, 3967, 3423, 3444, 3644, 3729, 3941, 4080, 4087, 4298, 4387, 4526, 4687, 4722, 5261, 5479, 5480, 5530, 5671, 5679, 5682, 5800, 5869, 5870, 5945, 5947, 5988, 6063, 6067, 6415, 6416, 6486, 6611, 6854 AND 6927.

1888 SOUTHERN COAL CO

Yorkshire 0-6-0T

Coal mining—and to some extent, cedar cutting—was the catalyst in the development of towns and villages along the NSW South Coast. Initially, tiny operations sprang up in a bid to provide fuel for metropolitan markets. By the 1890s, some larger companies, aided by their own deepwater jetties at Wollongong and Port Kembla, were sending coal out by the shipload.

One such enterprise was the Southern Coal Co which in January 1889 opened its Mount Pleasant Colliery, transporting its product by rail direct to Port Kembla. In readiness for the start-up of operations, the company had imported two little 0-6-0T locomotives from the Yorkshire Engine Co in England (Builder's Nos 428 and 429) of 1888 manufacture.

Just one year later, the company acquired the assets of the adjoining Corrimal Coal Co and set about modernising the rail operation, replacing an original 610 mm gauge system linking the mine with the NSWGR at Corrimal with a standard gauge railway serving new screens, this coming on stream from February 1890.

This extended the route availability of the two Yorkshire locomotives and not only did they haul

Corrimal Coal Co's No. 2 at work in 1965 just prior to its withdrawal from service after an active 77-year life. (Late Ron Preston)

Corrimal coal over the NSWGR tracks between there and the company's Unanderra coke ovens, but conveyed coal direct to Port Kembla—and, for a time, northwards along NSWGR to Bellambi, where the company once shipped coal from the Bellambi Point jetty via South Bulli Mining Co's connection.

The late Gifford Eardley reported in his book *Transporting the Black Diamonds* that the two Yorkshire locomotives went into service wearing a 'rich yellow livery set off to perfection by a black smokebox', earning them the nickname 'Yellowbellies'. Rationality prevailed, it seems, for the ravages of coal dust and soot saw the engines painted black after a relatively short time.

Both locomotives were serviced at Unanderra coke ovens until that plant closed circa 1912, when the engines were sent to Corrimal Colliery. Throughout that decade, both engines enjoyed periods on lease to the Port Kembla-based Electrolytic Refining & Smelting Co. They were also known to have worked coal miners' picnic trains and there is a photo of one engine and brakevan standing in Bulli station, a location well away from their normal sphere of operation.

In later years, all haulage over NSWGR metals was

entrusted to the government, hauling out of company 'exchange sidings', and the little engines generally remained at the Corrimal Colliery hauling coal between the screens and the sidings where, by 1963, author Peter Neve noted their general boiler condition was such that No. 1 was restricted to a 120 psi boiler pressure while No. 2 was devalued to just 80 psi.

A year later, Australian Iron & Steel acquired the business and soon afterwards, No. 1 was withdrawn and cut up. No. 2 soldiered on, shunting Corrimal Coke Works until November 1965, after which it was forwarded to the parent company's Cringila workshops and officially scrapped in March 1968.

SPECIFICATIONS

	IMPERIAL (METRIC)
CYLINDERS:	18 x 26 IN (46 x 66 CM)
BOILER PRESSURE:	140 PSI (965 KPA)
COUPLED WHEELS:	4 FT 0 IN (122 CM)
TRACTIVE EFFORT:	19 656 LB (87.3 KN)
GRATE AREA:	21 SQ FT (1.951 M²)
TOTAL WEIGHT:	75.9 TONS (77.4 T)
GAUGE:	1435 MM
ROAD NUMBERS:	1 AND 2

A Y-class locomotive after it emerged from VR's Newport Workshops following the 1904–09 rebuild programme. (V/Line archives, Len Whalley collection)

1889 VICTORIAN RAILWAYS

Y-class 0-6-0

By the mid-1880s the VR administration was faced with a large number of varying designs of locomotive, few of which were compatible. It had become apparent that a standardised approach to the motive power situation would result in definite economy of operation over the longer term.

As a result, various classes of a standard design were produced and used for express passenger, heavy freight and suburban passenger services. They were all designed under the direction of the VR's Chief Mechanical Engineer, Mr Richard Speight.

The first engines to appear were Y-class 0-6-0s in January 1889. They were built for heavy freight haulage and all 31 were running by October that year. Although the pattern engine had been built in England by Kitson & Co, the remaining 30 were constructed in Ballarat by the Phoenix Foundry.

Between 1904 and 1909, all were given new high pressure 1206 kPa boilers (in lieu of their original 965 kPa ones), which increased their tractive effort by almost a quarter. As the boiler line was increased, shorter cast iron chimneys were added, along with raised cabs.

On the whole, the Y-class excelled. They were regarded as 'free steamers' and reasonable riders considering their 0-6-0 configuration. In fact, they were not confined to goods traffic, often being employed on Melbourne race and excursion specials in the days before suburban electrification.

With the introduction of more powerful goods engines from 1918, the Y-class was gradually relegated to local transfer and shunting duties. Many

were later fitted with platforms which stretched the entire length of both engine and tender to enable ground shunters to ride and direct movements as required. These locomotives were seen in many rail yards, including Geelong, Ballarat, Bendigo and Melbourne.

Between 1924 and 1931, the Y-class received an additional 13 to their number when similarly styled 0-6-0 New R-class locomotives were reclassified 'Y'. These acted as replacements for some original Y-class after scrappings started in 1926. No. 397 was the first of the original fleet to go and nine more had vanished by the end of that decade.

By 1960, the class had been reduced to a mere two engines, both of which were subsequently preserved. Loco Y108 is a static exhibit in the ARHS's Newport Museum and Y112 has just been fully restored in Ballarat for Steamrail.

As an additional point of interest, Y109 was one of the few steam locomotives in Australia to be converted to diesel. This occurred in April 1954, when the frame and wheels were sold to a gypsum works at Nowingi to form the basis of a diesel-mechanical locomotive.

SPECIFICATIONS

	ORIGINAL	AS REBUILT
	IMPERIAL (METRIC)	IMPERIAL (METRIC)
CYLINDERS:	18 x 26 IN (46 x 66 CM)	18 x 26 IN (46 x 66 CM)
BOILER PRESSURE:	140 PSI (965 KPA)	175 PSI (1206 KPA)
COUPLED WHEELS:	4 FT 6 IN (137 CM)	4FT 6 IN (137 CM)
TRACTIVE EFFORT:	17 472 LB (77.8 KN)	21 840 LB (97.2 KN)
GRATE AREA:	21 SQ FT (1.951 M²)	21 SQ FT (1.951 M²)
TOTAL WEIGHT:	69.2 TONS (70.6 T)	69.5 TONS (70.7 T)
GAUGE:	1600 MM	1600 MM
ROAD NUMBERS:	(ORIGINAL) 383–441	
	(LATER NUMBERING) Y100–109, 111, 112, 114–121	
	(EX NEW R-CLASS) Y110, 113, 122v132	

An early photograph of 'New' A-class No. 416. Note the impressive collection of kerosene lamps. (V/Line archives, author's collection)

1889 VICTORIAN RAILWAYS

New A-class 4-4-0

The VR, in common with the NSWGR, favoured the 4-4-0 design for its passenger and main line express haulage. In all, nine 4-4-0 classes finally found their way onto VR metals. One long remembered was the Kitson-designed 'New' A-class express passenger type.

Fifteen were built between October 1889 and April 1891 by the Phoenix Foundry, part of the celebrated Richard Speight group of standard locomotive designs.

At first they were confined to the main lines, being based at Melbourne, Ballarat, Bendigo and Benalla. As such, they shared the express haulage with the old A-class Bissel-bogied Beyer, Peacock-built locomotives of 1884. Among their more important duties was the operation of the Sydney and Melbourne expresses in relay between Melbourne and Albury.

As the nineteenth century drew to a close, it became evident even more passenger locomotives would be needed. While the 'New' A-class was selected as the basis for these new engines, the opportunity was taken to fine-tune the design. As a test, loco 422's cylinders were converted to accommodate overhead

piston valves (the first locomotive on the system to be so fitted). The economy experienced from this move, both in operation and maintenance, saw virtually all subsequent new VR steam locomotives similarly equipped.

At the same time, the VR drawing office went to work on the 'New A' drawings and came up with a slightly heavier, more powerful 4-4-0 design which employed larger 48 x 66 cm cylinders and 1275 kPa boiler pressure. The prototype's dumpy leading Bissell bogie was replaced with a riveted-plate equalised bogie with outside wheel bearings. The coupled wheels were also provided with equalisation to better distribute axle forces.

Twenty of these locomotives were built at the Phoenix Foundry between August 1900 and November 1903 and entered service as the AA-class. Not all were the same, however, for from the eleventh delivery the fireboxes were increased 15 cm and the grate area enlarged some 0.200 m^2. Whereas the boilers were pressed to 1378 kPa, longer-range bogie tenders identical to those designed for the then under construction DD-class replaced the original 6-wheel variety.

Meanwhile, from 1901, the older 'New' A-class locomotives were gradually being rebuilt with higher-pressure 1206 kPa standard boilers, which increased their tractive effort by over 13 kN. New cabs were also fitted. After some of the more important branch

Improved 'New' A-class (AA-class) No. 550 following its 1903 rebuild. This was the first of the second rebuilt batch that came with the bogie-type tenders then under construction for the new DD-class. These tenders gave the engines a more balanced look and provided a greater operating range. (V/Line archives, Len Whalley collection)

lines were re-railed during the early 1900s, the locomotives were able to work as far afield as Echuca and Mornington.

With the introduction of larger 4-6-0 A2-class locomotives in 1907, the 'New' A and AA-classes lost much of their former appeal and many were relegated to assistant duties. Others entered short-transfer goods service but, as engines were always required for seasonal duties, they continued at the helm of show and race specials for many years.

By the early 1920s, the 'New' A-class boilers were once more wearing out, and class members were quickly withdrawn. Four were scrapped in June 1924, and by February 1925 all had vanished. The last to be scrapped was No. 412.

But some AA-class locomotives were able to 'keep their hand in' for, following the scrapping of three in 1919, four others (542, 544, 566 and 570) were rebuilt with Robinson superheaters and extended smokeboxes in 1923–24. These locomotives' boiler pressure was correspondingly reduced to 1206 kPa (which reduced internal stresses and lowered boiler maintenance).

The last four AA-class remained active until the Great Depression years and were finally scrapped in January 1932. The exception was 532, which was withdrawn in 1925 to become a stationary boiler at

Newport Workshops, a position it held until circa 1940.

SPECIFICATIONS

	ORIGINAL	AS REBUILT
	IMPERIAL (METRIC)	IMPERIAL (METRIC)
CYLINDERS:	18 x 24 IN (46 x 61 CM)	18 x 24 IN (46 x 61 CM)
BOILER PRESSURE:	140 PSI (965 KPA)	175 PSI (1206 KPA)
COUPLED WHEELS:	6 FT 0 IN (183 CM)	6 FT 0 IN (183 CM)
TRACTIVE EFFORT:	12 096 LB (53.8 KN)	15 120 LB (67.3 KN)
GRATE AREA:	21 SQ FT (1.951 M²)	21 SQ FT (1.951 M²)
TOTAL WEIGHT:	73 TONS (74.5 T)	75 TONS (76.5 T)
GAUGE:	1600 MM	1600 MM

	AA-CLASS AS BUILT	SUPERHEATED AA-CLASS
	IMPERIAL (METRIC)	IMPERIAL (METRIC)
CYLINDERS:	19 x 26 IN (48 x 66 CM)	19 x 66 IN (48 x 66 CM)
BOILER PRESSURE:	185 PSI (1275 KPA)	175 PSI (1206 KPA)
COUPLED WHEELS:	6 FT 1 IN (185 CM)	6 FT 1 IN (185 CM)
TRACTIVE EFFORT:	19 029 LB (84.9 KN)	19 125 LB (85.2 KN)
GRATE AREA:	21 SQ FT (1.951 M²)	21 SQ FT (1.951 M²)
TOTAL WEIGHT:	80 TONS 6 CWT (82.1 T)	93 TONS (94.8 T)
GAUGE:	1600 MM	1600 MM
ROAD NUMBERS:	'NEW' A-CLASS, 396–424 (EVEN NUMBERS ONLY)	
	AA-CLASS, 530–548, 550–570	

E-class 2-4-2T No. 512, as delivered by Melbourne manufacturer Munro & Co. It was later converted to 0-6-2T EE-class. (Author's collection)

E-class 2-4-2T

By the latter part of the 1880s, it had become increasingly obvious that the motive power working Melbourne's suburban traffic would soon need to be replaced due to ever-increasing weights of trains and the expanding services.

At that time the 63 modest locomotives of the N, M, L and C classes were hard pressed to maintain the traffic on offer so plans were prepared, under the then locomotive standardisation scheme, for a more powerful 2-4-2 tank type. The result became the E-class.

The initial pattern engine arrived from Kitson & Co in April 1889. After it proved successful, a further 70 were ordered locally from the Phoenix Foundry (45) and Munro & Co of Melbourne (25). These were all delivered between 1890 and 1894.

The class was placed on main line suburban passenger runs and quickly became firm favourites with locomotive crews and maintenance staff alike for both performance and reliability. They were the backbone of this service for nearly 20 years. From 1908, however, with the delivery of the more powerful DDe-class 4-6-2T locomotives, the elderly 2-4-2Ts were gradually relegated to the less difficult routes until electrification was introduced in the 1920s.

When a need for shunting locomotives arose, the original E-class design was adopted but configured to an 0-6-2T wheel arrangement. The initial five constructed by the Phoenix Foundry became the EE-class. In addition, 24 of the original E-class locomotives were converted to 0-6-2Ts between June 1898 and August 1924.

Although the EE's had a similar outward appearance to their prototype, they differed in that some were fitted with larger 46 cm cylinders and bigger boilers of 'New' A-class type. This increased their tractive effort by over 22 kN. In addition, the remaining E-class locomotives were rebuilt in 1907 with new specially-built boilers rated at 1102 kPa. Though their cylinders were not enlarged, their subsequent power increase represented about 9 kN over their previous performance.

As metropolitan electrification continued, many E's and EE's were withdrawn from service. Some were destined for additional lives when, in 1920 and 1921, the SAR purchased twenty 2-4-2Ts for its Adelaide suburban passenger services. These became that state's M-class, and were generally restricted to the Port Adelaide line because of their heavy axle load. They did not last long, most being condemned and scrapped during the later 1920s, the last one in traffic being 257 (ex-VR E372) which was condemned in May 1935.

The remaining E's and EE's on the Victorian system were also being scrapped at this time. The first one to go was the pattern engine, 426, and a total of 26 had been discarded by 1924. The remainder spent their later years as pilots (shunters) in yards, depots and workshops. The last 2-4-2T version in traffic was 506, which worked at the Newport Railway Workshops until withdrawn in 1953. (This

EE-class 0-6-2T No. 369 standing with VR's 'vintage train' at Newport Workshops on 4 October 1969. The train had been prepared for a railway exhibition at Spencer Street station over the following two days. (V/Line archives, Len Whalley collection)

locomotive is today preserved at the ARHS's North Williamstown Museum.)

The 0-6-2T version lingered a little longer, the last withdrawn being 371, on 15 November 1963, after a period shunting at Ballarat.

SPECIFICATIONS

	Imperial (Metric)
Cylinders:	17 x 26 in (43 x 66 cm)
Boiler pressure:	140 psi (965 kPa)
Coupled wheels:	5 ft 0 in (152 cm)
Tractive effort:	14 026 lb (62.4 kN)
Grate area:	17.8 sq ft (1.654 m²)
Total weight:	53.4 tons (54.5 t)
Gauge:	1600 mm
Road numbers:	(original) 12, 34, 36, 346–394, 426–460, 472–520 (even numbers only) (1923 numbering of those remaining): 350–381, 390 (No. 506 later un-classed and numbered 236) (SAR M-class): 256–275

1889 QUEENSLAND RAILWAYS

B15-class 4-6-0

The continuing increase in freight traffic in Queensland during the 1880s prompted the preparation of drawings for a more powerful 4-6-0 tender design. When the first 15 locomotives, ordered from the British firm of Nasmyth Wilson & Co, entered traffic between 1889 and 1890, it was thought that they would become the system's G-class, but because they were delivered during the reclassification of the Queensland locomotive fleet they became the B15-class. (The B signified three driving axles and the 15 was the cylinder diameter in inches.)

As these locomotives were so successful, another 21 were ordered, this time from the Queensland firm of Evans, Anderson, Phelan & Co. They were delivered between 1893 and 1896. An additional ten were ordered from the Yorkshire Engine Co in Sheffield, plus a total of 46 from Walkers Ltd of Maryborough, Queensland. Between 1900 and 1909, six similar locomotives were introduced to the privately-owned Chillagoe Railway & Mining Co in northern Queensland. One of these was sold new to QR and the rest followed when the government assumed ownership of the line in 1919. In all, 98

B15 No. 290 after its cosmetic restoration for preservation. (QR archives)

locomotives of this type were eventually operated by QR.

Reboilering started in 1903. By 1928, some 93 had received higher-pressure boilers and an extra 23 cm on their coupled wheels for passenger working. These became known as the B15 (converted) class. The five non-converted locomotives were written off in November 1934.

Even in the last decade of their service life, examples could be found at most principal depots, with a large number based in the Cairns area. Whereas others had kerosene lighting, the Cairns engines were equipped with electric lighting to work the Kuranda line and beyond.

B15 (converted) locomotives were also popular on sugar trains, and examples were regularly used as yard shunters in the Brisbane area until the last.

Withdrawals began as boiler and mechanical conditions dictated. Loco 290 (a converted engine) lasted for some time, shunting at Rockhampton. It finally broke down and was towed to Redbank Workshops on 26 September 1968 and retained by QR for preservation.

In addition, B15 (converted) 299 has been restored to operation by the Model Engineers and Live Steamers Association on behalf of the City of Maryborough. When not in use it stands at Maryborough railway station.

SPECIFICATIONS

	ORIGINAL	AS CONVERTED
	IMPERIAL (METRIC)	IMPERIAL (METRIC)
CYLINDERS:	15 x 20 IN (38 x 51 CM)	15 x 20 IN (38 x 51 CM)
BOILER PRESSURE:	140 PSI (965 KPA)	160 PSI (1102 KPA)
COUPLED WHEELS:	3 FT 0 IN (91 CM)	3 FT 9 IN (114 CM)
TRACTIVE EFFORT:	14 000 LB (62.3 KN)	14 769 LB (65.7 KN)
GRATE AREA:	12.8 SQ FT (1.189 M²)	12.8 SQ FT (1.189 M²)
TOTAL WEIGHT:	51.7 TONS (52.7 T)	55.4 TONS (56.5 T)
GAUGE:	1067 MM	1067 MM
ROAD NUMBERS:	3, 23, 42, 54, 95, 205–219, 235–244, 270–280, 289–338, 341–346, 539	

1889 VICTORIAN RAILWAYS

'New' R-class 0-6-0

Twenty-five of these locomotives, designed by Kitson under the VR's locomotive standardisation initiative of the late 1880s, were constructed by the South Melbourne firm Messrs Robinson Bros, Campbell & Sloss. They entered service between 31 December 1889 and 15 September 1891, all having been acquired for main line freight haulage.

The locomotives became the state's 'New' R-class because, except for their leading wheel spacing, they were very similar to the existing 0-6-0 R-class, introduced in 1879.

RY-class No. 461 at North Melbourne depot in 1927. (V/Line archives, Len Whalley collection)

The new locomotives became champions of Victoria's wheat haulage for many years; once they were all in service, many were allotted to Bendigo and Stawell depots.

Between 1905 and 1909, all were rebuilt with larger, high-pressure 1206 kPa boilers similar to those being fitted on the Y and 'New' A-class rebuilds. They all then became the RY-class, the letter 'Y' being introduced due to the their similarity in both capacity and appearance to another 1889 engine, the Y-class 0-6-0 discussed on page 82. In fact, they were so alike that 13 of the class were actually classified 'Y' between 1924 and 1931.

Withdrawals commenced in June 1926, when 451 and 459 were scrapped. Many more followed, with three going in 1927 and another in 1928. By 1936, all the RY-class had been scrapped, leaving the 13 reclassified Y-class to do yard shunting and pilot work. Some remained in Melbourne, Geelong and Bendigo yards until they were finally scrapped.

The last to go were 127 and 131 in September and June 1960 respectively.

SPECIFICATIONS

	ORIGINAL	RY-CLASS
	IMPERIAL (METRIC)	IMPERIAL (METRIC)
CYLINDERS:	17 x 26 IN (43 x 66 CM)	18 x 26 IN (46 x 66 CM)
BOILER PRESSURE:	140 PSI (965 KPA)	175 PSI (1206 KPA)
COUPLED WHEELS:	4 FT 6 IN (137 CM)	4 FT 6 IN (137 CM)
TRACTIVE EFFORT:	15 585 LB (69.4 KN)	21 840 LB (97.2 KN)
GRATE AREA:	17.8 SQ FT (1.654 M²)	17.8 SQ FT (1.654 M²)
TOTAL WEIGHT:	64.5 TONS (65.8 T)	71 TONS (72.4 T)
GAUGE:	1600 MM	1600 MM
ROAD NUMBERS:	447–495 (ODD NUMBERS ONLY)	
	Y-CLASS CONVERTS BECAME: 110, 113, 122–132	

1891 NEW SOUTH WALES
GOVERNMENT RAILWAYS

B55-class 2-6-0

Due to the success of the B205-class 2-6-0s of 1882, NSWGR ordered an additional 25 basically similar locomotives during 1885, this time from Dubs & Co. These locomotives carried several updated refinements which included a left-hand driving station (which was to become the norm on NSWGR), an enclosed steel cab, deeper, sloping smokebox designed to reduce lower tube blockages, and improved tenders.

The locomotives arrived a little later than expected, the first not entering service until 10 March 1891. However, all were operating heavy goods trains over the state's principal main lines by mid-August. The class was some 9 tonnes heavier than its B205-class prototype but operated identical routes and services.

Between 1903 and 1908, reboilering became necessary and they were given raised Belpaire boilers, standard smokeboxes and cast iron funnels.

As the heavier T-class 2-8-0s multiplied, the old 2-6-0s were shuffled out onto the flatter main lines and then onto light branch-line duties. During the early part of the century, most of them worked around Werris Creek and Narrabri. Others worked coal trains in the Newcastle area until they also were displaced by the T-class.

While all became the Z24-class in the 1924 renumbering system, their boilers were soon in need of replacement and, accordingly, withdrawals started in June 1929 with 2405. Eleven more quickly followed

B55-class No. 407, which later became 2422, as delivered in 1891. (Bruce Macdonald collection)

and during 1937 no less than ten were scrapped. However, the remaining engines were repaired and continued in their shunting and branch-line roles until sales to private railway operators thinned their ranks. One engine worthy of note was 2415, which was sold to BHP at Newcastle in November 1940, where it was promptly converted to an 0-6-0 saddle tank and worked as that railway's number 26 until it was scrapped in the mid-1960s.

Others were bought by coal mines and gravel works and another purchaser, the Bunnerong Powerhouse (Sydney), operated one until mid-1975.

The last of the departmental engines to be withdrawn was 2413 during November 1960. Used at Enfield locomotive depot in a shunting capacity, it was sold to Bunnerong Powerhouse with sister engines 2408 and 2414. In November 1975 all were preserved, 2408 and 2414 going to the Dorrigo Steam Railway and Museum and 2413 to the ACT Division of the ARHS (it is currently on loan to the Junee Railway Roundhouse). In addition, NSWRTM loco 2419 is on display at Goulburn roundhouse.

B55-class No. 2415 was sold to BHP's Newcastle works in November 1940 and on 28 July 1941 emerged as an 0-6-0 saddle tank, working there as No. 26 until scrapped in the mid-1960s. (BHP)

SPECIFICATIONS

	Imperial (Metric)
Cylinders:	18 x 26 in (46 x 66 cm)
Boiler pressure:	140 psi (965 kPa)
Coupled wheels:	4 ft 0 in (122 cm)
Tractive effort:	19 656 lb (87.3 kN)
Grate area:	21 sq ft (1.951 m²)
Total weight:	75.9 tons (77.4 t)
Gauge:	1435 mm
Road numbers:	(original) 55–78, 388–393, 407–410. (1924) 2401–2425

1891 New South Wales Government Railways

O446-class 4-6-0

As train loads had outgrown the capacity of the elderly 4-4-0 C79 class, the NSWGR badly needed heavier express passenger locomotives. Although fifty 4-6-0s were on order from Beyer, Peacock & Co in England, it soon became clear that they would be late arriving. Consequently, 12 Baldwin Locomotive Works standard 4-6-0s of generally similar size were ordered as an emergency measure.

Being a stock design, they were delivered soon afterwards and entered traffic between 28 July and 25 August 1891. While similar to those placed in service over the Baltimore & Ohio Railway in the USA, the NSWGR version was slightly lighter, fitted with the Australian-approved screw reverse in lieu of the US Johnson-bar arrangement, and was slightly narrower to suit the loading gauge.

These new locomotives, which were designated the O-class, immediately took over the difficult 1 in 33 Blue Mountains run; when the English-built

The pure North American lines of the domeless 2-6-0 design employed on the NSWGR are beautifully portrayed in this Baldwin Locomotive Works image. (Author's collection)

4-6-0 P-class arrived, their range was extended to Bathurst and Orange. The whole class was banned from passenger running after 452 was involved in a serious accident at Tarana which at first was blamed on the leading bogie axle boxes. (The subsequent inquiry found the accident had been caused by a broken rail.) Their speed limit was reduced to 65 km/h and the locomotives were captive to goods working until a serious shortage of locomotives presented itself after World War I.

An improved outside bearing leading bogie was fitted to all the O-class locomotives to enable their speed limit to be increased to 80 km/h for further passenger working, and they were returned to the Blue Mountains route. No further trouble was ever experienced. From that time, all engines were gradually fitted with domed superheater boilers (some with Belpaire fireboxes) and piston valves.

The arrival of heavier NN-class 4-6-0 express locomotives from 1914, and then 75 larger C36-class 4-6-0 engines during the late 1920s, considerably eased the passenger engine shortage and the O-class was transferred to the Binnaway area for branch line goods and passenger working. During this time, examples could be found working the Mudgee passenger trains through to Lithgow.

In the 1924 renumbering system, the Baldwins were classified Z23.

Loco 2305 was the first to be withdrawn in May 1933. By 1941, only six remained in traffic. They had all been retired by September 1946, with 2304 being the last to go. None remain today.

SPECIFICATIONS

	ORIGINAL	SUPERHEATED
	IMPERIAL (METRIC)	IMPERIAL (METRIC)
CYLINDERS:	21 x 24 IN (53 x 61 CM)	21 x 24 IN (53 x 61 CM)
BOILER PRESSURE:	160 PSI (1102 KPA)	160 PSI (1102 KPA)
COUPLED WHEELS:	5 FT 1 IN (155 CM)	5 FT 1 IN (155 CM)
TRACTIVE EFFORT:	22 209 LB (98.8 KN)	23 600 LB (105 KN)
GRATE AREA:	27.7 SQ FT (2.54 M²)	27.7 SQ FT (2.54 M²)
TOTAL WEIGHT:	90 TONS (91.4 T)	99 TONS (100.5 T)
GAUGE:	1435 MM	1435 MM
ROAD NUMBERS:	(ORIGINAL) 446–457	
	(1924) 2301–2312	

1891 NEW SOUTH WALES GOVERNMENT RAILWAYS

J483-class 2-8-0

In an effort to cater for the ever-increasing goods train loads over the steeply-graded Blue Mountains route, an order was placed with the Baldwin Locomotive Works in the USA for 20 standard North American 2-8-0 freight-type locomotives. The first entered traffic on 30 September 1891, and all 20 were operating within two months.

Unlike the bulk of the fleet, which was fitted with two standard cylinders, the final two locomotives were built as 4-cylinder compounds of Vauclain design. This design utilised normally wasted exhaust steam to provide a second power impulse through low-pressure cylinders. Although this design was somewhat similar to the Mallet compounding system, it permitted both the high- and low-pressure cylinders in the common casting to drive

J-class 492 (which became 2910) at Hornsby in 1911. (Late O.B. Bolton, Bruce Macdonald collection)

a single crosshead. The compounds were not a real success, however, and both engines were rebuilt as conventional 2-cylinder simples in 1896.

The design of the J-class was basically a goods version of the 4-6-0 O-class passenger engines that had appeared from the same builder's factory two months earlier. The husky 2-8-0s represented a vast increase in performance over previous locomotive types and, as with the O-class, their bogie tenders, while providing an increased fuel and water capacity, demonstrated considerable ride improvements.

The J-class gave splendid service over the Blue Mountains route (and beyond to Dubbo), its power availability being an increase of about 28 per cent on the principal existing goods locomotives, the A and B classes. As sufficient numbers of new English-built T-class 2-8-0s were commissioned during the latter half of the 1890s, the still-new J-class was moved westwards, mainly centred on Wellington depot. After the turn of the century, most were transferred to the Newcastle area for coal train haulage between Port Waratah, Hexham and Maitland. However, with continuing deliveries of T-class, the Baldwin locomotives were withdrawn in 1915.

For reasons never fully explained—given the proliferation of English-type T and TF classes—six J-class were shopped between 1916 and 1920, at which time they were fitted with superheaters and slightly larger piston valve cylinders. In addition, 2904 was equipped with the novel Southern valve gear in 1917 to gauge its effects prior to its introduction into service on the 120 K-class 2-8-0s the following year.

In their stronger form, the superheated J-class locomotives returned to the main line, being generally confined to the Central-West and North-West routes.

In 1924, the locomotives nominally became the Z29-class but, because some of the saturated locomotives were lying out of traffic, only the superheated locomotives and seven remaining saturated examples actually carried the new numbers. Scrapping of the saturated class members was completed between 1926 and 1930.

The superheated versions soldiered on until their boilers gave out. The last in service, 2918, was withdrawn in April 1935. By mid-December 1937, all had been scrapped.

SPECIFICATIONS

	ORIGINAL	SUPERHEATED
	IMPERIAL (METRIC)	IMPERIAL (METRIC)
CYLINDERS:	21 x 26 IN (53 x 66 CM)	22 x 26 IN (56 x 66 CM)
BOILER PRESSURE:	150 PSI (1034 KPA)	140 PSI (965 KPA)
COUPLED WHEELS:	4 FT 3 IN (130 CM)	4 FT 3 IN (130 CM)
TRACTIVE EFFORT:	26 976 LB (120 KN)	29 363 LB (130.7 KN)
GRATE AREA:	32 SQ FT (2.973 M²)	32 SQ FT (2.973 M²)
TOTAL WEIGHT:	100.6 TONS (102.6 T)	102 TONS (104.5 T)
GAUGE:	1435 MM	435 MM
ROAD NUMBERS:	(1889) 483–502	2904, 2908, 2910, 2914, 2916, 2918
	(1924) 2901–2920	

Double 32-class, 3241 and 3268 top the 1 in 40 Cooks Cutting (near Breadalbane) with a Down Cootamundra-bound goods on 13 October 1962. It was probably the last such movement seen on the line. (Leon Oberg)

1892 NEW SOUTH WALES
GOVERNMENT RAILWAYS

P6-class 4-6-0

Who would have thought, when the first examples of this locomotive type entered service on 10 February 1892, that representatives of the marque would still be operating 80 years later? Needless to say, this class, which finally totalled 191 locomotives, became one of Australia's most highly successful motive power types.

Manufactured by four separate builders over 19 years, the design was credited to NSWGR locomotive staff under then CME William Thow, who had recently moved to Sydney from South Australia. Those plans were prepared in close liaison with British builder Beyer, Peacock & Co. The 191 locomotives were built by Beyer, Peacock & Co (106), the Clyde Engineering Co in Sydney (45), the Baldwin Locomotive Works of the USA (20) and the NSWGR's own Eveleigh Workshops (20).

The initial 50 locomotives were delivered with 6-wheel tenders. Subsequent orders called for higher capacity (longer range) bogie 8-wheel tenders of a similar design to those fitted to the T-class 2-8-0 locomotives which had arrived in 1896.

At the suggestion of the builder, the last two of the first order were built as 3-cylinder compounds with twin low-pressure cylinders on the right side and a single high-pressure cylinder on the other. Due to starting difficulties, both were converted to conventional 2-cylinder simples in 1901. In April 1911, Beyer, Peacock delivered the numerically last engine of the series, which was equipped with a trial Schmidt superheater. This device, the first on the system, was so successful that all the engines were given it as they passed through the workshops between 1914 and 1939. In addition, they were fitted with 'more exacting' inside admission piston valves which replaced the former D-type slide variety.

Superheating, a form of reheating and drying of steam by directing it through additional tubes before passing to the cylinders, was introduced in Belgium in 1901 by locomotive engineer Wilhelm Schmidt. It became one of the world's greatest locomotive developments by providing both higher power and fuel savings in the order of 30 per cent.

Though the P-class was designed as an express passenger engine, it saw service throughout the state, working anything from expresses to pick-up freights. It soon won a reputation for being a faithful and reliable engine.

In 1924, all became the C32-class and, although

Two locomotives believed to have received brand-new Clyde Engineering-built rolling chassis during the mid-1950s, 3214 (left) and 3203, survive into preservation and are pictured slumbering in Goulburn locomotive depot on 17 July 1977. (Leon Oberg)

there were more powerful express locomotives in service, the class never lost its glory. Even in their twilight years they were regularly rostered on South Coast, Newcastle and Blue Mountains local and fast passenger services. Examples were also working in great numbers on country main and branch lines.

From the 1930s, many were fitted with heavy-duty raised frames in an effort to arrest fractures. By then, most of the early examples had been equipped with bogie tenders (though it must be pointed out some retained their old 6-wheel tenders so that they could be turned at locations with 15.4 m turntables).

New frames were still being built as late as 1954, when Clyde Engineering won a contract to construct five rolling chassis complete with cab sides. All the railways had to do was add reconditioned boilers. (These indeed could be considered new locomotives.)

It is interesting to observe that until a smash at Otford in 1956, all 191 locomotives were still in traffic. On that occasion, 3264, working a milk train, ploughed into the rear of a freight train. The engine was considered a total loss and was scrapped in January 1957.

With the impending dieselisation of the Broken Hill line and the electrification of the Blue Mountains line, more C32s began to be withdrawn. The arrival of the 48-class Co-Co branch-line diesel locomotives

from 1959 onwards marked the beginning of the end for the hard-working veterans and withdrawals began in earnest, particularly from country depots, as boiler and mechanical condition dictated.

Nevertheless, one of the class, 3246, holds the distinction of running the last steam-hauled regular passenger service in Australia. This service between Newcastle and Singleton eventually fell to diesel traction in July 1971. Five months later, the last remaining class member, 3229, was withdrawn from shunting duty at Goulburn, and on New Year's Eve was transferred to Enfield for eventual scrapping.

Only four of these popular, delightfully pro-portioned 4-6-0s remain: 3203 and 3214 in static NSWRTM custody, 3237 in active service with the Lachlan Valley Railway, and 3265, a Sydney Powerhouse Museum working exhibit which ran its initial road trial in June 2009.

Engine 3242 recorded the highest distance travelled by any Australian steam locomotive—a grand 3 802 024 km! Forty-six more of the class exceeded 3 200 000 km each. (Of course, these figures were obtained with equipment which during their lifetimes received several new boilers, at least one change of frame and in some cases, new tenders.)

Twenty-six similar locomotives were introduced on the Commonwealth Railways (CR) for Trans-

Locomotive 3229 shunting a mail train at Dubbo. (Leon Oberg)

Australian Railway service from 1914 (see page 166). As an aside, it is believed the NSWGR purchased at least one boiler from CR during the mid-1950s, fitting it to locomotive 3246 after some modifications were made to its frame.

SPECIFICATIONS

	ORIGINAL	SUPERHEATED
	IMPERIAL (METRIC)	IMPERIAL (METRIC)
CYLINDERS:	20 x 26 FT IN (51 x 66 CM)	21 x 26 IN (53 x 66 CM)
BOILER PRESSURE:	160 PSI (1102 KPA)	160 PSI (1102 KPA)
COUPLED WHEELS:	5 FT 0 IN (152 CM)	5 FT 0 IN (152 CM)
TRACTIVE EFFORT:	22 187 LB (98.7 KN)	25 990 LB (115.5 KN)
GRATE AREA:	27 SQ FT (2.508 M²)	27 SQ FT (2.508 M²)
TOTAL WEIGHT:	88.13 TONS (90.5 T)	110 TONS (112.2 T)
GAUGE:	1435 MM	1435 MM
ROAD NUMBERS:	(ORIGINAL) 69, 11, 12, 83, 84, 105, 130, 458 482, 503–521, 574–598, 679–700, 702–726, 786–800, 830–859, 910–927 AND 937 (1924) 3201–3391	

1892 NEW SOUTH WALES GOVERNMENT RAILWAYS

I17-class 2-6-2T

These 20 cumbersome-looking locomotives were a saddle-tank version of the successful B-55 class 2-6-0 freight engines constructed in 1890 by the same builder, Dubs & Co.

The locomotives were ordered for banking duties over the taxing 1 in 33 grades of the Blue Mountains. They entered service between January and May 1892, but were soon found unsuitable for their intended purpose because of their limited fuel capacity. As a result, some were transferred to Waterfall for banking duties while the bulk of the fleet went into mineral train working and hauled coal out of Newcastle and Illawarra district coal mines for some decades.

The I-class was eventually displaced on Illawarra coal haulage by the heavier J and T classes, and reduced to yard shunters at Darling Harbour with occasional trips (during peak periods) pulling excursion passenger trains to the Royal National Park south of Sydney.

The locomotives became the Z26-class during the 1924 renumbering system.

In later years, employment for these engines was found at Lithgow and Bathurst in shunting and push-up duties while others shunted the vast Port Kembla network until replaced by 70-class 0-6-0 diesel-hydraulics in the early 1960s. The first class member

The last 26-class engine in regular use was 2605, in the employ of the Commonwealth Portland Cement Co near Lithgow. (Graham Cotterall)

withdrawn was 2602 at Bathurst in September 1956. Lithgow engine 2610 followed in October, and by 1961 only nine remained. The last in government service was 2604, withdrawn at Bathurst in October 1970.

Meanwhile, the Commonwealth Portland Cement Co purchased 2605 in December 1966; it remained in regular cement haulage at Portland until replaced by a leased AI&S B-B diesel-electric in August 1982. It has since been preserved at the State Mine Railway & Museum in Lithgow. No. 2606 resides at the Thirlmere Railway Museum.

SPECIFICATIONS

	IMPERIAL (METRIC)
CYLINDERS:	18 x 26 IN (46 x 66 CM)
BOILER PRESSURE:	150 PSI (1034 KPa)
COUPLED WHEELS:	4 FT 0 IN (122 CM)
TRACTIVE EFFORT:	21 060 LB (93.7 KN)
GRATE AREA:	21 SQ FT (1.951 M²)
TOTAL WEIGHT:	65.9 TONS (67.2 T)
GAUGE:	1435 MM
ROAD NUMBERS:	(ORIGINAL) 17–22, 103, 127–129, 292, 293, 391, 394, 397–402
	(1924) 2601–2620

1892 TASMANIAN GOVERNMENT RAILWAYS

A-class 4-4-0

Built by Beyer, Peacock & Co at its Gorton foundry, these eight locomotives were ordered as 'additional motive power' following the takeover of the Tasmanian Main Line Railway Co in 1890. They entered passenger service over the main Launceston–Hobart and western routes between 1892 and 1902.

In many respects, the class was an improved passenger version of the Tasmanian Railways' Beyer, Peacock 4-4-0 B-class. The A-class was displaced from the elite main line running after the arrival of the M-class Beyer Garratts in 1912.

In 1908, Nos 2 and 4 were rebuilt with Belpaire boilers and enlarged smokeboxes and in that form were sometimes referred to as the Ab-class. More conversions were eventually carried out, with five being treated between 1927 and 1932. No. 7 was the last converted, in 1946. As rebuilt, the class boasted an additional 3.4 kN tractive effort and 68 kPa higher boiler pressure.

When the higher powered R-class Pacifics arrived in 1923, the class was relegated to secondary passenger and mixed trains.

Fame was bestowed upon No. 4 when it was called on to work no less than four Royal Trains over a period of 20 years. These included two visits by the

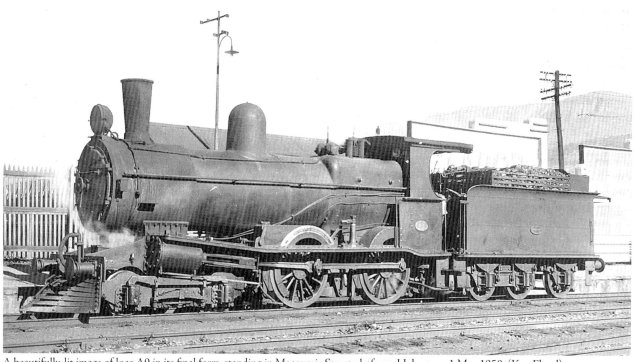

A beautifully-lit image of loco A9 in its final form, standing in Macquarie Street platform, Hobart, on 1 May 1950. (Ken Flood)

Duke of York, one by the Prince of Wales and, in 1935, the Duke of Gloucester.

Used extensively on passenger trains to the end, all eight 4-4-0s were withdrawn between 1952 and 1954 after the X-class diesel-electric Bo-Bo units were put into service. The A-class was left to rust in a siding at Turners Marsh until seven were sold for scrap in 1956. Fortunately, No. 4 was saved and in 1960 was placed in Launceston City Park. In the early 1990s the veteran engine was exchanged for a four-wheel U-class diesel and today resides in the Don River Railway, outside Devonport.

SPECIFICATIONS

	ORIGINAL	AS REBUILT
	IMPERIAL (METRIC)	IMPERIAL (METRIC)
CYLINDERS:	15½ x 22 IN (39 x 56 CM)	15½ x 22 IN (39 x 56 CM)
BOILER PRESSURE:	150 PSI (1034 KPA)	160 PSI (1102 KPA)
COUPLED WHEELS:	4 FT 7 IN (140 CM)	4 FT 7 IN (140 CM)
TRACTIVE EFFORT:	11 532 LB (51.3 KN)	12 301 LB (54.7 KN)
GRATE AREA:	15.7 SQ FT (1.463 M²)	15.7 SQ FT (1.463 M²)
TOTAL WEIGHT:	53 TONS (54.1 T)	55 TONS (56.1 T)
GAUGE:	1067 MM	1067 MM
ROAD NUMBERS:	2–9	

1893 WESTERN AUSTRALIAN
GOVERNMENT RAILWAYS

K-class 2-8-4T

Introduced for suburban work, this class of 24 heavy tank locomotives, all built by the Scottish firm Neilson & Co, entered service between October 1893 and August 1898.

As the initial deliveries were being commissioned in Australia, the British government obtained six engines intended for the WAGR off the factory floor, sending them to South Africa to ease a serious locomotive shortage on the Imperial Military Railways caused by the Boer War. These locomotives were Neilson builder's numbers 5897–5902. All were afterwards taken into Central South African Railways stock to become the C-class, numbered 203–208.

Back on the WAGR, where examples were centred on Kalgoorlie and the Collie branch line, the first re-powering of these engines was realised in 1915 when two were fitted with new superheater boilers. A further three had been treated by 1929. However, the original two were converted back to saturated steam about this time as the superheater equipment was deemed 'unsatisfactory', requiring heavy maintenance. The other three were reconverted by 1937.

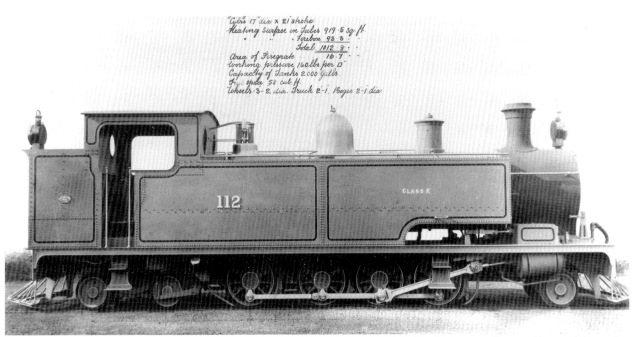

A Neilson & Co works photograph showing a K-class locomotive carrying the number 112, a number not actually carried by any class member in active WAGR service. (Westrail archives)

Following these attempts at re-powering, new high-pressure 1102 kPa boilers were fitted, which increased their tractive effort by over a quarter, and the fire grate area was reduced to 1.472 m².

During World War II, the class was worked to its limit and by the close of hostilities most were worn out and withdrawn for scrapping. During 1946–47, seven were cut up. While more followed slowly, others were shopped because of the need for cheap shunting power in the Perth area (and relief motive power for race-day passenger trains). These remained until as late as December 1964.

Meanwhile, Central South African Railways sold three of its 2-8-4T locomotives in 1904. Nos 204 and 208 went to Clydesdale Collieries and 205 went to Oogies Colliery. The other three were scrapped prior to Union in 1910. However, Clydesdale 204, which received a new high-pressure 180 psi (1240 kPa) boiler in 1939, was noted in service as recently as 1972.

SPECIFICATIONS

	IMPERIAL (METRIC)
CYLINDERS:	17 x 21 IN (43 x 53 CM)
BOILER PRESSURE:	120 PSI (827 KPA)
COUPLED WHEELS:	3 FT 2 IN (97 CM)
TRACTIVE EFFORT:	15 332 LB (68.2 KN)
GRATE AREA:	16.7 SQ FT (1.551 M²)
TOTAL WEIGHT:	53 TONS (54.1 T)
GAUGE:	1067 MM
ROAD NUMBERS:	34–41, 101–106, 186–195

1894 SOUTH AUSTRALIAN RAILWAYS

S-class 4-4-0

This class of 4-4-0 tender locomotives, which eventually numbered 18, was acquired by the South Australian Railways to work express passenger traffic over the state's less hilly broad-gauge lines. All were built in two distinct batches by the Gawler firm James Martin & Co, deliveries commencing in February 1894. The last six entered traffic during 1903–04.

The class became the staple motive power on the Broken Hill expresses between Adelaide and Terowie, and on the Melbourne expresses on the easier Tailem Bend to Serviceton portion of the route.

The class was found to be sound and reliable and two engines rose to fame when they were selected to haul Royal Trains—Nos 130 (in 1901) and 135 (in 1920).

All were built with saturated boilers but 133 was experimentally fitted with a superheated boiler in February 1923. While it ran in that form for a decade, no others were similarly equipped, despite the class being shopped for reboilering from 1914. At that time they received extended smokeboxes and large (longer range) bogie tenders, which greatly improved their already handsome appearance.

The S-class was replaced by larger Webb-introduced locomotives from the mid-1920s, being gradually withdrawn from elite main line services

The well-balanced lines of the S-class are shown to advantage in this photograph taken at Tailem Bend on 1 February 1954. (Late L.E. Bates, Doug Colquhoun collection)

and reduced to secondary branch lines such as those to Victor Harbor and Moonta. In later years, the survivors were used in the south-east of the state and in yard shunting until condemnations commenced with no fewer than six engines in 1956.

The last to go was 136, withdrawn at Tailem Bend in 1959. It lay for twelve months while moves were made to have it preserved. These finally fell through and the relic was scrapped in 1961.

SPECIFICATIONS

	IMPERIAL (METRIC)
CYLINDERS:	18 x 24 IN (46 x 61 CM)
BOILER PRESSURE:	150 PSI (1034 KPA)
COUPLED WHEELS:	6 FT 6 IN (198 CM)
TRACTIVE EFFORT:	11 812 LB (52.6 KN)
TOTAL WEIGHT:	61 TONS (62.2 T)
GAUGE:	1600 MM
ROAD NUMBERS:	11, 13, 14, 17, 26, 50, 127–137 AND 154

1896 WESTERN AUSTRALIAN GOVERNMENT RAILWAYS

N-class 4-4-4T

The rich gold strikes in Western Australia during the 1890s, particularly in the Kalgoorlie area, led to an immediate influx of fortune hunters. The WAGR made its fortune too, for as more and more people came to the goldfields, passenger train travel increased; before long, suburban services started in Kalgoorlie, for a time eclipsing those in metropolitan Perth. This led to the introduction of the N-class 4-4-4 tank locomotives.

Designed as a medium-range locomotive type and built by Neilson & Co of Scotland, the first five entered service in Perth during the early months of 1896. Shortly afterwards, following the start of the Kalgoorlie suburban services in November 1897, an order was placed with Robert Stephenson & Co for an additional 12 locomotives, which arrived late in 1898 and early 1899.

As traffic continued to increase, a further 15 were ordered, this time from Nasmyth, Wilson & Co, England. They were all running by 1901.

Despite a slackening of the Kalgoorlie services, brought about by a decline in gold prospecting, the Perth suburban services continued to expand. During 1907–08, ten Neilson-built 2-8-0 O-class tender locomotives were converted into N-class tank engines by the WAGR. (The O-class had been built at the same time as the early Neilson-built N-class and thus carried many standard parts.)

As the Kalgoorlie services continued to wane, the N-class locomotives were gradually transferred to Perth. The Kalgoorlie services ceased altogether in 1929, by which time the 4-4-4Ts had been allocated to East Perth, Midland Junction and Fremantle sheds. Soon afterwards, a decline in traffic caused by the Great Depression found many N-class locomotives surplus to requirements and they were withdrawn to 'await busier days'.

Those days did in fact arrive with World War II. All were shopped for light tone-ups and restored to traffic, and reports suggest that they worked harder than ever before.

But the moment of glory for the class did not last very long, for WAGR design teams had been working on a heavier, more powerful tank type for

Engine 207 carrying 201's number plates, in use as a steam cleaner at East Perth depot. Further evidence the engine is not 201 rests in the knowledge that this locomotive was never equipped with an electric lighting generation unit. (Philip G. Graham)

suburban work which, when delivered from 1945, became the Dm and Dd classes. The elderly N-class's lack of adhesive weight could not compete with the new locomotives on the heavy trains and by 1950 ten had been withdrawn.

A further 16 had gone by 1953 and, when diesel railcars arrived in 1953 and 1954, the days of the remaining 4-4-4Ts were numbered. By 1961, only two were left. The last engine in service was 207 (carrying 201's number plates), which was used as a steam cleaner at East Perth depot. It is now preserved at the ARHS's Bassendean Museum.

SPECIFICATIONS

	ORIGINAL	CONVERTED O-CLASS
	IMPERIAL (METRIC)	IMPERIAL (METRIC)
CYLINDERS:	15½ x 21 IN (39 x 53 CM)	15½ x 21 IN (39 x 53 CM)
BOILER PRESSURE:	160 PSI (1102 KPA)	160 PSI (1102 KPA)
COUPLED WHEELS:	4 FT 0 IN (122 CM)	4 FT 1.5 IN (126 CM)
TRACTIVE EFFORT:	13 454 LB (59.9 KN)	13 046 LB (58.1 KN)
GRATE AREA:	15.75 SQ FT (1.463 M²)	15.75 SQ FT (1.463 M²)
TOTAL WEIGHT:	44 TONS (44.9 T)	48.75 TONS (49.7 T)
GAUGE:	1067 MM	1067 MM
ROAD NUMBERS:	1, 19, 20, 25–27, 69–73, 132, 196–207, 256–283	
	(CONVERTED O-CLASS) 75–79, 85–87, 95 AND 96	

1896 NEW SOUTH WALES
GOVERNMENT RAILWAYS

T524-class 2-8-0

This class of 280 general freight locomotives was one of Australia's most trouble-free designs. Designated T524-class, the first to enter service was 528 on 15 May 1896. Within a matter of weeks, all five of the initial order were showing their prowess on heavy Blue Mountains goods traffic.

Designed by the NSWGR in close cooperation with Beyer, Peacock & Co, the T-class was in effect a goods version of the highly successful P6-class of 1892. It was created to replace the elderly 0-6-0 and 2-6-0 locomotive types then employed in heavy main-line goods service.

The pioneering T524-class was soon seen to be as exceptional and trouble free as the P6-class, and orders multiplied as traffic increased and repairs to the older 0-6-0 and 2-6-0 locomotives were truncated. In all, five builders were employed in construction of the T524-class: Beyer, Peacock & Co (151), the North British Co (84), Neilson & Co (10), the Clyde Engineering Co (30) and Dubs & Co (5). The last engine entered service on 13 June 1916.

Although the first 205 were built with saturated boilers, ongoing overseas locomotive developments enabled the remaining engines to be equipped with fuel-saving superheaters. This successful equipment was subsequently fitted to many of the

Lasting in its original saturated form throughout its long working life, 5069 was pictured at the Port Waratah (Newcastle) depot between coal train assignments in January 1962. It has survived into preservation. (Leon Oberg)

earlier deliveries as they passed through workshops. For identification purposes, the saturated version generally employed a short, snub smokebox. The superheated locomotives' smokebox was extended to house the header and, in the case of the later North British-built examples, carried equipment associated with 'automatic' ash disposal.

In 1924, the T524-class became the D50-class.

The Depression years, which saw a serious traffic downturn, halted further superheating conversions and no fewer than 72 saturated D50s were unceremoniously withdrawn because of their poor condition. Many of them were used in the testing of the Sydney Harbour bridge in 1932. While most were scrapped in 1939 to provide scrap for steel production from which war goods were manufactured, World War II itself caused a severe engine shortage due to the massive traffic increases. As a result, 14 long-stored D50-class locomotives were rebuilt with superheaters and returned to service.

With delivery of 25 D57-class 4-8-2s in 1929, the old 2-8-0s lost some of the glamour main line jobs. Many of the saturated type were then released for Newcastle district non-air coal train working while others became shunting locomotives at country depots.

Of the rest, diesels gradually replaced the 2-8-0s, most falling to the scrapper's torch during the 1960s. Some have been rescued for preservation, including the last engine in active revenue service, an original-outline saturated locomotive numbered 5069. It was also the last of its class in NSWGR operation, ending its days based at Port Waratah depot for coal train duties. Withdrawn in January 1973 at the very end of NSWGR steam operations, 5069 was sold, along with superheated 5132, to the Dorrigo Steam Railway and Museum. Saturated 5096 (the first locomotive built by the Clyde Engineering Co) has been preserved at Thirlmere Railway Museum, and

Boasting a new superheater and extended smokebox (to accommodate the equipment), and several other upgraded features including a more commodious Morts Dock turret tender, 5191 poses for official photographs outside Eveleigh Workshops in this November 1929 view. (Rail Corp archives)

Commonwealth Railways engine K.30 on delivery. Apart from their tenders, the K-class was visually identical to the North British-built NSWGR's T-class. (Former AN archives)

saturated 5112 was preserved at Bathurst when this book went to press.

In addition to the above locomotives, the British Railway Operating Division (ROD) seized ten T524-class locomotives intended for the NSWGR, under construction at the North British Co's Glasgow works, and redirected them to France for service in World War I. The ROD felt its need was greater than that of the NSWGR. The ROD numbered the locomotives 701–710 and they all became the property of the Belgian Railways after the war.

Commonwealth Railways interest

Meanwhile, Commonwealth Railways was constructing its Trans-Australian line between Port Augusta and Kalgoorlie and selected the NSWGR T-class design as the prototype for its initial freight engines. The CR ordered eight from the North British Co and they entered service between March and June 1916. These became the K-class on the CR and carried road numbers 27–34.

While similar to the T-class in all leading aspects, the CR locomotives were equipped with slightly larger diameter cylinders and lower pressure 1034 kPa boilers. In addition, their tenders were able to carry about half as much coal and water again as the T-class.

Most of them had been withdrawn before dieselisation arrived in the early 1950s. The last engine actually in service was K.34, which was withdrawn in March 1952. All were scrapped in the mid-1950s at Port Augusta, where old inhabitants of the town still recall watching contractors blow these and other locomotives to pieces using dynamite.

Footnote: The same basic design was selected by the East Greta Railway at South Maitland in 1912 for coal haulage. It differed in that it was redesigned as a tank engine. Beyer, Peacock & Co built 14 and the last remained in commercial coal traffic between Hexham and Stockrington Colliery until 22 September 1987. All still exist (see page 151).

SPECIFICATIONS

NSWGR LOCOMOTIVES

	Original Imperial (Metric)	Superheated engines Imperial (Metric)
CYLINDERS:	21 x 26 IN (53 x 66 CM)	22 x 26 IN (56 x 66 CM)
BOILER PRESSURE:	160 PSI (1102 KPA)	160 PSI (1102 KPA)
TRACTIVE EFFORT:	28 777 LB (128.1 KN)	33 557 LB (149.3 KN)
COUPLED WHEELS:	4 FT 3 IN (130 CM)	4 FT 3 IN (130 CM)
GRATE AREA:	29 SQ FT (2.694 M²)	29 SQ FT (2.694 M²)
TOTAL WEIGHT:	111.25 TONS (113.5T)	131.7 TONS (134.4T)
GAUGE:	1435 MM	1435 MM
ROAD NUMBERS:	(ORIGINAL) 68, 69, 71–74, 356, 522, 524–528, 531, 532, 534–573, 599–635, 671–678, 727–785, 1042–1061, 1254–1303 (1924 NUMBERS) 5001–5280	

CR K-CLASS

	Imperial (Metric)
CYLINDERS:	22 x 26 IN (56 x 66 CM)
BOILER PRESSURE:	150 PSI (1034 KPA)
TRACTIVE EFFORT:	29 609 LB (131.8 KPA)
COUPLED WHEELS:	4 FT 3 IN (130 CM)
GRATE AREA:	29 SQ FT (2.694 M²)
TOTAL WEIGHT:	115.13 TONS (118 T)
GAUGE:	1435 MM
ROAD NUMBERS:	27–34

Abt locomotive 3 in its resurrected life as a tourist locomotive, pictured at Dubbil Barril on 1 January 2006. (Kevin Waid)

1896 Mt Lyell Mining & Railway Company

Abt Type 0-4-2T

The 34 km railway which connects Queenstown with Regatta Point (outside Strahan), on the west coast of Tasmania, has been described by many as one of the most remarkable railways in the world.

Following discoveries of vast quantities of copper at Iron Blow, Mt Lyell, a 1067 mm gauge line was constructed through dense mountainous rainforest between 1894 and 1896. For 5.5 km, between Dubbil Barril and Halls Creek (peaking at Rindadeena), it had grades of 1 in 16 (6.25 per cent) to 1 in 20 (5 per cent) through curves as tight as four and five chains radius. To provide adequate power, which was denied by conventional wheel-friction traction, the famous Abt rack system was employed on this section.

This system, invented by the Swiss-born engineer Roman Abt, consisted originally of triple flat steel bars bearing staggered teeth on the upper edges and placed side by side to allow meshing with corresponding teeth on the locomotive. Abt's system was first used in the Harz Mountains between the central German villages of Tann and Blankenburg

as early as 1885. Abt later designed twin and even single rack railways, and the Mt Lyell system was of the double flatbar type.

An order was placed with Dubs & Co for four Abt-system rack locomotives to work the rich traffic offering. The design called for two outside cylinders to conventionally drive the coupled wheels while two additional cylinders were provided between the frames powering the cog system.

The first arrived in August 1896, well in time for the official opening of the line, initially as far as Teepookana port, in March 1897. The line was extended to Regatta Point in 1899 and by 1901 all four locomotives were in service.

The small 0-4-2Ts excelled themselves, operating faultlessly over the rugged route—so much so that a fifth was acquired in 1938 to cope with increasing traffic. By now Dubs & Co had become part of the North British Co so this engine carried that company's works plate.

The Mt Lyell railway boasted some 48 bridges, and some trains were banked in the rear as they clawed their way up the tremendous gradients. On the more level sections, speeds of 50 km/h could be attained, particularly west of Lowana and east of Halls Creek.

Passenger traffic was also catered for, most of the

A Sharp Stewart works photograph of a G-class locomotive. (Tasrail archives)

business being miners and their families. These good things came to an end in 1963, when this picturesque line was closed in favour of road transport and dismantled. Fortunately, most of the locomotives, which had been equipped for oil firing in their later years, were preserved in various places in Tasmania and Victoria.

But miracles do happen, and in July 1998 funding was forthcoming for the reconstruction of the line between Queenstown and Regatta Point. Abt locomotives 1 and 3 were removed from display at Zeehan and Queenstown for rebuilding. Abt 5 was later acquired from the Puffing Billy Railway's Menzies Creek Museum in Victoria and shipped to Tasmania in November 2003. The rebuilt line was officially opened as the West Coast Wilderness Railway on 3 April 2003, exactly 106 years after the official opening of the original line.

Locomotive Abt 2 remains on static display at the Tasmanian Transport Museum, Glenorchy.

SPECIFICATIONS

	IMPERIAL (METRIC)
CYLINDERS:	11½ x 20 IN (29 x 51 CM)
	11½ x 15½ IN RACK (29 x 39 CM)
BOILER PRESSURE:	(APPROX) 175 PSI (1206 KPA)
COUPLED WHEELS:	3 FT 0 IN (91 CM)
TRACTIVE EFFORT:	(APPROX) 17 000 LB (76 KN)
TOTAL WEIGHT:	24 TONS (24.4 T)
GAUGE:	1067 MM
ROAD NUMBERS:	1–5

G-class 0-4-2T

For working the rugged North East Dundas Tramway, Tasmanian Government Railways purchased two small 0-4-2 tank locomotives from Sharp Stewart of Glasgow, Scotland. They entered service during 1896 and 1898.

This line, laid to the narrow 610 mm gauge, was built to open up the Mt Read mining district. It ran through some of the remotest wilderness country found in the Tasmanian west coast region, passing through solid rock cuttings and around sharp curves with an average gradient of 1 in 40.

One of these quite powerful little locos featured in possibly one of Australia's worst boiler explosions. Shortly after entering service, G1 was standing in Zeehan yard on the morning of Wednesday 16 May 1899 when its boiler exploded, killing the crew. The force of the explosion is reputed to have flung the boiler 30 metres into the air to land some 230 metres away. Every component above the frame was torn away (except for the smokebox) and the engine was a total loss.

In 1900 a replacement locomotive of the same class arrived from the Sharp Stewart works, carrying the wrecked engine's road number.

Both G-class locomotives were rendered surplus after more powerful replacements arrived, and were sold to the Isis Central Sugar Mill in Queensland. While in their new employ they were converted to tender engines and, although numbered 9 and 10, were affectionately known as 'Tassie A' and 'Tassie B' due to their Tasmanian origins. Both remained in service until 1962.

'Tassie B' was eventually acquired by a rail preservationist for further use at a planned Sydney theme park. While held in a compound at St Marys in western Sydney, it was illegally cut up in 1991, along with a Fowler 0-4-2T and a near-new Perry boiler. 'Tassie A' found its way into a Childers service station yard following its retirement but all traces of it seem to have since vanished.

SPECIFICATIONS

	IMPERIAL (METRIC)
CYLINDERS:	12 x 16 IN (30 x 41 CM)
BOILER PRESSURE:	140 PSI (965 KPA)
COUPLED WHEELS:	2 FT 6 IN (76 CM)
TRACTIVE EFFORT:	8601 LB (38.3 KN)
GRATE AREA:	9.5 SQ FT (0.883 M²)
TOTAL WEIGHT:	19.7 TONS (20.2 T)
GAUGE:	610 MM
ROAD NUMBERS:	(TGR) G1, G2 AND 2ND G1 (ISIS CENTRAL) 9 AND 10

1897 WESTERN AUSTRALIAN GOVERNMENT RAILWAYS

R-class 4-4-0

The WAGR did not use many locomotives of the 4-4-0 type, unlike the other major Australian railway systems. In fact, only 36 locomotives in three classes on the WAGR had this wheel arrangement, and of these 14 were later converted to the 4-4-2 type.

Let us look at the most graceful of this state's 4-4-0 designs, the 24-member strong R-class, which was introduced between 1897 and 1899 for express passenger working. Built by Dubs & Co, these locomotives hauled the state's principal passenger services until heavier Baldwin-built Ec-class 4-6-2s gradually began arriving from 1902. Since they were considered a little heavy for branch-line working, 14 R-class locomotives were fitted with a trailing axle beneath the cab to reduce overall axle load. This tended also to improve their stability. In their new 4-4-2 form, the locomotives became the Ra-class for further mixed train work on the lighter branch lines.

Between 1924 and 1925, the ten original R-class locomotives were scrapped and the converted 4-4-2 engines again became the R-class. By 1932, six had been put into store and the remaining eight locomotives were mainly confined to the Eastern line between Perth and Northam. They were also utilised as bank engines on main line expresses over the heavily-graded Midland to Chidlow section.

Gradually they were all withdrawn from service, although 174, the last of the class in actual service, was saved from the indignity of the scrapyard when it was reconverted to its original 4-4-0 form. Painted in the royal blue livery of the class's heyday, 174 was placed outside the Railway Institute Library building at Midland Junction in 1956. In 1972, it was transferred a new Centrepoint shopping complex which was built on land formerly owned by the Midland Railway Co.

WAGR's R-class 146 after it was equipped with extended cab protection for the crew (on the tender) for reverse running. (former Westrail archives)

SPECIFICATIONS

	IMPERIAL (METRIC)
CYLINDERS:	16 x 22 IN (41 x 56 CM)
BOILER PRESSURE:	160 PSI (1102 KPA)
COUPLED WHEELS:	4 FT 9 IN (145 CM)
TRACTIVE EFFORT:	12 647 LB (56.3 KN)
GRATE AREA:	16.6 SQ FT (1.542 M²)
TOTAL WEIGHT:	55.8 TONS (56.9 T)
	RA-CLASS 57 TONS (58.2 T)
GAUGE:	1067 MM
ROAD NUMBERS:	(ORIGINAL R-CLASS) 144–155, 174–179, 227–232
	(RA-CLASS) 148, 150, 153, 154, 174, 175, 177, 178, 227–232

1898 VICTORIAN GOVERNMENT RAILWAYS

Na-class 2-6-2T

During the 1880s it became obvious that some kind of lower-cost, light, narrow gauge railway would have to be built in Victoria to open up the rich but sparsely populated areas of the state. After exhaustive investigations were made about the feasibility of such a scheme, work started during the mid-1890s on what became the 762 mm gauge Wangaratta to Whitfield railway. The line opened for traffic early in 1899.

Meanwhile, an order was placed with the Baldwin Locomotive Works in the USA for two 2-6-2 tank locomotives to work the railway. They arrived late in 1898 and promptly entered construction service. These locomotives became the Na-class.

The success of this pioneer railway soon led to the construction of more such lines and the next to appear was from Upper Ferntree Gully to Gembrook. This line, set in the heart of the state's Dandenong Ranges, was opened during 1900 and a further two Na-class locomotives were acquired. Unlike the initial two, they were constructed in the VR's Newport Railway Workshops, which continued to churn out Na-class locomotives to supply motive power for the Colac to Beech Forest line, which was opened in 1902 (and was further extended in 1911 to Crowes), and the Moe to Walhalla line, which was opened in 1910 and served the steep Baw Baw Ranges area.

By 1915, a total of 17 Na-class locomotives had been built. With the exception of Nos 2A and 3A, which were built for compound working, these little workhorses were all wonderfully trouble free and hard working.

The advent of motor vehicles and reliable roads led to the gradual decrease in tonnages hauled over all four lines, however, and eventually they were forced to close. A serious landslide in 1952 forced the closure of the Gembrook line beyond Belgrave, and in 1958, electrification and an extension of the Melbourne suburban broad gauge network replaced this last remaining section of the narrow gauge steam line. The Whitfield line had ceased operations in 1953 and the Walhalla line was closed the following year. Finally, the Crowes line was forced out of business in 1962, by which time most of the Na-class locomotives had been withdrawn or scrapped.

With the extension of electrification to Belgrave, a group of far-sighted enthusiasts saw the tourist potential of the Gembrook line. They successfully obtained permission to work on the Belgrave–Menzies Creek section and finally, in July 1962, proudly opened it for tourist business utilising Na-

An officially posed image of Baldwin-built 2-6-2T, No. 2A. (Jack Richardson collection)

Locomotives 6A and 7A power out of Belgrave with a heavy 10.30 am tourist train bound for Lakeside on 9 November 2005. (Stephen Relf)

class locomotives. This line was gradually extended to Emerald, then to picturesque Lakeside, following the rerouting of the railway beside the aforementioned landslide, and finally the 25 km to Gembrook.

Catering for some 250 000 visitors a year, a large collection of Na-class engines has been acquired for this business, including 3A from a Portsea park, for spares. This and 6A, 7A, 8A, 12A and 14A were transferred to the Emerald Tourist Railway Board (popularly known as 'Puffing Billy') upon its inception in 1977. The then manager of the workshops branch, Alan Gardner, reported in 2005 that all operational locomotives had progressively received new welded steel boilers, while 6A had also received a modern Lempor draft ejector based on the designs of renowned Argentinean-born steam engineer, the late Livio Dante Porta. Many locomotives employing this system, which in part reduces back-pressure, have experienced up to 20 per cent improvements in efficiency and power output.

SPECIFICATIONS

	IMPERIAL (METRIC)
CYLINDERS:	13 x 18 IN (33 x 46 CM)
BOILER PRESSURE:	180 PSI (1240 KPA)
COUPLED WHEELS:	3 FT 0 IN (91 CM)
TRACTIVE EFFORT:	13 008 LB (57.9 KN)
GRATE AREA:	9.3 SQ FT (0.864 M^2)
TOTAL WEIGHT:	34.35 TONS (35 T)
GAUGE:	762 MM
ROAD NUMBERS:	1A–17A

1899 QUEENSLAND RAILWAYS

PB15-class 4-6-0

Described as Queensland Railways' most successful pioneer locomotive type, the PB15, designed initially for mail train haulage, was in fact a passenger version of the 1889 B15-class.

Light enough to run over Queensland's entire 1067 mm gauge railways, the class-leader appeared in December 1899 from Walkers Ltd of Maryborough.

An early Stephenson's valve-geared PB15, No. 443, rolls through old Woolloongabba (Brisbane) yard in September 1966. (Ian Crellin)

The first 16 engines were highly successful as both a passenger and goods engines, and further orders were soon placed. By late January 1913, no less than 202 had been delivered, built by Walkers Ltd (92), Evans, Anderson, Phelan & Co (70), Toowoomba Foundry (20) and Kitson & Co (20).

QR's Ipswich Railway Workshops constructed a similar engine in 1924 for the Aramac Shire Council Tramway. Although it differed in respect of a slightly raised boiler and a larger tender, this engine was purchased by the QR in June 1958 and numbered 1052 and later 12.

The PB15s were the first Australian locomotives to employ American balanced slide valves. The class won the admiration of its crews, who reported a startling turn of speed despite the engine's limited 122 cm diameter driving wheels.

Apart from receiving 1102 kPa boilers in lieu of the former 1034 kPa vessels, and being fitted with extended smokeboxes, electric headlights and chimney alterations, the PB15s saw little major rebuilding. One surprising alteration, however, was carried out in May 1918 when 411 was converted to a 4-6-4 tank engine for suburban passenger work; it is believed to have been classified B15D. It had its tender restored in March 1922.

Until then, all PB15s had been fitted with Stephenson's link valve motion but, when still more light-type locomotives were required early in the 1920s, plans were prepared for an improved PB15 utilising Walschaerts valve gear. In fact, 30 were ordered from Walkers Ltd and these entered service between October 1925 and July 1926. One of these engines, 744, is remembered for its use on Cairns tourist trains, where it became known as *Miss Cairns*.

PB15 No. 743, one of the last 21 equipped with the more precise Walschaerts valve gear, pictured outside Southport depot on Australia Day 1964. (John S. Glastonbury)

With their modest firegrate and small boilers, some firemen claimed the PB15s to be rather touchy engines to fire. In the words of one retired driver, 'If the fireman was chatting to the driver or waving to girls when he should have been placing a fire, the pressure would slip back and you could rarely recover it again when working hard'.

'The PB15 was an engine you had to keep on top with all of the time,' he added.

The World War II years took their toll on the class and no less than 17 of the Stephenson type were scrapped during June 1942. A further 13 followed in January 1943.

It soon became apparent, however, that engine shortages would occur if scrapping continued. With the post-war building boom, 140 of the class survived to remain in service as at 1966. In fact, these locomotives, due to their light weight and outback roles, were not adversely affected by dieselisation in its early stages.

With the arrival of 62-tonne branch-line diesel-electrics throughout the 1960s, withdrawals began in earnest. On 30 June 1969, 26 engines were written off in one sweep of the pen; by the time the system had completely dieselised in August 1970, only seven remained in traffic, four of them working out of Mackay depot and three from Rockhampton. These

were officially condemned 12 months later.

A number of PB15s have been preserved, some of which are in working order. Walschaerts engines 732 and 738 are among them, the former being retained by QR for steam excursions, the latter being in the care of the Rosewood Railway Museum (west of Ipswich). No. 444 resides at The Workshops Rail Museum at North Ipswich while 446 (bearing '448' number plates) has been acquired by the Queensland Pioneer Steam Railway.

Interstate, the Bellarine Peninsula Railway at Queenscliff, Victoria, obtained loco 454 for tourist service.

SPECIFICATIONS

Imperial (Metric)

Cylinders:	15 x 20 in (38 x 51 cm)
Boiler pressure:	150 psi (1034 kPa) later 160 psi (1102 kPa)
Coupled wheels:	4 ft 0 in (122 cm)
Tractive effort:	11 250 lb (50.1 kN); later 12 000 lb (53.4 kN)
Grate area:	13.1 sq ft (1.217 m²)
Total weight:	56.3 tons (57.4 t)
Gauge:	1067 mm
Road numbers:	(Stephenson type) 12, 347–362, 385–394, 404–413, 434–509, 518–537, 540–609
	(Walschaerts) 5, 103, 126, 128, 143, 220, 286, 339, 340, 731–751

A Baldwin Locomotive Works photograph of the newly-assembled compound V-class 409. (V/Line archives, Len Whalley collection)

1899 VICTORIAN RAILWAYS

V-class 2-8-0

Built by the Baldwin Locomotive Works as a pattern engine and delivered in 1899, this locomotive type became the first 2-8-0 Consolidation on the VR system.

Entering service working coal traffic between Melbourne and Nyora for test purposes, the V-class was the heaviest engine in Victoria at the time, and was deemed a resounding success. An additional 15 were delivered by the Phoenix Foundry of Ballarat in 1902 and 1903. They were mainly used over the heavily-graded South Gippsland line.

All were constructed as 4-cylinder compounds of Vauclain arrangement with two outside low-pressure cylinders incorporating two high-pressure cylinders. Because drivers were allegedly abusing the equipment, admitting steam at full boiler pressure into the low-pressure cylinders just by keeping the starting valve closed, maintenance costs surged. As a result, all were rebuilt as 2-cylinder simples during 1912 and 1913, receiving 47 x 66 cm cylinders and new boilers with pressure reduced to 1240 kPa.

Described as 'comfortable engines to crew due to their generous cabs', the class was a favoured power source in the colder parts of the state, the Bendigo and Gippsland regions.

The first engine to be withdrawn was 413 during the early 1920s and by January 1930 all had been written off, pattern engine 499 being the last to go.

SPECIFICATIONS

	IMPERIAL (METRIC)	
CYLINDERS:	HIGH PRESSURE 13 x 26 IN (33 x 66 CM)	
	LOW PRESSURE 22 x 26 IN (56 x 66 CM)	
BOILER PRESSURE:	200 PSI (1378 KPA) LATER 180 PSI (1240 KPA)	
COUPLED WHEELS:	4 FT 6 IN (139 CM)	
TRACTIVE EFFORT:	26 400 LB (117.5 KN); LATER REDUCED TO 23 729 LB (105.6 KN)	
TOTAL WEIGHT:	91 TONS (93T)	
GAUGE:	1600 MM	
ROAD NUMBERS:	449–529 (ODD NUMBERS ONLY) 200–215 (AS RENUMBERED IN 1923)	

1900 EMU BAY RAILWAY COMPANY

Dubs 4-8-0

One of Australia's longest-serving private railway operators was the Emu Bay Railway Co, which operated a 1067 mm gauge railway through the rugged west coast region of Tasmania from 1897 to 1998. The line linked Burnie (formerly Emu Bay) and Melba (near Zeehan), passing through some of the state's most inhospitable terrain.

The operation was principally an ore-carrying railway, with its early history extending back to February 1878, when a 914 mm gauge wooden railway was opened between Emu Bay and Rouses Camp (near Waratah) to serve the nearby tin mines at Mt Bischoff.

The original company, the Van Diemens Land Co, which operated the early horse-drawn railway, was taken over by the Emu Bay & Mt Bischoff Railway Co in 1887. The new owners re-laid the line to a gauge of 1067 mm, with iron rails for steam locomotive haulage.

With vast copper finds in the Mt Lyell area and subsequent 'railway wars' between the government and private operators over who should ship the material, the powerful Emu Bay Co took over the Emu Bay & Mt Bischoff concern in 1897. Before long the company was permitted to extend the line to Zeehan, the extension being ready for traffic late in 1900.

Emu Bay No. 8 *Heemskirk*, in action on the Don River Railway in December 2005. (Kevin Waid)

The Emu Bay Railway had acquired a number of old locomotives but they were considered too light for the projected level of mineral traffic. Dubs & Co was therefore contracted to deliver three heavy 4-8-0 tender locomotives, which arrived at about the time the new extension was opened.

It soon became evident that these majestic, clean-looking locomotives would be equally successful working the company's passenger services. In fact, they ended their days in passenger service.

In 1910, Dubs & Co, which by that time had become part of the North British Co, was asked to deliver another 4-8-0. It was numbered 11 on the company's roster and entered service in 1911.

In steam's twilight years, the Emu Bay Railway introduced a prestige train, the *West Coaster*, to cater for the growing number of tourists exploring the Tasmanian west coast. Two 4-8-0s were painted in distinctive blue livery, converted to oil burners and named *Heemskirk* and *Murchison* to work the new 'matching blue painted train'.

Steam soon disappeared and on 2 November 1963, No. 8 *Heemskirk* became the last steam locomotive to work the service. Taken out of store for the occasion, No. 8 replaced No. 6 *Murchison*, which had developed leaking tubes at the last minute. However, trouble continued, with *Heemskirk* running out of fuel oil at

Ridgley on the return journey. The passengers returned to Burnie by bus, and a following ore train propelled the disabled locomotive and cars the remaining 17.5 km into Burnie some hours later.

Murchison and *Heemskirk* were both preserved, the former at the West Coast Pioneers Memorial Museum at Zeehan and the latter at the Don River Railway. *Heemskirk* was restored to its original coal-burning condition for the Emu Bay Railway's October 1997 centenary celebrations, making a successful trial run from Don to Burnie on 20 July 1997.

SPECIFICATIONS

	IMPERIAL (METRIC)
CYLINDERS:	17 x 22 IN (43 x 56 CM)
BOILER PRESSURE:	175 PSI (1206 KPA)
COUPLED WHEELS:	3 FT 9 IN (114 CM)
TRACTIVE EFFORT:	19 780 LB (88.1 KN)
GRATE AREA:	16 SQ FT (1.486 M²)
TOTAL WEIGHT:	71.85 TONS (73 T)
GAUGE:	1067 MM
ROAD NUMBERS:	6—8 AND 11

One of just a handful of known photographs of *Hagan's Patent.* (former Tasmanian Railways)

J-class 2-6-4-0

To provide additional motive power for the picturesque and rugged 610 mm North East Dundas Tramway, a single weird and wonderful locomotive specimen arrived in 1900 from its German builders, Lokomotivfabrik Hagans in Erfut.

This rather cumbersome locomotive was to become known as *Hagan's Patent.* The design featured an articulated 2-6-4-0 arrangement, with the first six coupled wheels being driven by the usual connecting rod, and the final four wheels powered by a separate rod transmitted through knuckle joints from the standard piston rod.

Despite being quite powerful for its size, the locomotive was destined to be the only one of its type to come to Australia. Contemporary reports indicated loads of 95 to 100 tonnes could be hauled by the engine up a 1 in 25 grade, quite a performance indeed on 610 mm gauge, although because of its weight the locomotive initially played havoc with the light rails of the day.

Despite two K-class Beyer-Garratts being acquired for the Zeehan narrow gauge system in 1910, *Hagan's Patent* continued in service until 1928, often being preferred for its greater haulage ability.

Recent research in Tasmania suggests the locomotive appears to have been withdrawn about 1928 and remained in Zeehan despite being offered for sale. It was reportedly stripped in Zeehan in 1948, although many parts remained in the yard. The spectacle plate was later recovered and is now on display at the Tasmanian Transport Museum in Hobart.

	IMPERIAL (METRIC)
CYLINDERS:	15 x 15 IN (40 x 40 CM)
BOILER PRESSURE:	195 PSI (1344 KPA)
COUPLED WHEELS:	2 FT 7½ IN (80 CM)
TRACTIVE EFFORT:	23 885 LB (106.3 KN)
GRATE AREA:	16 SQ FT (1.486 M²)
TOTAL WEIGHT:	41.5 TONS (42.3 T)
GAUGE:	610 MM

Mallet 0-4-4-0T

Unlike many other countries around the world, Mallet-type locomotives were few and far between in Australia. In fact, only three examples—all of the same design and dimensions—came to this country.

Mallet locomotives provided a crude means of spreading a locomotive's weight while at the same time providing as many driving wheels as possible for increased traction. In addition, they were articulated, the leading frame turning in isolation to the rear set of driving wheels, which were attached to the main chassis.

The first Mallet was acquired from the German industrial locomotive specialist Orenstein & Koppel by the Magnet Silver Mining Co in Tasmania. This locomotive (works number 882 of August 1901) entered service in December that year. The locomotive, carrying the number 1, was put to work hauling ore concentrates over the company's 610 mm gauge railway, which linked the mine with the Emu Bay Railway near Waratah.

Almost simultaneously, the Port Douglas Shire Council in far northern Queensland ordered an exact copy to haul goods and sugar cane over its approximately 13 km railway, which linked Mossman and Port Douglas. This locomotive, maker's number 943 of May 1902, entered service about three months later.

Increased mining activity at Mt Magnet led to an order for yet another Mallet, maker's number 2609 of October 1907. This locomotive, No. 3, entered service in January 1908.

Mt Magnet No. 1 remained active until the 1930s, when it was set aside and cannibalised for parts to keep its sister running until the mine closed towards the end of World War II. The locomotives

A delightful historic view of Mt Magnet No. 3, taken circa 1920. (Author's collection)

and equipment were sold at auction in 1946 and the operational No. 3 was acquired (along with the parts of No. 1) by the Boulder Gold Mine at Kalgoorlie, where it remained active until about 1972. After a period lying in a park at Middle Swan, the relic was acquired by Bennett Brook Railway, at Whiteman Park in Perth, where it is currently under restoration.

The Port Douglas locomotive remained active until withdrawn and scrapped circa 1948.

SPECIFICATIONS

	IMPERIAL (METRIC)
CYLINDERS:	(2) 8¼ x 12 IN (21 x 30 CM)
	(2) 12 x 12 IN (30 x 30 CM)
BOILER PRESSURE:	176 PSI (1210 KPA)
COUPLED WHEELS:	2 FT 1 IN (63 CM)
TRACTIVE EFFORT:	6460 LB (29.1 KN)
GRATE AREA:	7.5 SQ FT (.687 M²)
TOTAL WEIGHT:	17.5 TONS (17.8 T)
ROAD NUMBERS:	(MT MAGNET) 1 AND 3

1902 WESTERN AUSTRALIAN GOVERNMENT RAILWAYS

Ec-class 4-6-2

WAGR drivers had to be specially educated in the operation of compound steam locomotives after 20 Baldwin Locomotive Works Pacific-type locomotives were delivered to Fremantle in July 1901, entering service between August and October that year.

Based on Baldwin's very first Pacific-type, just introduced by Millars Timber Co of West Australia as *Jubilee*, the Ec-class was bought by the WAGR as 'emergency power' to keep trains running over 60 lb rails on the Eastern Goldfields Railway. The locomotives were the first on the system to employ compounding, two smaller high-pressure cylinders being mounted above larger low-pressure cylinders with the pistons connected to the one crosshead under the Vauclain system of steam expansion (allowing a unit of steam to perform two tasks and thus save on energy costs).

By existing standards, the Ec-class was a large engine. In service its efficiency was noteworthy, being able to haul almost 40 per cent greater loads between Northam and Southern Cross than the existing

An Ec-class displaying its distinctive Vauclain compounding. (Noel Inglis collection).

goods engines, at the same time saving an hour and a half in running time.

The Ec-class was so versatile that it was pressed into heavy Christmas holiday passenger service by year's end, and where two locomotives had previously been needed for such loadings, the new Compounds handled the chore singly. Ec-class locomotives were running into Kalgoorlie by 1903.

Apart from official engine management education, drivers were tutoring themselves after discovering they could gain more power in difficult haulage conditions by admitting steam at full boiler pressure into the low-pressure cylinders simply by keeping the starting valve closed. Because the high and low pressure cylinders were proportioned so that under compound operation there was a balanced thrust on their common crosshead, inducting high pressure steam into the large cylinders meant the force was unbalanced, producing excessive loads on the piston rods and crossheads and overstressing the frames.

As a result, the frames of some Ec locomotives began fracturing behind the cylinders. By the close of 1906, eight frames had been replaced and another repaired.

Between 1920 and 1923, nine of the class were lightened to work over lighter 45 lb rails, with 12 cwt (about two-thirds of a tonne) being shaved off the coupled wheel loadings. They became the Eca-class. However, they did not last long, for withdrawals started with converted engines 250 and 255 on 20 June 1923. The last engine in service was Eca 240,

withdrawn on 24 August 1925.

But the story did not end there, for a start had been made in Midland Workshops to rebuild the engines using their chassis, wheels, tenders and cabs. With new superheater boilers, conventional cylinders and Walschaerts valve gear, all 20 had been treated by December 1925, beginning with engine 250 in January 1924. The revised product, known as the L-class, became champions of pioneer lines and the remnants were only withdrawn with the arrival of the X-class diesels from 1954.

SPECIFICATIONS

	IMPERIAL (METRIC)
CYLINDERS:	HIGH PRESSURE 12 x 22 IN (30 x 56 CM)
	LOW PRESSURE 20 x 26 IN (51 x 56 CM)
COUPLED WHEELS:	4 FT 6 IN (137 CM)
BOILER PRESSURE:	200 PSI (1378 KPA)
TRACTIVE EFFORT:	16 000 LB (71.1 KN)
GRATE AREA:	20.5 SQ FT (1.89 M²)
TOTAL WEIGHT:	74 TONS 8 CWT (75.8 T)
GAUGE:	1067 MM
ROAD NUMBERS:	EC 236–255 (ECA CONVERSIONS WERE 237, 238, 240–242, 245, 250, 253 AND 255)

The Commonwealth Oil Corporation used four Shays to haul product over the 50 km standard gauge Blue Mountains Railway which linked the Main Western line with shale oil mining operations at Newnes in the Wolgan Valley. The largest of the four, No 4 was pictured at the terminus's locomotive servicing area soon after its delivery in 1910. (Author's collection)

Shay Locomotives

The classic off-centre-boilered Shay locomotives, the first three of which entered service in Australia during 1902, can be ranked with the Beyer-Garratt design as among the world's most remarkable.

The Shay geared locomotive was developed in the Upper Michigan Peninsula region of the USA where a medical practitioner, Ephraim Shay, gave up his business in the 1870s to establish a sawmill. Shay, also a capable engineer, set up his own wooden railway in an effort to cut logging costs and worked it by horses. This railway became known as the Harbor Springs Railway Co.

Concerned over wet weather stoppages to his timber output, Shay purchased a small conventional steam locomotive to haul his log skips. He quickly observed that the locomotive caused serious damage to his wooden trackwork, although the heavier bogie logging vehicles rode the rails with ease.

Shay studied the problem and, much to the amusement of his lumbermen colleagues, came up with a steam locomotive bearing bogies at either end. This contraption appeared during the mid-1870s and boasted a vertical boiler and drive shafting to the wheels.

Following trials, further experiments and alterations, it quickly aroused the interest of his neighbouring lumbermen, who looked on in awe as Shay continued to haul lumber out of his forests in any weather. His rivals asked him to build them locomotives too but Dr Shay refused, suggesting they contact the nearby Lima Machine Works, which had offered him every assistance during the construction of his own unit.

Lima did in fact construct a few locomotives for the lumbermen. As more people showed interest in this unorthodox design, however, Shay patented his engine and in 1881 gave Lima the rights of construction and further development.

Lima and Shay never looked back. Orders came from lumber operators, private railroaders and even government railway systems in nearly two dozen countries around the world. In fact, 2761 locomotives were built between 1880 and 1945 and saw service in such places as Siam (now Thailand), Japan, Chile, the Philippines, Hawaii, Canada, the USA and South America.

Over the years, Lima transformed Shay's basic vertical boiler 2-cylinder machine into a massive 3-cylinder conventional-boilered example of the finest engineering in the business. Lima's final Shay, built in 1945 for a West Virginian operator, produced no

An early photograph, taken near the Commonwealth Oil Corporation's 25-milepost at The Bluff, clearly demonstrates the nature of the Wolgan Valley railway. A Shay locomotive, thought to be the company's 80.6 tonne No. 3, works a Newnes Junction-bound mixed train through the rugged scene. (Author's collection)

less than a giant 265.8 kN tractive effort and weighed 182 tonnes. This engine is now preserved.

Not unlike a Beyer-Garratt, the Shay design made it possible to haul far greater payloads using a conventional boiler.

Australia also placed orders with Lima between 1902 and 1915, resulting in 18 Shay-type locomotives arriving for diversified working roles in virtually every state. Their jobs included timber mills in Victoria and Western Australia, sugar interests in Queensland, copper mines in Tasmania and shale oil haulage in the Wolgan Valley of New South Wales.

The weights of the Australian locomotives ranged from 14 tonnes to the large 98-tonne Wolgan Valley No. 4 machine, and their gauges ranged from 610 mm to the standard 1435 mm. Two were imported by the Lloyd Copper Co of New South Wales to the unusual gauge of 914 mm.

The classic and largest of the Australian Shays were the four once operated by the Commonwealth Oil Corporation's 50 km railway in the rugged Blue Mountains of New South Wales. Following the opening of its extensive shale oil mining operation at Newnes (in the Wolgan Valley) and the subsequent establishment of refineries, a standard gauge railway line was constructed to a very high standard through some of Australia's roughest country to link the works with the NSWGR's Great Western line at Newnes Junction, 142 km west of Sydney.

The company's line encountered grades as severe as 1 in 25 and traversed mostly inaccessible mountainous country with giant 610-metre sandstone cliffs and deep valleys.

Since conventional engine power was considered unsuitable for such a track, orders were placed with the Lima Works for three Shay locomotives, the first of which arrived in October 1906. Eleven months later No. 2 arrived, followed by No. 3 in 1908. The two later deliveries were heavier than the first.

As mining flourished and haulage increased, a final order was placed for a large 98-tonne unit of 179.8 kN tractive effort, which arrived late in 1910. Being much larger and more powerful than the earlier three, No. 4 appears to have worked the bulk of the traffic over the line. The smaller locomotives were retained for shunting at Newnes Works and for standby main-line use when No. 4 was out for maintenance.

The Commonwealth Oil Corporation closed down about 1923 and, although the rail link was maintained for a while to enable a railmotor to bring in supplies to Newnes, the Shay locomotives were left abandoned. A washaway finally closed the line and the whole scene lay ignored until the early 1950s, when a start was made to scrap the four locomotives. No. 4 lasted the longest, being cut up in 1956.

Shay locomotives were also popular with the Christmas Island Phosphate Co's mining railway

This photograph clearly shows the Shay system of vertical cylinders driving shafting to the wheels. This locomotive is a former Taiwan Forestry Commission Shay that was imported by the Puffing Billy Preservation Society for its Menzies Creek Museum in 1972. (Leon Oberg)

which was commissioned during 1914. Of standard gauge, this 17.5 km railway linked Flying Fish Cove in the south of the island with the Drumsite Quarry almost due north.

Christmas Island, some 2650 km west of Darwin in the Indian Ocean, is included here since its affairs (during much of the railway's operation) were administered by the Australian government, and at that time was an Australian territory.

The railway, which until its closure was operated by the British Phosphate Commission, once employed eight steam locomotives, four of which were Shays. Built by Lima, all were 3-truck machines boasting 30 x 38 cm cylinders and 91 cm diameter wheels. Capable of speeds to 18 km/h, one was seriously damaged in a Japanese air raid during World War II. Its salvageable parts went to keep its three sisters running until they were displaced by diesels in 1955.

All of this railway's steam locomotives were purchased by a Hong Kong scrap merchant in 1960.

In Australia, a few Shays have survived to become museum pieces. Among them is a little locomotive which was last used at Moreton Sugar Mill and was put together from parts of builder's numbers 2021 of 1908 and 2800 of 1914. Because it had originally been used over the Mapleton line, the historic locomotive was transferred to that town for further preservation following the closure of the mill late in 2003.

The Illawarra Light Railway Museum at Albion Park, New South Wales, was fortunate in obtaining the derelict remains of two 762 mm gauge Shays which last saw service on a timber tramway between Hampdon and Palmtree (near Toowoomba) in Queensland which closed in 1936. The museum is already striving to build one operational engine from these parts which had been ravaged by 40 years of exposure in a subtropical rainforest.

Remains of a 610 mm gauge Shay, 2823 of 1915, were also recently discovered partly buried in a QR embankment at Palmwoods. This locomotive had seen work on the Buderim Tramway. Parts of a 915 mm gauge Shay have also been reported at a Victorian address.

In Victoria, Shay interest was so intense that the Puffing Billy Preservation Society imported one 2-truck locomotive from the Taiwan Forestry Commission in 1972. It was formerly 14 of the Mt Arisan Railway and carries builder's number 2550 of 1912.

Since few Australian Shays were alike, the

following specifications will mean little, except to provide a comparison against more conventional motive power. The values relate to the four large Wolgan Valley machines.

SPECIFICATIONS

	WOLGAN NOS 1–3	WOLGAN NO. 4
	IMPERIAL (METRIC)	IMPERIAL (METRIC)
CYLINDERS:	(3) 12 x 15 IN (30 x 38 CM)	14½ x 15 IN (37 x 38 CM)
BOILER PRESSURE:	200 PSI (1378 KPA)	200 PSI (1378 KPA)
COUPLED WHEELS:	3 FT 0 IN (91 CM)	3 FT 0 IN (91 CM)
TRACTIVE EFFORT:	29 800 LB (132.6 KN)	40 400 LB (179 8 KN)
GRATE AREA:	22.5 SQ FT (2.090 M²)	27 SQ FT (2.5 M²)
TOTAL WEIGHT:	NO. 1: 65 TONS (66.3 T)	96 TONS (97.9 T)
	NOS 2 AND 3: 79 TONS (80.6 T)	
GAUGE:	1435 MM	1435 MM

1902 VICTORIAN RAILWAYS

DD-class 4-6-0

Designed as a light line, mixed-traffic locomotive, the DD-class was to become the numerically largest class on the VR, as no less than 261 units were built between 1902 and 1920. The builders involved in their construction were Newport Railway Workshops (138), the Phoenix Foundry (7), Beyer, Peacock & Co (20), the Baldwin Locomotive Works (20), Walkers Ltd (20), Thompsons (40), Ballarat Railway Workshops (8) and Bendigo Railway Workshops (8).

In their early days DDs worked the fast Adelaide expresses until they were replaced by the heavier A2-class 4-6-0s in 1907. Locomotive crews were delighted with this change because the earliest DDs were found to be short-winded at high speeds due to the unsatisfactory balance between their small boilers and rather generous cylinders. Subsequently, they were withdrawn from main line service in favour of the branch lines.

During their lengthy construction period, numerous modifications were made to the original design. For example, engines built after 1904 received full-width cabs instead of the narrow cabs on the early engines. In addition, those built at Newport in 1904 were fitted with raised running frames as opposed to the earlier low type.

In 1914, superheating, which greatly improved fuel efficiency, was introduced to the VR with DD.882, which had 25 cm larger cylinders (48 cm bore). A number of later deliveries were also built in this form.

With more and more superheated DDs becoming available for traffic, these more powerful engines returned to heavy main line work once again. But they were not destined to stay there long, because a few years later high-powered 8-coupled engines of the N and X classes arrived. Once again, the DDs were returned to secondary and branch-line roles.

Fame was bestowed on the class when DD.980 was selected to become the Commissioner's personal tour engine in 1916. The class was associated with this important duty for almost 50 years.

Meanwhile, superheated DD.1032 was loaned to the South Australian Railways over nine days early in September 1918 to run comparative tests against their basically similar 4-6-0 Rx-class. The advantages of superheating were spectacularly demonstrated.

From 1929, renumbering and reclassification of the DDs commenced with the original saturated engines becoming D1-class. The superheated engines became D2-class. Later that year, a start was made to further improve the superheated engines when they

Offshore locomotive manufacturers usually fully prepared at least one locomotive for archive photographs. The Baldwin Locomotive Works in the USA, which received a contract to construct 20 DD-class 4-6-0s for the VR, was no exception. An unidentified example is portrayed here. (Leon Oberg collection)

No. 664, one of 94 improved superheated D3-class as running in the early 1950s. (V/Line archives, Len Whalley collection)

were gradually rebuilt with larger boilers, which were basically similar to those of the K-class 2-8-0 freight locomotives. Ninety-four engines were eventually altered in this way and became the VR's D3-class.

Withdrawals and scrappings commenced in May 1929 when the original engine, D1.584, was cut up. By October of that year, a further five had gone and by 1951 a total of 120 had vanished. By now, the remaining D1-class engines were the principal shunting power at most of Victoria's yards. The D2s on the other hand were operating over branch lines and working some suburban freight services, while the D3s could be accounted for on some main lines as well as important branch lines.

The D3-class was a remarkable locomotive, being capable of hard work and bursts of speed up to 120 km/h. From a maintenance point of view, they were extremely trouble free and easy to work on.

The first D3 to go to scrap was former Commissioner's engine 639, at Ballarat North Workshops in June 1958. However, 639's number was to continue, for it was bestowed on its sister engine 658 for further use by the Commissioner. In what became a stroke of fate, this was the last of its class to be withdrawn and today it is available to work special trains under the care of Steamrail Victoria Limited, under its proper number.

D3.608 was under restoration at Ballarat when this book went to press, as was D3.646, for use over the Castlemaine and Maldon Railway.

One of the last D1s in active service was 552, which

was purchased by Australian Paper Manufacturers of Maryvale in October 1941. It lasted until replaced by two centre-cab Whitcomb diesel-electric units in 1949. Needing a standby for the new diesels, APM then acquired D2.604 in February 1956. This locomotive saw little main-line running and most of its life with APM involved generating steam for the factory. It was eventually donated to the ARHS for the North Williamstown Railway Museum.

Locomotive D3.635 is also preserved at North Williamstown. Twelve other D3s are preserved across the state, including representatives at Ballarat Railway Workshops, Bayswater, Bendigo, Lismore, Swan Hill and Seymour.

A 4-6-2 tank-engine copy of the DDs appeared in 1908 for metropolitan passenger service. These became the DDe-class and were so similar to the DDs that two were actually converted to tender engines in 1922–23 (see page 141).

SPECIFICATIONS

	D1-CLASS	D2-CLASS
	IMPERIAL (METRIC)	IMPERIAL (METRIC)
CYLINDERS:	18 x 26 IN (46 x 66 CM)	19 x 26 IN (48 x 66 CM)
BOILER PRESSURE:	175 PSI (1206 KPA)	165 PSI (1137 KPA)
COUPLED WHEELS:	5 FT 1 IN (155 CM)	5 FT 1 IN (155 CM)
TRACTIVE EFFORT:	19 334 LB (86 KN)	21 580 LB (96 KN)
GRATE AREA:	22.5 SQ FT (2.090 M²)	22.5 SQ FT (2.090 M²)
TOTAL WEIGHT:	94 TONS (95.9 T)	9 TONS (98.9 T)
GAUGE:	1600 MM	1600 MM
ROAD NUMBERS:	MANY ALTERATIONS WERE CARRIED OUT DURING THEIR LIVES BUT RESTRICTION OF SPACE LIMITS US TO PROVIDING THE ORIGINAL	

WAGR's Es304, as running in January 1950. (John Sullivan)

COMPLICATED NUMBERING, WHICH WAS AS FOLLOWS: 560 (PATTERN ENGINE), 531–569 (ODD NUMBERS), 571–581 (ODDS), 582–690 (ALL), 692–700 (EVENS), 761, 765, 873–912 (ALL), 943–982 (ALL) AND 1013–1052 (ALL). (NOS 761 AND 765 WERE ORIGINALLY DDE-CLASS NOS 712 AND 710 RESPECTIVELY.)

D3-CLASS

	IMPERIAL (METRIC)
CYLINDERS:	19 x 26 IN (48 x 66 CM)
BOILER PRESSURE:	170 PSI (1171 KPA) SOME 180 PSI (1240 KPA)
COUPLED WHEELS:	5 FT 1 IN (155 CM)
TRACTIVE EFFORT:	22 234 LB (98.9 KN)
GRATE AREA:	25 SQ FT (2.323 M²)
TOTAL WEIGHT:	99.5 TONS (101.5 T)
GAUGE:	1600 MM
ROAD NUMBERS:	D3 606–699

1902 WESTERN AUSTRALIAN GOVERNMENT RAILWAYS

E-class 4-6-2

This successful, long-lasting passenger engine class, introduced in 1902, eventually multiplied into 65 locomotives.

Intended for main line operations, the first 15 were supplied in 1902–03 by Naysmith, Wilson & Co. Almost immediately, Vulcan Foundry was given orders for an additional 30. Increasing passenger train weights and an extending network saw a final order placed with North British for 20 more, in 1912.

All of these locomotives were delivered with saturated-type boilers exhibiting somewhat higher than usual 180 psi (1240 kPa) boilers. Regarded as heavy locomotives, two of them, 336 and 346, underwent minor weight reduction in 1934 to allow them to run on light 45 lb lines. In this form they were known as the Ea-class. Both had been reconverted by 1939.

By then a start had been made on rebuilding the class with superheated boilers and all but 306, 336, 338 and 353 were progressively treated, increasing their usefulness by the degree of boiler pressure and cylinder sizes employed. To explain, some class members for a time retained their original 17 x 23 (43 x 58 cm) cylinder dimensions but employed 175 psi

Time was fast running out for Fs452, pictured shunting at Narrogin on 9 October 1968. (Peter Neve)

(1206 kPa) boilers. Others were equipped with 160 psi (1102 kPa) boilers which powered 19 x 23 (48 x 58 cm) cylinders. Eventually, all of the superheated Es-class engines were standardised with 18 x 23 (46 x 58 cm) cylinders and 1102 kPa boilers and used on main line passenger trains.

Four Es locomotives (340, 341, 354 and 355) were converted for use on light lines and these briefly became the WAGR's Eas-class for this service. All had been reconverted back to standard Es engines by 1937.

The story did not stop there, however, as eight worn-out E and Es class locomotives were returned to the WAGR's Midland Workshops in 1945 where their frames, cylinders and wheels formed the basis of a 'new' 4-6-4 Dm-class tank type aimed at modernising the Perth metropolitan passenger service. The first three engines employed in this form, 314, 309 and 317, briefly carried their original road numbers. These eight engines spawned the improved Dd-class, ten of which were built new in 1946 (see page 230).

The last of the Es engines were written off on 7 October 1963, although eleven were retained on the 'emergency reserve' until sent to scrap in September 1966. Loco Es308 is preserved at the ARHS Rail Transport Museum, Bassendean.

SPECIFICATIONS

	ORIGINAL IMPERIAL (METRIC)	SUPERHEATED Es IMPERIAL (METRIC)
CYLINDERS:	17 x 23 IN (43 x 58 CM)	18 x 23 IN (46 x 58 CM)
COUPLED WHEELS:	4 FT 6 IN (137 CM)	4 FT 6 IN (137 CM)
BOILER PRESSURE:	180 PSI (1240 KPA)	175 PSI (1206 KPA)
TRACTIVE EFFORT:	16 620 LB (73 KN)	20 527 LB (88.1 KN)
GRATE AREA:	19 SQ FT (1.766 M²)	18.8 SQ FT (1.732 M²)
TOTAL WEIGHT:	83 TONS 4 CWT (85.2T)	88 TONS (91.6T)
GAUGE:	1067 MM	1067 MM
ROAD NUMBERS:	291–355	

1902 WESTERN AUSTRALIAN
GOVERNMENT RAILWAYS

F-class 4-8-0

WAGR's fifty-seven F-class 4-8-0 locomotives were the main line goods version of the aforementioned E-class passenger type. Designed concurrently in the same mechanical staff office, the two types employed many similar parts including boilers, cylinders and tenders.

The initial 15 were delivered in 1902 by Dubs & Co. Because of their equally trouble-free nature (albeit exhibiting a slow plodding gait), North British Works delivered an additional 42 locomotives in two orders throughout 1912–13. At this time, boiler superheating was becoming widespread overseas and at the suggestion of the builder, two (366 and 367) were 'trial' equipped with Schmidt superheaters.

The steam and fuel saving advantages of superheating became apparent in service and between 1924 and 1945, all locomotives except 398, 401, 403 and 415 were fitted with superheaters and classified Fs. As with the Es, the superheated Fs engines came in several forms, some retaining their 43 x 58 cm cylinders and 1206 kPa boilers, others with 48 x 58 cm cylinders and 1102 kPa boilers. Yet others were standardised with 46 x 59 cm cylinders powered with 1206 kPa boilers.

Superheating also had its downside, being higher on maintenance, and many were reconverted to F-class after having this equipment removed towards the end of their service lives, where they were employed in yard shunting. The last examples remained in that capacity until the late 1960s.

	ORIGINAL	SUPERHEATED
	IMPERIAL (METRIC)	IMPERIAL (METRIC)
CYLINDERS:	17 x 23 IN (43 x 58 CM)	18 x 23 IN (46 x 58 CM)
COUPLED WHEELS:	3 FT 6.5 IN (108 CM)	3 FT 6.5 IN (108 CM)
BOILER PRESSURE:	180 PSI (1240 KPA)	175 PSI (1206 KPA)
TRACTIVE EFFORT:	21 115 LB (90.1 KN)	26 082 LB (119 KN)
GRATE AREA:	19 SQ FT (1.766 M²)	18.8 SQ FT (1.732 M²)
TOTAL WEIGHT:	81 TONS 8 CWT (83.1 T)	85 TONS 14 CWT (87 T)
GAUGE:	1067 MM	1067 MM
ROAD NUMBERS:	276–290, 356–367, 394–423	

1902 BELLAMBI COAL CO

Avonside 0-6-0ST

Prior to amalgamations and closures, up to 20 separate coal companies fought for a market share on the NSW South Coast. With coal mining in that area dating back the opening of a mine at Mt Keira in 1845, the railway as a mode of transport was seized upon by the early colonial industrialists and throughout the late 1800s individual railways and associated jetties sprang up along the coastal strip. Those early rail links predated the arrival of government railways in the area.

While most of the privately-owned coal railways employed the standard 1435 mm gauge, some mines used gauges as narrow as 610 mm.

One colliery that experienced several takeovers during its earliest years was the old South Bulli

Colliery at Bellambi. Its early developers constructed a 4.5 km standard gauge line between the Russel Vale Depot (loading area) and Bellambi jetty. In May 1901, the Bellambi Coal Co acquired all the colliery's assets and immediately set about developing the enterprise on a much larger scale. The railway was upgraded with many new sidings.

At the same time, BHP was developing a battery of 120 coke ovens adjacent to the main Illawarra railway line near Bellambi, and Bellambi Coal Co contracted to supply BHP with 80 000 tonnes of coal annually. All this material had to pass over the coal company's railway.

All the former South Bulli locomotives had come to the mine second-hand, and the colliery's new owners believed the available motive power to be inadequate for the company's emerging importance. The Avonside Engine Co of Bristol, England, which possessed a range of popular industrial designs, was asked to supply a new 0-6-0ST which arrived resplendent in green livery with polished brass dome in 1902. It quickly received the name *Green Frog*.

Due to the development in 1908 of an additional four square miles of coal land, and the interconnection of the South Bulli mine, combined annual output was projected to average 500 000 tonnes. In a bid to help move this coal, Avonside was asked in 1907 to supply an identical engine. A third was added to the fleet in 1909 as production continued to expand. These locomotives became, in order of arrival, No. 5 and (second) No. 4.

Upon the closure of BHP's Bellambi coke works, due to a newly-created battery opening at the

South Bulli No. 5 as running in its last decade of service. (Brian Chamberlain)

Australian Iron and Steel Works at Port Kembla, Bellambi Coal Co successfully negotiated running rights for its locomotive No. 5 and non-air coal hoppers to trundle all the way to Port Kembla. Permission was revoked two years later after the dinky locomotive continuously stalled with its allegedly overloaded trains on the 1 in 75 grade into Wollongong station. The company renegotiated its position and was allowed to operate its trains to Mt Pleasant siding, from which point government haulage was arranged.

Meanwhile, the bulk of the company's coal continued to be shipped out of Bellambi jetty. However, following World War II, exports gradually declined and the jetty was closed in 1952 in favour of the government's Port Kembla installation. From that time until the railway yielded to road transport in 1969, all coal over the Bellambi Coal Co's railway was conveyed to government 'exchange' sidings adjacent to the old BHP coke ovens.

The three Avonside locomotives remained until the end, the last in service being No. 4, withdrawn 5 April 1968. While its two sisters were unceremoniously scrapped during the 1969 autumn, No. 4 was set up in a children's park at nearby Corrimal by the local Lions Club.

SPECIFICATIONS

	IMPERIAL (METRIC)
CYLINDERS:	15 x 20 IN (38 x 51 CM)
COUPLED WHEELS:	3 FT 3 IN (99 CM)
BOILER PRESSURE:	150 PSI (1034 KPA)
TRACTIVE EFFORT:	13 846 LB (61.2 KN)
TOTAL WEIGHT:	APPROX. 48 TONS (49 T)
GAUGE:	1435 MM
ROAD NUMBERS:	(2ND) 1, (2ND) 4, 5

1902 SOUTH AUSTRALIAN RAILWAYS

F-class 4-6-2T

Until 1902, when this sturdy class of 4-6-2 tank engines appeared, the Adelaide suburban passenger traffic had been hauled by small 2-4-0T P-class locomotives. With train weights increasing steadily, particularly over the Port Adelaide route, the traffic was clearly beyond the modest capabilities, both in power and range, of those elderly little locomotives.

From the turn of the century, the CME's office started preparing drawings for a replacement, which led to a handsome, well-balanced and exceedingly simple T.S. Roberts-designed 60-tonne 4-6-2T of almost twice the power output of the P-class. Designated F-class, the first locomotive emerged from the SAR's Islington Workshops in April 1902. This one-off engine was so successful that it formed the pattern for no fewer than 42 more, and by October 1922 Islington had constructed 21, James Martin & Co had provided 12 and Perry Engineering accounted for the final ten.

Nicknamed 'The Dollies' in honour of popular Boer War vocalist Dolly Gray, the class was easily able to cope with the continually increasing workload, which included the torrid Adelaide Hills route, along with trips as far as Hamley Bridge, Sedan and Willunga.

There are reports that F-class locomotives even worked to Long Plains, and for a time during the 1920s one was stationed at Strathalbyn on a rotating basis to work the Milang train. No. 181 had its moment of glory on 16 July 1920 when it was decorated to work a Royal Train.

Equipped with Allen straight link valve gear, the leading coupled wheels were unflanged to provide more flexibility through tight curves. Over the years, many changes were made to the original design. At the close of World War II, the class-leader was equipped with an extended Drumhead smokebox and stovepipe chimney in a bid to improve steaming. In addition, this locomotive and six others were converted to burn oil fuel to overcome shortages of good NSW steaming coal.

The steady introduction of diesel railcars from the mid-1930s caused the class's eventual downfall. Initially, older suburban locomotive types were withdrawn and F-class engines started to gravitate into shunting and suburban freight haulage. The first engines to be condemned were the class-leader, 167, and 178, both of which were in need of general overhauls, on 23 January 1956.

Only a handful survived when broad gauge steam operations ceased in June 1967; the final F-class in actual SAR service was 170 at Islington Workshops, last steamed in November 1967.

Fortunately, several have been preserved—Perry engine 255 at the National Railway Museum, Port Adelaide; Martin engine 245 at Gawler; and Perry example 251, which is operated by SteamRanger on its 'Cockle Train' tourist run between Goolwa and Victor Harbor.

James Martin F-class product No. 239 at Mile End on 18 March 1953. (Doug Colquhoun)

SPECIFICATIONS

	IMPERIAL (METRIC)
CYLINDERS:	17½ x 24 IN (44½ x 61 CM)
COUPLED WHEELS:	5 FT 3 IN (160 CM)
TRACTIVE EFFORT:	17 260 LB (76.8 KN)
BOILER PRESSURE:	185 PSI (1275 KPA)
GRATE AREA:	18 SQ FT (1.670 M²)
TOTAL WEIGHT:	59 TONS (60 T)
GAUGE:	1600 MM
ROAD NUMBERS:	167–189, 236–255

C16-class 4-8-0

Although the 2-8-0 type locomotive had been in use in Australia since 1879 for heavy goods haulage, the QR improved upon it during 1903 when it introduced the 4-8-0 C16-class. No fewer than 405 locomotives in three classes subsequently bore this wheel arrangement.

The C16-class 4-8-0s had been designed around the turn of the century in an effort to provide an engine to handle the growing cattle and general goods

traffic. By 1917, the Ipswich Railway Workshops had constructed 51 and there were also deliveries from Walkers Ltd (45), the Toowoomba Foundry (15) and Evans, Anderson, Phelan of Brisbane (41).

By 1918, a total of 152 C16s were available for traffic.

They were not restricted to freight services. The southern mails to Wallangarra were among the regular passenger services worked by the class until more powerful types became available.

Following tests on superheated boilers in other states, two C16s were so equipped during 1918. The results were so successful that designs were prepared to incorporate superheating in similar 4-8-0s. The first appeared in 1920 and eventually 227 were constructed, being known as the C17-class. Further C16-class engines were also converted between 1923 and 1937.

With the outbreak of World War II, engine requirements on the narrow-gauge sections of the Commonwealth Railways far exceeded the numbers available and during mid to late 1942 eleven C16s were loaned to this system, where they became the CR's Nmb-class (Nos 55–65). All were returned between late 1943 and mid-1944.

During their active lives, some of the class received the Master Mechanics smokebox, a device which increased steaming. Others were fitted with

C16-class 38 with a passenger service outside Kalka on 13 April 1968. (David G Bailey)

improved cabs and tenders.

Withdrawals began in September 1934, with the retirement of six engines. In July 1950, loco 517 was seriously damaged in a collision at Oakhurst and also withdrawn. One hundred and forty-two still remained in traffic at the time. With impending dieselisation, however, large numbers were soon withdrawn and by 31 December 1969 only five remained. No. 38, the last engine in service, was retired after working a special to Toogoolawah on 10 May 1970.

C16-class 106 was retained by QR for preservation until October 2001, when it was delivered to the Toowoomba-based Darling Downs Historical Rail Society for restoration to active service.

SPECIFICATIONS

	ORIGINAL	SUPERHEATED
	IMPERIAL (METRIC)	IMPERIAL (METRIC)
CYLINDERS:	16 x 22 IN (41 x 56 CM)	16 x 22 IN (41 x 56 CM)
BOILER PRESSURE:	175 PSI (1206 KPA)	170 PSI (1171 KPA)
COUPLED WHEELS:	3 FT 9 IN (114 CM)	3 FT 9 IN (114 CM)
TRACTIVE EFFORT:	17 522 LB (78 KN)	18 085 LB (80.5 KN)
GRATE AREA:	18.5 SQ FT (1.719 M²)	18.5 SQ FT (1.719 M²)
TOTAL WEIGHT:	80.5 TONS (82.1 T)	82.4 TONS (83.9 T)
GAUGE:	1067 MM	1067 MM
ROAD NUMBERS:	4, 6–14, 19–22, 31, 34–39, 41, 43, 44, 51, 63–65, 67, 69, 72–74, 96–99, 105–111, 118, 131–133, 139–142, 167–172, 176, 178, 395, 414–433, 510–517, 614–675	

T-class 4-8-0

To cope with the early twentieth century's expansion of ore and freight traffic over the 1067 mm Broken Hill narrow gauge railway, the SAR instructed its Chief Mechanical Engineer, Mr T.S. Roberts, to supply drawings for a locomotive type with the power and range to handle the traffic.

He designed an engine of the 4-8-0 wheel arrangement which was much larger than anything yet seen in South Australia. This locomotive type was destined to become one of the SAR's most successful workhorses.

One pattern engine, numbered 180, was initially produced at Islington Railway Workshops and entered service in a trial capacity in February 1903. Its strength, flexibility and ease of operation made it an immediate success and led to large orders. By September 1917, there were 78 in service, built by James Martin (34), Walkers Ltd (40) and Islington Railway Workshops (4).

These locomotives initially worked over the northern lines hauling Broken Hill ore and goods trains to the border at Cockburn. By 1935, some were transferred to the state's south-eastern lines while others were sent to the isolated Eyre Peninsula system where they remained hauling gypsum, wheat and general goods trains until replaced by 830-class

Oil-burning T44 was working out its last days on hire to the Commonwealth Railways when caught working a Hawker to Quorn goods on 28 October 1969. (Graham Cotterall)

diesel-electric Co-Co units from 1963.

Meanwhile, the Tasmanian Government Railways had been looking for higher-powered engines for its system and negotiated a deal to purchase six T-class from the SAR during 1921–22. These worked heavy goods trains and were based at Devonport and Launceston.

All of the T-class engines were originally built with saturated-type boilers but, during routine rebuilding between June 1925 and May 1939, those remaining in South Australia received superheaters. In a bid to increase their range, all of their tender sides were raised from 1930, thus enlarging their coal capacity from 6 to 8 tonnes.

During a period of severe locomotive shortage over the productive broad-gauge Murray Lands

SAR's T198 prepares a train in Peterborough yard on 3 September 1969. (Len Whalley)

An extremely rare photograph showing one of the four SAR T-class seconded for wartime use on the Commonwealth Railways' Central Australia Railway, taking water at Coward Springs in late 1941. A warm spring located in the trees at left ran all year round and not only provided locomotive water, but frequently gave train crew and passengers a place to swim, the photographer told this author. (Late Norm Macauley)

lines, five T-class locomotives were converted to the 1600 mm gauge during 1922–23 and classified Tx. All were reconverted to narrow gauge in 1949.

World War II traffic increases over the Commonwealth Railways' narrow-gauge Quorn to Alice Springs Central Australia route were so great during the early 1940s that five of the SAR T-class (46, 50, 212, 247 and 256) were borrowed by that system. Although only on short-term loan, the CR classified these locomotives 'Nma' and numbered them 50 to 54. They were all returned to the SAR by late 1942.

The arrival in South Australia of 830-class branch-line diesel-electrics from 1962 spelled the beginning

of the end as far as the T-class was concerned. One of the class's last real stamping grounds was over the very line it was built for—the northern route to Cockburn on the NSW border. T181 was in fact used as far as Broken Hill on reclamation duties even after gauge standardisation in 1970.

On the Eyre Peninsula, two lasted in shunting service until March and April 1971. They were 48 at Thevenard and 241 at Port Lincoln.

In Tasmania, the T-class was not seriously affected by early dieselisation but the first major blow came early in 1957 as re-wheeled Ma-class Pacifics were issued to traffic. When the Roland branch line was closed later that year, those T-class locomotives not utilised in push-up or shunting service were withdrawn. Loco 219 was the first to go, in May 1957.

The last in service, 235, was withdrawn from shunting service at Devonport in September 1961. By mid-August 1963, all the TGR's T-class had been cut up.

Today 181 is preserved in Broken Hill; 224 at Millicent; 253 at the National Railway Museum, Port Adelaide; 186 is owned by the Pichi Richi Railway Preservation Society, Quorn, and 199, which sat derelict in a park in Peterborough for many years, was rescued for preservation in Peterborough. Another, 251, is owned by the Bellarine Peninsula Railway at Queenscliff and used for tourist service.

While in Commonwealth Railways service, the T-class was temporarily known as the Nma-class. Like all engines working on the wartime CR, they were frequently involved in accidents such as this one at Warrina in the winter of 1942, when the line collapsed beneath the train. (Late Norm Macauley)

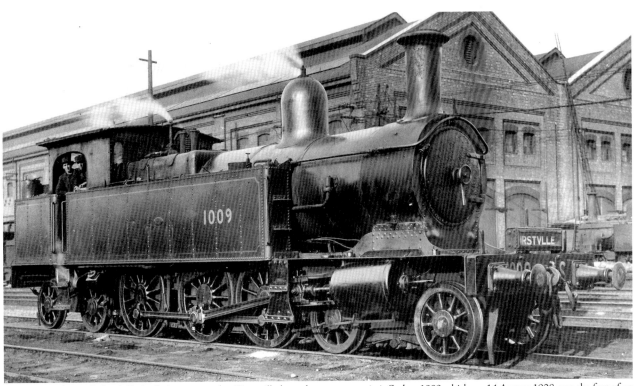

Preparing to depart Sydney's Eveleigh depot to work a Hurstville-bound commuter train is S-class 1009 which, on 14 August 1928, was the first of an eventual 77 of the class to be out-shopped as tender engines for branch-line service. For the record, this one became 3088T. (RailCorp archives)

SPECIFICATIONS

	ORIGINAL	SUPERHEATED
	IMPERIAL (METRIC)	IMPERIAL (METRIC)
CYLINDERS:	16½ x 22 IN (42 x 56 CM)	16½ x 22 IN (42 x 56 CM)
BOILER PRESSURE:	185 PSI (1275 KPA)	185 PSI (1275 KPA)
COUPLED WHEELS:	3 FT 7 IN (109 CM)	3 FT 7 IN (109 CM)
TRACTIVE EFFORT:	20 615 LB (91.7 KN)	21 903 LB (97.5 KN)
GRATE AREA:	17.3 SQ FT (1.607 M²)	17.3 SQ FT (1.607 M²)
TOTAL WEIGHT:	78.8 TONS (80.4 T)	81.3 TONS (83 T)
GAUGE:	1067 MM	1067 MM AND 1600 MM
ROAD NUMBERS:	23, 24, 44–48, 50, 51, 180–186, 197–258	
	(TO TX-CLASS:) 183 (BECAME 276), 199 (277), 252 (278), 243 (279), 220 (280)	
	TASMANIAN RAILWAYS: 219, 222, 223, 230, 235, 237	

1903 NEW SOUTH WALES GOVERNMENT RAILWAYS

S636-class 4-6-4T

The rapid expansion of the Sydney suburban services during the late 1890s saw a marked increase in the number of vehicles the existing 2-6-4T, 4-4-2T and 2-6-2T engines had to haul. Drivers were finding it increasingly difficult to keep to the timetabling of the day, so plans were prepared for a new and heavier 4-6-4 tank locomotive type to meet the need.

The first two of the S636-class entered service during August 1903; eventually 145 engines were delivered by Beyer, Peacock & Co (95) and Eveleigh Railway Workshops (50). By February 1917, all were in service.

Although these classic hard-working locomotives had saturated boilers, they soon made a name for themselves, being reliable free steamers, good riders and generally trouble free. They were intended for Sydney service but some were transferred to the Wollongong and Newcastle areas for further suburban passenger operations.

They became the C30-class during the locomotive renumbering of 1924.

With work progressing on the electrification of Sydney's main suburban lines (the first services beginning between Oatley and Sydney in March 1926), it became obvious to the administration that many of these gallant tank engines would soon be out of work, so plans were prepared to convert a substantial number to tender engines for country branch-line service.

Seventy-seven were converted to 4-6-0 C30T-class locomotives between August 1928 and July 1933. The Clyde Engineering Co and the NSWGR's Eveleigh Workshops handled the conversions.

The remaining 4-6-4Ts were released to work the outer Sydney suburban feeder routes, including those from Campbelltown, Camden, Carlingford and

Tank engine 3099 was looking rather work-worn when pictured charging out of Casula with a Campbelltown-bound commuter train on 7 December 1963. (Leon Oberg)

Penrith, while others soldiered on with Newcastle and Wollongong commuter trains. At least one, 3105, saw service out of Narrandera in the south of the state, and a photograph exists of it perched on its side following a derailment.

One job held by a C30-class until 20 February 1967 was the daily Wollongong to Moss Vale return passenger service.

With the exception of alterations to injector feed pipes and the provision on some of electric lighting, very few modifications were made to the 4-6-4Ts. However, 73 units had their boiler pressures increased to 175 psi (1205 kPa) from the early 1920s to the 1930s, some enjoying the increased pressure even after they were converted to tender engines.

Further improvements were made to 28 of the tender engines when they were fitted with superheaters and larger-capacity bogie tenders discarded from goods engines. Many, including some tank engines, were also provided with electric lighting.

The first engine withdrawn was tank engine 3012, in February 1957. While others quickly followed, some managed to linger as carriage shunters in the Sydney yard. But it was the introduction of two-car diesel railmotors on the Liverpool–Campbelltown and Newcastle–Maitland routes that spelled disaster for the hard-working 4-6-4Ts. After the Wollongong area commuter trains were dieselised in 1965, just 33 tank engines were left in service; most of these survivors went quickly after diesel-hydraulic 73-class shunting locomotives were introduced into Sydney yard from late 1970.

By mid-1971, only three remained operational, two of them in Bathurst shunting service.

Hebburn colliery had purchased 3013 in May 1967 for coal haulage work between its mines and

On a wintry afternoon in 1967, 4-6-4T No. 3046 works hard to accelerate a 5-car train away from Booragul, on its all-station journey from Toronto to Newcastle. Note how this locomotive was equipped with a steam-driven electric generator but lacked a headlight. (Late Ron Preston)

Boasting larger air reservoirs to handle non-air coal trains, former NSWGR tank engine 3013 rolls toward Weston in the NSW Hunter Valley with a loaded coal train from Hebburn No. 2 Colliery, on 12 March 1970. (Leon Oberg)

The tender C30T-class performed sterling work on the branches, and for decades examples could be found almost everywhere. But with dieselisation looming, withdrawals started with 3126T in December 1958. The gradual introduction of Alco 48-class and EMD 49-class branch-line diesels from 1959 and 1960 saw just 25 in traffic by mid-1967. The last 4-6-0 in government service was ex-Temora shunter 3144T, withdrawn in April 1972 after working a return enthusiast train from Wagga Wagga to Tumbarumba.

Some survive. Tender engine 3001T and tankers 3137 are preserved by the NSWRTM, tank engine 3085 is located at Goulburn roundhouse and 3112 is preserved in Canberra under private ownership. The Dorrigo Steam Railway & Museum play host to 3028T, 3046 and 3090T, while 3013 and 3026T are owned by the Lachlan Valley Railway. The ACT Division pf the ARHS owns 3016T and 3102T (the former being operational) and 3075T is statically preserved in a park beside Parkes Information Centre.

Footnote: Three 4-6-4 tank locomotives built by Beyer,

Superheated 3016, working an excursion train at Thirlmere station on 3 March, 2007. (Leon Oberg)

The first of three 15-class 4-6-4 tank locomotives built by Beyer, Peacock & Co for the South Maitland Railways to NSWGR S-class plans, pictured outside the railway's East Greta running sheds just before its September 1965 withdrawal from service. (Brian Chamberlain)

Peacock & Co for the South Maitland Railways to the NSWGR S-class plans became known as that railway's 15-class. Two were delivered in 1912 carrying the numbers 15 and 16 while the third (numbered 29 on the railway's roster) arrived in 1929. They were originally intended for passenger trains, but did little work in this capacity, being favourites in later years hauling the daily Cessnock goods. The last in service, 15, was withdrawn on 11 September 1965. All three were scrapped at East Greta eight years later.

SPECIFICATIONS

	ORIGINAL	SUPERHEATED C30T
	IMPERIAL (METRIC)	IMPERIAL (METRIC)
CYLINDERS:	18½ x 24 IN (47 x 61 CM)	19 x 24 IN (48 x 61 CM)
BOILER PRESSURE:	160 PSI (1102 KPA)	160 PSI (1102 KPA)
COUPLED WHEELS:	4 FT 7 IN (140 CM)	4 FT 7 IN (140 CM)
TRACTIVE EFFORT:	19 116 LB (85.1 KN)	21 424 LB (95.3 KN)
GRATE AREA:	24 SQ FT (2.23 M²)	24 SQ FT (2.23 M²)
TOTAL WEIGHT:	72.3 TONS (73.3 T)	99.13 TONS (101.2 T)
GAUGE:	1435 MM	1435 MM
ROAD NUMBERS:	(ORIGINAL) 158–163, 353, 354, 357, 360, 367, 636– 670, 801–829, 989–1016, 1062–1073, 1224–1253 (1924) 3001–3145 (C30T AT RANDOM)	

Superheated C30T-class 3011 at Bathurst locomotive depot in August 1963. The engine sports cylinder slide-bar covers to reduce Western Division sand scuffing the machinery, and a T-class bogie tender for extended range. (Leon Oberg)

Sandford's first locomotive was *Eskbank,* a modest little 28-tonne 0-4-0T affair (with crane attached) which came from the R. & W. Hawthorn Leslie & Co stable. It was pictured (minus crane) at Port Kembla in 1936 demonstrating its diminutive size against *Brolga,* one of the company's eight purpose-built 0-6-0ST steel plant locomotives. (Author's collection)

1905 William Sandford Ltd/G. & C. Hoskins Ltd

Industrial steam

Modern iron and steelmaking in Australia had its roots in the NSW Blue Mountains town of Eskbank (now Lithgow) in 1905, when entrepreneur William Sandford established William Sandford Ltd, Eskbank Ironworks.

As with most industrial concerns around the world at that time, railways became the dominant transport ingredient. While the business started in a small way, it was to eventually become a monolith under subsequent owners G. & C. Hoskins, Hoskins Iron & Steel Co Ltd, Australian Iron & Steel Pty Ltd and then Broken Hill Proprietary Co Ltd which, since 29 August 1928, when the No. 1 blast furnace was 'blown in', has been operating at Port Kembla on the NSW South Coast.

This entry attempts to profile Sandford's pioneering locomotives and those used by the company following subsequent takeovers and locations. It is a fascinating story of confusion and diversity, with locomotives being transferred between the company's many industrial and mining sites with seeming gay abandon.

Sandford's first locomotive was quite a modest affair, a rather small 28-tonne 0-4-0T locomotive (with crane attached) built new for the industrialist (from an existing design) by R. & W. Hawthorn Leslie & Co in 1905. Bestowed the name *Eskbank,* it was immediately pressed into wholesale works construction duties. It was joined by a slightly larger 29-tonne 0-4-0ST, built new by the same

manufacturer in 1906 and named *William Sandford,* whose initial job was to assist in the construction of the company's new blast furnace.

But Sandford's operation was on shaky ground and on 2 January 1908 his entire business was acquired by G. & C. Hoskins Ltd, under whose ownership the company quickly grew in stature, assisted by industrial development and railway-building activities throughout the state. Before long, a second blast furnace was built at Eskbank and the company contracted R. & W. Hawthorn Leslie & Co to construct a sister engine to *William Sandford.* It was delivered in 1913 and pressed into hot metal haulage carrying the name *Wallaby.*

A sister crane engine to *Eskbank* (also by R. & W. Hawthorn Leslie & Co) had been acquired in 1909 from a used machinery dealer. Known as *Shifter,* it was used for a brief period during 1912–13 at the company's Rhodes pipe plant. *Shifter* had the distinction of being the last locomotive to see service at Eskbank (Lithgow), its crane being useful in helping workers dismantle the works during 1931–33. *Shifter* was then forwarded to Port Kembla where, like *Esbank,* its last four years were spent with coke oven construction gangs. Both were condemned in the closing months of 1937, *Eskbank* being scrapped in February 1938 while *Shifter* lasted until it ingloriously fed the hungry blast furnaces in March 1939.

The bulk of G. & C. Hoskins' locomotive power was acquired second-hand, one being the diminutive 18.2-tonne Manning Wardle 0-6-0ST (B/No. 919 of 1884), which had been built new for the NSWGR's Campbelltown to Camden tramway. Purchased through an intermediary in September 1909, it was

Port Kembla 0-4-0ST jetty shunting locomotive *Wallaby*, caught between assignments awaiting a service at the AI&S locomotive workshops area, circa 1950. Its boiler was condemned in November 1962. (Late Jack Southern, Bruce Macdonald collection)

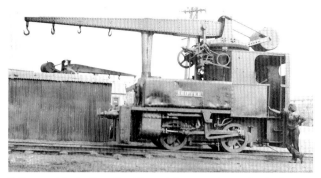

Shifter outside the Port Kembla works' water column, clearly showing its crane. (Bruce Macdonald collection)

put to work in the Lithgow works carrying the name *Bunyip*. In 1914, it was transferred to Springhill to help construct the company's rail link to Cadia ironstone mine and, until 1920, to work trains over this 18.5 km route.

Meanwhile, in a bid to obtain an independent source of metallurgical coking coal, G. & C. Hoskins in 1916 took an option over coal leases at Wongawilli, west of the South Coast town of Dapto. At the time, due to the unsuitability of Lithgow coals, the company had been railing South Coast coke produced at Coal Cliff from mainly Bulli and Mt Pleasant mines.

As part of the Wongawilli development, G. & C. Hoskins built a 4.7 km railway to the mine and associated coke works which left the NSWGR at Brownsville. The company then purchased a tiny 16.3-tonne 0-4-0ST Andrew Barclay (B/No. 167 of 1873) second-hand to work the trains. This locomotive arrived in Australia way back in 1874 for ore haulage under the ownership of British Tasmanian Charcoal Iron Coy at Port Lampriere in Tasmania. After that plant closed in 1876, the little engine is believed to have seen further service in NSW North Coast timber mills.

With the opening of the Wongawilli line on 25

October 1916, this 0-4-0ST was pressed into coke haulage at that mine, where in 1922 it was officially named *Wonga*. By now, the small locomotive was due for general overhaul, poor boiler and mechanical condition eventually dictating its withdrawal the following year. But *Wonga* must have been built under a lucky star, for in October 1927 it was 'tidied up a little' and forwarded to Berrima (where Hoskins was then developing a new cement-making plant) to shunt stone trains in Gingenbullen Quarry. It only operated there for a year, languishing in store at New Berrima until scrapped in 1942 to feed the parent company's blast furnaces at Port Kembla.

Wonga was replaced by the aforementioned *Bunyip* which, after a brief period at Lithgow, was taken to Wongawilli Colliery and Coke Works in 1928 and renamed *Tom Tit*. But it was found to be too light for the task, being forwarded to Port Kembla in September 1929 for jetty shunting, this time carrying the name *Rat*. It saw little service here either, being replaced by a heavier locomotive two years later, and was eventually scrapped.

Another Hoskins purchase was a short wheel-base 0-6-0T Kerr Stuart locomotive (B/No. 780 of 1908) which had been built for the Commonwealth Oil Corporation for shunting at nearby Newnes. The Hoskins family purchased the engine in 1912 for steel mill shunting. It was forwarded to Spring Hill

Dingo, the ex-NSWGR (N)67-class 0-6-0T No. 71, pictured at Lithgow where it hauled coal for the iron and steel works. It was later used in the demolition of the Lithgow plant, being transferred to Port Kembla in 1932 and quickly scrapped. (Bruce Macdonald collection)

Kangaroo as working at Port Kembla in 1936. (Bruce Macdonald collection)

in 1916 to help construct the company's railway to the Cadia iron stone deposits. Although it saw a few more years' service at Lithgow during the early 1920s, most of the period 1919–36 was spent working coke trains at the company's Wongawilli Colliery, carrying the name *Lithgow*. Following workshop attention, the engine spent a few years working the company's Bulli Colliery and, from January 1940, the Mt Keira Colliery, where it was bestowed the number 2nd No. 3. When the colliery's railway closed in November 1954, the engine was immediately scrapped.

To further assist with train working over the Wongawilli coal line, Hoskins acquired former NSWGR suburban passenger locomotive 4-4-2T M50 in December 1918 through A. Goninan & Co. It only lasted there several months, for the loco's 186 cm driving wheels were found to be too large for the grades and it was briefly forwarded to the company's Lithgow steel works. Here the wheels again proved too large for low-speed heavy-haul tasks associated with a steel mill, so the engine was dispatched to the Cadia railway where it worked until May 1927 (a year prior to the line's closure).

The veteran 4-4-2T's next eight years were spent in jetty shunting at Port Kembla and coal haulage between Wongawilli and the Port Kembla steel works, eventually receiving the name *Wallaroo*. Withdrawn in 1935, it was cut up for scrap the following year.

Another early Hoskins purchase was ex-NSWGR (N)67-class 0-6-0T number 71 (built in 1875 for suburban service by Sydney firm Vale & Lacy) in November 1913. This locomotive was named *Dingo* by its new owner and most of its time at Lithgow was spent hauling coal. It was also used in the demolition of the Lithgow plant, being transferred to Port Kembla in 1932, at which time it was scrapped.

At this time, G. & C. Hoskins' business was quite varied and included nearby limestone quarries and a pipe foundry in the Sydney suburb of Rhodes. In 1913, the latter works took delivery of a little 20.5-tonne 0-4-0ST Baldwin Locomotive Works product (B/No. 6114 of 1882) which was originally delivered to Berrima Colliery. In 1898 the engine was acquired by Bellambi Coal Co and spent most of its time up until its sale to Hoskins shunting Bellambi jetty. It eventually became known as *Rabbit*.

Lithgow was in turn replaced by a 37.5-tonne 0-6-0ST Beyer, Peacock & Co product (B/No. 1418 of 1873). This veteran engine, built for the Australian Agricultural Co's Sea Pit Colliery near Newcastle, was acquired by Hoskins in 1920. In February 1923 the locomotive was transferred to the owner's Lithgow steel works to shunt coal and coke trains, where it became known as *Koala*. Following the transfer of Hoskins' steel operations to the Australian Iron & Steel works at Port Kembla, *Koala* was forwarded to that site, initially to haul slag. Receiving a new boiler later that decade, *Koala* spent the next 16 years in general steel works and wharf shunting until withdrawn in October 1955 with a cracked cylinder. It was scrapped eleven months later.

At the time of *Koala*'s purchase, the Hoskins family managed to acquire an identical Beyer, Peacock & Co engine (B/No. 4558 of 1903) from Hebburn Colliery. Like the previous engine, this locomotive was forwarded to Lithgow where it worked at the blast furnace, bearing the name *Kangaroo*. It was one of the first locomotives transferred to the steel company's new Port Kembla plant in March 1928, spending the next ten years hauling hot metal.

Meanwhile, with World War II affecting Australian shipping (including the company's iron ore supplies from Whyalla), Australian Iron & Steel (which was acquired by the Broken Hill Proprietary Co Ltd on 17 October 1935) turned to local supplies in many parts of the state, including Cadia (which was a principal Hoskins iron ore supply throughout Lithgow days). Thus *Kangaroo* spent five months working line 'reconstruction' trains over the Spring Hill to Cadia line, commencing June 1941. Upon its return to Port Kembla, the locomotive found light shunting work around the expanding steel mill area, including wharf work. Withdrawn from service in April 1957 following the arrival of new 61-tonne English Electric B-B diesels, *Kangaroo* was quietly scrapped three months later.

Also transferred to Port Kembla were original locomotive *William Sandford* (which had been renamed *Possum* by G. & C. Hoskins) and its sister engine, *Wallaby*. Both took up residence at their new quarters in August 1932 where they were pressed into general shunting. Although the former was condemned in 1935 and scrapped, in March 1933 *Wallaby* had been sold to the South Kembla Colliery. But it was to return to Australian Iron & Steel ownership six months later following the purchase of that colliery. For the next 12 years it became an entrenched Port Kembla jetty shunting locomotive, its light weight and short wheelbase being ideal for the task.

Through most of the 1950s, records indicate the little 0-4-0ST saw more time under repairs than operating; with aggressive plant dieselisation well

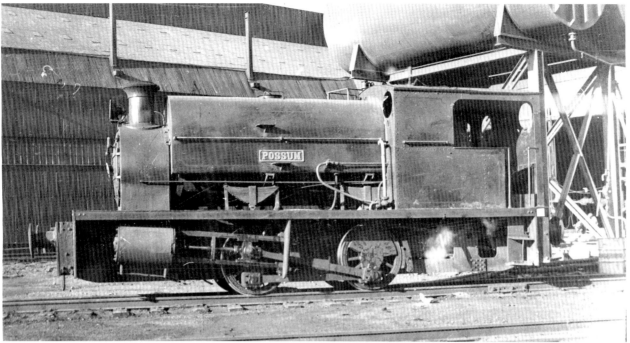

Possum, a 42-tonne 0-4-0ST built by Manning Wardle in 1912 for the British firm Vickers Maxims Ltd of Barrow on Furness. Operating there as *Cyclops*, the locomotive arrived at Lithgow in February 1919, was transferred to Port Kembla in 1928 where it was pictured, remaining there until withdrawn in 1964. (Late Colin Oakley)

An outstanding study showing the Walschaerts valve gear and dome-mounted safety valves on the Beyer, Peacock-built *Platypus*, taken at Port Kembla on 27 April 1950. (Late Jack Southern, Bruce Macdonald collection)

underway, the maintenance staff lost interest in the engine and its boiler was condemned in November 1962. But the story did not end there, for the locomotive was once again shopped, this time for static preservation. After spending 15 years standing on a plinth outside the company's visitors centre, *Wallaby* today languishes at the Illawarra Light Railway Museum Society's Albion Park operation centre.

Another G. & C. Hoskins acquisition of interest was *Platypus*, a 35.3-tonne 0-4-0ST, also of Beyer, Peacock manufacture (B/No. 5639 of 1912). Purchased for general heavy haulage at the Lithgow works, the locomotive was transferred to Wongawilli Colliery in 1924. After seeing further work at Lithgow, *Platypus* was forwarded to the company's new Port Kembla plant in April 1929. Some of

its life from the early 1940s was spent under lease to nearby industrialists John Lysaghts, and to the Electrolytic Refining & Smelting Co. It eked out its days shunting the No. 2 jetty at Port Kembla, finally being withdrawn in August 1956 due to poor boiler condition. With new diesels being delivered at the time, the relic was scrapped the following January.

Then came *Possum*, a heavy 42-tonne 0-4-0ST which Manning Wardle had built in 1912 for the British firm Vickers Maxims Ltd, of Barrow on Furness. Operating there as *Cyclops*, the locomotive arrived at Lithgow in February 1919 where it was re-named. This locomotive was among the first to be sent to the new Port Kembla plant, taking up residence in August 1928. It remained here until withdrawn in June 1964 upon the arrival of English-Electric Bo-Bo diesel-electric locomotive D30. After a period held as a standby loco, *Possom* was finally retired in October 1967 and, following a short period in store, was cosmetically restored for preservation in the grounds of the Lithgow and District Historical Society's Eskbank House museum.

Footnote: Two other steam types were employed by the company—the *Iron Duke* of 1920 manufacture and the celebrated B-class which appeared from 1929 and was captive to the Port Kembla plant. Due to their significance, those types have been listed as separate entries (see pages 171 and 207).

A true relic of the past: No. 5 at Hexham on 24 November 1971, prior to its rescue for preservation. (Leon Oberg)

1907 RICHMOND VALE RAILWAY

0-6-4T

During the closing months of 1885, nine large tank locomotives appeared in England for use over the Mersey Railway linking Liverpool with Birkenhead. Because this line boasted grades of 1 in 27, a powerful design was needed to which, because of the number of tunnels over the route, the builders, Beyer, Peacock & Co, fitted steam-condensing apparatus.

When the line was electrified in 1903, the now mostly surplus 0-6-4Ts were offered for sale. Three eventually went to Alexandria docks, two to Shipley Colliery and the other four came to Australia for John Brown's Richmond Vale Railway (outside Newcastle) for coal haulage.

Prior to their dispatch to Australia, all were overhauled by their original builder, at which time their condensing apparatus was removed, steam braking provided (replacing the typical UK vacuum-type braking) and cabs fitted. The date the first engines arrived is disputed (some say 1905, others 1907), but whichever it was they were put to work

hauling the heavy Pelaw Main to Hexham coal traffic. They received the numbers 5 to 8 in Brown's steadily increasing locomotive roster; the last engine arrived in Australia in 1908, having been retained for a time for use on Mersey Railway plant trains.

Their promised efficiency did not live up to expectations and their cabs were found to be hot. When new Kitson 2-8-2 tank locomotives arrived from 1908, the Mersey tanks were largely relegated to minor shunting roles and by 1919 they had all reached the major overhaul stage. Instead of overhauling them, Brown purchased a number of ex-ROD 2-8-0 war engines, which arrived in Australia from 1924. The 0-6-4Ts later found themselves set aside as the 1929–31 Great Depression reduced mining activity.

But all cycles change. With a gradual improvement in the world's economy from the early 1930s, coal mining surged, the nearby Cessnock Colliery buying 0-6-4T No. 6 for yard shunting. Carrying the number 1, it proved 'too rigid for the track' and was little used, according to a surviving account. It was advertised for sale in 1934 but, when no buyer was forthcoming, it lay for many years near Kalingo Colliery's locomotive

A2-class No. 824, one of the initial batch of Stephenson valve gear locomotives. (V/Line archives, author's collection)

shed until its boiler was removed in the early 1950s. Its remains were eventually scrapped where they lay.

Of the remainder, No. 7 lost its boiler (for use in a colliery stationary steam generation plant) in 1932 and its remains lay derelict for over 30 years. No. 8, withdrawn by 1934, remained in store at Wallis Creek until transferred to Pelaw Main depot in 1960 to escape metal thieves, but it was eventually scrapped there in September 1968 (a main driving wheelset surviving to become an exhibit at Richmond Main Museum).

The class-leader, No. 5, was the real survivor for, after its Depression years' withdrawal, it was moved to Hexham in July 1942, finding further use as a buffer stop until advertised for disposal in 1973. The preservation group, the NSW Rail Transport Museum, was fortunately the successful tenderer and today the relic stands within that organisation's giant Thirlmere Railway Museum.

SPECIFICATIONS

	IMPERIAL (METRIC)
CYLINDERS:	21 x 26 IN (53 x 66 CM)
BOILER PRESSURE:	150 PSI (1034 KPA)
COUPLED WHEELS:	4 FT 7 IN (140 CM)
TRACTIVE EFFORT:	25 017 LB (111.3 KN)
GRATE AREA:	21 SQ FT (1.951 M²)
TOTAL WEIGHT:	67.8 TONS (69.2 T)
GAUGE:	1435 MM
ROAD NUMBERS:	5–8 (BEING NOS 1, 4, 7 AND 9 ON THE MERSEY RAILWAY)

1907 VICTORIAN RAILWAYS

A2-class 4-6-0

Around the turn of the century, the VR, in common with other Australian systems, was experiencing rapidly increasing passenger loads, which meant that double-heading of many services became necessary. New, more powerful locomotives were obviously the answer. Accordingly, drawings were prepared for a large 120-tonne 4-6-0 express type which was to become one of Australia's most successful locomotive types.

A pattern engine built at Newport Railway Workshops steamed into traffic as the A2-class on 2 December 1907. It was so well received that a further 124 were constructed at Newport between 1908 and 1915. All were all equipped with saturated boilers and Stephenson's link motion.

Considered a heavy engine type, however, boasting an 18-tonne axle load, the A2-class's route availability was limited to the principal main lines.

When the need for even greater motive power arose, the A2 design was selected but the opportunity was taken to improve the new batch with more modern features such as superheated boilers and Walschaerts valve gear. In all, 60 of these improved locomotives were constructed by VR at its Newport, Ballarat and Bendigo workshops and delivered between 1915 and 1922.

Visually, the two types differed slightly. The running plates on the earlier Stephenson (or

The more refined styling of the Walschaerts valve gear engines is evident in this portrait of superheated engine 956. (V/Line archives, author's collection)

saturated) locomotives climbed above the cylinders in a series of steps, levelling out behind the smokebox. The improved superheated locomotives, with upright cylinders, needed revised running plates and these climbed in a more graceful arc from the buffer beam (see photographs). To distinguish between the two types, the saturated Stephenson locomotives theoretically became the A1-class under the VR's 1923 renumbering system. However, since many of them had received superheaters while retaining the Stephenson motion, only 70 actually became A1-class. Gradually these too were rebuilt, locomotive 808 being the last to be converted in October 1949.

With the elimination of the A1-class, the locomotives became A2 Stephenson and A2 Walschaerts engines.

Many modifications were made to the class over the years. Smokebox deflectors were introduced in 1934 and an ACFI water-feed heater was experimentally fitted to 973 in 1935 (remaining in place until removed 12 years later). In November 1945, engine 942 was out-shopped as an oil-burner; with subsequent coal shortages due to prolonged industrial disputes, similar equipment was bestowed upon 56 more. Another alteration to the basic theme was the fitting of Boxpok balanced coupled wheels to 944, 948, 964, 986 and 992.

While the introduction of the S-class Pacifics on the North-eastern line to Albury made inroads into A2-class operations from 1928, their biggest blow

came in 1951 with the arrival of the first British-built R-class Hudsons. These quickly displaced the double-heading of the A2 class now required on the important *Overland* interstate expresses and other main line services. As if in anticipation of these new engines, four A2s had by then been withdrawn, the first being 878 in March 1946.

Surplus main line rail had in the meantime been 'gravitating down' to improve the branch lines, and the elderly A2-class started to forge yet another name for itself in secondary roles. But the writing was already on the wall—with so many R-class already available and the arrival of main line diesels exactly a year later, withdrawals began in earnest in 1953–54 when no fewer than 89 were withdrawn.

The class's last regular main line passenger duty was between Flinders Street and Leongatha, south-east of Melbourne, the remaining engines operating light goods services or enthusiast passenger specials. The last A2 in traffic was 986, withdrawn on 2 December 1963 following a light engine run from North Melbourne depot to Newport.

Today, 884 and 995 are preserved at the ARHS's Railway Museum, North Williamstown; 964 is preserved at Reservoir (Edwardes Park); 986, which resided in a Warragul park for several decades, is undergoing restoration by Steamrail while 996 is located at Echuca.

	Original	Superheated
	Imperial (Metric)	Imperial (Metric)
Cylinders:	21 x 26 in (53 x 66 cm)	21 x 26 in (53 x 66 cm)
Boiler pressure:	200 psi (1378 kPa)	185 psi (1275 kPa)
Coupled wheels:	6 ft 1 in (185 cm)	6 ft 1 in (185 cm)
Tractive effort:	25 131 lb (111.8 kN)	27 107 lb (120.6 kN)
Grate area:	29 sq ft (2.694 m²)	29 sq ft (2.694 m²)
Total weight:	117.5 tons (119.9 t)	121.7 tons (124.1 t)
Gauge:	1600 mm	1600 mm
Road numbers:	(1923 numbering only) Stephenson engines: 816–939	
	Walschaerts engines: 940–999	

1908 Richmond Vale Railway

Kitson 2-8-2T

We have already seen how Newcastle-region coalmining magnate John Brown imported four ex-Mersey Railway 0-6-4T locomotives in 1907 for use over his Richmond Vale Railway (see page 135). Although they were robust and capable engines, surviving accounts indicate that they possessed rough riding characteristics and, due to their chassis inflexibility, occasionally derailed while negotiating uneven curves.

Brown asked the Leeds firm Kitson & Co to design a 2-8-2 tank engine more suited to his railway. Brown must have wanted to be sure the design was going to work for him before committing too much expense up-front, because he ordered just one locomotive which arrived in Newcastle during the latter part of 1908.

Boasting steam brakes (because Hunter Valley coal trains then comprised non-air wagons), the engine was fully British in appearance with shallow smokebox, small cast chimney and long (saturated steam) boiler. Another feature of the intelligent design was the raised side tanks, which provided easy access to the Stephenson's inside link motion.

The locomotive was initially based at Pelaw Main shed for heavy Hexham line service. But being British in every way, crews starting their first Australian summer aboard the big engine soon expressed their concern at the heat inside the partly enclosed cab. But those were the fledgling days of the unions, and despite crew concerns two similarly-styled locomotives were ordered in 1910, both of which entered traffic the following year.

Carrying the road numbers 9 to 11, all three locomotives were provided with names of running sheds located on the Brown railway. Thus number 9 became *Pelaw Main*, 10 *Richmond Main* and 11 *Hexham*.

No. 9 *Pelaw Main* outside Hexham's loco servicing shed on 24 November 1971. (Leon Oberg)

The three green-painted 2-8-2Ts handled the bulk of Brown's main line coal traffic until the arrival from the mid-1920s of ex-British Railway Operating Division (ROD) 2-8-0 tender locomotives. The three Kitsons were then pressed into Pelaw Main and Richmond Main miners' passenger traffic, a role they maintained for the next 20 years, only punctuated with shunting duties and extended trips into the workshops for overhauls.

By the mid-1940s the RODs started to take over passenger services too, so all three Kitson engines were returned to heavy coal service until *Hexham* was withdrawn in 1949. Towed to the company's 'fodder shed', it remained there, the target of metal thieves, until officially scrapped in September 1968.

Nos 9 and 10 were much luckier, as both received major overhauls during the mid-1950s for continued coal haulage. By 1970, however, the two 2-8-2Ts lay rust-streaked on a scrap line at Hexham along with a host of ex-RODs, for by then the only colliery that remained in the once awe-inspiring Brown organisation was Stockrington. But since the remaining few RODs were running on their original boilers, the Department of Labour and Industry, which authorised all privately-owned pressure vessels, gradually condemned them. This led to the old Kitsons being once again shopped and pressed, firstly, into Hexham shunting and afterwards, main line Stockrington colliery service, two jobs they were destined to maintain for several more years.

The axe fell on *Richmond Main* after it steamed into Hexham shed following a shunting shift on 3 November 1976. Its boiler and firebox were considered condemnable. *Pelaw Main* remained in traffic a further three years; according to the depot's daily traffic diary, it last ran on 7 December 1979. Although the veteran's boiler was sound, the company, now part of Coal & Allied Industries, told this author that some pressing mechanical repairs were becoming necessary and, because of the availability of its South Maitland Railways 10-class 2-8-2Ts, the work was considered unnecessary.

The Richmond Vale Railway eventually closed on 22 September 1987. Both surviving locomotives were snapped up by the nearby Richmond Vale Preservation Society whose operations are centred at that former mine.

SPECIFICATIONS

IMPERIAL (METRIC)

CYLINDERS:	20 x 26 IN (51 x 66 CM)
BOILER PRESSURE:	180 PSI (1240 KPA)
COUPLED WHEELS:	4 FT 7 IN (140 CM)
TRACTIVE EFFORT:	27 229 LB (121.2 KN)
GRATE AREA:	23.6 SQ FT (2.192 M²)
TOTAL WEIGHT:	90 TONS (91.8 T)
GAUGE:	1435 MM
ROAD NUMBERS:	9 PELAW MAIN, 10 RICHMOND MAIN, 11 HEXHAM

1908 EAST GRETA RAILWAY COMPANY

Avonside 13-class 0-8-2T

The East Greta Coalmining Co, formed in 1892 to win the vast coal reserves of the Maitland–Cessnock area, entered the railway business with the running of its first train in June 1902. The line was laid to the standard gauge and initially developed to transport coal from company-owned mines.

As other collieries sprang up in the area, the East Greta Railway quickly became the transport authority and before long a double track was provided between Maitland (East Greta sidings) and Cessnock's outskirts.

The company initially purchased an assortment of locomotives, including small 0-4-0 and 0-6-0 types and two larger and chunkier 0-8-0 saddle tanks.

With mining activity extending beyond Cessnock, most of the existing engine power was hard-pressed to lift the loaded coal trains over the 1 in 70 Caledonia bank, so in 1908 an order was placed with the Avonside Engine Co of Bristol for two impressive, heavy 0-8-2 tank locomotives. The first to arrive was numbered 13 on the company's expanding roster and entered service in December 1908. The second, No. 14, started hauling coal trains three months later.

Featuring Walschaerts valve gear and Belpaire boilers, the two locomotives proved good buys and a third was ordered. This arrived in 1911 and was numbered 1 in place of the company's original locomotive which had by then been withdrawn.

A severe coal slump in the 1930s created by the Great Depression saw a huge reduction in mining activities and a serious fall-off in train running. Contemporary reports suggest that locos 13 and 14

No. 14 simmering outside the Hetton Bellbird Coal Co's Hexham engine shed on 23 November 1971, just months before its withdrawal. (Leon Oberg)

saw little service during the 1930s and while No. 1 remained in 'fairly constant use' it was sold to the Bulli Coal Mining Co in 1937. This colliery was purchased by Australian Iron & Steel (now One Steel) in 1938 and the locomotive was transferred to the company's Wongawilli Colliery to haul coal trains between there and Brownsville exchange sidings (near Dapto). In September 1939, the engine was forwarded to the Clyde Engineering Co's Granville plant for heavy boiler work. It remained working at Wongawilli until returned to Bulli Colliery where a new, heavier rail layout had been installed, in February 1952, immediately after receiving a complete overhaul. It was eventually withdrawn in December 1959 due to a firebox foundation ring fracture and was cut up after standing derelict for about six years.

No. 14 was sold to the Hexham-based Hetton Bellbird Coal Co in 1936 for shunting service. Continuing in traffic until 1972, the still-operational locomotive was obtained by the Dorrigo Steam Railway & Museum for preservation in 1975.

Locomotive No. 1, in the employ of BHP at Bulli Colliery during the mid-1950s. (Arthur Reynell)

An official photo following the 1926 out-shopping of former East Greta Railway's Avonside 0-8-2T BHP 13 as a chunky 0-6-0T. (BHP)

No. 13 underwent a complete transformation following its sale to BHP's Newcastle steelworks in October 1945. Numbered 29 by BHP, the old 0-8-2T was rebuilt as an 0-6-0 tank engine and its boiler was slightly shortened. Because of this, the locomotive was prone to priming. A former BHP traffic manager, Roy Mullard, told this author that to correct the problem, company steam engineers tracked a revised steam delivery pipe from on top of the Belpaire firebox, where the steam was drier, over the top of the boiler into the dome. It was then threaded into the regulator valve and the locomotive's main steam pipe.

BHP 29's main duties were to haul coal and cart iron ore from the ships to holding dumps. It was eventually scrapped in 1961 after full dieselisation.

SPECIFICATIONS

	IMPERIAL (METRIC)
CYLINDERS:	20 x 24 IN (51 x 61 CM)
BOILER PRESSURE:	140 PSI (965 KPA)
COUPLED WHEELS:	3 FT 10 IN (91 CM)
TRACTIVE EFFORT:	23 374 LB (104 KN)
GRATE AREA:	20.7 SQ FT (1.923 M²)
TOTAL WEIGHT:	60 TONS (61.2 T)
GAUGE:	1435 MM
ROAD NUMBERS:	1, 12 AND 14 AT EAST GRETA

DDe-class 4-6-2T

With Melbourne's suburban passenger traffic growing unabated into the first years of the twentieth century, authority was given by the transport ministry to construct a pattern 4-6-2 tank locomotive in a bid to find a suitable solution to the shortage of motive power.

The VR drawing office decided to model the new locomotive on an already tried and proven prototype, the graceful and well-proportioned DD-class tender locomotives, the first of which appeared in 1902.

The pattern tank version was built at the Newport Railway Workshops and delivered in June 1908. As expected, due to the outstanding performance of the DD-class tender engines, the tank version proved a resounding success and by June 1913 a total of 58 engines had been delivered.

All were built at Newport and became known as the DDe-class.

These 4-6-2Ts were so similar to the DD-class tender engines that two actually 'changed sides' to become tender engines, due to Melbourne metropolitan electrification. (The tank engines were deliberately designed for easy conversion should the occasion arise.)

Most of the class went through life unaltered. However, three were given superheated boilers in 1923 and 1936 to operate the Mornington and Werribee passenger services. In later years, three engines were equipped with cow-catchers, both front and rear, for service over the same lines.

In company with all other VR locomotives, the

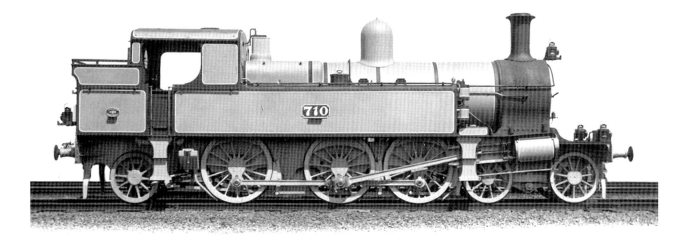

D4-class 710 in immaculate 'upon delivery' condition. It was one of two later converted to tender engines. (VR archives, author's collection)

DDe-class underwent a reclassification in 1924, at which time it became the system's D4-class. But with sales, conversions and withdrawals (due to metropolitan electrification) reducing their ranks, only 38 actually received new numbers.

Scrapping started in June 1924 when no fewer than ten fell victim to the scrapper's torch. Four more followed in 1925. The State Electricity Commission purchased locomotive 704 in September 1926 for use at Yallourn—it was finally broken up in July 1938.

Further electrification project openings resulted in the remaining D4s being displaced from the passenger scene and pressed into suburban goods and transfer working, and car and wagon shunting. Some spare engines were allotted to Ballarat to work the Newlyn branch.

Twenty-five survived until 1951 when scrappings again started in earnest with D4.282. Another 23 gradually followed but fortunately D4.268 was spared for preservation at Newport Museum.

SPECIFICATIONS

	IMPERIAL (METRIC)
CYLINDERS:	18 x 26 IN (46 x 66 CM)
BOILER PRESSURE:	185 PSI (1275 KPA)
COUPLED WHEELS:	5 FT 1.75 IN (156 CM)
TRACTIVE EFFORT:	20 190 LB (89.9 KN)
GRATE AREA:	22.5 SQ FT (2.090 M²)
TOTAL WEIGHT:	69 TONS (70.4 T)
GAUGE:	1600 MM
ROAD NUMBERS:	(ORIGINAL DDE) 702–720, 732–750, 772–796 (EVEN NUMBERS) AND 701–749 (ODD NUMBERS). NOTE: DDE 712 AND DDE 710 BECAME DD 761 AND DD 765 (TENDER ENGINES) RESPECTIVELY. (RENUMBERED AS D4) 250–287

1909 NEW SOUTH WALES GOVERNMENT RAILWAYS

N928-class 4-6-0

This class of five heavy 4-6-0s was in effect an enlarged and more powerful version of the successful P6-class of 1891, and appeared between December 1909 and April 1910.

Designed by the highly productive CME William Thow (the designer of the P6), the N-class was built to add both pace and power to express trains, then growing heavier due to their increased numbers of vehicles.

Although only five in number, the N-class was intended initially to work over both the Southern and Main Northern lines but, because of a slight dynamic imbalance between larger driving wheels, modest cylinders and slightly underpowered saturated boilers, all five were gradually transferred for use on the generally level tracks that radiated out from Junee.

Their power problem was easily fixed when, between May 1919 and March 1926, all were provided with 24-element Schmidt superheaters which increased their tractive effort from 106.5 kN at 80 per cent boiler pressure to 118.6 kN at 85 per cent. At the same time, each locomotive's cylinder diameter was increased by 1.3 cm and more precise piston valves fitted.

In 1924, the locomotives were renumbered and became the 34-class.

The gradual introduction of 36-class 4-6-0s to Southern express workings from the late 1920s gave the administration the incentive to entrust the 34-class to North Coast running. After all, weren't they now more powerful and better suited for hilly terrain? But problems of a different nature presented themselves, one of the hardest to rectify being a multitude of broken engine springs, brought about by the severe pitching and swaying of the rather top-heavy locomotives on the perpetually curved coastal railway. After just a couple of years' service (1929–31) wheeling the express and mail trains to South Grafton, all were returned to the flat and basically straighter lines of the Riverina district.

Remaining at Junee depot for the rest of their lives, the 34-class found work hauling fast perishable fruit and mail trains between Narrandera and Junee. When spare, these locomotives were rostered as 'bankers' on heavily loaded interstate expresses, running as far as Wagga Wagga, Albury, Cootamundra and occasionally to Goulburn.

All had been commissioned with T524-class 16 590 litre bogie tenders. With the success of similarly-styled but larger 18 200 litre tenders on the newer 35-class, five new ones were built for the C34s to improve their range.

Early in their lives, civil engineers expressed their concern at the 34-class's extreme coupled wheel hammer blow while running at express speed. In 1924, when the 36-class 4-6-0s were being designed, engineers successfully fine-balanced the similar 34 and 35 class coupled wheels for use beneath the newer engines, and the legacy of that work reduced

After an early career that took them firstly to the Main Northern Line and later to the North Coast, the 34-class finally settled in at Junee in southern New South Wales. The 10-car *South West Mail* on Good Friday 1956 was worked to Narrandera by 3401, shown here during a stop at Ganmain. (Late Ron Preston)

the coupled wheel forces by almost three quarters. Some 34s also received new cabs with square side windows during rebuilds.

Due to the large number of more modern express-type locomotives available, 3405 was withdrawn when its boiler gave out in October 1950. The last engine in operation was 3402, stopped in August 1957. It sat in scrap sidings at Enfield until sold to a metal contracting firm in 1962; despite last-minute efforts to save the relic for preservation, the locomotive was destroyed soon afterwards.

During their lives, all managed between 1.25 and 1.5 million kilometres in operation.

SPECIFICATIONS

	ORIGINAL	SUPERHEATED
	IMPERIAL (METRIC)	IMPERIAL (METRIC)
CYLINDERS:	21 x 26 IN (53 x 66 CM)	21½ x 26 IN (55 x 66 CM)
BOILER PRESSURE:	180 PSI (1240 KPA)	180 PSI (1240 KPA)
COUPLED WHEELS:	5 FT 9 IN (175 CM)	5 FT 9 IN (175 CM)
TRACTIVE EFFORT:	23 929 LB (106.5 KN)	26 649 LB (118.6 KN)
GRATE AREA:	28.5 SQ FT (2.648 M²)	28.5 SQ FT (2.648 M²)
TOTAL WEIGHT:	108.5 TONS (110.7 T)	114 TONS (116.3 T)
GAUGE:	1435 MM 1435 MM	
ROAD NUMBERS:	(ORIGINAL) 928–932	
	(1924) 3401–3405	

K-class 0-4-0 + 0-4-0

The Tasmanian Government Railways had the distinction of operating the world's first Garratt-type locomotive, a diminutive 0-4-0 + 0-4-0 Beyer, Peacock & Co-built engine, two of which were ordered in 1909 for use over the 610 mm gauge North East Dundas Tramway.

Surviving accounts indicate that these locomotives, known as the K-class, cost approximately $6900 each, arrived late in 1909 and were assembled in the railway workshops at Zeehan early in 1910.

Ordered to augment the single member of the 2-6-4-0 J-class, *Hagan's Patent* (see page 111), it soon became apparent that despite being basically a good design, the Garratts possessed a fault that would have to be rectified in any follow-up designs. The problem lay with their cylinders, which were positioned inwards. Enginemen complained of extremely hot cab floors due to a set of cylinders being placed underneath the floor.

The construction of an aerial ropeway from Williamsford to Rosebery led to the closure of the Nickel Junction to Williamsford section of the North East Dundas Tramway in 1929. The remainder of the 610 mm gauge railway was closed in sections up to 1938–39 and both Garratts were put into store at Zeehan.

During 1947 Beyer, Peacock & Co negotiated the repurchase of class-leader K1 for exhibition in its Gorton Works in Manchester. Being in poor condition, K1 was made complete with parts from sister engine, K2, then dismantled and sea-freighted to England.

Beyer, Peacock works photograph of K1. (Manchester Museum of Technology)

The closure of Beyer, Peacock & Co in 1966 saw the veteran sold to the Festiniog 597 mm gauge railway in Wales. After lying beneath a tarpaulin awaiting restoration and planned regauging for use over that tourist railway, it was finally transferred on loan to the National Railway Museum at York (UK). Externally restored in pristine grey and black livery, the locomotive was returned in April 1995 and restored for use by the Welsh Highland Railway in April 1995. It was steamed in September 2004 and now operates tourist trains.

The remains of K2 lay in the grass at Zeehan for at least a quarter of a century. During that time, the tanks were purchased, then the boiler. The cab and stripped engine units were finally scrapped in the 1960s.

SPECIFICATIONS

	IMPERIAL (METRIC)
CYLINDERS:	(2) 11 x 16 IN (28 x 41 CM) HIGH PRESSURE
	(2) 17 x 16 IN (43 x 41 CM) LOW PRESSURE
BOILER PRESSURE:	195 PSI (1344 KPA)
COUPLED WHEELS:	2 FT 7½ IN (80 CM)
TRACTIVE EFFORT:	17 900 LB (79.7 KN)
GRATE AREA:	14.8 SQ FT (1.375 M²)
TOTAL WEIGHT:	34 TONS (34.5 T)
GAUGE:	610 MM
ROAD NUMBERS:	K1 AND K2

Barclay 0-4-0T / 0-6-0T

The Commonwealth Portland Cement Co Ltd, which in 1901 acquired a closed cement and lime works (on the western fringe of the NSW Blue Mountains) decided, right from the very start, that a standard gauge rail link was going to be a top priority.

The plant, initially opened under the ownership of the Cullen Bullen Lime & Cement Co in 1883, had employed a light 915 mm gauge 1.8 km railway to link its works with Portland rail siding. This pioneering company collapsed during the 1890s depression.

The new owners believed that re-laying the rail link to the standard gauge would eliminate 'nuisance' transhipping in Portland yard and ensure faster customer delivery. Whereas the first two locomotives used by the new company were low-powered 0-6-0ST engines of Hudswell Clarke and Robert Stephenson construction, three Andrew Barclay products were acquired between 1911 and 1916, the first (No. 3) and last (No. 5) being 0-6-0T products which exerted an average 20 000 psi (88 kN) tractive effort, approximately twice the power rating of the Hudswell Clarke and Robert Stephenson locos.

No. 3 in Portland works yard on 20 April 1974. (John S. Glastonbury)

The remaining Barclay purchase was of 0-4-0T configuration and was less popular with the crews due to its low 10 400 psi (45 kN) output. With just two driving axles, combined with the regular occurrence of mists and fogs in the area, it was prone to slipping on the short, steep 1 in 38 grade out of the factory yard. Not surprisingly, this Barclay, known as CPC No. 4, was scrapped in 1957. No. 5 began to suffer from boiler problems from the early 1970s and, although a repaired boiler was actually fitted in 1976, the locomotive did not re-enter service; a NSWGR 26-class 2-6-2ST, No. 2605, was bought instead.

By that time Barclay No. 3 was also in poor order and, with the arrival of 2605, it ended its days mostly as a standby engine.

By late 1982 the poor condition of the steam locomotives dictated radical thinking and, in August 1982, the company's administration approached Australian Iron & Steel at Port Kembla for help. A 282 kW B-B diesel-electric unit, D10, was provided and worked the line until its closure five months later. While D10 was returned, Barclay No. 3 found a temporary home with the Central West Railway Preservation Society before being sold to the Dorrigo Steam Railway and Museum late in 1997. No. 5 was last seen by this author in storage at Wodonga for the Tallangatta Valley Tourist Railway, while 2605 was conveyed to nearby Lithgow for preservation.

SPECIFICATIONS

No. 3

IMPERIAL (METRIC)

CYLINDERS:	16 x 24 IN (41 x 61 CM)
BOILER PRESSURE:	160 PSI (1102 KPA)
COUPLED WHEELS:	3 FT 6 IN (106 CM)
TRACTIVE EFFORT:	18 724 LB (83.5 KN)
TOTAL WEIGHT:	41 TONS 10 CWT (42.5 T)
GAUGE:	1435 MM
ROAD NUMBERS:	3, 5

1912 SILVERTON TRAMWAY

A-class 4-6-0

From its inception in 1888, the 58 km Silverton Tramway linking Broken Hill with Cockburn (on the NSW–South Australia border), used a collection of 45-tonne Y-class 2-6-0 locomotives to haul its ore, goods and passenger trains.

These little engines exchanged their trains at the border with similarly-designed South Australian locomotives and could haul 605 tonnes between Broken Hill and Cockburn (and 385 tonnes on the return). However, increasing mine production called for greater train payloads and late in 1910 the Silverton Tramway asked Beyer, Peacock & Co of Manchester, England, to recommend a more powerful design and to quote on two locomotives.

Thus the Tramway's A-class was born, with two

The survivor, No. 21, at Peterborough depot on Australia Day 1953, while on lease to the SAR. (National Railway Museum, Port Adelaide archives)

examples arriving in Port Pirie (South Australia) in 1912. At Broken Hill, the new fat-boilered superheated 4-6-0 locomotives were found to be free steamers which could haul 837 tonnes to Cockburn and return with 586 tonnes. They also became popular on the interstate *Broken Hill Express* (which exchanged engines at the border).

Because water and coal capacities were not a major problem on the Tramway, the A-class was equipped with similar 6-wheel tenders as the Y-class.

Their popularity led to the acquisition of two more in 1915, and these four A-class locomotives plodded over their given beat for nearly 40 years. During a major rebuild in that time, their cylinder stroke was increased by 50 mm, which increased the tractive effort by 7.7 kN.

Despite the arrival of four semi-streamlined W-class 4-8-2s in 1951, the elderly A-class remained on the books. For several years during the early 1950s, two at a time were leased on a rotating basis to South Australian Railways for shunting duties at Peterborough. Others were used for sporadic shunting at Broken Hill and work train duties over the Silverton Tramway until their deteriorating condition dictated their demise. The final one in service, No. 21, last steamed on 28 October 1960 (two months before Alco DL531 diesels eliminated steam on the railway altogether).

Fortunately, locomotive 21 has been preserved and today can be found at the National Railway Museum, Port Adelaide.

SPECIFICATIONS

	ORIGINAL	AS REBUILT
	IMPERIAL (METRIC)	IMPERIAL (METRIC)
CYLINDERS:	16½ x 20 IN (42 x 51CM)	16½ x 22 IN (42 x 56 CM)
COUPLED WHEELS:	4 FT 3 IN (130 CM)	4 FT 3 IN (130 CM)
BOILER PRESSURE:	185 PSI (1275 KPA)	185 PSI (1275 KPA)
TRACTIVE EFFORT:	15 801 LB (70 KN)	17 381 LB (77.7 KN)
GRATE AREA:	17 SQ FT (1.61M²)	17 SQ FT (1.61M²)
TOTAL WEIGHT:	59 TONS 2 CWT (61.1 T)	59 TONS 8 CWT (61.8 T)
GAUGE:	1067 MM	1067 MM
ROAD NUMBERS:	18–21	18–21

1912 SYDNEY WATER BOARD

Vulcan 0-4-0ST

Typical of US industrial designs for small standard gauge rail operators were the two 27-tonne 0-4-0ST locomotives delivered to the NSW government's Sydney Water Board in 1912.

Built by the Vulcan Iron Works at Wilkes Barre, Pennsylvania, for construction duties at the Board's Potts Hill reservoirs, the locomotives were later sold to the Emu Prospect & Gravel Co to work the newly opened Greystanes branch. In 1924 and 1926 they were progressively transferred to the company's Emu Plains gravel mining quarry. The company had started mining gravel beside the Nepean River at Emu Plains in the 1880s; when a connection with the NSWGR was established around 1910, horses initially hauled the gravel trucks.

The line was expanded after the steam locomotives

A battered 1023 working in Enfield's No. 2 roundhouse, attached to the tender from a Standard Goods engine, in 1958. (Late Ron Preston)

arrived, eventually reaching a length of about 2.5 km. In 1936, No. 2 was withdrawn from service (replaced with a NSWGR 25-class 2-6-0) and used as a source of spare parts for its sister engine.

Meanwhile, the Vulcan Iron Works received another order from the NSW PWD to supply two identical 0-4-0STs for railway construction duties. These were commissioned late in 1916, just months prior to the NSWGR taking over full responsibility for railway construction. The two new engines were absorbed into the NSWGR's fleet, initially as the V-class, and put to work building the network of goods-only lines in Sydney. Renumbered 1022 and 1023 under the state's renumbering system, the engines spent much of the 1930s working a government blue metal quarry at Kiama until required for war duty. In 1943, No. 1023 and its sister were leased to the US Army for work at the Sandown (Sydney)-based US Quartermaster's store.

Following hostilities, the two diminutive engines found employment shunting locomotives and tenders around the sprawling multi-roundhouse complex at Enfield locomotive depot. The first withdrawn for scrap was 1023, in June 1964. Its sister 1022 lingered on in depot shunting until October 1970, when it was withdrawn for preservation by the NSWRTM.

The story did not end there, however, for in March 1967 the Emu Plains gravel railway closed (following a takeover) and its Vulcan No. 1 locomotive was acquired by the Steam Tram & Railway Preservation Society for planned use in Parramatta Park. But it was in such poor order that the Society arranged a swap in October 1970 with the NSWRTM's 1022. After an overhaul, 1022 was in regular use until a mysterious fire on 7 June 1993 destroyed the Society's passenger carriage (tram) fleet and seriously damaged its motive power, including 1022. The locomotive is today undergoing a major overhaul at the NSWRTM's Valley Heights Blue Mountains complex.

SPECIFICATIONS

	IMPERIAL (METRIC)
CYLINDERS:	12 x 18 IN (30½ x 46 CM)
COUPLED WHEELS:	3 FT 0 IN (914 MM)
BOILER PRESSURE:	150 PSI (1034 KPA)
GRATE AREA:	14 SQ FT (1.31 M²)
TRACTIVE EFFORT:	22 219 LB (98.8 KN)
TOTAL WEIGHT:	26 TONS 18 CWT (27.3 T)
GAUGE:	1435 MM
ROAD NUMBERS:	WATER BOARD/EMU GRAVEL: 1 AND 2
	NSWGR: V1217 AND V1218; LATER 1022 AND 1023

Steam action on Tumulla bank west of Bathurst on 4 July 1965 as two 53-class, 5384 and 5480 (with a third 53-class pushing at the rear), stagger up the 1 in 40 gradient with an Orange-bound goods train. (Leon Oberg)

1912 NEW SOUTH WALES GOVERNMENT RAILWAYS

TF939-class 2-8-0

Continually expanding goods traffic over the NSWGR called for even more purpose-built locomotives to answer the haulage task. Although North British was hard at work building vast numbers of Thow-designed T524-class 2-8-0s, it was felt that certain improvements could be made to the extraordinary design by adding several 'tried and proven' Great Western Railway features.

These included boilers that tapered from the firebox to the mid-ring, extended 'self-cleaning' smokeboxes, piston valves and exhaust injectors. Cosmetically, the design allowed for a raised running board, arcing in a single step immediately behind the front buffer beam.

All these features were to some extent the handiwork of Thow's assistant (and eventual successor), Ernest Lucy, who had been recruited from the GWR in 1906.

Despite vast numbers of locomotives continuing to be manufactured offshore (with an outstanding order for 83 T-class yet to be delivered by North British), the Sydney-based Clyde Engineering Co had proved it was up to the task. It had successfully built 75 heavy main line locomotives of the P and T classes for the NSWGR between 1906 and 1911.

When it came time to order this new, improved TF-class 2-8-0, Clyde Engineering received the contract to construct the initial 30, the first one going into traffic on 26 April 1912. Successive orders saw no fewer than 180 in traffic by 2 November 1917. Thirty of them were built in three small batches by the NSWGR's own Eveleigh Workshops.

But not everything came up smelling of roses. Enginemen were complaining about the riding quality of the new TFs and the problem was traced to poorly balanced coupled wheels, brought about largely by the use of knuckle joints on the second driver (rods). Lucy had to defend his design before a Parliamentary inquiry.

Because the TFs were troublesome steamers made worse when the superheater equipment corroded, many were operated in saturated form with their boiler pressures reduced to 150 psi (1033 kPa).

In 1924, the TF locomotives became the D53-class.

By the end of the Great Depression, many of their boilers were giving out and, since the non-tapered superheated boilers fitted to the earlier T-class were proving so successful (see page 99) a new common boiler for use across the standard goods engine fleet was unveiled—a compromise design incorporating features of the taper boiler and the T class boiler. The noticeable change was the increase in the width of the 'water legs'; the space between the inner and outer fireboxes which was larger in the standard boiler compared to the T-class boiler, and was the same size as the water legs in the taper boiler. Therefore, the grate area of the standard boiler was smaller than the T-class boiler but the same as the TF.

However, a lack of funds saw only 166 receive these new boilers. The rest were scrapped for wartime

The last of the class, 5490, assists Beyer-Garratt 6036 near Hawkmount with a Broken Hill to Sulphide Siding (Newcastle) concentrate train on 13 December 1969. (Graham Cotterall)

metal in 1939–40, with the exception of 1122 which had destroyed itself in a spectacular runaway at Lawson in 1923. This engine was officially scrapped in April 1928.

Other modifications carried out over the years included the provision of specially-balanced coupled wheels to 24 engines for mail and fruit express workings. Another was fitted for a short time with outside bearing axleboxes on its leading pony wheels.

Others were equipped with large-capacity tenders, some of which were converted to freight vehicles to carry welded rails following the withdrawal of steam. In this form, two tender chassis were welded together at the inner ends. Many wagons remained in traffic under the ownership of Rail Services Australia until 2000, when they were sold to Chicago Freight Car Leasing for conversion at Goulburn workshops into high-speed container flats for national use.

The D53-class worked over the state's main trunk lines and, just prior to dieselisation, the greatest number were to be found on the Western Division.

The first superheated engine to be withdrawn was 5402, which was involved in a runaway at Dombarton crossing loop in January 1957. With new diesels arriving, repairs were not a consideration and withdrawals of more class members began in earnest

as mechanical and boiler condition dictated. By July 1969, only 39 remained, most working Hunter Valley coal trains.

Amazingly, general repairs were still being made to key engines as late as October 1971; the last in service was 5365, withdrawn at Port Waratah in January 1973.

Several have been preserved, including 5353 in the Dorrigo Steam Railway & Museum; 5367 at the Lachlan Valley Railway Society's Cowra museum; and 5461 which is a static exhibit at the NSWRTM's Valley Heights roundhouse.

Ka-class

Twenty-six similar locomotives were acquired by Commonwealth Railways between September 1918 and June 1920 for service over the Trans-Australian Railway. They were built in two batches by Walkers Ltd of Maryborough, Queensland (20), and Perry Engineering of Mile End, South Australia (6). They were classified Ka and numbered 35–54 and 56–61.

They differed from their NSWGR counterparts in that their boilers were pressed to a lower 1034 kPa. In addition, the cylinder diameter was a slightly larger 56 cm.

A view forward from the galloping cab of NSWR 5461 (now preserved) working a Southern Line goods between Carrick and Towrang. (Leon Oberg)

The six Perry engines received superheaters during 1943, three of which had modified front ends and stovepipe chimneys. The national coal strike of 1949 forced three to be converted to burn oil fuel but they were reconverted to coal within months.

The high salt content of the South Australian bore water played havoc with locomotive boilers and the first Ka to be withdrawn was Ka38 in March

1925, after less than a decade of service. It lay at Port Augusta, yielding parts to sister engines until scrapped in 1958. Twelve others were retired during World War II.

The introduction of diesel-electric GM-class units in 1951 sounded the death knell for the eight remaining engines and withdrawals started again in earnest, the last in steam being Ka53 and Ka58, withdrawn in April 1952. Scrap teams moved in later that decade and began by blasting their boilers open with dynamite. None remain.

SPECIFICATIONS
NSWGR TF

	Original Imperial (Metric)	Superheated Imperial (Metric)
CYLINDERS:	21 x 26 IN (53 x 66 CM)	22 x 26 IN (56 x 66 CM)
BOILER PRESSURE:	160 PSI (1102 KPA)	160 PSI (1102 KPA)
TRACTIVE EFFORT:	28 777 LB (128.1 KN)	33 557 LB (149.3 KN)
COUPLED WHEELS:	4 FT 3 IN (130 CM)	4 FT 3 IN (130 CM)
GRATE AREA:	28.75 SQ FT (2.671 M²)	28.75 M² (2.671 M²)
TOTAL WEIGHT:	112.5 TONS (114.8 T)	124.5 TONS (127 T)
GAUGE:	1435 MM	1435 MM
ROAD NUMBERS:	(ORIGINAL) 939–998, 1017–1026, 1056–1203	
	(1924) 5301–5490	

CR Ka

	Imperial (Metric)
CYLINDERS:	22 x 26 IN (5 x 66 CM)
BOILER PRESSURE:	150 PSI (1034 KPA)
COUPLED WHEELS:	4 FT 3 IN (130 CM)
TRACTIVE EFFORT:	29 609 LB (131.8 KN)
GRATE AREA:	28.75 SQ FT (2.671 M²)
TOTAL WEIGHT:	132.5 TONS (135.2 T)
GAUGE:	1435 MM
ROAD NUMBERS:	35–54, 56–61

Commonwealth Railways' Ka56 clearly shows its NSWGR parentage—right down to its tapered boiler. (Author's collection)

Locomotive SMR31 stands in the East Greta locomotive depot yard in May 1983, following its very last shop visit. (Leon Oberg)

1912 East Greta Railway

10-class 2-8-2T

The East Greta Railway, later known as the South Maitland Railways, was once one of the largest privately-owned rail operations in Australia. It was built initially to serve vast coal interests and over time became the haulage authority for a large number of mining companies in the Maitland–Cessnock area of New South Wales. At the height of operations, trains ran over high-quality duplicated trackage between East Greta (Maitland) and Caledonia.

It would be hard to find a railway of this size anywhere that operated such a vast assortment of locomotives. Some were bought second-hand from the NSWGR while others were purchased from rail-laying contractors. However, when reliability entered the equation, a number were purchased new, the most remarkable of these being the 14 sturdy 2-8-2 mineral tank locomotives built in various batches by Beyer, Peacock & Co in Manchester between 1912 and 1925.

Known as the 10-class, the design was basically a tank-engine version of the NSWGR's T-class 2-8-0 tender locomotives, with some features of the earlier P-class 4-6-0s, both of which had initially been produced by Beyer, Peacock. Retaining their saturated boilers all of their lives, the 10-class was more productive than their NSWGR counterparts

in that their pressure was rated at a more useful 1240 kPa in lieu of the prototype's 1102 kPa.

The 10-class proved itself in rugged coal work. They rode like tourist coaches, steamed with ease and were fastidiously maintained in top mechanical condition in the company's elaborate workshops at East Greta.

With a slump in coal production during the 1950s, class-leader No. 10 was withdrawn from service and set aside. As further cuts were made in train running following continuing fluctuations in coal production, only five 2-8-2Ts remained in service by 1967. But in typical coal industry fashion, fortune returned and the resultant upward swing in export orders created a critical shortage of locomotives. Thus three Richmond Vale Railway ex-ROD 2-8-0 tender locomotives were called on to work the expanding number of trains while a start was made to rebuild the withdrawn 10-class.

Over time, Coal & Allied (the railway's then owner) returned all of the 10-class to active service and in so doing constructed several new conventional-riveted, and all-welded boilers in the East Greta Workshops. This was a fortunate move because as mining waned again, rationalisation of engine power over Coal & Allied's Richmond Vale (Hexham to Stockrington Colliery) Railway saw 10-class locomotives transferred there on a rotating basis from 1974.

But all good things do come to an end and Coal & Allied withdrew steam from the old South Maitland

Railways line on Friday 10 June 1983, the remaining traffic going to the NSW State Rail Authority. However, the Hexham to Stockrington line remained steam hauled until 22 September 1987, making it the very last commercial steam worked railway in Australia.

Fortunately, all fourteen 10-class locomotives have been preserved, some in operational order. The Hunter Valley Training Co, a railway equipment rebuild organisation that was established at East Greta locomotive workshops, retains No. 10 while No. 18, after a period on hire to Sydney-based 3801 Ltd for use on its regular 'Cockatoo Run' tourist train between Port Kembla and Moss Vale, was forwarded to Braemar Engineering (Mittagong) on 21 May 2003 for a complete rebuild and eventual tourist operation in the NSW Hunter Valley region, being out-shopped in April 2006. The Richmond Vale Railway Museum controls locos 19, 22, 24, 25 and 30 while Nos 17, 20, 23, 26, 27, 28 and 31 belong to the Hunter Valley Railway Trust and are held at Branxton.

SPECIFICATIONS

	IMPERIAL (METRIC)
CYLINDERS: 20 X 26 IN	(51 X 66 CM)
BOILER PRESSURE:	180 PSI (1240 KPA)
COUPLED WHEELS:	4 FT 3 IN (130 CM)
TRACTIVE EFFORT:	29 363 LB (130.7 KN)
GRATE AREA:	29 SQ FT (2.694 M²)
TOTAL WEIGHT:	83.5 TONS (85.2 T)
GAUGE:	1435 MM
ROAD NUMBERS:	SMR10, 17–20, 22–28, 30 AND 31

M-class 4-4-2 + 2-4-4

Following the Tasmanian Government Railway's experimental operation in 1909 of the world's first Garratt locomotive, the administration quickly saw the value of articulation and ordered further engines for its 1067 mm gauge mainline railway.

Four locomotives were acquired from Beyer, Peacock & Co in England, two for passenger service, designated M-class, and the other two for freight haulage, becoming the system's L-class.

The M-class was the world's first Garratt built for express passenger service. Soon after delivery in 1912, an M-class engine became the first articulated locomotive to attain the speed of 88 km/h, which was quite fast at that time considering it was running over a narrow gauge railway.

Designed with eight simple cylinders (four outside and four inside), the M-class boasted the same boiler as the L-class (see next entry) to enable interchangeability if required during periods of workshop maintenance.

The M-class spent their entire career working out of Launceston Depot and from new they worked the main expresses between Launceston and Hobart. In later years they operated the night mails between Launceston and Antill Ponds and return.

Following the introduction of the R-class Pacifics in 1923, class-leader M1 was withdrawn around 1925. It was eventually cut up for scrap at Launceston about 1950.

Its sister engine, M2, remained operational until 1931 but, instead of succumbing to a quick demise, it remained in store for a further 20 years. It was last in existence at Mowbray, where it was finally cut up by a Sydney scrap firm about 1951.

Handsome and well balanced, M1 poses for its maker's camera prior to delivery to Tasmania. (Manchester Museum of Technology)

	Imperial (Metric)
Cylinders:	(8) 12 x 20 in (30 x 51 cm)
Boiler pressure:	160 psi (1102 kPa)
Coupled wheels:	5 ft 0 in (152 cm)
Tractive effort:	24 576 lb (109.4 kn)
Grate area:	33.9 sq ft (3.149 m²)
Total weight:	95 tons (96.9 t)
Gauge:	1067 mm
Road numbers:	M1 and M2

1912 Tasmanian Government Railways

L-class 2-6-2 + 2-6-2

In company with the two M-class Beyer Garratt passenger locomotives described above, the Tasmanian Government Railways acquired two Garratts for freight operation. These locomotives, which arrived in 1912, were designated L-class and were quickly seen to be a 'vast improvement' on the then most powerful Tasmanian locomotive type, the relatively new E-class of 1907.

Like the M-class, these new L-class locomotives were based at Launceston depot; they were initially used to haul freight trains between Launceston and Hobart as well as passenger trains when required.

During 1936, both engines were withdrawn for scrapping after they were rendered surplus following the arrival of sufficient numbers of more powerful Q-class 4-8-2 engines. However, a serious locomotive shortage brought about by World War II traffic increases caused both engines to be shopped for major overhauls in 1943, and they were returned to active service.

Their reprieve did not last long, as L2 was taken out of service in 1944 with the arrival of Commonwealth Government-financed Australian Standard Garratts. No. L1 was withdrawn in 1945.

Both lay idle at Launceston for some years, eventually being towed to TGR's locomotive graveyard at Mowbray, only to be brought back to Launceston once more for the removal of useful parts and brass boiler fittings. The boiler of L2 was sold and the remains of both engines again returned to Mowbray, where a Sydney scrap metal dealer cut them up about 1951.

	Imperial (Metric)
Cylinders:	(4) 15 x 22 in (38 x 56 cm)
Boiler pressure:	160 psi (1102 kPa)
Coupled wheels:	3 ft 6 in (107 cm)
Tractive effort:	30 171 lb (134.3 kn)
Grate area:	33.9 sq ft (3.149 m²)
Total weight:	90 tons (91.8 t)
Gauge:	1067 mm
Road numbers:	L1 and L2

1912 Western Australian Government Railways

D-class 4-6-4T

With the existing suburban-type N-class 4-4-4T locomotives hard-pressed to meet the ever-increasing Perth suburban requirements, in 1911 an order was placed in England with the North British Locomotive Co for 20 large, powerful tank locomotives to meet the need.

These D-class locomotives arrived between July and September 1912 and proved to be one of the most successful types seen on the WAGR. Their design was so sound that, when a need arose a decade or so later, the Chief Mechanical Engineer of the day explored the possibility of re-powering the class.

From 1932 onwards, all but locomotives 372, 380, 386 and 387 were rebuilt with superheated boilers,

Locomotive L1 on completion at Beyer, Peacock's British works. (Manchester Museum of Technology)

D-class locomotive 369. (former Westrail archives)

which increased their tractive effort by 6.83 kN, and became the Ds-class.

In a further bid to increase the class's usefulness, Ds.377 was experimentally fitted with larger side tanks in 1944. These were extended forward, coming flush with the smokebox front, and the locomotive was again reclassified, to become the Dsm-class.

Although no further conversions were made, the success of these tanks saw similar-styled ones fitted to the Dm-class 4-6-4T suburban tank locomotives then under construction in the WAGR Midland Workshops. These eight Dm locomotives were rebuilds of the 1902-introduced E-class Pacific tender locomotives.

This ongoing experimentation, which included the establishment of the best features on subsequent new locomotives, meant that the original and successful D-class became superseded by their protégés.

When new diesel railcars arrived for Perth suburban traffic in 1953, the ranks of the old 4-6-4s began to thin and by 1964, they had all been withdrawn.

SPECIFICATIONS

	ORIGINAL	SUPERHEATED
	IMPERIAL (METRIC)	IMPERIAL (METRIC)
CYLINDERS:	17 x 23 IN (43 x 58CM)	18 x 23 IN (46 x 58 CM)
BOILER PRESSURE:	175 PSI (1206 KPA)	160 PSI (1102 KPA)
COUPLED WHEELS:	4 FT 6 IN (137 CM)	4 FT 6 IN (137 CM)
TRACTIVE EFFORT:	17 233 LB (76.7 KN)	18 768 LB (83.5 KN)
GRATE AREA:	18.63 SQ FT (1.731 M²)	18.63 SQ FT (1.731 M²)
TOTAL WEIGHT:	65.5 TONS (69.9 T)	70 TONS (71.4 T)
GAUGE:	1067 MM	1067 MM
ROAD NUMBERS:	368–387	

C-class 4-6-2

Early in the twentieth century, the movement of traffic over the Western Australian-based Midland Railway Co's line became increasingly difficult for the 4-4-0 type locomotives then in service to cope with. As the problem could only be overcome by using new and more powerful engines, an order was placed with Kitson & Co of Leeds for five light Pacifics, which all arrived in 1912.

The Midland Railway Co had become Western Australia's transport success story and in a short time built 446 kilometres of 1067 mm gauge railway which connected with the WAGR at both Midland Junction and Geraldton. This link was opened to traffic in 1894.

These C-class Pacific locomotives operated faultlessly for nearly 50 years. A feature of their design was the typical North American bar-frame styling (which provided chassis flexibility), along with many other US features. (In fact, they were uncannily similar to the 12 Baldwin C-class 4-6-0s delivered to the WAGR during 1902.)

Four of the new Midland Pacifics were built with saturated boilers, but were given superheated versions in 1935. No. 18 had been built with this equipment. No. 18 was also the first locomotive in Western Australia to be fitted with an electric headlight.

The C-class operated all forms of traffic over the Midland line. However, during the 1920s, larger 4-8-0 and 2-8-2 type locomotives arrived on the scene, relegating the C-class to mail train and other lighter duties.

A maker's works photograph of the Midland Railway Co's first C-class locomotive, which originally carried the number 11. It was later renumbered 14. (former Westrail archives)

The first to be withdrawn was No. 14, which was taken out for boiler repairs in 1954. Steadily they all followed and were sold for scrap—with the exception again of No. 18, which remained as a standby engine to the diesels that arrived in 1958 until it was scrapped in 1963.

SPECIFICATIONS

	ORIGINAL	SUPERHEATED
	IMPERIAL (METRIC)	IMPERIAL (METRIC)
CYLINDERS:	16½ x 22 IN (42 x 56 CM)	16½ x 22 IN (42 x 56 CM)
BOILER PRESSURE:	160 PSI (1102 KPA)	160 PSI (1102 KPA)
COUPLED WHEELS:	4 FT 1 IN (125 CM)	4 FT 1 IN (125 CM)
TRACTIVE EFFORT:	15 646 LB (69.6 KN)	16 624 LB (74 KN)
GRATE AREA:	21.14 SQ FT (1.964 M²)	21.14 SQ FT (1.964 M²)
TOTAL WEIGHT:	77 TONS (78.6 T)	77.14 TONS (79.1 T)
GAUGE:	1067 MM	1067 MM
ROAD NUMBERS:	14–18 (ORIGINALLY 11–15)	

1913 NSW PUBLIC WORKS DEPARTMENT

Hunslet 2-6-0

Until 31 December 1916, the NSW PWD was the government's railway route construction authority. For this purpose it owned a nondescript fleet of discarded, surplus steam locomotives which had been seeing service hauling infrastructure trains (sleepers, rails and ballast) associated with the growing network.

The fleet included braces of tiny 0-4-0ST and 0-6-0T Manning Wardle and Vulcan locomotives, and 0-6-0 tender locomotives, some of which dated back to 1871.

With an extensive amount of work on the books and the promise of further route extensions, the PWD believed it would be better served with a unified fleet of new locomotives and accordingly placed an order in 1912 with the Leeds-based Hunslet Engine Co for eight 2-6-0 tender locomotives. They were given the road numbers PWD 1–8 on their arrival. The fifth and eighth members of the fleet were the first placed in service (February 1913) and all were operational by May that year.

Following the transfer of line construction duties to the NSWGR, the economic value of these relatively new locomotives—now known as the G-class—was deemed to be 'too good' for lowly, slow-moving work trains and towards the end of World War I some were joining older British-built low-powered B-class 2-6-0 locomotives in Hunter Valley coal haulage while others were pressed into metropolitan freight workings, including the haulage of locomotive coal to Enfield and Eveleigh depots.

However, this Hunslet was a rather rigid locomotive and did not operate well in curvy country. Eventually, a permanent home was found for the fleet based at Narrabri West depot, whose multitude of radiating branch lines mostly boasted wide-radius curves.

As major overhauls came due from 1930, the opportunity was taken to standardise the fleet, which from August 1924 had become the 27-class through the provision of standard 25-class boilers. Their original 9450 litre (2100 gallon) tenders were replaced with larger capacity 16 425 litre (3600 gallon) T-class bogie tenders, which almost doubled their coal supply from 5588 kg (5.5 tons) to 9652 kg (9.5 tons). All had been treated by October 1942.

Dieselisation elsewhere on the network and the resultant cascade effect, which saw more useful, higher-powered steam locomotives of the 30T-class become available for branch line work, led to the Hunslets' initial demise. The first to be withdrawn were 2706 and 2702, in October and November 1957 respectively, after both had been forwarded to Eveleigh workshops for attention. The transfer of new 48-class diesel-electrics to the Narrabri West region

The immaculately preserved Hunslet 2705 prepares to depart Thirlmere with a NSWRTM tourist train for Buxton on 21 May 2006. (Leon Oberg)

from 1960 marked the end, and the last locomotive in service, 2705, was subsequently selected for active preservation. The beautifully maintained relic works tourist trains out of Thirlmere Railway Museum to this day.

SPECIFICATIONS

	IMPERIAL (METRIC)
CYLINDERS:	18 x 24 IN (45.7 x 61 CM)
BOILER PRESSURE:	160 PSI (1102 KPA)
COUPLED WHEELS:	4 FT ½ IN (123 CM)
TRACTIVE EFFORT:	20 520 LB (91.2 KN)
GRATE AREA:	21 SQ FT (1.95 M²)
TOTAL WEIGHT:	80.7 TONS (81.6 T)
GAUGE:	1435 MM
ROAD NUMBERS:	ORIGINAL PWD 1–8 (ORIGINAL NSWGR NUMBERS 1204–1211 BECAME 2701–2708)

1914 Broken Hill Proprietary Co

Industrial steam

The huge Broken Hill Proprietary Co, formed on 13 August 1885, was a rail operator right from its earliest days.

From its humble beginnings at Broken Hill in far western New South Wales, the company formed by mineral speculators who virtually by accident stumbled upon vast reserves of lead, zinc, silver and later gold, realised that railways would have to play a major role in hauling their wealth to markets. For this reason the young BHP became a shareholder in the Silverton Tramway, the transport authority which built a link between the growing Broken Hill and the South Australian Railways at Cockburn, on the state border.

A large smelting plant was established at Port Pirie by the company and this too employed a small railway within its confines.

With signs shortly after the turn of the century of diminishing reserves in Broken Hill, BHP started to seek diversification. As company engineers had become highly skilled in the metallurgy of ferrous and nonferrous metals, the company decided to turn its experience towards iron and steel production, particularly since Australia had been moving deeper into the industrial age. That move eventually found three large steelmaking plants in operation, two in New South Wales and one in South Australia. The first works to open was the company's Newcastle plant, which was blown-in during March 1915.

As in most of the world's steel industries, railways were destined to play a huge role at BHP's new plant and, for construction work at Newcastle, the NSWGR supplied a surplus 1870-vintage 0-6-0 tender engine, E17-class No. 40. This had last been used by a rail-building contractor and had been in storage.

However, problems arose with the veteran's limited curvature, so it was rebuilt as an 0-6-0 saddle tank. Surprisingly, the locomotive, known at the Newcastle plant as 'Old Lizzie', remained with the company until the virtual end of steam, although during that period it underwent one further rebuild at which time it received an enclosed BHP-pattern cab.

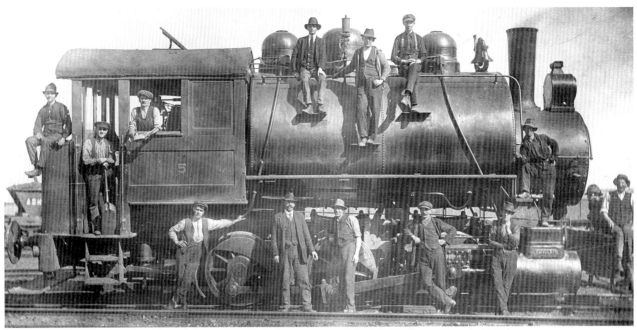

No. 5 'The Doll', in its original saddle-tank form. In 1939, the locomotive was rebuilt by BHP as a side tank. (BHP)

Throughout the bulk of its time with BHP, 'Old Lizzie' was used to convey shipping to the wharf and haul general cargo and coal to and from Morandoo Siding, located outside the BHP main gate. The veteran was eventually scrapped in 1960.

Meanwhile, BHP Newcastle had placed orders with the Pittsburgh industrial locomotive specialist H.K. Porter & Co for three chunky 48-tonne 0-4-0T locomotives with a surprisingly short wheelbase of just 213 cm. The success of these locomotives, which were delivered in 1914–15, led to additional orders with Porter. Between 1915 and 1924, nine similar locomotives entered steelworks traffic. These classic machines boasted a tractive effort of 14 418 lb (64.1 kN) and a boiler pressure of 150 psi (1034 kPa).

Porter also delivered a larger 61-tonne 0-6-0ST engine of 20 763 lb (92.1 kN) in 1915. This powerful engine was numbered 5 on the BHP roster. It was rebuilt as a side-tank engine in 1939 and remained in that guise until scrapped in 1961.

According to the old hands whose job it was to service the company's locomotives, No. 5, which was affectionately known as 'The Doll', used to 'go walkabout on occasions' (suffering from steam blowing through the regulator valve in the dome and then into the cylinders). One day, the locomotive's fire

'The Doll' following its 1939 rebuild as a side-tank engine. (Bruce Macdonald)

BHP Newcastle's very first product built on site from new parts was loco 21, which appeared in 1930. By 1946, staff had constructed eight more new locomotives to suit the exacting needs of a large steel mill. (BHP)

had been lit inside the engine shed and someone left the locomotive in forward gear. When enough steam had been raised, the locomotive began creeping. 'It walked out through the shed, derailed, kept going down a flight of three or four steps, steamed out through some double doors and ended up with its sooty nose poking out into the plant,' recalled former BHP Newcastle traffic manager, Roy Mullard. This engine's normal job was to haul open-top metal pots out of the blast furnace area; when it was later replaced by a BHP-built 0-4-0T Porter type, 'The Doll' was assigned to coal haulage.

Mr Mullard said the 0-4-0 Porters were notoriously rough riders and locomotive foreman Harry Bagley decided to equip No. 13 with coil springs in the hope it would improve the ride. 'But

with the new springs it used to rock and roll and bounce around so badly that it split points and lost traction. After persevering with the springing for a while, Bagley refitted the conventional semi-elliptical springs,' he recalled.

He said the original Porters had a small 'webby' frame that used to fracture easily. Its weakest spot was where the frame was cut away to carry the cylinders and heavy buffer beam.

The company's machine shop built new frames for the Porters from solid section, cut with a profile burner. No more problems were ever experienced.

Mr Mullard remembered how Bagley wanted to change the motion on all of the Porters during the 1940s from Johnson bar-activated Stephenson inside valve gear to screw reverse-activated Walschaerts

The writing was well and truly on the wall for steam's future at Newcastle works when standard 0-4-0T, BHP4, was utilised to haul brand-new Cooper-Bessemer diesel-electric BHP32 onto the plant in July 1954. (Roy Mullard)

One of the very few photographs taken of a 915 mm gauge Orenstein & Koppel at work in Newcastle steel works. Pictured is the company's first No. 7 posing with a rake of 4-wheel coke buggies, circa 1918. (Bruce Macdonald collection)

outside valve gear. To replace eccentrics or repair the valve gear on a Porter, the locomotive had to be lifted from the rear to drop the wheels out. Although a model was tested in the plant, no conversions were ever done, due to the high cost.

Most of the Newcastle operations were over the standard 1435 mm gauge but space limitations deep inside the works saw the narrow 915 mm gauge selected for a railway which linked the coke ovens and blast furnaces. Two new narrow-gauge Orenstein & Koppel 0-4-0T locomotives were acquired in 1915 specifically to haul the 4-wheel coke buggies; these Lilliputian machines became (1st) Nos 7 and 9 on the motive power roster.

The Orenstein & Koppels were considered rather light for the service and a spare parts problem existed. All of this was overcome in 1930 when that rail link was replaced with a new standard gauge route to serve a more modern coke oven battery. Both tiny locomotives were withdrawn and lay boarded-up in storage in the spares depot until scrapped about six years later.

Formerly a NSWGR 24-class 2-6-0 tender engine, BHP26 displays the work of creative in-house engineering, operating on 6 October 1958 in its much chunkier 0-6-0ST form. (Ken Winney)

The 915 mm gauge was also used in connection with BHP's ingot moulding system and associated delivery lines. Since H.K. Porter had supplied one 915 mm gauge 0-4-0T in 1915, American-designed locomotives continued to be the favoured locomotive type for this traffic right up until the end of steam. Three of these 38-tonne locomotives, Nos 8, 15 and 18, were imported. Each exerted a slightly greater tractive effort, 14 550 lb (66.1 kN) more than their standard gauge counterparts due to their similar mechanical and boiler proportions driving smaller driving wheels.

An additional engine, No. 30, was assembled in BHP's workshops in 1946 from what old hands described as 'bits and pieces'. At that time also, No. 18 was withdrawn and scrapped. This locomotive was smaller than its sisters and incapable of successfully lifting the ingot buggies.

Neil Bulbert, who in 1987 was working as foreman, remembered these vehicles were 'such bad runners'. They were equipped with brass axleboxes running in grease but the heat from the ingots would dry the boxes out and make them hard to haul. 'No. 18 was disliked so it generally stood pilot,' he said.

The remaining narrow-gauge fleet soldiered on until diesel-electrics replaced them in 1960. While No. 30 was scrapped virtually immediately, the remaining pair met their fate in 1966.

Meanwhile, the growth of the steel mill in the early decades of the twentieth century had been so impressive that yet more standard gauge locomotives were needed. The NSWGR was again asked to supply surplus engines but, because World War I was still making huge demands on the railways, no suitable power was on hand. The NSW PWD answered BHP's call and in December 1917 sold

BHP25 running at Whyalla steel plant in 1965 as that plant's B2. Two Porter-type locomotives were forwarded to BHP's Whyalla plant in 1962 to work slag traffic. (Late Ron Preston)

the company a near-new Manning Wardle 0-4-0ST which had last seen service in rail construction work on the NSW North Coast. Originally carrying PWD No. 62, the engine became BHP's No. 11. It soon received the nickname 'Coffee Pot' due to the gurgling sounds that regularly came from deep within while standing still.

In 1934, No. 11 underwent a total rebuild and emerged from the BHP shops with new boiler, slidebars, re-designed cab and allied components. Surviving reports indicate it was a bad steamer, and Roy Mullard recalls with a chuckle that all the new drivers were assigned No. 11—if the new hand could

successfully operate the loco, he remained a driver.

The locomotive's main task was to work rodmill traffic (coils) from the mill to Rylands wire plant until it was transferred to a BHP subsidiary, Commonwealth Steel Pty Ltd at nearby Waratah. It was there named *Minerva*.

Another locomotive of interest, also built originally for the NSWGR, was 0-6-0 tender engine 99 of the A93-class. It gravitated to BHP in 1915 after having worked under the ownership of a rail-laying contractor. It became BHP's No. 6. As with the company's similarly-styled No. 1 engine, this veteran was rebuilt and emerged from the company's

Narrow-gauge H.K. Porter product of 1915, No. 8, standing in the ingot cooling area in the early 1950s. (Late Tony Maston)

An early photograph showing BHP11 'Coffee Pot' prior to its 1934 rebuild. Several imported H.K. Porter 0-4-0Ts, including BHP2, are posed behind it. No. 11 came to BHP in 1917 from the NSW Public Works Department. (BHP)

shops as a rugged-looking saddle tanker. Surviving accounts reveal this locomotive was forwarded to the company's John Darling Colliery in 1927 for shunting service. About 1948, it returned to the steelworks for rebuild and remained at the plant in general service until standard-gauge dieselisation forced its withdrawal and scrapping in 1961.

Further steelworks upgrades through the 1930s led to a continuing need for additional locomotives. Since nothing suitable seemed to be available from the NSWGR, the company decided to become a locomotive manufacturer and overcome its motive power needs in-house. The plans of the imported

0-4-0T Porter design from 1914–15 were dusted off and formed the basis for the company's standard steelworks shunter. The first company-built engine emerged in June 1930, carrying the number 21. The Great Depression halted any further deliveries until 1935 when, with the formation of a number of BHP subsidiaries and a general surge in the economy, steel production once again bounded ahead. By August 1942, the company had built eight 0-4-0Ts, all of which remained in service until full dieselisation.

At that stage, a large number of the steam fleet remained in excellent condition and were considered 'too good' to simply scrap. BHP had decided to

Affectionately known by the Newcastle BHP traffic department as the 'Fighting Faggot', No. 22 specially posed for photographs in 1948 the day it emerged from the workshops rebuilt as a saddle tank. (BHP)

construct a steel works at Whyalla, South Australia, and although new diesel-hydraulic locomotives had been ordered for that plant's new standard gauge railway, two Newcastle Porters, 21 and 25, were forwarded to Whyalla in 1962 for works slag traffic. These trains required steam power to tip the slag 'skulls' and the two steam locomotives, now renumbered B1 and B2, remained in that service for three years until air-tipping was commissioned. Both were quickly scrapped.

Commonwealth Steel at Newcastle acquired No. 4 for works shunting in 1962. It survives today in the care of the Dorrigo Steam Railway & Museum.

In addition, the Emu Sand & Gravel Co at Emu Plains in Sydney's west purchased 12 and 16 during 1962–63 for gravel haulage, and both remained in traffic until the railway closed in April 1967. Although 12 was broken up late in 1967, No. 16 survives, and after working for a time as a shunter with the NSWRTM at Thirlmere Railway Museum, the relic today forms the basis of a small railway museum at St Mary's Tourist Information Centre in western Sydney.

It seems as though the BHP locomotives possessed distinct personalities, for despite the stable of Porters- and company-constructed 0-4-0Ts, BHP continued to acquire second-hand locomotives from whomever it could, whenever it could. One classic was the 'Fighting Faggot', a dainty 0-4-0ST which had been built for the Sulphide Corporation by Henry Vale. It came to the BHP works in 1933, where it was numbered 22 on the roster. In true company fashion, the locomotive was almost instantly rebuilt and emerged from the workshops as a conventional side-tank engine.

It remained in this form until the late 1940s, when it was accidentally hit from the front by another train. The weight behind was sufficient to open the locomotive's plate frames and its boiler dropped down onto the driving axles. It was subsequently overhauled, emerging from the workshops once again as a saddle-tank engine, and remained in traffic until dieselisation, finally being sold to Commonwealth Steel in 1960 to become that company's *Minerva 2*.

Another interesting company-owned locomotive came from the NSWGR in November 1940. Formerly B-class 2-6-0 tender engine 2415, it too underwent a complete rebuild to suit BHP's individual doctrine and most of its service was spent as a chunky-looking 0-6-0ST. Numbered 26, this locomotive, remembered for its excellent ride and steaming qualities, was used principally to haul limestone, iron ore and other ingredients to established dumps. It was withdrawn early in 1961 and scrapped several years later.

Apart from the occasional hiring of government-owned locomotives, principally to work at BHP collieries, two 0-6-0ST locomotives were borrowed from the subsidiary, Australian Iron & Steel Co of Port Kembla, in 1952. The two locomotives, *Bandicoot* and *Bronzewing*, which could be spared due to the recent introduction of diesels, were acquired to arrest a desperate motive power shortage caused by post-war building booms. They were put to work hauling metal from Nos 1 and 2 blast furnaces to the open hearth. They remained at Newcastle until February 1955, when new 492 kW Cooper-Bessemer Bo-Bo diesel-electric locomotives were introduced. With the commissioning of these five units, the writing was on the wall for steam. After the arrival of sufficient 410 kW Cummins-powered centre-cab Bo-Bo diesels from July 1960 (see page 278), steam quickly vanished.

The last steam locomotives in regular service on BHP's Newcastle plant appear to have been Nos 8 and 15, two narrow-gauge ingot train engines. They were finally scrapped in 1966. Standard-gauge No. 3 remained as a steam generation unit, being hauled around the works to wherever its boiler-powered pile-driving equipment was required. Listed as derelict in 1966, it is thought this locomotive was cut up along with Nos 8 and 15.

Although this small story can only scratch the surface of BHP's diverse and interesting fleet, the study of these locomotives is extremely rewarding. Old hands readily recall the days before World War II when every driver would be issued with a bottle of Brasso and a quantity of cotton waste to keep his individual locomotive spotless. 'You could lose a bonus if you worked a dirty locomotive,' recalled Roy Mullard. He remembered vividly the heavy workload of the post-World War II years, when the driver was required to drive *and* fire his engine. After that date two men were rostered to each locomotive, the second man acting as both fireman and lookout.

Space limitations and the huge variety of types in use at Newcastle restricts a listing of comparative specifications, and those given here describe the most-used types—the 0-4-0T Porters. On historic grounds, a complete list of every steam locomotive used at BHP Newcastle follows, and it comes by courtesy of that company.

PORTER SPECIFICATIONS

	STANDARD GAUGE IMPERIAL (METRIC)	NARROW GAUGE IMPERIAL (METRIC)
CYLINDERS:	15 x 24 IN (38 x 61 CM)	15 x 20 IN (38 x 51 CM)
BOILER PRESSURE:	150 PSI (1034 KPA)	150 PSI (1034 KPA)
COUPLED WHEELS:	3 FT 9 IN (114 CM)	3 FT 4 IN (104 CM)
TRACTIVE EFFORT:	14 400 LB (64.1 KN)	13 500 LB (60.3 KN)
GRATE AREA:	16 SQ FT (1.486 M²)	16 SQ FT (1.486 M²)
TOTAL WEIGHT:	45–48 TONS (45.9-49 T)	37 TONS (38.3 T)
ROAD NUMBERS:	2–5, 12–14, 16, 17, 19–21, 23–25, 27–28	8, 9, 15, 18, 30
GAUGE:	1435 MM	915 MM

BHP NEWCASTLE LOCOMOTIVES IN RUNNING NUMBER ORDER

LOCO	TYPE	MAKER	B/NO	AT BHP	REMARKS
1	0-6-0ST	HENRY VALE	5	1914–60	EX NSWGR E40
2	0-4-0T	H.K. PORTER	5525	1914–61	
3	0-4-0T	H.K. PORTER	5288	1914–66	CUT-UP 1968
4	0-4-0T	H.K. PORTER	5685	1915–62	TO COMSTEEL
5	0-6-0ST	H.K. PORTER	5762	1915–62	
6	0-6-0ST	BEYER PEACOCK	1675	1915–61	EX NSWGR A99
7 (1ST)	0-4-0T	ORENSTEIN & KOPPEL	6270	1915–36	NARROW GAUGE
7 (2ND)	0-4-0T	BHP	4	1936–61	
8	0-4-0ST	H.K. PORTER	5834	1915–66	NARROW GAUGE
9 (1ST)	0-4-0T	ORENSTEIN & KOPPEL	6731	1915–30	NARROW GAUGE
9 (2ND)	0-4-0T	BHP	5	1937–60	
10	0-4-0ST	VULCAN IRON WORKS	2894	1917–61	
11	0-4-0ST	MANNING WARDLE	1898	1917–52	EX PWD 62
12	0-4-0T	H.K. PORTER	6415	1919–63	TO EMU GRAVEL
13	0-4-0T	H. K. PORTER	6411	1919–61	
14	0-4-0T	H. K. PORTER	6412	1919–61	
15	0-4-0ST	H. K. PORTER	6413	1919–66	NARROW GAUGE
16	0-4-0T	H. K. PORTER	6596	1920–62	TO EMU GRAVEL
17	0-4-0T	H. K. PORTER	6597	1920–60	
18	0-4-0ST	H. K. PORTER	6670	1921–46	NARROW GAUGE
19	0-4-0T	H. K. PORTER	6940	1924–61	
20	0-4-0T	H. K. PORTER	6941	1924–60	
21	0-4-0T	BHP	1	1930–62	TO WHYALLA B1
22	0-4-0T	HENRY VALE	64	1933–60	TO COMSTEEL
23	0-4-0T	BHP	2	1935–62	
24	0-4-0T	BHP	3	1936–62	
25	0-4-0T	BHP	6	1938–62	TO WHYALLA B2
26	0-6-0ST	DUBS & CO	2637	1940–61	EX NSWGR 2415
27	0-4-0T	BHP	7	1942–62	
28	0-4-0T	BHP	8	1942–62	
29	0-6-0T	AVONSIDE	1541	1944–61	EX SMR NO. 13
30	0-4-0ST	BHP	9	1946–62	NARROW GAUGE
31	0-6-0ST	CLYDE ENGINEERING	457	1952–55	LOAN, EX AIS
(32)*	0-6-0ST	H.K. PORTER	7160	1952–55	LOAN, EX AIS

(* UNDERSTOOD TO HAVE NEVER CARRIED THE ROAD NUMBER)

Hudswell Clarke 0-6-0

Few steam locomotive types were as successful at handling heavy Queensland sugar industry trains as the nine legendary 0-6-0 tender locomotives from Leeds (UK) manufacturer, Hudswell Clarke & Co.

The first engine was imported by the Colonial Sugar Refinery (CSR) for its Homebush Mill (near Mackay) in 1914. It was based on a tender version of a 1911-delivered 0-6-0T design used at Mulgrave Mill and operating as *Adelaide*. (*Pyramid* was added to the fleet some years later.)

The new 23-ton tender version boasted two 21.5 x 30 cm cylinders. This pioneering 0-6-0 locomotive was transferred to the CSR's Victoria Mill at Ingham when Homebush Mill closed in 1922, subsequently receiving the name *Homebush* in honour of its heritage.

Prior to this locomotive entering service in Australia, CSR had eleven similarly-styled locomotives delivered to its Lautoka, Rarawai and Lambasa mills in Fiji between 1912 and 1914. Another engine was ordered in 1914 for Australia's Childers Mill, but delivery is thought to have been delayed until 1919 due to World War I transport problems.

By 1914, Hudswell Clarke had come up with a larger, heavier (29.7 tonne) design with two 4 x 30 cm cylinders. Despite Goondi Mill having ordered an example that same year, its delivery too was delayed until 1919, when the locomotive was forwarded via Sydney, eventually arriving at its intended destination the following year. In all, 12 of these 0-6-0 locomotives were acquired by CSR for Australian and Fijian sugar train haulage up until 1938, some of them being supplied without tenders.

Hudswell Clarke was able to offer an even larger model, a 35-ton (including tender) version with two 25 x 30 cm cylinders. The first of these appeared in 1938. Overall, nine of them saw service in CSR's Australian and Fijian plantations, the last (known as *Coronation*) entering traffic at Victoria Mill in 1952.

The convenience of dieselisation eventually swept these handsome locomotives aside and the last mills to use the famous 0-6-0s were Victoria and Macknade. Between the two they mustered six locomotives throughout the 1976 season and, one day in October, *Cairns* charged into Victoria Mill

Victoria Sugar Mill's Hudswell Clarke, *Townsville*, was in immaculate condition when pictured steaming towards its mill with a loaded cane train in August 1972. (Ken Winney)

yard with a record 177 full bins for 925 tonnes tugging at its drawbar—a record for a steam-hauled Australian mill train.

Victoria Sugar Mill management thought enough of the locomotive type to retain *Homebush* for operation during local festivals and visits by special dignitaries. In all, 13 examples of the three types have been preserved in Victoria, New South Wales and Queensland, several of them in working order.

Hudswell Clarke's first locomotive was built in 1880 and construction ceased as recently as 1961. By that time, the company had built more than 1600 steam locomotives, examples going to many state-owned and private railways on a diversity of gauges throughout the world.

SPECIFICATIONS

	TYPE 1*	TYPE 2**
	IMPERIAL (METRIC)	IMPERIAL (METRIC)
CYLINDERS:	8½ x 12 IN (21.5 x 30 CM)	9½ x 12 IN (24 x 30 CM)
BOILER PRESSURE:	160 PSI (1102K PA)	160 PSI (1102 KPA)
COUPLED WHEELS:	2 FT 0 IN (61 CM)	2 FT 2.5 IN (67.3 CM)
TRACTIVE EFFORT:	4624 LB (21.2 KN)	5231 LB (23.3 KN)
GRATE AREA:	6 SQ FT	7.5 SQ FT
TOTAL WEIGHT:	23 TONS (23.5 T)	29 TONS (29.7 T)
GAUGE:	610 MM	610 MM
	*B/No. 1067	**B/Nos 1098 AND 1099

	TYPE 3***
	IMPERIAL (METRIC)
CYLINDERS:	10 x 12 IN (25 x 30 CM)

BOILER PRESSURE:	160 PSI (1102 KPA)
COUPLED WHEELS:	2 FT 2½ IN (67.3 CM)
TRACTIVE EFFORT:	5796 LB (24 KN)
GRATE AREA:	8.7 SQ FT
TOTAL WEIGHT:	35 TONS (35.8 T)
GAUGE:	610 MM

***B/Nos 1701, 1706, 1838, 1861–1863

1914 NEW SOUTH WALES GOVERNMENT RAILWAYS

NN-class 4-6-0

Designed and built at NSWGR's Eveleigh Railway Workshops, this class of thirty-five 4-6-0 express passenger locomotives was ordered for the state's top express passenger trains. The locomotives were constructed in two batches, the first entering service in August 1914. All were working by November 1923.

The NNs were part of a package that included the construction of more commodious 12-wheel carriages for express working when the existing P6-class 4-6-0s of 1892 vintage were no longer strong enough to singly pull the heavier trains.

Totally English in appearance, which was not

Locomotive 3526, out-shopped by the Thirlmere Railway Museum for tourist train service in mid-2004 after sitting lifeless for three decades, is pictured nearing Thirlmere with a passenger train on 5 March 2006. (Leon Oberg)

surprising since the locomotive was designed under the direction of the NSWGR's new Great Western-educated CME, Ernest Lucy, the NN was not one of the Railway's better engines due to its rough riding qualities and poor steaming. All were improved somewhat from 1924, when their coupled wheels were rebalanced and overall axle loads revised downwards.

In 1924, the locomotives became the C35-class and, soon afterwards, were ousted from the more important express trains by larger C36-class 4-6-0s. They were all eventually transferred to the northern area of the state for North Coast and Northern Tablelands working. They remained in that capacity until gradually ousted by diesels from the late 1950s.

Further improvements were made from December 1937 when the class was progressively rebuilt with slightly larger (internal circumference) boilers which increased slightly the firebox heating surface. In addition, they were rebuilt with new enclosed cabs instead of the former chilly cut-away type, new frames and valances. The lower frame height at the front allowed access to the valve gear from above and at the rear, which also acted as a frame stiffener.

By the late 1950s, some survivors had been relegated to goods traffic including long-distance coal trains between Port Waratah and Muswellbrook.

Some were even fitted at this time with higher capacity, better-riding turret tenders handed down from scrapped goods locomotives. The first engine to be withdrawn was 3533 in February 1959. Eight more followed over the next two years.

The last engine running in commercial service was class-leader 3501, which worked an enthusiast special in August 1968. That locomotive managed to run a creditable 3.2 million kilometres during its 54-year service life, the greatest distance of any class member. Today, only one remains, 3526, which was turned out by the Thirlmere Railway Museum for tourist train service in mid-2004.

SPECIFICATIONS

	IMPERIAL (METRIC)
CYLINDERS:	22½ x 26 IN (57 x 66 CM)
BOILER PRESSURE:	180 PSI (1240 KPA)
COUPLED WHEELS:	5 FT 9 IN (175 CM)
TRACTIVE EFFORT:	29 186 LB (129.9 KN)
GRATE AREA:	30.5 SQ FT (2.833 M²)
TOTAL WEIGHT:	(ORIGINAL) 124.75 TONS (127.3 T)
	(AS REBUILT) 128 TONS (129.5 T)
GAUGE:	1435 MM
ROAD NUMBERS:	(ORIGINAL) 1027–1041, 1304–1323
	(1924) 3501–3535

An early view of Commonwealth Railways' G6 standing in the Port Augusta locomotive workshop area. (AN archives)

1914 Commonwealth Railways

G-class 4-6-0

A Commonwealth Act of Parliament passed in September 1911 was the outcome of an extensive four-year survey of a projected railway line to link Port Augusta in South Australia with Kalgoorlie in Western Australia. As no state or private operator would consider operating such a link, and most importantly because it was seen as an important defence initiative, the Commonwealth Railways came into being.

The 'first-sod turning ceremony' took place at Port Augusta in September 1912. Some months later work started at the Kalgoorlie end and slowly, like pincers, the line reached out, crossing the arid, waterless Nullarbor Plain. Eventually, a 1691 km ribbon of standard-gauge steel linked the two centres and a whole new industry was born.

To assist with construction of the railway, six Q-class 4-4-0 locomotives were purchased from the NSWGR together with one 2-6-0 (American-built) K-class locomotive, No. 295. As the line slowly grew, CR's executives began looking for suitable motive power to work the planned services.

The Railway's progressive Engineer in Chief, Henry Deane, originally intended to introduce diesel-electric traction from the very beginning. Despite this power being in its infancy, Deane was quick to emphasise the high cost of hauling coal and water across the remote route. While the time taken debating the issue during a series of inquiries saved steam's day, as Deane prophetically said, 'it was an exercise in marking time.'

So much time had been lost, in fact, that the only way to have enough locomotives available for the railway's opening was to adopt an existing design. Since the NSWGR was enjoying marked success with its P6-class 4-6-0 passenger locomotives, the CR selected this type for its passenger haulage and an order for four was placed with the Clyde Engineering Co in Sydney. A further 12 were ordered from the US-based Baldwin Locomotive Works. All arrived about the same time and entered traffic between March and August 1914 as the G-class.

Some were pressed into construction train service at both ends of the line, the Western Division locomotives having to be shipped to Perth partly dismantled, then conveyed to Parkeston for reassembly.

An order was also placed with the North British Co for eight locomotives based on the prolific NSWGR T-class 2-8-0s. Due to wartime pressures, delays were guaranteed, so an additional ten G-class 4-6-0s were ordered from the Toowoomba Foundry in Queensland as a stopgap measure. These arrived between June 1916 and August 1917.

A total 26 G-class locomotives were available for service when the railway was unceremoniously opened two months later. The inaugural train left Port Augusta hauled by G22 on 22 October 1917.

Strangely, all the Gs were built with saturated boilers, but equipped with slightly higher capacity tenders. Commonwealth Railways' maintenance staff soon found the high mineral salt content of the bore water available along the route was playing havoc with the boilers, boiler repairs at one time accounting for an amazing 87 per cent of all locomotive maintenance. The problem was only arrested with the introduction of barium carbonate treatment plants at watering points.

Withdrawals commenced as early as February

1925, when G8 was stopped for repairs. Locomotive G10 followed five months later and both became spare parts engines. About 1930, a decision was made to re-power the class with superheated boilers and the first engine treated was G24, which emerged from the Port Augusta workshops in August 1933. In a bid to differentiate it from its brethren, this locomotive was reclassified Ga.

Another six were similarly converted but when the high-powered C-class 4-6-0s appeared from January 1938, no further conversions were carried out and the remaining saturated engines were withdrawn spasmodically as their general condition dictated. When GM diesels arrived in October 1951, only four G-class remained active, along with all seven Ga-class.

With dieselisation, the survivors were relegated to workshop and yard shunting, and most were withdrawn during 1952. However, G2 remained functional as a Port Pirie Junction shunting engine until September 1958. Fortunately, the class-leader, G1, had been secreted away inside the Port Augusta carriage shed and in 1969 was released for preservation. Today it can be found basking in the National Railway Museum, Port Adelaide.

SPECIFICATIONS

	ORIGINAL	AS REBUILT
	IMPERIAL (METRIC)	IMPERIAL (METRIC)
CYLINDERS:	20 x 26 IN (51 x 66 CM)	21 x 26 IN (53 x 66 CM)
BOILER PRESSURE:	160 PSI (1102 KPA)	160 PSI (1102 KPA)
COUPLED WHEELS:	5 FT 0 IN (152 CM)	5 FT 0 IN (152 CM)
TRACTIVE EFFORT:	22 187 LB (98.7 KN)	25 990 LB (115.7 KN)
GRATE AREA:	27 SQ FT (2.508 M²)	27 SQ FT (2.508 M²)
TOTAL WEIGHT:	106 TONS (108.1 T)	110 TONS (112.2 T)
GAUGE:	1435 MM	1435 MM
ROAD NUMBERS:	1—26	GA-CLASS 6, 9, 17, 19, 23, 24, 26

1915 BROKEN HILL PROPRIETARY CO

Baldwin 4-6-0

The formation of the now giant Broken Hill Proprietary Co in August 1885 indirectly paved the way for the growth of Hummock Hill (now Whyalla) in South Australia.

Although no one could have foreseen it at the time, the Middleback Ranges, which skirt the western edge of the Spencer Gulf, were to yield some of the richest iron ore in Australia (up to 68 per cent metallic iron). Mining there came about through

BHP's need for suitable iron ore to be used as a flux in its lead-silver smelting operations at Port Pirie. The smelters, built to treat the high-grade minerals being won at Broken Hill, started production in 1897 with ore brought in from the Broken Hill area. But a more reliable economic supply was paramount, so the company commissioned several exploratory expeditions nearby and the vast Middleback Ranges deposits were located.

Leases were acquired in November 1899. The first need was transportation. While a narrow-gauge 1067 mm railway, commissioned in 1901, was being built to link Iron Knob quarry with Hummock Hill, a distance of 56 km, the product was hauled out by bullock drays. From Hummock Hill it was then ferried across the Spencer Gulf by barge.

BHP's first locomotive to be used over the Iron Knob Tramway was an 0-6-0ST Nasmyth, Wilson & Co engine transferred from the company's Broken Hill operations. This was followed by an 0-6-0T Andrew Barclay product. Later, two Beyer, Peacock engines joined the scene.

Up to this time, iron ore mining had been only a small-time operation. Now, with the need to diversify operations due to difficulties in the lead-silver-zinc mines at Broken Hill, the company's directors decided to build a steelworks, and a Bill enacted in Federal Parliament in November 1912 allowed work to start. Although the site first mooted was Hummock Hill (close to the ore supplies), a swampy site beside Newcastle harbour in New South Wales, which had been obtained during the 1890s for a projected smelter, was ultimately decided upon, being handy to most raw materials, manpower and markets. When commissioned in March 1915, Iron Knob iron ore fed the modest single furnace. To work the larger trainloads out of Iron Knob quarry, two 81-tonne 4-6-0 tender locomotives had been purchased from the Baldwin Locomotive Works the previous year. Carrying the road numbers 4 and 5, these large-boilered engines could manage loads of up to 360 tonnes against the Beyer, Peacock 2-6-2T No. 2's 180 tonnes.

Continuing expansion of the Newcastle steel-works, which included construction of additional blast furnaces, required even greater payloads over the Iron Knob tramway. As a result, two larger 2-8-2 locomotives, capable of handling a huge 2650 tonnes, were obtained from the Baldwin Works in 1920. The commissioning of two more 2-8-2s in 1928 and 1938 reduced BHP's elderly 4-6-0s to yard shunting

Baldwin Locomotive Works-built BHP5 standing in Whyalla yard early in its career. (BHP)

duties and the haulage of company water trains to the mines (Iron Baron had opened in 1930).

With the arrival of Clyde-built GM diesel-electrics for main line ore train service in November 1956, steam was quickly removed from the tramway and scrapped. A survivor was the 4-6-0 class-leader No. 4, which for many years was used as a mobile steam generation plant for pile driving, and later as a distillation plant. Its last dramatic fling was experienced in May 1965, when it worked a special railway enthusiast charter train to Iron Knob. It was finally condemned in June 1969 and presented tenderless to the ARHS for preservation today in the National Railway Museum, Port Adelaide.

SPECIFICATIONS

	IMPERIAL (METRIC)
CYLINDERS:	16 x 22 IN (41 x 56 CM)
BOILER PRESSURE:	180 PSI (1240 KPA)
COUPLED WHEELS:	3 FT 8 IN (112 CM)
TRACTIVE EFFORT:	18 432 LB (82 KN)
GRATE AREA:	17.9 SQ FT (1.663 M²)
TOTAL WEIGHT:	65 TONS (66.3 T)
GAUGE:	1067 MM
ROAD NUMBERS:	4 AND 5

1918 VICTORIAN RAILWAYS

C-class 2-8-0

This class of 26 heavy freight locomotives, the first of which entered service in March 1918, was the most powerful locomotive type in Australia at its time of introduction.

It was designed by VR's celebrated CME W.M. Shannon, and known by administration as the H-class while on the drawing boards.

Painted red and chocolate, the pattern engine, C1, began operating over the North-Eastern line between Melbourne and Seymour. An additional 25 engines were constructed at the Newport Railway Workshops and all were running by December 1926.

Superheaters were provided from the outset and the easier to maintain Walschaerts valve gear was employed. Although built for heavy goods haulage, the C-class was found to possess a fine turn of speed too, and the locomotives were soon authorised to work passenger trains up to 96 km/h. They were also the first non-passenger engine to be equipped with automatic staff exchanges due to their frequent use on express goods and fast fruit services.

In 1929, C5 became the first Victorian locomotive to be fitted with a high-capacity compound air compressor.

Locomotive C2 in original condition. (V/Line archives, Len Whalley collection)

During World War II, the class started working passenger services of a heavier type because the existing passenger engines could not cope with the increased density of traffic. Up until then, the C-class had been considered a rather 'short-winded' engine. However, when an oil-burner was fitted to C15 in 1946, its boiler's steam generation was improved so all 26 were converted. After crews complained of smoke drift problems, deflector plates were added from June 1948 onwards.

The C-class operated over all Victoria's main lines, although they still continued to run out of steam if pushed too hard, particularly on long rising grades. Main line dieselisation from 1952 was the C-class's downfall, with C20, then due for heavy overhaul, being the first withdrawn in June 1954. Gradually the class was removed from the main lines and, with little work left for them and new S-class diesel-electrics on the way, the rest were gradually withdrawn.

All have been scrapped with the exception of C10, which is preserved at the ARHS's North Williamstown Railway Museum.

Interestingly, the VR stores division kept several brand new C-class boilers for many years afterwards and in 1982 allowed their sale to Steamrail Victoria Ltd, an organisation which regularly operates steam-hauled tourist trains throughout Victoria. There are hopes the relic might operate again under the hand of this dedicated body.

SPECIFICATIONS

	IMPERIAL (METRIC)
CYLINDERS:	22 x 28 IN (56 x 71 CM)
BOILER PRESSURE:	200 PSI (1378 KPA)
COUPLED WHEELS:	5 FT 0 IN (152 CM)
TRACTIVE EFFORT:	38 397 LB (170.9 KN)
GRATE AREA:	32 SQ FT (2.973 M²)
TOTAL WEIGHT:	128.5 TONS (131.1 T)
GAUGE:	1600 MM
ROAD NUMBERS:	C1—26

1918 NEW SOUTH WALES GOVERNMENT RAILWAYS

K1353-class 2-8-0

The 120 locomotives of NSWGR's K1353-class were a further modification of the T and TF class 2-8-0s, which by 1917 numbered no fewer than 470 engines.

Originally 300 K-class were envisioned, largely to completely replace the low-powered 6-coupled A and B classes which dated back to the 1870s–1880s. As with the TF-class, the new locomotives employed the tapered boiler, but all were superheated from new. Several innovations were incorporated into the design such as the novel, though complicated, Southern valve gear, bland higher-capacity tenders and, in the case of about 30, outside bearings on the leading pony trucks. Other improvements included

One of the last 55-class in service, 5593 was pictured at Port Kembla shortly before its March 1966 withdrawal. (Late Colin Oakley)

rocking firebars, drop grates and ashpan dampers.

All emerged from the Clyde Engineering Co's Sydney works between 29 November 1918 and 13 March 1925. These locomotives became the D55-class during the 1924 renumbering system.

The engines worked over the state's main lines but as they were a little heavier than their T-class (D50) prototype, they were restricted over some branch lines.

As they became due for boiler renewals during the mid-1930s, all D55s were equipped with the non-tapered D50-class superheated vessels which had become standard replacement parts on all rebuilt D50 and D53-class (T and TF) locomotives. The superheated engines from the three classes (D50/53/55) became known as the 'standard goods engines', being given identical loads and operating conditions.

In September 1946, No. 5502 was converted to burn fuel oil. With industrial action threatening in the NSW coal fields, 14 more were similarly treated over the next 15 months. In 1949, the miners' unrest developed into an all-out strike so another fifty-five D55-class engines were hurriedly converted to oil-burners to meet the state's freight needs.

Unlike the coal-fired members of the class, which had to relay their trains at principal depots due to servicing requirements, the oil-burners could be used almost continuously, running trains the full distance between Sydney and Junee. But there was a downside and retired (former) Commissioner's driver, the late Jack Thorburn, recalled how the trailing coupled wheels' axlebox bronze bearings used to prematurely run out of lubricant and subsequently fail due to the radiated heat from the pulsating oil-burning equipment in the fire grate immediately above.

Another problem was that when the axleboxes' horn cheeks wore (there was no adjustment), they were able to move longitudinally, which put strain on the connecting rods; in turn, because these were attached to Southern valve gear, the valve timing suffered, affecting haulage capabilities.

Of the 70 engines converted, 15 were changed back to coal firing once the coal strike was resolved. As something of an insurance against another strike, most of the oil-burners were then placed in store at city and country depots, the first being 5518, in April 1951. Following the decision to dieselise, most of the class was scrapped during the 1954–57 period, exceptions being the handful converted back to coal after that period. To better enable them to work fruit express and mail trains, locos 5531 and 5605 were fitted with specially balanced coupled wheels, increasing their operational speed from 55 to 65 km/h. Both were occasionally rostered to work the Cooma mail trains between Goulburn and Cooma.

The last of the breed in service, 5597, was finally withdrawn in July 1967 after working metropolitan trip and ballast trains. All have been scrapped with the exception of 5595, now exhibited at the Thirlmere Railway Museum. This locomotive managed to travel 1.66 million kilometres during its 43 years of service, further than any other engine in the class.

	IMPERIAL (METRIC)
CYLINDERS:	22 X 26 IN (56 X 66 CM)
BOILER PRESSURE:	160 PSI (1102 KPa)
COUPLED WHEELS:	4 FT 3 IN (130 CM)
TRACTIVE EFFORT:	33 557 LB (149.3 KN)
GRATE AREA:	28.75 SQ FT (2.671 M²)
TOTAL WEIGHT:	127.5 TONS (130.1 T)
GAUGE:	1435 MM
ROAD NUMBERS:	(ORIGINAL) 1353–1454, 5603–5620.
	(1924) 5501–5620

1920 G. & C. HOSKINS LIMITED

Iron Duke 4-6-4T

One little-known railway in New South Wales ran the 18.5 kilometre distance between Spring Hill and Cadia in the state's central west. The railway was built by Lithgow iron and steel magnates, G. & C. Hoskins, to haul ironstone.

Shortages of ironstone due to the pressures of World War I saw Hoskins begin explorations to locate more suitable and easily obtained sources.

The serious investigations quickly revealed several promising deposits, one of them being at Cadia, near Orange (the location of one of Australia's first high grade copper mining enterprises in 1858).

In those days, rail transport was a key ingredient in any development so in February 1916 the company began building a standard 1435 mm gauge railway to link its new mine with the NSWGR at Spring Hill. The line was completed in 31 months.

To aid construction, a former NSWGR 0-6-0ST, P293, a Manning Wardle product built in 1884 for the Camden Tramway, was brought in. The railway's second locomotive was another ex-NSWGR veteran, M50, a 4-4-2T Beyer, Peacock & Co suburban tank engine of 1891 manufacture.

Neither of these was really suitable, being too low powered, so Hoskins began looking around for something more reliable. The search resulted in a contract being signed with the Clyde Engineering Co in Sydney for a new, sturdy 75-tonne 4-6-4T. Named *Iron Duke* (after one of the two district copper mines) and readied for traffic early in 1920, this locomotive was based upon a NSWGR S-class 4-6-4 suburban tank engine.

Whereas the S-class employed plate frames,

The *Iron Duke*, standing in the spartan locomotive servicing area provided at Springhill, some time in the 1920s. (RailCorp archives)

however, the *Iron Duke* was constructed with American-type bar frames and smokebox saddle. Another interesting feature was the use of outside bogie frames and bearings in a marginal bid to provide easier maintenance.

When comparing the *Iron Duke's* leading specifications with its NSWGR S-class prototype, the two types read identically, right down to the theoretical tractive output. However, while the S-class was a perfect performer, it seems the *Iron Duke* left much to be desired for, although a neater-looking locomotive, surviving accounts from two crew members reveal that it was despised, particularly in the steaming department. The crew believed the engine's different grate arrangement was the cause.

With the impending transfer of the Hoskins family's iron and steel making operations to Port Kembla in 1929 (thus forming Australian Iron & Steel), the Cadia railway closed in June 1928 and the locomotives were transferred to Port Kembla. *Iron Duke* was initially employed hauling iron ore from the jetty. It was then pressed into coal train haulage from Wongawilli Colliery (west of Dapto) and when not engaged in this duty could be found shunting the Port Kembla by-products coke ovens.

Iron Duke was finally withdrawn from service by Australian Iron & Steel in May 1957 as dieselisation of the company's considerable railways advanced. It was not destined to last long, being broken up for scrap on 29 July that year. Just a handful of photographs remain of this unique locomotive.

Footnote: Miners have returned to Cadia, in October 1998 commissioning what promises to be Australia's second richest gold mine. Proven reserves have been discovered in a 5.5 km long, 600 m deep ore body.

SPECIFICATIONS

	IMPERIAL (METRIC)
CYLINDERS:	18½ x 24 IN (47 x 61 CM)
BOILER PRESSURE:	160 PSI (1102 KPA)
COUPLED WHEELS:	4 FT 7 IN (140 CM)
TRACTIVE EFFORT:	19 116 LB (85.1 KN)
GRATE AREA:	24 SQ FT (2.23 M²)
TOTAL WEIGHT:	73.5 TONS (75 T)
GAUGE:	1435 MM

C17-class 4-8-0

Introduced in 1920, this class was basically an improved version of the earlier C16-class, its main feature being a more efficient superheated boiler.

In fact, the C17 was destined to become one of the most versatile locomotive types in Queensland, with no fewer than 227 constructed over the following 33 years. Unsurprisingly, modifications were carried out with each new order and the final 40 (which were affectionately known as 'Brown Bombers' because of their chocolate brown livery) were fitted with roller bearings.

The locomotives were built by the Ipswich Railway Workshops (16), Walkers Ltd (138), Evans, Anderson, Phelan (28), Sir W.G. Armstrong Whitworth & Co (25) and the Clyde Engineering Co (20). The last in service was a Walkers engine, delivered as late as September 1953.

C17-class locomotives saw service in virtually every corner of the state. Over the years they worked everything from air-conditioned expresses to cane trains, suburban passenger services and freight trains. Although designed as a goods engine, they were regarded as the most powerful all-lines locomotive type in the state.

Records reveal nearly 100 operated in the Northern Division before dieselisation, when they were gradually withdrawn, the first to go being 261 on 21 October 1952 (even before the delivery of the final ten). Five C17s at Rockhampton and one, 979, at Mackay lasted until the QR was fully dieselised but they were all condemned on 26 August 1970.

Today, some twenty-six C17s are preserved in parks and museums all over the state with another two in New South Wales. QR holds two under cover at Redbank Workshops, 2 and 1000, for historical purposes. No. 2 represents the original version; 1000 is a modern one. No. 802 has been restored to working order at Mary Valley, Gympie, where it has been joined by its stored sisters 45 and 253 (under restoration); 974 is kept in a trafficable condition for enthusiast train workings, and 812 has been restored to operation by the Ravenshoe-Atherton Insteam Locomotive Co after languishing in Rotary Park, Atherton, for more than 20 years. In addition, 720, 763 and 935 are awaiting restoration at the Rosewood Railway Museum while 967 now resides at Gympie

C17 No. 940 blasts out of Gowrie Junction with Stephenson's PB15.551 with a Chinchilla–Toowoomba goods train on 30 September 1967. (Graham Cotterall)

after its 2003 restoration to service at Beaudesert.

In New South Wales, 934 can be found hauling tourist trains at the awe-inspiring Zig Zag Railway outside Lithgow.

Commonwealth Railways NM-class

In addition to the 227 built for QR, in 1925–27 the Commonwealth Railways acquired 25 of these 4-8-0s in two batches from Thompson & Co of Castlemaine, Victoria, for use over the Central Australia Railway, which at the time was being extended to link Port Augusta with Alice Springs. The first entered service in June 1925 and they had all been delivered by December 1927 as the NM-class. The final engine in the fleet, 38, was delivered to the North Australia Railway to haul construction trains between Katherine and Birdum, but it tended to derail on the light track and was sent to Darwin with the intention of returning it to the CAR. This was not to be and the engine remained on the NAR until withdrawn in June 1956.

During the severe coal strike of 1949, eighteen NMs were converted to burn a mixture of oil and coal. All were changed back to coal shortly after the strike ended, with the exception of NM22.

The first to be withdrawn was NM23 in January 1954. When NSU diesels arrived later that year, three more were withdrawn and they were all out of service by October 1956, with NM22 being the last to run. Scrapping commenced in October 1958.

Loco NM25 is operated by the Pichi Richi Railway Preservation Society at Quorn while NM34 resides in the National Railway Museum, Port Adelaide.

Commonwealth Railways' Nm21. (AN archives)

	ORIGINAL	REBUILT
	IMPERIAL (METRIC)	IMPERIAL (METRIC)
CYLINDERS:	17 x 22 IN (43 x 56 CM)	17 x 22 IN (43 x 56 CM)
BOILER PRESSURE:	160 PSI (1102 kPA)	175 PSI (7206 kPA)
COUPLED WHEELS:	3 FT 9IN (114 CM)	3 FT 9 IN (114 CM)
TRACTIVE EFFORT:	18 085 (80.5 kN)	21 017 (93.5 kN)
GRATE AREA:	18.5 SQ FT (1.719 M²)	18.5 SQ FT (1.719 M²)
TOTAL WEIGHT:	79.7 (81.3 T)	82.9 TONS (84.6 T)
GAUGE:	1067 MM	1067 MM
ROAD NUMBERS:	(QR): 2, 15, 17, 24, 25, 29, 32, 33, 45, 46, 55, 57, 62, 68, 121, 138, 145–147, 165, 166, 179, 182, 187, 188, 226, 245–259, 261, 263, 264, 308, 705–730, 752–767, 772–791, 802–826, 831–840, 858–863, 917–948, 955–1000 (CR): 15–28, 31–38	

1920 BROKEN HILL PROPRIETARY CO

Baldwin 2-8-2

The continuing expansion of the Broken Hill Proprietary Co's Newcastle steelworks called for steady iron ore production increases at the company's Iron Knob mine in the South Australian Middleback Ranges. This growing appetite for iron ore was putting a strain on the modest 56 km 'tramway' linking Whyalla with the mine site. Clearly, larger trains would have to be run to cater for the expanded production requirements.

Although BHP had taken delivery of two 66.3-tonne Baldwin 4-6-0s in 1915, locomotives of much greater capacity seemed to be the answer. The Baldwin company's sales team recommended a 147.9-tonne 2-8-2 (Mikado) tender design which was capable of developing 166.8 kN, almost double the older Baldwin capacities. Accordingly, two were ordered in 1919.

These chunky locomotives, which boasted superheaters and pistons driven by Walschaerts valve gear, were the most powerful in Australia when delivered late in 1920. They also were the first in this country to carry the 2-8-2 wheel arrangement.

With the development of Hoskins' steelworks at Port Kembla (which later formed Australian Iron & Steel), a further market was to hand for Middleback Ranges iron ore and the Iron Baron mine was developed, a spur line being opened in December 1930.

Initially only lighter-type locomotives could work the spur line; when an additional 2-8-2 was ordered for the main line, older and smaller locomotive power was thus released for the new branch. This third

Baldwin 2-8-2 No. 6 at Whyalla shortly after its delivery in 1920. (Author's collection)

2-8-2 differed slightly from the first two in that it was 11 tonnes lighter.

Although the 2-8-2s were rated to haul 600 tonnes, one special test in the 1930s proved the design was capable of hauling as much as 2650 tonnes. While trains of that weight did not become commonplace, double-heading of the 2-8-2s did after a track strengthening program. In fact, surviving company records show that a record train of 3838 tonnes was hauled out of Iron Knob in 1937 by two Mikado locomotives.

The final 2-8-2 was purchased in 1938. It differed slightly again from the three before it. The locomotive, although of similar lighter weight to the third engine, was equipped with an extended long-range tender which made its all-up weight identical to the initial two. In addition, as a trial, it was fitted with an exhaust steam injector. Records reveal that this equipment was not a success and shortly afterwards it was replaced with a standard Sellers lifting injector.

With the arrival of two 977 kW EMD model G-12 diesel-electric main line locomotives during November 1956, steam haulage of the ore trains quickly ceased and the Mikados were withdrawn and scrapped. No. 7 remained the longest, eventually being scrapped in 1958. Only the tenders were retained, the tanks being removed to carry water, and their frames forming flat-top vehicles for use with BHP's rail-laying train.

SPECIFICATIONS

	IMPERIAL (METRIC)
CYLINDERS:	21 x 24 IN (53 x 61 CM)
BOILER PRESSURE:	200 PSI (1378 KPA)
COUPLED WHEELS:	4 FT 0 IN (122 CM)
TRACTIVE EFFORT:	37 485 LB (166.8 KN)
GRATE AREA:	41.3 SQ FT (3.837 M²)
TOTAL WEIGHT:	145 TONS (147.9 T); No. 8: 134 TONS (136.7 T)
GAUGE:	1067 MM
ROAD NUMBERS:	6–9

6D9½-class (Hunslet) 4-6-0T

A small Hunslet Engine Company World War I steam locomotive is today wooing the thousands of visitors who daily swarm through the Australian War Memorial in Canberra. The 1916-built 610 mm gauge 4-6-0T locomotive has taken up pride of place in the memorial's fabled Anzac Hall, virtually rubbing shoulders with the likes of Lancaster bomber G *for George* and a raft of other relics that includes tanks and trucks.

The locomotive was one of 155 built for the British War Department to the 600 mm (and afterwards) 760 mm gauges for service in France and the Middle East.

The War Memorial example assisted the Allied forces on the European Western Front, transporting troops and supplies where required. It survived the war to be repatriated to Britain for resale. Fifteen of its war order sisters (some of which did not see war service) were destined to haul sugar cane in Queensland after they were regauged to 610 mm.

Six initially arrived in Australia in October 1920, having been purchased by the London-based Agent-General for the Queensland Government, the first going into service on the Innisfail Tramway as No. 6 of the 6D9½-class. The others were distributed among the government's Proserpine, North Eton, Babina and South Johnstone sugar mills. The locomotives were so well received in Queensland that a further example was built brand new in 1925 (maker's number 1498) for the Australian Estates & Mortgage Co's Kalamia Mill, operating there as *Northam*.

The Australian War Memorial's locomotive initially saw Australian employment at the Gin Gin Sugar Mill, Wallaville, until 1967. The relic then passed into the hands of a Brisbane-based scrap metal merchant. But Charlie McClelland, of the Melbourne bayside suburb of Frankston, was able to acquire the engine and after building a short length of track and a wooden carriage, periodically steamed the locomotive to entertain his friends.

In 1994, a NSW cotton farmer purchased this Hunslet and stored it in a machinery shed on his farm at Wee Waa in the state's north-west until the

Australian War Memorial Anzac Hall gallery staff with the exceptionally-presented Hunslet locomotive (builder's number 306) on 12 April 2005. (Leon Oberg)

Australian War Memorial bought it in 2001.

The Hunslet, which carries War Department number 306, underwent meticulous restoration work in the Memorial's conservation complex in Canberra's suburban Mitchell. Four more survive in Queensland, one at The Workshops Museum in Ipswich; one at the Proserpine Historical Society Museum; another at the Durundur Railway Woodford, while the fourth is in private hands.

SPECIFICATIONS

	IMPERIAL (METRIC)
CYLINDERS:	9½ × 12 IN (24 × 30 CM)
BOILER PRESSURE:	160 PSI (1102 KPA)
COUPLED WHEELS:	2FT 0 IN (61 CM)
TRACTIVE EFFORT:	5776 LB (25 KN)
GRATE AREA:	3.95 SQ FT (0.34 M²)
TOTAL WEIGHT:	14 TONS 1 CWT (14.2 T)
GAUGE:	610 MM
ROAD NUMBERS:	INNISFAIL TRAMWAY: 1, 2 AND 6. TWELVE OTHERS CARRIED NUMBERS OR NAMES AS APPLIED BY INDIVIDUAL MILLS.

1922 QUEENSLAND RAILWAYS

C19-class 4-8-0

This class, which eventually numbered 29 locomotives, was the most powerful conventional steam type ever to run on the Queensland Railways. When introduced, they were considered to be one of the world's largest locomotives running on 1067 mm gauge.

The first C19 arrived in 1922, one of ten designed as a superheated version of the similarly-styled but saturated C18-class of 1914. Ten more were built by QR's extensive Ipswich Workshops in 1927 and were followed by a further six from Walkers Ltd of Maryborough. The last entered service in 1935.

The class mainly worked the heavily-graded routes, including the Main, Southern, Northern and Western lines. Even though designed for heavy goods haulage, they were also used extensively on passenger and mail train services over the steeper lines.

A striking view of C19 No. 702 as delivered. (QR)

The resounding success of this class led to the earlier C18s being converted to superheated locomotives. Unlike the C19s, which were built with the more accurate piston valves, the converted C18s initially retained their original D-type slide valves. But the higher steam temperatures created by superheating provided lubrication problems and thus the three C18s were also given piston valves and larger diameter cylinders, and reclassified as C19s.

Some locomotives boasted individual identities. Ipswich-built 702 was named *Centenary* and fitted with a small kerosene-type headlight converted to electricity. During the 1940s, No. 796 boasted a unique vertical-sided regulator dome. In addition, 196 to 201 were equipped with Capuchion funnels.

Dieselisation seriously eroded the C19s' role and for some years they were relegated to hauling workers' trains and performing menial shunting service. During the 1955–56 financial year, no fewer than eight were withdrawn. Despite further scrappings, engines working in the Toowoomba area continued to be overhauled for a while but, as more and more diesel-electrics were introduced, all C19s were eventually withdrawn. The last in traffic, 700, was withdrawn on 26 February 1964.

No. 700 appears to have been produced beneath a lucky star, for in December 1934 it was chosen to work a Royal Train conveying the Duke of Gloucester from Wallangarra to Brisbane and on to Nambour. This locomotive was retained for preservation by QR and is currently stored at the Redbank Workshops.

SPECIFICATIONS

IMPERIAL (METRIC)

CYLINDERS:	19 x 23 IN (48 x 58 CM)
BOILER PRESSURE:	160 PSI (1102 KPA)
COUPLED WHEELS:	4 FT 0 IN (122 CM)
TRACTIVE EFFORT:	23 525 LB (104.7 KN)
GRATE AREA:	21.37 SQ FT (1.985 M²)
TOTAL WEIGHT:	97 TONS (98.9 T)
GAUGE:	1067 MM
ROAD NUMBERS:	692–704, 792–801, 196–201

1922 VICTORIAN RAILWAYS

K-class 2-8-0

A serious post-World War I shortage of light freight-type locomotives led to the preparation of drawings for what was destined to become one of the VR's most trouble-free locomotive types.

The VR's celebrated Chief Mechanical Engineer, Mr Alfred Smith, headed the design team whose efforts led to an order for ten 2-8-0 locomotives to be known as the K-class from the VR's Newport Workshops. The first entered traffic in August 1922.

The locomotives were used virtually everywhere in the state, operating over both main and branch lines. As late as 1940, the design was considered so reliable that engines were still being ordered; by October 1946, a total of 53 had been built.

One that could not be saved was K170, pictured between yard shunting assignments at Wodonga in 1975. (John Adamson)

Although the later examples were basically similar to the earlier engines, they were provided with several modern detail alterations. In addition, the final seven were equipped with better balanced Boxpok coupled wheels. They were all fitted with staff exchangers.

The K-class, which was highly regarded by its crews, seemed to have worked on all 1600 mm gauge tracks throughout the state at some stage. There is even a photograph of K157 at the head of a Commissioner's special train at Picola.

The gradual introduction of T-class Bo-Bo diesel-electrics from 1955 marked the beginning of the end for this hard-working 2-8-0 type and withdrawals and scrappings soon commenced. K142 was the first to go in August 1958, and others quickly followed. However, some were put into service as yard pilots and fitted with shunters' steps.

Others were brought out of store in country locations to help transport the wheat harvest during the early 1970s while some, like K157 and K162, were retained as shunters at Ballarat Workshops, the latter engine lasting until 29 March 1979.

While a number were provided to various municipalities and organisations for park or museum preservation, four, K153, K183, K184 and K190, are today in the care of Steamrail, an enthusiast organisation involved in the running of regular charter and vintage train steam tours in Victoria. Although not all are operational, some have seen service on a rotating basis.

The Victorian Goldfields Railway, Maldon, owns

two, K157 and K160, while K163, K174, K177 and K191 are part of the Mornington Peninsula Preservation Society's Moorooduc-based fleet. K165 stands in the North Williamstown Railway Museum and K176 awaits cosmetic restoration at the Seymour Steam Railway and Museum after being salvaged in poor order from a Deniliquin park. Nine more are scattered through country Victoria.

SPECIFICATIONS

	Imperial (Metric)
Cylinders:	20 x 26 in (51 x 66 cm)
Boiler pressure:	175 psi (1206 kPa)
Coupled wheels:	4 ft 7 in (140 cm)
Tractive effort:	28 127 lb (125.2 kN)
Grate area:	25.75 sq ft (2.4 m²)
Total weight:	104.6 tons (106.9 t)
Gauge:	1600 mm
Road numbers:	140–192

1922 TASMANIAN GOVERNMENT RAILWAYS

Q-class 4-8-2

This class, introduced in 1922, finally totalled 19 locomotives and became the mainstay of Tasmania's heavy freight services for well over a quarter of a century. Designed by the TGR and constructed by the Perry Engineering Co of Adelaide, South Australia, the first batch of six locomotives was running by

The last member of the class, Q19, poses for official photographs on delivery from the Clyde Engineering Co's Granville factory in 1945. It was one of four upgraded through the provision of higher-pressure 1240 kPa boilers. (Roydon Burk collection)

the end of 1923. An additional three were delivered during 1929 by Walkers Ltd, Queensland.

Designed as a 'mountain type', these heavy locomotives were restricted to the state's heaviest lines which included the Fingal, main Launceston to Hobart, Western and Derwent Valley routes.

The design was so efficient and versatile that, beginning early in the 1930s, a further ten were ordered, this time from the Clyde Engineering Co. These went into traffic between 1936 and 1945. Although the locomotives from the three manufacturers were very similar, progressive detail changes were made, including roller bearings to final deliveries and thermic siphons inside the fireboxes to improve steaming. The final four were supplied with 1240 kPa boilers which could provide a bonus 15.1 kN tractive effort. In practice, however, boilers used to be swapped between locomotives and there was no operational distinction made between the different types.

While nominally a goods engine, Q-class locomotives were frequently pressed into the haulage of country passenger trains and, following the introduction of X-class diesel-electrics from late 1950, some found employment at the head of selected Hobart suburban services.

As the number of X-class locomotives increased, making inroads into the remaining heavy steam-hauled goods services, the Qs battled on, even finding employment here and there as shunting engines. But all good things come to an end and, as

mechanical and boiler condition dictated, they began to be withdrawn, the first to go being Nos 8 and 9, in 1956. A further four were retired by 1959 and they were all put out of service after the Y-class diesel-electrics arrived.

The last two in regular service were Nos 4 and 12, last seen hauling suburban passenger trains in the Hobart area. Both were withdrawn and condemned in December 1963. (It is of interest that No. 12 was seen working a passenger turn later that month, despite having been officially condemned.)

All were subsequently scrapped with the exception of No. 5, which was retained for preservation in the Tasmanian Transport Museum, Glenorchy.

SPECIFICATIONS

	Nos 1–15	Nos 16–19
	IMPERIAL (METRIC)	IMPERIAL (METRIC)
CYLINDERS:	20 x 24 IN (51 x 61 CM)	20 x 24 IN (51 x 61 CM)
BOILER PRESSURE:	160 PSI (1102 KPA)	180 PSI (1240 KPA)
COUPLED WHEELS:	4 FT 0 IN (122 CM)	4 FT 0 IN (122 CM)
TRACTIVE EFFORT:	27 200 LB (121 KN)	30 600 LB (136.2 KN)
GRATE AREA:	32.5 SQ FT (3.019 M²)	32.5 SQ FT (3.019 M²)
GAUGE:	1067 MM	1067 MM
ROAD NUMBERS:	1–19	

Locomotive R2 in original condition at Hobart roundhouse in the mid-1920s. (Michael Dix collection)

1923 Tasmanian Government Railways

R-class 4-6-2

In a bid to replace its elderly and by now hard-pressed A-class 4-4-0 locomotives, in the early 1920s the Tasmanian Government Railways contracted the Perry Engineering Co of Adelaide, South Australia, to construct a suitably powerful express locomotive type.

At the time, Perry Engineering was constructing six TGR-designed Q-class 4-8-2 locomotives to replace ageing power over TGR main lines. The new 4-6-2 Pacific-type passenger locomotives for TGR were virtually identical to the Q-class but with slightly shorter boilers and larger diameter driving wheels.

Only four of these Pacifics were ordered and were delivered in 1923 as the system's R-class. Reputedly capable of speeds up to 96 km/h, the locomotives saw service over the Western, Derwent Valley, Hobart to Launceston and Fingal lines.

With the emphasis on some mainland railways

Locomotive R4 prepares to depart Hobart station with the *Launceston Express* soon after it and a sister engine were equipped with VR-inspired streamlining. (Author's collection)

on streamlined and named trains, the TGR was not going to be left out in the cold. In 1937, after introducing new main-line steel carriages to work the Hobart to Launceston express, streamlined R3 and R4 were designated to work the train. TGR streamlining was a plagiarised version of that equipped to the Victorian Railways' S-class Pacifics, and to most with an artist's eye was not nearly as stylish. This less stylish appearance did not prevent the R-class performing sterling work on this intercity service, negotiating the line's 1 in 40 grades and twisty terrain with relative ease.

During World War II, locomotive maintenance came second to getting the job done so the streamlining on Nos 3 and 4 deteriorated to the point where parts were reportedly falling off and it was removed altogether.

New X-class diesels marked the beginning of the end for these hard-working locomotives and all four were withdrawn as major mechanical and boiler overhauls fell due. R2 and R4 were retired in March and August 1956 while the last in service was R1, which was withdrawn at Launceston in October 1957. All had been scrapped by 1959.

SPECIFICATIONS

	Imperial (Metric)
Cylinders:	20 x 24 in (51 x 61 cm)
Boiler pressure:	160 psi (1102 kPa)
Coupled wheels:	4 ft 7 in (140 cm)
Tractive effort:	23 738 lb (105.6 kN)
Grate area:	32.5 sq ft (3.019 m²)
Total weight:	98 tons (100 t)
Gauge:	1067 mm
Road numbers:	1–4

The Final Flutter

None of the locomotives used by the many privately-owned timber mill railway and tramway companies in Australia could quite match the contraption built in 1923 for the Rhodes Timber Co's Mt George Tramway, located in mountainous country south of the NSW North Coast town of Taree.

Aptly known as *The Final Flutter*, this weird-looking locomotive was intended to operate over the company's standard-gauge, mostly wooden-railed right of way, where the grades were reputed to be as steep as 1 in 10 in places and a classic zig-zag was provided for added variety.

During its railway years, the Rhodes Timber Co owned two steam locomotives. The first was constructed from 'bits and pieces' cannibalised from worn-out locomotives and steam equipment, and was apparently a total disaster in operation. The second, although professionally built by Tulloch Ltd at Rhodes, was little better. The highly original work of art which became *The Final Flutter* was assembled to the design and/or shape of a Climax-geared locomotive, largely from scrap steel and oddments. It boasted a former NSWGR F-class boiler and a vertical 2-cylinder engine unit which had once been used in a Sydney Harbour tug-boat. A large gear wheel fitted to the projecting end of the engine's crankshaft engaged a pinion which attached to a shaft leading to a gearbox mounted on the frames. A drive shaft ran from this gearbox to drive bevel gears attached to each of the locomotive's two 4-wheel bogies.

The cab was basically a galvanised iron shed. A large spark-arrestor chimney anchored by stay-wires completed the front end. Finally, a large commercial-type water tank was fitted above the trailing bogie.

On its first run, *The Final Flutter*, working in reverse, waddled off toward the logging area. At the first rising grade, the water in the boiler inclined away from the firebox crown and the lead fusible plug gave out. Not to be outfaced, the crew repaired the damage and finally set off for home. But according to noted locomotive historian Gifford Eardly, writing in the ARHS's monthly *Bulletin*, the locomotive took off and raced out of control, smashing rails as it went. He added that although the crew had activated the brakes on all eight wheels, the chains and brake gear

The Final Flutter, featuring a NSWGR F-class boiler teamed with a shanty-style cab for its hapless crew. (Bruce Macdonald collection)

were torn away due to the swinging bogies. The crew jumped!

Surprisingly, the engine did not derail and afterwards was taken into the mill's workshop and dismantled. The boiler was later sold to another sawmill.

Since the steam locomotives were such failures, the company decided to put its future motive power faith in 4-wheel-drive motor vehicles specially fitted with rail wheels. The tramway finally closed in 1948. Portions of the route can still be traced beneath thick undergrowth.

1100-class Bo-Bo

The growth of energised suburban lines following the opening of Melbourne's first electrification project between Flinders Street and Essendon on 28 May 1919 led to the construction of two Bo-Bo electric locomotives at the Newport and Jolimont Electric Workshops. The first entered service in July 1923, the second in August.

Powered by suburban electric passenger equipment, these locomotives, numbered 1100 and 1101, were so successful that an additional ten were ordered. The opportunity was taken to slightly modify the original rather spartan steeple-cab design which boasted just a single pantograph. These new box-cab double pantograph units were built in the

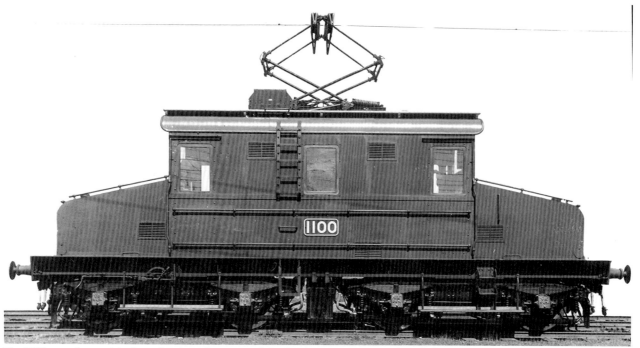

No. 1100, one of two original steeple-cab single pantograph Bo-Bo electric units, pictured just before its 1923 release to service. (VR archives, author's collection)

same workshops and delivered between December 1928 and December 1929 and. The new units were 5.2 tonnes heavier than the initial two.

The box-cab units initially became 1100-class and were numbered 1102 to 1111; they were reclassified E-class (for electric) in later years and received former E-class steam locomotive classification plates.

The 12 locomotives were employed on all classes of suburban workings, from metropolitan goods and shunting service to passenger rolling-stock shunting.

The original two locomotives were withdrawn from service during the early 1950s due to their need for new electrical equipment. No. 1100 was dismantled in July 1953, followed by 1101 a month later. Their remains were dispatched to Spotswood reclamation depot.

Meanwhile, the ten box-cab E-class soldiered on until the late 1970s, when withdrawals started. The last one was stopped in 1984. Four have been

preserved, 1102 statically by the ARHS's North Williamstown Railway Museum, and 1106, 1108 and 1109 by Steamrail Victoria Ltd.

SPECIFICATIONS

	IMPERIAL (METRIC)
ELECTRICAL EQUIPMENT:	1500 DC
TRACTION HORSEPOWER:	600 (448 kW)
STARTING TRACTIVE EFFORT:	24 400 LB (108.6 kN)
CONTINUOUS TRACTIVE EFFORT:	14 160 LB (63 kN)
TOTAL WEIGHT:	Nos. 1100, 1101: 50 TONS (51.1 T)
	Nos. 1102–1111: 55.1 TONS (56.2 T)
GAUGE:	1600 MM
ROAD NUMBERS:	(1ST BATCH) 1100, 1101
	(2ND BATCH) 1102–1111

1923 CORRIMAL COAL CO

Burra 0-4-0ST

Weighing just 7.5 tonnes, this diminutive 0-4-0ST locomotive was constructed for the Corrimal Colliery's isolated 610 mm gauge mountainside railway by the British firm, Hawthorn Leslie & Co.

The quaint locomotive was ordered through the Sydney-based Austral Engineering & Supply Co Ltd in April 1923 and by the close of July that same year had been completed. It arrived at Corrimal Colliery, complete with diamond-stack chimney, on 26

The first of ten upgraded 1100-class, pictured upon completion in 1928. These box-cab locomotives featured twin pantographs. (V/Line archives, author's collection)

Burra at work on the Illawarra Light Railway and Museum's popular Albion Park tourist railway. (Leon Oberg)

November 1923 and was bestowed with the name *Burra*. (Folklore has it the locomotive was to have been named *Kookaburra*, but this name would not fit on the rather small saddle tanks.)

Burra was intended as a replacement for the company's original 0-4-0WT Krauss locomotive (former Tasmanian Government Railways H-class locomotive No. 2) which had worked the railway since its opening in 1908.

Apart from a period out of service in 1945 awaiting a Clyde Engineering Co general overhaul, at which time it received a new boiler, *Burra* spent 43 years hauling coal skips and colliery materials along the company's approximately 1.6 km rail link.

Australian Iron & Steel Pty Ltd acquired the mine in March 1964 and within a few years the new owners closed *Burra*'s little railway and withdrew the relic for scrap. However, the company's then director of public affairs, Bill Fancourt, headed a successful delegation to AI&S management to have the little locomotive preserved outside the company's visitors centre, and *Burra* was mounted on a plinth in February 1968, with many of its valves and fittings welded closed.

Rationalisation of the visitors centre a decade later saw *Burra* donated to the Illawarra Light Railway and Museum at nearby Albion Park with a view to returning the veteran to working order. Assisted by a federal government employment grant, members expended some 20 000 voluntary hours on its total rebuild. Bill Fancourt was among a number of dignitaries present on 8 October 1995 when *Burra* was majestically returned to active service. Other guests present on that day were Hugh Bradford (who drove the locomotive at the colliery in 1940), Bill Leitch, who fired for Mr Bradford at that time, and Fred Worthington (the engine's 1964 driver).

SPECIFICATIONS

	Imperial (Metric)
Cylinders:	8 x 12 in (20.5 x 30 cm)
Boiler pressure:	160 psi (1102 kPa)
Coupled wheels:	2 ft 0 in (61 cm)
Tractive effort:	4096 lb (17.9 kN)
Grate area:	4 sq ft (0.36 m²)
Total weight:	7.5 tons (7.6 t)
Gauge:	610 mm

The second Fowler locomotive, carrying the builder's number 17732 and bearing the *Wee Georgie Wood* name plates, standing at Tullah circa 1950. (Ralph Proctor)

1924 North Mt Farrell Mining Co

Wee Georgie Wood
0-4-0T

Few railways in Australia have been engendered with as much pioneering aura as the 10 km, 610 mm gauge North Mt Farrell Mining Company's Tullah Tramway in Tasmania. Until 1962, this railway was the only transport link between the west coast silver-lead mining and sawmilling township of Tullah and the outside world, its sinuous curves linking the town with Farrell Siding on the Emu Bay Railway.

With grades up to 1 in 14 and some curves as sharp as one chain radius, the Tullah Tramway, when installed in 1902, used timber rails and was worked by horses. In 1908 the company decided to modernise and strengthen the line with railway infrastructure suitable for steam operation.

Among the earliest locomotives to work the line was an 0-4-0T Krauss, which entered service just prior to Christmas 1908. This little 8-tonne engine was no match for the pioneering nature of the railway,

which resulted in its almost daily derailment.

In 1924, a replacement engine arrived, a small 0-4-0T John Fowler product (No. 16203), which was affectionately given the name *Wee Georgie Wood* after the then popular, diminutive English music hall comic/performer.

A virtually identical Fowler, No. 17732 (it differed in boiler manhole location), was acquired in 1927. Some say it was known as *Mary*.

By the late 1940s, *Wee Georgie Wood* was in need of major repairs. In anticipation of this, its sister 17732 was forwarded to the Emu Bay Railway's workshops at Burnie for a full general overhaul in December 1947. Two years later, 16203 was withdrawn and the *Wee Georgie Wood* name plates were transferred to the overhauled 17732. As the company searched for a replacement for 16203, the opportunity arose to purchase an ex-Mt Lyell Railway 10-tonne Krauss 0-4-0T which was located at the Commonwealth Carbide Co's property at Ida Bay. It continued to carry its road number 9 at Tullah.

Reporter L.B. Manny, writing in the ARHS monthly *Bulletin* in April 1960, in describing a trip over the tramway behind the Krauss locomotive said the train required one hour to travel the 10 km: 'The locomotive's water tanks needed replenishment three times during the journey, which could be punctuated at any moment by derailments because the twisting route did not possess curves, they were kinks—a series of straight rails which curved when they joined!'

A road replaced the railway in 1962 and both remaining locomotives were preserved. Today, 17732 (which confusingly acquired 16203's builder's plates) operates out of Tullah on alternate Sundays between September and Easter over a 1.8 km section of restored track under the care of the Wee Georgie Wood Steam Railway. Krauss No. 9 was awaiting overhaul as a relief engine as this book went to press.

SPECIFICATIONS

	IMPERIAL (METRIC)
CYLINDERS:	7 x 12 IN (18 x 30.5 CM)
BOILER PRESSURE:	180 PSI (1240 KPA)
COUPLED WHEELS:	2FT 0IN (610MM)
TRACTIVE EFFORT:	3600 LB (15.9 KN)
GRATE AREA:	4 SQ FT (0.36 M²)
TOTAL WEIGHT:	7.3 TONS (7.4 T)
GAUGE:	610 MM

1924 STATE ELECTRICITY COMMISSION OF WESTERN AUSTRALIA

Electric Bo-Bo

The Western Australia State Electricity Commission became something of a pioneer when it imported a single 1067 mm gauge 44.5-tonne Bo-Bo electric locomotive from Metropolitan Vickers Electrical Co Ltd of Manchester, England, in 1924.

Up to that point, electricity as a locomotion source had been seen as something of a novelty in Australia, even though it had been used successfully in several European countries.

The locomotive, which experienced its trial run on 2 May 1924, was required to haul coal trucks between East Perth railway siding and the powerhouse, a distance of almost a kilometre. Despite the little unit's modest 448 kW power output, the gearing was sufficiently low to allow it to haul 400 tonnes up a 1 in 46 gradient at 20 km/h.

This locomotive, believed to have been a duplicate of 78 others used at one time on the electrified railways

The State Electricity Commission of Western Australia 1067 mm gauge 44.5-tonne Bo-Bo electric locomotive transferring coal to the East Perth power station. (ARHS Western Australia Division archives)

of South Africa, remained in service until March 1969 when the powerhouse was converted to burn oil fuel. The Bo-Bo was subsequently donated to the Australian Railway Historical Society for exhibition at its Bassendean (Perth) Railway Museum.

Footnote: In 1973–74, when a looming oil crisis promised industrial doom and gloom, a decision was taken to reconvert the East Perth power station back to coal. The railway was re-laid and a small 15-tonne WAGR Z-class Drewry Car Co diesel shunting unit employed until the facility was closed in 1981.

SPECIFICATIONS

	IMPERIAL (METRIC)
ELECTRICAL EQUIPMENT:	600 V DC METROPOLITAN VICKERS
TRACTION HORSEPOWER:	600 (448 KW)
MAXIMUM TRACTIVE EFFORT:	21 450 LB (95.4 KN)
TOTAL WEIGHT:	43.12 TONS (44.5 T)
GAUGE:	1067 MM

No. 110, the only N-class member to receive a booster. (V/Line archives)

1925 Victorian Railways

N-class 2-8-2

Built under the expert direction of the Victorian Railways' CME Alfred Smith, this class was destined to become one of the most successful all-lines locomotives on the VR system.

Designated N-class, it was the first (Mikado) 2-8-2 design used by any government railway system in Australia. The 2-8-2 wheel arrangement eventually became extremely popular with designers as it allowed the use of much larger fire grates than was possible with the 2-8-0 form.

The N-class was acquired for heavy freight haulage over main lines. The first engine appeared on 25 May 1925 and by 13 July 1931 there were 30 in traffic, all of them constructed in the VR's Newport Workshops.

Following post-World War II traffic increases and a general shortage of motive power due to an overwhelming need for heavy overhauls, the N-class drawings were dusted off and 70 new locomotives were ordered. Fifty were constructed in England by the North British Co and delivered between August 1950 and April 1951.

Newport Workshops had been authorised to construct the remaining 20 but, because orders had also been placed for main line diesel locomotives of the B-class, only three of the 20 were actually built. These were fitted with highly balanced Boxpok coupled wheels and entered service from July 1950.

At the same time the neighbouring South Australian Railways system was also experiencing a severe locomotive shortage. Between January and May 1951, SAR acquired ten of the comparatively new North British-built N-class engines from Victoria. These became the SAR's 750-class and operated anything from heavy goods services to race-day specials. Being lighter than the SAR's own modern goods type, the 750s were very useful working the lighter routes such as the Truro and Spalding branches. Several could be found at Tailem Bend for use over the many Mallee lines that radiated out of that district.

In Victoria, dieselisation meant that heavy overhauls ceased on the N-class and withdrawals of the original engines started in the mid-1950s. The first to be cut up was 419 in December 1958, followed by five more in 1960. The last N-class engine was withdrawn on 14 October 1966. No. 432 was spared for preservation and can be found today in the North Williamstown Railway Museum. (This was the last steam locomotive to be built at Newport Workshops.)

Dieselisation of the SAR's broad gauge lines also spelled the end for the 750-class. Withdrawals started in the late 1950s and the first to be condemned was 751 (ex VR 475) in July 1961. Some engines continued in their regular branch line role for a few more years but by 1964 engine 752 was the only example operational, seeing regular use on the Mile End to Truro goods. It was finally withdrawn on 8 October 1967. All but one was subsequently cut up. The survivor was 752 (ex VR 477), now at the National Railway Museum, Port Adelaide.

	ORIGINAL	LATER ENGINES
	IMPERIAL (METRIC)	IMPERIAL (METRIC)
CYLINDERS:	20 x 26 IN (51 x 66 CM)	20 x 26 IN (51 x 66 CM)
BOILER PRESSURE:	175 PSI (1206 KPA)	175 PSI (1206 KPA)
COUPLED WHEELS:	4 FT 6 IN (137 CM)	4 FT 7 IN (142 CM)
TRACTIVE EFFORT:	28 648 LB (127.55 KN)	27 749 LB (123.55 KN)
GRATE AREA:	31 SQ FT (2.88 M²)	31 SQ FT (2.88 M²)
TOTAL WEIGHT:	120.65 TONS (123 T)	124.65 TONS (127.1 T)
GAUGE:	1600 MM	1600 MM
ROAD NUMBERS:	(ORIGINAL VR): 110–139 (RENUMBERED 400–429 IN 1950) (POST-WAR VR DELIVERIES): 430–432, 450–499 (SAR): 750–759, WHICH WERE VR 474, 471, 477, 465, 461, 485, 491, 490, 494 AND 495 RESPECTIVELY.	

1925 NEW SOUTH WALES GOVERNMENT RAILWAYS

C36-class 4-6-0

The sheer magnitude of the NSW main line system and the time it took to service locomotives en route were two circumstances mitigating against running efficient passenger trains in the 1920s. Celebrated NSWRG CME Ernest Lucy had designed a fleet of comfortable main line carriages but, by and large, the vintage P6-class 4-6-0 locomotive fleet then in use was not capable of wresting the ultimate economies of scale out of that rolling-stock. Their tenders were small and the inside Stephenson's valve gear, which was in general use, was found to attract abnormal grime and needed a pit for crews to properly oil. Small smokeboxes resulted in a build-up of ash blocking off lower tubes, which depreciated the effectiveness of steaming qualities. In addition, train weights were taxing the old locomotives to such an extent that uneconomic double-heading had become common.

These shortcomings clearly prevented the NSWGR from running faster, more efficient trains. While 2- and 3-cylinder Pacific-type locomotives had been mooted as early as 1921, Lucy's design team eventually reworked the plans for the NN-class (of 1914) to come up with a slightly more powerful, heavier and much more efficient answer to the immediate need, the NN2-class.

Advertised around the globe, no fewer than 13 locomotive builders tendered for the job to build the initially planned 35 engines. In the end, the NSWGR's Eveleigh Workshops was contracted to construct 25 and the Clyde Engineering Co at Granville the balance.

But all did not go well with the Eveleigh order for, after it delivered its first example in January 1925, the workshops' lack of speed in construction soon saw the contract reduced to ten engines and the balance, along with an additional 40, being given to Clyde.

All 75 had been delivered by November 1928; the last one in service was Eveleigh product 3610.

While under construction the locomotives were expected to become the NN2-class, but because of the NSWGR's 1924 renumbering system, they appeared as the C36-class. This class was destined to become one of Australia's finest types once it had overcome some initial teething problems.

Following early goods and then Sydney metropolitan passenger trials, the class-leader was put to work on the state's top main line express routes, eventually relaying at principal depots. These locos excelled themselves in this capacity, being free steamers and really fast, good riders with ample reserves of fuel. Many old Southern drivers claimed they were faster than the crack C38-class Pacifics which arrived in later years and were reputed to have reached speeds in excess of 150 km/h.

The C36s worked the Wollongong, Albury,

Locomotive 3674 with original cab and round-top firebox. It bears the smaller diameter leading wheels mounted in a bogie of revised equalised design as fitted to locomotives 3661 onwards. (RailCorp archives)

'One-off' Giesl-equipped reboilered locomotive 3616 arrives in Parkes yard from Orange on 5 July 1962. (Leon Oberg)

Bathurst, Brisbane and Werris Creek routes and, when heavier rails were laid, began working to Canberra, Dubbo and Parkes.

A number of in-service modifications were carried out during the class's lifetime. In the 1930s, two were fitted with trial smoke deflectors and became the only NSWGR locomotives to have this arrangement. Later on their lubrication equipment was altered, and from 1953 onwards all but two were progressively rebuilt with new Belpaire 1378 kPa boilers and improved cabs. These boilers also carried modern smokebox-mounted throttle valves, first introduced to the NSWGR on the C38.

Their coupled wheels were also subject to improved balancing and during rebuilding heavier coupling rods were provided. The rebuilds increased their in-service weight by a little over 1 tonne.

In 1957, No. 3616 was provided with a Giesl exhaust ejector. Dr Adolph Giesl-Gieslingen's rectangular chimney above a slot-shaped blast pipe nozzle, although 'invented in theory' in 1924 and used as part of his doctoral thesis five years later, was not taken up seriously by the world's railways until steam traction, like the C36-class, was on the decline.

Despite the opportunity to equip (but not test) his ejector to a German locomotive at Floridorf Locomotive Works in 1940, the veteran designer had to wait until 1947 to trial his theories. The Chesapeake & Ohio Railroad of the USA fitted Giesl's exhaust and complete front end modifications to a shunting locomotive. While tests proved the doctor's theories, the idea was still not yet adopted.

Another four years were to pass before main line tests could be carried out on the invention. In 1951, when the equipment was fitted to an Austrian 2-8-4,—it not only increased the locomotive's power

output by 25 per cent but demonstrated a small coal saving as well. Austrian Railways subsequently fitted hundreds of steam locomotives with the ejector, as did East German, Czechoslovakian and East African rail systems. Worldwide, several thousand were eventually equipped, ranging from huge Beyer-Garratts to tiny narrow-gauge locomotives.

The Giesl ejector was based upon carefully calculated blastpipe nozzle and chimney sizes which were determined by the characteristics of the locomotive. The blast arrangement had seven exhaust steam jets located one behind the other. The steam, passing upwards fan-like, was calculated to fit the chimney exactly, narrowing towards its base. The jets presented a large surface area to draw gases from the firebox. Careful mathematical proportioning ensured a good draught on the fire while allowing a lower pressure of exhausting steam.

Despite the lower exhaust pressure, the fire in a Giesl-equipped locomotive was found to burn strongly with a reduction in cylinder back pressure. This meant that poorer quality coal could be burned.

Although all these claims were found to be true in 3616's case, no other engines in the class were fitted with the chimney due to expanding dieselisation.

It was that same dieselisation that truncated the rebuilds of two original round-boilered locomotives, 3622 and 3663, last in use at Taree depot. They were withdrawn at Eveleigh in September 1958. Retirements of rebuilt engines soon followed, and by 1962–63 most of the remaining engines were working goods (and some mail) trains on the Sydney–Albury, Lithgow to Dubbo/Parkes and Gosford–Werris Creek routes. By January 1968, their active number had been reduced to 28, at which time they fell foul of a driver's union ban which claimed

In this classic 1959 view, the five cars forming the air-conditioned No. 28 Up Central West were hurried through lush grazing land between Sodwalls and Rydal by reboilered 4-6-0 No. 3655. (Late Ron Preston)

a lack of certain creature comforts such as 'sufficient room to stow tucker boxes'. Enginemen also disliked the locomotives' rather stiff 19-turn reversing screws. A jammed screw regularly needed a hefty tap from a coal pick to free it.

Despite this, severe shortages of haulage power occasioned by a bumper wheat harvest led to six locomotives being taken out of store and fitted with power reverse equipment, trailing sand boxes and special lockers on the tenders to house the crew's personal belongings. These six re-entered service from March 1968 and operated for up to 18 months.

The last engine in regular traffic was 3642, withdrawn from Broadmeadow depot in September 1969. This locomotive, along with 3616, had been retained for special excursion services for a few years and in October 1972 worked a special train into South Australia to mark the opening of the rail link from Whyalla to Port Augusta.

Both engines were finally retired due to poor mechanical and boiler condition and forwarded to Thirlmere Railway Museum in the early 1970s where they joined 3609 as static exhibits. In 1979, No. 3642 was hauled to Goulburn locomotive depot for boiler change and restoration. After many months of part-time work, the engine was out-shopped in November 1981 and following a further recent overhaul, continues to work regular steam-hauled excursion traffic.

Footote: The C36-class design was adopted by Commonwealth Railways for express train haulage between Port Pirie and Kalgoorlie. Eight locomotives, bearing long-range 6-wheel bogie tenders, were built for CR by Walkers Ltd in 1938 (see page 215).

SPECIFICATIONS

	ORIGINAL	REBUILT
	IMPERIAL (METRIC)	IMPERIAL (METRIC)
CYLINDERS:	23 x 26 IN (58 x 66 CM)	23 x 26 IN (58 x 66 CM)
BOILER PRESSURE:	180 PSI (1240 KPA)	200 PSI (1378 KPA)
COUPLED WHEELS:	5 FT 9IN (175 CM)	5 FT 9 IN (175 CM)
TRACTIVE EFFORT:	30 498 LB (135.7 KN)	33 887 LB (150.8 KN)
GRATE AREA:	30.5 SQ FT (2.83 M²)	30.5 SQ FT (2.83 M²)
TOTAL WEIGHT:	159 TONS (162.2 T)	160.3 TONS (163.5 T)
GAUGE:	1435 MM	1435 MM
ROAD NUMBERS:	3601–3675	3601–3621, 3623–3662, 3664–3675

1926 BROKEN HILL PROPRIETARY CO

E-class Bo-Bo

The Broken Hill Proprietary Co turned to a 600V DC electric overhead wire system from 1926 as part of a complete modernisation of its Iron Knob quarry in South Australia. In looking for suitable motive power to work the trains on this system, BHP turned to the little 22.7-tonne steeple-cab 1067 mm gauge 74 kW E-class Bo-Bo locomotive, and four were progressively imported from Metropolitan Vickers' Trafford Park, Manchester, works between 1928 and 1936.

BHP's subsequent development of a limestone

Bo-Bo electric locomotive E7 working in Iron Knob quarry in 1965. (Late Ron Preston)

quarry on a coastal cliff at Rapid Bay (about 170 km south of Adelaide) during the early years of World War II to provide calcium carbonate for steel making in the company's Whyalla steelworks, then under construction, saw an order placed with Metropolitan Vickers for two more of these rugged Bo-Bo electric locomotives. But with the war raging across Europe, the manufacturer was too busy keeping up with domestic orders to fill BHP's order

In 1940, Metropolitan Vickers agreed to deliver the electrical equipment and main frames necessary to construct the two units and licensed Adelaide's Perry Engineering to fabricate the locomotives. The first unit was delivered to Rapid Bay in July 1942, a month before the operation's start-up date.

Perry Engineering assembled a further two identical locomotives under licence in September 1954; these were delivered to the Iron Knob quarry operation. Thirteen months later, the Rapid Bay railway was replaced by road transport and the two little locomotives which operated at that location were set aside and eventually scrapped.

The Iron Knob rail operation lasted another decade but it finally fell to road haulage in July 1968. Fortunately, two of these distinctive electric locomotives are preserved, the class-leader in the National Railway Museum, Port Adelaide and a Perry-built unit, E7, in Iron Knob's main street.

SPECIFICATIONS

	IMPERIAL (METRIC)
ELECTRICAL EQUIPMENT:	METROPOLITAN VICKERS 600V (DC)
TRACTION HORSEPOWER:	96 (74 kW)
TOTAL WEIGHT:	22 TONS (22.7 T)
MAXIMUM TRACTIVE EFFORT:	(APPROX) 5500 LB (24.5 kN)
GAUGE:	1067 MM
ROAD NUMBERS:	E1—E8

1926 VICTORIAN RAILWAYS

G-class 2-6-0 + 0-6-2

Although the VR thought about buying Garratts on at least two occasions, only one type actually appeared on the system, the G-class 2-6-0 + 0-6-2s. Only two were ordered from Beyer, Peacock & Co. They arrived in April 1926, to be given the numbers 41 and 42.

These engines were ordered as replacements for the older Na-class 2-6-2Ts, which had been forced to double-head in VR's struggle to handle the increasing freight train loads over the exacting 762 mm gauge routes radiating from Moe and Colac.

The class-leader was transported to Colac to work the 70 km narrow-gauge branch line to Crowes, while G42 was sent to Moe for the 42 km Walhalla route.

An official pre-service portrait of G42. (V/Line archives, author's collection)

Being powerful, flexible and boasting Walschaerts valve gear, we can only speculate as to just how many more would have been acquired had earlier proposals to construct narrow gauge lines from Benalla to Tatong, and from Tallangatta to Cudgewa, come to fruition. (These routes were subsequently built to the regular VR 1600 mm gauge.)

The Garratts were fitted with outside frames and mechanical lubricators and were able to work trains over their assigned lines unassisted. In addition, they produced reported savings of around 40 per cent in fuel and water.

As more reliable roads were constructed into Victoria's hinterland, the need for light, narrow-gauge pioneer railway lines gradually waned. When the Moe line was closed in 1954, G42 was transferred to Colac to assist its sister engine until that line ceased operating in 1962.

Loco G41 lay idle for some time but was eventually cut up for scrap in October 1964. G42 was saved from this fate for, after its last steaming in June 1962, it was held in store for another year, when it was transferred to the Puffing Billy Preservation Society's museum at Menzies Creek. After painstaking restoration work lasting some two decades, the little Garratt took its first tentative steps in steam outside the society's workshops early in March 2004, preparatory to entering tourist traffic the following month.

SPECIFICATIONS

	Imperial (Metric)
Cylinders:	(4) 13¼ x 18 in (34 x 46 cm)
Boiler pressure:	180 psi (1240 kPa)
Coupled wheels:	3 ft 0 in (91 cm)
Tractive effort:	27 860 lb (124.0 kN)
Grate area:	22.6 sq ft (2.1 m²)
Total weight:	70.15 tons (71.6 t)
Gauge:	762 mm
Road numbers:	G41 and G42

1926 RICHMOND VALE RAILWAY

Robinson 2-8-0

The Robinson 2-8-0 of England's Great Central Railway, introduced in 1911 as class 8K, was destined to become one of the world's most simple locomotive designs. Robinson eventually built 126 examples for his railway's heavy freight haulage.

In fact, the design was so sound, trouble free and easy to maintain that the British Government's World War I Railway Operating Division (ROD) selected the type for war service in Europe. Between 1917 and 1920 the government financed the construction of 521 engines, which were built in various workshops throughout the country. As it happened, three of those locomotives did not strictly pass into government hands, for at the war's end, these and many others were offered for sale, most being snapped up by British railway companies. Australian coal mining magnate John Brown, urgently needing reliable motive power for his 28 km Richmond Vale Railway just north of Newcastle, New South Wales, also took an interest in the surplus engines and duly instructed his Fenchurch Street office to negotiate the purchase of three. Although the sale went through in 1923, delivery was not made immediately, all three being loaded aboard one of Brown's coal ships, the SS *Boorara*, which eventually arrived in Sydney in February 1926.

Further expansion of the mines led Brown to acquire additional ex-ROD locomotives. In five separate transactions, a total of thirteen 2-8-0s were acquired, the last arriving in Australia late in 1927. One of those, a Kitson engine, had been fastidiously repainted and presented by Sir W.G. Armstrong Whitworth & Co as a 'demonstrator'.

The Brown locomotives were numbered in the Richmond Vale Railway's 12–24 series and their sheer reliability became a legend in Australia. At that

Ex-ROD (Brown) No. 15 had just one more month's life remaining when pictured in Hexham yard on November 1971. (Leon Oberg)

time, the Richmond Vale Railway was serving seven collieries, with coal trains working to Hexham where export facilities had been established for shipping.

As the Great Depression started to bite in 1929, some ex-RODs started to fall by the wayside, with parts of failed locomotives being used to keep sister engines operational. Leaking superheater elements were among the first components to give trouble—the remedy was simply to remove them, thus converting the locomotives to saturated steam.

At that time, locomotive 18 lost its boiler altogether and for 37 years its remains lay in storage, yielding further spare parts until is was finally cut up for scrap in 1969.

World War II saw the need for additional coal supplies and most of the ex-RODs were shopped for major overhauls. By 1942, ten were back in service. But the coal industry was extremely fickle, and subsequent gradual mine closures and a serious slump in coal orders during the mid-1960s once again found many Richmond Vale locomotives placed in store as their boiler and mechanical condition deteriorated. By then, management had been looking at the economies of acquiring diesel locomotives and, in a bid to cut costs, E.M. Baldwin of Castle Hill prepared drawings for a 62-tonne jackshaft drive 0-8-0 unit that employed the frames, driving wheels, connecting and coupling rods of the RODs. The

tender was also factored into the design as a braking vehicle.

The closure of Richmond Main Colliery in 1967 saw the end of the railway beyond Stockrington Colliery and, operating under the new control of Coal & Allied Industries, only engines 13, 15, 23 and 24 remained in service by 1970. It was thought that these were the last remaining RODs left working anywhere in the world.

A boiler failure on loco 15 in December 1971 marked the end of an era and, since all the boilers were original, the remaining locomotives went fast. The last in operation was 23, which was withdrawn at Hexham in May 1973. Soon afterwards, tenders were called for the purchase of all but one of the remaining RODs. While scrap merchants acquired most, British preservationists expressed an interest in 20 and 24. These two were held in store until the high cost of transport back to England saw their claim transferred to the Newcastle district preservation group, the Hunter Valley Steam Railway & Museum (now Dorrigo Steam Railway & Museum), late in 1975.

Loco 23 is located at a diverse mining and railway museum centred on the old Richmond Main colliery.

SPECIFICATIONS

	IMPERIAL (METRIC)
CYLINDERS:	21 x 26 IN (53 x 66 CM)
BOILER PRESSURE:	185 PSI (1275 KPA)
COUPLED WHEELS:	4 FT 8 IN (142 CM)
TRACTIVE EFFORT:	30 303 LB (134.9 KN)
GRATE AREA:	26.25 SQ FT (2.439 M2)
TOTAL WEIGHT:	123 TONS (125.5 T)
GAUGE:	1435 MM
ROAD NUMBERS:	12–24

1926 SOUTH AUSTRALIAN RAILWAYS

500-class 4-8-2

When Commissioner W.A. Webb was appointed to the SAR late in 1922, he immediately set about rehabilitating the state's railways, particularly the broad gauge system.

Mr Webb, formerly of the Missouri, Kansas & Texas Railroad in the USA, was particularly concerned about South Australia's underpowered 4-4-0 and 4-6-0 locomotives, some of them dating back to 1894 but still performing prime main line service, where double- and even triple-heading was common.

'Big power' was Webb's credo and within four years he acquired some of Australia's mightiest locomotives. Among the first to appear was a brutish-looking 4-8-2 which became the 500-class. Ten were ordered from Sir W.G. Armstrong Whitworth & Co in England, a firm of ship-building engineers. The first entered traffic on 4 June 1926 and all ten were running by 28 October that year.

The 500-class was ordered for heavy express passenger and freight service over the Adelaide–Murray Bridge section of the Main South Line. This route featured the solid Mt Lofty Ranges with grades of 1 in 45 and 200-metre radius curves.

The power of the locomotives had to be seen to be believed and crews who up until then had been accustomed to tractive efforts of 95.68 kN now had to manage 226.95 kN. Couplings started breaking and rails began to spread, causing derailments. Initially it was thought that a heavier than expected axle loading on the locomotives was the cause, but the trouble was later traced to faulty equalising of weight over the driving wheels.

In May 1928, No. 506 was experimentally fitted

The gradient is 1 in 49 as locomotive 501 nears Eden Hills deep in the formidable Adelaide Hills with a Tailem Bend-bound goods train, on 27 January 1952. (Ron Lennard, Len Whalley collection)

A lovely original study of locomotive 603 at Tailem Bend locomotive depot on 28 January 1952. (Late Lionel Bates, Graham Cotterall collection)

with a booster to drive a newly created 4-wheel trailing truck. This US-inspired addition was seen to be a boon when starting heavier loads and could be activated in mountainous country when conditions dictated. All 500-class locomotives were subsequently so equipped. The booster generated an extra 35.6 kN of starting tractive effort.

During the late 1930s, the SAR embarked upon an image-building policy, and the bold piping and plumbing on the 500s was replaced by semi-streamlined casing on all but two of the class members. Valances, too, were added, and the giant locomotives looked grander than ever.

The supremacy of the 500s was challenged with the introduction of 900-class diesel-electric locomotives in 1951. When another diesel-electric type, the 930-class, arrived in 1955, two 500s (502 and 507) were immediately withdrawn. By July 1962, all had been taken out of service, the last two left in traffic being the class-leader, 500, and 504. The latter is now in the National Railway Museum, Port Adelaide.

SPECIFICATIONS

	IMPERIAL (METRIC)
CYLINDERS:	26 x 28 IN (66 x 71 CM)
BOILER PRESSURE:	200 PSI (1378 KPA)
COUPLED WHEELS:	5 FT 3 IN (160 CM)
TRACTIVE EFFORT:	51 076 LB (227.3 KN)
GRATE AREA:	66.6 SQ FT (6.187 M2)
TOTAL WEIGHT:	222.3 TONS (226.8 T)
GAUGE:	1600 MM
ROAD NUMBERS:	500–509

1926 SOUTH AUSTRALIAN RAILWAYS

600-class 4-6-2

This was the second design in a group of three delightfully-proportioned locomotives developed in conjunction under the auspices of newly-appointed SAR Commissioner Mr W. A. Webb as a means of modernising his state's broad gauge railways.

While the 500-class 4-8-2s were designed to work heavy trains through the demanding Adelaide Hills, Webb believed it imperative that heavier, more powerful motive power be provided to economically work the express passenger services between Adelaide, Serviceton and Terowie. Thus the mighty 600-class 4-6-2 was born.

In company with the 500s, the ten members of the 600-class were built in England by Sir W.G. Armstrong Whitworth & Co. The first entered traffic on 10 May 1926 (a month earlier than the first 500) and all were running within three months.

As did the 500-class, the new locomotives experienced teething troubles, particularly in regard to weight distribution over the coupled wheels caused by faulty springing. The SAR had to have the spring buckles redesigned to correct the weight transfer through the equalisers.

Despite this meticulous correctional work, the 600s had to be withdrawn from the Terowie run following further evidence of track pounding, which was traced to their high 23.62-tonne axle load. Subsequently the 600s were confined to the

An immaculately turned out class-leader 700, steaming into history at the head of an enthusiast special on 2 June 1968. (Graham Cotterall)

Serviceton, Mount Gambier (after it became a broad gauge line), Victor Harbor and Port Pirie routes for virtually the rest of their lives, working both passenger and fast freight trains.

Modifications over the years included the fitting of new steel boilers from July 1939, which were pressed to an extra 103 kPa and increased their tractive effort by 12 kN. Five were fitted with automatic stokers during the late 1940s, and the remaining engines were converted to burn a mixture of both coal and oil. In addition, they acquired smoke deflectors.

With the arrival of diesel-electrics from 1951, the usefulness of the 600s gradually diminished and they were withdrawn as mechanical or boiler condition dictated. Withdrawals started with 607 and the last engine in actual service was 603, condemned on 6 July 1961. All had been scrapped by the end of February 1963.

SPECIFICATIONS

	ORIGINAL	AS REBUILT
	IMPERIAL (METRIC)	IMPERIAL (METRIC)
CYLINDERS:	24 x 28 IN (61 x 71 CM)	24 x 28 IN (61 x 71 CM)
BOILER PRESSURE:	200 PSI (1378 KPA)	215 PSI (1481 KPA)
COUPLED WHEELS:	6 FT 3 IN (160 CM)	6 FT 3 IN (160 CM)
TRACTIVE EFFORT:	36 557 LB (162.7 KN)	39 600 LB (174.8 KN)
GRATE AREA:	55 SQ FT (5.11 M2)	55 SQ FT (5.11 M2)
TOTAL WEIGHT:	197 TONS (200.9 T)	198.5 TONS (201.3 T)
GAUGE:	1600 MM	1600 MM
ROAD NUMBERS:	600–609	

1926 SOUTH AUSTRALIAN RAILWAYS

700-class 2-8-2

The 700-class was the third of a collection of modern, powerful locomotive designs instigated by SAR Commissioner W.A. Webb in the 1920s. As with the 500 and 600 classes, the new 700-class was based on North American practice and built in England by Sir W.G. Armstrong Whitworth & Co.

The 700s arrived in Port Adelaide in March 1926 and were soon assembled. The class-leader, 700, had its first trial over the Northern Line on 27 April 1926 (thus making it the first of the three new classes to actually run). As trials continued, it was found that faulty compensation of the coupled wheels produced an abnormally high axle load for the light 27 kg lines over which the engines were expected to run. But, in company with the 500 and 600 classes, this problem was quickly overcome through a correction within the equalising arrangement and the 700s became one of Australia's most successful medium-powered locomotive types.

The usefulness of the 700s led to the creation of a revised version in 1928, which became the 710-class. Initially 30 were ordered from the Department's own Islington Workshops. The class-leader arrived in October 1928 and all were running by August 1929. Besides being slightly heavier, the new engines embodied several improvements over the 700 prototype, including smokebox regulators (the first such use in Australia), a cross-compound air-compressor and boosters driving the trailing truck.

It must be mentioned that when the 710 was on the drawing board, locomotive 706 was equipped with a booster (from May 1927) to gauge the efficiency of this apparatus in branch-line traffic.

The increased axle load on the trailing truck caused by the booster equipment quickly became a problem, and the order for 30 of the new class was reduced to just ten. In a bid to increase the class's route availability, the boosters were removed from all 710s, as well as 706, during the 1930s.

Following World War II, a number of the original 700s were converted to burn fuel oil because of severe coal shortages. In fact, two engines were converted to burn a mixture of coal and oil. The remaining five coal-fired engines were then equipped with coal pushers from September 1948. With the exception of 708, all the oil-burning engines were converted back to coal in their final years.

The first two 700-class condemned were 703 and 707, in June 1959. Their overhauls were not warranted because ten 830-class branch-line Alco diesels had been ordered. Soon afterwards, further withdrawals were made and the last engine in traffic was class-leader 700, which steamed into history at the head of an enthusiast special on 2 June 1968.

While no 710s were retained for preservation, 702 survives in the National Railway Museum, Port Adelaide.

SPECIFICATIONS

	700-class	710-class
	IMPERIAL (METRIC)	IMPERIAL (METRIC)
CYLINDERS:	22 x 28 IN (56 x 71 CM)	22 x 28 IN (56 x 71 CM)
BOILER PRESSURE:	200 PSI (1378 KPA)	200 PSI (1378 KPA)
COUPLED WHEELS:	4 FT 9 IN (145 CM)	4 FT 9 IN (145 CM)
TRACTIVE EFFORT:	40 418 LB (179.9 KN)	40 418 LB (179.9 KN)
GRATE AREA:	47 SQ FT (4.366 M2)	47 SQ FT (4.366 M2)
TOTAL WEIGHT:	171.15 TONS (174.6 T)	175.75 (179.3 T)
GAUGE:	1600 MM	1600 MM
ROAD NUMBERS:	700–709	710–719

1926 QUEENSLAND RAILWAYS

B.18¼-class 4-6-2

Designed to become the principal express and passenger locomotive on Queensland's railways, the B.18¼-class also became the first Pacific-type on the system. The first of a batch of 17 was introduced in 1926 and all class members were running by 1930. They were constructed within the QR's Ipswich Workshops.

Possessing an impressive turn of speed, the locomotives quickly earned the respect of their crews as easy to handle, tireless performers and good riders. As a result, further orders were placed for six in 1935 (utilising second-hand tenders) and then 60 more, which were delivered by Walkers Ltd and Ipswich Workshops between 1936 and 1947.

These later locomotives were slightly more sophisticated than the original 17, as they were equipped with improved cabs and higher-pressure boilers. Eventually, some had larger tenders fitted in a bid to further extend their operational range.

Initially they operated express and fast fruit express trains until somewhat superseded on the more important runs from 1951 by an improved, more modern version, the BB.18¼-class.

The colour scheme of the class bears mention because in their early days they were painted Prussian blue, with a natural metal finish on the boilers. In 1949, all were painted green and lined out in red and silver.

The efficiencies resulting from dieselisation provided a body blow to the B.18¼s, for the locomotives were then asked to work anything from sugar cane trains to suburban services, ballast trains to slow freight. The first to be withdrawn was 910 in March 1967. Eleven followed within the next 15 months, while the last engines in service, 770, 849 and 881, were used until July 1970.

It is significant to mention that engine 84 holds the highest distance record for any QR steam locomotive. It steamed 2 356 574 km during its commercial career. No. 771 was retained by QR for preservation.

SPECIFICATIONS

	ORIGINAL	IMPROVED
	IMPERIAL (METRIC)	IMPERIAL (METRIC)
CYLINDERS:	18¼ x 24 IN (46 x 61 CM)	18¼ x 24 IN (46 x 61 CM)
BOILER PRESSURE:	160 PSI (1102 KPA)	170 PSI (1171 KPA)
COUPLED WHEELS:	4 FT 3 IN (130 CM)	4 FT 3 IN (130 CM)
TRACTIVE EFFORT:	21 316 LB (94.9 KN)	22 648 LB (100.8 KN)
GRATE AREA:	25 SQ FT (2.323 M2)	25 SQ FT (2.323 M2)
TOTAL WEIGHT:	93.25 TONS (95.1 T)	100.5 TONS (102 T)
GAUGE:	1067 MM	1067 MM
ROAD NUMBERS:	16, 18, 27, 28, 30, 40, 50, 52, 84, 227–232, 768–771, 827–830, 841–852, 864–881, 887–916	

B.18¼-class 848 at Monkland on 1 May 1965. (David G. Bailey)

1927 STATE ELECTRICITY COMMISSION OF VICTORIA

Electric Bo-Bo

Probably few readers will be fully aware of the tremendous role railways played in connection with the State Electricity Commission (SEC) of Victoria's Latrobe Valley operations.

Formed by the Victorian government in 1921 to develop the valley's vast brown coal reserves, the SEC's first need was a reliable transport system. Until the government rid itself of the operation in 1993 under the banner of privatisation, up to 60 locomotives (steam, diesel, petrol and electric) were at one stage employed by the Commission.

Brown coal was first discovered at Morwell North about 1879 and within ten years the Great Morwell Coal Mining Co had started open-cut mining on the north bank of the Latrobe River. Forced into liquidation after a bushfire destroyed its new briquette plant, the mine was taken over by the Victorian Mines Department in 1899.

In 1917, prodded by the Institute of Victorian Industry, a state government advisory committee recommended the establishment of a brown coal-fired 50 MW electricity generating plant near the Morwell coal reserves. As a result, the SEC was formed in 1921 and took over brown coal mining from the Mines Department in 1924.

The transport of coal from the open-cut mine was originally undertaken by horse-drawn vehicles, with an aerial ropeway taking the mineral onwards to the Yallourn power station. But from January 1925, second-hand steam locomotives were acquired to work out of the open-cut mine over a newly laid 1067 mm gauge railway.

By December of that year, six steam engines were in constant service but due to fires in the pit (caused by sparks from the locomotives) the horses were returned to the fold, allowing executives time to ponder a more reliable form of haulage. They came up with the decision to build a new electric railway and in February 1927, after relaying the line to the narrower 900 mm gauge, commissioned the first of three German-built Bo-Bo electric locomotives together with ten 20-tonne capacity side-tipping coal trucks.

Built by Henschel, with electrical equipment supplied by Siemens, the new railway operated on an 1100 volt DC system, fed from an overhead trolley wire placed 3.4 to 4.4 metres above the rail.

Known as the 46-ton locomotive type, the three Bo-Bo units were joined by four more in 1928. As mining and SEC's generating capacity grew, so too did the railway. This led to 17 more similarly-powered Bo-Bo units being commissioned between 1929 and 1952, these locos being built in Australia by Kelly & Lewis with electrical equipment from Australian General Electric.

Beginning in 1950, a larger design known as the 60-ton locomotive type was introduced. Thirteen

The very first Bo-Bo unit, the Henschel-Siemens 21, with a train being loaded by an overhead dredge. This locomotive was retired in June 1970 after a working life of 43 years. (SEC archives)

of these were acquired over a 4-year period from Henschel-Siemens. They were rated at 760 kW and exerted a maximum tractive effort figure of 174 kN, making them almost twice as powerful as the older 46-ton machines. The completion of that order provided locomotive power for a new briquette factory development at Morwell, including a 20 km railway which was officially opened in June 1955.

Steadily increasing payloads over the railway led to the acquisition of three more locomotives from Henschel-Siemens in 1963. Numbered 121 to 123, these 760 kW units became the 62-ton type; they were fundamentally a refined version of the 60-ton units, but exerted slightly more tractive effort.

The new units were fitted with regenerative braking (a device which reverses the generator field, thus acting as a retarding force) and equipped for

One of 17 electric locomotives from the second distinct Kelly & Lewis deliveries, SEC 35, which was introduced in 1942 and retired in April 1970. It is pictured outside SEC's locomotive servicing area. (SEC archives)

multiple-unit operation. A final two identically powerful 63-ton locomotives were acquired in 1968 from Japanese builder Hitachi.

A policy to replace the open-cut railways with a conveyor belt system was adopted from 9 February 1968, and the first locomotives to be withdrawn were the 46-ton plants. The first 12 were 'officially' retired on 15 April 1970, followed by eight more on 25 June of the same year. The remaining four class members, locos 27, 37, 40 and 41, were retained for shunting and track lifting operations although, in a letter to this author dated July 1982 from SEC's then manager, area administration, Mr J.C. Hutchinson, it was revealed that 27 was used for parts to keep the other three running.

The increasing use of conveyor systems and a greater reliance upon road transport decimated the railway throughout the 1980s. In 1992, SEC made the decision to scrap the remaining 13 km of electric railway between Yallourn and Morwell due to the reported 'high cost of the lengthy lead time and high cost of acquiring spare parts'.

Under subsequent privatisation, the transport component of that haulage was tendered out and the government expected to see a heavy-haul road system put in place. The Dandenong-based firm, Cooks Construction, did tender for road haulage, but in the same document came up with an alternative: 'scrap the electric railway and overhead reticulation system, upgrade the railway and employ diesel locomotives'.

The diesel railway option was accepted and Cooks

The first of a 1963 Henschel-Siemens order for what became the 63-ton type, 121 is shown at Yallourn in 1964. (SEC archives)

The last of the Henschel-Siemens units, SEC 123 *Electric Blue*, at Yallourn on 18 April 1993. (Darren Hodges)

Construction was contracted from 10 September 1993 to provide the transport service. In a bid to have suitable equipment available for the start-up, the company acquired four DH-class diesel-hydraulic locomotives (DH4, DH5, DH24 and DH56) from the Queensland Railways in June 1993; after being regauged from 1067 mm to 900 mm, they were put into service. (Another two were later purchased.) For the next few years twin DH-class units handled 900-tonne 16-vehicle trains over the rail system.

The electric locomotives were quickly scrapped after this, except for unit 37, which went to the North Williamstown ARHS Railway Museum, and 125, retained for the Morwell Powerworks.

The railway finally closed in October 2000. Three of the former coal wagons were used to construct passenger carriages at the nearby Walhalla Goldfields Railway where a former SEC diesel locomotive is operating tourist trains.

SPECIFICATIONS

	IMPERIAL (METRIC)	IMPERIAL (METRIC)	IMPERIAL (METRIC)	IMPERIAL (METRIC)	IMPERIAL (METRIC)
BUILDER:	HENSCHEL	KELLY & LEWIS	HENSCHEL	HENSCHEL HITACHI	
ELECTRICAL EQUIPMENT:	SIEMENS	AGE	SIEMENS	SIEMENS HITACHI	
RATED HORSEPOWER:	461 (344 kW)	461 (344 kW)	1019 (760 kW)	1019 (760 kW)	1019 (760 kW)
STARTING TRACTIVE EFFORT:	30 000 LB (133.5 kN)	30 000 LB (133.5 kN)	39 000 LB (173.6 kN)	40 000 LB (178 kN)	40 000 LB (178 kN)
CONTINUOUS TRACTIVE EFFORT:	26 000 LB (115.7 kN)	26 000 LB (115.7 kN)	33 000 LB (146.9 kN)	34 800 LB (154.9 kN)	34 800 LB (154.9 kN)
WEIGHT:	46 TONS (46.9 T)	46 TONS (46.9 T)	60 TONS (61.2 T)	62 TONS (63.2 T)	62 TONS (63.2 T)
GAUGE:	900 MM	900 MM	900 MM	900 MM	900 MM
ROAD NUMBERS:	21–27	28–44	101–113	121–123	124–125

Wiluna, as it appeared circa 1942. (Noel Inglis collection)

1928 Public Works Department (Western Australia)

Barclay 4-6-0

The railway construction task was always one of the least-lamented duties associated with locomotive operations.

In some states, private companies acted as rail construction contractors, often importing locomotives to their own desired design to facilitate the task. In other states, the governments themselves were the railway construction authorities, often placing the work in their public works portfolios. Very often their locomotives were 'hand-me-downs' from sister railway departments, and quite often of low power or nearing the ends of their economic lives.

In 1927, the Railway Construction Branch of Western Australia's Public Works Department was employing four elderly 44.5-tonne 4-6-0 G-class and one larger L-class in its expanding rail-building activities. With further rail-building works on the drawing boards, particularly in the state's south, the department signed a contract with Andrew Barclay of Kilmarnock late in 1927 for the supply of two modern 4-6-0 locomotives. These steamed into traffic the following July carrying the names *Wiluna* and *Nornalup*.

Of chunky 'square-rigged' configuration, appearing to some extent like austere war machines, these two 61-tonne engines nevertheless were effective companions for the department's earlier steeds.

With the Great Depression firmly affecting departmental finances, the PWD's railway construction branch was merged with the WAGR in January 1931, the two Barclay 4-6-0s classified as Q-class and provided with the running numbers 62 and 63 respectively.

Continuing in infrastructure work, the engines were employed in many locations, including for a time at the railway department's own Banksiadale sawmill until the class-leader was withdrawn from traffic in October 1949. Engine 63 managed to soldier on for another four years, when both were eventually scrapped.

SPECIFICATIONS

	IMPERIAL (METRIC)
CYLINDERS:	14½ x 20 IN (37 x 51 CM)
BOILER PRESSURE:	165 PSI (1137 KPA)
COUPLED WHEELS:	3 FT 3 IN (99 CM)
TRACTIVE EFFORT:	14 100 LB (63 KN)
GRATE AREA:	15.5 SQ FT (1.455 M²)
TOTAL WEIGHT:	60 TONS (61 T)
GAUGE:	1067 MM
IDENTIFICATION:	WILUNA AND NORNALUP, WHICH BECAME WAGR 62 AND 63

1928 Victorian Railways

S-class 4-6-2

These magnificent 3-cylinder locomotives have vanished into the realm of folklore despite being one of Australia's finest locomotive types. The loco, which had just four representatives, was designed under the

Edward Henty, alias S302, poses for its portrait late in 1937, upon receiving streamlining and an accompanying long-range tender to work the Albury expresses. (V/Line archives, Len Whalley collection)

direction of Victorian Railways' CME Alfred Smith for premier express passenger operations. All were built at the VR Newport Workshops, emerging between 1928 and 1930.

After an exhausting series of trials, the new locomotives, which became the S-class, immediately replaced the older A2-class 4-6-0s on the prestigious Melbourne–Albury line. When an all-steel set of new carriages was launched by the state Premier, Mr A. Dunstan, on 17 November 1937, all four locomotives had been streamlined and painted blue to match a state-of-the-art train introduced at that time as the *Spirit of Progress.*

At this time the locomotives received large 6-wheel bogie tenders of sufficient capacity for them to operate a crack non-stop service from Melbourne's Spencer Street station to Albury, 190 miles (305 km) distant. The S-class gained an international reputation as an exciting performer and the route offered some really fast sustained running.

VR deliberately encouraged this aura when it commissioned a now classic publicity photograph which showed the streamlined *Spirit of Progress* running a pre-service trial to Geelong with a biplane seemingly being left behind in the train's wake.

The S-class's centre cylinder was driven by conjugated valve gear, introduced five years earlier by Sir Nigel Gresley on his famous LNER A1-class Pacifics in England. It consisted of a clever series of valve extensions and a heavy-duty rack driving a conjugated crosshead. While effective, it was vulnerable to wear and heat expansion, which tended to cause valve-timing difficulties. Not only that, but the entire system had to be dismantled whenever work had to be carried out on the centre cylinder's valve.

All four locomotives were converted to burn oil fuel during 1951–52, and their tenders altered to carry 9100 litres of oil together with 57 300 litres of water.

The coming of the streamlined diesel age on the VR in July 1952 spelled the beginning of the end for the classic S-class locomotives. The newfangled B-class diesel-electrics quickly took charge of the *Spirit of Progress* and reduced the S-class to secondary passenger services and fast goods duties. In this capacity their sphere of operation was restricted to the heavier-railed Geelong and Albury routes, due to their high 23.5-ton axle loads.

As more diesels arrived, the S-class locomotives quickly vanished, S301 being withdrawn on 16 October 1953. S303 followed in May 1954 and on 17 September 1954 the last one, class-leader S300, was withdrawn. The furthest-travelled was S302 which remarkably endured the immense stresses of 2 327 370 km of very fast travel. All were all too quickly scrapped. An increasing number of people say it was 'sheer vandalism' that, despite at least one attempt, an example was not preserved for posterity.

	IMPERIAL (METRIC)
CYLINDERS:	(3) 20½ x 28 IN (52 x 71 CM)
BOILER PRESSURE:	200 PSI (1378 KPA)
COUPLED WHEELS:	6 FT 0 IN (183 CM)
TRACTIVE EFFORT:	41 675 LB (185.5 KN)
GRATE AREA:	50 SQ FT (4.645 M²)
TOTAL WEIGHT:	223.85 TONS (228.3 T)
GAUGE:	1600 MM
ROAD NUMBERS & NAMES:	S300 MATTHEW FLINDERS, S301 SIR THOMAS MITCHELL, 302 EDWARD HENTY, S303 C.J. LATROBE

1928 BROKEN HILL PROPRIETARY CO

Davenport Bo-Bo

This small 28-tonne diesel-electric locomotive was purchased initially to shunt iron-ore vehicles on the floor of the BHP's Iron Knob quarry in South Australia. It was acquired under a modernisation scheme that two years earlier, in 1926, saw the introduction of electric shunting locomotives.

Designed and built by the Davenport Locomotive Works (USA) and delivered in 1928, the 1067 mm gauge unit was originally powered by two Red Seal 6-cylinder petrol engines, each with a rating of 105 hp (74.6 kW). At first identified by the company as PE1, this one-off unit provided the flexibility to operate over trackage where no electric overhead was available because of maintenance or track shifting.

After three decades of service, PE1 was withdrawn from the quarry and converted to diesel-electric operation for service within BHP's new Whyalla

steelworks. Its Red Seal petrol engines were replaced with two Mack Lanover 673-series diesel engines, each with a rating of 170 hp (127 kW). In this form, it re-entered service on 31 August 1966 carrying number DE10.

Its initial duties included the haulage of screened ore and other vital steel-making ingredients over the 3.5 km narrow-gauge railway which linked the ore treatment plant at Hummock Hill with Nos 1 and 2 blast furnaces. However, the demands of the furnaces were greater than the locomotive's rather modest capacity and a Clyde GM main line unit had to be called in until a Walkers B-B diesel-hydraulic was acquired for the line in March 1968. (Five Walkers units had earlier been commissioned for the standard gauge tracks within the steelworks.)

For a time, DE10 acted as a standby unit until finally it was returned to the workshops to be converted to run on the steel mill's standard gauge, its new bogies being fashioned from withdrawn Metropolitan Vickers electric locomotives last used in the Iron Knob quarry. The company's traffic department hoped DE10 would blend with the Walkers units to form a regular works roster. But, despite its use on all four designated shunting areas within the plant, the only job the veteran could manage with any degree of success was the ingot shunt. Since there was usually a spare DH-class available to do this, it saw very little service until withdrawn altogether in 1981.

After an extended storage outside the diesel repair shop, DE10 was eventually donated to the Pichi Richi Railway Preservation Society for exhibition at its Quorn museum.

Equipped with bogies specially configured for standard gauge and salvaged from a quarry electric locomotive, DE10 (as it appeared in its final form) is shown shunting the ingot area in March 1975. (BHP Archives)

IMPERIAL (METRIC)	
POWER UNIT:	(2) RED SEAL 28H
TRACTION HORSEPOWER:	264 (197 KW)
STARTING TRACTIVE EFFORT:	13 200 LB (58.7 KN)
CONTINUOUS TRACTIVE EFFORT:	7 600 LB (33.8 KN)
TOTAL WEIGHT:	27.5 TONS (28 T)
GAUGE (ORIGINAL)	1067 MM (FROM 1968, 1435 MM)
ROAD NUMBER:	PE1 (FROM 1966, DE10)

1928 TYERS VALLEY TRAMWAY

Climax Bo-Bo

The Tyers Valley Tramway, a typical Australian bush timber railway, was located in the Gippsland area of Victoria and operated out of Collins Siding on the VR's 762 mm gauge Moe–Walhalla line. The tramway opened on 12 January 1928, a converted Fordson tractor being used for motive power until a steam locomotive arrived later that year.

The 80 km, 762 mm gauge line served eight sawmills and featured 24.5-metre radius curves. It was laid with a mixture of 19, 20 and 21 kg/m rails.

The company did contemplate buying a 2-6-0 + 0-6-2 Beyer-Garratt similar to the VR G-class which had just come into service on the Walhalla line, but considered such a locomotive would be too heavy. Instead, an order was placed with Alfred Harman of Port Melbourne for a small, geared steam locomotive.

It proved troublesome from the start, and three tractor appliances were used over the network until an order with the Climax Manufacturing Co in the USA for a more substantial bogie-powered geared locomotive could be filled. This locomotive, maker's number 1694, eventually arrived on 6 September 1928. Everything went well until 1933, when the locomotive began to break axles, when it was discovered that they were too light for the power being placed upon them. Tractors again came to the rescue; on one occasion, tests were carried out with an Na-class tank locomotive borrowed from VR with a view to purchasing it.

In 1934, the Climax locomotive again broke an axle and, in derailing, turned onto its side. During its subsequent rebuild, high-tensile steel axles better suited to the conditions were fitted.

This delightfully-proportioned locomotive, which weighed 25 tonnes, boasted two 23 x 30 cm cylinders activated by Stephenson's link motion driving through tail shafts to the two 4-wheel bogies bearing 71 cm wheels. The total wheelbase of the engine was 644 cm and the boiler was registered at 200 psi (1378 kPa). Its rated tractive effort was 10 910 lb (49 kN).

Serious floods in 1935 and bushfires in 1939 provided significant setbacks to the district's once-buoyant timber industry, and it never really recovered. By 1949, output was the lowest ever and, on 5 August of that year, the line was closed. The Climax and the initial Harman locomotive were stored in a shed at Tyers Junction until the Climax engine was rescued in 1950 by the Forestry Commission and sent to work at the state sawmill at nearby Erica. It was eventually donated to the Puffing Billy Preservation Society and, after some decades on exhibition at the diverse Menzies Creek museum, was returned to active tourist service late in 1988 following some six

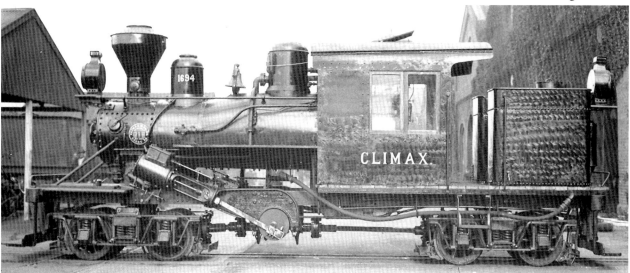

The Climax locomotive at VR's Newport workshops when new. (former VR archives)

years (and 10 000 hours) of dedicated restoration work by staff and members. It is just one of a handful of serviceable Climax locomotives in the world.

The Harman engine was scrapped in 1954.

SPECIFICATIONS

	IMPERIAL (METRIC)
CYLINDERS:	(2) 9 x 12 IN (23 x 30 CM)
BOILER PRESSURE:	200 PSI (1378 KPA)
COUPLED WHEELS:	2 FT 3½ IN (71 CM)
TRACTIVE EFFORT:	10 910 LB (49 KN)
GRATE AREA:	14 SQ FT (1.31 M²)
TOTAL WEIGHT:	24.7 TONS (25 T)
GAUGE:	762 MM

1929 NEW SOUTH WALES GOVERNMENT RAILWAYS

D57-class 4-8-2

The NSWGR's Chief Mechanical Engineer, Ernest Lucy, shared South Australian Railways' Commissioner W.A. Webb's desire for super-power steam locomotives to more efficiently move heavier trains. In Lucy's case, the move to super-power was to become one of his most controversial; it almost destroyed him after fiery questions were continually raised in Parliament for many years afterwards.

Although Lucy's team had been working on the mammoth engine's design for some years, the Commissioner's official approval to design and build the D57-class was not given until May 1927. Following the calling of tenders, which attracted interest throughout the world, the Clyde Engineering Co in Sydney was awarded a contract ten months later to build 25 of the new 232-tonne locomotives.

The class-leader emerged for its initial trial run in August 1929. Its design unveiled a host of newfangled features including the incorporation of a third cylinder operated by Gresley conjugating gear. This patented gear, perfected in England by esteemed LNER mechanical engineer Sir Nigel Gresley, eliminated a third set of valve gears. The D57 was also fitted with one-piece cast steel frames imported from North America, Delta trailing truck, power-assisted reverse gear and automatic coal stokers which fed the massive 65 sq ft (6.039 m²) firebox.

Boasting a 67 per cent tractive effort increase over the state's then largest goods engines, the D50, D53 and D55 classes, the D57-class was destined to remain the NSWGR's most powerful non-articulated locomotive type. However, since these engines were almost 95 per cent heavier than their replacements, their poorer power to weight ratio generated much of the said design's controversy for, despite their brute size and some 90-tonnes weight sitting over the driving wheels, the D57-class was extremely light on its feet.

Another problem which surfaced in Parliament was these engines' alleged ability (caused as it was by indifferent driving) to pull the draw-gear out of what in reality were the rather flimsy hook-coupling wagons of the day. Vehicles with heavier headstocks, automatic

Engine 5714 shows its might as it pauses at Emu Plains in 1932. The locomotive is in 'as delivered condition' with the cross-compound air pumps mounted on the boiler side. (Late Tony Maston)

Truly a big engine: 5715 in original condition, pictured circa 1930. (Author's collection)

drawgear and improved grade-control braking had to be procured which, of course, overcame the 'problem'.

Early and continuing teething troubles centred on a lack of strength in the engines' coupling rods and eccentric crank pins. In many cases, a dangerously flailing, broken or severely bent side-rod would destroy or at best damage the frame-mounted high-capacity air-compressors and brake rigging. One of the first modifications carried out on the class was the repositioning of the vulnerable air pumps to a position adjacent to the smokebox. But revised-strength side-rods were also found to be deficient. Parliament's opposition members continued to have a field day.

The D57s, due to their weight and lengthy wheelbase over which all wheels were flanged, also made a habit of rolling rails over in some yards and depots. As if all these difficulties weren't enough, their extreme width and 24-tonne axle loadings meant that routes had to be specially prepared for the locomotives before they could operate. Some bridges and rails had to be strengthened, platforms needed to be cut back and special facilities were required at

depots, including 90 foot (27.4 metre) turntables, resulting in the D57s being confined to the Sydney–Thirroul, Sydney–Junee and Sydney–Lithgow lines throughout their working lives.

Other modifications included the employment of heavier axle-box and big-end lubricants and associated alterations which eliminated overheating of these parts early in their careers. The coal capacity of one tender was also increased.

With the electrification of the Lithgow line in 1957, no further major overhauls were carried out and withdrawals started with 5702 in October 1957. Loco 5711 was the last of the class in service, withdrawn after working a freight train from Goulburn to Cootamundra on 2 March 1962 (five months after its official withdrawal date). This engine is now under static restoration at the NSWRTM's Valley Heights roundhouse, the remainder having been scrapped. Nevertheless, their memory lingered through the 1960s after some of their huge tenders were coupled into sets and employed as water trains based at Werris Creek.

SPECIFICATIONS

	IMPERIAL (METRIC)
CYLINDERS:	(3) 23¼ x 28 IN (59 x 71 CM)
BOILER PRESSURE:	200 PSI (1378 KPA)
COUPLED WHEELS:	5 FT 0 IN (152 CM)
TRACTIVE EFFORT:	64 327 LB (286.3 KN)
GRATE AREA:	65 SQ FT (6.039 M²)
TOTAL WEIGHT:	227.75 TONS (232.3 T)
GAUGE:	1435 MM
ROAD NUMBERS:	5701–5725

For a work-stained 5717, it was trip's end as it dropped into Lithgow with a Down goods during the early 1950s. This engine represents the class's final form, with the air-compressor clinging to a refashioned smokebox side. (Arthur Reynell)

The Belpaire boiler version of the handsome X-class showing loco X39, complete with smoke deflectors, posing for official photographs upon its completion. (V/Line archives)

1929 Victorian Railways

X-class 2-8-2

This class of 29 heavy main line freight locomotives, introduced in 1929, was regarded as the most powerful type on the VR until the arrival of *Heavy Harry*, the mighty H-class 4-8-4 of 1941.

All 29 X-class were built at the VR's Newport Workshops as an enlarged and improved version of the earlier 2-8-0 C-class, and designed to be easily converted to standard gauge should the need arise.

All locomotives were running by 1947, the later deliveries arriving with Belpaire boilers. With their hefty 172.3 kN tractive effort, it was no longer found necessary to double-head goods trains. To provide even more power, boosters were fitted to all but locomotive X36 which produced an extra 40 kN tractive effort. This equipment included the provision beneath the cab of a small 2-cylinder steam engine to drive the booster fitted to the locomotive's trailing truck.

The X-class was possibly one of the VR's more highly-rated engines and the harder the locomotives were driven the better they steamed and performed. On the debit side, they required expert driving and firing for maximum results. Many a fireman finished his shift complete with the proverbial blistering 'sunburn' because he failed to cover his arms or legs from the white-hot rays that emanated from the large 3.9 m² firebox.

In 1949, X32 was further improved with the fitting of a German-built pulverising coal-burning plant. Although all these engines were earmarked for similar conversion, impending dieselisation saw the plans shelved, along with the intention to build an additional 15 new units. Meanwhile, one highlight of X32's career was its emergency operation of the crack *Spirit of Progress* between Melbourne and Albury with no loss of time, an incredible performance for a goods-type engine. The locomotive was fitted with the pulverising plant at the time.

As diesels quietly made inroads into X-class territory, they were relegated to short-hop transfer goods haulage. They were economically useless in this capacity, however, for they were main line engines of the first order, and scrapping soon started, X43 being the first to go in 1957. The last in service was X36, which was removed from the register in May 1961 and retained for preservation in the ARHS's North Williamstown Railway Museum.

The Belpaire boiler last used in X30 continued to steam on for a further 47 years at the Carter, Holt, Harvey Pinepanels plant in Oberon, New South Wales. It was installed to provide steam to dry timber entering the factory and then help press the finished particleboard, undergoing its initial certification on 4 December 1959. Although still in good internal condition, it was replaced with a gas-fired unit as recently as April 2006. This boiler has been promised to a Victorian preservation body.

SPECIFICATIONS

	Imperial (Metric)
Cylinders:	22 x 28 in (56 x 71 cm)
Boiler pressure:	205 psi (1413 kPa)
Coupled wheels:	5 ft 1 in (155 cm)
Tractive effort:	38 712 lb (172.3 kN)
	Booster added 8900 lb (40 kN)
Grate area:	42 sq ft (3.902 m²)
Total weight:	185.35 tons (189 t)
Gauge:	1600 mm
Road numbers:	27–55

B-class 0-6-0ST

When Hoskins Iron & Steel Co established a new steelworks at Port Kembla in 1929, forming Australian Iron & Steel Pty Ltd (AI&S), the only motive power available to the works consisted largely of low-power nondescript locomotives which had been used in connection with the family's former Lithgow operations.

With the effects of the crippling Great Depression yet to hit, aspirations running high and a new plant guaranteeing space for future expansion, the opportunity was taken to invest in a new, reliable, purpose-built locomotive. Industrial locomotive specialists in the US city of Pittsburgh, H.K. Porter & Co, had the perfect engine, an 0-6-0ST of 62.5 tonnes. Initially, just one engine was ordered; it arrived in Port Kembla in November 1929.

As with other heavy steelworks locomotives, this 0-6-0ST, named *Bandicoot*, found employment in a multitude of roles including jetty shunting and Wongawilli coal train haulage. However, the company had over-borrowed, and on 17 October 1935 the

Broken Hill Proprietary Co acquired all ordinary shares in the business. The combination of new ownership and a country coming out of recession saw considerable expansion and modernisation at Port Kembla and, with annual steel production having reached 120 000 tonnes the previous year, four more 0-6-0STs were ordered, this time from the Clyde Engineering Co in Sydney. Delivered between 1936 and 1938, they were named, in order of construction, *Brolga*, *Bronzewing*, *Baradine* and *Burrawa*.

With the commissioning of another blast furnace a final three 0-6-0STs were constructed within the AI&S's own machine shops. Two of them, *Bellbird* and *Badger*, entered traffic in 1943 and the third, *Bantam*, was completed in 1944. While all eight locomotives were basically similar, several detail differences existed and their weights in working order varied. For instance, the later engines were equipped with higher saddle tanks that provided additional water capacity. In addition, the AI&S-manufactured locomotives possessed ornate, flared chimneys in lieu of the earlier stovepipe type.

A veteran driver recalled how when *Bantam* was new, it would not steam: 'They altered the blast pipe by sharpening the exhaust and fitted the firebox with a brick

Bellbird was one of the final three B-class locomotives constructed in Australian Iron & Steel's own machine shop during the later years of World War II. (Late Colin Oakley)

arch which corrected the problem.' He remembered how all B-class were equipped with steel crossheads running on steel guide bars: 'Originally they had white metal and bronze slippers which lasted just six months. The AI&S modification lasted six years!'

While always intended for internal works use, surviving records indicate some of the Porters were pressed into Wongawilli coal haulage during the 1940s but their operations lasted only for a short time.

Fitted with steam brakes, heavy automatic couplings and large buffer faces to eliminate buffer-lock on sharp curves, the 0-6-0STs remained operational more than two decades into plant dieselisation thanks to the need for steam to work slag-dumping trains. However, these vehicles were converted to air operation by early 1972, allowing for the use of diesel locomotives, with the result that the first B-class was withdrawn in August 1971, the remaining seven following in December that year. With other new diesels on the plant by then, older B-B D9-type units were cascaded down the motive-power pecking order to take over the slag haulage.

The 0-6-0STs were stored beside the company's coke ovens and once in a while fitters would perform minor maintenance on them in anticipation of further use. But a decision in favour of complete dieselisation saw six cut up for scrap during mid-1975. Of the two survivors, *Bronzewing*, after being exhibited at the Thirlmere Railway Museum for more than two decades, was returned to BHP Steel Port Kembla for overhaul, where it was steamed early in 1996 for company public relations use. *Badger* can be found at the Dorrigo Steam Railway & Museum.

Footnote: Both *Bronzewing* and *Bandicoot* were on loan to BHP Newcastle between 1952 and 1956, to arrest that plant's serious post-war locomotive shortages.

SPECIFICATIONS

	Imperial (Metric)
Cylinders:	18 x 24 in (46 x 61 cm)
Boiler pressure:	180 psi (1240 kPa)
Coupled wheels:	3 ft 4 in (102 cm)
Tractive effort:	27 994 lb (124.6 kN)
Grate area:	21 to 25 sq ft (1.951 to 2.323 m²)
Total weight:	61 to 67 tons (62 to 68 t)
Gauge:	1435 mm

Msa-class 2-6-0 + 0-6-2

The ten articulated locomotives in this class were the first Garratt type to be designed and constructed entirely in Australia. They were built at the WAGR's Midland Railway Workshops and the first entered service in February 1930, designated Msa-class.

The WAGR had long been to the forefront of Garratt technology, for back in 1912 it took delivery of six Ma-class 2-6-0 + 0-6-2 machines which became the world's second Beyer-Garratt type. (The first type had been delivered to the TGR three years earlier.) The early WAGR saturated steam Beyer, Peacock & Co locomotives were followed in 1913–14 by seven identical superheated Garratts which became the Ms-class.

The local Msa-class, while basically similar in outline, was an improvement of the superheated Ms-class. While only 4 tonnes heavier, the new locomotives boasted nearly 91 kN extra tractive effort.

They were initially designed to operate over light 20 kg/m rails, working both mixed and goods services in the south-west, but were also used on the Bunbury coal trains. In later years boiler pressure of the Msa-class was reduced by 100 kPa, altering its tractive effort figures to equal the earlier Ms-class.

Although the prototype Ma and Ms classes were written off between 1947 and 1955, the Msa-class lasted as late as 1961, when one was noted working a railway picnic special to Busselton.

All were written off in 1963 and eventually scrapped, with one of the fleet having its final moment of glory at Springhill Army Base outside Northam when it was used for artillery target practice.

Footnote: It is relevant to mention that the Australian Portland Cement Co at Geelong, Victoria, imported two 72.1-tonne 2-6-0 + 0-6-2 superheated Garratts to the same basic design of the WAGR Ms, in 1936 and 1938. Those locomotives were required to work over a 5.6 km, 1067 mm gauge railway with grades as steep as 1 in 36 that linked the company's limestone quarry and the Fyansford cement works. Steam traction was replaced with a single EMD G-8 diesel-electric locomotive in 1956, and Garratt No. 2 was subsequently preserved at the Puffing Billy Museum at Menzies Creek in Victoria.

Msa-class leader 466 outside Midland workshops in February 1930. It was the first Garratt-type locomotive to be built in Australia. (Westrail archives)

SPECIFICATIONS

	IMPERIAL (METRIC)
CYLINDERS:	(4) 13¼ x 20 IN (32 x 51 CM)
BOILER PRESSURE:	175 PSI (1206 KPa)
COUPLED WHEELS:	3 FT 3 IN (99 CM)
TRACTIVE EFFORT:	26 784 LB (119.2 KN)
GRATE AREA:	27 SQ FT (2.508 M²)
TOTAL WEIGHT:	74.1 TONS (75.6 T)
GAUGE:	1067 MM
ROAD NUMBERS:	466–475 (RENUMBERED IN 1948 AS 491–500)

1930 EMU BAY RAILWAY

Beyer-Garratt
4-8-2 + 2-8-4

The three locomotives of this class were ordered by the Electrolytic Zinc Co of Australia for use over the 88 mile (140 km) Emu Bay Railway on Tasmania's west coast.

Huge in all respects, and certainly larger, heavier and more powerful than any locomotive in Tasmania at that time, the three 4-8-2 + 2-8-4 locomotives were built by Beyer, Peacock at Manchester in 1929. All arrived on the one ship on 14 February 1930 and progressively entered service following a trial run by the class-leader, No. 12, on 9 March 1930.

According to Beyer, Peacock & Co documents acquired by the author, these superheated locomotives were designed to haul 400 tons (406 tonnes) on 50 lb/yard rail over 1 in 40 gradients. On one test, Beyer, Peacock noted that 496 tonnes was lifted from a standing start on such a gradient. At the time of their

delivery, more than 100 000 tonnes of zinc, lead and copper ore was being hauled annually over the railway, which linked Rosebery to Burnie.

The trio was taken out of service during the early 1960s, largely replaced by surplus Australian Standard Garratts purchased from the TGR and Queensland Railways. The first one withdrawn was locomotive 13, stopped in August 1961 and scrapped almost immediately. No. 12 was the last in service, withdrawn in August 1963 and scrapped in September 1964. No. 14, which was stopped in June 1962, was not cut up until June 1964.

SPECIFICATIONS

	IMPERIAL (METRIC)
CYLINDERS:	(4) 16½ x 22 IN (42 x 56 CM)
COUPLED WHEELS:	3 FT 7 IN (110 CM)
BOILER PRESSURE:	180 PSI (1240 KPa)
TRACTIVE EFFORT:	42 630 LB (188 KN)
GRATE AREA:	43.6 SQ FT (3.980 M²)
TOTAL WEIGHT:	132.6 TONS (134.7 T)
GAUGE:	1067 MM
ROAD NUMBERS:	12–14

One of the Emu Bay Beyer-Garratt locomotives standing in Burnie yard. (Roydon Burk collection)

The massive bulk of SAR's 232-tonne 720-class is shown to advantage in this study, taken at Tailem Bend depot in September 1954. (Douglas Colquhoun)

1930 South Australian Railways

720-class 2-8-4

Despite adverse publicity in Parliament and the press regarding the suitability of SAR Commissioner Webb's big-engine policy, plans were prepared in 1929 for an intended 30 heavy freight locomotives. Massive in all proportions, the new locomotive type was to become the 720-class.

To provide even more starting power, Webb specified a booster-powered 4-wheel trailing truck, which also fractionally reduced the axle loading at the rear of the engine. Like all Webb engines, the 720s were based on American practice.

Of the 30 originally mooted, only five were initially ordered from the SAR's Islington Workshops, the first entering traffic on 26 November 1930. Originally intended for the state's broad-gauge lighter lines as a more powerful answer to the earlier 700/710-classes, the new 232-tonne locomotives began to spread the rails, particularly on curves, and thus had to be confined to the heavier main lines.

Islington Workshops was authorised to construct an additional five of this class during the mid-1930s, and these entered traffic between October 1938 and May 1939. During their construction, the order was increased by a further seven, and all 17 were running by August 1943. However, the final seven differed in that they were provided with streamlined valances

and most of the external boiler plumbing and fittings was enclosed in an attractive outer casing. They also boasted large 6-wheel bogie tenders and all in all were a really impressive engine.

With a severe shortage of coal during the national coal strike of 1949, all but three were converted to burn an oil-coal fuel mixture. They were changed back to coal in 1952, but were again converted to oil the following year, and in 1954 most were fitted with full oil-burning equipment.

With the 'second wave' of dieselisation during the mid-1950s, the 720s were quickly withdrawn. The first one condemned was 734 in March 1958. These and subsequent withdrawals sat in store at Islington for several years and, in what amounted to a book entry, the last six condemnations were made official on 14 April 1960. All have been scrapped.

SPECIFICATIONS

	Imperial (Metric)
Cylinders:	22 x 28 in (56 x 71 cm)
Boiler pressure:	215 psi (1481 kPa)
Coupled wheels:	4 ft 9 in (145 cm)
Tractive effort:	43 450 lb (193.4 kN)
Grate area:	46.8 sq ft (4.348 m²)
Total weight:	227.4 tons (232 t)
Gauge:	1600 mm
Road numbers:	720–736

Qunaba Mill's 0-6-2T *Flash* at work in 1965. (Late Ron Preston)

1934 Perry Engineering

Sugar industry
0-4-2 / 0-6-2T

Although most of the steam locomotives engaged in the intensive Queensland sugar tramway industry were imported from Britain or Europe, the Australian firm Perry Engineering Co Ltd began marketing a 610 mm gauge engine as early as 1934.

Designed by Perry's chief engineer, the late Mr L.C. Leslie, and based on an earlier company industrial design, the first engine, an 0-6-2T, was purchased in May 1934 by the Kalamia Sugar Mill.

By October 1951, no fewer than 19 had been delivered to Queensland sugar mill and council operators, six of this number built to the more flexible 0-4-2T wheel arrangement.

Perry Engineering's roots dated back to 1897 when a young Englishman, Samuel Perry, arrived in South Australia and purchased a small blacksmithing business in Hindley Street, Adelaide. Initially building horse carriages and trolleys, the business quickly grew and in 1908, with a view to future expansion, Perry purchased about 5 hectares of land at Mile End. A few years later he received an order

from the SAR to construct 12 steam locomotive boilers and in 1912 began moving his Hindley Street operations to a new workshop at Mile End. By 1913, his entire business was being conducted from the new site.

Two years later, Perry Engineering acquired the long-established locomotive building firm James Martin & Co of Gawler, which at that time was the largest engineering company in South Australia. With this acquisition, Perry's fame and fortune grew, and before long the firm was building locomotives for the Commonwealth, South Australian and Tasmanian railway systems.

In particular to assist with the Tasmanian contract for Q and R class 4-8-2 / 4-6-2s, the company acquired the services of Mr Leslie, a consulting engineer based in Melbourne. While working in that capacity, Mr Leslie had designed a chunky 0-4-0T industrial locomotive type for the 1067 mm gauge Victorian State River & Water Supply Commission's railway. Eight appeared during 1923–27 for use in the construction of the Hume Weir. The Melbourne & Metropolitan Board of Works acquired an additional nine in 1928 for the Silvan Dam's construction.

Flushed with success, Perry Engineering finally gained the full-time services of Mr Leslie. Soon after taking up duty, he designed a 610 mm gauge version of his earlier locomotive for cane and industrial use. Weighing 19 tonnes and boasting enough water and coal/fuel capacity to give the locomotives a wide range, the type became a firm favourite with 12 sugar mills.

All were built with saturated boilers and a generous heating surface of 31.59 m². With a tractive effort of 32 kN, the little locomotives ultimately earned big reputations for their power and reliability.

With dieselisation, all were gradually withdrawn, the last two in service being an 0-6-2T at Qunaba Mill (withdrawn after the 1979 season) and a similar engine at Marian Mill (held for yard shunting work until December 1982).

Only three of these engines (all 0-4-2Ts) have actually been scrapped, the rest finding places in enthusiast-sponsored museums and preservation schemes almost nationwide. Of the more meticulously-restored examples, a 0-6-2T built in 1949 for Tully Mill can be seen working at the Illawarra Light Railway Society's Albion Park Museum, Qunaba Mill's 0-6-2T *Flash* is at The Workshops Rail Museum at North Ipswich. North Eton Mill's Nos 6 and 7 have found a home on the Lake Macquarie Light Railway at the outer Newcastle (NSW) suburb of Toronto where one has been restored to working order. A Marian Mill 0-6-2T operates at Chinderah near Murwillumbah, NSW; South Johnson Mill's No. 9 is operational at Gisborne Steam Park (Vic); Babinda Mill's No. 7 operates at Heyfield, Victoria; Qunaba Mill's *Skipper* is at the National Railway Museum, Port Adelaide, while Inkerman Mill's *Adelaide* operates at the Bennett Brook Railway (WA).

SPECIFICATIONS

	IMPERIAL (METRIC)
CYLINDERS:	10 x 14 IN (25 x 36 CM)
BOILER PRESSURE:	180 PSI (1240 KPA)
COUPLED WHEELS:	2 FT 4 IN (71 CM)
TRACTIVE EFFORT:	7200 LB (32 KN)
GRATE AREA:	7.2 SQ FT (4.819 M²)
TOTAL WEIGHT:	19 TONS (19.4 T)
GAUGE:	610 MM

Ruston & Hornsby 0-4-0 / 0-6-0

The British firm of Ruston & Hornsby, based in Lincoln, exported no fewer than 90 principally 4-wheel 0-4-0 diesel-powered industrial locomotives to Australia between 1935 and 1960.

This company was established in September 1918 when Ruston, Proctor & Co and Richard Hornsby & Sons merged. Although general engineers, both firms had dabbled in locomotive construction, particularly during World War I when they delivered light 4-wheel gasoline units to armament manufacturers. The former had been involved in limited steam locomotive manufacture while the latter firm had experimented with heavy oil or paraffin locomotives since the 1890s.

The merged company commenced diesel production with a vengeance from 1931, with many hundreds of locomotives built to several standard designs being delivered to railway operators large and small across the globe. Research indicates that no fewer than 14 different R&H designs eventually arrived in Australia, ranging from 3.6-tonne locomotives in the 'dinky' 13.4 kW 610 mm gauge through to a 115 kW 28-tonne standard gauge type. In addition, at least four locomotives were imported second-hand from South Africa and the UK.

The earliest R&H unit to see service in Australia seems to have been a 5.5-tonne 610 mm gauge unit delivered to the Marvel Loch Gold Mine, Western Australia, in 1935. The most widely used model was the 20DL, twenty-eight of which were delivered to several operators, including 13 to the NSWGR in 1950–51. The NSW units were acquired to haul spoil trains in connection with the Eastern Suburbs Railway construction, specifically between Sydney's Domain and a proposed station at Martin Place.

They were officially known as 20DLU units, the 'U' denoting underground use. When construction of that line was halted in August 1952 due to a shortage of funds, the units were stored for a while at Sydenham prior to their dispatch to the Water Supply workshops, Chullora, where it is known at least four survived for eventual preservation.

Other 20DL and 20DLU locomotives found employment at collieries and sugar mills.

Built new for the Melbourne & Metropolitan Board of Works in 1949, the 2-cylinder 4-wheel DM 30DL product is shown operating at the Illawarra Light Railway Museum Society in March 2006. Eventually finding its way to a Melbourne machinery dealer, the locomotive was sold to Leighton Contractors Pty Ltd on 18 January 1972 for a tunnel construction project at Warriewood (NSW), later finding work at the Belconnen sewerage tunnel (ACT). The museum has a second, slightly smaller unit which was built as a 20DLU in 1951 for the Eastern Suburbs Railway and later used by the NSW Metropolitan Water, Sewerage & Drainage Board. (Kevin Waid)

Fifteen slightly larger 30DL locomotives also came to Australia, the largest number going to Victoria's Melbourne & Metropolitan Board of Works. Others found employment in collieries, sugar mills and at Mt Isa Mines.

There was also a 3-cylinder 40DL model; a 1953 survivor, used initially at Titanium Alloy Manufacturing Co, Cudgen (NSW), spent the years from 1958 to 1976 hauling sugar cane at CSR's Condong Sugar Mill in northern New South Wales. When that mill closed, the locomotive was employed by the NSW Co-operative Sugar Mill Association from 1978 to 1994, and in 2004 was donated to the Illawarra Light Railway Museum Society at Albion Park (NSW) where it is undergoing restoration.

The second most widely-used R&H model in Australia was the 48DL (or 48DLU), 20 of which arrived on these shores for roles in organisations as diverse as sewage treatment works, sugar mills and, again, collieries. Gin Gin Sugar Mill in Queensland even imported two second-hand from Rhodesia.

Several R&H locomotives have found their way into preservation and tourist train service. They include a Bingera Sugar Mill 1956-built 48DL and a 1954 model Caledonian Colliery-owned 30DL, both

of which were acquired by the Nambour-based Big Pineapple tourist attraction, the latter engine being loosely reconfigured to resemble a steam locomotive.

The largest units of all were four standard-gauge Model 165DS machines built for heavy industry. The Shell Oil Refinery in Sydney obtained a November 1953-built machine to shunt rail tankers at its Clyde terminal. The engine became redundant following the commissioning of a bulk fuel terminal and was sold in 1964 to the then Commonwealth Railways for workshop shunting at Port Augusta, where it became DR1. It is preserved at the Richmond Vale Railway Museum in the NSW Hunter Valley along with a 1952-model 20DLU and a 1956-built 30DLU ex Nymboida Colliery, both built for 610 mm gauge.

Simsmetal purchased two second-hand from the NSW PWD, while ICI South Australia bought one unit for shunting at its Osborne (Adelaide) plant. This locomotive (maker's no. 304475), which left the company's works in December 1951, was earlier exhibited at the Festival of Britain. It was replaced at ICI (now Penrice Soda Products) in the late 1980s with an AN 500-class, and is now a National Railway Museum, Port Adelaide, exhibit.

A Ruston & Hornsby 3-cylinder Model 40DL as used by Condong Sugar Mill, located on Murwillumbah's northern outskirts. (Brian Chamberlain)

This Ruston & Hornsby locomotive (B/No. 304475 of 1951) typifies the company's larger products. It was pictured at ICI's (now Penrice Soda Products) Port Adelaide plant on 31 January 1980. The unit now basks in the National Railway Museum, Port Adelaide. (Leon Oberg)

Ruston & Hornsby 88DS (B/No 326064 of 1952) which was delivered to the Helensburgh-based Metropolitan Colliery in 1953 for standard-gauge yard shunting work. It was transferred to BHP's Port Kembla steel works in 1982 and sold in February 1983 to the Unanderra firm Westweb Civil Engineering, where it was cut up for scrap in May 1988. (Brian Chamberlain)

SPECIFICATIONS
(FIGURES DENOTE LARGEST 165DS DESIGN)

	IMPERIAL (METRIC)
POWER UNIT:	RUSTON 6VPHL
TRACTION HORSEPOWER:	150 (113 KW)
MAXIMUM TRACTIVE EFFORT:	13 600 LB (60.5 KN)
TOTAL WEIGHT:	28 TONS (28.6 T)
GAUGE:	1435 MM

1936 SOUTH AUSTRALIAN RAILWAYS

620-class 4-6-2

Commissioner Webb of the SAR had established firm groundwork for improved train operations on his system, but despite his good work, elderly S-class 4-4-0 and Rx-class 4-6-0 locomotives were still treading much of the broad-gauge network in the 1930s.

By the mid-1930s Webb needed light-line replacements for these locos, because traffic over the state's branch lines was increasing as the effects of the crippling depression earlier that decade were becoming a bitter memory. Accordingly, drawings were prepared for a light-lines Pacific to be known as the 620-class.

Ten were ordered from the Islington Workshops. Since South Australia's centennial celebrations coincided with the arrival of the first of the class, 620, the locomotive was specially streamlined, fitted with a chrome steel grille, painted a striking green and exhibited at the Wayville Showgrounds in Adelaide.

On 16 June 1936, three months after it emerged from the workshops, 620 was released for trials and worked under speed to Gawler and return. The locomotive entered revenue service ten days later.

None of the subsequent deliveries was streamlined, and all ten were running by late March 1938.

A novel feature of these locomotives was their Baker valve gear (reputed to be able to achieve squarer valve settings); as the maintenance costs of this equipment proved to be very high, no other locomotives on the SAR were so fitted.

The 620s operated over all but the lightest of the state's branch lines and were favourites with the crews when used on Adelaide suburban services. Their long-stroke cylinders, ample boiler capacity and large grates gave these locomotives considerable

Locomotive 621 with a Tailem Bend-bound passenger train at Murray Bridge in 1971. (Graham Cotterall)

sustaining power.

Smoke deflectors were subsequently fitted while, in August 1949, two were converted to oil-burners. In addition, 620 lost its streamlining.

Before dieselisation finally overtook the class in the mid-1950s, its last stronghold was the Adelaide–Tailem Bend and Gladstone–Willunga lines. The first to be withdrawn was 620 in July 1961, and all ten were written off by September 1969. Local enthusiasts spearheaded 621's return to service for special tourist train operations, and today the sturdy locomotive is the centrepiece in the ARHS's SteamRanger tour operations which are centred on the Victor Harbor line.

Loco 624 has been preserved at the National Railway Museum, Port Adelaide.

SPECIFICATIONS

	IMPERIAL (METRIC)
CYLINDERS:	18½ x 28 IN (47 x 71 CM)
BOILER PRESSURE:	200 PSI (1378 KPA)
COUPLED WHEELS:	5 FT 6 IN (168 CM)
TRACTIVE EFFORT:	24 683 LB (109.8 KN)
GRATE AREA:	33.4 SQ FT (3.103 M²)
TOTAL WEIGHT:	140.75 TONS (143.6 T)
GAUGE:	1600 MM
ROAD NUMBERS:	620–629

1938 COMMONWEALTH RAILWAYS

C-class 4-6-0

In a bid to cut travelling times between Adelaide and Kalgoorlie, the Commonwealth Railways completed construction of a new standard-gauge railway between Port Augusta and Port Pirie in 1937. This extension was built to connect the CR with neighbouring South Australian Railway's broad gauge line from Adelaide to Port Pirie and thus eliminate the need to traverse the slow, more circuitous narrow gauge railway between Terowie and Port Augusta. The master plan was to speed up trains and introduce new, heavier carriages over both routes.

The CR administration was quick to realise, however, that any speed-up of services on the Trans-Australian Railway would not be possible with the existing G and Ga class 4-6-0 locomotives. More powerful engines were clearly the answer.

In keeping with CR's earlier motive-power acquisitions strategy, the NSWGR was approached to provide the drawings of its successful C36-class 4-6-0 design, 75 of which were at that time handling with ease the state's express passenger duties. Modifications to the design to suit CR's needs were few. Cab roof ventilation was added while extra boiler washout plugs were included in the firebox. A cow-catcher hung from a bufferless bufferbeam and automatic couplings were fitted.

Commonwealth Railways' C65, showing to advantage its monster 6-wheel tender. (Author's collection)

The major change, in a bid to increase fuel and water capacity for the long desert hauls, was the addition of enormous 6-wheel bogie tenders capable of carrying 18 tonnes of coal and 56 360 litres of water. (The C36-class tender carried 14.2 tonnes and 28 400 litres.) This added 48 tonnes to the locomotive's all-up weight.

The Queensland heavy engineering firm, Walkers Ltd, was the successful tenderer for eight locomotives and the first entered service as No. 63 in January 1938. All were running by late April of that year. The C-class was the largest steam locomotive ever constructed by Walkers.

The C-class's capabilities were quickly capitalised upon, for not only could CR increase its passenger loadings to 510 tonnes, it could also prune as much as 10.5 hours off the *Trans-Australia Express* timetable in both directions.

During the C-class's years of operation, a number of small modifications were made to improve performance. For instance, slide-bar cover plates were fitted to reduce sand damage to the valve gear. High-mounted smoke deflectors were added to lift smoke from the cab while at least two, 65 and 68, received cowling over the full length of their boilers. The Commissioner must have liked the result because engine 68 was for many years his personal tour engine.

Between July and August 1949, locos 63, 65, 67, 68 and 69 were converted to burn oil fuel in a bid to overcome the national coal strike, and huge 15 900 litre tanks were fitted to their tenders. All were returned to coal-burners a few months later as the emergency passed.

The arrival of GM-class diesel-electrics from September 1951 spelled the end for the hard-working C-class, the first to go being the last built, loco 69, in January 1952. Five more were withdrawn the following month and those remaining were used as shunters at Port Pirie and Kalgoorlie. For a time, another stood pilot at Cook in case of a diesel failure.

With additional diesels on hand, 63 was withdrawn in February 1956 and the last engine operational, 65, was withdrawn in September 1957. It was retained for some years in case floodwaters made the Trans-Australian Railway impassable to diesel-electrics.

Sadly, none were spared scrapping, although some tenders were retained as water carriers for CR's weed-killer train, and two L-class Mikado locomotives, 80 and 81, were fitted with C-class tenders in 1952 for the construction of the Stirling North–Brachina standard gauge line. Some tender bogies could still be found beneath service rolling stock at Port Augusta and Stirling North as recently as January 1998.

SPECIFICATIONS

	IMPERIAL (METRIC)
CYLINDERS:	23 x 26 IN (58 x 66 CM)
BOILER PRESSURE:	180 PSI (1240 KPA)
COUPLED WHEELS:	5 FT 9 IN (175 CM)
TRACTIVE EFFORT:	30 498 LB (135.7 KN)
GRATE AREA:	30.5 SQ FT (2.833 M²)
TOTAL WEIGHT:	207 TONS (211.1 T)
GAUGE:	1435 MM
ROAD NUMBERS:	62–69

1939 QUEENSLAND RAILWAYS

DL-class 2-6-0DM

Although the NSWGR had commissioned the diesel-powered *Silver City Comet* in 1937, and other states including Queensland had been using internal combustion railmotors since the 1910s, the Queensland Railways DL-class was the first diesel-powered locomotive type to run on an Australian government railway. Introduced in 1939, the DL-class preceded serious dieselisation in Australia by about a decade.

Designed to work over the steeply graded and lightly laid Etheridge line in remote northern

DL.2 *Forsayth* at Townsville in July 1973. (Peter Watts)

Queensland, the first DL-class unit appeared as an 0-6-0DM. Initial trials close to Brisbane found the unit to be a rough rider so it was returned to its builder, Ipswich Railway Workshops, and a leading pony wheel was added.

Out-shopped once again, this time as a 2-6-0DM, the locomotive was finally transferred north, where it replaced light railmotors unable to cope with the modestly expanding traffic. (Floods had damaged the Etheridge line so severely in 1927 that even the lightest steam locomotives were banned from the route.)

Powered with a 114 kW Gardner engine and employing mechanical transmission, DL.1 was joined by a sister unit in 1954, after increasing traffic over the nearby Forsayth line again began taxing the railmotors. DL.2 came from the British firm Robert Stephenson & Hawthorn. On entering service, the unit was named *Forsayth*.

As traffic in the area continued to increase, an additional two were ordered from the Queensland firm Walkers Ltd. They entered service in 1961 and were named after stations along the route they were to work: DL.3 becoming *Mt Surprise* and DL.4 *Almaden*. Both were wired for multiple-unit operation, the original two subsequently receiving this facility.

The final two locomotives appear to have been only a stop-gap for, later in the 1960s, the lines over which they worked were progressively rebuilt with heavier rails capable of carrying 1620-class diesel-electric locomotives. All the DLs were subsequently withdrawn and for a time their future looked bleak. However, their duty was not finished, for by mid-1982 DL.1 and DL.3, both now boasting enclosed cabs (of different designs), could be found shunting at Wallangarra and Ipswich shops while DL.2 and DL.4 were working out of Townsville. One of the latter pair was regularly on hand at Ayr, a sub-depot

to Townsville. DL.4 was to rise in status on 6 May 1988 when it was sent north to work a *Gulflander* service over the isolated but world-famous 152 km Normanton–Croydon line while the regular railmotor was being overhauled.

Despite being written off on 14 October 1987, all four remain: DL.1 is exhibited at The Workshops Rail Museum at North Ipswich, DL.2 has been plinthed in Forsayth; DL.3 operates at the ARHS's Rosewood Railway Museum and DL.4 is at Normanton.

SPECIFICATIONS

	IMPERIAL (METRIC)
POWER UNIT:	GARDNER
TRACTION HORSEPOWER:	153 (114 kW)
MAXIMUM TRACTIVE EFFORT:	7035 LB (31 kN)
TOTAL WEIGHT:	17 TONS (17.5 T)
GAUGE:	1067 MM
ROAD NUMBERS:	DL.1–DL.4

1939 TASMANIAN GOVERNMENT RAILWAYS

Ds-class 2-6-4T

Seriously in need of suburban tank engines to work expanding Hobart services, in 1939 the TGR turned to the New Zealand Railways, which had surplus home-grown Wf-class 2-6-4T locomotives available at short notice. Forty-one of these had been built between 1904 and 1928 for suburban passenger and branch-line service. The initial four Tasmanian acquisitions were joined in 1944 by another four.

Classified Ds, the 'new' locomotives, built by the New Zealand Railway Workshops and by A. & G. Price Ltd of Thames, New Zealand, offered more than twice the tractive effort and a better turn of speed with much heavier trains than could be offered by TGR's elderly Beyer, Peacock-built suburban tank engines, the 2-4-2T D-class, which dated back to 1891.

Regarded as good riders and, with their outside Walschaerts valve gear, convenient to maintain, the Ds-class also saw service on shunting rosters and a handful of branch lines, including (1949–51) Ds7 on the Don Junction–Melrose link where crews had long complained of the chilly conditions when running tender first because of the lack of turning facilities at Melrose.

However, their new life in Tasmania was short, for Ds2, Ds3 and Ds6 went into storage from 1949

Locomotive Ds2 newly assembled at Launceston in 1939. (Brian Chamberlain collection)

and were scrapped circa 1951. Engines Ds1 and Ds4 were sold to the Mt Lyell Railway in 1952, where they worked for several more years; the last engine in TGR traffic was Ds7, which was set aside in 1957 and scrapped in May the following year.

SPECIFICATIONS

	IMPERIAL (METRIC)
CYLINDERS:	14 x 22 IN (55 x 71 CM)
BOILER PRESSURE:	200 PSI (1378 KPA)
COUPLED WHEELS:	3 FT 9 IN (114 CM)
TRACTIVE EFFORT:	16 289 LB (72 KN)
GRATE AREA:	15.4 SQ FT (1.40 M²)
TOTAL WEIGHT:	43.7 TONS (44.5 T)
GAUGE:	1067 MM
ROAD NUMBERS:	DS1–DS8

1941 VICTORIAN RAILWAYS

H-class 4-8-4

The Victorian Railways' single H-class engine, or 'Heavy Harry' as it was affectionately known, was the largest on the system and the heaviest non-articulated steam locomotive ever used in Australia. It was originally bought to eliminate double-heading of the important *The Overland* interstate express.

At the time 'Heavy Harry' was being built, the A2-class 4-6-0 locomotives of 1907 vintage were used to pull this interstate express. They could not cope single-handed with the heavy grades over much of the route and VR realised it was time to generally upgrade the service by re-powering the train and strengthening the bridges.

Initially three H-class locomotives were ordered from VR's Newport Railway Workshops but, following the delivery of class-leader H220 in February 1941, work on the others had to be suspended because available funds and manpower efforts had to be redirected to World War II support requirements. Nor were the necessary bridge repair works on the Western line able to be carried out.

Despite the wartime austerity, 'Heavy Harry', being Victoria's biggest locomotive (and the state's answer to Webb's super-locomotives on the SAR and Lucy's D57-class on the NSWGR) and thus a source of great pride, was unveiled to the public at Spencer Street station. Among its features were double chimneys, three cylinders, American-styled bar frames and a giant 6.3 m² grate area which was fed automatically by a steam-operated worm, and a combustion chamber with thermic siphon to ensure high steaming rates. 'Heavy Harry' carried the highest boiler pressure 220 psi (1516 kPa) of any Australian locomotive at the time, only being eclipsed by the NSWGR's celebrated C38-class Pacifics at 245 psi (1688 kPa) two years later.

The impressive bulk of H220 is evident in this study of the locomotive at Wodonga, circa 1952. (Arthur Reynell)

VR's S-class 3-cylinder Pacifics employed Gresley conjugate valve gear to the centre cylinder, but the H-class's designing engineers came up with an improved and simplified version of levers in response to the administration's concerns about the trouble maintenance staff were experiencing with the S-class's motion, not to mention the time taken to dismantle the valve gear when work was necessary on the centre cylinder.

The successful system used on the H-class was made possible because the engine's centre cylinder was set forward of the outer two. This had another positive advantage, in that the centre crank drove the leading driving wheel while the outside two drove the second axle. This divided drive system produced a better balanced engine free of the rotational hammer-blow experienced with other 3-cylinder types, whose three cylinders were usually located directly on the one plane with the connecting rods all driving the same axle.

No. 220, which soon after its arrival was equipped with smoke deflectors, spent almost all of its life hauling fast freight trains over the North-eastern line between Melbourne and Wodonga. Occasionally it had the opportunity to demonstrate what it was really capable of, when called upon to replace a failed Pacific streamliner on passenger working.

'Heavy Harry' was taken out of service in April 1958 following the arrival of S-class Co-Co diesel-electrics, and lay in store at Newport for many years before saved for preservation within the North Williamstown Railway Museum. Surviving records indicate that the big engine ran a creditable 1 314 976 km during its relatively short working life.

SPECIFICATIONS

	IMPERIAL (METRIC)
CYLINDERS:	(3) 21½ x 28 IN (55 x 71 CM)
BOILER PRESSURE:	220 PSI (1516 KPA)
COUPLED WHEELS:	5 FT 7 IN (170 CM)
TRACTIVE EFFORT:	55 008 LB (244.8 KN)
GRATE AREA:	68 SQ FT (6.3 M²)
TOTAL WEIGHT:	260.05 TONS (265.3 T)
GAUGE:	1600 MM
ROAD NUMBER:	H220

1943 NEW SOUTH WALES GOVERNMENT RAILWAYS

C38-class 4-6-2

Regarded as Australia's ultimate in steam design and construction, this class of 30 heavy Pacifics was built to work the NSWGR's top express services. The locomotives were so successful in this role that a number were still working passenger expresses 14 years after serious dieselisation began.

The C38-class was designed by the NSWGR's principal design engineer (later CME), Harold Young, in the late 1930s. As did the D57-class (the design of which included some input from Mr Young), the massively-proportioned C38 incorporated a cast steel chassis. This design also embodied cast Boxpok coupled wheels for improved rotational balance, and the Delta trailing truck.

A contract to assemble five locomotives (with some key parts supplied from the railway's own Eveleigh

An August 1943 scene inside the Clyde Engineering Co's Granville, NSW, erecting shop as three 38-class engines and a TGR Q-class (foreground) near completion. Undergoing in-steam adjustments on that day was 3803, flanked by 3804 and 3805 nearest wall. (Author's collection)

works), was awarded to the Clyde Engineering Co at Granville. Construction coincided with delays caused by World War II and the class-leader, 3801, did enter service until 22 January 1943.

The locomotive initially possessed just one main teething problem—nobody could maintain steam in its 1688 kPa boiler. Two firemen were assigned to the engine during 3801's early Southern line trials, and travelling inspector the late Jack Bowen recalled how 'some gun passenger firemen brought in from Eveleigh in February 1943 even tried using long handle shovels'.

Mr Bowen, who was appointed to Goulburn depot for the introduction of the C38s, recalled that the problem was solved when an imported Bathurst fireman insisted on inspecting the locomotive's blast pipe. He demonstrated how the blast pipe's shape made it impossible for the steam to cleanly clear the chimney's apron, which affected the smokebox's vacuum action on the fire grate. When the blast pipe nozzle was altered, 3801 erupted as a good steam locomotive should.

In an emotional interview many years later, the then retired Harold Young acknowledged that he was a great lover of the racehorse and his C38-class was deliberately designed to be 'his racehorse'. And it surely was, for its wheels were equipped with roller bearings, its throttle linkage activated a valve in the smokebox-mounted superheater-header, its valve gear was provided with Franklin power reverse equipment and its valve timings were so meticulous

Locomotive 3808 rolls through Casula with No. 50 Moss Vale to Sydney passenger on 7 December 1963. (Leon Oberg)

Immaculately preserved by the Powerhouse Museum, non-streamlined 3830 prepares to depart Sydney station with an excursion train on 24 September 2005. An interesting original feature of the C38 all-steel boiler design was the connection between the inclined round boiler and the tapered square-top (Belpaire) firebox throat plate. The difficulty of connecting the two was overcome by fitting what became known as a Belpaire ring, which was flanged from flat plate. (Leon Oberg)

that experienced drivers all agreed the 38-class was an 'excitement machine' in all respects.

All five of the Clyde-built locomotives were semi-streamlined.

As the last of the five were emerging from the Clyde plant, a decision was made to build 25 more. Because the streamlined casing was adding to routine maintenance time, the new locomotives were deliberately non-streamlined, and construction responsibilities were kept in-house, with the Department's Eveleigh Workshops constructing the even-numbered ones and Cardiff Railway Workshops (Newcastle) the odd-numbered ones.

All C38s were running by 27 September 1949. They were designed as replacements for the 1925 vintage C36-class 4-6-0s and were capable of running heavier trains at faster speeds. For instance, a C38 could manage up to 450 tons over the 1 in 75 grades of the Main Southern line.

Due to its high 22.5 ton axle load, the C38-class was to some extent restricted in its steam-days route availability and was only rostered to work over the Sydney–Albury, Sydney–Dubbo, Sydney–Newcastle and Sydney–Thirroul lines. It

also operated for a short time over the North Coast line until track problems surfaced.

The C38 was designed to be fired with the very best 14 000 BTU Abermain coal, and engineering apprentice schools in the 1940s–50s were told coal consumption was regarded as about 2.8 lb per horsepower rating or some 43 hp per square foot grate area. This provided an economically achievable 2021 hp. NSWGR tests at the time demonstrated that while higher outputs were achievable, fuel consumption at such output became an 'uneconomical' factor.

This class also boasted the highest boiler pressure, 245 psi (1688 kPa), of any steam locomotive in Australia.

The C38 locomotives were destined to become the only Pacifics on the NSWGR. In their heyday, all were painted a distinctive verdant green, but with dieselisation the work required to keep the livery waxed was considered unwarranted, and all except 3813 were painted standard black. Subsequent representations from railway enthusiast groups saw green livery restored to 3801 and 3830 during the 1960s. In addition to their normal duties, these locomotives were used by the Department and by

Locomotive 3827 storms through Murrays Flat station while working the Down Goulburn day train on 26 October 1963. (Leon Oberg)

enthusiast bodies for special occasions.

Although the arrival of the 42 and 43 class diesel-electrics in 1955–56 initially robbed the C38s of some of the prestige work, notably the *Melbourne Limited* and *Central West* expresses, these classic 4-6-2s remained proud and purposeful until mid-1958, when sufficient numbers of Alco 44-class diesel-electrics had arrived. Some then began to appear on goods services, a job they performed with startling success, for the strength and performance they brought to the task was awe inspiring. A C38 would regularly climb the 1 in 66 Wingello bank with a regulation 595-tonne goods train with the valve gear about 5.1 turns off full forward. When pressed, some members of the class, including 3830, have been noted climbing the same grade with an overloaded 612-tonne train with the valve gear set almost 5.8 turns back.

The first engine to be withdrawn was 3826, after it collided with a 265-tonne Beyer-Garratt at Glenlee Junction while hauling the *Melbourne Express* in 1961. Gradually accidents claimed another few victims, with 3817 branded a 'hoo-doo engine' by the Sydney press in 1963 when it collided with a Garratt at Geurie. It was 3817's third serious roll-over accident.

By 1962 a number of these locos, including class-leader 3801, had been withdrawn at Eveleigh for scrapping. However, increasing tensions between the USA and Cuba, coupled with the uncertainties of diesel supplies should a conflict erupt, saw all serviceable members of the class shopped for general overhauls. As tensions evaporated, future heavy overhauls were abandoned and the C38s again started falling by the

wayside as mechanical condition dictated. The class-leader was again withdrawn, but enthusiasts were determined to save this grand streamliner and raised much of the hard cash required to overhaul it. No. 3801 was subsequently destined to work enthusiast and departmental specials throughout New South Wales, and even to Perth in 1970.

The last 38-class engine in regular service was 3820, which was withdrawn at Broadmeadow in December 1970. For a time afterwards this engine joined several other trafficable C38s in promotional and excursion service. By then, heavier rails and bridge improvements had seen the route availability of the C38s extended to include Parkes and Broken Hill and parts of the north-west.

As Australia was preparing for its Bicentennial in 1988, State Rail of NSW's then chief executive David Hill insisted on restoring 3801 for the occasion. Out-of-work apprentices performed much of the toil in Newcastle and, after its return to service in 1987, the locomotive visited every mainland capital served by rail in 1988. Until recently, the locomotive was maintained and operated by 3801 Limited, a non-profit NSW company charged with commercially running heritage trains.

The company's staff also rebuilt sister engine and Powerhouse Museum exhibit 3830 in October 1997, fittingly winning an Institution of Engineers Australian Division engineering excellence award for their efforts. That engine had been out of service for 30 years. Loco 3801 is today undergoing another rebuild (including new boiler) under the guidance of the NSWRTM,

S-class No. 542 at Collie in April 1968. (Philip G. Graham)

who also house 3820. Key parts of 3813 also still exist, sadly in broken-down form.

SPECIFICATIONS

	IMPERIAL (METRIC)
CYLINDERS:	21½ x 26 IN (55 x 66 CM)
BOILER PRESSURE:	245 PSI (1688 KPA)
COUPLED WHEELS:	5 FT 9 IN (175 CM)
TRACTIVE EFFORT:	36 273 LB (161.4 KN)
GRATE AREA:	47 SQ FT (4.366 M²)
TOTAL WEIGHT:	201.2 TONS (205.2 T)
GAUGE:	1435 MM
ROAD NUMBERS:	3801–3830

1943 WESTERN AUSTRALIAN GOVERNMENT RAILWAYS

S-class 4-8-2

During the mid-1930s, drawings were produced by the WAGR for a mixed traffic high-powered locomotive type capable of hauling fast passenger and goods traffic. World War II delayed its construction and it was not until 1942, by which time the war had caused an acute engine shortage, that building was started in the Midland Railway Workshops.

The first S-class steamed into service in February 1943, and ten were in traffic by November 1947. They were all named after mountains in Western Australia.

Able to haul 640 tonnes on a 1 in 80 grade, the locomotives were initially put to work over the Eastern Goldfields line on both passenger and freight trains, but after the war were used on heavy freight service in the south-west in addition to the eastern route. All were equipped with a semi-streamlining cowling hood running the entire length of the locomotive's top, but in later years the rear half was removed due to maintenance considerations.

Another alteration made in later years was the rebuilding of the tenders, which decreased their coal capacity from the original 9 to 7 tonnes. This enabled the water capacity to be increased from 15 900 litres to 22 700 litres, providing a far greater operational range. The normal brake system in use in Western Australia was vacuum, but the S-class had steam brakes on the locomotive and vacuum brakes on the tender.

Although ten were written off in June 1971, some continued running right up until Christmas Eve 1971, the last day steam was used commercially by the WAGR. The last S-class engine in service on that day was 548. Today, its sister engine 549 is preserved at the ARHS's Bassendean Rail Transport Museum in full working order while 542, which was displayed by Westrail outside Perth terminal for some two decades, was returned to service by the ARHS in 1995 for heritage train operations. No. 547 was acquired by the Bellarine Peninsula Railway, which operates tourist trains out of Queenscliff, Victoria.

	IMPERIAL (METRIC)
CYLINDERS:	19 x 24 IN (48 x 61 CM)
BOILER PRESSURE:	200 PSI (1378 KPA)
COUPLED WHEELS:	4 FT 0 IN (122 CM)
TRACTIVE EFFORT:	30 685 LB (136.6 KN)
GRATE AREA:	40 SQ FT (3.716 M²)
TOTAL WEIGHT:	119 TONS (121.4 T)
GAUGE:	1067 MM
ROAD NUMBERS:	541–550 (FINAL)

1943 QUEENSLAND RAILWAYS

AC16-class 2-8-2

The dramatic increase in traffic over QR lines following the outbreak of World War II led to the demand for twenty 2-8-2 medium-powered locomotives. All arrived in 1943, imported under a lend lease arrangement with the US Army, and built by the Baldwin Locomotive Works to a standard 1067 and 1000 mm gauge design. Similar locomotives saw service in India, Greece, Malaysia and Thailand, on various rail gauges.

While these AC16-class locomotives were intended for heavy freight service, early tests were also carried out with fast freight and even passenger trains. But as their tenders possessed coil springs and were inclined to roll alarmingly at higher than slow goods speeds, a speed limit of just 48 km/h was imposed.

This remained the situation until 1959, when spare tenders from withdrawn C16-class locomotives (which were equipped with conventional leaf springs) were fitted to the class, enabling the maximum permitted speed to be increased to 80 km/h. This move also gladdened the firemen, who were now able to scoop coal off a raised shovel plate rather than from floor level.

In their new form, AC16s began working passenger trains, including *The Midlander* west of Bogantungan.

Another early weakness in the class was the fitting of cast iron tyres, which were thrown at regular intervals and ultimately replaced with a steel version.

Another interesting story recalls how all AC16s were provided with US-type re-railing ramps which hung from a hook midframe. Because the locomotive's flexibility was superior to any other on the indifferent track work of the day, the ramps were all 'filched by marshalling yard staff' to re-rail wagons. In the words of one veteran engineman, the locos never needed them.

All AC16s were finally purchased outright from the US government by QR and, despite being rather hot to fire due to their large grate and firehole door arrangement, became a highly regarded locomotive type.

The first to be written off was 225A, in October 1957. More followed as boiler and mechanical condition dictated but 218A lasted at Rockhampton until 30 June 1969.

Locomotive 218A under the Mackay coal stage on 21 January 1964. (John S. Glastonbury)

No. 221A was retained by QR for preservation, bearing an original tender. After more than three decades it was restored to running order, making its return test run from Ipswich Workshops to Granchester on 12 May 2003. No. 218A was bought by the Lithgow Zig Zag Cooperative in New South Wales for eventual service over its scenic tourist railway.

SPECIFICATIONS

	IMPERIAL (METRIC)
CYLINDERS:	16 x 24 IN (41 x 61 CM)
BOILER PRESSURE:	185 PSI (1275 KPA)
COUPLED WHEELS:	4 FT 0 IN (122 CM)
TRACTIVE EFFORT:	20 128 LB (89.6 KN)
GRATE AREA:	27.7 SQ FT (2.573 M²)
TOTAL WEIGHT:	94.05 TONS (95 9 T)
GAUGE:	1067 MM
ROAD NUMBERS:	216A–235A (THESE WERE US ARMY NUMBERS)

1943 COMMONWEALTH LAND TRANSPORT BOARD

ASG-type (Garratt) 4-8-2 + 2-8-4

When enemy bombs rained down on Darwin in 1942, and hostile action was rising to a crescendo in the Pacific to the north of Queensland, World War II became much more of a reality to Australia than ever before.

The federal wartime controller of both rail and road transport—the Commonwealth Land Transport Board—declared the need for additional locomotives to move men and equipment over the nation's 1067 mm gauge railways. The Board called for a powerful design capable of negotiating Queensland's minimum 8.7-tonne axle loading and hauling a far greater payload.

The WAGR submitted plans for three Garratt types and, although some states were against the idea, the Board approached Beyer, Peacock & Co for prices for these articulated designs. However, talks broke down and authority was subsequently given to build 65 light Garratts made to this Australian design. The locomotive type became known as the Australian Standard Garratt (ASG). WAGR influences abounded in the design and in many respects it followed that railway's recently introduced S-class 4-8-2, right down to the semi-streamlining along the boiler.

The 65 engines were scheduled to be constructed by the following Australian builders: Newport Railway Workshops (G1–G10 and G31–G36), Islington Railway Workshops (G11–G20, G44 and G45), Clyde Engineering Co (G21–G25, G37–G43 and G51–G65) and Midland Railway Workshops (G26–G30 and G46–G50).

The first engine emerged from Newport Railway Workshops (Victoria) in September 1943 after a record minimum construction period of only four months.

The ASGs which initially entered service in Queensland impressed many people with their

ASG locomotive G23 was taking shape when pictured inside the Clyde Engineering Co's Granville plant in 1944. (Author's collection)

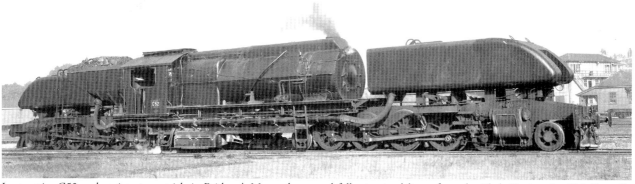

Locomotive G52 undergoing steam trials in Brisbane's Mayne depot yard following its delivery from the Clyde Engineering Co's Granville (NSW) plant. (QR)

hefty capabilities. But trouble was just around the corner, for their unflanged leading coupled wheels (a standard feature on comparable locomotives built at that time by Beyer, Peacock & Co) were found to leave the rails at awkward times. As other faults came to light, including flexible steam pipes, crews began to despise them and serious industrial action developed, with attempts being made to cancel construction altogether.

The Board resolved to continue with the project, hoping that the faults would be overcome.

In all, the QR officially placed 23 of the class on its books although, due to the action by crews, they were all withdrawn by September 1945 and stored (the AC16s from the USA were seen to be better propositions). One ASG locomotive never turned a wheel while another saw just two months' service.

The last engine actually assembled, G57 (which cost $34 000) from the Clyde Engineering Co, appeared in December 1945. There should have been another five from Clyde and a further three from the Newport Railway Workshops, but they were never built.

There were similar industrial disputes on the WAGR, where 25 Garratts were operating. A Royal Commission was even established to hear the enginemen's complaints.

Withdrawals commenced in Western Australia in the early 1950s. Because the SAR required extra motive power for Leigh Creek coal traffic and Broken Hill ore haulage (that state had ten 400-class Beyer-Garratts on order), six WAGR ASGs (G26, G29, G30–G32 and G49) were sold to SAR in 1952. These locomotives became SAR's 300-class and were numbered 300–305. They were largely used for training crews and fitters on articulated locomotives. After the Beyer-Garratts on order arrived in 1953, the ASGs, which were proving troublesome, saw little use. As most had sat out of service for some time, all were condemned on 24 February 1956. This was merely a book entry.

In Tasmania, the position was marginally better after a number of alterations were made to the initial eight engines. Although not firm favourites with the crews, a further six locomotives were bought from

A 1950 view of Tasmanian Railways' G6 standing outside Launceston workshops in pristine condition as executives and staff undertake a pre-service inspection. (Roydon Burk collection)

Newly-delivered G6 standing in South Burnie in 1950. (Roydon Burk collection)

the QR in 1949. The last ASGs to operate on the TGR were withdrawn in October 1957.

Tasmania's Emu Bay Railway operated a total of five ASGs, taking delivery of the first two ex-QR locomotives, G16 and G23, in 1949. Because the Emu Bay crews were used to Beyer-Garratts, there were no major dramas and the locomotives performed rather well after in-house modifications, which included fitting extended sandboxes and vacuum brakes.

A third, G17, was acquired from Queensland in 1953. Eight years later, the company was able to purchase the out-of-service G25 from the TGR as a replacement for Beyer-Garratt No. 13. After G25's brakes failed on the steep descent into Burnie on 20 February 1962, the locomotive overturning in the process, Emu Bay management arranged the purchase of G12 which again, miraculously at that late stage, remained intact on the TGR. Emu Bay's locomotives (in order of purchase) became 16–18, 20 and 20A respectively. They were all used on heavy freight and ore haulage, and in the last years of steam some worked passenger traffic when more suitable engines were not available.

The arrival of Walkers-built diesel-hydraulic locomotives in 1963 spelt the end for steam on the Emu Bay Railway and the last four operational ASGs on that system were withdrawn in September 1963. All had been cut up by 1966.

Parts of the remaining TGR locomotives tended to linger on. The driving wheels of some were used beneath four 4-6-2 M-class, and a number of boilers were sold to dairies and timber mills across Tasmania. One ASG water tank still resides in the former Hobart railway yards while another was noted at the Ipswich Railway Workshops Museum in 2005.

In October 1946 the Australian Portland Cement Co at Fyansford, Geelong, took delivery of G33 from Commonwealth Disposals for heavy cement haulage over its steeply-graded 4 km, 1067 mm gauge railway. As on the Emu Bay Railway, Portland Cement crews were used to Beyer-Garratts, so this locomotive tended to be well liked. In 1957, the company acquired a Bo-Bo diesel-electric and the ASG, which carried the road number 3, was withdrawn and boarded up. While it never again saw revenue service, it did receive an overhaul for standby service in 1965, then was steamed on 10 September 1966 for a visiting railway enthusiast tour. The railway closed soon afterwards and the locomotive was donated to the ARHS's North Williamstown Museum.

In hindsight, the major failing with the ASG would appear to be cost cutting at a time when the nation was in real crisis. Today's locomotive students believe the major design defect was a lack of equalisation in the suspension. Compensation was a standard feature in American design but not in British practice.

SPECIFICATIONS

	IMPERIAL (METRIC)
CYLINDERS:	(4) 14¼ x 24 IN (37 x 61 CM)
BOILER PRESSURE:	200 PSI (1378 KPA)
COUPLED WHEELS:	4 FT 0 IN (122 CM)
TRACTIVE EFFORT:	34 521 LB (153.6 KN)
GRATE AREA:	35 SQ FT (3.252 M²)
TOTAL WEIGHT:	119 TONS (121.4 T)
GAUGE:	1067 MM
ROAD NUMBERS:	G1–G65 (NOTE: G34, G36 AND G39–G43 WERE NEVER ASSEMBLED).

1943 COMMONWEALTH DEPARTMENT OF SUPPLY

79-class Bo-Bo

Commonwealth Railways' DE90 (ex 7921) shunting at Port Pirie yard on 25 January 1968. (Len Whalley)

Many readers who travelled through Sydney terminal from the late 1940s will remember a stable of drab-looking black-painted centre-cab diesel-electric locomotives busily going about carriage shunting duties. For more than two decades, examples of this type stood alone among the regular steam-powered shunting fleets of the day and intrigued many rail travellers.

Their history dated back to 1943 when the then Commonwealth Department of Supply, in association with the US Army, imported four standard General-Electric 40-ton units for use at the St Marys munitions factory in western Sydney. They were among a large number built for the US Army and carried US road numbers 7920 to 7923.

Towards the end of the war, directors of BHP's Australian Iron & Steel company at Port Kembla were becoming interested in works dieselisation in a bid to improve locomotive efficiencies, and 7922 was loaned to the company during April 1945 for evaluation trials. While at the plant, the little unit worked all classes of train, from ladles to ingot traffic. While it was considered too light for steel service, the economies it displayed eventually led to dieselisation of the steelworks from 1950.

Following cessation of wartime hostilities, all four 79-class were absorbed into the NSWGR motive-power rosters and used in passenger carriage shunting, principally in Sydney yard. Almost immediately, the federal government rightly claimed ownership and the Department of Supply transferred 7921 and 7922 to South Australia to work equipment trains

between the expanding Woomera rocket range site and the Commonwealth Railways' exchange siding near Wirrappa.

The two Woomera units were absorbed into Commonwealth Railways (now Australian National) stock in 1950 but prior to that were noted working goods and mixed trains between Port Pirie and Woomera during the winter of 1949, at the height of a national coal strike.

The locomotives became DE90 (ex 7921) and DE91 (ex 7922) on the CR and were principally employed shunting locomotives at Port Augusta and Port Pirie. In later years they saw active service with railway construction trains, DE90 for example, seeing thousands of hours' work on the Whyalla line in the early 1970s.

After a further decade spent shunting at Port Augusta's railway workshops, both units were withdrawn. Today DE90 (bearing its original number, 7921) is an active exhibit at the Thirlmere Railway Museum in NSW while 7922 is preserved at the National Railway Museum, Port Adelaide.

Meanwhile, the two NSW units, which had been officially transferred to the NSWGR, were sold to the British Phosphate Commission on 31 October

The British Phosphate Commission's 9402 (ex 7923) at work on Christmas Island in 1981. (Author's collection)

1974 for use over that authority's Christmas Island phosphate railway. Both were in 'average to poor condition' when forwarded to their new owner and a report to the author from the transport manager during the mid-1970s indicated that 9401 (renumbered from 7920) was able to perform only 40 per cent of its capabilities due to the 'deteriorated state of its electrical system and engines'.

The Commission conveyed 9401 to the Perth engineering firm F.R. Tulk for complete rebuilding to give it a low maintenance life of ten years. This August 1979 rebuild included the replacement of the original twin Caterpillar-type D17000 engines with two Caterpillar-type D3306 plants. This increased the locomotive's traction output from 254 kW to 298 kW. The unit also received an upgraded electrical system, roller bearings replaced the former friction type, pneumatic equipment was substituted for older mechanical linkages to the throttle controls, while the former steam locomotive-type air-braking equipment was exchanged for the latest available equipment. More efficient main generator and slightly lower geared traction motors were also provided.

Appearance-wise, Tulk provided a low-profile configuration which gave improved operator visibility. The sister unit was similarly rebuilt and initially the two could be seen working as a pair on the commission's 20 km standard-gauge railway. At that time the railway was moving 1.4 million tonnes per annum, collecting material from four loading bridges. By mid-1987, this had fallen to the equivalent of 860 000 tonnes a year (about eight trainloads a day), and the writing was on the wall for the railway. It closed on 31 December that year, 9401 having been fully overhauled only three months beforehand. The unit—minus engines, generators and traction motors—was subsequently placed on exhibition outside Drumsite school. As this book closed for press, 9402 remained at Drumsite in a complete state. It had been used to dismantle the railway.

SPECIFICATIONS

	ORIGINAL	TULK REBUILDS
	IMPERIAL (METRIC)	IMPERIAL (METRIC)
POWER UNIT:	CATERPILLAR D1700	CATERPILLAR D3306
TRACTION HORSEPOWER:	340 (254 kW)	400 (298 kW)
STARTING TRACTIVE EFFORT:	17 600 LB (78 kN)	18 500 LB (82 kN)
CONTINUOUS TRACTIVE EFFORT:	13 000 LB (58 kN)	13 500 LB (60 kN)
TOTAL WEIGHT:	39.2 TONS (39.7 T)	39.2 TONS (40 T)
ROAD NUMBERS:	7920–7923	9401 (EX 7920)
		9402 (EX 7923)
	(CR UNITS DE90 [EX 7921] AND DE91 [EX 7922])	

520-class 4-8-4

This class, which finally numbered 12 engines, was designed as a light lines broad gauge express passenger and freight locomotive. The first of the class entered service on 10 November 1943.

Of massive proportions, in keeping with the SAR's long-held big-engine policy, these locomotives were capable of speeds up to 112 km/h, but were designed in such a way that they could operate over light 27 kg/m rails.

All were constructed at the SAR's Islington Workshops. Originally there were to be 20 engines but with thoughts turning to diesels, the final eight were never authorised for building and the last 520-class entered service on 19 December 1947.

There were two distinct types in the class. After the first three had been delivered, the cowling above the smokebox was revised and grille ventilators installed. This improved the locomotive's general aesthetics considerably.

The 520-class was quite a powerful locomotive which over the years was subjected to many exhaustive trials. Surviving records describing one of these tests show that an indicated 2600 horsepower (1950 kW) was produced at 112 km/h with a 510-tonne load. This can be considered a fine achievement with 52 x 71 cm cylinders. The locomotive was found to be a steady rider and surprisingly economical on fuel.

The 520-class regularly operated between Adelaide and Port Pirie, Terowie and Tailem Bend, and worked over all but the lightest lines in the state.

Following complaints from firemen that coal would not shake forward in the tenders when it was running low, the possibility of installing coal pushers was investigated but, as coal supplies were so uncertain at the time (1948), all locomotives were converted to burn fuel oil.

Despite the proliferation of diesels, the big locomotives remained at their post until their boilers gave out from the late 1950s. With the multiplication of new 930-class main line diesel-electrics, three were condemned in July 1961 and another two went a year later. Gradually the rest followed, only locos 520 and 526 remaining operational until 1971.

All have been scrapped except for 520, which operates tourist trains as part of the ARHS's

Locomotive 523, which proved to be a survivor, at Murray Bridge. (Philip G. Graham)

SteamRanger program, and 523, which is preserved at the National Railway Museum, Port Adelaide.

SPECIFICATIONS

	IMPERIAL (METRIC)
CYLINDERS:	20½ x 28 IN (52 x 71 CM)
BOILER PRESSURE:	200 PSI (1378 KPA)
COUPLED WHEELS:	5 FT 6 IN (168 CM)
TRACTIVE EFFORT:	32 582 LB (145 KN)
GRATE AREA:	46 SQ FT (4.181 M²)
TOTAL WEIGHT:	200.5 TONS (204.5 T)
GAUGE:	1600 MM
ROAD NUMBERS:	520–531

1945 WESTERN AUSTRALIAN GOVERNMENT RAILWAYS

Dm and Dd class 4-6-4T

With the supreme effort required to maintain its interstate train services during the lengthy hostilities of World War II, the Perth metropolitan passenger services tended to be neglected.

While this was certainly no reflection upon the WAGR whose resources, by virtue of the massive extra war traffic, were stretched to the limit, the fact remained that many of Perth's suburban passenger trains were still in the hands of low-powered locomotives. These included the 4-4-4T N-class, the small-wheeled 4-8-4T K-class and a small fleet of 20 4-6-4T Ds-class locomotives, all of which were between 30 and 50 years old.

Train services became ever slower and more unreliable as loads steadily increased, to the point that during the latter stages of the war the WAGR came to the realisation that something must be done to ease the situation.

Money was tight, but inventive engineers thought an improved Ds-type 4-6-4T might be an answer. Salvation lay in the WAGR's E/Es-class tender locomotives, which had reached the stage where complete rebuilds were needed to make them fit for further service. Their chassis, cylinders and wheels were salvaged to form the basis of a new Baltic tank locomotive.

Known as the Dm-class, eight smart engines emerged from the railway's Midland Workshops between March and November 1945. Exerting a similar power output and having the same leading dimensions as the older Ds-type, the new engines boasted a slightly increased water

Dd 591 working a metropolitan goods train at East Perth in April 1968. (Philip G. Graham)

and coal capacity and were 2 tonnes heavier.

These eight locomotives hardly scratched the surface, however, and still more were needed post-war to cater for the ever-increasing traffic. The Department ordered an additional ten from Midland Workshops, this time built from new materials, which allowed the opportunity to be taken to redesign the valve gear and make other subtle improvements. These new locomotives became the Dd-class and were delivered between April and November 1946. They quickly attracted the nickname the 'Donald Ducks'.

Although built for Perth suburban passenger (and transfer freight) service, the Dm/Dd-classes could occasionally be found working as far afield as Bunbury and Merredin when tender-engine shortages arose.

The introduction of diesel railcars on some metropolitan passenger services from 1953 did not hamper the new engines to any degree. Rather, they replaced older 1912-vintage Ds-class engines. But the arrival of new and large diesel railcars in 1968 was a different story, and the stylish Dm/Dd engines went quickly. Dm 581 was the first to go, being cut up on 15 March 1968. Five Dd's stored at Northam

immediately followed. The remaining locomotives were largely used on shunting duties until the closure of Midland steam depot in May 1971, when all but one were written off.

Two survive. Dd 592 is displayed today at Gosnelle City Markets after running special tourist trains until September 1994. Dd 596 is exhibited at the ARHS Bassendean Rail Transport Museum.

SPECIFICATIONS

	IMPERIAL (METRIC)
CYLINDERS:	8 x 23 IN (46 x 60 CM)
COUPLED WHEELS:	4 FT 6 IN (137 CM)
BOILER PRESSURE:	160 PSI (1102 KPA)
TRACTIVE EFFORT:	18 768 LB (82 KN)
GRATE AREA:	18.6 SQ FT 1.719 M²)
TOTAL WEIGHT:	DM71.9 TONS (72.4 T); DD 72.6 TONS (73.1 T)
GAUGE:	1067 MM
ROAD NUMBERS:	DM 581–588; DD 591–600

Loco U657 at Midland Junction shed in January 1950. (John Sullivan)

1946 Western Australian Government Railways

U-class 4-6-2

As we have seen, after World War II the WAGR was in dire need of extra locomotives. An answer to its problem came with the news that a number of Pacific-type engines were surplus at the North British Locomotive Co's Glasgow works. Fifty-five 4-6-2s had been ordered by the British Ministry of Munitions, to have been forwarded to the Sudan Railways, but the fall of the Axis powers rendered them surplus.

The WAGR immediately snapped up 14 and they entered traffic between November 1946 and April 1947, designated U class.

These locomotives, which burnt fuel oil, operated the bulk of the state's country crack expresses right up until 1955, by when the majority of the new X-class diesel-electrics had made their presence felt. The U-class was then relegated to goods working and gradually, as mechanical and boiler problems dictated, they were withdrawn. By August 1957, all were out of service.

Ut664 soon after its 1957 conversion as a tank engine. (former Westrail archives)

But 664, which had been converted to burn coal in December 1954 and remained like this until it was withdrawn in November 1956, was not scrapped. Soon afterwards it was shopped for an overhaul and converted to an oil-burning 4-6-4 tank engine for Perth suburban services. In that form, 664 became the Ut-class and was able to maintain diesel railcar schedules on most routes until it was withdrawn in December 1959.

A serious coal shortage threatened the state early in 1961 when, much to the delight of local enthusiasts, the Ut engine and five of the original U-class were recommissioned for several months until the pressure eased. Ut664 was restored to running condition again in November 1966 and worked ballast specials until 1969.

U655 and Ut664 are both preserved in the ARHS's Bassendean Rail Transport Museum. They were officially written off in September 1970, being the last members of their classes in service.

SPECIFICATIONS

	U-class	Ut-class
	Imperial (Metric)	Imperial (Metric)
Cylinders:	18 x 24 in (46 x 61 cm)	18 x 24 in (46 x 61 cm)
Boiler pressure:	180 psi (1240 kPa)	180 psi (1240 kPa)
Coupled wheels:	4 ft 6 in (137 cm)	4 ft 6 in (137 cm)
Tractive effort:	22 032 lb (98 kN)	22 032 lb (98 kN)
Grate area:	26 sq ft (2.415 m²)	26 sq ft (2.415 m²)
Total weight:	107.7 tons (109.9 t)	80 tons (81.6 t)
Gauge:	1067 mm	1067 mm
Road numbers:	651–664	664

DD17-class 4-6-4T

Although some tender-type locomotives were used in Brisbane's suburban services, the brunt of this traffic was worked by tank-type locomotives.

By the mid-1940s, however, the tank locomotives of the 1905-vintage D16-class had almost reached the end of their economic lives and a new and powerful design was prepared as a replacement. The design employed the best features of both the later D17 4-6-4Ts (an improved D16) and the recently acquired Baldwin-built US Army AC16-class tender engines.

The 12 new 4-6-4Ts, built at the Ipswich Railway Workshops, were equipped with roller bearings, superheaters, self-cleaning smokeboxes, mechanical lubricators and electric lighting. Issued to traffic between 1948 and 1952 as the DD17-class, they represented a 15 per cent increase in power over the older D17-class.

Virtually their entire lives were spent working out of Brisbane's Mayne depot. After diesel-electrics assumed command of the metropolitan passenger operations in the 1960s, the DD17-class was pressed into transfer goods work and shunting duties.

The first of the class to be written off was 1048 in November 1966. The last engine in service, 1046, was condemned during October 1969.

Today, 1051, fully restored to its blue livery by QR and officially named *Blue Baby*, is an operational locomotive for Queensland heritage rail tour

DD17 1051 as preserved by QR. (QR)

programs. Locos 1046, 1047 and 1049 are at the Lithgow Zig Zag tourist railway, with 1049 presently operational.

SPECIFICATIONS

	IMPERIAL (METRIC)
CYLINDERS:	17 x 24 IN (43 x 61 CM)
BOILER PRESSURE:	180 PSI (1240 KPA)
COUPLED WHEELS:	4 FT 3 IN (130 CM)
TRACTIVE EFFORT:	20 808 LB (92.6 KN)
GRATE AREA:	18.5 SQ FT (1.719 M²)
TOTAL WEIGHT:	62 TONS (63.2 T)
GAUGE:	1067 MM
ROAD NUMBERS:	949–954, 1046–1051

1949 AUSTRALIAN PAPER MANUFACTURERS

Whitcomb B-B

In company with many of Australia's leading industrial operations, Australia Paper Manufacturers, the nation's largest producer of cardboard and packaging paper products, operates a private railway to convey its raw materials and finished products.

The largest APM mill is situated at Maryvale, some 6 kilometres north of Morwell in Victoria's La Trobe Valley, and close to supplies of raw materials. Maryvale Mill employs about 1100 people and it is here that the largest company-maintained railway operates.

Constructed in 1938, the railway's initial motive-power needs were filled by a petrol-powered 78 kW 4-wheel unit of Malcolm Moore manufacture, acquired in 1939. The little locomotive was soon found to be too light for the link with the VR's main line outside Morwell so an 0-6-4T steam locomotive was purchased in 1940 from South Australian Railways. Formerly No. 42 of that system's K-class, it was relieved just one year later by a former VR D1-class 4-6-0 steam locomotive, 552.

But modernisation, always a catchcry with APM, soon saw company engineers looking toward internal combustion locomotives. During the late 1940s, an order was placed with Whitcomb Locomotive Works of Rochelle, Illinois, for two B-B centre-cab diesel-electrics.

Whitcomb had been building industrial and mining locomotives since 1906 and was able to offer APM an already tried design, one which had appeared in 1942 for the US Navy.

The first unit, No. 1, appeared in 1949 and its sister locomotive was commissioned the following year. They boasted a centre-cab design for good all-round vision and their bogies were equipped with just the one traction motor. Drive to the adjacent axle was initially by chain, but nuisance chain breakages occurred so the wheels were soon joined by siderods.

The APM units arrived with Hercules 6-cylinder engines, two of which provided all-up power of 283 kW per locomotive. In 1964, both locomotives were rebuilt with twin Detroit 6-cylinder diesel engines, which increased output to 298 kW for a maximum tractive effort of 113 kN.

APM's No. 1 locomotive standing in the mill's yard on 9 February 1979. (Leon Oberg)

Originally commissioned in emerald green livery, the pair ran during later years in safety yellow with black visibility stripes. Their maximum speed was 32 km/h.

Both locomotives were withdrawn in 1987 and scrapped. They were replaced with branch-line V/Line diesel-electrics until March 1993, when the rails into the plant were strengthened to handle the weight of mainline locomotives and unit trains. The company now trades as PaperlinX.

SPECIFICATIONS

	IMPERIAL (METRIC)
POWER UNIT:	2 × HERCULES 6-CYLINDER
TRACTION HORSEPOWER:	360 (268 kW)
MAXIMUM TRACTIVE EFFORT:	25 000 lb (111 kN)
TOTAL WEIGHT:	49.5 TONS (50.5 T)
GAUGE:	1600 MM
ROAD NUMBERS:	1 AND 2

1948 TASMANIAN GOVERNMENT RAILWAYS

V-class 0-6-0DM

Although all Australian government railway systems were dabbling in internal combustion power plants to drive railmotors and, in some cases, small shunting locomotives, Tasmanian Government Railways stole a march on the others after World War II by ordering four standard Drewry 0-6-0 diesel mechanical units.

These locomotives were narrow-gauge versions of that British manufacturer's emerging catalogue item which on British Rail became Class 04 (later 03).

The units entered Tasmanian service toward year's end and, apart from the NSWGR's 79-class Bo-Bo centre cabs (which in reality were imported for factory shunting at St Marys by the Commonwealth Department of Munitions), were the first diesel locomotives bought new by an Australian government rail system.

The class had swollen to eight examples by 1955. Wanting still more, however, the TGR decided to go it alone and over a 10-year period beginning in 1959, built four in its own Launceston workshops. While largely employing imported mechanical and electrical components, they made history in that they were the first locomotives actually built from scratch by the TGR. While some visual differences also existed between the original and home-grown locomotives,

Built in 1953 for the Mt Lyell Mining & Railway Co and sold to the TGR in 1963 as its V13, this locomotive, pictured at Burnie in January 1971, now belongs to the West Coast Wilderness Railway and operates as D2. It has been equipped for Abt rack operation and is based at Regatta Point. (Peter Watts)

the latter were geared much lower, which improved their maximum tractive effort for starting trains, and rode on roller bearings (the earlier units were subsequently converted).

But these new locomotives came at a price for existing locomotives V1 and V8, which lost their diesel engines in 1962 to new units and were instead equipped with Gardner 6-cylinder 153 hp engines last used in salvaged DP-class ex-passenger rail cars. Four-speed gear boxes that came with these engines replaced the original 5-speed variety, with the revised units becoming the VA-class. In 1970, V3 and VA8 were undergoing overhauls at Launceston and, in an effort to release the better one quickly into service, creative scheduling saw V3 receive VA8's mechanical components, thus creating VA3. When VA8 emerged two years later, it reverted back to its V8 number because it now carried V3's original mechanicals. Both VA1 and V8 are today preserved by the Bellarine Peninsula (tourist) Railway, Victoria. For the record, V8 was the last of the breed in actual Tasrail service, being withdrawn as the Railton shunter in April 1987.

Meanwhile, the Tasmanian Mt Lyell Mining & Railway Co bought two V-class from Drewry in 1953, selling one to the Emu Bay Railway Company in 1962 to carry the number 22. The other went to the TGR in 1963 to become V13. Both are now under the ownership of the West Coast Wilderness Railway, the former running there as D1 and the latter, equipped for Abt rack operation, as D2. Others preserved are V2 and the frame of V6 at the Don River Railway, Devonport; V9 (for parts) and V12 at the Emerald Tourist Railway Board (Puffing Billy), Victoria, and V4 and V5 at the Hotham Valley Railway in Western Australia, where they joined a basically similar loco originally imported by the SEC of Western Australia to shunt coal from Robb Jetty into the South Fremantle powerhouse as SEC1.

SPECIFICATIONS

	IMPERIAL (METRIC)
POWER UNIT:	GARDNER 8L3
TRACTION HORSEPOWER:	204 (150 KW)
MAXIMUM TRACTIVE EFFORT:	22 960 LB (101 KN)
TOTAL WEIGHT:	30 TONS (30.5 T)
GAUGE:	1067 MM
ROAD NUMBERS:	(TGR) V1–V13; (V13 NOW WCWR D2)
	(TGR) VA1, VA3* AND VA8*
	(*AT NO STAGE DID THESE UNITS OPERATE CONCURRENTLY)
	(EMU BAY RAILWAY) 22 (NOW WCWR D1)

1949 SOUTH AUSTRALIAN RAILWAYS

350-class Bo-Bo

From a government railways' point of view, the South Australian Railways administration had always been something of an innovator. While other rail systems were talking about diesels throughout the 1940s, the SAR actually did something about it.

As there was no diesel manufacturing base in Australia at that time, SAR designed its own small hood-type shunting locomotive and contracted the English Electric Co's UK Preston works to supply a pair of 6KT diesel (World War II-era landing craft) engines and associated electrical equipment/traction motors to complete the task.

The first entered service on 7 June 1949, the second 14 days later. Initially, the two little locomotives worked in Adelaide shunting yards and hauled transfer goods trains. Soon after their arrival, however, a national coal strike saw them used on Adelaide suburban passenger services.

They were not really a success due to the low power of their 350 hp (260 kW) engines and one was forwarded to Mt Gambier during the 1950s for shunting service. In August 1967 and January 1968, locos 350 and 351 were respectively made captive to SAR's Islington Workshops, where they ended their days shunting rolling stock and dead locomotives around the plant.

The 350-class was the only locomotive on the SAR to employ a gravity feed fuel tank. It possessed an overhead 'header' tank in addition to its main storage. Should such a locomotive run out of fuel, its entire fuel system had to be primed. In addition, the 350-class was unusual in that it was possible to push-start the unit in the event of a flat battery. A former senior fitter at Mile End, Roger Hall, recalled that if a 350 were pushed in excess of 20 km/h, the driver could 'drop in the contactors and use the traction motors as generators to turn the engine over'. Mr Hall said the engine oil and fuel pressures had to be individually hand-primed beforehand.

Both were withdrawn as shunters at Islington Workshops during the late 1980s. Today 350 is operating over SteamRanger's Victor Harbor Tourist Railway while 351 is preserved at the National Railway Museum, Port Adelaide.

Boasting rather bland and dumpy styling, class-leader 350 stands in Mile End yard on 7 February 1978. (Leon Oberg)

Pm710 stands in Collie locomotive depot beside W915 on 27 February 1971. (Bob Grant)

SPECIFICATIONS

	IMPERIAL (METRIC)
POWER UNIT:	ENGLISH ELECTRIC 6KT
TRACTION HORSEPOWER:	350 (250 kW)
STARTING TRACTIVE EFFORT:	3 400 LB (106 kN)
CONTINUOUS TRACTIVE EFFORT:	4 800 LB (21.3 kN)
TOTAL WEIGHT:	49.1 TONS (51 T)
GAUGE:	1600 MM
ROAD NUMBERS:	350 AND 351

1950 WESTERN AUSTRALIAN GOVERNMENT RAILWAYS

Pm & Pmr class 4-6-2

Intended for express passenger service, the Pm-class Pacifics were a post-war, more modern version of the older Pr-class 4-6-2s which were then WAGR's leading passenger locomotives.

Introduced on 4 January 1950, a total of 35 Pm-class locomotives were acquired from the North British Locomotive Co of Glasgow and all were running in passenger service by September that year.

They were found to be rough riders at speed because of their rigidity, so compensating beams initially were fitted to their coupled wheels in an attempt to correct the problem. This only marginally improved the situation, so all were reduced to freight service and only permitted to work passenger trains when no other engine was available.

While under construction in Glasgow, 16 of the engines had been given roller bearings on their coupled wheels and reclassified as the Pmr-class. One other engine was converted later by the WAGR.

Their lives were principally spent working on the Great Southern and Eastern Goldfields routes and their associated branches. With dieselisation of the Goldfields line, the class was confined to the Southern and South Western lines until there too they were displaced by diesels.

Five Pm-class and three Pmr-class were written off in September 1970 and the remainder saw their last service over the Narrogin–Collie and Perth–Bunbury sections. The last locomotives in traffic were withdrawn and stored in mid-1971. Today, Pm701 is preserved at Bassendean Rail Transport Museum; Pm706 is owned by Hotham Valley Railway member, Colin Taylor; Pmr721 is on exhibition at the Old Railway Station Museum, Northam; Pmr729 is at Coolgardie Railway Station Museum; Pmr735 resides at Tuart Hill; and Pmr720, which was acquired by the South Australian tourist railway society, Steamtown Peterborough, has been restored to work periodically between Peterborough and Eurelia.

SPECIFICATIONS

	IMPERIAL (METRIC)
CYLINDERS:	19 X 26 IN (48 X 66 CM)
BOILER PRESSURE:	175 PSI (1206 kPA)
COUPLED WHEELS:	4 FT 6 IN (137 CM)
TRACTIVE EFFORT:	25 855 LB (115 kN)
GRATE AREA:	35 SQ FT (3.252 M²)
TOTAL WEIGHT:	109 TONS (111.2 T)
GAUGE:	1067 MM
ROAD NUMBERS:	PM 701–714, 716–719
	PMR 715, 720–735

The class-leader, 5801, taking on water at Yass Junction circa 1952. (Arthur Reynell)

D58-class 4-8-2

World War II was taking an enormous toll on the NSWGR—locomotive maintenance was behind schedule due to the considerable amount of extra traffic on offer, and additional heavy goods locomotives were desperately needed.

The NSWGR's design team, who over the years had suggested a selection of Mallets using the D57-class boiler design, finally adopted an improved D57-class 4-8-2 design when approval was given in 1943 to build 25 new heavy freight locomotives. The opportunity was taken to incorporate some of the more modern features from the successful C38-class, such as smokebox regulators, air-whistles and padded seating in the sedan-type cabs (see page 219). The most fundamental engineering alterations were smaller cylinders, which enabled the locomotives to meet the general loading gauge, and the provision of rack and pinion valve gear to operate the centre cylinder.

Construction of the locomotives was to have been divided between the NSWGR's Eveleigh and Cardiff workshops. Wartime delays, manpower and material shortages all took their toll on production and the first one did not appear until January 1950. Unfortunately, it was soon found to be inferior to the older D57-class, in more ways than one. Its smaller cylinders made it somewhat underpowered in the eyes of the administration, and the engines could really only be operated at their best with a three-quarters load. The use of a rack and pinion drive gear

was another partial failure, because soot and grime lodged in the brass teeth and caused premature wear, despite the equipment being enclosed inside a steel cover.

The D58s were employed mainly on the Western line to Lithgow, but were also used to a limited extent on the Main Southern line to Goulburn and Junee. Interestingly, perusals of surviving early 1950s repair books at Goulburn depot reveal that the locomotives were really quite trouble free, and the few occasions when bookings had to be made generally pointed only to warm big and little end bearings.

With impending dieselisation and planned Blue Mountains electrification to Lithgow, it was decreed that no further D58s of the 25 originally envisaged were to be constructed after the thirteenth arrived in October 1952. Thus a scheduled general overhaul to 5803 was cancelled in October 1956 and the last two running, 5808 and 5813, were stopped in July 1957, just one month after the Lithgow line was energised. The locomotives were stored at Chullora and Enfield and lay in situ until tenders were called for their disposal in 1963. A Sydney scrap metal firm moved in and cut all engines up where they stood, the first to go being 5807 at Chullora. By late February 1964, all had sadly vanished.

However, 5813's boiler saw further use in a Dorrigo timber mill and some tenders were used for more than a decade as part of a water train consist based at Werris Creek. Another tender body was sent to Canberra to store locomotive diesel fuel. It remains there to this day, while several cabs from the non-assembled engines form picnic shelters at Thirlmere Railway Museum.

	IMPERIAL (METRIC)
CYLINDERS:	(3) 21½ x 28 IN (55 x 71 CM)
BOILER PRESSURE:	200 PSI (1378 KPA)
COUPLED WHEELS:	5 FT 0 IN (152 CM)
TRACTIVE EFFORT:	55 007 LB (244.8 KN)
GRATE AREA:	65 SQ FT (6.039 M²)
TOTAL WEIGHT:	227.75 TONS (232.3 T)
GAUGE:	1435 MM
ROAD NUMBERS:	5801–5813

1950 QUEENSLAND RAILWAYS

Garratt-type 4-8-2 + 2-8-4

This class of 30 Beyer-Garratt locomotives was the most powerful steam locomotive type seen on the QR system. Ten were built at the Gorton works of Beyer, Peacock & Co and the final 20 came from their associate, the Franco-Belge Corporation in France. The first locomotive entered service on 22 August 1950 but the type was never classified.

The initial engine, distinctively painted maroon and gold, was exhibited at the Rockhampton Central Queensland Industries Fair and then went into regular service in that area. As further deliveries were made, the locomotives became regulars on the Brisbane–Toowoomba line but, due to excessive heat within the Victoria Tunnel in the Little Liverpool Range, they had to be withdrawn from this route and confined to the Brisbane–Bundaberg line.

With expanding dieselisation, some of the Garratts were transferred to Rockhampton depot to operate the heavy Dawson Valley coal trains until a more direct dieselised route was commissioned in the late 1960s.

Although introduced for freight services, tests were conducted with passenger trains and examples were reported to have sometimes worked the *Sunlander Express*, the *Rockhampton Mail* and the *Midlander*.

The first to be withdrawn was 1092 in May 1964. Gradually the others followed and no less than 22 were condemned during the 1967–68 financial year. The last engine in traffic was 1096, stopped in March 1970.

Fortunately, one example, 1009, has been preserved. After residing in the QR Redbank Museum for over two decades, the locomotive was overhauled and returned to service midway through 1995 to work a restored QR heritage train and other privately-sponsored rail tours.

SPECIFICATIONS

	IMPERIAL (METRIC)
CYLINDERS:	(4) 13 x 26 IN (35 x 66 CM)
BOILER PRESSURE:	200 PSI (1378 KPA)
COUPLED WHEELS:	4 FT 3 IN (130 CM)
TRACTIVE EFFORT:	32 771 LB (145.8 KN)
GRATE AREA:	39 SQ FT (3.623 M²)
TOTAL WEIGHT:	137 TONS (139.7 T)
GAUGE:	1067 MM
ROAD NUMBERS:	1001–1010, 1090–1109

Newly assembled and painted, Garratt 1105 poses for official pre-service publicity photographs in 1950. (QR archives)

Original pattern Commonwealth Engineering-built locomotive D3, wearing Australian Iron & Steel livery on 12 July 1972 (Leon Oberg)

1950 AUSTRALIAN IRON & STEEL

D1/D16-type Bo-Bo

When Charles Hoskins relocated his ironworks from Lithgow to Port Kembla in 1929, forming Australian Iron & Steel Pty Ltd (AI&S), the move was aimed at bringing his operations closer to its raw materials, on a site capable of huge on-going development and with a deep sea port. As with the Lithgow operation, railways played an important role in the steadily growing operation.

Unfortunately, Hoskins' move to Port Kembla coincided with the economic woes of the Great Depression. Because the owners had somewhat over-capitalised, poor early returns under the prevailing conditions eventually led to a mutual agreement with the Broken Hill Proprietary Co, which acquired all ordinary share capital in 1935. Under BHP's stewardship, modernisation and expansion was continuous and from 1945 management began to take an interest in dieselisation as a means of providing improved locomotive availability and operating economies.

In April 1945, the company managed to stage a trial throughout the plant with General-Electric Bo-Bo 7922, one of four locomotives imported by US defence authorities for use at the St Marys

munitions factory during World War II. Although much too light for Port Kembla works service, its obvious versatility led to serious investigations of more suitable locomotives.

Because no Australian locomotive maker had acquired manufacturing rights to overseas products, AI&S staff members made a number of trips to the USA and the UK and, through contacts and experience gained, finally decided to build eight 544 kW Bo-Bo locomotives to an AI&S-influenced design, using power equipment imported from the UK firm English Electric. Sydney rolling-stock builder Commonwealth Engineering undertook to assemble the units.

Entering service on 4 May 1950, the class-leader, D1, became Australia's very first main line diesel locomotive type. Its arrival followed massive reorganisation of newly-acquired nearby collieries that laid claim to the rich Wongawilli seam, including the commissioning of Nebo Colliery near Mt Kembla. The new diesels and their accompanying 61-tonne all-steel bogie coal wagons, which started arriving in 1950, totally revolutionised coal train haulage, not only at AI&S, but in New South Wales generally.

Weighing 87 tonnes and geared for only 34 km/h, early tests showed the new diesel could haul 3060 tonnes on level ground and, on the 1 in 50 Brownsville bank (Wongawilli line), it actually lifted a 1430-

Wearing BHP Port Kembla livery, D19 trundles through the complex on 21 October 1986. (Leon Oberg)

tonne train from a standing start. The locomotives were equipped with EE's 8-cylinder normally-aspirated SRKT diesel engine; this powered an EE819 generator which in turn energised four 101 kW axle-mounted traction motors. As more were delivered they were put to work within the rambling steel plant.

Expansion and modernisation continued. A new blast furnace was built and flat products mills constructed. AI&S acquired an additional 12 similarly-styled Bo-Bo units in four contracts, delivered at staggered intervals between December 1959 and September 1964. By then EE had set up a manufacturing plant in the Brisbane suburb of Rocklea and all of these units were constructed there, boasting a cleaner, more refined look. In addition,

A remarkably rare sight inside the steelworks—three 589kW locomotives handling the one ingot. Because the locomotives lacked multiple unit control, all were manned for the special heavy shunt into the No. 1 soaking pit area involving locomotives D19, D27 and D16 on 11 December 1979. (Leon Oberg)

EE had further developed the engine, which was up-rated by some 45 kW. These locomotives were identified as D16–D19 and D26–D33.

The entire fleet remained in everyday traffic until a serious steel slump descended on Australia during the early 1980s and led to the closure of three Port Kembla blast furnaces. (One was later restored.) Two locomotives, including the class-leader, were withdrawn on 4 August 1982 and by the end of October 1983 seven original D1-type class units were lying in store.

Although steelmaking conditions slowly improved, no further use was found for the pioneering Bo-Bos in the plant, due in part to the gradual modernisation of operations. For instance, when a new slab-caster replaced ingots in the mid-1980s, several shunting jobs were eliminated. However, the company's Sheet Steel & Coil Division (formerly Lysaghts) locomotives had reached the end of their economic lives, so D7 was re-liveried and returned to service at that plant.

No. D6, retained for a time by the company for historic purposes, which included hauling employee picnic trains and visiting groups around the works. While D7 was sold to a Canberra industrialist in fully operational condition during 2001, No. D1 was forwarded to Thirlmere Railway Museum on permanent loan and periodically sees service shunting.

Of the Rocklea-built Bo-Bos, the first unit withdrawn was the class-leader, D16, following a works accident in 2001. Six sisters remained serviceable as at January 2010 with two others, D31 and D32, stored for their parts.

SPECIFICATIONS

	D1-TYPE	D16-TYPE
	IMPERIAL (METRIC)	IMPERIAL (METRIC)
POWER UNIT:	ENGLISH ELECTRIC 8SRKT	ENGLISH ELECTRIC 8SRKT
TRACTION HORSEPOWER:	730 (544 KW)	790 (589 KW)
STARTING TRACTIVE EFFORT:	57 000 LB (254 KN)	52 500 LB (234 KN)
CONTINUOUS TRACTIVE EFFORT:	25 000 LB (111) KN	30 000 LB (133 KN)
TOTAL WEIGHT:	84.3 TONS (86 T)	91 TONS (93 T)
GAUGE:	1435 MM	1435 MM
ROAD NUMBERS:	D1–D8	D16–D19, D26–D33

X-class Bo-Bo

The Tasmanian Government Railways was the first government-owned railway system in Australia to introduce main line diesel-electric motive power. Ten Bo-Bo units were initially ordered from English Electric of Preston, England, in 1948 and were delivered from October 1950. Subsequent contracts resulted in a total of 32 units being delivered by mid-December 1952, the first 20 coming from the Vulcan Foundry (Lancashire) and the remaining two from the Dick Kerr (Preston) workshops.

Initially the locomotives were placed on main line freight services out of Hobart but as further examples were commissioned they began replacing steam on the long-distance passenger services. Steam traction afterwards remained on secondary service and selected branch lines only. In 1957, goods diagrams and locomotive rosters were reorganised to make better use of diesel, resulting in reductions (and withdrawals) of steam locomotives on an as yet unrivalled scale.

Initially restricted to 64 km/h, suspension modifications to all X-class units during the early 1960s enabled their speed limit to be increased to 72 km/h. In addition, five were upgraded from 1961 with higher capacity generators and traction motors. The locomotives involved, 9, 12, 14, 22 and 28, were reclassified XA and provided with numbers from 1 to 5 respectively.

Age finally caught up with the veterans, the first X-class being withdrawn in October 1980 and the first XA in May 1983. The conversion of rolling stock to air brakes and the influx of 830-class Alcos and ZB-class EEs allowed for the gradual withdrawal of the X and XA classes. The last two were taken out of service in August 1988. Most were withdrawn due to poor mechanical condition, although two were destroyed in January 1986 when they tumbled off the Emu River bridge at Burnie following a fatal level crossing collision.

Several have been preserved. Class-leader X1 now resides in the Tasmanian Transport Museum, Glenorchy; X4 is with the Don River Railway, Devonport; X10 and X18, which were bought by the Derwent Valley Railway Preservation Society for tourist train operations out of New Norfolk, were joined in 2003 by a vandalised X30, the sole

A now historic picture showing XA1 and XA3 leading the larger Y3 while preparing a train in Hobart yard on 14 October 1974. (Peter Watts)

surviving Dick Kerr-built member of the class. It had been acquired in 1988 by the local Lions Club as a centrepiece for a planned rail-themed display around St Marys railway station. In addition, X3 and X20 crossed Bass Strait and are preserved by the Bellarine Peninsula Railway at Queenscliff, Victoria.

SPECIFICATIONS

	IMPERIAL (METRIC)
POWER UNIT:	ENGLISH ELECTRIC 6SRKT
TRACTION HORSEPOWER:	600 (447 KW)
STARTING TRACTIVE EFFORT:	33 500 LB (138 KN)
CONTINUOUS TRACTIVE EFFORT:	12 700 LB (57 KN)
TOTAL WEIGHT:	56.9 TONS (58 T)
GAUGE:	1067 MM
ROAD NUMBERS:	1–32 (XA1–5 WERE PREVIOUSLY X9, X12, X14, X22 AND X28 RESPECTIVELY.)

BB18¼-class 4-6-2

When the QR required additional passenger locomotives following World War II, the administration based the new design on the later series B.18¼-class, which appeared from 1936.

The new Pacifics, designated BB18¼-class, incorporated many modern features, including roller bearings and anti-vacuum devices. The latter were equipped to prevent the superheater elements burning out when the locomotives were standing.

The first order for 35 was placed with the Vulcan Foundry of England. The initial two entered service on 3 February 1951, quickly earning their places on premier express and passenger services. They were

The second locomotive in the BB18¼-class, 1012, poses for official photographs in 1951. (QR archives)

every bit as successful as their earlier prototype, but more refined, being quick off the mark, fast runners and free steamers. Accordingly, a further 20 were ordered, this time from the local firm Walkers Ltd; by 1958, all 55 locomotives in the class were in service.

Their sphere of operation included the Southern and Central Divisions and they were based mainly at Mayne (Brisbane), Toowoomba and Rockhampton. After the Cairns line was upgraded later that decade, their route availability was further extended.

An early in-service modification was made to the locomotives' springing and equalisers, as occasional nasty derailments had been occurring on points.

Diesels made inroads into BB18¼-class territory during the 1960s. The class had to work whatever was available and could be found at the head of anything from suburban passenger services to cane trains.

The first engine withdrawn was 1045 in November 1966. Further withdrawals quickly followed and no less than 13 were condemned on 30 June 1969, by far the largest mass condemnation of the class.

However, two units in service in Mackay lasted until complete dieselisation and both have been preserved; 1037, after languishing in a local park, has been removed for complete rebuild, but as an oil burner. The Mackay Heritage Railway Association, undertaking this work, has also acquired 1086 from a park in Emerald. No. 1089, the last government-owned steam locomotive to enter service in Australia, was retained by QR for preservation and after many years on exhibition in the now closed Redbank Railway Museum entered Ipswich workshops for rebuild and is expected to join QR heritage engine 1079. No. 1072 hauls tourist trains at the Zig Zag Railway at Lithgow, while 1077 (carrying 1015's numbers) is displayed at Winton.

SPECIFICATIONS

	IMPERIAL (METRIC)
CYLINDERS:	18¼ x 24 IN (46 x 61 CM)
BOILER PRESSURE:	170 PSI (1171 KPA)
COUPLED WHEELS:	4 FT 3 IN (130 CM)
TRACTIVE EFFORT:	22 648 LB (100.8 KN)
GRATE AREA:	25 SQ FT (2.323 M²)
TOTAL WEIGHT:	101 TONS (103.1 T)
GAUGE:	1067 MM
ROAD NUMBERS:	1011–1045, 1070–1089

L-class 2-8-2

Part of Australia's contribution to the United Nations Relief and Rehabilitation Administration for assistance to Nationalist China during the late 1940s involved help with that country's railways. Accordingly, the Commonwealth government ordered 50 Mikado-type 2-8-2 locomotives of standard gauge (based on SAR's 700-class, which appeared in 1926) from the Clyde Engineering Co, and planned to ship them to China during 1951–52.

In 1949, with these locomotives' construction in full swing, the Chinese Nationalist government fell to the Communists and Australia's obligation ceased. However, the vexed problem of how to dispose of the locomotives already under construction surfaced. While the NSWGR wanted locomotives, these were slightly outside its loading gauge.

The Commonwealth Department of Supply had been able to successfully reduce the original order from 50 to just 20, and the Commonwealth Railways, despite its decision to dieselise its standard gauge, reluctantly agreed to take ten as the L-class. The administration thought they might be useful to help haul coal trains from Leigh Creek once that railway was rebuilt to standard gauge.

The CR L-class came too late, however, for while they were being built that railway's GM1-class diesel-electrics were being manufactured on Clyde Engineering's very same factory floor. Despite this, the class-leader entered service in April 1951 and the tenth engine was delivered in July 1952.

At least one L-class did see service hauling construction trains on the delayed Leigh Creek standardisation project, but further diesel orders put paid to the steam operation of those trains and the L-class saw very little useful work. They were largely employed on shunting duties and in standby roles. While officially withdrawn between December 1956 and May 1959, two were maintained on standby status into the early 1960s in case of flood.

Details of their disposal are rather sketchy. A couple were cut up during the early 1960s and tenders were called for the disposal of the remainder around 1966. Two boilers were subsequently sent to New Guinea for steam generation while the boiler from 82 was forwarded to Kuala Lumpur in 1968.

Meanwhile, the remaining ten locomotives sitting

Several L-class, including L81 and L82, leave Clyde Engineering's Granville complex on delivery to South Australia. (former CR archives)

in Clyde Engineering's Sydney yard were acquired by South Australian Railways, which absorbed them into its fleet as the 740-class. They had first to be regauged to 1600 mm, and entered traffic between March 1952 and October 1953. Despite their smaller-capacity tenders, the 740-class worked goods trains in conjunction with their 700-class prototype over the state's lighter broad gauge routes.

The SAR's 740s saw many kilometres of useful service until dieselisation rendered them redundant. Although all ten remained operational in 1961, after 745 was stored in January 1962 others went with a rush, seven being condemned in July 1963. The last example in service was 747, withdrawn on 7 July 1964 and condemned on 25 November 1965.

Although an unused L-class tender (last used in a poison train) was sighted in Spencer Junction (Port Augusta) as recently as January 1998, neither an L nor a 740 locomotive was preserved.

Footnote: In 1946, Clyde Engineering hoped to sell the identical locomotive type to the South Maitland Railways (SMR). A Clyde Engineering letter to the SMR, dated 2 October 1946, that has been sighted by this author, furnished details of the locomotives it was building for China.

SPECIFICATIONS

	Imperial (Metric)
Cylinders:	22 x 28 in (56 x 71 cm)
Boiler pressure:	200 psi (1378 kPa)
Coupled wheels:	4 ft 9 in (145 cm)
Tractive effort:	40 418 lb (180 kN)
Grate area:	47 sq ft (4.36 m²)
Total weight:	165 tons (168.3 t)
Gauge:	1435 mm (L-class)
	1600 mm (740-class)
Road numbers:	(CR) L80–L89; (SAR) 740–749

1951 WESTERN AUSTRALIAN GOVERNMENT RAILWAYS

W-class 4-8-2

Designed by Beyer, Peacock & Co, no fewer than 60 locomotives of this class entered service in Western Australia between April 1951 and June 1952. They were acquired as replacements for the elderly G-class 2-6-0 and 4-6-0s to work the state's branch lines, some of which were just 20 kg/m. Designed specifically for the low-heat, crumbly Collie coal, the locomotives' boilers incorporated combustion chambers, thermic siphons and arch tubes. Master Mechanics spark arrestors were provided in the smokeboxes. Other features included self-emptying ashpans, self-cleaning smokeboxes, roller-bearing axle-boxes to all wheels and power reverse equipment.

Being free steamers, exceptionally good riders, economical to operate and maintenance friendly,

W955 rides the Collie turntable in this delightfully moody commercial steam-age April 1968 image. (Philip G. Graham)

the W-class, although nominally a goods engine, was regularly assigned to the prestigious *Australind Express* train.

The W-class was not seriously affected by the introduction of diesels and, although there were 120 of those available by early 1970, the W-class continued operating at full strength. Their stronghold was in the south-western area where they operated mainly goods services. Diesels inevitably broke through, however, and late in 1970 the first withdrawal was made.

By March 1972, only eleven remained operational, steam working finally ceasing in Western Australia on Christmas Eve of that year.

Understandably, W-class locomotives became extremely popular with preservationists and no fewer than 15 were saved from the scrappers. In Western Australia, W903, W908, W920, W945 and W947 have been acquired by the Pinjarra-based Hotham Valley Railway for tourist traffic/parts; W919 is statically preserved at Esperance; W943 slumbers in Collie Railway Museum and W953 resides at the Bassendean Rail Transport Museum.

Interstate, W901 and W907 were acquired by Steamtown Peterborough; the Quorn-based Pichi Richi Preservation Society bought W916 (for spare parts), W931, W933 and W934, while W924 is in the care of The Ghan Preservation Society at MacDonnell Siding, 10 km south of Alice Springs.

But the story does not stop here, for in an intriguing twist, in 1990 the Pichi Richi Preservation Society acquired ex-Silverton Tramway Co W22 from the Puffing Billy Preservation Society of Victoria. The Broken Hill-based Silverton Tramway had acquired four W-class locomotives in 1951 which were basically identical except for the provision of streamlined cowling above their boilers (see page 251). With initial plans to return the Silverton relic to active tourist train service, it was discovered the work to restore the engine was too great; instead, the former WAGR W916 which, as mentioned, had been bought for its spare parts, was shopped. Using a combination of parts from the two locomotives, W916 was returned to service in 2003 carrying the number and styling of W22. The original W22 is stored at the Society's Quorn compound.

SPECIFICATIONS

	IMPERIAL (METRIC)
CYLINDERS:	16 x 24 IN (41 x 61 CM)
BOILER PRESSURE:	200 PSI (1378 KPA)
COUPLED WHEELS:	4 FT 0 IN (122 CM)
TRACTIVE EFFORT:	21 760 LB (96.8 KN)
GRATE AREA:	27 SQ FT (2.508 M²)
TOTAL WEIGHT:	101.11 TONS (103.1 T)
GAUGE:	1067 MM
ROAD NUMBERS:	901–960

R701 was showing its age when captured on film working No. 13 Ballarat–Maryborough goods on 19 January 1965. (John S. Glastonbury)

1951 VICTORIAN RAILWAYS

R-class 4-6-4

Designed to replace VR's successful but ageing A2 class 4-6-0s which dated back to 1907, the R-class Hudsons were handicapped from the start by the simultaneous deliveries of main line diesel-electrics.

Seventy of these 4-6-4 giants were built by the North British Locomotive Co and entered service from 19 July 1951. The last into traffic, R707, arrived in August 1954 complete with experimental Stug pulverising coal-burning equipment. Although the trials were resoundingly successful and plans were in place to retrofit the entire fleet with the equipment, continuous diesel ordering resulted in a change of policy. The equipment was removed from R707 in 1957.

The R-class quickly took over the A2-class's more important express passenger diagrams, eliminating double-heading on some of the heavier expresses. However, with new B-class Co-Co diesels arriving midway through commissioning of the big 4-6-4s, their resounding effectiveness was dulled somewhat by the efficiency of the interlopers and the R-class was relegated to the less important services and freight trains.

The first to be withdrawn was R755, after it was badly damaged in a serious accident at Broadmeadows in September 1960. The locomotive was officially cut up two months later. Three more succumbed in 1961 and another five in 1962. Engines R707 and R761 remained in good enough condition to enjoy a brief period of special passenger tour train working during the early 1970s; when they were eventually withdrawn, enough storage space could fortunately be found for them, and others, outside Newport Workshops, allowing time for preservation groups to arrange suitable restoration projects.

Today, R700, R711 and R761 are owned by Steamrail Victoria Ltd; R704 is exhibited at North Williamstown Railway Museum; R707 is operated by Newport-based R707 Operations which also owns R753. In addition, R766 was being converted to standard gauge, as this book closed for press, for lease to the NSW Hunter Valley Railway Trust, which intends basing it in Sydney for tourist operations carrying traditional London, Midland & Sottish (UK) Coronation Red livery. (The R-class, like many modern Victorian steam types, was originally designed for gauge conversion.)

As an interesting aside, Steamrail Victoria's R711 was returned to commercial service in May 1999 by the now defunct West Coast Railway Limited. The restoration was carried out at Ballarat Workshops and included the fitting of a performance-enhancing double chimney. It was also configured for multiple unit operation with non-crewed diesel locomotives. A special control stand was rigged into the locomotive's cab operating all diesel controls except dynamic braking.

SPECIFICATIONS

	Imperial (Metric)
Cylinders:	21¼ x 28 in (54 x 71 cm)
Boiler pressure:	210 psi (1446 kPa)
Coupled wheels:	6 ft 1 in (186 cm)
Tractive effort:	31 648 lb (140.8 kN)
Grate area:	42 sq ft (3.9 m²)
Total weight:	187 tons (190.7 t)
Gauge:	1600 mm
Road numbers:	700–769

1951 Tasmanian Government Railways

H-class 4-8-2

In common with other Australian state railway systems, the TGR required urgent post-war motive power, both to meet fast development and to replace worn-out stock.

Suitable main line locomotives were needed quickly and no time could be lost in designing them, so the CME of the day visited Britain and researched what the principal builders had to offer. He eventually settled on eight of a 4-8-2 Mountain-type freight locomotive design, an improved version of a pre-war design that was at the time being supplied by the Vulcan Foundry to the Gold Coast Railway in Africa.

The new locomotives all arrived on the one ship in October 1951 and became the TGR's H-class. They were slightly larger than the existing Australian-built Q-class 4-8-2s and were equipped with a higher pressure boiler. Despite the H-class having a higher tractive effort, the H and Q classes were given identical load ratings by the TGR.

All eight locomotives, like the new X, M and V classes, were delivered in green livery, a welcome change after the drab all-black engines that until then had been working on the system.

Because the X-class diesel-electrics were being delivered concurrently with the H-class, these beautifully-balanced 4-8-2s were restricted to operating in certain areas. They worked the northern portion of the Main, Fingal and Western lines as far as Wynyard, and were also used on Western line passenger duties, two being repainted red in 1956 for that purpose.

H2 at Launceston in September 1968. (Philip G. Graham)

When general overhauls became due from 1961, the class was gradually withdrawn from service because new Y-class diesel-electrics were coming on stream. H2 and H4 were set aside that year, followed by the class-leader in 1962.

The remaining locomotives saw limited service on goods trains out of Launceston and Devonport throughout the 1960s, with H2 being overhauled and returned to service in 1967.

The TGR's centenary celebrations in February 1971 were marked by a steam extravaganza, with several classes of locomotives being used on special trains throughout the state to the delight of local and visiting railway enthusiasts. The H-class was represented by H2 and H5. While the latter engine was withdrawn during June 1971, H2 remained in service, frequently being used on suburban passenger trains, the Launceston and Western Junction passenger and on special workings. It was eventually withdrawn in September 1975 after hauling a ballast train.

With the operational takeover of the Tasmanian rail system by the federal government in 1978, the new owners had no further use for steam locomotives and all were disposed of.

Today, the class-leader is exhibited in the Tasmanian Transport Museum at Glenorchy. H2 and H5 reside at the Derwent Valley Railway Preservation Society's New Norfolk complex while a tenderless H6 is in a Perth (Tasmania) park and H7 is part of the Don River Railway (Devonport) collection.

H3, H4 and H8 were towed to Mowbray for scrapping in December 1978.

SPECIFICATIONS

	Imperial (Metric)
Cylinders:	18 x 24 in (46 x 61 cm)
Boiler pressure:	200 psi (1378 kPa)
Coupled wheels:	4 ft 0 in (122 cm)
Tractive effort:	27 540 lb (122.6 kN)
Grate area:	34 sq ft (3.159 m²)
Total weight:	111 tons (113.2 t)
Gauge:	1067 mm
Road numbers:	1–8

1951 COMMONWEALTH RAILWAYS

GM1-class A1A-A1A

Commonwealth Railways, operator of the arid Trans-Australian Railway, had been actively investigating dieselisation since 1913 (well before its first services started between Port Augusta and Kalgoorlie).

Steam traction was ultimately employed on the CR when the line opened in 1917, but boiler repairs became a real burden to the railway, the corrosive effects of the saline desert bore-water accounting for up to 80 per cent of all locomotive repairs.

During the late 1940s CR entered negotiations with the Clyde Engineering Co, a leading Sydney steam locomotive and rolling-stock builder. Following several trips overseas by CR and Clyde executives, the builder managed to secure a manufacturing licence agreement with the powerful La Grange, Illinois-based Electro-Motive Division (EMD) of General Motors Corporation. This firm at the time had a variety of tried and proven diesel-electric designs operating in North America, including its streamlined Bo-Bo F7 model.

Prominent in establishing the manufacturing deal was ex-South Australian Railways CME Fred Shea. He believed Australia, with its plethora of worn-out steam locomotives coupled with the post-war traffic boom, was a rich and untapped market for reliable new diesel-electrics.

Armed with a contract for eleven diesel-electric locomotives, Shea's first task was to redesign the F7 and produce a stretched, lowered version more in keeping with Australia's tighter loading gauge. This was done through the repositioning of overhead radiators to the side walls and the relocation within the engine room of the ancillary equipment.

To reduce the locomotive's axle load to 19.5 tonnes, the unit's extra length made it possible to fit two 3-axle bogies in lieu of the US version's 4-axle bogies. However, the axle for the centre wheels of each Australian bogie was a non-powered idler axle, making the unit's wheel arrangement A1A-A1A.

The resultant 110-tonne locomotives, which appeared between September 1951 and July 1952, became Commonwealth Railways' GM1-class; all eleven were powered by EMD's proven but (then) ageing 16-cylinder 567B diesel engine which exerted 1119 kW for traction purposes.

These sturdy machines were an overnight success

A pristine, fully overhauled GM1, after it emerged from its most recent rebuild, basking in Port Augusta's Spencer Junction yard on 27 November 1997, awaiting entry into active service with ASR. (Leon Oberg)

and, apart from reducing all CR's standard gauge steam operations to shunting, construction or standby use, spawned a variety of EMD/Clyde diesel locomotives that eventually saw service in all mainland states and several overseas countries as well.

Over the years their engines were upgraded. Their 'B'-type crankcases were provided with 'C' insert liners, which allowed cooling water to be fed into the engine from a water gallery within the engine rather than in the crankcase. This eliminated the fears of cracking caused by corrosion and fatigue within the crankcase cooling water area, as had been experienced in high mileage locomotives in the USA.

As the Commonwealth rail system gradually expanded following the formation of Australian National Railways (AN) in 1978, so too did the class's operational sphere. This was further aided by brief inter-system locomotive operations, which for a time saw these ultra-reliable locomotives haul trains as far afield as Perth and Lithgow.

The first locomotive withdrawn was GM5, which was badly damaged in a serious four-locomotive head-on collision at Port Augusta station on Good Friday 1987. Soon afterwards, sister units GM4 and GM9 rolled onto their sides with their engine blocks cracked open following a derailment at Crystal Brook. Their age and the high cost of repairs dictated their withdrawals too.

Amazingly, when the still-active class-leader,

GM1, was retired for preservation at Port Augusta station mid-1989, it had covered almost 7.5 million kilometres in an exemplary 38-year working life.

The last locomotive in traffic was GM10, used as a shunter at Port Augusta Workshops until 13 September 1994. However, the story did not end there, for GM1, which due to vandalism was returned to Port Augusta Workshops for 'its own safety', was in 1997 overhauled on the orders of then Federal Transport Minister John Sharp. This author had brought the plight of the locomotive to Mr Sharp's attention in 1996 and argued it should be returned to original, pristine operating condition and kept in Canberra by the Commonwealth as a public relations locomotive. AN's Port Augusta Workshops was given the work, which included the fitting of a fully overhauled 567C diesel engine suitably down-rated to meet the limited capabilities of the locomotive's electrical system.

The unit underwent a series of trials during the late spring of 1997. However, before the locomotive could be forwarded to Canberra, the Federal Government sold AN, the mainland intrastate operations going to a consortium (which included GM1's builder, Clyde Engineering) to be known as Australia Southern Railroad. This company assumed control on 8 November 1997. Unfortunately, the sale coincided with the re-registration of GM1 and ASR insisted that since it was 'on AN's books' the

Former Commonwealth Railways GM10 wears the colours of Southern Shorthaul Railroad. In this form the unit has been worked in three states, principally in metropolitan trip train and wagon exchange service. The veteran locomotive was pictured in Goulburn on 26 July 2004, well away from its original stamping ground. (Leon Oberg)

unit technically belonged to them and within weeks put the relic to work hauling wheat and other general freight. Although seeing little service in recent years, it fortunately does remain operational.

Of the others, GM2 resides in the National Railway Museum, Port Adelaide, and GM3 is on permanent loan to Clyde Engineering. After it received a light overhaul and a repaint in original CR colours, the unit was named *Ray E. Purves* in honour of the Clyde Industries chairman and managing director who was responsible for obtaining the first EMD manufacturing licence outside the USA. The locomotive is now Clyde's Bathurst works shunting and public relations locomotive.

GM10 remained in store at Port Augusta shops until sold to Great Northern Railroad (Melbourne) in August 1998 and returned to active service. It now has a permanent home with Rail Heritage West Australia's Bassendean's Rail Transport Museum.

Footnote: Two US F7 567B-engined Bo-Bo locomotives came to Australia second-hand from the Western Pacific Railroad in March 1968, imported by the Mt Newman Mining Co in Western Australia's Pilbara region. They were used initially for rail construction duties, and later for shunting work and train haulage. Both have been preserved locally, one in operational condition.

SPECIFICATIONS

	IMPERIAL (METRIC)
POWER UNIT:	EMD 16-567B
TRACTION HORSEPOWER:	1500 (1119 kW)
STARTING TRACTIVE EFFORT:	48 400 LB (215 kN)
CONTINUOUS TRACTIVE EFFORT:	31 000 LB (138 kN)
TOTAL WEIGHT:	108 TONS (110 T)
GAUGE:	1435 MM
ROAD NUMBERS:	GM1–GM11

1951 SILVERTON TRAMWAY

W-class 4-8-2

The economies of working larger and heavier trains were quickly becoming apparent to directors of the Silverton Tramway in far-western New South Wales, a 58 km mineral railway built during the late 1880s and linking Broken Hill's rich mines with the South Australian Railways at Cockburn.

The post-World War II minerals boom was taxing the tramway's ability to economically shift the tonnage it was now required to handle. The company's largest locomotives were four members of the 4-6-0 A-class, which were augmented by a collection of elderly, small Y-class 2-6-0s, most of which had been acquired during the 1890s.

The only member of the class cut up for scrap was loco W23, pictured at Railwaytown with an older A-class in 1965. (Late Ron Preston)

Clearly, larger and more powerful engines were required, and the company placed an order in 1950 with Beyer, Peacock & Co (the suppliers of all engines to the railway in the past) for four heavy 4-8-2 tender engines, similar to 60 on order to WAGR.

But the tramway almost did not receive their locomotives because they and their ship were nearly lost at sea during their voyage from Liverpool docks to Port Pirie aboard the SS *Belpareil* in mid-1951 (along with TGR's eight H-class 4-8-2s). An obscure account accidentally unearthed during the 1980s revealed that, when anchored in the Mediterranean Sea off Port Said awaiting a convoy through the Suez Canal, 'a frightful storm blew up producing waves which crashed over the ship's decks'.

The pitching and rolling of the ship soon started to take its toll on the locomotives, which were being carried on the open between deck. With each giant wave came scraping, creaking and groaning from the moored locomotives. As the crew members summoned to further lash the engines and tenders worked frantically, an extreme wave suddenly snapped the lashings of one locomotive which immediately lurched sideways, totally out of control. It slithered into the ship's side with a shudder which could be felt all through the vessel, protruding over the plating by 25 cm, but held from ripping the sides from the ship by the ribbing. One sailor was trapped in the space between the engine and the plate sides. The only way

out was to crawl between the wheels, but because of the storm to do this would have meant instant death. He spent the remainder of the night in that perilous position, feeling the cold wash of the sea on the plates behind his back.

Morning saw the sea flatten out, making it possible to move the runaway. Using huge snatch bolts and a powerful winch, the locomotive was gradually inched back into its original position.

The *Belpareil* arrived safely in Port Pirie in October 1951, where all of the W-class were assembled and operated as one train to Broken Hill, with two of the engines in steam.

Exerting a tractive effort of 97 kN, the new W-class provided an increase of 20 kN over the elderly A-class on the line. They were capable of hauling 1020 tonnes over a 1 in 100 gradient and 610 tonnes over a 1 in 60 grade.

Throughout their lives the four class members wore distinctive green livery and carried semi-streamlining, somewhat similar to WAGR's S-class 4-8-2s. During the early 1950s, all were hired out to the SAR on a rotating basis, being based at Peterborough. This was a period of extreme narrow-gauge engine shortage which was relieved from June 1953 with the delivery of new 400-class Beyer-Garratts which, as far as their running gear was concerned, were almost a copy of the W-class.

Working the Broken Hill expresses in addition

to their freight train chores, the W-class gave exceptional service to the tramway until replaced by three 653 kW Alco diesel-electrics from December 1960. All were placed in store inside the company's Railwaytown locomotive shed and only one ever ran again, being used to head special trains for visiting rail enthusiasts.

With the elimination of the Silverton Tramway's narrow-gauge Cockburn route (via Silverton) because of the East–West gauge-standardisation project in 1970, all four members of the class were disposed of. W22, which was freighted to Victoria's Puffing Billy Preservation Society at Menzies Creek, today resides at South Australia's Pichi Richi Railway (having given its number and certain cosmetics to ex-WAGR W-class W916, which now operates tourist trains); W24 is preserved at Broken Hill's Sulphide Street Station Museum and W25 was forwarded to the ARHS's Port Dock Station Railway Museum. Sadly, W23 was cut up for scrap in 1970.

During their decade of active service, all managed to cover some 360 000 km; the furthest travelled engine was W25 (the last one actually in traffic) which accumulated an impressive 379 689 km.

SPECIFICATIONS

	IMPERIAL (METRIC)
CYLINDERS:	16 x 24 IN (41 x 61 CM)
BOILER PRESSURE:	200 PSI (1378 KPA)
COUPLED WHEELS:	4 FT 0 IN (122 CM)
TRACTIVE EFFORT:	21 760 LB (96.8 KN)
GRATE AREA:	27 SQ FT (2.508 M²)
TOTAL WEIGHT:	102 TONS (104 T)
GAUGE:	1067 MM
ROAD NUMBERS:	W22–25

900-class A1A-A1A

The ten diesel-electric locomotives of this class were the first main line units to be operated by the SAR. They were introduced to the system after an elaborate ceremony on 10 September 1951 at the railway's Islington Workshops.

Because they were planned in the days prior to any Australian engineering firm having stitched up manufacturing licence agreements with existing overseas diesel-electric builders, these 900-class locomotives were designed and built by the railway department itself. All mechanical and electrical components were subcontracted to the UK firm English Electric.

All were in broad-gauge service by July 1953.

The 900-class locomotives were built to replace steam power over the heavily-graded Adelaide–Tailem Bend line. They quickly took over the 500-class 4-8-4 steam working of *The Overland* interstate expresses, and became firm favourites for heavy interstate freight work.

Resplendent in maroon livery and silver-like stainless steel panels, the class-leader was named *Lady Norrie* after the wife of the then state governor, Sir Willoughby Norrie.

Each locomotive was powered by a 1184 kW 16-cylinder diesel engine while all units were fitted with acoustic panels to absorb noise. Their top speed was 118 km/h.

Gradually ousted from the top interstate traffic by newer Alco-powered 930-class locomotives later

Locomotive 901 in Mile End Locomotive Depot yard following a service of 7 February 1978. (Leon Oberg)

that decade, the 900-class eventually found its niche principally working express passenger and goods traffic over the easy grades of the Port Pirie line. They also became regular power on the Peterborough run.

Due to ageing technology and a shortage of spare parts, 903 was withdrawn on 1 May 1979 when it became due for full overhaul and rewire. All remaining units had been retired by June 1985.

The class-leader, 900, today resides at the National Railway Museum, Port Adelaide. Nos 907 and 909, after being saved by the South Australian ARHS, were disposed of to the Port Pirie-based Australian Railway Locomotive & Rollingstock Co for planned reactivation. The other seven have been cut up as scrap.

SPECIFICATIONS

	IMPERIAL (METRIC)
POWER UNIT:	ENGLISH ELECTRIC 16SVT
TRACTION HORSEPOWER:	1588 (1184 kW)
STARTING TRACTIVE EFFORT:	44 800 LB (196 kN)
CONTINUOUS TRACTIVE EFFORT:	34 000 LB (151 kN)
TOTAL WEIGHT:	119.6 TONS (122 T)
GAUGE:	1600 MM
ROAD NUMBERS:	900–909

1951 VICTORIAN RAILWAYS

F-class 0-6-0DE

Buoyed by the promise dieselisation held for improved locomotive availability, the Victorian government turned to English Electric in the UK for help when needing shunting locomotives for both its Victorian Railways shunting operations and State Electricity Commission exchange siding transfer needs.

English Electric had been developing a range of rigid-framed 0-6-0 shunting locomotives since the 1930s. While early examples had mechanical transmissions, ongoing developments saw a reliable electric transmission available in the UK midway through World War II.

The British Ministry of Supply promptly ordered 20 for war service, some of which were sent to Holland, Belgium and France during the closing stages of hostilities. Six units delivered after the war ended were acquired by the London Midland & Scottish Railway and the type soon became know as the 'ultimate' shunting locomotive. The design was adopted by British Rail in 1949 and at one

Locomotive F209, an original VR delivery, rests at Melbourne's Dynon locomotive depot on 7 February 1979. (Leon Oberg)

stage 106 units were in standard-gauge service throughout Britain. Another 25 were built new for the Netherlands Railways Company between 1949 and 1954 as their class 511. (These joined ten LMS-built British Ministry of Supply units that had been phased into Netherlands service following hostilities.)

It was this basic 260 kW design that was adopted by the Victorian government although, tipping the scales at 50 tonnes and equipped for 1600 mm gauge, they were slightly heavier than their British counterparts.

Ten were issued to Victorian Railways and the remaining six went to the SEC. However, the SEC's need for so many broad-gauge shunting units was questionable, as some actually spent more time working in VR yards. All had passed into VR hands by May 1971.

Collectively, the distinctive little end-cab machines, which were fitted with sideboards to protect shunting staff getting 'tangled up' in their steam locomotive-type motion, became the F-class. One used to have its daily moment of glory at Melbourne's Spencer Street station when it transferred *The Overland* express train between the station and the nearby car sheds for cleaning.

The last unit in VR operation was F211, which ended its days as workshop shunter at South Dynon depot late in 1986. It was initially mounted on a short portion of line outside that complex but today basks in the ARHS North Williamstown Museum with F216 (preserved as SEC2). Three others also survive: F202 at Seymour; F208 (carrying an earlier number F317) operational with a Newport preservation body, and F212 operational at Maldon.

SPECIFICATIONS

	IMPERIAL (METRIC)
POWER UNIT:	ENGLISH ELECTRIC 6KT

TRACTION HORSEPOWER:	350 (250 kW)
STARTING TRACTIVE EFFORT:	33 000 lb (146.9 kN)
CONTINUOUS TRACTIVE EFFORT:	11 000 lb (48.9 kN)
TOTAL WEIGHT:	49.5 tons (50.8 t)
GAUGE:	1600 mm
ROAD NUMBERS:	(ORIGINAL) F310–319 AND BECAME F201–216 IN 1960, INCLUDING ABSORPTION OF SEC UNITS

1951 NEW SOUTH WALES GOVERNMENT RAILWAYS

40-class A1A-A1A

Although the NSWGR had been operating two Bo-Bo 79-class diesel-electrics in shunting capacities since World War II, the 20-member strong 40-class represented the railway's first serious attempt at main line dieselisation.

This basically 'off the shelf' American Locomotive Co design was imported from that manufacturer's Montreal, Canada, factory, with the first two entering service between Enfield and Broadmeadow on 30 November 1951.

The 40-class derived from a type which originated in North America in 1946, when the first of what eventually amounted to 352 Bo-Bo 1119 kW locomotives, produced in four and a half years, went

into service. The diesel engine was then up-rated to 1193 kW and about 1600 more locomotives were manufactured.

The Australian 40-class stemmed from the later North American up-rated RSC3 model, of which 19 entered service in Canada and the USA between November 1950 and June 1952. For Australian service, minor structural alterations, mainly to the cab profile, were required to meet the NSWGR's less-generous loading gauge.

As additional locomotives arrived, the 40-class began to take over former steam-hauled express goods and fruit trains and worked as far north as South Brisbane and south to Albury. By April 1952, all 20 were running, usually working through loads as paired units.

Although basically intended for goods haulage, the 40-class ran successful early tests with the *Brisbane Limited Express* passenger services. Over the following few years they infiltrated into long-distance passenger diagrams during holiday times, including the haulage of Sunday tour specials to Canberra.

The class was introduced in green livery but 4001 and 4002 were repainted royal blue in connection with HM Queen Elizabeth's 1954 Royal Tour of New South Wales. These locomotives became famous when they worked three royal trains between Sydney and Newcastle, Sydney and Bulli, and Bathurst to Sydney.

A rather smokey 4009 at Goulburn on 19 November 1962. (Leon Oberg)

Cliffs, Robe River Iron Associates (now part of Pilbara Rail) customised the pair of 40-class bought second-hand from A.E. Goodwin Ltd. Here we see 9401 (formerly NSWGR 4006) shunting at Cape Lambert on 31 July 1979. (Peter Watts)

The class's arrival coincided with the delivery of new D59 and AD60 class steam locomotives. Needless to say, the new diesels were more popular with the crews for they were cleaner, fast and very capable. Despite their higher capital cost, the administration was impressed by their capacity to work virtually non-stop for up to 23 hours each day. Thus the die was cast, and dieselisation of the NSWGR became a reality.

With the introduction of additional diesel-electric locomotive types later that decade, the 40-class became a regular light passenger engine over the North Coast, North and Southern lines. The *North Coast Daylight Express* became a regular 40-class roster. Others could be found working the *Kempsey Mail.*

During their first decade of service, engine reliability was improved with the conversion of their original air-cooled turbo-superchargers to water cooling.

History was made in mid-1961 when 4017 logged the first million miles (1.6 million kilometres) for the class in only nine years. Soon all had exceeded this total. Not long afterwards, investigations were made into the possibility of repowering the class. Being of A1A-A1A wheel configuration, unsurprisingly problems were arising with driving wheel wear. Because only the outside wheels of each bogie were powered, they were wearing faster than the unpowered centre pair. Coupled with a low adhesive weight when compared to a similar locomotive where all axles were powered, nuisance wheelslip was a characteristic of the class.

The 40-class performed yeoman service for the department nonetheless, and it was not until there was a serious electrical fire in 4014 in May 1968 that any reductions were made to the number in traffic. Six months later, 4007 suffered a similar fire and joined its sister engine at Chullora Workshops as a provider of spare parts. By January 1970, another two had been retired. Shortly afterwards an order was placed with A.E. Goodwin Ltd for 20 larger Co-Co units as replacements for the entire class, with the A1A-A1As successfully being offered as trade-ins.

In March 1970, No. 4004 became the first to be dispatched by Goodwin for stripping and subsequent scrapping. Others followed, a limited number of their parts being retained for the new main-liner Co-Cos.

However, life was not over for all of the 40-class. Early in 1971, the Western Australian iron ore miner, Cliffs, Robe River Iron Associates, began construction of a 162 km mining railroad linking Cape Lambert with the mine site at Mt Enid. Placing an order with A.E. Goodwin in Sydney (the holder of Alco's Australian licence) for six heavy M636 locomotives, the contractors setting up the mine and railway also sought two second-hand locos for railway construction purposes. The units selected were trade-ins 4002 and 4006, which were overhauled, painted yellow, renumbered 261.002 and 261.001 respectively and despatched to Darling Island on 8 August 1971 for shipping to the Pilbara.

After the railway was commissioned, the two units passed from the contractor's hands to the mining company, which used them as shunting locomotives, generally working together at Cape Lambert. Robe River renumbered them, 4006 becoming 9401 and 4002 becoming 9405.

With the increasing weight of the unit ore trains, their A1A-A1A wheel arrangement provided too much wheel slip so the company removed the centre freewheeling axles of each bogie to increase adhesion. Their equalisers were then extended, effectively turning them into Bo-Bo units.

Both locomotives were retired late in 1980 and preserved locally.

Meanwhile, the end had come for the remaining NSWGR units and on 13 December 1971 the last in service, 4015, was withdrawn. Class-leader 4001 was undergoing restoration to full running order by the Thirlmere Railway Museum as this book was being prepared. It has been in static preservation for more than three decades.

SPECIFICATIONS

	IMPERIAL (METRIC)
POWER UNIT:	Alco 244 12-cylinders
TRACTION HORSEPOWER:	1600 (1193 kW)
STARTING TRACTIVE EFFORT:	49 700 lb (221 kN)
CONTINUOUS TRACTIVE EFFORT:	46 000 lb (205 kN)
TOTAL WEIGHT:	111 tons (113 t)
GAUGE:	1435 mm
ROAD NUMBERS:	(NSWGR) 4001–4020
	(Cliffs) 9401 (ex 4006) and 9405 (ex 4002)

M-class 4-6-2

In addition to the eight Mountain-type H-class locomotives ordered during the TGR CME's post-war visit to Britain, ten light passenger-type steam locomotives were bought from Robert Stephenson & Hawthorn Ltd. These locomotives were similar to a 1000 mm gauge design which had just been delivered to the Indian and Burma railways as the YB-class.

All ten arrived in Hobart on the freighter *Christen Smith* on 12 March 1952 and became the M-class. They were towed to Launceston for commissioning, following which most were allotted to operate across northern Tasmania. A total of five were based at Launceston shed at one stage.

As diesel-electric X-class locomotives had already made giant inroads into the state's railway network, the 4-6-2s were somewhat restricted from the very start, and in 1957 four of them were fitted with smaller 122 cm diameter coupled wheels salvaged from withdrawn Australian Standard Garratts. This modification enabled them to operate heavier trains over the steeply-graded North Eastern line. The converted locomotives became the MA-class and the entire fleet subjected to a seemingly irrational road number reshuffle.

By 1960, the TGR had surplus steam power so M-class locomotives were withdrawn as they needed major attention. The engine renumbered as M1 (originally delivered as M7) was the first to go, followed by M2 (formerly M10) in 1961.

Four M and two MA-class survived until June 1971, two of which (MA4 and M6) were used as steam cleaning plants at Launceston and Hobart respectively.

The TGR returned M3 to service in 1972, after which the locomotive saw extensive use on Hobart suburban passenger trains, the Launceston–Western Junction passenger and special tour trains. It was withdrawn in late 1975.

It is satisfying to relate that the entire class has been preserved. M1, which wastefully ran just 143 000 km during its lifetime, awaits restoration at the Derwent Valley Railway, as does MA1. Locomotive M2, after residing for some decades at Stanley Caravan Park, was bought tenderless by the Tanfield Railway (in north-east England) during the early 1990s, while MA2, MA4, M3 and M4 are at

Locomotive M6 operational at Queenscliff in Victoria in September 2002. (Leon Oberg)

the Don River Railway, Devonport. Loco MA3 is at Margate; M5 inhabits the Tasmanian Transport Museum, Glenorchy; while M6 was acquired by the Bellarine Peninsula Railway at Queenscliff, Victoria and regularly works tourist trains.

SPECIFICATIONS

	M-CLASS	MA-CLASS
	IMPERIAL (METRIC)	IMPERIAL (METRIC)
CYLINDERS:	16 x 24 IN (41 x 61 CM)	16 x 24 IN (41 x 61 CM)
BOILER PRESSURE:	180 LB (1240 KPA)	180 PSI (1240 KPA)
COUPLED WHEELS:	4 FT 7 IN (140 CM)	4 FT 0 IN (122 CM)
TRACTIVE EFFORT:	17 091 LB (76 KN)	19 584 LB (87 KN)
GRATE AREA:	21.3 SQ FT (2.0 M²)	21.3 SQ FT (2.0 M²)
TOTAL WEIGHT:	97 TONS (99 T)	95 TONS (97 T)
GAUGE:	1067 MM	1067 MM
ROAD NUMBERS:	(ORIGINAL) M1—M10	
	(MA-CLASS) MA1—MA4 (ORIGINALLY M8, M1, M6 AND M2 RESPECTIVELY)	
	(FINAL M-CLASS DISPLACEMENT) M1 (WAS M7), M2 (WAS M10), M3, M4, M5, M6 (WAS M9)	

1952 MULGRAVE SUGAR MILL

Bundaberg Fowler 0-6-2T

The many sugar producers along the Queensland coast have always held an interest for the true railway enthusiast. Up until the early 1980s, steam locomotives, sometimes of tiny proportions, trundled their laden rakes of wagons of raw sugar cane to the mills over many kilometres of principally 610 mm gauge track.

Among the steam locomotives to operate in this capacity were small engines from American, German, British and, more recently, Australian builders. One of the most favoured was the English Fowler, a product of John Fowler & Co of Leeds. The company was formed in 1850 by John Fowler, the inventor of the steam plough, who produced this and other steam-powered items for agriculture, including traction engines and road rollers. Their continued interest in agricultural equipment led to a substantial business later on with light locomotives.

About 130 Fowler locomotives were sold to the Queensland sugar mills and a number of other industrial concerns in Australia.

No.1 *Jumbo*, a 1952 Bundaberg Foundry 0-6-2T product based on a Fowler design, used at the Millaquin Sugar Co's Qunaba mill, was one of the last in commercial cane service. (Late Ron Preston)

In 1935, John Fowler & Co ceased making steam locomotives but, as there was still a need for them in Australia, the plans were obtained by the Bundaberg Foundry in Queensland. Because no real rival to the sugar industry light steam locomotive seemed possible as the 1950s dawned, the Bundaberg Foundry started marketing its own product (a re-designed version) and the first sale was made to the Mulgrave Sugar Mill early in 1952. Within 12 months, a total of eight had been delivered to Queensland sugar mills, including Mossman Central, Bingera, Proserpine, Pleystowe and Millaquin.

All were built to the 0-6-2T wheel arrangement except for No. 3, which was constructed as an 0-4-2T to suit its customer's need for a more flexible chassis arrangement.

Dieselisation came fast to the canefields and, although the maker's plates had been cast for a planned ninth engine, the Bundaberg Foundry began constructing diesels from its No. 10 number onwards. The eight steam locomotives gave extremely good service and three (maker's numbers 1, 3 and 6) remained in service throughout much of the 1970s.

All still remain, although as museum pieces. Perhaps the first to be given a tourist-train role was No. 4, which left Bingera Mill in 1974 for Goulburn. Soon afterwards it was transferred to the Lachlan Vintage Village at Forbes, where it saw several more years hauling tourist trains before being sold to Echuca interests, on the Murray River.

Nos 1 and 3 belong to the Australian Sugar Cane Railway (in Bundaberg's Botanical Gardens), Nos 2 and 6 are at the Ballyhooley Tourist Railway at Port Douglas, while No. 8 is held by a Murumba Downs enthusiast.

The Australian Narrow Gauge Railway Museum Society at Woodford operates No. 5. This sturdy locomotive had moments of fame when it was loaned to the Moreton Central Sugar Mill at Nambour in 1997, 1999 and 2000 and put to commercial use hauling sugar cane trains between Howard Street (exchange) yard and the mill as part of the district's annual mid-August Sugar Festival celebrations. Gulliver Media Australia, a maker of television documentaries, hired the locomotive for filming at several mills (from Nambour in the state's south to Mossman in the far north) during August–September 2000.

No. 7 loco was last noted operating at the Coal Creek Museum at Korumburra in Victoria.

	IMPERIAL (METRIC)
CYLINDERS:	10 x 14 IN (25 x 35 CM)
BOILER PRESSURE:	180 PSI (1240 KPA)
COUPLED WHEELS:	2 FT 4 IN (71 CM)
TRACTIVE EFFORT:	7200 LB (32 KN)
GRATE AREA:	7.2 SQ FT (0.670 M²)
GAUGE:	610 MM

1952 NEW SOUTH WALES GOVERNMENT RAILWAYS

45-class Co+Co

With the promise of increasing train loads over the NSWGR's steeply graded Blue Mountains, partly brought about by planned coal mine outputs in that area, a decision was made during the early 1950s to electrify the railway to Lithgow. With planning underway, forty 2535 kW 1500V (DC) 46-class locomotives were ordered from the UK (see page 303) to work that route, which at the time was the domain of hard-working Mountain-type D57 and D58 class steam locomotives.

In a bid to train enginemen in the 'newfangled' motive power, the NSWGR administration decided to construct a one-off locomotive to the same basic plans as the 46-class. Completed at its Chullora Workshops from parts (including body) generally supplied and fabricated by local firm Commonwealth Engineering, this locomotive was numbered 4501.

Weighing in at 108 tons (the same as those on order), the locomotive in reality saw little commercial use until wiring extended further into outer suburban stations. For instance, when western electrification reached Penrith in October 1955, engine 4501 was used for a time to haul local passenger trains. When the first 46-class locomotives were commissioned eight months later, 4501 became a regular in the training of crews while it assisted north-bound steam-hauled goods trains over the difficult North Strathfield to Hornsby route. Because of its then green and cream paint job, the steam drivers quickly bestowed on it the nickname 'Green Beetle'.

In 1957, the locomotive was permanently based at Flemington electric car sheds where it was employed as a shunter. Four years later, 4501 underwent an identity change, officially becoming 7100 from October 1961 to make the 45-class series available

The rather boxy 7100 (ex 4501), which is today preserved by the NSWRTM at Thirlmere Railway Museum. (Leon Oberg).

for a new order of heavy Alco diesel locomotives. Under this new identity, 7100 soldiered on at Flemington car sheds with little drama until 1968, when it received an overhaul, several tonnes of added ballast, and was provided with necessary main line-safe working equipment for heavy coal service over the then newly-electrified Glenlee coal mine railway (outside Campbelltown).

But failures dogged the veteran to the point where the administration eventually lost patience, and it was condemned in June 1974. After a period of storage outside Chullora workshops, the relic was donated to the NSW Rail Transport Museum and today is located at Thirlmere Railway Museum.

SPECIFICATIONS

	IMPERIAL (METRIC)
ELECTRICAL EQUIPMENT:	AEI 1500 V (DC)
MAXIMUM HORSEPOWER:	2700 (2045 KW)
STARTING TRACTIVE EFFORT:	72 600 LB (323 KN)
CONTINUOUS TRACTIVE EFFORT:	38 700 LB (173 KN)
TOTAL WEIGHT:	108 TONS (110 T)
GAUGE:	1435 MM
ROAD NUMBERS:	4501 (RENUMBERED 7100, OCTOBER 1961)

1952 NEW SOUTH WALES GOVERNMENT RAILWAYS

AD60-class
4-8-4 + 4-8-4

Although the NSWGR had considered standard-gauge Garratts on four separate occasions from 1920 when new express passenger engines were required, articulated locomotives did not arrive on the system until 30 July 1952, when the first of an order for 25 monster AD60-class Beyer-Garratts entered service.

Designed and built by Beyer, Peacock & Co to haul feeder freight service to main lines where larger locomotives could take over the loads, these massively proportioned locomotives, which weighed 265 tonnes, boasted a light 16-tonne axle load.

Although 40-class diesel-electrics were now arriving and 40 electric locomotives were on order for Lithgow electrification, an additional 25 Garratts were ordered. Shortly afterwards, however, the success of the 40-class caused the NSWGR to change its motive power policy to the detriment of steam, and to contact Beyer, Peacock & Co in an effort to cancel the second Garratt contract.

But work was well advanced on the 12 engines 6026 to 6037, and the department was forced to accept ten of them—five as complete locomotives and the other five broken down into spare parts. The last locomotive actually assembled, 6040, entered traffic on 2 January 1957.

Interestingly, the locomotives were employed in heavy main line running from the outset, particularly over the Sydney–Broadmeadow, Lithgow and Junee routes.

The AD60-class boasted a tractive effort of 265 kN and was regarded as the most powerful locomotive in the Southern Hemisphere in its day. Some interesting, if unofficial feats have been performed by these locomotives. One demonstration of their brute power was witnessed by the author one

North-bound main line trains faced a steep grade as they left Fassifern. In 1966, a 600-ton general goods from Gosford thunders through the village with the four cylinders of 6018 working under full steam. (Late Ron Preston)

Engine 6042 the second (ex 6010) at Parkes locomotive depot on 17 May 1975. (Leon Oberg)

evening when a 1220-tonne double-diesel freight failed on a 1 in 66 grade section of Wingello bank. A Garratt working a freight in the other direction was quickly summoned to clear the section. It lifted the entire load, now in the order of 1450 tonnes with the added weight of the two dead diesels, without a hint of wheelslip!

After electrification was extended to Lithgow in June 1957, displaced 60-class operations were extended to Dubbo, Coonamble, Parkes and Werris Creek. They were also pressed into branch-line working which, for a brief time, included runs to Crookwell and Captains Flat.

To further increase their usefulness, particularly on main lines where a lack of turning facilities existed, 31 were equipped with dual controls from August 1958; many were fitted with increased coal-carrying capacity (from 14 to 18 tonnes) and larger cylinders, which increased their tractive effort to more than 280 kN.

Continuing dieselisation through the late 1950s led to the preparation of drawings in February 1957 for the conversion of some of these Garratts into conventional locomotives. The proposal was to use individual engine units and equip each one with a D59-class boiler, a new cab, fittings and a standard goods turret tender. In this form the proposed locomotives would exert a 32 140 lb (142.7 kN) tractive effort.

Although 6012 was withdrawn in February 1955 after just two year's service (officially 'as a source of spare parts' despite five unassembled locomotives having been acquired as spare parts), the conversions did not take place and the rest of the class remained in constant traffic over the Southern, Western and Northern lines until a serious accident at Geurie in 1963 claimed engine 6003.

Few further major overhauls were carried out as dieselisation was well under way and those Garratts not provided with dual-controls were effectively the first to go. The AD60s spent their last days working between Gosford, Newcastle and Newdell but, with continued dieselisation of the system throughout the early 1970s, they were withdrawn one by one. The last in traffic, 6042 (which in reality is 6010, due to an August 1968 Cardiff Workshops 'creative' identity swap, according to author and former works manager at Cardiff, the late Ron Preston), was also the last steam locomotive in government service in Australia. It was withdrawn with due ceremony in March 1973.

Several have been preserved. No. 6029 was acquired as an operational engine by the federal government in 1974 for the National Museum of Australia in Canberra. While awaiting the construction of the museum, the relic was placed in the care of the Canberra Division of the Australian Railway Historical Society and, until its front tubeplate was condemned in 1981, spent seven years working excursion trains (including one into Victoria).

Since then, 6029 has languished in the Society's

extensive Canberra Railway Museum. Museum members, along with the federal government, reaffirmed their desire in 1994 to see the locomotive running and, according to society life member and engineer Stephen Buck, a specially-funded feasibility study revealed the locomotive could be repaired. The Society remains quietly confident that funding, including grants moneys, will eventually flow. To this end, the Society has already acquired a 60-class boiler from a Victorian timber mill, one of several sold by the NSWGR to commercial interests during the 1960s. Mr Buck said he was encouraged after a detailed inspection found the boiler to be in 'almost works condition'.

Other preserved 60-class include 6039 at the Dorrigo Steam Railway and Museum and 6040 at the Thirlmere Railway Museum, while the engine bearing the 6042 numerals presently rests inside the remains of the Lachlan Vintage Village complex at Forbes.

SPECIFICATIONS

	ORIGINAL	AS MODIFIED
	IMPERIAL (METRIC)	IMPERIAL (METRIC)
CYLINDERS:	(4) 19¼ x 26 IN (49 x 66 CM)	(4) 19.9 x 26 IN (50 x 66 CM)
BOILER PRESSURE:	200 PSI (1378 KPA)	200 PSI (1378 KPA)
COUPLED WHEELS:	4 FT 7 IN (140 CM)	4 FT 7 IN (140 CM)
TRACTIVE EFFORT:	59 559 LB (265 KN)	63 016 LB (280.4 KN)
GRATE AREA:	63.5 SQ FT (5.899 M²)	63.5 SQ FT (5.899 M²)
TOTAL WEIGHT:	263.5 TONS (269 T)	264.25 (270 T)
GAUGE:	1435 MM	1435 MM
ROAD NUMBERS:	6001–6042 AT RANDOM	

D59-class 2-8-2

Among the many locomotives acquired by the NSWGR to meet expanding post-war goods haulage needs were 20 oil-burning lightweight Mikados. These locomotives, acquired from the Baldwin-Lima-Hamilton Corporation in the USA, were that recently merged company's standard design for developing nations, except for their customised cabs and tenders. The NSWGR required shorter tenders to enable the locomotives to use the system's small 18.3 metre turntables.

All 20 being delivered in completed form, the first entered service on 30 August 1952 and all were running by 31 March 1953. Initially, the class was placed into service over the Sydney–Broadmeadow route; as more locomotives were made available, they gravitated to North Coast and Northern Tablelands routes until these lines were dieselised in the early 1960s.

In 1962, a start was made to convert them all to coal-burners and, in March class-leader 5901 emerged from the Cardiff Railway Workshops for trials. With the exception of three, including 5918 which had been withdrawn basically for spare parts during July 1957, the rest were similarly converted over the following years in response to the cheaper cost of coal as a fuel.

Locomotive 5917 as a coal-burner. (Leon Oberg)

Although they ran several trials over the Main Southern line as far as Junee during the 1950s, the D59s did not enter regular 'short' south working (between Sydney and Goulburn) until May 1966. But this was steam's twilight years and, with encroaching dieselisation over that line, withdrawals started again in June 1969 when 5903 was stopped due to its mechanical condition.

After the Goulburn line was dieselised in October 1969, the few remaining locomotives worked out their lives as push-up engines based in Bathurst and on the Northern line, working out of Broadmeadow depot, until December 1972. The two surviving oil-burners, 5908 and 5916, remained operational as shunters on the far North Coast centres of Casino and Grafton. After they were retired in January 1971 and December 1970 respectively, both saw further service at Broadmeadow generating steam for the locomotive depot at half their operational boiler pressures. In August 1974, engine 5916 was transferred to Eveleigh Carriage Works for similar service. Both were towed to Thirlmere Railway Museum in 1977, and after thirty-two years were forwarded to Goulburn in November 2009 where one is expected to be sectioned.

The last locomotive in commercial traffic was 5910, withdrawn in December 1972 and for a time saw heritage train work out of the Thirlmere Museum.

No. 5917 was purchased by a consortium of enthusiasts who eventually formed the active Lachlan Valley Railway Society based at Cowra, and following a recent overhaul, is available for tourist service.

Locomotive 5920 is part of the vast Dorrigo Steam Railway & Museum collection.

SPECIFICATIONS

	IMPERIAL (METRIC)
CYLINDERS:	21 x 28 IN (53 x 71 CM)
BOILER PRESSURE:	200 PSI (1378 KPA)
COUPLED WHEELS:	5 FT 0 IN (152 CM)
TRACTIVE EFFORT:	34 986 LB (155.7 KN)
GRATE AREA:	47 SQ FT (4.36 M²)
TOTAL WEIGHT:	150.25 TONS (153.25 T)
GAUGE:	1435 MM
ROAD NUMBERS:	5901–5920

1952 VICTORIAN RAILWAYS

B-class Co-Co

Although four Australian rail systems had by 1952 pressed diesels into main line service, Victorian Railways had been looking at such a move since the late 1940s. Their people were watching the developments of both British and US types and finally, when calling tenders, expressed the desire for British-type bi-directional locos.

The newly established General Motors licence holder, the Clyde Engineering Co, was the successful tenderer. That company proposed a dual-cab Co-Co version of an A1A-A1A design then under construction for Commonwealth Railways.

Victorian Railways commissioned its first Co-Co in July 1952, to become that state's B-class, eventually numbering 26 locomotives. The locomotive worked under its own power on standard gauge works bogies from Sydney, changing to Victorian broad gauge bogies at Wodonga.

All had been delivered within two years and their impact was such that steam operation of all principal express passenger services and many freight trains in Victoria ceased forever. Their commissioning saw the total withdrawal of both the S-class 4-6-2 and H-class 4-8-4 locomotives, and of hosts of X, N, K and A2 class members.

Despite the arrival of more modern diesel types in subsequent years, the B-class continued to work important trains, allocated exclusively to the broad gauge throughout their VR lives except for the class-leader, B60 *Harold Clapp*, which was specially transferred to the Melbourne–Albury standard gauge route for 18 days in May 1975 to honour the centenary year of the former Chief Commissioner, the late Mr Harold Clapp. While working over that elite route, the unit logged a stunning 10 369 km.

Age and their early technology finally caught up with the veterans. But instead of retiring them, VR (now V/Line) decided to fully upgrade the class for the planned introduction of high-speed country intercity passenger services. Plans were formulated to return all 26 units (subsequently reduced to 13) to the original builder and re-power them with turbo-charged 12-cylinder 1827 kW diesel engines, and give them modern modular electrics, air-conditioning, updated traction motors and control stands. Their twin round-noses were retained in the upgraded package.

B62 standing outside Dynon (Melbourne) depot following a service on 11 May 1976. (Leon Oberg)

The first treated, B73, was forwarded to Clyde Engineering's Rosewater plant early in 1982 after it was severely damaged in an electrical fire. It was returned to V/Line rebuilt and renumbered as A73. (Others converted to the A-class specifications were B60, B62, B66, B70, B71, B77, B79, B81 and B85; an account of this type appears on page 396.)

Some B-class units soldiered on in government service until the last one, B61, was taken off the register on 6 January 1993. This unit covered the greatest distance of any class member, accumulating 6 292 131 km in its almost 41 years of service. However, enthusiasts could not see a classic and rather unique design go to the scrappers so easily. The West Coast Railway, operators of the private Warrnambool passenger service, bought this unit as well as B64, B65, B75, B76 and B80, some for parts. While B75 was on-sold to Great Northern Railway late in 1999, B80 was overhauled, placed on standard gauge and leased to several NSW and Victorian private rail operators from the spring of 2000. All four remaining West Coast Railway units were sold to CFCLA for Southern Shorthaul Railroad on 17 August 2004, mostly for eventual use in New South Wales, B61 and B65 being absorbed into the latter company's ownership.

Steamrail acquired B63, and a member of that organisation secured B72. Seymour Loco Steam Preservation Group obtained B74 and equipped it with standard gauge bogies for lease work, including a stint from November 2000 in NSW grain workings

into Port Kembla. Unit B83 is at the ARHS's North Williamstown Museum.

SPECIFICATIONS

	IMPERIAL (METRIC)
POWER UNIT:	EMD 16-567B
TRACTION HORSEPOWER:	1500 (1119 KW)
STARTING TRACTIVE EFFORT:	60 000 LB (267 KN)
CONTINUOUS TRACTIVE EFFORT:	40 000 LB (178 KN)
TOTAL WEIGHT:	111 TONS (113 T)
GAUGE:	1600 MM
ROAD NUMBERS:	B60–B85

1952 QUEENSLAND RAILWAYS

1210/1300/1150-class Co-Co

This family of ten diesel-electric 820 kW Co-Co locomotives was the first main line diesel type on the Queensland Railways and was part of an order from US-based International General Electric incorporating the manufacture of two distinct locomotive types (ten hood and ten streamlined).

Seven hood units were the first to arrive as deck cargo on the Norwegian-owned SS *Christen Smith* and initially became the 1210-class. The first one was issued to traffic on 6 November 1952, some eleven months

The trial run of what was then numbered 1210 (later class-leader 1150) at Warwick station on 21 January 1953. (Late Tony Maston)

later than planned. The delay was reputed to have been caused by a prolonged US steel strike and the need at that time for that country's efforts to be directed toward the manufacture of defence equipment.

Built in Erie, Pennsylvania, all ten were running within four months, the final three having been delivered in Sydney and railed to Brisbane aboard flat vehicles. When commissioned, they carried the numbers 1210–1219. (The streamlined locomotives were not delivered until July 1953—see page 268.)

Dieselisation brought many advantages to the QR. The arrival of the 1210-class coincided with a record wheat harvest so the class was issued to the Darling Downs region to haul the grain to port. At the time, QR claimed diesels saved the running of 106 trains (or 16 960 train kilometres) over the Toowoomba to Brisbane section—a very favourable introduction indeed!

However, they highlighted one unanticipated problem, the lightweight drawgear in use on goods rolling stock at the time. Consequently, until stronger equipment could be fitted, diesel loads were somewhat restricted for fear of breakage.

As additional diesel types were commissioned, the 1210s were used mainly between Brisbane and Cairns and Toowoomba, and quickly replaced steam on the *Sunshine Express*, reducing running times by two hours and 45 minutes.

In common with a number of early QR diesel locomotive types, the 1210s were renumbered in 1956, at which time they became the 1300-class. At this time, an additional three locomotives were on order from A. Goninan & Co, Broadmeadow (which had just acquired the Australian GE licence) and in 1965 all 13 locomotives became the 1150-class.

History was made in 1962 when 1156 (formerly 1306 and 1216) became QR's first diesel locomotive to log a million miles (1.6 million km) after a little under ten years' running.

The first of the class to be written off was 1155, on 13 April 1977, but six survived until 4 February 1988. Their later days were generally spent working in the Townsville area. Today, 1159 is located at the Workshops Rail Museum, Ipswich, while 1150 is undergoing restoration to working order by the ARHS, Townsville.

SPECIFICATIONS

	IMPERIAL (METRIC)
POWER UNIT:	COOPER-BESSEMER FVL 12T
TRACTION HORSEPOWER:	1100 (820 kW)
STARTING TRACTIVE EFFORT:	59 200 LB (263 kN)
CONTINUOUS TRACTIVE EFFORT:	31 000 LB (138 kN)
TOTAL WEIGHT:	89 TONS (90.4 T)
GAUGE:	1067 MM
ROAD NUMBERS:	(FINAL SERIES) 1150–1162

Baguley locomotive (maker's number 3378 of 1954) working at Mossman sugar mill as *Mowbray* on 12 October 1975. (Peter Watts)

1952 COLONIAL SUGAR REFINERY

Drewry 0-6-0DM

The narrow gauge steam locomotives used throughout Australia's east coast sugar mills needed on average almost four hours to raise enough steam from cold before they could be put to work.

Despite the development of mostly crude petrol-powered locomotives during the 1920s–1930s, they were in no way suitable for heavy main line canefields haulage due to their low power, light adhesive weight, crude mechanical transmissions and less than modest speed. However, they did make extremely useful yard shunters and work-train locomotives because of their immediate availability.

But steam for heavy and reliable cane haulage remained the staple diet of the mills despite its cost of operation until 1951 when, following major sugar industry expansion, the Drewry Car Co (London), in association with E.E. Baguley Ltd of Burton-on-Trent, delivered the first of an initial four 17.7-tonne 610 mm gauge 0-6-0DM units to the CSR's big Victoria Mill at Ingham. Their acquisition

coincided with the construction of a new tram line to Abergowrie.

Powered with 104 kW Gardner 8LW diesel engines, CSR soon found these locomotives could indeed do the main line work of a steam locomotive and in 1953 acquired a heavier 20.5-tonne unit for its Hambledon Mill at Cairns. (This was transferred to Victoria Mill in 1955.)

Two other mills purchased 17.7-tonne Drewry diesels, the South Johnstone Mill at Innisfail (three units) and Kalamia Mill at Ayr (one).

Other, basically similar Baguley locomotives were supplied to sugar mills and the Queensland Railways' Innisfail Tramway in two different power and weight ranges through the Railway Mine & Plantation Equipment Co Ltd of the UK. The two QR units eventually passed into sugar mill ownership; DL12 is still seeing navvy use at South Johnstone Mill, numbered 10, while DL13 became the former Moreton Mill's first *Jamaica* before being scrapped in 1994.

While no more of this type were imported, they did pave the way for a highly successful Australian-based diesel canefields locomotive industry that stormed the marketplace from 1954.

	IMPERIAL (METRIC)
POWER UNIT:	GARDNER 8LW
TRACTION HORSEPOWER:	135 (104 kW)
MAXIMUM TRACTIVE EFFORT:	8288 LB (41.9 kN)
TOTAL WEIGHT:	14.8 TO 17.5 TONS (15 TO 17.7T)*
GAUGE:	610 MM

(* KALAMIA MILL'S UNIT WEIGHED 20.1 TONS [20.5 T].)

1953 QUEENSLAND RAILWAYS

1200-class Co-Co

Until electric locomotives arrived in Queensland from 1988, these ten streamlined 1200-class diesel-electric locomotives remained the only true cab-type locomotives in the state.

Manufactured at English Electric's Bradford, UK plant and delivered from July 1953, they were ten of an order for 20 diesel-electrics of two different types acquired to gauge the effects of dieselisation on the system.

The other locomotive type acquired at that time was the GE-built 1210-class hood unit (which afterwards became the 1150-class).

The 1200-class quickly found employment working the state's top expresses such as the *Sunshine Express* (later *Sunlander*) and *Inlander* and, despite their relatively low power, ran them to faster schedules than before.

As the years passed, all were eventually ousted from those exacting passenger roles by more modern locomotive types, at which time they gravitated into general goods service working under the 'pool system' (with other units), mainly on the coastal route. Eventually, more than two decades on, age caught up with the veterans and, given the proliferation of more powerful modern locomotive power and the need of heavy overhauls and rewires from the late 1970s, class members were gradually retired.

The first to be withdrawn was 1202, which was officially written off on 13 April 1977. Four more followed on 6 March 1979.

Despite these withdrawals, 1208 received a replacement engine and generator out of sister unit 1206 in August 1983. However, by then its usefulness had dwindled and it was finally withdrawn on 20 March 1984. After lying in store at Redbank (with sister locomotives being scrapped around it), the veteran was shopped for modifications aimed at overcoming problems crews had earlier expressed which related to poor rearward vision when coupling up to trains. Accordingly, the full-width body behind the cab was removed and a narrow hood structure substituted. A twin sealed-beam headlight was swapped for the original British-made Stone's 'round' type.

'New' body parts came from withdrawn EE locomotives of the 1250-class, including 1252, 1253 and 1624, and even from Clyde GM, 1492. Because the locomotive now loosely resembled both a 1200-class and 1250-class, it was given a new road number

Streamlined 1203 at Rockhampton on 28 July 1973. (Peter Watts)

commensurate with its new guise. Thus, locomotive 1225 was born and quickly earned the nickname 'Hybrid.' After its first test run to Grandchester and return on 16 January 1985, the locomotive was put to work over the Wallangarra route and provided with similar load tables as the A1A-A1A 1400-class (slightly less than the 1200-class). Locomotive 1225 eventually was withdrawn for preservation late on 4 February 1988.

Class-leader 1200 was acquired by the Queensland Division of the ARHS for preservation, and a QR employee living in Toowoomba purchased the nose/cab of one 1200-class for his backyard. Both 1200 and 1225 (also in the care of the ARHS) remain in store at Redbank.

SPECIFICATIONS

	IMPERIAL (METRIC)
POWER UNIT:	ENGLISH ELECTRIC 12SVT
TRACTION HORSEPOWER:	1280 (954 KW)
STARTING TRACTIVE EFFORT:	50 000 LB (962 KW)
CONTINUOUS TRACTIVE EFFORT:	30 500 LB (136 KN)
TOTAL WEIGHT:	90 TONS (91.4 T)
GAUGE:	1067 MM
ROAD NUMBERS:	1200–1209 (1208 REBUILT AS 1225)

PVH1 0-8-0DH

This North British-built locomotive (Builder's No. 27084/1953) not only became the first diesel-hydraulic in Australia but was also destined to be the only diesel locomotive in the country to boast the 0-8-0 wheel arrangement.

It was imported by Tasmania's Emu Bay Railway Co for main line ore train haulage duties out of Burnie, arriving aboard the sea freighter *Hertfordshire* on 18 September 1953. While it did not immediately enter service due to sea-water damage sustained on its voyage, the locomotive was eventually commissioned as PVH1. It was later bestowed the next available road number in the (until then) strictly steam locomotive roster, No. 21.

This pioneering diesel unit was powered by a 4-stroke 12-cylinder Paxman engine, which drove through a Voith L37V torque converter to a reversing gearbox to steam locomotive-type siderods via a jackshaft. Capable of 35 mph (56 km/h) in high range, the unit paved the way for two classes of Australian designed and built diesel-hydraulic locomotives, the 10 and 11 classes, which collectively numbered eleven units.

With the introduction of the first three of those

The Emu Bay Railway's PVH21 shunting Burnie on 11 October 1974. (Peter Watts)

L-class 1152 awaits its next assignment out of the Latrobe Valley as it rests at Warragul on 8 February 1979. (Leon Oberg)

locomotives from 1963, No. 21 was relegated to Burnie yard shunting duties until temporarily transferred to Rosebery in 1968–69. While there it assisted with the relaying of the Rosebery to Melba Flats railway prior to the commencement of copper and pyrites traffic from the Mt Lyell mine in 1970.

Following modifications to the cab windows and the fitting of automatic couplers, 21 became the prime source of motive power for moving ore trains of up to 1500 tonnes through the Burnie unloader, continuing to be used for this task until early 2001 when it was replaced by an 11-class. No. 21 was then sold to the Derwent Valley Railway and made its last and longest main line run on 29 July 2001, when it ran from Burnie to New Norfolk for preservation. On that trip the locomotive was plagued with overheating problems, one of the problems that had afflicted it in its time running trains on the Emu Bay Railway.

SPECIFICATIONS

	IMPERIAL (METRIC)
POWER UNIT:	DAVEY PAXMAN 12 RPHXL SERIES 2
TRACTION HORSEPOWER:	530 (395 kW)
STARTING TRACTIVE EFFORT:	31 000 lb (138 kN)
CONTINUOUS TRACTIVE EFFORT:	20 380 lb (91 kN)
TOTAL WEIGHT:	42 TONS (42.8 T)
GAUGE:	1067 MM
ROAD NUMBER:	PVH1 (LATER 21)

1953 VICTORIAN RAILWAYS
L-class Co-Co

With general increases in coal output, industrial output and settlement in the Gippsland region of Victoria, east of Melbourne, there were considerable increases in traffic on the VR. Electrification of this vital link became more of a matter of urgency than luxury, particularly as large tonnages of brown Yallourn coal were being railed daily to Melbourne.

Twelve Bo-Bo electric locomotives had been operating around the generally flat metropolitan area since the early 1920s but locomotives of at least twice their tractive effort would be required for coal haulage because almost 128 km of somewhat hilly line was to be electrified between Dandenong and Traralgon in the 1950s.

The English Electric Co in England was thus contracted to supply 25 Co-Co 1790 kW electric locomotives, the first of which arrived in Melbourne toward the end of January 1953. Although all had been delivered by August 1954 as the system's L-class, electrification of the route they were intended for was not complete until 1956. Because there were now too many electric locomotives for the work available, some dozen units were stored at the Newport Railway Workshops for a time.

The smooth-riding L-class was quite a powerful locomotive type; load capabilities released at the time by VR reported that a single unit could haul 1120 tonnes at 48 km/h over 1 in 110 grades. In passenger service, they were capable of speeds up to 120 km/h.

Several modifications were made to the class over

Garratt 406 hurries a Broken Hill to Port Pirie ore concentrate train through undulating country near Huddleston on 11 December 1969. (John S. Glastonbury)

the years, but perhaps the most noteworthy was the trial lowering in 1976 of 1171's nose for better crew visibility. No further nose conversions were carried out. However, due to the large number of traction motor failures diagnosed as being caused by electric current collection problems in the pantographs, Brecknell-Willis pantographs were fitted to most of the L-class from the early 1980s.

With so many units for just one short length of electrified track, a general overhaul to 1164 was not considered necessary when it fell due and it was removed from the register on 7 November 1984.

Falling traffic, the high cost of maintaining the 1500 V (DC) overhead, along with an abundance of diesels, led to the decision to withdraw electric traction over the line in 1987. Class-leader 1150 worked the last electric passenger train to Traralgon on 13 June and goods haulage ceased within days.

Today, 1150 resides in the North Williamstown Museum, 1160 and 1169 can be found at Steamrail's Newport compound and 1162 has been made a fully operational heritage locomotive. The rest were quickly scrapped.

SPECIFICATIONS

	IMPERIAL (METRIC)
ELECTRICAL EQUIPMENT:	ENGLISH ELECTRIC 1500 V (DC)
TRACTION HORSEPOWER:	2400 (1790 KW)
STARTING TRACTIVE EFFORT:	47 000 LB (209 KN)
CONTINUOUS TRACTIVE EFFORT:	25 200 LB (112 KN)
TOTAL WEIGHT:	97.5 TONS (99.5 T)
GAUGE:	1600 MM
ROAD NUMBERS:	1150–1174

400-class 4-8-2 + 2-8-4

With tonnages steadily increasing from both the Leigh Creek coalfields and the Broken Hill lead, zinc and silver mines, it was little wonder that the SAR was experiencing severe motive-power problems early in the 1950s. At the time, the railway's principal narrow gauge goods engine was the T-class 4-8-0 locomotive, a design which dated back to 1909.

Authority was given in 1951 for the purchase of ten oil-fired 1067 mm gauge Beyer-Garratts to overcome the problems. Garratts were favoured because their high power and light axle load made it unnecessary to provide the expensive track and bridge strengthening which would have been required had larger conventional locomotives been selected.

All were built under licence by the French firm Société Franco-Belge de Matériel de Chemins de Fer. As an added attraction, they were designed to be convertible to 1600 mm gauge should the occasion arise.

The SAR had earlier purchased six Australian Standard Garratts from the WAGR as a stop-gap measure, and also as a means of training crews in operating the new articulated Garratts. After the first imported 400-class Garratts entered service on 1 July 1953, the stop-gap 300-class locomotives quickly lost favour and were withdrawn.

All of the imported Garratts were running by 6 February 1954.

With a new standard gauge Commonwealth-

The 41-class, although offering rather spartan crew comforts and operating principles, was visually quite a balanced design, as evidenced by this image of 4102 caught working out its last months shunting Chullora Workshops on 16 December 1974. (Leon Oberg)

owned railway being built soon afterwards to the coalfields, the 400-class was generally confined to the Broken Hill line plus occasional trips south from Peterborough to Terowie. Displaying its versatility, the class frequently worked the Broken Hill express passenger trains.

The 400-class was withdrawn en masse during the latter half of 1963 following the arrival of 830-class diesel-electrics. Though three continued to run for a time, scrappings started with 405 in June 1966. With little work, the remainder were held in storage at Peterborough until 1969, when some were returned to active traffic to tide the railway over while the 830-class diesels were equipped with 1435 mm bogies for the soon-to-open East–West standard gauge project. The last Garratt in traffic was 404, withdrawn on 10 January 1970.

Today, 409 is in the National Railway Museum, Port Adelaide, while Lithgow's Zig Zag Railway's 402 is to be loaned to Steamtown Peterborough (SA) for reactivation.

SPECIFICATIONS

	IMPERIAL (METRIC)
CYLINDERS:	(4) 16 x 24 IN (41 x 61 CM)
BOILER PRESSURE:	200 PSI (1378 KPA)
COUPLED WHEELS:	4 FT 0 IN (122 CM)
TRACTIVE EFFORT:	43 520 LB (193.7 KN)
GRATE AREA:	48.8 SQ FT (4.534 M²)
TRACTIVE EFFORT:	43 520 LB (193.7 KN)
TOTAL WEIGHT:	149 TONS (152 T)
GAUGE:	1067 MM
ROAD NUMBERS:	400–409

1953 NEW SOUTH WALES
GOVERNMENT RAILWAYS

41-class Bo-Bo

The NSWGR turned to joint English manufacturers British Thompson-Houston (which supplied the electrical equipment) and Metropolitan Cammell Carriage & Wagon Co for a small class of ten centre-cab Bo-Bo diesel-electric locomotives. Their acquisition was basically a trial to gauge how medium-weight diesels would perform in metropolitan freight haulage.

Entering service from December 1953 as the 41-class, the locomotives were pressed into a multitude of jobs in the Sydney region, including the haulage of coal trains out of Narellan (between Campbelltown and Camden).

The 83.5-tonne locomotives were powered with twin Davey Paxman 6-cylinder diesel engines. In operation, their crews discovered cooling to the trailing engines to be wanting, and the locomotives often suffered from electrical irregularities. Thus, they were not very popular and when 4106 was involved in an accident in the mid-1950s at Botany which resulted in a fire, it was set aside at Chullora Workshops where it yielded parts for its sisters.

The others gradually fell by the wayside during the 1960s and the last in traffic was 4102, withdrawn on 30 June 1975 following a crankcase explosion during a shunting assignment. While all its sisters had at that time been scrapped, 4102's career was not yet over, for it passed into the hands of the Thirlmere Railway Museum. In the early 1990s it was forwarded to State Rail's Meeks Road (XPT) depot for engine overhaul as a part-time venture. (The depot's fitters were familiar with Paxman-powered XPT locomotives.) Then depot head John Shields told this author the locomotive arrived with a 'shaft poking out of the block'.

Meeks Road fitters overhauled the locomotive's operational engine, along with a spare one from the Thirlmere Railway Museum, and had the relic up and running within a year. No. 4102 has since been returned to Thirlmere.

SPECIFICATIONS

	Imperial (Metric)
Power unit:	(Twin) Davey Paxman RPHL V6
Traction horsepower:	720 (535 kW)
Starting tractive effort:	36 700 lb (161 kN)
Continuous tractive effort:	22 800 lb (102.3 kN)
Total weight:	82.5 tons (84.5 t)
Gauge:	1435 mm
Road numbers:	4101–4110

1954 Victorian Railways

J-class 2-8-0

This class of 60 locomotives, which was a progression of the 1922-introduced K-class 2-8-0, was ordered by Victorian Railways from the UK firm Vulcan Foundry of Newton-le-Willows.

The first locomotive entered service in March 1954 and all were running by December of that year, the last engine in the series, 559, having the distinction of being the last steam locomotive ever to enter service with VR. They were all shipped as deck cargo, fully assembled, and offloaded at Williamstown. Designated J-class, the locomotives were engineered in such a way that they could be converted to standard gauge should the occasion arise.

The first 30 were built as coal-burners, the remainder being equipped for oil firing. They quickly replaced the ageing D2 and D3 4-6-0s on branch and light lines.

The J-class was the last steam type to remain intact on the VR during the changeover from steam to diesel traction and despite being relatively new, many were relegated to shunting duties. It was not until 17 November 1967 that any scrapping started, and J523 was the first to go. Gradually others followed, some being put into store at country and metropolitan locations for seasonal service as heavy wheat harvests dictated.

Through the early 1970s at least two were used as shunting power and limited wheat train haulage in western Victoria; the last in regular VR use was J549, used spasmodically as a pilot until late 1972. (However, J515 was resurrected in May 1976 to shunt Newport Workshops following the failure of the regular diesel.)

Some have been preserved, J515 having been fastidiously restored to running order by the Seymour Loco Steam Preservation Group. This group has now turned its attention to J512, having recovered it from

J503 on its commissioning in 1954. (V/Line archives, Len Whalley collection)

Alexandra. It is expected to be converted to standard gauge. J516 is under restoration at Healesville for the Yarra Valley Tourist Railway; J549 is used by the Victorian Goldfields Railway, Maldon, and privately owned J541 is under contract restoration at the Puffing Billy Museum at Menzies Creek. Others statically preserved include J507 at Mulwala in New South Wales; J524 at Donald; J536 at Newport; J539 at Dimboola; J550 at Warragul and J556 at the ARHS's North Williamstown Railway Museum.

SPECIFICATIONS

	IMPERIAL (METRIC)
CYLINDERS:	20 x 26 IN (51 x 66 CM)
BOILER PRESSURE:	175 PSI (1206 KPA)
COUPLED WHEELS:	4 FT 7IN (140 CM)
TRACTIVE EFFORT:	28 127 LB (1251.7 KN)
GRATE AREA:	31 SQ FT (2.88 M²)
TOTAL WEIGHT:	112.75 TONS (115 T)
GAUGE:	1600 MM
ROAD NUMBERS:	500–559

1954 WESTERN AUSTRALIAN GOVERNMENT RAILWAYS

X-class 2-Do-2

Quality British steam locomotive builder Beyer, Peacock & Co teamed up with Metropolitan Vickers Electrical Co Ltd to supply 48 unusual 2-Do-2 779 kW X-class diesel-electric locomotives for Western Australian Government Railways from 1954. This was the largest single order for diesel motive power yet placed by an Australian railway. The units entered service from March 1954 up to 1956.

The 2-Do-2 wheel arrangement was something akin to steam locomotive practice in that the leading 4-wheel bogie 'steered' the unit through the curves while the eight driving wheels, attached to the rigid main frame, provided the traction. No only did this arrangement cause rough riding, but only just half of the locomotive's all-up 80.2-tonne weight was available for adhesion, which contributed to wheel slip. Like many early diesel locomotives, the X-class was fitted with a marine-type diesel engine, this one being a Crossley 8-cylinder HST Vee-type re-engineered for locomotive use. Being Crossley's first foray into a 'traction' type engine, it had a few teething problems—it was prone to vibration, its early weight-saving aluminium heads cracked, and oil consumption caused considerable concern. In addition, ring failures began causing costly cylinder damage—a problem that was to remain with the class for at least two decades.

The locomotives had some advantages though. Due to their relatively light weight spread over so many wheels, they were able to tread the entire WAGR network, where some lines were laid with rail as light as 20 kg/m. When enough were eventually available to assume control of the state's top express runs including the *Westland*, *Albany Express* and *Kalgoorlie Express*, the X-class decimated steam-era timetables. For instance, the previous 17-hour *Kalgoorlie Express* schedule was reduced by four hours.

While under construction, the final 16 were wired for multiple-unit control and fitted with

X1010 rolls through heavy earthworks established in the late 1960s for the standard gauge with a passenger train. (Ken Morgan)

'intercommunication' doors at each end, and became known as the XA-class. In later years, WAGR decided to wire ten of the original X-class for multiple-unit control but as these ten were not provided with the end-access doors they became the XB-class.

Despite alleged faults, these well-proportioned dual-cab locomotives continued to tread the system's 1067 mm gauge network until late 1972 when two units in poor condition, 1015 and 1029, were withdrawn to supply parts for sister locomotives. On 17 November 1976 both were written off.

Withdrawals started in earnest from the early 1980s with the closure of many light branch lines. The last X in service was 1031, retired in January 1986, and the last XB running, 1017, was withdrawn on 17 October 1986. With 2 623 473 km behind it, 1017 had the eventual honour of running the furthest distance of any X/XA/XB.

Of the remaining XAs, some were equipped with Westinghouse air-brake equipment (Westrail gradually moved over to this universal system after having employed the vacuum type of braking since its inception), and could be found working Perth suburban passenger rolling stock until the last unit, XA1402, made its second last trip for Westrail at the head of the 17.10 Perth–Armadale 'local' on 30 March 1988. The following day, it worked a freight train from Forrestfield to Midland and closed the chapter on the class for the WAGR.

One X-class and five XA units have been preserved. Class-leader X1001 and XA1402 reside at the Bassendean Rail Transport Museum; XA1401 was sold to a group of Hotham Valley Tourist Railway members and restored to running order; XA1405 was acquired by the ARHS and is today undergoing restoration at Midland workshops; XA1411 now belongs to a Hotham Valley Tourist Railway member, and XA1415 resides in a Narrogin park.

SPECIFICATIONS

	Imperial (Metric)
Power unit:	Crossley HST V8
Traction horsepower:	1045 (779 kW)
Starting tractive effort:	26 000 lb (116 kN)
Continuous tractive effort:	12 000 lb (53 kN)
Total weight:	78.6 tons (80.2 t)
Gauge:	1067 mm
Road numbers:	X-class: 1001–1032
	XA-class 1401–1416
	XB-class: 1004, 1006, 1008, 1017, 1018, 1020, 1022, 1024, 1027 and 1032

1954 Clyde Engineering

Sugar/Industrial 0-6-0DH

Up until the early 1950s, the steam locomotive had reigned supreme on the sugar mill tramway systems, the loads to be hauled being well within the capabilities of the multitude of steam types in use. While lightweight petrol and diesel-mechanical locomotives had arrived in the canefields from the 1930s—some from the Fowler and Simplex companies—their diminutive size limited them to light duties.

In 1950, massive expansion within the industry led to the need for large numbers of high-powered locomotives. Although Perry Engineering in South Australia and the Bundaberg Foundry were successfully marketing 0-4-2T and 0-6-2T steam types which amply covered the power requirements, sugar mill directors began looking at developments in the diesel world and in 1952 CSR purchased four 104kW diesel-mechanical 0-6-0 units from the Drewry Car Co of England.

Diesels, being ready at the touch of a button, certainly beat waiting several hours for steam locomotives to raise steam after light-up. The sugar industry immediately sat up and took notice for here, at last, was a diesel locomotive capable of hauling steam locomotive loadings.

About that time, two respected Australian manufacturers entered the field with reliable products, the first being the Clyde Engineering Co, which marketed its own design, an 18-tonne loco (model DHI-71) powered with a GM 6-cylinder 127 kW diesel engine. This rigid wheelbase model proved popular; since the unit's introduction at Hambledon Mill in March 1954, no fewer than 80 were built for three gauge configurations: 74 sold to Queensland and Fiji sugar mills, five to the British Phosphate Commission on Nauru and one to Utah at St Marys in western Sydney. The last of this model, delivered to Racecourse Co-operative Mill at Mackay in May 1971 (as No. 7 *Broadsound*) was experimentally equipped with hydrostatic drive. It was later converted to the more conventional hydraulic drive.

Responding to ever-increasing train loads in the canefields, Clyde Engineering came up with a larger and more powerful HG3R model in 1961. Weighing

Two 1067 mm gauge DHI-71s, *Colevale* and *Airdale*, at Pioneer Sugar Mill on 20 September 2002. (Chris Walters)

Marian Sugar Mill's HG3R model, No. 26 *Bassett*, at the mill on 21 September 2002. (Chris Walters)

up to 24 tonnes, the look-alike was powered with a GM Detroit V8 diesel engine rated at 196 kW. Thirty-three have been built, the last appearing in June 1975 for Isis Central mill.

Scrappings of the DHI-71 model have started. All the Nauru units have gone, as has an early (1954) Tully Sugar Mill unit. Several of Isis Sugar Mill's six DHI-71s, converted into cabless 'booster units', were restored to original configuration following their sale to the Fiji Sugar Corporation in 1974. However, while many DHI-71s and HG3Rs remained operational into the new century, their

limited speed and tractive effort (compared to new, faster 1990s units) have become a hindrance in mills with long single-line entries. As a result, preservations have started, with an aged unit, *MacDesme*, one of five acquired by Pioneer Sugar Mill for 1067 mm gauge, being restored to running in 2003 at the Mackay Heritage Railway.

SPECIFICATIONS

Model	Imperial (Metric) DHI-71	Imperial (Metric) Model HG3R
Power unit:	GM 71-series	GM Detroit

Traction horsepower:	170 (127 kW)	263 (196 kW)
Tractive effort:	8750 lb (39 kN)	10 000 lb (44.5 kN)
Gauges:	610, 915, 1067 and 1435 mm	610 mm
Total weight:	18 tons, some 14 tons	24 tons (24.5 t)
	(18.4 t, some 14.3 t)	

1954 Commonwealth Railways

NSU-class A1A-A1A

Few Australian railway operators had as much continuous 'poor country' to traverse as the federal government's Commonwealth Railways. The arid, desolate saltbush land of Australia's interior, with its contrasting floods, sandstorms and burning heat for weeks on end, has always made life very tough for railwaymen, be they train crews or track maintenance staff. The narrow gauge section of the Central Australia Railway, which once linked Port Augusta and Marree, was the epitome of such harshness. Much of the route passed through sheer desert wilderness.

It is little wonder that diesel-electrics were considered for this section as early as the 1940s, and for the sister North Australian Railway which once linked Darwin with Larrimah. Eventually, 14 lightweight NSU-class diesels were ordered from the Birmingham Carriage & Waggon Co in England during the 1950–51 financial year. Powered with marine-type Sulzer engines, CR hoped some would arrive by late 1952. But materials delays in England forced the CR to continue using steam until the second half of 1954.

On 12 June 1954, NSU class-leader 51 was officially unveiled at Port Augusta 23 days after being unloaded from a ship at Port Adelaide. It was named *George McLeay* after the Federal Minister for Shipping and Transport. Although acquired for 1067 mm gauge service, two sets of standard gauge bogies were acquired and 51, following the handover ceremony, hauled an official train onto the Trans-Australian Railway (to Bookaloo) and return. In addition, 54 worked for some months over the standard gauge Port Augusta–Port Pirie section and was used for shunting appraisals.

At the same time 52 was engaged in crew training and, with ceremonies over, Nos 51 and 54 were in regular service working the narrow gauge Alice Springs route by 24 June. All 14 were running within two months and, although traffic had increased somewhat, did not replace all steam traction until the line was standardised between Port Augusta and Marree in 1956. This released 63 and 64 for use over the North Australian Railway. No. 63 worked there until it was replaced by 53 in November 1967. The NSUs were eventually replaced on the NAR by newer NT-class units (see page 338) which had been ordered to provide motive power to cope with the increased Frances Creek iron ore traffic, and had been returned to the south by October 1971.

The Frances Creek ore traffic (and the modest amount of general goods on offer) kept the NTs in full operation on the NAR until a serious accident in the Darwin harbour yards in November 1972 reduced their number by three. To fill this gap, two NSU locomotives were again forwarded north and remained there until ore traffic declined. Both were returned late in 1974, along with some of the NTs.

With the host of more modern locomotives by this time available for use over the CAR, NSU-

Locomotives NSU55 and NSU52 stand in Alice Springs yard on 11 September 1973. (Peter Watts

class locomotives began to fall by the wayside when forwarded to Port Augusta Workshops for attention. The first withdrawals were 59, 63 and 64, removed from the register in October 1981. But the writing was on the wall for many of CR's narrow gauge locomotives with the commissioning of a new all-weather standard gauge railway between Tarcoola and Alice Springs in October 1980. In a surprise move, two NSUs (56 and 58) were forwarded to Gladstone depot for use over the former SAR narrow gauge Wilmington line. About that time, 53 and 56 were sent to Peterborough for the Quorn line. The remaining few units were stored in Marree where three (59, 63 and 64) were made available to contractors engaged in the removal of the old CAR narrow gauge line, one for spare parts.

The very last NSU in commercial service was loco 58, which worked out of Gladstone shed until the 1987 winter. Amazingly, all 14 NSUs still exist in some form, 51, 52 and 54 at the Pichi Richi Railway, Quorn; 61 at the National Railway Museum, Port Adelaide; 53 beside the Stuart Highway outside MacDonnell Siding promoting the Old Ghan Heritage Railway which also contains 58 (operational), 59 and 64. Locos 55 and 62 are at Steamtown, Peterborough; 56, 57 and 60 are with the Marree Progress Association at Marree station while 63 sits on a plinth at old Adelaide River station.

SPECIFICATIONS

	IMPERIAL (METRIC)
POWER UNIT:	SULZER 6 LDA 28
TRACTION HORSEPOWER:	850 (634 kW)
STARTING TRACTIVE EFFORT:	22 400 LB (100 kN)
CONTINUOUS TRACTIVE EFFORT:	15 300 LB (68 kN)
TOTAL WEIGHT:	60 TONS (61.5 T)
GAUGE:	1067 MM
ROAD NUMBERS:	51–64

1954 BROKEN HILL PROPRIETARY CO
Cooper-Bessemer Bo-Bo

Due to post-war building booms and the nation-wide need for more steel products, BHP, which was operating no fewer than 30 locomotives within its 100 kilometres of railway at its Newcastle plant, urgently required more motive power. With two 0-6-0ST steam locomotives on loan from its sister plant at Port Kembla since 1952, the decision was made to purchase diesels, due to their resounding success at Port Kembla. Not only were these new locomotives much more readily available, but pollution was starting to worry company executives.

Accordingly, three General Electric Bo-Bo units were ordered through the Australian engineering firm A. Goninan & Co, which also assembled them. They were based on GE's 71-tonne switcher design, a locomotive introduced in the USA during 1946 and tailor-made for industrialists because of its heavy construction and excellent vision.

The first locomotive, 32, entered service at BHP in July 1954. Powered by a Cooper-Bessemer 6-cylinder 492 kW engine, the three locomotives replaced steam in the coal exchange traffic, working billet loads from the mills and running traffic over

BHP 34 shunting in Morandoo siding, Port Waratah, on 2 May 1981. (Leon Oberg)

the nearby BOS, Lysaghts and Stewart & Lloyds plants.

Early teething problems included the need for the diesel engine to be hand-primed to raise lubrication oil pressure before actual starting. According to a leading hand responsible for their commissioning, if this was not done the engine could start dry of oil and damage the bearings. No. 33 suffered that problem soon after it entered traffic, he recalled.

Early modifications included the addition of train air-brake lines. (The locomotives had been delivered with only engine independent air.) Load-bearing pedestals with wear plates were mounted each side of the bogies to stabilise the unit after the bogies had been offset 457 mm to suit the small radius curves which abounded within BHP's extensive plant.

Another two were delivered by A. Goninan & Co in December 1956, making the class total five.

They were not a popular locomotive. BHP transport staff recalled that their weight distribution was uneven, with much of it sitting over the engine end. Thus the wheels beneath the cab tended to spin, damaging the traction motors. Parts, particularly traction motors, were scarce in later years and some spares were even acquired from Queensland Railways.

Although major overhauls of the locomotives continued into 1982, massive rationalisation of BHP's Newcastle plant soon afterwards (due to a world-wide steel slump) saw loco 36 withdrawn in mid-1985 because of a broken crankshaft. No. 32 suffered a similar fate exactly one year later. The last unit in service was 34, which remained operational until January 1990.

Today, class-leader 32 is preserved in the BHP Museum (which was established on site following the closure of that plant in October 1999) while 34 is maintained in operational condition by the Richmond Vale Railway. The other three have been scrapped.

SPECIFICATIONS

	IMPERIAL (METRIC)
POWER UNIT:	COOPER-BESSEMER FWL-6T
TRACTION HORSEPOWER:	660 (492 KW)
STARTING TRACTIVE EFFORT:	57 000 LB (254 KN)
CONTINUOUS TRACTIVE EFFORT:	20 000 LB (89 KN)
TOTAL WEIGHT:	70 TONS (71.4 T)
GAUGE:	1435 MM
ROAD NUMBERS:	32–36

1955 COMMONWEALTH ENGINEERING
Sugar/Industrial 0-4-0/0-6-0/B-B

Commonwealth Engineering (Comeng) developed a light locomotive suitable for narrow gauge sugar service about the same time as did the Clyde Engineering Co (see page 275). But Comeng's earliest offerings were equipped with mechanical transmission instead of the hydraulic transmission used by Clyde.

Comeng's first six units were powered with Gardner 8LW series diesel engines rated at 112 kW and designed for use over 13.5 kg/m rail and to negotiate curves as tight as 30 metres radius. Five were supplied to the Mulgrave Sugar Mill at Gordonvale and the other to the South Johnstone mill at Innisfail. Comeng's order books quickly filled as operators saw the economic benefits of diesels over their long-established steam fleets.

As with other sugar locomotives, the Comeng design called for outside frames and the units were powered through a jackshaft, which transmitted drive to the wheels by means of cranks and outside coupling roofs.

Unlike Clyde Engineering, whose 0-6-0DH was being produced as a one-size-fits-all, Comeng was customising its product with a number of options tailored to suit the customer. Rolls Royce, Caterpillar and General Motors engines—ranging in power from 82 kW to 209 kW—have been used. Transmission type, locomotive weight and wheel arrangement could all vary depending on the purchaser's requirements.

All locomotives delivered up until 1957 were mechanical transmission, but in that year Comeng's first hydraulic unit was delivered to Kalamia Mill and after that sales of both types were made.

Up until 1966, a total of 76 locomotives had been sold to sugar mill tramways, most of which were to the 0-6-0 wheel arrangement. Of the three 0-4-0s produced, one went to Haughton Sugar Mill at Giru and was named *Invicta*, another went to Kalamia Sugar Mill as *Ivanhoe*, and the third to the Commonwealth Department of Supply at St Mary's in Sydney. It was later sold to the (now closed) Fairymead Sugar Mill as No. 72.

No further Comeng cane locomotives appeared

Originally built in 1957 as 0-6-0DM *Mowbray* for Mossman Sugar Mill, this little unit was later rebuilt as a diesel-hydraulic and renamed *Mossman*. It was pictured on 16 April 2002 roaming the mill yard with yet another more recent improvement, its upgraded cab. (Chris Walters)

Comeng's unique bogie unit, 51 *Finch Hatton*, approaches Racecourse Sugar Mill on 22 September 2002 wearing a modified cab. It is currently in store at North Eton mill. (Chris Walters)

between 1966 and 1975, which was the year the company sold the first of its redesigned and once popular F-model units. After a second F-model appeared in 1977, Comeng unveiled its new bogie B-B unit, a large 21 to 24.5 tonner based in many ways upon the F-model. Surprisingly, only one unit was ever sold, despite the design's lighter overall axle loads. It went to

the Cattle Creek Mill at Finch Hatton.

During the late 1980s and early 1990s, several 0-6-0 units were converted into 18-tonne brakevans. This was an easy task for mill engineers, for the original brakevans built for the industry were constructed by Comeng (and Clyde) using locomotive chassis and wheels.

The well-proportioned, towering lines of the V-class are exemplified in this study of 1218 on shed at Midland depot on 22 February 1971. (Bob Grant)

1955 Western Australian Government Railways

V-class 2-8-2

The highly-refined V-class was the last steam locomotive type to enter service on the Western Australia Government Railways. It consisted of 24 locomotives which were built to a Beyer, Peacock & Co design by the British firm Robert Stephenson & Hawthorn Ltd of Darlington.

They were the most advanced locomotives in the state and equal to anything then in the country. Fitted with roller bearings, power reverse and Walschaerts valve gear, the class was not only functional, but also good looking. The engines were also equipped with thermic siphons, a firebox resource that drew water from the lower part of the boiler near the rear tubeplate and conveyed it almost vertically upwards to the hotter crownsheet. Because the water-filled siphons were right in the midst of the fire, the more heat was absorbed through radiation, with claims, particularly from US users, that boiler performance could be enhanced by up to 10 per cent.

The V-class entered traffic between April 1955 and November 1956 and initially worked heavy coal trains from the Collie area. Later on they gave yeoman service on equally heavy freight trains, particularly over the Great Southern line from York to Albany, and again to Collie. The locomotives were still working at Collie nearly 15 years later when diesels finally ousted them. The last V-class in revenue traffic was retired in August 1972.

However, 1220 lasted a little longer, working enthusiast specials. It is now in the ARHS's Bassendean Rail Transport Museum. Several others have been preserved. No. 1213, which was overhauled by Willis Light Engineering of Perth during the late 1990s, entered sawn timber haulage between Lyall and Pemberton in 1999, a distance of 21 kilometres, under the ownership of Ian Willis. Mr Willis also uses the locomotive in public locomotive driving exercises over the Pemberton Tramway Co.

A non-operational 1215 resides at Collie, and 1209 belongs to the Bellarine Peninsula Railway for service out of Queenscliff, Victoria.

SPECIFICATIONS

	IMPERIAL (METRIC)
CYLINDERS:	19 x 26 IN (48 x 66 CM)
BOILER PRESSURE:	215 PSI (1481 KPA)
COUPLED WHEELS:	4 FT 3IN (130 CM)
TRACTIVE EFFORT:	33 633 LB (1496.7 KN)
GRATE AREA:	40 SQ FT (3.716 M²)
TOTAL WEIGHT:	134.5 TONS (137.5 T)
GAUGE:	1067 MM
ROAD NUMBERS:	1201–1224

Showing its British heritage to full advantage, Hebburn Colliery's 2-6-2T, carrying its final road number, rolls through the company's No. 1 colliery yard in December 1965. (Late Ron Preston)

1955 Hebburn Colliery

Stephenson 2-6-2T

Delivered in August 1955, this relatively powerful 76-tonne 2-6-2T had the potential to answer many decades of locomotive procrastination for the owners of Hebburn Colliery, between Maitland and Cessnock in the Hunter Valley of New South Wales. It was ordered new from UK firm Robert Stephenson & Hawthorn Ltd to an existing design and built in that company's Newcastle-on-Tyne plant.

The colliery's directors believed that the locomotive would be a reliable replacement for the long line of unsuitable, sometimes life-expired, second-hand or hired locomotives which had been used since the company started coal mining in 1903.

In reality, the elegant 2-6-2T was little better than the 14 or so engines that came before it. For a start, it was an old design, two examples (36 and 37) having been built in 1920 for the Alexandra (Newport & South Wales) Dock & Railway, and which became Great Western Railway locomotives 1205 and 1206. In fact, the Hebburn engine was built just one year before the last Welsh example was scrapped.

Despite its business-like lines and strong general construction, the locomotive was not a good steamer and tended to lack the suspension flexibility needed to traverse the often indifferent 4 kilometres of track that linked the company's collieries with the South Maitland Railway's exchange siding at Weston.

When cylinder problems developed in February 1967, the engine, with little more than 60 000 km on the clock, was stored, and its place taken by a worn-out 2-6-4T veteran hired from the nearby Richmond Vale Railway (RVR). The day after it arrived, this engine needed attention. Eventually, the ongoing reliability woes drove the company to buy 4-6-4T 3013 from the NSWGR in May 1967, a move which finally provided some motive power stability.

The Robert Stephenson & Hawthorn engine was never repaired and was quietly cut up for scrap after some six years resting beneath coal-loading chutes at Hebburn No. 2 colliery. When Hebburn Colliery closed soon afterwards, 3013 found employment working out of the RVR's Hexham depot.

SPECIFICATIONS

	Imperial (Metric)
Cylinders:	19 x 26 in (48 x 66 cm)
Boiler pressure:	160 psi (1102 kPa)
Coupled wheels:	4 ft 7 in (140 cm)
Tractive effort:	21 843 lb (95.5 kN)
Grate area:	20.8 sq ft (1.925 m²)
Total weight:	75 tons 2 cwt (76.1 t)
Road number:	4 (later renumbered 1 'new series')

GM12-class Co-Co

In 1951 and 1952, the Commonwealth Railways acquired eleven A1A-A1A 1119 kW diesel-electric locomotives from the Clyde Engineering Co to dieselise its torrid Trans-Australia Railway. Those pioneering main line locomotives paved the way for the manufacturer's wholesale assault on the Australian locomotive marketplace, with an order following in 1951 from Victorian Railways and another in 1953 from the Commonwealth Government to supply nine almost identical GM1-class units for the 1676 mm gauge North West Railway of Pakistan under the internationally-administered Colombo Plan.

While the locomotives for Pakistan were in the development stage, General Motors was able to replace the EMD 16-567B diesel engine used in the earlier CR and Victorian deliveries with the much improved 567C version. This engine's main difference was its new crankcase, which successfully eliminated

cracks that had developed (in the USA) within high-mileage 567B engines due to corrosion and fatigue in the cooling-water area. The crankcase also increased engine speed from its original 800 rpm to 835 rpm. Coupled with an improved fuel injection system, the 567C engine lifted power output from the main generator to a more useful 1305 kW.

Commonwealth Railways, itself needing more diesels to work trains over the newly-laid standard gauge line to serve the Leigh Creek coal deposits, turned to this 1305 kW Co-Co Pakistani version when placing orders for five units late in 1954. Weighing 116 tonnes, these and subsequent deliveries brought about by steadily increasing freight haulage over the Trans-Australia Railway saw no fewer than 36 in service by December 1967. These were further improved with the provision of a single traction motor blower. (Each traction motor on the CR GM1, VR B-class and the Pakistani locomotives originally possessed its own 5 hp traction motor blower.)

The final eleven were further improved by the fitting of dynamic braking to better stabilise

One of the final eleven GM-class units equipped with dynamic brakes, GM40, wearing Australian National Railways lettering, rests between assignments in Port Augusta's Spencer Junction yard on 3 February 1980, with then near-new 2237kW AL-class unit AL22. Within hours, both were hurtling westward, Kalgoorlie-bound at the head of a heavy freight train. (Leon Oberg)

Dynamic-braked GM45, presenting the striking colours of the US-dominated Australian Railroad Group (now Genesee & Wyoming Australia). (Leon Oberg)

increasing tonnages on the Leigh Creek coal route, a job they continued to play in, admittedly, a decreasing role right up until 1997, despite the proliferation of modern higher-powered motive power types.

While both the A1A-A1A and Co-Co variants worked side by side on the CR system, the latter version became known as the GM12-class. Following the formation of Australian National Railways in 1978, the obvious imbalance of the two traction motor configurations was overcome in working timetables, with the early GM1-class described as the F-type (for four traction motors) and the GM12 locomotives as the S-type (for six motors). Visually, the GM1 type boasted three portholes along the body sides while the GM12s were equipped with four.

Occasionally though, things would get mixed up. At one stage during the 1970s, GM26 spent a lengthy period between workshop visits with a GM1-series 567B engine in its chassis, effectively depreciating its traction output.

Gradually over the years, the GM12s were seen in most mainland states. Due to reciprocal intersystem motive power deals through the 1980s, examples gradually filtered into Perth and to Lithgow in New South Wales. Others were leased on several extended periods to Victorian Railways to arrest severe motive power shortages over the Melbourne–Albury standard gauge line while some could be found well into the early 2000s operating over Western Australia's standard gauge Leonora route while filling serious locomotive shortages.

In a surprise move, two dynamic-brake units, GM42 and GM43, were issued to the broad gauge network from March 1992, where they saw diversified service including interstate superfreight train assistance between Adelaide and Tailem Bend, Penrice limestone haulage and Mt Gambier freight workings. They were returned to standard gauge after the Adelaide–Melbourne line was standardised in mid-1995, and they and some remaining GM12 remnants moved into wheat haulage over the Tailem Bend to Adelaide portion of the route, a role some continue to enjoy.

Withdrawals began with GM29 late in 1985, the result of a level crossing collision on the Marree line. Gradually others followed and the last to receive a general overhaul under AN ownership was GM46, out-shopped from Port Augusta on 9 July 1995. Although by then relegated to 'lesser duties', examples did continue to tread their originally intended routes, with one regularly rostered to work the weekly

Adelaide–Cook fuel train as late as 1998.

One off-beat use for derelict GM14 saw it feature in a series of 25 kph freight rolling-stock crash compression tests in Whyalla during 1996. We can report that the locomotive won.

For many years, AN's Port Augusta Workshops staff were concerned by cracking and bending in GM-class noses. Knowing their chassis were the strongest of any locomotive type they had encountered, engineers, with help from the original manufacturer, started preparing plans during the early 1990s to rebuild and re-power 14 GM12s with EMD 16-645E3B engines, D67 traction motors and EM2000 computers. These units were to receive raked AN-class cabs, the result planned to become the GMX-class.

However, these plans, along with another to convert about four derelict GM12-class to engineless 'tractive effort booster units', were shelved pending the sale of the railway, the South Australian intrastate freight and workshops component (including the remaining GM12-class units) to a consortium led by US-owned Genesee & Wyoming Inc. This firm became the Australian Railroad Group, assuming full responsibility from 8 November 1997. Due to initial locomotive shortages, the new owner rejuvenated some stored GM12s in readiness for the state's wheat season. Many remained running into 2007.

This owner also started shopping class members, beginning with GM44 (which had been involved in a destructive Port Adelaide rollover). It emerged for trials in August 1999. Workshop attention continued and in a surprise May 2005 move, ARG forwarded out-of-service GM30 to the Forrestfield (Perth) Workshops for a 2237 kW rebuild. Expected to be renumbered GN3401, it had not emerged for trials when this book closed for press in April 2007. However, it is known the locomotive has been fitted with a US-sourced EMD 16-645E3B (turbocharged) engine, modern electrics including wheel-creep technology and upgraded radiators. It is believed the unit will retain its original 'bulldog' nose/cab although its roofline is expected to look more like a CL-class.

ARG considered eleven GM12s to be surplus to its initial needs and in July 1998 sold them to the Melbourne-based locomotive leasing and shunting company Great Northern Railroad. The units involved were GM12, GM14, GM18, GM19, GM25, GM26, GM27, GM28, GM33, GM35 and GM41, some of which were derelict and acquired solely for

NSWR 42-class 4206 rides the turntable at Goulburn Locomotive Depot on 16 December 1979, overseen by an impressive collection of 422-class box-cab EMD units: (from left) 42215, 42212, 42211, 42208, 42216, 42205 and 42217. Former SAR Alco 847 and NSWGR's similarly-styled 4896 can be glimpsed as well. (Leon Oberg)

parts. Fully operational GM22, which had earlier been bought by Port Pirie Council for preservation, was also acquired by Great Northern, swapping it for the cosmetically restored non-operational GM28 (carrying the number GM22). While some were leased back to ARG to cover seasonal locomotive shortages, others went through several ownerships, with GM19 now under overhaul in Goulburn for Rail Power P/L, and GM35 finding a home on a property in the Mudgee district of New South Wales.

Following the company's 2003 collapse, Great Northern Railroad's locomotives passed into the ownership of Chicago Freightcar Leasing (Australia) on 2 December 2003. GM22 and GM27 have been re-liveried in Southern Shorthaul Railroad colours and all see constant service in New South Wales.

In addition to these, GM36 is owned by the Seymour Loco Steam Preservation Group (Victoria) and through 2005–06 was enjoying extensive commercial lease service with QR National.

Mentioning QRN, while that authority acquired ARG on 1 June 2006, all of the surviving GM12-class fleet (except for rebuilt GM30) remained under the direct ownership of Genesee & Wyoming Australia's Adelaide office.

NSWGR 42-class

In NSW that state's government-owned railway system ordered six of these Co-Co 1305 kW single-cab machines for its prestige long-distance express passenger services in 1955. Differing from the GM12s only in respect of appointments, gearing and minor body detail, and the provision of spartan driving (hostler) controls in the rear end, they were introduced between November 1955 and December 1956 as the 42-class.

These 120-tonne locomotives initially worked trains as important as the Sydney–Melbourne *Intercapital Daylight*, *Melbourne Limited* and *Brisbane Limited* expresses. After Victoria's *Spirit of Progress* began running through to Sydney following 1962 gauge standardisation, 42-class locomotives made regular appearances on that train for another two decades, often working in pairs to Albury.

The bulk of the 42-class's working life was spent on the Main Southern line. As newer locomotive types were progressively added to the system, the 42s could be seen working anything from slow bulk wheat trains to fast interstate freighters.

All were withdrawn by the winter of 1983, although 4204, now owned by the Lachlan Valley (Tourist) Railway saw some immediate limited service. It has since been resurrected and repainted, running a heritage train to Dungog on 13 February 2010.

Two others have been preserved, 4201 at Thirlmere Railway Museum and 4206 at Dorrigo Steam Railway and Museum. No. 4203, after sitting at the entrance to a Cowra caravan park for more than a decade, was scrapped in December 2000, some mechanical parts going to Great Northern Rail Services and Lachlan Valley Railway. But its memory lingers, for the nose/cab and portion of the rear end were sold as a 'compressed' centrepiece for an Emu Plains hotel.

Victorian Railways S-class

A copy of the 42-class was introduced by Victorian Railways for mainline freight service from August 1957. Ten 116-tonne units were initially acquired for broad gauge freight service; then, with the Albury to Melbourne standard gauge project nearing completion in 1960, an additional eight were ordered to work express passenger and interstate goods trains over that route. The last arrived in December 1961, one month prior to the standard gauge line's opening.

By then, ongoing refinements saw the final deliveries upgraded with fuel-intake improvements which increased their power rating to 1342 kW.

Forced withdrawals started in February 1969 as a result of the horrific and fatal *Southern Aurora* collision at Violet Town crossing loop, where S314 and S316 met head-on. They were so badly damaged that both were scrapped, their salvageable parts going into replacement X-class hood units.

With the arrival of more modern locomotive types throughout the 1970s and 1980s, the standard gauge S-class was gradually reassigned to the broad gauge, where they worked everything from the *Overland* to wheat and steel traffic.

Age finally caught up with the remaining S-class in May 1987 when S304 was withdrawn, yielding parts to sister units. It was eventually cut up at Spotswood Reclamation Centre in April 1992. Others gradually followed, some having achieved more than 6.6 million kilometres of hard use. One, S311, had an eleventh-hour moment of glory at Easter 1992 when it was re-equipped with standard gauge bogies and worked the very last overnight *Sydney Express*, returning the following evening with the final return Melbourne movement.

Four potentially operational units, S300, S302, S311 and S312, were acquired in 1993 by the privatised passenger-carrying West Coast Railway, with some overhauled and repainted in that company's attractive corporate two-tone blue and white livery. They remained in service hauling company passenger trains between Melbourne and Warrnambool until the company's lease expired mid-2004. Locomotive S302 was then sold to V/Line Passenger and S312 to emerging company Rail Power Pty Ltd; the other two were disposed of to Chicago Freight Car Leasing Australia on 17 August 2004 for use in New South

Originally VR's class-leader, S300 poses at Dynon depot (Melbourne) on 19 February 1995, wearing its striking but now defunct West Coast Railway livery. (Leon Oberg)

VR's S304 *George Bass*, wearing traditional livery (albeit work-worn) at South Dynon on 11 May 1976. (Leon Oberg)

Wales and Victoria.

Four other units, S301, S306, S307 and S310, survived in V/Line seasonal grain haulage long enough to become part of that railway's sale to the private company, Freight Victoria, in April 1999. Most thought their future was limited but no—all four were shopped and restored to full-time front of train operations in January 2000, much to enthusiasts' delight. Their surprise rejuvenation was due to the company's increased traffic responsibilities, which included log and grain haulage interstate. (The firm became Freight Australia from 1 March 2000.)

Loco S303 has also been given immortality, having been meticulously restored by the Seymour Railway Heritage Centre, while S317, initially overhauled by Great Northern Rail Services, now belongs to Southern Shorthaul Railroad.

The Melbourne-based Steamrail has restored S313 to active excursion service, the unit seeing further commercial freight work during 2001 while on brief lease to Freight Australia.

Meanwhile, S308, which in the mid-1990s was used for a fitter's training aid at South Dynon depot, perspex panels having replaced some fittings to give students better perceptions of a locomotive's internal operation, has since gone to the ARHS's North Williamstown Railway Museum.

SPECIFICATIONS

GM12-CLASS

IMPERIAL (METRIC)	
POWER UNIT:	EMD 16-567C
TRACTION HORSEPOWER:	1750 (1305 kW)
STARTING TRACTIVE EFFORT:	63 500 lb (282 kN)
CONTINUOUS TRACTIVE EFFORT:	50 000 lb (238 kN)
TOTAL WEIGHT:	114 tons (116.3 t)
GAUGE:	1435 mm (two on 1600 mm for brief period)
ROAD NUMBERS:	GM12–GM47

NSWGR 42-CLASS

IMPERIAL (METRIC)	
POWER UNIT:	EMD 16-567C
TRACTION HORSEPOWER:	1750 (1305 kW)
STARTING TRACTIVE EFFORT:	78 300 lb (348 kN)
CONTINUOUS TRACTIVE EFFORT:	61 250 lb (272 kN)
TOTAL WEIGHT:	120 tons (122.4 t)
GAUGE:	1435 mm
ROAD NUMBERS:	4201–4206

VR S-CLASS

IMPERIAL (METRIC)	
POWER UNIT:	EMD 16-567C
TRACTION HORSEPOWER:	1800 (1342 kW)
STARTING TRACTIVE EFFORT:	65 300 lb (282 kN)
CONTINUOUS TRACTIVE EFFORT:	53 500 lb (238 kN)
TOTAL WEIGHT:	114 tons (116.3 t)
GAUGE:	1435/1600 mm
ROAD NUMBERS:	S300–S317

Typifying EMD's G-12 styling, Queensland Railway's 1407 prepares to depart Mackay with a goods train on 4 August 1978. (Peter Watts)

1955 QUEENSLAND RAILWAYS

1230/1400/1450-class A1A-A1A

By 1955, all Australian railway systems had tried dieselisation and were making serious decisions about the future of steam. In fact, by this time Commonwealth Railways was almost totally dieselised and Victorian Railways was also operating large numbers, both systems standardising on General Motors products. NSWGR had six Co-Co 42-class GMs on order.

In its belief that Queensland Railways' vast system would be an ideal marketplace for GM products, that manufacturer's Australian representative, the Clyde Engineering Co of Sydney, initiated a clever sales promotion early in 1955, offering QR a 977 kW hood-type A1A-A1A unit on a 'try and buy if satisfied' basis.

The locomotive type was EMD's 'developing nations' G-12 model. Even before the demonstration unit had been delivered (on 30 May 1955), QR had ordered two more. Formal purchase of the prototype followed six months later, by which time QR had signed a contract for another ten.

The first three, which were numbered 1230–1232, became the 1230-class, but rationalisation of the system's diesel numbering in 1956 with the arrival of the additional ten saw these locomotives become the 1400-class, numbered 1400–1412.

Totally reliable, their only real drawback was

that, since only the two outside axles of each bogie were powered (with the centre axle being used to spread the locomotive's weight), wheel-slip problems developed, particularly over the steeply-graded Toowoomba line.

Clyde re-jigged the design to better suit the conditions and later that year was able to offer QR an improved Co-Co (all axles powered) version. Contracts were again signed, this time for ten new units.

Delivered during 1957–58 as the 1450-class, these locomotives were longer than their prototype to provide enough room beneath the chassis to accommodate longer bogies carrying the extra traction motors. The 1450-class could be readily identified in service by its rather long nose.

Although plans had been drawn up to extend the frames of the 1400s to accommodate Co-Co bogies (and an associated electrical upgrade), the locomotives were banned from the hilly Toowoomba route as the 1450-class proved its worth. The 1400s generally spent their remaining years working over the northern coastal strip, with half being based at Mayne for the South-eastern District and the other half appointed to Townsville for use in the Northern Division, while the entire 1450-class was generally allocated for South-eastern District service.

No units of the 1400/1450 class remain in commercial service, the first 1400 written off being 1406 on 12 May 1987 (it was subsequently stripped bare behind the cab and used as a workshops diesel engine transfer unit). The first 1450-class to go was 1458, on 18 May 1988. All had been decommissioned by November 1988.

The 1450-class's extra length to accommodate Co-Co bogies is perfectly evident in this picture showing 1458 at Mayne depot in July 1985. (Leon Oberg)

While 1400 belongs to the ARHS for preservation and 1407 is part of the QR heritage fleet at Ipswich, Co-Co units 1450 and 1455 have been retained for this fleet, the latter technically for spare parts after spending many years sitting outside QR's Redbank Workshops to provide energy to test locomotive traction motors.

BHP DE-class

BHP acquired seven basically similar G-12 units for use in South Australian mineral service. Purchased in three contracts, the initial four (acquired between November 1956 and August 1957) arrived to replace steam haulage on the 1067 mm gauge Iron Knob and Iron Baron iron ore railway.

These locomotives differed from QR's early 1400-class in the provision of Bo-Bo (4-wheel) bogies with all axles powered, providing 100 per cent adhesive weight.

Expanding production from BHP's Middleback Ranges mines saw an additional unit commissioned in June 1961. When the company began developing mineral sand mining operations further down the Eyre Peninsula, constructing a new standard gauge railway between the mine site near Coffin Bay and the port at Proper Bay (Port Lincoln), two more G-12 Bo-Bo units were purchased for that line. Arriving in November 1965, they differed in that they were equipped with standard gauge bogies and Farr Dynavane filtering systems to keep sand dust out of their main engine rooms. Only one of them was destined to entered traffic at Port Lincoln, and remained there until exchanged late in 1968 for two lower-powered G-8 model 652 kW units which had been made surplus when road transport replaced rail haulage in the Iron Knob quarry. The other G-12 was held at Whyalla for ore train haulage.

A number of modifications were made to the

BHP units DE06 and DE04 in their original G-12B form, but bearing Abdel-Malek silencers, prepare to depart Whyalla ore plant with an empty train for Iron Monarch in 1975. (BHP Whyalla)

Demonstrating their Morrison Knudsen G-14 rebuilt form, DE4 and DE7 leave Iron Baron with a Whyalla-bound ore train on 27 February 1995. (Leon Oberg)

BHP units over the years. Engineers increased the cab upper sections from 1971 to improve headroom for enginemen while adding noise absorption materials to cab bulkheads. From February 1973 the units were progressively fitted with a revolutionary sound-suppression unit to reduce engine noise inside the cabs to something 'more bearable', for tests on the locomotives had recorded noise levels of up to 108 decibels. With the new equipment, designed by BHP Whyalla's special project engineer Samir Abdel-Malek, readings fell to 87 decibels. This was a remarkable breakthrough after earlier warnings to BHP by the locomotives' manufacturer that any tampering with exhaust flow would almost certainly reduce performance. Although details of the design

remain 'classified', equipment measuring 274 x 91 x 61 cm was placed on top of each locomotive's hood, and company engineers told this author performance had not been impaired in any way.

In the design of the unit, expensive sound-measuring equipment was imported from Denmark to determine the major frequencies which were responsible for the bulk of the noise, and tape recordings made inside the cabs were analysed in BHP's laboratory. Here the frequencies which were predominant could be ascertained and a silencer designed to reduce the noise at those frequencies.

In 1992, BHP instigated a plan to further upgrade its Bo-Bo units when it commissioned Morrison Knudsen (Australia) to remanufacture them as G-14

Former Kowloon Canton Railway unit 54, pictured at Melbourne's Dynon depot on 3 June 2009 carrying CFCLA's number TL154. (Leon Oberg)

units. The first locomotive so reworked, DE09, was initially accepted for traffic on 7 June 1993.

Boasting modern microprocessor control equipment, AC alternators in place of the original DC generators and upgraded traction motor cooling, the 12-567C diesel engines were improved by reboring the cylinders and including stronger 645E parts. In their new form the locomotives produced 1045 kW.

Morrison Knudsen also took the opportunity to redesign the locomotives, effectively making them end-cab units. An air-conditioner was placed on the front platform and, in an effort to improve visibility, closed circuit TV installed in the cabs. Five G-12 units (DE03, DE04, DE07, DE08 and DE09) were rebuilt along with DE01, one of the original 653 kW G-8 units. The last unit treated, DE03, arrived from Morrison Knudsen on 10 March 1995.

The two non-rebuilt G-12s continued to see service over the ore railway until a serious head-on collision outside Iron Baron mine on 23 November 1996 destroyed DE06. The collision also involved the rebuilt G-14s DE04 and DE07 (which were repaired). Disaster struck again on 28 April 2002 when DE08 and DE09, working an empty Down train, collided with four stationary loaded hoppers which had broken away from an earlier Up train between Iron Baron and Iron Duke mines. Both were scrapped within months. By then (from 1 December 1999), the four remaining operational DE-class units had been sold to Australian Southern Railroad, which had negotiated a deal to handle rail services for BHP. From early 2003, these were renumbered 1301–1304.

Then, in a move that surprised many, the remaining originally-styled unit, DE05, was forwarded to Forrestfield, Perth, in 2003 as a narrow gauge depot shunter carrying the revised number 1251. It remained there as this book went to press, but under the ownership of QRN-West.

Kowloon Canton Railway imports

But the story does not end here, for in an extraordinary 2005 move, Chicago Freight Car Leasing (Australia) managed to acquire four of the five standard gauge G-12 Bo-Bo locomotives built in Sydney between 1955 and 1957 by the Clyde Engineering Co for the Hong Kong-based Kowloon Canton Railway (KCR). CFCLA needed additional lease power for its steadily growing clientele. The recently overhauled air-conditioned locomotives were landed in Port Adelaide for reactivation work by Bluebird Engineering (Islington) on 22 December 2005. They are finding service in 2007 as terminal yard shunters in several states.

Manager, customer relations, with KCR, Winnie Hong, told this author the locomotives were originally acquired by her railway to replace steam working on both passenger and freight trains by day and engineering (maintenance) trains by night. After electric multiple-unit trains took over passenger rosters from 1982, the G-12s were captive to freight and engineering trains at KCR East Rail, particularly between Kowloon Freight Terminal and Lo Wu marshalling yard.

The five locomotives received scheduled overhauls every six years until withdrawn in 2004. Class-leader 51 was donated to the Hong Kong Railway Museum while units 52–55 returned to Australia to become CFCLA's TL-class 152–155. Several have already been commissioned.

SPECIFICATIONS

	1400-CLASS Imperial (Metric)	1450-CLASS Imperial (Metric)	BHP G-14B Imperial (Metric)
Power unit:	EMD 12-567C	EMD 12-567C	EMD 12-645E
Traction horsepower:	1310 (977 kW)	1310 (977 kW)	1400 (1045 kW)
Starting tractive effort:	36 288 lb (161 kN)	54 432 lb (242 kN)	54 000 lb (240 kN)
Continuous tractive effort:	28 000 lb (125 kN)	42 000 lb (187 kN)	33 200 lb (150 kN)
Total weight:	76 tons (77.5 t)	90 tons (91.8 t)	70.2 tons (72.0 t)
Gauge:	1067 mm	1067 mm	1067 mm/1435 mm
Road numbers:	1400–1412	1450–1459	

(BHP) DE03–DE09 (DE03, DE04 and DE07 renumbered 1302–1304 respectively)
(CFCLA) TL152–TL155

T-class Bo-Bo

This class was introduced by VR in 1955 as part of its $160 million rehabilitation program to replace old Y, E, A2 and D3 classes on branch lines. Many of these steam locomotives were then up to 60 years old.

The diesel-electric order consisted of 27 EMD (Developing Nations) G-8 model Bo-Bo locomotives built to a modified plan by the Clyde Engineering Co. These locomotives possessed lengthened underframes with 26 ft 6 in (7.77 metres) bolster centres in lieu of the US version's 25 ft 0 in (7.6 metres) centres because it was originally intended to equip the class with rounded J-cabs at both ends (as then used on Irish State Railways).

Clyde Engineering prepared an initial drawing (No. 2305434 dated 31 August 1954) for the dual-cab type but the plan as such was abandoned. Instead, VR contracted the builder to manufacture an 'Australian' G-8 locomotive type employing the lengthened chassis of the proposed design. This conveniently enabled a platform to be provided behind the B-end hood.

Victorian Railways' class-leader T320 eventually arrived in Melbourne on 2 August 1955 after making a powered delivery run over both NSW and Victorian metals (exchanging standard gauge delivery bogies at Wodonga for new 1600 mm gauge trucks).

This 69-tonne design, whose 8-567C engine exerted 653 kW for traction purposes, was a huge success. However, it did have one small fault, in that it needed to use turntables at terminating stations due to the provision of a single control stand. To rectify this problem, Clyde custom-fitted dual control stands with the delivery of the seventh and subsequent locomotives. All 27 of this order were running by December 1956. As more funds became available, ten additional T-class were ordered, the first entering service in June 1959. While mechanically and electrically similar to the first 27, the builder had re-designed the cab, raising it above the hood line to provide additional headroom.

Because early T-class locomotives were equipped with a right-angled speed increaser drive to the cooling fan, which was found to be high on maintenance, locomotives from road number T357 onwards were provided with deeper radiators and a direct-drive system to eliminate the problem. The last ten of this type were also equipped with higher-capacity generators.

But orders did not stop there. When VR needed more diesels to eliminate steam altogether, the manufacturer further 'Australianised' the design and from the 48th delivery in February 1964 came up with a low-profile nose. This eliminated the expense of a second control stand and meant that the driving station could be favourably located for driving long-end leading, the low nose providing adequate vision when operating short-end first.

Since the US parent had an improved 8-645E engine package available for these light-type locomotives (which exerted 708 kW to the rail), these engines were employed in the final deliveries, increasing the weight of each locomotive to almost 82 tonnes. In all, 51 low-profile units were ordered. Although early deliveries came with the original 653 kW engine, the final 19 were constructed with an improved and more powerful 708 kW prime mover.

As the last deliveries were being made, VR decided to specially equip the final five for Melbourne hump yard shunting. Fitted with special low-speed controls and an extra 10 tonnes ballast weight for added adhesion, these became the H-class, although delivered bearing T-class number plates. All had been delivered by March 1969.

In their heavier form, the five H-class units were initially restricted to the heaviest main lines and, while spare units could occasionally be seen working goods trains to Wodonga and Geelong, they became regulars on Bacchus Marsh commuter trains until their hump shunting days ceased and all were forwarded to Geelong for local export grain train transfer duties. In January 1989, following widespread track upgrading works made necessary due to the proliferation of heavier main line locomotives, all speed limit restrictions on the H-class were lifted and the units were placed in general service and pooled with their T-class prototype.

The steady closure of Victorian branch lines through the 1980s saw large numbers of T-class withdrawn, rebuilt for other duties, sold or scrapped. However, there was life after death for some original flat-top units. Since V/Line wanted to improve and increase its commuter train services, large numbers of Melbourne suburban electric train carriages were refurbished by Clyde Engineering, which was also contracted to remanufacture 13 T-class locomotives

'Second series raised cab version' T352 was brand-new and on delivery to VR when pictured at Delec depot, Sydney, on 20 September 1959. (Arthur Reynell)

T369, representing the revised low-profile nose styling of the 'third series' T-class, in the employ of the now defunct West Coast Railway. It was pictured at Dynon depot on 4 December 2001. (Leon Oberg)

T371, a 'third series' unit, wearing Freight Australia's corporate livery in 2003. (Leon Oberg)

A pair of H-class acquired specifically for hump yard shunting, H1 and H3, arrive at Dynon depot at shift change on 11 May 1976. (Leon Oberg)

with stronger 8-cylinder 645E 640 kW engines. The units were given chopped noses for added crew vision, larger, raised and more comfortable isolated cabs, and given head-end power to provide train lighting, air-conditioning, etc. The first locomotive treated was T336, which emerged in May 1984 as P11 of the P-class (see page 397).

Australian National Railways acquired six late-model 708 kW units from V/Line, being T401 and T403–T407, taking delivery of the first in October 1992. While T403 was bought for spares, the operational units became that railway's CK-class and have been employed as shunters and bankers through the Adelaide Hills and, more recently, to haul wheat and Penrice limestone trains. All CK locomotives passed into the ownership of a consortium led by Genesee & Wyoming, the buyers of AN's mainland freight and workshops component, from 8 November 1997. Although their number had diminished by one with the earlier withdrawal of CK2 as a source

of spare parts, some were placed on the narrow gauge after the company acquired a contract to supply all BHP Whyalla's rail services from 1 December 1999.

While four surplus flat-top T-class (less bogies), T322, T323, T324 and T343, were snapped up in 1987 by a Geelong electrical engineering firm and in 2007 continue to provide power to test rotating the high-capacity equipment that regularly passes through its workshop, several Victorian enthusiast groups have acquired early T-class units for tourist and preservation schemes. The Seymour Loco Steam Preservation Group acquired class-leader T320, intermediate model T357 and low-nose unit T378; T334 and T411 are with the Mornington Rail Preservation Society, Crib Point; T341 has been bought by the Yarra Valley Tourist Railway, Healesville; T342 went to the South Gippsland Tourist Railway, Korumburra; T356, T364 and T395 to Steamrail, Newport, and T367 to the North Williamstown Railway Museum.

AN acquired six late-model 708 kW V/Line T-class units from October 1992, placing them into the CK-classification. The class-leader, CK1 (formerly T401), leads DE1 out of Whyalla with empty ore wagons bound for Iron Duke, on 5 February 2001. (Leon Oberg)

Pacific National-liveried T-class T379 and T371, loading a grain train at Henty on 29 April 2006. (Leon Oberg)

For a time T387 found a home at South Australia's Yorke Peninsula Rail Preservation Society for tourist service over the Wallaroo–Kadina line but later came into the ownership of Chicago Freight Car Leasing (Australia) for commercial operations in Victoria.

V/Line locomotive inspector Paul Moore managed to procure locos T372, T373, T376, T377 and T381 from V/Line in 1994 and formed Great Northern Rail Services, where all units, except T372 (which was scrapped for its parts) saw service. He later acquired original flat-top unit T345 from a rail preservation group for rebuild. His meticulously maintained motive power not only saw service with National Rail, in Victorian shunting and ballast train service, but also on leased duty to other operators, appearing from time to time in South Australia and New South Wales.

A 2003 victim of increasing insurance costs and falling traffic due to a nationwide drought, Great Northern Rail Services sadly went into liquidation, most locomotives being absorbed into the CFCLA roster. In January 2004, the business arm was acquired by the Southern Shorthaul Railroad consortium, which on 17 August 2004 also added locomotives T363, T369 and T385 to its register. These had earlier belonged to the West Coast Railway.

By early 1996, only 13 T-class remained under V/Line ownership and these, T371, T374, T379, T382, T388, T390, T393, T396, T399, T400, T402, T408 and T409, along with the entire H-class, were sold to Freight Victoria, buyer of the government-owned Victorian freight business. Within a year, this US-parented firm had aggressively secured new business, renaming itself Freight Australia. Several previously stored T-class were returned to traffic, some equipped with standard gauge wheelsets for operation in several states. Freight Australia was taken over by Pacific National in 2004.

BHP DE-class

Another pioneer operator of the G-8 model was BHP, which in 1956 obtained two 'Mark 1' units, DE01 and DE02, from the Clyde Engineering Co for iron-ore train haulage between Iron Knob and Whyalla and shunting duty in the quarry floor. When the quarry railway closed in favour of road transport in 1968 these 1067 mm gauge locomotives were transferred to standard gauge and fitted with dynamic brakes for use at BHP's mineral sand railway linking Proper Bay and Coffin Bay on the Eyre Peninsula, replacing a heavier G-12 model Clyde unit.

A downturn in traffic caused by the importation of sand from Japan saw DE01 returned to Whyalla steelworks in 1975. Following an overhaul and the fitting of a larger cab, it was held as a standby unit to a small stable of Walkers-built diesel-hydraulic locomotives.

In 1994, BHP saw an opportunity to upgrade and re-power several of its G-12 locomotives

BHP's Whyalla-based G-8 model DE01 after undergoing an MKA rebuild in March 1994 to emerge as a G-14 type. Note the driver operating the locomotive from the front steps using a remote control pad. (BHP)

and contracted Morrison Knudsen (Australia) to undertake the work at its Whyalla plant. BHP's G-8 model DE01 was also selected to undergo a rebuild and emerged in G-14 form, exerting a more useful 1045 kW from a spare rebored 12-657C engine (effectively making it a 12-645E power plant).

This unit was bought by Australia Southern Railroad (now ARG) on 1 December 1999 after that firm won a contract to handle all rail services for BHP Whyalla. Four years later it was renumbered 1301 in keeping with the operator's four-numeral identification system.

The other unit, DE02, continued to haul irregular sand trains until 1989 when a storm damaged the Proper Bay outloader. DE02 was eventually returned to Whyalla in 1993, where it became semi-derelict as parts were taken from it to maintain other units. Officially deregistered on 10 October 1997, the unit's remains were sold to NREC-Alco, who in 2006 rebuilt the relic in Adelaide for SCT Logistics, employing the Series-3 T-class cab/low nose configuration. Renumbered T414, the creation retained its 8-567C engine. Also rebuilt under SCT ownership was derelict CK2 (which reverted to its original VR number, T404). Both are expected to be used for standard gauge shunting and transfer duties.

Australian Portland Cement

Struck by the success of the T-class, VR customer Australian Portland Cement Co, based at Fyansford, near Geelong, bought a copy in 1956 for its 1067 mm gauge quarry transfer service. Although boasting a flat 'Mark-1' top, this locomotive was based more on the G-8s delivered to BHP than on the first series T-class, for it came with plate-steel pilots, chopper couplings and chains, narrow steps, a single-note Westinghouse whistle and no marker lights. It was also equipped with dynamic braking, equipment which would later be fitted to the two BHP locomotives.

Numbered D1, this locomotive was acquired by VR in 1967 after a conveyor system replaced the cement company's railway. In VR service, this unit became T413 after modifications were made to various appointments; it was based at Wodonga, where its dynamic brake was an advantage on the steeply-graded Cudgewa line with grades as steep as 1 in 30.

Loco T413 was purchased during the late 1990s by a group of Geelong railwaymen and restored to pristine operational condition. In 2006 it was seeing infrastructure train lease work around Melbourne.

'Series 1' styled T413 began life as Australian Portland Cement Co's D1, where its dynamic brake was an advantage on the steeply graded line from the Geelong plant to North Geelong exchange siding. Bought by VR in 1967, the same equipment was seen to be an advantage for the Cudgewa line, which forged through extremely steep country. T413 is pictured working that line just prior to the route's 1970s closure. (Graham Cotterall)

SPECIFICATIONS

	IMPERIAL (METRIC)
POWER UNIT:	EMD 8-567C (FOR FIRST 79) AND 8-645E
TRACTION HORSEPOWER:	875 (652 kW) FOR FIRST 79 AND No. 413; 950 HP (708 kW) FOR Nos. 399–412 AND H-CLASS
STARTING TRACTIVE EFFORT:	37 000 LB (164.5 kN)
	38 080 LB (169.6 kN) LATER UNITS
CONTINUOUS TRACTIVE EFFORT:	23 000 LB (102.5 kN)
	28 000 LB (124.6 kN) LATER UNITS
TOTAL WEIGHT:	67–71 TONS (66.7–72.5 T)
	80 TONS (81.6 T) FOR H-CLASS
GAUGE:	(VR) 1435 MM AND 1600 MM
	(BHP) 1067 MM AND 1435 MM
	(APC) 1067 MM
ROAD NUMBERS:	(VR) T320–T346 AND T413 (MARK 1 TYPE)
	T347–T366 (MARK 2 TYPE)
	T367–T412 (MARK 3 TYPE)
	H1–H5 FORMER HUMP SHUNTING UNITS
	(BHP) DEO1–DEO2 (DEO1 RENUMBERED 1301 IN 2003)
	(APC) D1 (TO VR AS T413)
	(AN) CK1–CK5

1955 SOUTH AUSTRALIAN RAILWAYS

930-class Co-Co

To assist in the dieselisation of the difficult Adelaide–Tailem Bend line, the SAR introduced the first of six 1194 kW main line broad gauge diesel-electrics in December 1955.

The locomotives, built under licence to the American Locomotive Co (Alco) of the USA by A.E. Goodwin Ltd of Sydney, were an export model known as the World Series Model DL-500B which had at the time attracted orders from several countries. Alco claimed it could build them to rail gauges ranging from 1000 to 1678 mm.

Designated 930-class, SAR's six new locos quickly replaced remaining steam working over the Tailem Bend route and also began working further eastwards to Serviceton.

Buoyed by the success of these units, Goodwin Ltd was able to market a bi-directional version when the SAR next tendered for additional locomotives. Seventeen of this revised type, built by Alco, had already appeared on the Spanish National Railways in 1954 as its class 1600.

The dual-cab SAR units started to arrive in 1957, the model retaining its streamlined cab at the front in

The SAR's single-cab World Series Model DL-500B as exampled on loco 935, nearing Mallala on 1 February 1980. (Leon Oberg)

The classic lines of the dual-cab World Series Alco model are exemplified in this view showing [then] Bathurst-based 4475 and 4474 with an Up wheat train near the former rural station, Gemella, on 7 February, 1975. (Leon Oberg)

Locomotive 954, an SAR (later Australian National Rail) version of the dual-cab World-series package, pictured at Mile End on 3 February, 1982. (Leon Oberg)

The 'B' end of the dual cab World-series Alco locomotive is purely functional and, some might say, an afterthought, unlike the pleasing lines of its streamlined 'A' end. Two NSWGR 44-class, 4457 (wearing a short-lived no-frills livery) and 4448, coupled nose to nose and working an Up interstate express goods near Breadalbane on 9 January 1973. (Peter Watts)

The last 930-class in regular traffic was 961, which remained long enough to pass into Genesee & Wyoming ownership. It was soon sold as an active unit to Silverton Rail in May 2001 and promptly renumbered 44s1. The locomotive was pictured at Broken Hill depot on 22 September 2003. (Leon Oberg)

addition to a fully-equipped 'flat' cab at the No. 2 end. In this form it was 2.5 tonnes heavier than the prototype. The SAR acquired a total thirty-seven 930-class locomotives for broad gauge service (31 of them bi-directional). The last one entered traffic in June 1967.

The takeover of the non-metropolitan portions of the SAR by the federal government in 1978 eventually resulted in motive-power shuffles, and several dual-cab 930-class units were provided with standard gauge ex-NSWGR bogies during mid-

1982. They spent about a decade in AN ownership running to Broken Hill, Port Augusta and Whyalla while based at Peterborough.

Rationalisation and the arrival of more modern locomotive types eventually saw the demise of the 930-class. While most have been scrapped, heritage locomotive 961 remained in general standard gauge wheat service on the acquisition of AN's mainland freight and workshops portion on 8 November 1997 by a consortium led by Genesee & Wyoming (eventually forming the Australian Railroad Group). It was sold as an active unit to Silverton Rail in May 2001 and promptly renumbered 44s1, only to be acquired by CFCLA in 2005.

Class-leader 930 resides at the National Railway Museum, Port Adelaide, and 958 and 963 belong to the ARHS's SteamRanger rail tour organisation, the former in operational condition.

NSWGR 44-class

The NSWGR, which had been acquiring small numbers of Australian-built diesel-electric locomotive types for appraisal, was drawn to the potential versatility of the SAR's dual-cab 930-class Co-Co and ordered ten units. Entering service from 17 July 1957 as the 44-class, the NSWGR units were up-rated to produce 1343 kW. Although dogged by early but minor teething troubles that in many cases stemmed from operator unfamiliarity, additional batches followed, and by 22 January 1968 there were no fewer than 100 in service.

The gradual arrival of these units brought about the total dieselisation of the North Coast line during the late 1950s and the heavily-graded Unanderra–Moss Vale line in the early 1960s. The 44-class accounted directly for the withdrawal of some 280 steam locomotives of various types.

The 44-class was truly a universal locomotive. In New South Wales it worked everything from the *Southern Aurora* and *Indian Pacific* expresses to heavy, plodding limestone and pick-up trains. In its heyday, the class could be found working to all corners of the main line network—Broken Hill, Dubbo, Albury, Cooma, Nowra, South Brisbane and Wallangarra.

Forced withdrawals started as a result of a head-on collision at Robertson in May 1972, which destroyed 4462 and a later Alco type, 4525. In November 1974, locos 4476 and 4478 were involved in a violent and fatal head-on collision west of Condobolin. The badly damaged units were gradually stripped

at Chullora Workshops for re-usable parts and the remains scrapped.

During the late 1970s, withdrawals of early 44-class units needing rewiring and major overhauls started in earnest as newer locomotive types came onto the scene. However, 4403 and 4468 survived to work the last CityRail locomotive-hauled passenger service in the state on 10 July 1994. These units were officially withdrawn following an enthusiast farewell tour soon afterwards. Along with other surplus locomotives they were offered for sale in December 1994; while most were acquired by scrappers, many survive.

Today, 4401 is operated by rail tour group 3801 Limited; 4403 operates out of Junee Roundhouse Museum; 4420 is at Dorrigo Steam Railway and Museum; 4464, 4473 and 4486 were acquired by the Lachlan Valley Railway's Alco Group; 4465 is at Werris Creek, and 4490 is operational at the Thirlmere-based NSWRTM.

And while locos 4458, 4461, 4463, 4472, 4488, 4497 and 4498 were saved from scrap and largely reactivated for a lease programme by the Hunter Valley Railway Trust, all passed into the ownership of the principal user, Independent Railways of Australia (IRA), from April 2009. Interestingly, 4498 was equipped with an LP gas injection system in a bid to improve combustion and reduce exhaust emission.

Official railway life continued for several others held back from the sale for after lying in store at Chullora for almost four years, 4468, 4471, 4477 and 4483 were transferred to the government's Rail Services Australia division for potential ballast/work train locomotives. These were subsequently acquired by Chicago Freight Car Leasing (Australia) and continued in regular work until 4468 was deemed surplus to needs in late 2009 and sold to the ACT Division of the ARHS for heritage train service, and 4483 on-sold to IRA in February 2010. The balance have been sold to P&O Trans Australia.

SPECIFICATIONS

	SAR/AN 930-CLASS		NSW 44-CLASS
	IMPERIAL (METRIC)		IMPERIAL (METRIC)
POWER UNIT:	ALCO 251B	ALCO 251B	
TRACTION HORSEPOWER:	1600 (1194 KW)		1800 (1343 KW)
STARTING TRACTIVE EFFORT:	57 000 LB (254 KN)		50 200 LB (224 KN)
CONTINUOUS TRACTIVE EFFORT:	42 900 LB (191 KN)		47 100 LB (209 KN)
TOTAL WEIGHT:	104 TONS (106 T)		106 TNS (108 T) AND 110 TNS (112 T)
GAUGE:	1435 MM AND 1600 MM		1435 MM
ROAD NUMBERS:	930–966 (930 BECAME 967)		4401–44100

A. Goninan B-B

John Lysaghts, one of Australia's leading industrial companies, set up business in Australia in 1884 specifically to manufacture wire netting products. The Bristol (UK)-administered company initially traded from premises in the Sydney suburb of Five Dock.

Although business grew steadily, most of the firm's raw materials had to be railed long distances to meet company needs. However, with the formation of BHP's steel plant at Newcastle, manufacturing works soon appeared near that point.

Business continued to grow with new products coming on stream and soon BHP gained a shareholding in Lysaghts, setting up another plant at Port Kembla in 1929. This new outlet was situated right beside the newly-created Hoskins Kembla steelworks, which had just transferred its activities from Lithgow.

Railways quickly became one of Lysaghts' first needs, and both the Newcastle and Kembla plants developed many kilometres of standard gauge track to convey raw materials and finished products.

Initially, steam locomotives provided the motive power but in Port Kembla the economies of dieselisation of the nearby steelworks (from 1950) found Lysaghts directors purchasing two small 268 kW centre-cab B-B diesel-electrics from the American General Electric Co catalogue. Weighing 46 tonnes, the model was GE's standard post-1940 industrial design. In a bid to keep the unit's weight as low as possible, just one traction motor was provided to each bogie, the adjacent free axle being powered by connecting rods.

Both units were assembled by GE's Australian licence holder, A. Goninan & Co in Broadmeadow near Newcastle, the first being delivered in May 1955. These units were named *Ann* and *Primrose*; a third, *Helen Mary*, was added to the Port Kembla fleet in December 1962, all being named after company director Mr D.R. Lysaght's daughters.

As business continued to expand, and because the company's remaining steam locomotive required replacement, a fourth diesel-electric built to a higher-powered Bo-Bo design, JL4, was acquired in 1967, at which time the early B-B units were provided with a number, in order of delivery, becoming JL1–JL3.

The B-B units were geared for a maximum speed of 32 km/h and were in constant service transferring coil steel from the nearby AI&S works, and over the NSW SRA's railway to Lysaghts' Port Kembla North plant. For that latter service, they were wired for multiple-unit control.

Age finally caught up with the veterans and the first to be withdrawn was *Primrose* in December 1987. *Helen Mary* followed early in 1989 and the survivor, *Ann*, which had been completely rewired during a general overhaul in October 1985, remained in traffic until 23 September 1989. It was purchased by the Dorrigo Steam Railway and Museum. The others were scrapped.

SPECIFICATIONS

	IMPERIAL (METRIC)
POWER UNITS:	TWO CUMMINS H6 BI
TRACTION HORSEPOWER:	360 (268 KW)
TOTAL WEIGHT:	45 TONS (46 T)
GAUGE:	1435 MM
ROAD NUMBERS:	JLI ANN, JL2 PRIMROSE, JL3 HELEN MARY

Helen Mary and *Ann* at the John Lysaghts works on 20 July 1975. (Leon Oberg)

43-class Co-Co

In the early 1950s the NSWGR was feeling its way cautiously with dieselisation, acquiring motive power from a variety of sources in an attempt to gauge the best for its needs. Initially, 20 Alco-powered A1A-A1A hood units, known as the 40-class, were imported in 1951 from the Montreal Locomotive Works, Canada, for main line work. These were followed in 1953 by ten British-built Bo-Bos for metropolitan freight transfer work. Soon afterwards the administration purchased six EMD Co-Co units, which became the 42-class, from the Clyde Engineering Co for express passenger service.

Acquisition of the 43-class was immediately followed by the purchase of six similarly-styled Alco-powered General Electric locomotives, introduced in September 1956, which became the 43-class. Built in Newcastle by A. Goninan & Co for Alco and GE's then Australian agent Australian Electrical Industries, these locomotives were rather unusual in that, despite their design originating in the USA, only two similarly-styled cab units were ever built in that country, for the Erie Railroad.

All six had been delivered by June 1957 and they initially worked side by side with the EMD-powered 42-class in express passenger trains.

Those assignments included the newly created *Sydney to Melbourne Daylight Express* and the pre-electrification *Central West Express* between Sydney and Orange, along with the *Melbourne Limited* and *Brisbane Limited* expresses.

Although not popular with crews, the 43-class did pave the way for a long line of Alco-powered locomotives for NSWGR main line and branch line service. With the introduction of those newer types, the 43-class was transferred to Broadmeadow depot for use principally over the North Coast and Northern Tablelands routes. They remained at that depot until the last, occasionally venturing onto the main Sydney–Albury line which, if nothing else, kept crews on that route familiar with their operation.

Although their Alco 244 engines were improved from the late 1950s with the provision of more reliable water-cooling of the turbo-superchargers in lieu of the former air-cooling, generally speaking the 43-class was incompatible haulage-wise with other main line units due to their lower haulage capacity. When 4301 was partially stripped in Chullora Workshops as part of its regular general overhaul in August 1974, the decision was made to dispatch it to the yard, where its parts eventually helped to keep sister units on the road.

The last engine running was 4306, withdrawn on 2 October 1979 and forwarded to Thirlmere Railway Museum for preservation. It was eventually returned to active operation in June 1996.

Streamlined 4302 teams up with brand-new Alco 442-class No. 10 while working a north-bound goods train out of Broadmeadow yard in August 1972. (Peter Watts)

SPECIFICATIONS

	IMPERIAL (METRIC)
POWER UNIT:	ALCO 244 (12-CYLINDER)
TRACTION HORSEPOWER:	1600 (1193 KW)
STARTING TRACTIVE EFFORT:	71 000 LB (316 KN)
CONTINUOUS TRACTIVE EFFORT:	42 900 LB (191 KN)
TOTAL WEIGHT:	105.5 TONS (107.6 T)
GAUGE:	1435 MM
ROAD NUMBERS:	4301–4306

Locomotive 4633 at Delec shed on 26 May 1979. (Leon Oberg)

1956 NEW SOUTH WALES GOVERNMENT RAILWAYS

46-class Co+Co

The electrification of the formidable Blue Mountains line in New South Wales was probably the NSWGR's greatest single achievement since early railway route duplication.

Long-suffering enginemen, weary from battling the 1 in 33 grades of the mountains with poor quality coal and sluggish engines, found a renewed interest in their work. While the railway administration stood to gain considerable savings once the expense of the infrastructure was met, the travelling public also received a much cleaner, faster service.

The question of electrification was first raised in the early 1950s, when coal mining companies started developing plans to mine on the western rim of the mountains. By October 1955, 1500 V (DC) electrification had reached the outer suburban station of Penrith. Exactly one year later, the Valley Heights section was opened and by February 1957, electrification had reached as far as Katoomba. Finally, the descent into Lithgow past the silent and historic Zig Zag was completed, and electric services began on 9 June 1957.

Meanwhile, orders had been placed with Metropolitan Vickers and Beyer, Peacock & Co in Britain for 40 NSWGR-designed 2819 kW 46-class Co+Co electric locomotives to work the line. While these were being built, the NSWGR was training its crews in the operation of such units with a 45-class Co+Co main liner of June 1952 manufacture (see earlier entry).

The first 46-class entered traffic during June 1956 and was an instant success in respect of its sheer power and clean operation. They were all in traffic within two years.

The class's route availability was extended to Gosford from January 1960, to Newcastle in 1984 and to Port Kembla a year later following electrification of those lines.

All 40 remained in service until January 1977, when the horrific Granville accident claimed the lives of 83 commuter passengers and destroyed 4620. The locomotive's battered remains were officially scrapped at Chullora Workshops in 1980.

The proliferation of more modern electric classes from the late 1970s eventually led to the mass withdrawal of the 46-class, and by January 1996 most lay in various states of disrepair until scrappings started in earnest in 1998. Some have survived, however, 4638 being retained as an official heritage locomotive and housed at the NSWRTM, Thirlmere. An early moment of glory came in June 1998 when it was temporarily renumbered 4620 for the filming of *The Day of the Roses* TV mini-series, which looked at the Granville rail disaster.

Others preserved are 4601 by the NSWRTM, Valley Heights; 4602 by the Dorrigo Steam Railway and Museum; 4615 by the Sydney Electric Train Society, and 4627 by the Hunter Valley Railway Trust, Branxton.

SPECIFICATIONS

	IMPERIAL (METRIC)
ELECTRICAL EQUIPMENT:	AEI 1500 V (DC)
TRACTION HORSEPOWER:	3400 (2535 KW)
STARTING TRACTIVE EFFORT:	75 300 LB (335 KN)
CONTINUOUS TRACTIVE EFFORT:	40 800 LB (181 KN)
TOTAL WEIGHT:	108 TONS (110 T)
GAUGE:	1435 MM
ROAD NUMBERS:	4601–4640

800-class Bo-Bo

Up until 1956, South Australian Railways had been employing a fleet of elderly steam locomotives, including Rx and S class tender engines, in the bulk of its broad gauge shunting yards. With these engines' increasing need for expensive overhauls, the administration began looking toward diesels as replacements, particularly as experience since 1951 with its new English Electric 900-class main line diesel-electrics had shown definite economies.

Although the 900-class construction had to be carried out by the SAR due to the lack of a local EE manufacturer at the time, the British firm seized the opportunity in the mid-1950s to establish a plant in the Brisbane suburb of Rocklea. The SAR was the first customer when in 1955 it ordered ten heavy Bo-Bo locomotives for broad gauge shunting.

Classified 800-class, these end-cab locomotives' body design closely followed the eight Bo-Bo EE-powered locomotives commissioned by Australian Iron & Steel at Port Kembla in 1950. Initially road-trialled on specially built standard gauge bogies between Clapham and Kagaru, each unit's delivery was originally intended as a light engine movement over the standard gauge NSWGR, changing to broad gauge bogies at Wodonga. In the event, some actually hauled freight trains while running the Albury to Melbourne section.

Powered by EE's 6-cylinder SRKT model turbocharged 544 kW diesel engine, class-leader 800 entered service on 30 May 1956, and all were running by 31 August 1957. Although nominally a shunting locomotive, the units were regularly seen in busy Gilman yard and on transfer freight services throughout the Port Adelaide area and to Mile End and Dry Creek.

Capable of 100 km/h and described as 'extremely good riders', examples were also noted working suburban passenger services, and one was frequently rostered to work the Islington Workshops workers' trains. During periods of extreme motive-power shortages during the 1960s, the class even worked goods trains in multiple over both the Wallaroo and Terowie lines.

With the federal government's takeover of South Australia's non-metropolitan rail services in 1978, the 800-class came under the control of the newly-

A spick and span 807 outside Mile End workshops on 30 December 1971. (Peter Watts)

created Australian National Railway Commission. While their working did not vary, the new authority purged itself of the EE-powered equipment first.

In 1987, 806's engine failed, but because it possessed excellent electrical wiring, it received the engine out of 809, which at the time needed a re-wire, and emerged from the workshops on 12 January 1988 bearing the number 809. (The original 809 was dismantled for parts and scrapped as number 806.)

By 1992, all had been withdrawn. Today 801 is exhibited in operational condition at the National Railway Museum, Port Adelaide.

SPECIFICATIONS

	IMPERIAL (METRIC)
POWER UNIT:	ENGLISH ELECTRIC 6SRKT
TRACTION HORSEPOWER:	660 (497 kW)
STARTING TRACTIVE EFFORT:	40 900 LB (182 kN)
CONTINUOUS TRACTIVE EFFORT:	23 000 LB (102 kN)
TOTAL WEIGHT:	72 TONS (73 T)
GAUGE:	1600 MM
ROAD NUMBERS:	800–809

D9-type B-B

As part of a massive $78 million expansion and modernisation scheme announced in 1955 for the Port Kembla steel milling firm Australian Iron & Steel, the company's extensive railway system went under the microscope.

As part of that upgrade, an order was placed for seven B-B diesel-electrics. Since the company had been obtaining satisfactory service from its original English Electric-powered Bo-Bo units, it

Locomotive D20 shows its unique cooling and propulsion features as it rolls by the AI&S strip mill on 11 December 1979. (Leon Oberg)

seemed reasonable in the interests of operator and maintenance staff familiarity to again turn to this manufacturer's products.

Unlike the position in 1950, when AI&S was forced to import parts and contract an outside firm to construct its pioneering D1/D16-type Bo-Bo locomotives, English Electric had just established a manufacturing plant at Rocklea in Brisbane. The first unit was tested to nearby Greenbank early in August 1956.

Because of their low 29 km/h speed limit, a powered delivery over NSWGR tracks from Brisbane to Port Kembla was not possible, so for each unit's delivery the traction motors were disengaged to allow towing at full track speed.

The class-leader, bearing the number D9, entered traffic on 8 September 1956, and all seven were operating within 12 months.

Increased production throughout the works, including the commissioning of a sinter machine and an extra coke oven battery in addition to new wharf facilities within the Inner Harbour during 1960, saw the need for an additional six units, all commissioned between May and September of that year.

Of typical AI&S end-cab design, these D9 locomotives were externally interesting in that they featured a rather large cooling fan situated in the nose section. Equipped with only one traction motor to each bogie, the adjacent axle was powered by connecting rods.

Each locomotive was fitted with EE's 6-cylinder SRKT diesel engine, which provided a small 282 kW for traction. Because of their low power and the availability of many higher-powered locomotives, the class lost a certain grace in later years. In periods of steel output downturns it was not uncommon to see a row of the D9-type stored.

With threatened severe steel industry downturn set to overwhelm AI&S, a decision was made late in 1981 to suspend any further overhauls on the initial six class members and they were set aside at Steelhaven. Because some were in serviceable condition, the administration decided in mid-1982 to release four for either sale or lease.

No. D10 was leased to Blue Circle Cement's Portland plant from August 1982, but it attracted bitter industrial (crewing) problems and was returned to AI&S on 28 January 1983 after little use. The unit was then leased to Blue Circle Southern Cement for several months, beginning 24 February 1986 when that company's own Bo-Bo locomotive was out of service for a general overhaul.

The steel downturn continued and by late January 1983, D20 was the only locomotive of the class in service at the AI&S plant, being used in connection with inner harbour shunting. While contractors started cutting up a number of the stored locomotives where they lay (beginning with D21 in March 1988), some units were saved.

By 1989, AI&S had become BHP Steel; the former Lysaghts plant also became part of the restructure, and was renamed the Sheet Steel & Coil Division. With the withdrawal of Lysaghts' three centre-cab 268 kW B-B units, D23 and D24 were lightly overhauled and became their replacements, taking up rejuvenated duty early in 1989.

Others also found new homes. No. D9 was leased to the Lachlan Valley Railway, Cowra; D11 was sold to Simsmetal for use at Mascot, several years later going to the Dorrigo Steam Railway and Museum; D20, D21, D23 and D24 went to the Lithgow State Mine Museum (the latter for its parts), while D25 found a new home as a shunter at the ACT Division of the ARHS's Canberra Railway Museum.

SPECIFICATIONS

	IMPERIAL (METRIC)
POWER UNIT:	ENGLISH ELECTRIC 6SRKT
TRACTION HORSEPOWER:	378 (282 KW)
STARTING TRACTIVE EFFORT:	42 000 LB (187 KN)
CONTINUOUS TRACTIVE EFFORT:	13 600 LB (60 KN 9.8 KM/H)
TOTAL WEIGHT:	60 TONS (61 T)
GAUGE:	1435 MM
ROAD NUMBERS:	D9–D15, D20–D25

F-class A1A-A1A & G-class Co-Co

Western Australia's Midland Railway Co, operator of a 420 km, 1067 mm gauge railway linking Midland Junction with the farming and grazing communities along the northbound route to Walkaway, turned to the English Electric Co of Australia for seven light 42-tonners. At the time this railway was running about ten steam-hauled freight trains every seven days in addition to a weekly overnight passenger service.

Arriving throughout 1958 and known as that railway's F-class, these locomotives were basically a scaled-down version of the earlier SAR 6-cylinder 800-class but, to enable them to tread light rail, were equipped with two 3-axle A1A-A1A bogies.

Not long afterwards a comprehensive track strengthening programme was initiated over the full length of this railway, and in 1961 the company placed a follow-up order with EE for two heavier Co-Co units powered by 8-cylinder engines. These locomotives duly arrived two years later, becoming the railway's G-class. Both the F and G classes retained their classifications following the system's acquisition by WAGR on 1 August 1964. As the route was progressively laid with heavier rail to support the weight of more modern diesels, the F and G-classes tended to be used along the south-west route to Pemberton and Collie.

The G's were also pressed into Perth suburban passenger working in addition to stints at the head of the *Australind* passenger train. No. G51 was withdrawn and scrapped following an engine failure in April 1990. Its sister lasted in active service a further eleven months before it was saved from scrapping by the WA Division of the ARHS and 'sub-let' to the Hotham Valley Railway, which repaired the veteran and out-shopped it in original Midland Railway livery. The unit made its first tourist trip in May 1994.

The first F-class was retired in October 1984 and by April 1987 just F43 was left working, being a regular sight hauling transfer goods trains around the Perth area until May 1990, when repair costs made its continued use uneconomic. Of the seven F-class, three have been scrapped; F40 was acquired

F41 trundles over a bridge outside Williams with a Narrogin-bound goods train on 19 July 1979. (Peter Watts)

from a collector in 2004 by rail operator South Spur Rail Services (now part of P&O Trans Australia). F41 is displayed in original Midland livery at Moora (an old Midland Railway station); F43 is in the ARHS Bassendean Rail Transport Museum while F44 was sold to ALCOA where its engine and frame were converted to act as a pump at a caustic dam. It has since gone into private hands and at last report its remains resided on an Oakford property.

Of the G-class, G50 has been preserved by the WA ARHS while G51 was scrapped.

SPECIFICATIONS

	F-CLASS	G-CLASS
	IMPERIAL (METRIC)	IMPERIAL (METRIC)
POWER UNIT:	EE 6SRKT	EE 8SVT
TRACTION HORSEPOWER:	660 (497 kW)	950 (697 kW)
CONTINUOUS TRACTIVE EFFORT:	36 800 lb (160 kN)	54 000 lb (240 kN)
TOTAL WEIGHT:	63.9 tons (64.7 t)	75 tons (76 t)
GAUGE:	1067 mm	1067 mm
ROAD NUMBERS:	F40–46	G50, G51

1250-class Co-Co

This class was one of Australia's more unusual diesel designs, having among other things a full-width streamlined cab married to the manufacturer's standard hood design at the rear to provide greater accessibility during maintenance. Initially, Queensland Railways ordered five units from English Electric's Rocklea plant.

Engineering-wise, the 1250-class was an Australianised version of QR's imported 1200-class of 1954, taking advantage of the UK manufacturer's ongoing engine and electrical improvements.

Loco 1258 and a smaller sister EE unit, 1621, sun themselves outside Townsville locomotive depot on 25 July 1973. (Peter Watts)

The class-leader was released during a ceremony at the company's works on 22 July 1959, and 36 hours later was working a goods train between Brisbane and Toowoomba. As more units were delivered, their sphere of influence also included the North Coast line to Cairns, along with trips to Wallangarra.

These locomotives were powered by an English Electric 12SVT 1290 kW engine with 962 kW available for traction. All axles were motorised.

After the Mt Isa line was rebuilt to cope with the increased output from the mine, another 12 units were progressively ordered, and further improved by the fitting of multiple-unit control equipment and a 1440 hp engine with 1174 kW available for traction. These locomotives were delivered from September 1960 to July 1963.

With control-system voltage incompatibility making multiple-unit control impossible between EE locomotives and US types, EE locomotives were the first to be withdrawn following the arrival of more modern US-type locomotives during the 1970s and 1980s.

The first written-off was 1252, on 13 November 1981, as a result of serious fire damage suffered while hauling a Central Division goods train. No. 1253 suffered a similar fate about a year later. The last locomotives in service were 1255 and 1257, withdrawn on 16 November 1987.

No. 1263, the only member of the class to retain its original British Stone's headlight, is stored by the ARHS at Townsville, while QR heritage locomotive 1262 resides at the Workshops Rail Museum at North Ipswich, with hood doors and cowlings suspended above the unit to illustrate in cut-away style the internal workings of a diesel-electric locomotive.

SPECIFICATIONS

	ORIGINAL	FINAL 12
	IMPERIAL (METRIC)	IMPERIAL (METRIC)
POWER UNIT:	EE 12SVT	EE 12SVT
TRACTION HORSEPOWER:	1290 (962 kW)	1440 (1174 kW)
STARTING TRACTIVE EFFORT:	50 000 LB (222 kN)	57 000 LB (254 kN)
CONTINUOUS TRACTIVE EFFORT:	38 500 LB (173 kN)	41 500 LB (185 kN)
TOTAL WEIGHT:	85.9 TONS (87.9 T)	87.5 TONS (88.75 T)
GAUGE:	1067 MM	1067 MM
ROAD NUMBERS:	1250–1254	1255–1266

1959 NEW SOUTH WALES GOVERNMENT RAILWAYS

48-class Co-Co

Every once in a while the perfect, totally reliable locomotive comes along—a type that can be everything to everyone. Alco's Model DL-531, designed for developing nations, was just such a unit for, although rated at 671 kW, it was constructed from Alco's Model DL-500 World Series parts capable of withstanding higher 1343 kW load factors. Thus, because of the lower stresses, the DL-531 simply kept on going.

Already operating in Peru, Pakistan and Brazil, the model made its first Australian appearance on the NSWGR in September 1959 as that system's 48-class. Twenty units were ordered from Alco's Australian manufacturer, A.E. Goodwin Ltd, as replacements for elderly branch line steam locomotives. The 20 enabled light lines radiating out of Werris Creek and Casino to be fully dieselised.

Found to be incredibly trouble free and fuel efficient, repeat ordering saw 165 in operation by October 1970. During its 11-year manufacturing period, the class was refined with improved electrics, a slightly higher-rated engine and larger fuel tanks, which gave the locomotives the ability to assist on main lines. In fact, 48-class locomotives have worked to every nook and cranny of the state. They dieselised the Illawarra line and the Hunter Valley coal trains, and large numbers were based for many years at country depots such as Goulburn, Bathurst and Junee for both branch line and main line service.

South Australian move

The SAR also needed reliable motive power for use over the broad gauge (1600 mm) Murraylands branch lines that radiated out of Tailem Bend. Like the NSWGR, it too had earlier taken delivery of larger World Series Alcos, and in 1959 ordered ten DL-531s which could operate on light 20 kg/m rails as they had an axle load of only 12.75 tonnes.

Further orders were made, and by February 1970 the system had 45 units, 15 for the state's 1067 mm narrow gauge, 17 for the broad gauge and 13 for the newly-commissioned 1435 mm standard gauge linking Broken Hill with Port Pirie.

The neighbouring Silverton Tramway, once the operator of the 59 km, 1067 mm gauge line between Broken Hill and Cockburn (on the South Australian border), purchased three similar but less luxurious units for ore haulage. The first, loco 27, arrived in December 1960 and within a few months the other

two, 28 and 29, were also running. Steam operations on that line ceased immediately.

The opening of the East–West standard gauge project in 1970 effectively reduced the Silverton Tramway to a shunting authority and so, needing fewer locomotives, the company sold its class-leader to the SAR where it was renumbered 874.

The standard gauge project marked the start of extensive Model-531 intersystem travels. In July 1974, the SAR loaned three such units, 847–849, to the NSWGR to arrest a severe locomotive shortage on that system. They were pooled with their 48-class prototypes and used virtually state-wide until returned to Australian National Rail (the SAR's new owner since 1978) in December 1980. (Some were to return again in 1981 to work construction trains on the Sandy Hollow–Gulgong railway.)

ANR's acquisition of all non-metropolitan lines in South Australia (and of Tasmanian Railways) included the takeover of all but two 830-class (830 and 845 were retained for more than a decade by the metropolitan South Australian Transport Authority service). Under ANR ownership, the 830-class was trialled as shunting units in remote areas including Marree and Parkeston, but crew comforts were lacking due to their small and cramped cabs; this later led to the removal of a second control stand.

At the time of ANR's formation, Tasmanian rolling stock was in dire need of replacement. Indeed, the TGR was in danger of complete closure. To help relieve the situation, air-braked freight rolling stock was forwarded to Tasmania to replace the vacuum-brake equipment that had been the norm since 1900. To haul those air-braked trains, twenty 830-class Alcos were gradually shipped to the Apple Isle, where they were pressed into log, container, coal and general freight working. The first to arrive were 858

A pair of original Silverton Tramway DL531s, 29 and 28, prepare to depart Broken Hill's Railwaytown headquarters with a narrow gauge ore train for Cockburn on 8 June 1966. The line at the time travelled to the South Australian border via Silverton. (Leon Oberg)

SAR broad gauge example, 833, shunting at Tailem Bend on 29 January 1980. (Leon Oberg)

Originally built as Silverton Tramway's 27, this unit became the SAR's 874, which on 17 September 2001 was out-shopped with a low-profile nose and numbered T01 for West Australian woodchip traffic into Albany. It was fashioned using the nose and cab from accident-damaged DA3. Now ARG's 907, it spent some time afterwards working grain trains in New South Wales before once again heading west. (Leon Oberg)

and 865, which entered service in April 1980. Crews and maintenance staff, used to English Electrics, tended to shun their new charges.

Tasmanian enginemen also complained of 'fumy and cramped cabs that offered poor visibility'. The arrival of the 830s in Tasmania turned into a slow, drawn-out affair and it was six and a half years before all 20 units were delivered. By then their role had been played out, due in part to their unpopularity (many were allegedly worn out when they arrived) and in part to the presence of higher-powered 2350/2370-class Queensland Co-Co EE units. From the winter of 1987, tenders were called for the return to the mainland of six 830s (the programme was cancelled after three had been shipped).

In October 1989, tenders were called for the disposal of nine. Silverton Rail, as the operation had become in New South Wales, took advantage of this, acquiring 857 and 864 to operate, and 856 and 862 for parts. The bodies of the latter two remained in Tasmania and were subsequently scrapped. While most 830s were cut up in Tasmania, AN did return five more to the mainland where they saw continued service over narrow, standard and broad gauge networks, including the isolated Eyre Peninsula system. By then, AN had plans to withdraw its ageing EE 500 and 800 class Bo-Bo yard-shunting locomotives, and turned to the 830-class for replacements because of its strength at slow speeds.

AN, wanting to phase in driver-only shunting operations, selected locomotive 849 as the 'guinea pig', out-shopping it as DA1 in July 1991. The design has been credited to Graham Haywood of AN's Islington Workshops, who based the work on the Montreal

Locomotive Works' 1967-released low-nose RS-11 series. This nose was provided for added trackside visibility for the crew. To increase cab room, a control stand was removed and the area air-conditioned.

To date seven 830s have been converted. The first two employed original nose sections and cabs with 3-piece windscreens. But from DA3 onwards, further revised cabs and noses were fabricated, producing a more pointed look, with the higher cab roofs providing better access for air-conditioner cables. The 3-piece windscreens were replaced from DA4 onwards by two tinted bullet-proof screens as used in the Clyde-built DL-class. Although technically converted for shunting service, these units have seen considerable mainline service, hauling everything from wheat to gypsum and limestone, mostly on the standard gauge.

While the first six DAs were spawned by the 830-class, AN purchased at auction two 48s from NSW State Rail in December 1994, 4826 for parts and 4813 to convert as DA7. By then, this unit and those mainland 830-class units still 'on the books' had passed into the ownership of a consortium led by Genesee & Wyoming Inc (eventually forming the Australian Railroad Group). Loco DA7 had the distinction of launching the company's new black/red/yellow livery when commissioned in April 1998. Two units were also forwarded to Genesee & Wyoming's then Great Western Railroad in Western Australia, one being former Silverton Tramway locomotive 27 (SAR 874), which used the nose and cab from accident-damaged DA3, and was out-shopped for 1067 mm gauge trials from Forrestfield to Avon yard on 17 September 2001. It was styled as a DA but numbered T01 for West Australian use. Twelve days later, T02 (aka AN 849 and DA1) ran its trial and both units were transferred, albeit for a short time, to Albany for woodchip haulage.

With those companies coming together under the ownership of the Australian Railroad Group, the locomotives today carry the numbers 907 and 901 respectively and for a time in 2005 were hauling grain into Gunnedah in north-western New South Wales.

ARG delivered three surplus 830-class, 833, 838 and 845, to Australian Transport Network Access in Melbourne on 1 June 2000, initially for southern New South Wales branch line grain operations. This came as a result of the company's acquisition of an Australian Wheat Board Ltd grain haulage contract which saw the first main line train leave Junee for Port Kembla 14 days later. The company, along with these locomotives, today belongs to Pacific National.

After almost a decade's service, ARG sold its assets to Queensland Railways National (QRN) in June 2006 and as part of the deal picked up narrow gauge 852, which was quickly rostered into iron-ore shunting at Esperance. The rest of the surviving 830s and the seven DA-type rebuilds remained with a re-badged Genesee & Wyoming Australia.

NSW rationalisation

Meanwhile, the aforementioned December 1994 NSW State Rail locomotive auction which followed the commissioning of new 82 and 90 class locomotives saw four units, 4814, 4816, 4820 and 4836, acquired by the Australian Traction Corporation (Austrac) based at Junee in southern New South Wales. Three of those units were rebuilt, the company making its first foray into commercial rail operations between Griffith, Junee and Sydney on 3 November 1997. Austrac also made history on 5 November 1998,

when 4836 worked a company train into Melbourne, becoming the first of this class to visit that capital city. The three operational units today see spot lease service under the ownership of Junee Rail Workshops following Austrac's exit as an accredited train operator in 2003.

Sales continued, with 4812 going to the Kooragang Island (Newcastle) oilseed crushing company, Cargill (Australia), in February 1997 for shunting service and renumbered CAR1. A company spokesperson told this author the locomotive's high-tension circuits were modified, limiting it to operate in first 'gear' only. It now belongs to Junee Railway Workshops for a planned rebuild programme.

Six units, 4811, 4815, 4825, 4829, 4838 and 4843, were sold to Silverton Rail, some finding initial work as bankers on National Rail Corporation (NRC) trains between Adelaide and Tailem Bend, from late 1995 through to mid-1997. The Silverton locos were reclassified from March 1999 as the 48s-series.

Despite these sales, the first State Rail 48-class withdrawals were due to fires and accidents, the first to go being 4863, destroyed in a head-on collision at Breeza on 2 February 1985. The strong chassis of another accident victim, 48131, was put to further use in 1995 when it was converted at Bathurst Workshops to a match truck for an accident crane's boom. Life for the remainder of the State Rail fleet was not over, however. Many units in the 4885–48165 series were progressively upgraded from late 1996 and equipped with air-conditioners and sound-deadening materials. Locos 4848 and 4871 were provided with low-profile full-width nose/cabs for metropolitan trip train and shunting and ran their trials to Botany on 2 September 1998 numbered PL1 and PL2 respectively. They provided the template for another six basically similar conversions which began appearing from April 2000. Others converted were

Former NSWGR Mark 1 48-class, 4816, now in spot lease service by Junee Railway Workshops. (Leon Oberg)

RailCorp's 4827 which is equipped with a catalytic exhaust scrubber allowing it to work infrastructure trains inside tunnels. (Leon Oberg)

4870 (PL3), 4868 (PL4), 4881 (PL5) 4867 (PL6) and 4856 (PL7).

The aftermath

Preservationists and heritage bodies have acquired many 48/830-class examples. In Tasmania, the Don River Railway bought 866 and the parts of several others; 4803 is operated by the NSW Rail Transport Museum; 4807 is in tourist train use out of Canberra; 4821 operates at Goulburn Railway Heritage Centre, 4822 resides at Dorrigo Steam Railway and Museum while 4833, acquired from a scrap firm by a band of enthusiasts, has been meticulously restored and regularly works 3801 Limited excursion and service trains under the trading name Goodwin Alco.

One hundred and thirteen 48-class remained with FreightCorp when the Patrick Corp/Toll Holdings bought the business on 21 February 2002 as part of the FreightCorp/National Rail Corporation privatisation. But seven mainly inoperable units, 4804, 4809, 4828, 4830, 4837, 4841 and 4842, were on-sold to Silverton Rail on 20 February 2003, joining four hulks collected by that firm in 1998 and 1999. Of these, 4809 was sent to Forrestfield WA for planned (but aborted) reactivation using a Caterpillar engine. But 22 remain in NSW government ownership, stored 4801 and 4805, and operational 4819 and 4827, the latter forming part of the RailCorp infrastructure fleet which sport exhaust scrubbers to enable them to operate work trains inside tunnels.

In addition, 4886, 4897, 4899, 48100. 48110, 48111, 48113, 48115, 48116, 48124, 48125, 48142, 48145, 48148-48150, 48154 and 48157 were taken over from PN by the NSW Department of Transport on 1 July 2009 for lease to GrainCorp re-numbered 48201-48218. Locos 4846, 4859, 4864, 4872, 4878 and 4884 were later added, becoming GPU01-GPU06.

SPECIFICATIONS

	IMPERIAL (METRIC)
POWER UNIT:	Alco 251C (SIX CYLINDER)
TRACTION HORSEPOWER:	900 (671 kW)
STARTING TRACTIVE EFFORT:	49 500 LB (220 kN)
CONTINUOUS TRACTIVE EFFORT:	40 200 LB (179 kN)
TOTAL WEIGHT:	70 TONS (71.5 T) (LATER NSWR UNITS) 74.5 TONS (76 T)
GAUGE:	(NSW) 1435 MM
	(SAR/AN) 1067 MM, 1435 MM AND 1600 MM
	(SILVERTON) 1435 MM (ORIGINALLY 1067 MM)
ROAD NUMBERS:	(NSW) 4801–48165 (AS BUILT)
	PL1–PL7 (FORMERLY 4848, 4871, 4870, 4868, 4881, 4867 AND 4856)
	(SILVERTON) 48s28–48s38) SILVERTON 27 BECAME SAR 874 AND ARG T01/907
	(SAR/AN) 830–874 (830 BECAME 875)
	(AN) DA1–DA7 (FORMERLY 849, 832, 835, 839, 875, 836 AND 4813 RESPECTIVELY)
	(ARG) DA1 BECAME T02, THEN 901; DA2 - 902; DA4 - 903; DA5 - 904; DA6 - 905; DA7 - 906 AND 874 - T01 AND NOW 907. (NOTE DA3 WAS SCRAPPED)
	GRAINCORP FLEET: 48201-48218; GPU01-GPU06

W-class 0-6-0DH

Like many of Australia's heavy engineering firms, Tulloch Ltd, at Rhodes in Sydney, had made its name as a builder of rolling stock. But by the late 1950s the firm reckoned it would join its rivals and become a locomotive builder too.

Tulloch Ltd's first creation was an 0-4-0 diesel-mechanical 95 kW unit which was sold to Sims scrap-metal dealers in 1958 to shunt that firm's Mascot yard. This tiny standard gauge locomotive still exists, having been bought and upgraded in 1988 for electric carriage shunting by Skitube in the heart of the NSW Snowy Mountains.

Following this relatively slow start, Tulloch Ltd lifted its sights and offered the Australian railways a much more sophisticated 0-6-0DH based on established European practice. Tasmanian Railways became the first customer and in 1959–60 took delivery of two 1067 mm gauge centre-cab 260 kW W-class locomotives for intended use over light rural branch lines.

This locomotive type spawned a larger, almost look-alike 490 kW version for Victorian Railways. Between December 1959 and December 1961, no fewer than 27 Mercedes Benz-powered 12-cylinder 48.5-tonne 0-6-0DH units were delivered. Each was fitted with Krupp 2W1D46 transmission. As it happened—not by design—these locomotives also became the W-class, 25 of them being issued to the broad (1600 mm) gauge and the final two to the standard gauge for use principally at Dynon car sheds.

Interestingly, one of the standard gauge units had been built to demonstrate the model's prowess to the NSWGR and for some seven months was used in transfer freight operations in the Sydney metropolitan area. During that time the unit operated in NSWGR colours and was numbered 7101. In June 1961, the locomotive was returned to Tulloch and, after a repaint, sold to VR to become W266.

The VR W-class saw service in many Victorian yards until a move to larger trains and rationalisation of rail centres rendered them redundant. The last in service was W244, withdrawn and preserved with W241 at Geelong in 1994. Both today see lease service hauling Melbourne metropolitan infrastructure trains. Others to survive include W243 and W255 at the ARHS North Williamstown Railway Museum,

One of the two standard gauge units dedicated to Melbourne yard operations pictured at South Dynon depot on 7 February 1979. (Leon Oberg)

W250 at the Yarra Valley Tourist Railway and W260 in the River Murray Heritage Centre at Tocumwal in New South Wales.

For the record, the two Tasmanian W-class were scrapped at Launceston in 1981 after 'ordinary careers'.

SPECIFICATIONS

	IMPERIAL (METRIC)
POWER UNIT:	MERCEDES BENZ MB 820B
TRACTION HORSEPOWER:	650 (490 kW)
STARTING TRACTIVE EFFORT:	32 250 LB (149.5 kN)
CONTINUOUS TRACTIVE EFFORT:	29 200 LB (131.2 kN)
TOTAL WEIGHT:	48 TONS (48.5 T)
GAUGE:	1435 MM AND 1600 MM
ROAD NUMBERS:	W241–267 (NOS 266 AND 267 DELIVERED TO STANDARD GAUGE)

A-class Co-Co

As a means of dieselising the difficult Midland–Northam section of the WAGR, two 977 kW Co-Co type diesel-electric locomotives were acquired from the Clyde Engineering Co in June and July 1960.

Introduced as the A-class, the design was an improved Co-Co version of the EMD G12 model delivered six years earlier to Queensland Railways. The WAGR type also boasted a further refined body and cab.

Exerting an extra 116 kN tractive effort over WAGR's elderly British-built X-class diesel-electrics, the success of the A-class soon led to the acquisition of more units. Three were delivered in late 1962, while another, 1506, arrived the following June for use with the Jarrahdale bauxite trains. It became the first WA locomotive equipped with a dynamic brake.

With their route availability extended to Kalgoorlie, a total of 14 had been pressed into service by December 1965, the last two being financed by the Western Mining Co to haul iron ore from Westmine, in the rugged Koolanooka hills, to Geraldton. These two locomotives were also equipped with dynamic brakes.

Powered with EMD's proven 567C 12-cylinder engine, eight of the class were built at Clyde's Sydney plant and towed to Western Australia. For the remainder, Clyde contracted Commonwealth Engineering at Bassendean, Perth, to undertake final assembly (including construction of the bodywork) of 1507–1512, which became the first diesel-electrics built in that state.

Five improved A-class were subsequently acquired between August and November 1967. Known as the AA-class, these were equipped with EMD's new 645E engine, which added an extra 142 kN for traction, improved electrics and controls. These were followed by six AB-class units between October 1969 and March 1970, which differed from the AA's in the fitting of a larger fuel tank and Alliance couplers to enable them to work both vacuum and air-braked trains. The AA's and AB's were built in Sydney. (The earlier A and AA units were subsequently fitted with Alliance couplers in place of their original 'chopper' type.)

In poignant testimony to their quality, the A/AA and AB classes continued in traffic for more than three decades until A1503 was withdrawn for an overhaul in March 1994. While the three classes could be found working the entire system, the AA's and AB's were favoured on the wheat lines whereas the A's generally worked south-west timber trains in addition to Perth metropolitan goods services.

In January 1998, A1502–1510 and AB1533 were sold to Tranz Rail, which had recently purchased the Tasmanian component of Australian National Railways. All left Fremantle the following month bound for the company's Hutt Workshops (in New Zealand) for planned overhauls. However, five, including the AB, were scrapped in 2001 while A1507, which was forwarded to Tasmania for its spare parts in September 1998, eventually suffered this fate also. Only four units, A1502, A1503, A1504 and A1510, remained at Hutt as at late 2004, and were then sold through an intermediary company to South African

The classic G-12 body modified in several ways as the WAGR A-class, including the provision of high-roofed cab, dynamic brake module and cut-away valance. A1513 was pictured at Caron with a stock train on 13 August 1979. (Peter Watts)

interests. In 2006 they were undergoing overhauls and re-gauging to 1000 mm in the USA.

The remaining A/AA/AB units soldiered on until made redundant by new EMD S-class locomotives, and in September 1998 seven of them, A1512, AA1515–1519 and AB1532, were shipped out of North Fremantle wharf bound for new owners, Ferrocarril de Antofagasta a Bolivia, in Chile. They operate there as 1431–1437 respectively.

The last A-class unit in Westrail service was A1514. This unit, along with A1501, A1511 (which was a shunter at the Clyde maintenance facility), A1513 and A1514, survived to pass into the ownership of the Australian Railroad Group (ARG) on 2 December 2000. Both today operate on South Australia's Eyre Peninsula, numbered 1203 and 1204 under the ownership of Genesee & Wyoming Australia.

ARG also acquired AB-class locomotives 1531 and 1534–1536 at that time. As this book was being prepared there were plans to rebuild them under the ownership of Queensland National-West and confusingly renumber them 1501–1504.

Class-leader, the real 1501, has been earmarked for the ARHS museum.

SPECIFICATIONS

	A-CLASS	AA AND AB CLASSES
	IMPERIAL (METRIC)	IMPERIAL (METRIC)
POWER UNIT:	EMD 12-567C	EMD 12-645E
TRACTION HORSEPOWER	1310 (977 kW)	1500 (977 kW)
STARTING TRACTIVE EFFORT:	54 432 LB (242 kN)	60 000 LB (267 kN)
CONTINUOUS TRACTIVE EFFORT:	45 000 LB (200 kN)	50 820 LB (226 kN)
TOTAL WEIGHT:	90 TONS (91.5 T)	93/97 TONS (95/99 T)
GAUGE:	1067 MM	1067 MM
ROAD NUMBERS:	A1501–1514	AA1515–1519, AB1531–1536

General Electric Bo-Bo

These chunky 71-tonners are a larger and more-refined version of A. Goninan & Co's 45-tonne centre-cab B-B locomotives constructed in 1954 for John Lysaghts of Port Kembla.

Five were initially ordered by BHP Newcastle during 1959 to replace steam operations on its narrow (915 mm) gauge ingot system. The first, numbered 37, was delivered by the builder in July 1960. The design was based on a US GE standard industry type (suitably modified for BHP) dating back to 1940. Hundreds of units in various power outputs and sizes were built in that country, all employing the basic centre-cab theme.

Unlike BHP's earlier Cooper-Bessemer standard gauge units, the new Bo-Bo locomotives were built to an extremely narrow 221 cm body width to enable them to operate within the very tight confines of the plant's narrow gauge system.

Deemed to be an immediate success, eleven more were acquired in two batches, but for use on the company's standard gauge railway. Their delivery over the following two years led to the cessation of all BHP's commercial steam operations.

Until 1963, all Goninan's Bo-Bos had been powered with twin 6-cylinder 213 kW Cummins supercharged diesel engines. When orders were placed for a further five locomotives to help with steadily expanding production, they came equipped with twin 195 kW Rolls Royce engines. Intriguingly, despite their standard gauge service, these locomotives continued to be built to the narrow 221 cm width, but locomotive crews started complaining that they were experiencing vision difficulties when pushing rakes of wide-bodied 300-tonne capacity metal cars and coal hopper vehicles. Accordingly, the final locomotive of that order, a Cummins super-charged unit numbered BHP54, was delivered in January 1966 with a full-width 297 cm wide chassis and cab.

The company started rebuilding earlier narrow locomotives that month to the wider configuration, starting with BHP45, and all units numbered BHP42 onwards were eventually treated, the earlier ones being retained for the narrow gauge.

Ten years passed before any additional locomotives

One from the original batch of narrow gauge, narrow body units, BHP38, as running in February 1981. (Leon Oberg)

of this class arrived at the Newcastle works. These had been ordered in 1974 to assist with a projected increase in traffic over both the standard gauge and narrow gauge systems, particularly in connection with the commissioning of a new No. 2 bloom mill. Because the new mill had not been finished when the new locomotives were received (BHP55 in September 1977 and BHP56 in November 1977), both were stowed until late 1979 and early 1980 respectively. They were delivered with turbo-charged Cummins engines.

The No. 2 bloom at that time relied on ingots for its production so BHP56 was built to the narrow configuration for the 915 mm gauge network. It had been in service just a few months when it was involved in an accident with BHP40, badly damaging the new unit's cab.

It is interesting to note that the steel company was poised to hire two of these Bo-Bo units to the NSWGR for shunting service in the Newcastle area in the mid-1970s to arrest a period of severe government locomotive shortage. But the NSWGR crews alleged that 'the brake position was out of line with the hand and the seats were uncomfortable'. Since many other alterations would also be required, including vigilance control, the initiative was dropped.

Despite a looming downturn in steel-making at Newcastle, BHP ordered another two standard

The last unit acquired by Newcastle BHP was BHP58, shown shunting inside the plant on 29 April 1987. (Leon Oberg)

gauge Cummins-powered units during the late 1970s. While this author understands moves were made (in vain) to cancel the contract, their delivery during December 1982 and April 1983 coincided with the predicted steel slump. At the time six older Bo-Bo units had been placed in storage, beginning with locos BHP40 (from the narrow gauge), BHP46 and BHP51 on 1 November 1982.

Some of the stored locomotives were eventually returned to service but extensive rationalisation of the plant, which included the provision of slag granulators and continuous slab casters, saw the reliance on rail reduced considerably. The rail network had gradually fallen from a 1981 peak of 110 km to just 45 km. For instance, the slab casters alone led to the total elimination of the 22 km, 915 mm gauge system in June 1991 and the five narrow gauge units were cannibalised for their re-usable parts.

Eight BHP units remained operational when the Newcastle works officially closed on 30 September 1999, the four remaining Rolls Royce-powered units having by then been equipped with turbo-charged Cummins engines. All were offered for sale soon afterwards and BHP58 quickly found a home at Heggies Transport, Port Kembla. BHP50, after shunting wagons for scrap contractors at BHP

A long way from its original home, ex-Newcastle unit BHP49 at Loongana Lime Pty Ltd's Parkeston (WA) plant on 8 December 2001. (Leon Oberg)

throughout 2000, has been working since February 2001 at Cockburn Cement's (which until July 2006 was Loongana Lime) Rawlinna limestone quarry. Its initial job was to prepare 2500-tonne limestone trains which were forwarded to the company's Parkeston plant. BHP49 was acquired seven months later to shunt the latter works. Both remain in service.

Locos BHP47 and BHP52 were delivered to the Dorrigo Steam Railway and Museum for preservation in April 1994 while BHP42, BHP43, BHP53 and BHP54 have gone to the Richmond

BHP51 has a new life under Manildra Group ownership. The newly-liveried unit, numbered MM03, was pictured working the company's Manildra, New South Wales, plant soon after entering service in 2005. (Tim Gray)

Vale Railway Museum, the latter two taking up residence as late as July 2002.

Of the four remaining locomotives, BHP55 and BHP57 were sold to the Australian Traction Corporation on 30 July 2002, as anticipated lease power, leaving the BHP plant in mid-August for road haulage to the Junee Roundhouse maintenance centre. The former was noted in centre shunting service bearing the name *Folly* in November 2005.

The final two, BHP48 and BHP51, found new homes in December that year with the Manildra Group, returning to their original builder for an overhaul. They now carry the numbers MM03 and MM04 respectively and were allocated to Manildra and Gunnedah plants for shunting.

Industrialists adopt concept

Meanwhile, other Australian industrialists had been purchasing copies of this rugged Bo-Bo type. In November 1964 the Sulphide Corporation (later Pasminco) of Cockle Creek (south of Newcastle) took delivery of one un-numbered full-width Rolls Royce-powered unit for shunting over the company's 5 kilometres of sidings. The locomotive remained in service until early 2003, when it was stopped for a planned overhaul. But this was halted some months later and the unit allocated to the Dorrigo Steam Railway and Museum for preservation just prior to the plant's closure on 12 September, 2003.

John Lysaghts at Port Kembla acquired a Cummins-powered locomotive on 12 April 1973 to assist three smaller B-B GE units in the transfer of steel products from the nearby BHP Port Kembla North plant. This locomotive, known as JL4, was withdrawn in March 1989 and scrapped 14 months later.

Southern Portland Cement (which subsequently became Blue Circle Southern Cement Ltd) acquired two 81.5-tonne wide-bodied 537 kW Cummins turbo-charged units in July 1967. Until then, SPC had been hiring steam locomotives from the NSWGR to shunt at its Marulan South limestone quarry and at the Berrima cement works. No. D1 was commissioned at Marulan South and D2 stationed at Berrima. One of the latter locomotive's duties was to haul coal from the nearby Berrima colliery (closed to rail in the mid-1970s). While D2 was upgraded and re-engined during 1987, D1 was withdrawn after suffering a traction motor fire when working as a 'ballast plough' on 20 January 1999. It was eventually donated, along with some spare parts, to the Goulburn Rail Heritage Centre on 31 January 2001. Loco D2 was withdrawn on 24 June 2003, being the very last of this family of centre-cab Bo-Bo locomotives to operate at its original address. It now works at Manildra Starches' Nowra plant with BHP58.

The Sulphide Corporation's Rolls Royce-powered Bo-Bo unit shunts an inward-bound coal train in the company's Cockle Creek exchange siding on 21 August 1975. (Leon Oberg)

Blue Circle Southern Cement's Marulan South-based D1 was in use day and night. This image shows it preparing a lime train on 24 June 1983. (Leon Oberg)

SPECIFICATIONS

	Imperial (Metric)
Original power unit:	BHP36—47 and 54: twin Cummins NHSB16
	BHP48—53 and Sulphide: Rolls Royce C6TFL
	BHP55—56: Cummins NT855-L2
	BHP57—58: Cummins NT855-L4
	SPC1 and 2: Cummins NT380-C1
	Lysaghts JL4: Cummins NT335-B
Traction horsepower:	540 (403 kW) to 720 (537 kW)
Starting tractive effort:	(from) 48 000 lb (213.5 kN)
Continuous tractive effort:	(from) 20 380 lb (91 kN)
Total weight:	75 tons (76.5 t) to 81 tons (81.5 t)
Gauge:	915 mm and 1435 mm
Road numbers:	(BHP) 37—58
	(Lysaghts) JL4
	(SPC) D1, D2
	(Sulphide Corp) No road number allocated

1960 NEW SOUTH WALES GOVERNMENT RAILWAYS

70-class 0-6-0DH

The acquisition of the ten diesel-hydraulic locomotives of this class was an early attempt to dieselise some of the NSWGR's shunting yards.

Becoming the 70-class, the locomotives were ordered from Sydney-based manufacturer Commonwealth Engineering, a firm well known to the NSWGR as a passenger and goods rolling-stock builder. The firm had also been building underground mining, industrial and sugar locomotives for almost a decade.

The first unit entered service in August 1960, the first three years of their lives being spent working metropolitan transfer goods trains and in yard shunting in Sydney. Caterpillar diesel engines powered the steam locomotive-style driving wheels through Voith L420rU2 transmissions.

All ten were transferred to Port Kembla in 1963 to replace a diversified collection of small vintage steam locomotives in transfer steel and wharf shunting duties. They did that job so efficiently that some were deemed spare and for a short time could be found working short-haul coal trains in pairs, and singularly on selected workers' trains. They remained in the Port Kembla area for the rest of their working lives.

The first withdrawn was 7009, on 10 February 1984. A greater emphasis on unit trains and the rationalisation of wharf and yard shunting activities led to further withdrawals and the remaining shunting work was placed in the hands of 73-class diesel-hydraulic locomotives soon afterwards.

While 7004's key hydraulic transmission parts were salvaged during scrapping at Port Kembla for use in Emu Bay Railway units, locos 7007, 7008 and 7010 are today preserved by the Dorrigo Steam Railway and Museum and 7006 is with the Thirlmere Railway Museum, under private ownership.

SPECIFICATIONS

	Imperial (Metric)
POWER UNIT:	Caterpillar D397
TRACTION HORSEPOWER:	550 (372 kW)
STARTING TRACTIVE EFFORT:	32 200 lb (149.4 kN)
CONTINUOUS TRACTIVE EFFORT:	25 600 lb (113.2 kN)
TOTAL WEIGHT:	48 tons (48.5 t)
GAUGE:	1435 mm
ROAD NUMBERS:	7001–7010

1960 NEW SOUTH WALES GOVERNMENT RAILWAYS

49-class Co-Co

As a means of replacing steam traction over the Parkes to Broken Hill line in western New South Wales, at the time only lightly laid, the NSWGR turned to EMD's G-8 locomotive type when ordering six diesel-electrics in 1959. In essence, this model was identical to units supplied to VR from June 1959, but in a bid to further spread the locomotive's all-up weight, the maker, the Clyde Engineering Co, custom-designed the NSWGR model, adding Co-Co bogies instead of the VR's Bo-Bo trucks.

The first of these 49-class locomotives was delivered on 15 September 1960; with the arrival of the sixth in March 1961, traffic over the Broken Hill line was officially fully dieselised.

But the NSWGR did not stop there. Due to the class's reliability working through the harsh, hot and dusty conditions experienced in the far west of the state, several further contracts were let and by September 1964 eighteen locomotives had been delivered, all based at Parkes depot. This allowed the dieselisation of other Western Division branches, along with a certain amount of main line work to Lithgow and Dubbo. In addition, examples occasionally worked over the cross-country line to Cootamundra.

Locomotives 7007 and 7005 on a Port Kembla transfer trip. (Graham Cotterall)

Now in the employ of Chicago Freight Car Leasing (Australia), KL81 was formerly the NSWGR's 4910 and continues to see service across much of the State. (Leon Oberg)

Powered by EMD's reliable 567C 8-cylinder diesel engine rated at 652 kW for traction purposes, the final six units differed from the earlier deliveries in that their sideframe skirts were removed to allow better access to underneath plumbing and equipment.

Despite the opening of the East–West standard gauge in 1970 and the upgrading of the Parkes–Broken Hill route to carry main line locomotive types, the 49-class largely remained on the Western Division for another two decades. By then, 4915 had been withdrawn at Cardiff Workshops for its parts, following collision damage. It was officially scrapped in 1989, making it the only class member to as yet face the torch.

In November 1989, the 17 remaining units were transferred to Sydney for local, Illawarra and Tahmoor coal train haulage. They were gradually withdrawn and in July 1994, units 4907 and 4913 were sold to Manildra Starches as MM01 and MM02 respectively. This firm also acquired 4906 and 4911 for planned grain train haulage, on-selling 4906 to the Northern Rivers Railroad (NRR) in November 2000. NRR had already acquired seven others but following this company's acquisition by the Queensland government in 2003, two were disposed of to the Seymour Heritage Rail Centre in July 2004.

Three of the remaining NSWGR-owned units were surprisingly sent to Melbourne in October 1994 for eight months' construction train duties on the National Rail Corporation's standard gauge railway through western Victoria.

The class's final fling came late in 1995, when most remaining units were returned to traffic in Sydney to release other locomotives to handle that year's bumper wheat harvest. Locomotive 4904 was continuing as wheel-lathe shunter at Delec in late 1999 before it, 4910 and 4917 were sold to Melbourne-based Great Northern Rail Services. They were delivered on 5 May 2001. While Chicago Freight Car Leasing (Australia) managed to secure those three units, overhauling them to become KL80–82 respectively, two former NRR locomotives, 4903 and 4906, have since received overhauls and been provided with low profile noses; they are used today by Patrick Rail on Sydney metropolitan freight transfer duties.

While originally preserved as a heritage locomotive, 4908 is now owned by P&O Trans Australia working infrastructure trains while 4916 and 4918 are active heritage exhibits with the NSWRTM and 3801 Ltd respectively.

SPECIFICATIONS

	IMPERIAL (METRIC)
POWER UNIT:	EMD 8-567C
TRACTION HORSEPOWER:	875 (652 kW)
STARTING TRACTIVE EFFORT:	44 240 lb (197 kN)
CONTINUOUS TRACTIVE EFFORT:	37 200 lb (165 kN)
TOTAL WEIGHT:	78.5 tons (80 t)
GAUGE:	1435 mm
ROAD NUMBERS:	4901–4918; CFCLA UNITS: KL80 (EX 4904), KL81 (EX 4910) AND KL82 (EX 4917) RESPECTIVELY.

Carrying its most recent number, 2150, Tasrail's Y1 was pictured shunting in Burnie on 26 February 1999. (Chris Walters)

1961 Tasmanian Government Railways

Y-class Bo-Bo

These eight end-cab Y-class locomotives were a more Australianised, upgraded version of the Tasmanian Government Railway's pioneer main line X-class diesel-electrics and closely followed the design of the F-class of Western Australia's Midland Railway.

Initially, three were ordered from the railway's Launceston Workshops, the first entering main line goods service just before Christmas 1961. Although just half a tonne heavier than the X-class, the original engine type had been improved sufficiently by this time to exert an additional 150 kW of power output. Up-rated traction motors were also employed.

Within a short time, early deliveries started working log trains. Later that decade, examples could be seen hauling the *Tasman Limited* express service.

Additional orders saw eight running by the close of 1971, with all diesel engines and traction equipment used in their production supplied by English Electric. While the locomotive employed an unstressed superstructure, considerable use was made of aluminium in a bid to reduce all-up weight.

In company with all TGR locomotives, the Y-class was fitted with vacuum braking. But following the railway's takeover in 1978 by Australian National Railways, large numbers of air-braked mainland freight wagons were sent to Tasmania in a bid to upgrade rail services. Two Y-class units were modified

for air-brake operation in 1986 and utilised mainly for shunting duties. The vacuum-brake units ended their days working cement traffic between Goliath Cement, Railton and Devonport, being replaced initially by air-braked sister units.

With the conversion of vehicles to run air-braked cement services, the last revenue vacuum train ran on 15 July 1991 when Y6 hauled a Railton–Devonport cement train. The following day this locomotive hauled two sister units and the few remaining vacuum-braked wagons to Launceston Workshops for storage.

By mid-1994, the six vacuum Y-class had been heavily vandalised. Three were sold to preservation societies and restored to running condition, with Y2 at the Derwent Valley Railway, New Norfolk; Y4 at the Tasmanian Transport Museum, Glenorchy; Y6 (together with the stripped hulk of Y8) at the Don River Railway, Devonport, while Y3 resides in the Queen Victoria Museum and Art Gallery at Launceston.

Following the sale of Australian National, the two air-braked units, Y1 and Y5, and the remains of Y7 passed into the hands of the Australian Transport Network in November 1997, Y1 and Y5 subsequently being renumbered 2150 and 2151 respectively. Both remain in service as shunt locomotives.

The derelict remains of Y7 were retrieved from storage in 2001 and converted for use as an engineless remote-control driving cab on Devonport–Railton cement shuttles. Renumbered DV1, it entered service in October 2001.

	IMPERIAL (METRIC)
POWER UNIT:	EE 6SRKT
TRACTION HORSEPOWER:	800 (597 kW)
STARTING TRACTIVE EFFORT:	37 000 LB (164.6 kW)
CONTINUOUS TRACTIVE EFFORT:	34 000 (151.3 kW)
TOTAL WEIGHT:	58 TONS (59 T)
GAUGE:	1067 MM
ROAD NUMBERS:	TGR) Y1–Y8
	(ATN) 2150 (EX Y1), 2151 (Y5) AND DV1 (Y7)

1962 BROKEN HILL PROPRIETARY CO

DH-class B-B

Walkers Limited, an engineering foundry based in the Queensland city of Maryborough, had its roots in Ballarat, Victoria. Trading then as the Phoenix Foundry, it built hundreds of steam locomotives of various types for Victorian Railways.

On shifting to Maryborough during the late nineteenth century, Walkers soon received contracts from Queensland Railways and the Federal Government-owned Commonwealth Railways to build steam locomotives, its huge 211-tonne 4-6-0 C-class of 1938 for the CR being perhaps the firm's finest creation.

With serious dieselisation of Australia's railways taking place from the early 1950s, other engineering firms were obtaining licences to build tried and proven overseas locomotive types, and for a time Walkers found it difficult to compete. The company persevered and began developing diesel-hydraulic locomotives (most railway systems in Australia had commissioned diesel-electrics) and in 1956 offered a 610 mm gauge unit to the Queensland sugar industry, unfortunately not a success. BHP, however, turned to Walkers for three 427 kW centre-cab diesel-hydraulic locomotives when seeking motive power for its new Whyalla steelworks. They were delivered during April and May of 1962.

These locomotives' initial role was in works construction service; after the steel rolling mills came on stream in 1964, all three locomotives found full employment. With steel-making facilities completed by mid-1965, two additional locomotives were acquired from Walkers in August–September of that year.

Designated DH-class (short for diesel-hydraulic), these standard gauge locomotives were phased into all shunting and heavy transfer work throughout the steel plant, operating in four distinct areas—slag haulage, ingot transfer, steel ladle traffic, and cargo shunting to the government railway's exchange sidings.

A sixth DH-class was acquired on 7 March 1968 exclusively to work the trains over the narrow gauge (1067 mm) link from Hummock Hill raw materials blending area to Nos 1 and 2 blast furnaces' trestle bins some 3 kilometres distant.

As built, all DH-class units were powered with twin Cummins 913 kW turbo-charged NRTO.6BI diesel engines driving Voith torque converters. From March 1976, the fleet was gradually rebuilt with

After receiving its Cummins Model 908 V8 engines and Niigata torque converters, DH4 displays the class's unusual angular lines while posing for this study at Whyalla works on 9 February 1978. (Leon Oberg)

newer Cummins Model 908 V8 engines and Niighata torque converters. In addition to this new power equipment, each locomotive's cab was equipped with improved facilities and operator vision.

The introduction of a continuous slab-caster at the Whyalla works in 1992 spelt the virtual end for the plant's 70 km internal standard gauge railway. By the following year, the system had fallen to just 20 km and DH-class withdrawals had started with DH2, which eventually went to scrap in February 1994. The numerically last three units were cut up between September 1997 and February 1998, and at that stage only one, DH1, remained available for actual service. It was retained as a little-used back-up on the blast furnace trestle bins' narrow gauge link.

Late in 1999, Australian Southern Railroad was contracted to handle all Whyalla-based rail operations (for the company now trading as One Steel) and purchased the active locomotive fleet outright. Thus DH1, the last trafficable class member, came under the ownership of the new authority from 1 December 1999, eventually going to scrap in Port Augusta late September 2004.

SPECIFICATIONS

ORIGINAL

	IMPERIAL (METRIC)
POWER UNIT:	CUMMINS NRTO.6BI
TRACTION HORSEPOWER:	573 (427 kW)
STARTING TRACTIVE EFFORT:	48 000 LB (213 kN)
CONTINUOUS TRACTIVE EFFORT:	46 000 LB (204 kN)
TOTAL WEIGHT:	70 TONS (71.4 T)
GAUGE:	1435 MM AND 1067 MM
ROAD NUMBERS:	DH1—DH6

B-class 0-6-0DH

Designed by Commonwealth Engineering (Queensland) Pty Ltd and fabricated and assembled at the company's Bassendean plant, the ten diesel-hydraulic locomotives of this class were acquired for 1067 mm gauge yard shunting duties.

The initial order was for five locomotives which entered traffic at Midland and West Perth yards between March and August 1962. Another five followed in 1965, but their upper cab profiles were altered to enable them to clear the cranes used on Fremantle wharves. All were operational by November 1965.

After rather uneventful lives, the entire class was officially written off on 28 September 1984. Despite wholesale scrappings throughout 1988, however, several units managed to survive.

Class-leader 1601 has been preserved at the Rail Transport Museum, Bassendean, and was seen in shunting service at the neighbouring United Goninan factory for a period during the 1990s.

Of the rest, 1603 is on display at the Subiaco Railway Markets; 1608's remains, after being retained for private presentation at Bellevue, were in 2006 noted sharing space with derelict transport items on a Middle Swan property. Locomotive 1610 is owned by the Boulder Loop Line Railway at Boulder.

SPECIFICATIONS

	IMPERIAL (METRIC)
POWER UNIT:	CUMMINS VT12BI
TRACTION HORSEPOWER:	473 (348 kW)
STARTING TRACTIVE EFFORT:	23 000 LB (102 kN)
CONTINUOUS TRACTIVE EFFORT:	18 000 LB (80 kN)
TOTAL WEIGHT:	38.6 TONS (39.1 T)
GAUGE:	1067 MM
ROAD NUMBERS:	B1601—1610

B-class locomotive 1609 shows its chunky styling as it rests with 1605 between assignments at Perth's Forrestfield depot in July 1980. (Peter Watts)

45-class Co-Co

This class of 40 heavy Co-Co 1343 kW locomotives was basically a cheaper, more utilitarian, hood version of the popular streamlined World Series Alco medium-power diesel-electric locomotives first delivered to SAR in 1955.

Known as Alco's Model DL-541, the units were ordered from A.E. Goodwin Ltd by the NSWGR during 1961 for general main line haulage and designated 45-class. It was reasoned that the hood design would improve maintenance turnaround time.

Class-leader 4501 underwent its initial load trials between Sydney and Broadmeadow on 6 June 1962. Further trials followed to Albury and over the Unanderra–Moss Vale line where the ruling grade is 1 in 30.

As additional units arrived, the class was phased into blue ribbon interstate express freight working between Sydney and Albury; by September some had been phased into *Southern Aurora* and *Spirit of Progress* express passenger service.

All were running by January 1964 and soon afterwards large numbers of the later deliveries were transferred to the Western Division where they successfully replaced main line steam traction. (Some were equipped with longer traction motor cables to enable them to work the steeply graded and abnormally curvy Oberon branch line.)

The 45-class was powered with a 12-cylinder Alco model 251C diesel engine, similar to that fitted to the NSWGR's streamlined 44-class of 1957. Dual driving stations were provided to enable the locomotives to operate in either direction from the single cab.

The first 45-class withdrawal occurred as early as May 1972, when 4525 was seriously damaged in an accident at Robertson. It was almost immediately written off, together with the unit it rammed, World type 44-class, 4462. Both locomotives were twisted hulks as a result of the collision.

The final 15 years of the 45-class's life were virtually all spent working in the Northern Region Broadmeadow depot. The units were favoured power for a time on heavy unit coal trains, and they worked in volume over the North Coast and northern inland routes. They continued to tread the main lines even after the crews' union imposed, from 28 June 1984, a non-metropolitan ban on their cab conditions, which were alleged to be noisy, and draughty in winter. Largely unfazed by the ban, the railway administration simply rostered the locomotives as non-driveable trailing units in multiple-engine lash-ups.

In a bid to appease the crews, six were eventually shopped for modifications, which included new door latches, soundproofing, improved windows, better heaters for winter and fans for summer. In addition, one set of driving controls was removed, making room for a fold-up table on which the second crew member could maintain train journals. The first unit treated, 4507, was released from Cardiff Workshops in October 1988, later becoming a 451-class member. However, the modified units soon became

Wearing the multicoloured livery of the NSW State Rail Authority, 4516 arrives at the Port Waratah coal loader complex on 13 May 1983. (Leon Oberg)

The former Australian Traction Corporation (Austrac) rebuilt 4537 with a low-profile nose in 1995, registered the attractive creation as 103 and leased it to BHP Port Kembla for almost a decade. It today belongs to Patrick Rail and was pictured at Goulburn on 30 November 2006, just days after receiving an overhaul including a 1491kW engine and the operating company's livery. (Leon Oberg)

the 35-class and the bulk of their work was spent in shunting at Yeerongpilly depot in Brisbane, and banking heavy trains over the 1 in 40 grades of the Liverpool Range.

Most saw service (although punctuated by seasonal fortunes) until new 82 and 90 class EMD locomotives were commissioned from July 1994. The last in actual traffic was 3505, used for National Rail Corporation shunting and trip train working until 11 September 1995. Most were sold to scrappers at State Rail's monster locomotive auction in December 1994, but some survived, including 4520, which has been fully restored to work heritage trains, and 4521, acquired by the Dorrigo Steam Railway and Museum. Loco 4514 was bought privately but in late 2004 was

on-sold to Patrick Rail for container haulage.

Commercially, 4537, also bought privately at the auction, was overhauled and equipped with an external muffler/exhaust system and low-profile nose for improved driver visibility by the former Junee-based private railway firm Australian Traction Corporation (Austrac). In June 1995 it was leased to BHP Steel Port Kembla, carrying the number 103. Austrac acquired two others, 4503 and 3505, for a rebuild programme (3505 still awaits reactivation).

Silverton Rail owns 3532, and has rebuilt it at Broken Hill as 45s1. This unit has been extensively used in ballast and Sydney transfer freight work. Chicago Freight Car Leasing Australia own 4502 and 4528.

The first of four 'tractive effort booster units', BU1, clearly displays its 600-class parentage while resting in Spencer Junction yard on 28 February 1995. (Leon Oberg)

Additionally, 4501 is operated by 3801 Ltd and 4520 by the NSWRTM as heritage units.

SAR 600-class

The SAR also turned to the Alco model DL-541 when requiring locomotives for its new standard gauge Broken Hill to Port Pirie line. Initially two were ordered for construction trains and entered service in April and August 1965 as the 600-class. Another five were acquired as the railway neared completion. After trains started running over the route in 1970, the 600s worked the brunt of the traffic, which included Broken Hill ore concentrate trains and *Indian Pacific* express passenger services.

With the Federal Government's takeover of SAR's country lines in July 1978, re-rostering of motive power over the locomotives' old stamping ground eventually saw four being made available for service in New South Wales from July 1982 to October 1985 as part of a through-working scheme involving Australian National, VR and the NSW State Rail Authority. While in New South Wales, the 600s were based at Goulburn depot, principally to work limestone trains over the Port Kembla–Marulan South line and ballast trains on the Illawarra line.

When AN extended its standard gauge to Adelaide in the late 1980s, the 600-class's route availability was further advanced. They also began appearing on Leigh Creek unit coal trains and general goods services to Port Augusta and Whyalla.

Over the years, the 600s were improved with the fitting of dynamic brake silencers and sunroofs. From 1988, at least five were fitted with 1491 kW engines. In a further bid to raise power from their engines it was planned to equip loco 605 with a Napier turbo-supercharger the following year, raising its traction power rating to 1640 kW (2200hp). High-level anecdotal evidence suggests the parts went missing in the transfer of these locomotives' maintenance responsibility to Dry Creek in 1989, and the upgrade did not take place.

Many were at the end of their economic usefulness by 1994, with 601 already withdrawn for certain scrap. Motive-power theorists then did some sums. Whyalla manufacturer Morrison Knudsen Australia was rebuilding AN's eight AL-class EMDs as the ALF-class, and the rebuilt locomotives were deemed to possess the theoretical horsepower, when running in pairs, to haul 160-car Leigh Creek coal trains but could not support this with adhesion. Morrison Knudsen thus was called upon to rebuild four 600-class units,

601, 604, 605 and 606, as engineless 'tractive effort booster units' to boost the ALFs' tractive effort by 15 per cent. The class-leader made its first revenue trip on 6 August 1994. In this form, a 30-tonne concrete block was placed in the 'engineroom' for ballast, electric dynamic brakes retained (but of an EMD variety) and the original six AEI traction motors were replaced with four EMD D77 type, effectively turning the 600s (now BU 1–4) into A1A-A1A units.

In traffic, one BU unit was coupled between two ALF-class locomotives. However, the scheme was short-lived for, following a litany of interface problems and the discovery that the units became dead weight above 80 km/h, all four were stored at Dry Creek motive power depot by February 1996.

With AN's sale and the eventual formation of the Australian Railroad Group on 8 November 1997, the BU units were returned to MKA's Whyalla plant for storage. However, ARG, faced with motive power shortages, decided to give the experiment another try, taking delivery of BU1 on 18 February 2000. Following several trials, it was put to work with ALF units on Tailem Bend wheat trains, the added tractive effort expected to offer a bonus in the slow, hilly and twisting Adelaide Hills which feature over the bulk of that route. But the idea was soon discarded and all units were noted by this author stored at Islington workshops in June 2009 under National Railway Equipment Corporation (NREC) ownership (a company which acquired the MKA business). However, they had just days left for scrapping started the following month despite revelations of a scheme to rebuild them as powered locomotives. The remaining three 600s continued working in their conventional form until sold in 2004 to South Spur Rail Services (becoming part of Coote Industrial in 2007 which was acquired by P&O Trans Australia in March 2010) where they see regular service working infrastructure trains.

SPECIFICATIONS
IMPERIAL (METRIC)

POWER UNIT:	Alco 251C (12 cylinders)
TRACTION HORSEPOWER:	1800 (1342 kW)
STARTING TRACTIVE EFFORT:	74 250 lb (330 kN)
CONTINUOUS TRACTIVE EFFORT:	68 000 lb (302 kN)
TOTAL WEIGHT:	111 tons (113 t)
GAUGE:	1435 mm
ROAD NUMBERS:	(NSW) 4501–4540 (ex 45-class 3505, 3507, 3513, 3518, 3527, 3532)
	(SAR/AN) 600–606 (600 renumbered 607), then BU1–BU4 (ex 601, 604, 605, 606)

C1703 and sister unit C1702 in Forrestfield depot yard (Perth) in February 1991. (Jeff Austin)

1962 WESTERN AUSTRALIAN GOVERNMENT RAILWAYS

C-class Co-Co

This small class of just three locomotives was a direct development (and customised version) of the successful Queensland Railways improved 1145 kW 1250-class of 1959.

The Western Australian units dispensed with the full-width streamlined nose-cab styling married to the standard hood body of their prototype. WAGR opted for a conventional American-style 'set-back' cab on the same hood body/chassis package. Weighing slightly more than the 1250-class, the C-class was fitted with heavier-duty traction motors and slightly larger 102 cm wheels.

All three entered service in August 1962 and were employed in 1067 mm passenger service. Despite the gradual introduction of more modern locomotives and the withdrawal of many passenger services over the years, all managed to remain active until March 1992 in a fairly diversified career which towards the end included work at Avon yard and Geraldton, then Forrestfield.

They were also used for a time on Perth suburban passenger services until these were electrified in January 1992.

The introduction of the GE-built P-class saw the curtain fall on the C-class. No. 1702 was the last to run, working an oil train from Forrestfield to Leighton and return on 20 March 1992. All three locomotives have survived, 1702 and 1703 for tour train working under the auspices of the Hotham Valley Railway. Class-leader 1701 was originally

acquired by that organisation for spare parts, but was spruced up (including a repaint in original WAGR green) late in 2003 for display purposes at Pinjarra.

SPECIFICATIONS

	IMPERIAL (METRIC)
POWER UNIT:	EE 12CSVT
TRACTION HORSEPOWER:	1535 (1145 kW)
STARTING TRACTIVE EFFORT:	54 000 lb (240 kN)
CONTINUOUS TRACTIVE EFFORT:	45 500 lb (203 kN)
TOTAL WEIGHT:	90 (92 T)
GAUGE:	1067 MM
ROAD NUMBERS:	C1701–1703

1962 QUEENSLAND RAILWAYS

1600-class Co-Co

As a means of dieselising the extremely light pioneer lines west of Alpha (on the Central Division) and Roma (on the South-Western Division), Queensland

Locos 1616 and 1613 at Redbank workshops on 22 July 1991. (Peter Watts)

Railways signed a contract with English Electric of Rocklea in January 1962 for 12 diesel-electric locomotives.

Weighing 62 tonnes and of Co-Co wheel arrangement, the first examples appeared eleven months later. Although found to be slightly overweight, necessitating modifications by the builder, subsequent success in their sphere of operation led to an additional six units being ordered in March 1963. The entire class of 18 had been delivered by January 1964.

Of end-cab configuration, the 1600-class came equipped with Delta-type bogies for improved riding over the poorly ballasted branch lines. All were powered with EE's 6-cylinder 625 kW diesel engine.

These locomotives paved the way for 34 improved Co-Co units of the 1620-class, which were acquired from EE between January 1967 and May 1969. These differed both in internal layout and visually, being fitted with a hood nose which contained the electrical equipment (see page 348).

The 1600s started falling by the wayside due to horrific accidents, the first to be written off being 1607, destroyed on 6 February 1981 in an accident in the Drummond Ranges. Ten months later, 1610 was completely burnt out following a fatal rollover at Hannams Gap. Overturning fuel tankers ruptured on top of the derailed unit and the locomotive was virtually melted away.

By January 1991, fourteen still remained operational but the writing was on the wall. The last reported 1600-class commercial working was by 1603, which hauled an empty livestock train from Fields siding to Rockhampton on 14 April 1991.

Today, five remain: 1603 is stored by QR at the Workshops Rail Museum, Ipswich, 1604 operates at the ARHS Rosewood Railway Museum; 1613 is preserved at Longreach Powerhouse Museum; 1614 is located at the Archer Park Museum in Rockhampton, while 1616 has been acquired by the QPSR Swanbank Railway near Ipswich for use over its 7.5 km tourist railway.

SPECIFICATIONS

	IMPERIAL (METRIC)
POWER UNIT:	ENGLISH ELECTRIC 6CSRKT
TRACTION HORSEPOWER:	838 (625 KW)
STARTING TRACTIVE EFFORT:	41 500 LB (184.5 KN)
CONTINUOUS TRACTIVE EFFORT:	30 000 LB (133 KN)
TOTAL WEIGHT:	61.7 TONS (62.5 T)
GAUGE:	1067 MM
ROAD NUMBERS:	1600–1617

1963 QUEENSLAND RAILWAYS
1700-class Co-Co

Dieselisation had played a major role in speeding up transport over Queensland's main lines since 1952. Nevertheless, as the 1960s dawned, no manufacturer really had the answer to reliably deliver this to the state's pioneer branch lines, none of which could bear the heavy weight of a modern diesel-electric.

Even the Clyde Engineering Co/EMD's 68-tonne Model G-8, a locomotive type designed to satisfy developing nations' railways, was deemed to be too heavy. A lighter product was needed and Clyde Engineering happened to have just the design—more by good luck than good planning, for in mid-1962 the builder had just reworked its popular G-8 after South Australian Railways had called tenders for its 500-class shunting units. (Clyde was prepared to open a factory at Elizabeth to build these and other locomotives.)

While the order did not eventuate, the design was available to satisfy Queensland Railway's needs and the first unit was delivered in June 1963. It became the ultra-light lines 1700-class.

A host of space and weight-saving initiatives were employed in the design. The G-8's nose was eliminated and an end-cab substituted. In a bid to further reduce the weight to 60 tonnes, narrower than normal (CD36) traction motors, specially designed by the builder for this application, were employed.

Teamed with the same 8-567C 652 kW diesel engine used in the G-8, this locomotive's generator package was encouraged to drive Co-Co bogies (in lieu of the G-8's Bo-Bo type) which resulted in an even greater power output. (This lightweight design helped Clyde win a subsequent contract to build 75 Y-class shunting locomotives for Victorian Railways.)

Locomotive 1701 was sporting a forward-mounted air-conditioner when pictured at Brisbane's Mayne depot on 14 March 1997. (Leon Oberg)

Constructed under contract to Clyde in Comeng's Salisbury plant in Queensland, twelve 1700s had been commissioned by November 1963 and put to work over branch lines west of Toowoomba. They were restricted to a maximum of 80 km/h, although capable of 112 km/h.

Regarded as being amazingly reliable locomotives, only accidents caused premature withdrawals, the first two affected being 1706 at Bindango while working the *Westlander* on 6 November 1987 and, more recently, 1705, which suffered a bowed chassis in a severe yard collision in Maryborough during November 1995.

Converted to driver-only status during the 1990s and displaced from the Toowoomba, Roma and Charleville districts by heavier locomotives, the 1700-class's last service was mainly restricted to shunting in the Brisbane area and yards northwards. No fewer than seven were disposed of as scrap in September and October 2002, a last-minute effort by a private buyer saving 1707 (minus bogies) at that time for preservation. No others remain.

The 1700-class design led to QR's introduction of a slightly heavier and more powerful 745 kW 1720-class look-alike version in 1966, which by May 1970 totalled 56 units (see page 345).

Both types of Emu Bay Railway Walkers-built diesel-hydraulic locomotives are represented in this image, which shows 1002 sandwiched between the later 11-class units 1102 and 1106 working a freight at Ridgley in April 1982. (Peter Watts)

steam working over its 128 km West Coast 1067 mm gauge railway.

In addition to the locomotives, Walkers supplied a host of spare parts, some going into the construction of a fourth unit within the Tasmanian Government Railways' Launceston Workshops in 1966.

QR DH-class

Seeing obvious potential in the design, Walkers Ltd continued to develop the product and in November 1966 offered Queensland Railways the use of one demonstration 347 kW hood locomotive for yard shunting service. Tested initially in Maryborough, and afterwards in Brisbane, the locomotive was eventually purchased by QR in February 1968. Contracts were prepared for more and by 1974 no fewer than 73 of this type were in service in most of Queensland's shunting yards.

Known as the DH-class, these B-B locomotives were powered with Caterpillar diesel engines and featured a crawl-speed shunting control which permitted extremely fine control of the locomotive's power output during shunting movements. Some units were even used for freight services over the lightest of QR's 1067 mm gauge lines, including the Etheridge railway to Forsayth.

The combination of heavier unit trains and widespread yard rationalisation by rail systems saw

SPECIFICATIONS

	IMPERIAL (METRIC)
POWER UNIT:	EMD 8-567CR
TRACTION HORSEPOWER:	875 (653 kW)
STARTING TRACTIVE EFFORT:	40 000 LB (178 kN)
CONTINUOUS TRACTIVE EFFORT:	33 600 LB (150 kN)
TOTAL WEIGHT:	59 TONS (60 T)
GAUGE:	1067 MM
ROAD NUMBERS:	1700–1711

1963 EMU BAY RAILWAY

Diesel-hydraulic B-B

By the early 1960s, Walkers Ltd of Maryborough was gaining a foothold in the Australian diesel locomotive market. Following Walkers' success with sales to BHP, Tasmania's Emu Bay Railway placed an order for three 522 kW hood-type, Paxman-powered diesel-hydraulic units for heavy ore haulage.

Arriving in August 1963, these three 10-class locomotives made real inroads into the company's

The locomotive type that started a trend: QR's DH10 at Mayne depot on 29 July 1973. Some 73 were acquired by the rail authority over a 6-year period. (Peter Watts)

saw virtually all of these locomotives withdrawn from service around 1990–91. Loco DH7 was acquired by Mt Isa Mines in February 1991, carrying the re-number 5804, where it joined a low-nose, largely pressurised 373 kW Caterpillar unit that had been built new for the company on 23 March 1972 for yard shunting.

Locomotives DH55 and DH32 were sold to the Relk Corporation of Malaysia, and re-gauged to 1000 mm in QR's shops prior to delivery in August 1991 and February 1993 respectively.

Another four, DH4, DH5, DH56 and DH24 were delivered to Cooks Construction of Dandenong, Victoria, in June 1993 after that company received an SEC contract to haul brown coal between Yallourn and Morwell. Renumbered CC01–CC04 respectively, they were regauged to 900 mm. (Another two non-operable units, DH24 and DH36, followed in 1995.) Following the takeover of brown coal train haulage by the National Logistics Coordinators Group several years later, all six were eventually returned to Queensland, with CC04 rebuilt as Isis 6 for Isis Mill and CC03 rebuilt in 2004 as Tully No. 8. CC01 and CC02, still gauged at 900 mm, are owned by Mackay Sugar and remain stored at North Eton Mill. The two inoperable units (DH24 and DH36) are at Tully Mill, where reports suggest one good unit is to be created from their remains.

Locos DH5, DH59 (and DH23 for parts) operate at Victoria's 962 mm gauge Puffing Billy Railway, where DH59 confusingly carries number DH31.

These sales were small by comparison to the 32 units which have been sold to Queensland sugar mills, where already 28 have been upgraded and re-gauged to 610 mm. Loco DH67 has been converted by Isis Mill to a brake vehicle, but in such a way that it can be rebuilt as a locomotive should the need arise.

In addition, 13 DH-class locomotives were delivered to Vietnam Railways during 1993–95, and

The NSWGR's 7332 poses between shunting assignments in Port Waratah yard on 16 March 1974. (Leon Oberg)

examples were noted running that country's *Victoria Express* between Hanoi and Lao Chi in late 2004.

Other DH-class units have been leased to businesses and sold to enthusiast bodies for preservation or tourist train service, including DH2 at the Workshops Rail Museum, Ipswich; DH38, owned by the Queensland Division of the ARHS for use at the Rosewood Railway Museum, and DH14 at the Ghan Preservation Society's tourist railway at MacDonnell in the Northern Territory.

Despite these wholesale disposals, QR retained DH71–73, three units fitted with automatic couplers, for shunting or emergency train haulage during floods, DH71 intended a source of spare parts. Two more, DH37 and DH45 were leased to freight-forwarders QRX for shunting at Cairns in 1994, returning to QR in 2001 for infrastructure use. Both have been absorbed into the track machine roster and re-numbered MMY37 and MMY45 respectively. No others remain in QR service.

NSW 73-class

The NSWGR was also in need of shunting locomotives in the 1960s and until this diesel-hydraulic B-B came along, nothing viable seemed to be to hand. It ordered an initial 20, calling them the 73-class. These differed from the Queensland units in that they were powered with a Caterpillar 485 kW diesel engine and boasted low-profile noses to provide better visibility.

The first unit appeared in October 1970 and the eventual delivery of the whole 20 led to the elimination of all steam shunting over the entire North Coast strip, the Sydney metropolitan area and Goulburn yard. Their impact was profound and an additional 30 were acquired. When the last one was delivered in March 1973, all remaining steam yard-shunting operations throughout the state ceased.

The first NSW unit withdrawn, but not until February 1987, was 7330. After that, others quickly followed, and the only one in government ownership today is the class-leader, 7301, which was retained as the CountryLink XPT Meeks Road depot shunter. While 7322 and 7334 were utilised until 1998 as shunters at Lithgow, they (and 7333) were sold to Colin Rees Transport for shunting in Sydney and Melbourne. All three passed into the ownership of QR National in 2005.

Another two, 7307 and 7321, are working commercially in Sydney for Patrick PortLink, the Manildra Group has 7315, 7319 and 7340 while 22 units have been acquired by Queensland sugar

Top: Starting life as the NSWGR's standard gauge 7314, Proserpine Sugar Mill's No. 12 shows the result of its radical sugar industry rebuild while working a 610 mm gauge cane train at Glen Isla on Saturday 21 September 2002. (Chris Walters)

Middle: Wearing its third hat, Isis Sugar Mill's No. 6 rests at the mill between shifts on 8 September 2001. This loco was formerly CC04 on the Cooks Constructions roster and originally QR's DH28. (Brad Peadon)

Bottom: Cook's Constructions units CC03 and CC02 (formerly QR DH56 and DH5 respectively) at Yallourn on 27 June 1993. (Darren Hodges)

interests for conversion to 610 mm gauge canefields use. To date, thirteen have been rebuilt for this purpose by Walkers Ltd, Bundaberg Foundry Engineers Ltd, Tulk Goninan Ltd (Mackay), and Pleystowe and Pioneer sugar mills.

The Wimmera Container Line became a first-time locomotive owner in August 2008 when it acquired 7334 from QRN. The unit was bought to shunt wagons at the company's work yard outside Horsham, in western Victoria.

From the preservation perspective, 7320 and 7324 reside in Canberra; the Dorrigo Steam Railway and Museum has 7329 and a former (discarded) Manildra unit 7335; 7344 belongs to 3801 Ltd while the Hunter Valley Railway Trust at Branxton owns 7350.

Emu Bay Railway 11-class

Following the resounding success of its four 10-class B-B locomotives, the Emu Bay Railway acquired an additional seven B-B units in two contracts to cater for new traffic, taking delivery of the first five in January 1970 and the balance during mid-1971. These locomotives were built to the improved NSWGR low-profile nose configuration and became Emu Bay's 11-class. The 11-class was powered with Caterpillar's V12 D398B 530kW turbocharged engines rather than the 10-class's turboharged Paxman 12YHXL prime movers which were set for 395 kW. The 11-class weighed in at 55.8 tonnes, four tonnes heavier than its predecessor, was almost one metre longer and equipped for multiple-unit operation.

While the 10-class's original pneumatic control gear was replaced during 1969-1970 with electro-pneumatic equipment which facilitated multiple unit working within both classes, all were re-engined between 1980-1992 with the D398B Caterpillar power plants.

In 1996, the then Pasminco-owned Emu Bay Railway was hauling 650 000 tonnes per annum, requiring two trains each weekday to Hellyer mine, one to Rosebery and another to Melba. This latter service had been introduced to serve a newly-won contract with Copper Mines of Tasmania (which replaced the Mt Lyell Mining & Railway Co as the operator of the Queenstown copper mine in 1995).

Ownership of the Emu Bay Railway passed to Australian Transport Network on 22 May 1998 with little initial effect on daily operations. But the closure of the Hellyer mine in June 2000 substantially cut traffic levels and all four 10-class were set aside. (Loco 1002 was reactivated in April 2001, operating

'as required' until the end of that year.)

The remaining concentrate trains were converted to air-brake operation, resulting in the withdrawal of the vacuumed-braked 11-class on 23 March, 2002. Their place was taken by 91.5-tonne rebuilt 2140-class (ex-QR 1300-class) Co-Co diesel-electrics.

It is of interest to note that the furthest-travelled 10-class, 1003, had accumulated about 1 million kilometres in a little over 30 years while all 11-class units had covered around 2 million.

Further life fortunately awaited the 10-class. In April 2001, loco 1001 was sold to the Victorian-based Walhalla Goldfields Railway for 962 mm gauge tourist train service, 1002 went to the Don River Railway Society (Tasmania), and 1003 and 1004 were acquired that month by the Zig Zag Railway at Lithgow in New South Wales.

The 1100-class was offered for sale in March 2002. Loco 1101 found an active new home with the Cairns-based Kuranda Steam Trains Group in March 2003 (along with temporary lease work with Pacific National Queensland). It has since been joined by 1105.

Western Australian purchases

The Walkers diesel-hydraulic product had become extremely popular and in 1971 the WAGR ordered two 484 kW Cummins-powered low-nose M-class locomotives for narrow gauge shunting service in Forrestfield hump yard. Arriving in January 1972 and weighing 53 tonnes, these units were followed in April 1973 by three similar-styled but lighter 44.7-tonne Caterpillar-powered locomotives which because of the power change became the MA-class.

With the closure of the hump yard in the 1980s, the M-class moved into general yard shunting until overhauls were needed. Two Ms and an MA were written off in January 1994 and stored, which left MA1862 working at the Claisebrook electric carriage sheds. CSR bought the four stored units in mid-1994 by for conversion into sugarcane locomotives.

SPECIFICATIONS

Operator & road numbers	Power unit	Output: imperial (metric)	Weight: imperial (metric)
QR DH-class DH1–73	Caterpillar	465 hp (347 kW)	40 tons (40.6 t)
NSWGR 73-class 7301–7350	Caterpillar	650 hp (485 kW)	49 tons (51 t)
Emu Bay 10-class 1001–1004	Paxman	670 hp (522 kW)	49 tons (51 t)
Emu Bay 11-class 1101–1107	Caterpillar	670 hp (522 kW)	54 tons (55.8 t)
WAGR M-class 1851, 1852	Cummins	650 hp (485 kW)	52 tons (53.8 t)
WAGR MA-class 1861–1863	Caterpillar	650 hp (485 kW)	43 tons (44.5 t)
Mt Isa Mines 303 (later 5803)	Caterpillar	500 hp (373 kW)	48 tons (49 t)
Cooks Constructions CC01–CC04	Caterpillar	464 hp (347 kW)	40 tons (40.6 t)
Gauge		All ran originally on 1067 mm except for the 73-class which was 1435 mm	

Y-class Bo-Bo

When calling tenders for light shunting power early in 1962, Victorian Railways specified diesel-powered locomotives in the 448–485 kW range, with either electric or hydraulic transmission. Manufacturers were also invited to tender for fixed-frame 0-6-0 or bogie designs; should the latter design be adopted, the VR would supply the bogies and traction motors.

The Clyde Engineering Co's tender for a 448 kW GM model G-6B was selected. It was an end-cab hood design under which went the refurbished Bo-Bo powered bogies salvaged from redundant VR electric passenger suburban carriages, some of them dating back to 1927.

The contract, signed in December 1962, called for 25 locomotives, which were delivered from September 1963 as the Y-class. The design bore a basic resemblance to Queensland Railways' 1963-commissioned 1700-class Co-Co units.

Although the Y-class was nominally acquired as shunting power, VR had a novel habit of using whatever locomotives it had on hand for any given service and soon the class was working commuter traffic, including trains between Spencer Street and Werribee, in addition to main line freight trains.

Before long the Y-class had multiplied to 50 units, replacing remaining steam power in country shunting yards. However, the later locomotives were equipped with stronger EMD traction-motor windings to overcome the burn-out problem seen in earlier deliveries. As a means of protecting the 105 kW traction motors, output from the main generator was also reduced, from 960V to 810V.

The Y-class's prowess in working over the lightly laid, far-flung branch lines to more efficient schedules led to yet further acquisitions when, between December 1967 and August 1968, an additional 25 were commissioned. This final batch differed slightly in that they were equipped with EMD's up-rated 559 kW 645E diesel engine instead of the original 567C type.

These 75 locomotives were to be found scattered throughout Victoria and two even appeared on the standard gauge Melbourne to Albury line. While they were principally used as shunting power, they also worked ballast trains and, on several occasions during extreme locomotive shortages, were photographed by this author operating in multiple with main line units on interstate goods trains.

Initially, most were restricted to 64 km/h but after roller bearings replaced brass bearings within the traction motor armatures their speed was increased to 72.4 km/h. The exception was the last unit delivered, Y175, which was specially built to run at 100 km/h to work Commissioner's trains.

Most Y-class in Victoria had been withdrawn by the mid-1990s, and only 14 units (some non-operational) changed hands with the acquisition of V/Line Freight by the US-led Freight Australia in April 1999. They were Y115, Y118, Y119, Y122, Y124, Y142, Y147, Y151, Y152, Y157, Y165, Y169, Y171 and Y174. Four others, Y129, Y156, Y161 and

VR's Y139, an original 567C-engined type, as seen running in September 1972. (John M. Wilson)

Y163, were sold to the short-lived National Express Group PLC in July 1999, upon the privatisation of Victorian passenger interests, for car shunting at Melbourne and Geelong. These have been returned to the government, which had earlier held another eight back from sale.

Freight Australia's units came under the ownership of Pacific National with FA's sale to that business on 1 September 2004. By then, others not subject to the earlier FA sale had been disposed of: Y127 on lease by 707 Operations to Victorian Goldfields Railway, Maldon; Y133 to the Seymour Loco Steam Preservation Group; Y134 and Y136 are with EDI Cardiff (NSW) and Newport respectively; Y135 is at South Gippsland Tourist Railway, Korumburra; Y137 at the ARHS North Williamstown Museum; Y148 at BlueScope Steel, Long Island; Y159 with the Central Highlands Tourist Railway, Daylesford; Y164 at Steamrail, Newport, and Y168 (and derelict Y109) with Victorian operator, El Zorro Transport.

Footnote: The WAGR also adopted the basic design when it sought shunting power in 1965 (see page 342).

SPECIFICATIONS

	IMPERIAL (METRIC)
POWER UNIT:	EMD 567C/645E
TRACTION HORSEPOWER:	600/650 (447/485 kW)
STARTING TRACTIVE EFFORT:	35 850 lb (159 kN)
CONTINUOUS TRACTIVE EFFORT:	12 000 lb (53 kN)
TOTAL WEIGHT:	64–66.2 TONS (65.6–68 T)
GAUGE:	1435 mm AND 1600 mm
ROAD NUMBERS:	Y101–175

1964 QUEENSLAND RAILWAYS
1270-class Co-Co

Until 1964, English Electric locomotives in use throughout Australian were based upon the British parent company's designs. With Queensland Railways signalling its intentions to buy high-power diesel-electrics to modernise its coal haulage in central Queensland, leading EE British engineer, Stan Lyons (who designed British Rail's famous twin-engined 'Deltic') seized the opportunity to design a locomotive that would more aggressively take on the big US builders.

Locomotive 1271 rubs shoulders with EMD 1508 at Rockhampton depot arrival road on 28 July 1973. (Peter Watts)

Lyons had come to realise that Australian EE equipment was operating at lower power ratings, reliability and load factors than equivalent locomotives in his homeland. Observing the inroads US builders had made into the Australian marketplace, Lyons came up with a main line design that mirrored the North American road-switcher's hood design using British power equipment.

Unveiled as QR's 1270-class, the design (and its eventual derivatives) went like wildfire. Thirty 1270s were acquired in two contracts, starting in October 1964, initially for Moura to Gladstone coal service. The first 12 were powered by the same engines, generators and traction motors as QR's (1959) 1250-class. Improved EE548 traction motors (with slightly lower gear ratio) became available from locomotive 1282 onwards, increasing the maximum tractive effort by 6400 lb (28.4 kW), and the final six were equipped with 1100 kW dynamic brakes. All had been delivered by August 1966. From time to time, some 1270s also gravitated into mainline freight and Brisbane suburban passenger service.

With continuing coal mine development at Blackwater and South Blackwater (east of Emerald) under way, these locomotives paved the way for QR's later (1967) 45 similarly styled 1300-class coal units. These employed higher-power 1339 kW engines in addition to the EE548 traction motors, and other refinements.

Increasing unreliability of the English Electric classes in coal traffic resulted in their replacement with Clyde EMD diesel power during the 1980s. By the time of the coalfields electrification in 1986–87, all 1270s were being used in general traffic. The cascading effect of this significant event led to the class's final downfall, and despite indications that Brazilian interests were looking at the class (and the 1460s), all 1270s had been set aside at Redbank Workshops by late January 1989.

Workshops Rail Museum at Ipswich, the latter on display. All others were cut up by contractors at Redbank Workshops by the end of January 1992.

SPECIFICATIONS

	IMPERIAL (METRIC)
POWER UNIT:	ENGLISH ELECTRIC 12SVT
TRACTION HORSEPOWER:	1535 (1144 kW)
STARTING TRACTIVE EFFORT:	41 500 LB (185 kN)
CONTINUOUS TRACTIVE EFFORT:	40 200 LB (179 kN)
TOTAL WEIGHT:	90 TONS (91.4 T)
GAUGE:	1067 MM
ROAD NUMBERS:	1270–1299

1964 QUEENSLAND RAILWAYS

1460/1502-class Co-Co

Since the introduction of the 91.4-tonne 1450-class EMD locomotives during 1957–58, several changes had taken place on the Queensland Railways. They included the provision of heavier drawgear in goods vehicles and a bridge replacement programme that better suited heavier, more powerful diesel locomotives.

Accordingly, QR signed a contract with the Clyde Engineering Co in 1963, for 12 improved 1450-class Co-Co locomotives. By then, Clyde had refined the chunky American G-12 model's body styling and was able to offer a rounded 'Australianised' version complete with dual controls, updated generators and control equipment.

Introduced in April 1964, these locomotives became QR's 1460-class and by August 1966 a total of 42 (numbered 1460–1501) had been delivered, all from the Salisbury (Brisbane) plant of contractor Comeng. Six were equipped with dynamic brakes, the first use of this technology on the QR. The second unit of the order, 1461, was painted gold by QR to mark the railway's centenary in 1965.

Firm favourites with their crews, 1460-class locomotives were soon seen working the entire coastal main line strip, handling everything from slow freight to express passenger traffic. They were also to be seen in Brisbane metropolitan passenger and freight traffic.

The maker continued to refine the model and in 1967, when EMD's improved 645E engine became available, obtained further orders from QR. Twenty-nine locomotives (numbered 1502–1530) were equipped with this engine and became known as the 1502-class. All had been delivered by August 1969.

Over the years, several of these locomotives were severely damaged in accidents. Most were repaired, except for 1492, which was set aside in February 1982 following a serious level crossing accident at Bohle (Townsville). Following electrification of the coastal line later that decade, other 1460s started to fall by the wayside and in September 1990, Nos 1484 and 1494 were sold to South African Steel for use at Pretoria. Those units were renumbered and named 666-50 *Tienie* and 666-51 *Dennis* respectively, painted green, fitted with vacuum brakes, driving controls more suited to the new company and low-profile front hoods for improved driver visibility. Their buffer beams were strengthened to haul heavy coal trains.

By mid-1991, most of the 1460s had been stored at QR's Redbank Workshops, and although South African interest in the units continued, no further disposals were made until the US company, Wisconsin Central (which formed Tranz Rail after having recently acquired the New Zealand Railways), bought seven 1460s (1467, 1468, 1472, 1473, 1481, 1485 and dynamic-braked 1499) and 1521 in September 1995. The purchases were negotiated to help Tranz Rail cope with its dramatic

One of six 1460s equipped with dynamic brakes (note cooling grid on the nose) for working on Hughenden line phosphate rock haulage. Loco 1500, pictured in QR service on 14 July 1991, was delivered to Tranz Rail (New Zealand) on 27 May 1997. It was subsequently disposed of to a US-based manufacturing firm for rebuilding on behalf of an African customer. (Leon Oberg)

Twenty-five surplus 1460/1502-class locomotives were sold to Tranz Rail (New Zealand) between 1995 and 1997. Nineteen of them entered service there. Twelve of those, plus a further four that did not run in that country, were subsequently forwarded to the company's Tasmanian operation. One of the latter, 2010 (ex QR 1466), was pictured at Devonport on 30 October 2006, rigged for driverless radio-control shunting. Sent soon afterwards to Melbourne for rebuild, the stripped unit has been stored 'pending instructions'. (Leon Oberg)

10.7 per cent increase in freight volume in the year to 30 June 1995. Tranz Rail returned in April 1997 for another seventeen 1460/1502 locomotives which were shipped over the following few months.

Although a small number of these locomotives were provided with low-profile noses to allow for driver only operation in New Zealand where they became the DQ-class, problems soon arose with alleged excessive in-cab noise and rough riding.

With Wisconsin Central's acquisition of Tasrail (forming the Australian Transport Network) on 14 November 1997, a decision was made to replace that system's English Electric motive power with EMD units. Twelve of the modified DQ-class locomotives were shipped from New Zealand to Tasmania. The first to arrive were 2001 and 2002 (ex-QR 1521 and 1522 respectively) on 2 September 1998. The last four to arrive in Tasmania (2009–2012) had never actually run as DQs, being especially prepared for the Tasmanian task.

The first batches delivered to Tasmania were found to exceed the legal (state) workplace noise limit of 85 decibels, and extensive soundproofing work was undertaken to bring them below the legal maximum.

Three non-modified QR-class locomotives were also sent to Tasmania to work as slave units. Plans to send more DQ locomotives to Tasmania were dropped after the first 12 deliveries. As well as noise and rough riding issues, the imports were plagued by generator failures.

This left ten of the original purchase of 25 in New Zealand, consisting of four DQs, three QRs and the three untouched dynamic brake-equipped units. The latter three were planned to be converted into DQT-

class turbo-charged rebuilds, a scheme which never eventuated.

In 2004, QR 2079 and QR 2085, together with four similarly-powered ex-Westrail A-class and the remains of 1500 and 1501, were purchased by international lease and loco remanufacturing firm, NREC, for rebuilding. In November 2005 they were all shipped to the USA for remanufacture and delivery to an eventual African customer. The remains of 1499 were cut up in August 2005.

Following the shipping of the second order to Tranz Rail, only one 1460-class remained in Queensland, the gold-liveried 1461, which had been at Mayne depot in Brisbane for stationary training purposes until earmarked for preservation. At the time, twenty-five 1502-class members were continued and provided useful service for a further two and a half years. On 9 December 1999 they were withdrawn and stored operational at Redbank Workshops, having been made surplus by the cascading effect following the arrival of new 2260 kW Clyde-Walkers AC4000-class units.

However, life in a new form was emerging for some when they were selected for employment on QR's standard gauge arm, Interail, which was officially launched in Casino in May 2002. The converted locomotives became the 423-class and six had been so modified by 31 March 2005, principally in Hunter Valley coal traffic (see page 431).

With 1526 soldiering on as a shunter at Redbank locomotive workshops, seven of its sister units (1506, 1512, 1517, 1519, 1523, 1525 and 1530) were shipped out to Chile in the winter of 2005 for service on Ferrocarril Antofagasta a Bolivia's 911 km railway

1512, 1517, 1519, 1523, 1525 and 1530) were shipped out to Chile in the winter of 2005 for service on Ferrocarril Antofagasta a Bolivia's 911 km railway from the Pacific port of Antofagasta to Socompa on the Argentine border. The remaining 12 were still stored at Redbank workshops as at March 2006.

SPECIFICATIONS

	1460-CLASS	1502-CLASS
	IMPERIAL (METRIC)	IMPERIAL (METRIC)
POWER UNIT:	EMD 12-567C	EMD 12-645E
TRACTION HORSEPOWER:	1310 (977 KW)	1500 (1119 KW)
STARTING TRACTIVE EFFORT:	54 432 LB (242 KN)	60 000 LB (267 KN)
CONTINUOUS TRACTIVE EFFORT:	42 000 LB (187 KN)	50 820 LB (226 KN)
TOTAL WEIGHT:	90 TONS (91.5 T)	90 TONS (91.5 T)
GAUGE:	1067 MM	1067 MM
ROAD NUMBERS:	1460–1501	1502–1530

1964 SOUTH AUSTRALIAN RAILWAYS

500-class Bo-Bo

With the economic lives of most of South Australian Railways' remaining steam shunting locomotives drawing to an end, the administration decided in the early 1960s to build its own in-house diesel-electric replacements.

Having obtained excellent work from its class of ten 800-class English Electric-built Bo-Bo units, which arrived from May 1956 for heavy shunting and yard transfer work, it seemed natural to turn to this equipment for the new locomotives.

The SAR was no newcomer to diesel-electric locomotive manufacturing, having built ten main line 900-class A1A-A1A machines during 1951–53 and two 350-class Bo-Bo shunters in 1949, all of which were powered with EE equipment shipped out from England. SAR sourced the parts required for its new locomotives from EE's Rocklea plant and initially built 15 at its Islington Workshops, unveiled as the 500-class, when class-leader 500 ran its initial trial to Penfield on Anzac Day 1964.

The design perpetuated the 800-class's reliance on an end-cab and, although of modest power output (being equipped with EE's 4-cylinder 410 kW gross diesel engine), the locomotive type was a resounding success. So much so, a total of 34 were built, the last one, 533, being commissioned on 1 July 1969.

The 500-class was loosely a scaled-down customised 800-class and weighed 57 tonnes. It was capable of 64 km/h in traffic.

Soon after entering service, the class-leader was transferred to the Broken Hill to Port Pirie standard gauge railway then under construction for use on construction trains, and remained in that job for 19 months. As gauge standardisation neared completion, the final seven units of the class were built for use on that gauge and were subsequently commissioned in Peterborough and Port Pirie for yard working. In addition to their extensive use in the Adelaide metropolitan area, the broad gauge locomotives were issued to Naracoorte, Tailem Bend, Murray Bridge, Gladstone, Peterborough, Wallaroo and Port Pirie yards. Some were even phased into the haulage of Islington Workshops workers' trains.

When the Federal Government acquired all of SAR's non-metropolitan operations in 1978, the 500-class came as part of the package. After a time, the new owners (Australian National Railways) transferred some to Port Augusta standard gauge yard for shunting, replacing GM-class main liners. Upon the completion of Adelaide gauge standardisation in 1983, some 500-class units were re-gauged for Islington and Dry Creek yard use. Although not equipped with multiple-unit control when built, two were provided with this facility under AN ownership for work out of Dry Creek North yard.

The first withdrawn was 513 after suffering a severe engine failure in traffic in 1987. It was scrapped in August 1988. At least seven more were scrapped the following year. Commercially, 533 was sold to Morrison Knudsen (Australia) for shunting service at its Whyalla manufacturing plant.

Several operational units survived to be acquired by Australian Southern Railroad from 8 November 1997, and in March 1999 examples could be found shunting at Port Augusta and at ASR's Dry Creek motive power centre. Two more, 508 and 527, had one last moment of fame when they were forwarded to Katherine and Tennant Creek in February 2002 for Alice Springs to Darwin railway concrete sleeper

Locomotive 506 rolls through Mile End yard on 1 February 1980. (Leon Oberg)

plant shunting service. On 1 June 2006, unit 527 came under the ownership of QRN-West and was shunting Western Australia's Forrestfield Workshops in January 2007, while three sisters, 508, 517 and 532, are today with Genesee & Wyoming Australia following the sale of ARG.

Meanwhile, 507 is used by SteamRanger Tours for shunting service while 515 is exhibited at the National Railway Museum, Port Adelaide.

SPECIFICATIONS

	IMPERIAL (METRIC)
POWER UNIT:	ENGLISH ELECTRIC 4SRKT
TRACTION HORSEPOWER:	500 (373 KW)
STARTING TRACTIVE EFFORT:	31 320 LB (139 KN)
CONTINUOUS TRACTIVE EFFORT:	30 000 LB (133 KN)
TOTAL WEIGHT:	56 TONS (57 T)
GAUGE:	1435 MM AND 1600 MM
ROAD NUMBERS:	500–533 (500 LATER BECAME 534)

1965 WESTERN AUSTRALIAN GOVERNMENT RAILWAYS

H-class Bo-Bo

When the decision was made in the early 1960s to provide a standard gauge railway across Australia, the project meant the conversion of two existing state-owned narrow gauge railways. One of those was the Perth to Kalgoorlie section of the WAGR, a distance of 657 kilometres.

To assist with the rail link's construction, the WAGR ordered five 641 kW hood-type Bo-Bo locomotives in 1963 from English Electric's Rocklea plant in Queensland. Freighted by sea to Fremantle the following year, each locomotive was hauled dead on narrow gauge transfer bogies to the standard gauge materials depot at Upper Swan. From here they were eventually pressed into standard gauge construction service under the railway building contractor's control.

Although officially delivered to WAGR in September 1964, the first unit actually in service was No. 3 in January 1965. All became the WAGR's H-class. A construction feature of these rather front-heavy looking ('Brahman bull') locomotives was the provision of engine-room pressure ventilation.

On completion of the standardisation project, the H-class was pressed into local freight transfer service,

Ex-WAGR locomotives H3 and H2 at Specialialized Container Transport's Islington (Adelaide) complex on 5 December 2001. (Leon Oberg)

rail maintenance and ballast train service as required. Despite their seemingly lowly service status, the class was geared for 105 km/h and powered by EE's 6-cylinder CSRKT-model diesel engine.

Although H4 was scrapped in October 1992, the remaining four continued to shunt Forrestfield yard until their withdrawals early in 1996. Life for some continued in 1997 when freight-forwarding firm Specialialized Container Transport acquired H1, H2, H3 and H5 for terminal shunting, and they were reactivated for service in Kewdale (Western Australia), Islington (South Australia) and North Dynon (Victoria).

The Mt Goldsworthy Mining Co in Western Australia's Pilbara acquired two similar locomotives, initially pressing them into standard gauge rail construction service. It took delivery of both on 1 December 1965. After the company's heavy iron ore railway finally came into service, linking Goldsworthy mine with the export port at Finucane Island, the two locomotives (which became the company's B-class) were pressed into shunting service. They were also rostered to work supply trains.

In 1968, a serious accident involving GML1 and a larger main line unit practically destroyed the former. As a replacement, EE supplied a complete body and frame, less diesel engine and bogies, in December 1970 (maker's number 232). This and salvaged parts from the damaged unit formed a new GML1 locomotive.

The haulage capacity of the Goldsworthy engines differed from those of the WAGR due to their gear ratio, which was 55:16 while that of WAGR was 75:17.

Although AI&S steelworks at Port Kembla considered acquiring both Goldsworthy units during the mid-1980s for spare parts, the two units continued to serve their mining masters well after the absorption of the railway into what became BHP Iron Ore from 1 March 1991. Under the new ownership the locomotives were renumbered GML21 and GML22 and in 1993 helped construct a 28 km extension from Shay Gap to Yarri.

GML22 was eventually stopped on 31 October 1993, GML21 fifteen days later. Both were preserved in February 1995, carrying their original numbers, GML1 in operational condition at the Pilbara Railway Museum and GML2, whose traction motors were sold to BHP Steel, Port Kembla in 1995, statically in Port Hedland.

SPECIFICATIONS

WAGR H-class Goldsworthy units

	Imperial (Metric)	Imperial (Metric)
Power Unit:	EE 6CSRKT	EE 6CSRKT
Traction horsepower:	860 (641 kW)	860 (641 kW)
Starting tractive effort:	53 700 lb (239 kN)	40 300 lb (179 kN)
Continuous tractive effort:	37 700 lb (168 kN)	29 200 lb (130 kN)
Total weight:	72 tons (73 t)	72 tons (73 t)
Gauge:	1435 mm	1435 mm
Road numbers:	H1–H5	GML1 and 2

1965 Hamersley Iron Pty Ltd

Alco C628 Co-Co

The Pilbara region of Western Australia, a vast area covering some 435 000 square kilometres, is one of the world's richest places for minerals. Just four decades ago it was renowned only for its inhospitable coastal fringe, its rocky escarpments, deep gorges, arid spinifex and endless kilometres of desert shimmering away eastwards towards the Northern Territory border. The area was swept by strong winds and experienced temperatures up to 52°C. Consequently, there were no major industries except a few small mining concerns, a few thousand cattle and around half a million sheep.

From 1 July 1938 an export ban had been in place on Australian iron ore so that the country's only known, small reserves could be conserved for domestic use. In 1960, the Commonwealth Government, acting on advice from the Department of National Development, eased the embargo as an incentive to exploration and the Pilbara region, which was already known to possess some iron, became the target for intensive exploration.

It was not long before thousands of millions of tonnes of high-grade iron ore were discovered, drawing giant financial groups into the area. Japan, which was experiencing rapid expansion, became the biggest buyer.

In a flurry of activity, four mining companies quickly established major operations, all building substantial railways to transport their minerals overland for export. Three were constructed to heavy-duty American standards, with rails weighing up to 62 kg/m, then the heaviest in Australia.

The giant Hamersley Iron mining company had purchased two Bo-Bo locomotives second-hand from the USA in 1965 to work construction trains, and now ordered three Alco model C628-series Co-Co units for heavy mineral haulage through Alco's Australian licensee, A.E. Goodwin Ltd. Hamersley's urgent need saw the locomotives built at the works of

Utilitarian in every way, heavy C628 locomotive 2003 in Hamersley Iron's Seven Mile yard in August 1979. (Peter Watts)

the parent company, Alco Products in Schenectady, and shipped out as deck cargo aboard the *Katsura Maru*, which left San Francisco on 11 August 1965 and reached Dampier on the last days of that month. Two further Sydney-built units were delivered in June 1967.

These locomotives were the largest diesels in the country, the heaviest and most powerful Alcos ordered for export anywhere in the world. Weighing in at 176 tonnes, the first two were assigned rail construction duties upon commissioning from mid September that year. When the standard gauge line between the port and Mt Tom Price was commissioned, two locomotives working in multiple were rated to haul a load of 12 000 tonnes.

Based on a design popular in the USA, the Hamersley C628s were slightly modified for Australian conditions, with 18 200 litre fuel tanks instead of the domestic 9100 litre type, and were fitted with Alertor vigilance control equipment, a Chicago-developed electric system which worked on the principle that the driver would make some body movement every 20 seconds. These movements were read by an antenna located in the seat. Footboards for shunters were also provided.

Capable of 115 km/h and standing 6.2 m tall and 22 m long, all five were powered with Alco's 251 series turbocharged engine which developed 2051 kW for traction.

Hamersley subsequently acquired larger, updated C636 model locomotives, but all C628s continued in regular service until 2005 was withdrawn on 14 March 1981. The last in traffic was 2003, used as a shunting unit at Seven Mile Yard until 31 August 1982. All were then placed in the hands of Hamersley Iron's Salvage Department and tendered for sale. No. 2003 was eventually saved for static preservation (carrying its original number, 2000) outside the company's main gate at Seven Mile. All others were scrapped.

SPECIFICATIONS

	IMPERIAL (METRIC)
POWER UNIT:	ALCO 251C (16 CYLINDERS)
TRACTION HORSEPOWER:	2750 (2051 KW)
STARTING TRACTIVE EFFORT:	120 000 LB (534 KN)
CONTINUOUS TRACTIVE EFFORT:	84 000 LB (374 KN)
TOTAL WEIGHT:	72.5 TONS (176 T)
GAUGE:	1435 MM
ROAD NUMBERS:	2001–2005 (NOTE: 2003 ORIGINALLY DELIVERED AS 2000, AND RENUMBERED IN 1972)

NT-class Co-Co

Satisfied with the service their A1A-A1A Sulzer-powered NSU-class locomotives had given over the narrow gauge sections of Commonwealth Railways since 1954, the administration chose another, more powerful Sulzer locomotive type when needing additional motive power.

The requirement had arisen due to steadily increasing business over the Central Australia Railway, linking Marree with Alice Springs. CR initially ordered three NT-class units in 1964 from Tulloch Ltd of Rhodes in Sydney, a design based on a Sulzer Bros double-ended locomotive in traffic on the Nigerian Railways.

The class-leader, NT65, was officially handed over with due ceremony in Port Augusta on 12 May 1965 and named *Gordon Freeth* in honour of the then Federal Minister for Shipping and Transport.

Although the NT-class was only 9 tonnes heavier than the older NSU-class, an additional 336 kW were packed into the power unit thanks to ongoing engine developmental work. This included a faster-running 800 rpm engine instead of the earlier 750 rpm type. (CR's load tables rated one NT-class as equal to double NSU-class.) As a means of excluding dust from the engine-room, the locomotive bodies were fully pressurised.

As the three were being delivered, traffic projections relating to the Frances Creek ore traffic in the Northern Territory led to a follow-up order for another three, which entered service on the North Australia Railway between November 1966 and January 1967. The continued increase in this ore traffic led to another seven being ordered, and all 13 NT-class had been delivered by late September 1968. At that stage, eight were to be found on the NAR while five, including the last two of the final order, worked on the CAR system.

When higher-powered NJ-class Clyde/GM locomotives arrived in 1971, all southern NTs were sent to the northern line where their regular service included triple-working of the ore trains in continuous block loads. This continued to be the case until a serious accident in Darwin in November 1972 forced the withdrawal of NT70, NT71 and NT75, the worst-damaged unit, NT75, being scrapped almost immediately.

Triple-headed NT-class locomotives 69, 74 and 71 with a Frances Creek ore train sitting in Darwin yard on 20 July 1973. Note the special covers over the locomotives' engine-pressurising intake-fan hatches designed to stop monsoonal rain entering the units. (Peter Watts)

Two older NSU-class were sent to Darwin to replace them but ore traffic was declining, the mine closing altogether in 1974. Despite this, CR maintained a service until NT69 ran the last train on 30 June 1976, the line's demise being an early victim of the National Rail Corporation's formation and erosion of 'uneconomic railway routes'. The NAR locomotives (and operational rolling stock) were gradually transferred to Marree and Port Augusta workshops. Some NTs were overhauled and reassigned to the CAR line, allowing for the retirement of older NSU locomotives. The commissioning of a new standard gauge Alice Springs line in 1980 saw most NTs stored, the survivors being transferred to former SAR depots Gladstone and Peterborough for the Wilmington and Eurelia lines respectively. This allowed the transfer of Alco 830-class locomotives to Tasmania. Three NTs (Nos 69, 73 and 74) were forwarded to Port Lincoln in 1984/1985 for gypsum, wheat and shunting service, the last two running until September 1988 after some 830s were returned from Tasmania. However, the Peterborough division's NT67 and NT76 remained operational until 1989, the latter being acquired by the Pichi Richi Railway at Quorn. The rest were scrapped.

SPECIFICATIONS

	IMPERIAL (METRIC)
POWER UNIT:	SULZER BROS 6 LDA 28C
TRACTION HORSEPOWER:	1300 (969 kW)
STARTING TRACTIVE EFFORT:	47 500 LB (211 kN)
CONTINUOUS ACTIVE EFFORT:	34 000 LB (151 kN)
TOTAL WEIGHT:	68.5 TONS (70 T)
GAUGE:	1067 MM
ROAD NUMBERS:	65–77

1965 NEW SOUTH WALES GOVERNMENT RAILWAYS

421-class Co-Co

With A.E. Goodwin delivering large numbers of GR, Clyde Engineering was forced into countering this position by coming up with its own dual-cab EMD.

With a little re-jigging the maker was able to offer a bi-directional version of NSWGR's 42-class (see page 284) in December 1965 in answer to a contract for ten locomotives. These became the 421-class. Up-rated to 1342 kW, the design retained the older 42-class's round nose at the leading end, the rear cab being of 'flat end cab' construction.

Although super reliable early in their careers, crews rightly regarded these locomotives as extremely rough riders due to their bogie pins being placed off centre. This factor provided added overhang and resultant pitch and roll, something that seemingly could not satisfactorily be overcome by improving the spring rates and dampers, which kept breaking away from the bogies. In the end, the fitters discarded the dampers altogether.

Initially used over the Main Southern line, the entire class was transferred to Bathurst in 1970 to work *Indian Pacific* expresses and freight trains over the newly-commissioned East–West standard gauge railway. However, their pitch and roll, teamed with the lighter nature of the track as it was then between Parkes and Broken Hill, quickly saw them replaced by the aforementioned dual-cab Alcos which tended to ride much better, due in part to their heavily

One of five Interail (QR National)-owned units, 42105, as running in November 2004, wearing the multi-coloured livery of the former Northern Rivers Scenic Railway, where it had been engaged in tourist train service. (Leon Oberg)

equalised, conventionally-centred bogies.

The 421-class was returned to the Main Southern line and for a brief period during the mid-1980s entered NSW/Victoria running.

Gradually, regular maintenance was reduced and reliability problems arose. When examples started to give trouble the class was completely withdrawn during December 1986 and January 1987, no matter that some had just received full overhauls. After lying in store at Junee (with unit 42107 returned to limited service in 1989), they were offered for disposal in 1990. While scrappers managed to acquire three, the better four (42103, 42105, 42107 and 42109) were bought that year by the Northern Rivers Scenic Railway, for which company they eventually entered service, principally in northern New South Wales. Their work included hauling the company's flagship *Ritz Rail* tourist train between Murwillumbah and Casino from its inception late in 1997. The shell of 42106 was also acquired, with a view to restoration. On 31 May 2002, all of the company's interests, along with the 421-class, were acquired by Queensland Rail, now branded QR National, marking that operator's move into the standard gauge national network. The 421s are today heavily engaged in coal haulage on the lower North Coast.

Units 42101 and 42102 were snapped up by private preservationists.

SPECIFICATIONS

	IMPERIAL (METRIC)
POWER UNIT:	EMD 16-567C
TRACTION HORSEPOWER:	1800 (1342 kW)
STARTING TRACTIVE EFFORT:	72 600 lb (323 kW)
CONTINUOUS TRACTIVE EFFORT:	60 900 lb (271 kN)
TOTAL WEIGHT:	108 tons (110 t)
GAUGE:	1435 mm
ROAD NUMBERS:	42101–42110

K-class Co-Co

We have already seen how Stan Lyons' drive to standardise English Electric's Australian designs to more aggressively take on the big US builders (see QR 1270-class) was a masterstroke. Wholesale orders from QR were immediate.

With gauge standardisation becoming a reality in Western Australia in the 1960s (being part of the decades-old Bill Wentworth east–west common gauge aspiration), the WAGR, which had its first taste of EE locomotives in 1962 with its C-class, turned to the Lyons 1339 kW Co-Co package when seeking motive power to run passenger and goods trains over the Perth to Kalgoorlie portion of the national rail link.

Because the Koolyanobbing iron ore mine was due to come on stream in 1967, nine K-class locomotives were acquired between January 1966 and December 1968. The earliest deliveries were pressed into rail construction service and, for a time, grain train haulage between Merredin and Kwinana's storage silos.

After the Koolyanobbing mine opened in mid-1967, four of these 110-tonne locomotives became staple motive power on 8160-tonne ore trains between there and BHP's Kwinana steel plant.

English Electric delivered three copies to Goldsworthy Mining Ltd between October 1966 and March 1967 for iron ore train haulage over the company's original 110 km railway between Finucane Island and Goldsworthy mine in the Western Australian Pilbara. This was the first of four mining companies to establish large-scale iron ore mines in that area during the latter part of the 1960s.

An additional locomotive, K202, was supplied by WAGR to tide Goldsworthy over following a serious collision in 1968. This locomotive became Goldsworthy's GML6. At the same time, Goldsworthy placed an order with EE for a WAGR replacement, which became that system's K210 when delivered in December 1968.

In 1972, the Goldsworthy railway was extended a further 69 kilometres to Shay Gap. This development took in the mining areas of Sunrise Hill and Nimingarra and led to the purchase of two new locomotives from EE on 1 March 1972. They became GML7 and GML8. As

A picture taken immediately after the K-class's introduction, showing locomotives K208, K201 and two sisters quadruple-headed at the head of a Koolyanobbing iron ore train. (English Electric; author's collection)

demand increased and new continuous-roster workings were introduced, an additional K-class unit, K203, was purchased from the WAGR in July 1986. It became Goldsworthy's GML9.

Extensive upgrading of the Goldsworthy railway was undertaken between 1992 and 1995 following its acquisition by BHP, and it was quickly absorbed into the old Mt Newman network. Now totalling some 207 km and serving the new Yarrie mine, the upgrading included the continuous welding of 130 km of mechanical-jointed 50 kg/m rails and the relaying of 77 km of heavier 66 kg rails reclaimed from the Mt Newman line. This enabled 190-tonne GE locomotives and heavier trains to work the Goldsworthy route, and the well-worn EE units were withdrawn for scrap.

However, BHP Steel at Port Kembla (as AI&S had become) needed additional locomotives to work expanding West Dapto (Wongawilli) coal and spoil

traffic. This company had been an exclusive operator of EE motive power since 1950 and one of its units was a customised main line 132-tonne end-cab Co-Co unit. The steel plant's management completed a deal to buy six of the GML units (and the engine out of GML4, a July 1990 rollover victim). These arrived by sea at Port Kembla on 24 November 1992.

The first made operational was GML9 (ex WAGR K203), renumbered D51 by BHP Steel. By mid-1996, four had been pressed into heavy coal service. However, not all were then available for traffic because GML8, now D50, was withdrawn in December 1995 following a works collision. The remainder continued hauling coal, the last in BHP service being D49, used until its engine was damaged after dropping a valve working coal from Dendrobium Mine in June 2003.

Apart from the sales to Goldsworthy Ltd, the first Westrail unit to be withdrawn was K204 following a

Two of the four K-class actually reactivated at BHP Port Kembla for coal work, D50 (formerly WAGR K202/Goldsworthy Mining GML6) and D47 (GML5) with a spoil train nearing Wongawilli on 5 April 1994. (Leon Oberg)

shunting accident at West Merredin in March 1995. The remaining six were being used in transfer goods service to Kwinana and Leighton in addition to freight hauls to Avon and Merredin. They were prime shunting power at Merredin, Avon and Esperance yards and were sometimes used on the Cobblers Pool quarry trains during the mid-1990s.

Most still linger in private ownership, K201, K207, K208 and K209 having been acquired by freight forwarder Specialized Container Transport for terminal shunting in several states, while private operator South Spur (now P&O Trans Australia) operates K205, K206 and K210 in transfer and rail maintenance work.

This company also purchased all BHP's Port Kembla units in March 2002. Locos D47, D49 and D51 were reactivated in Port Kembla and for a while operated Bombo ballast trains and other infrastructure services in NSW before being sent to the company's Midland (Perth) operations base. Because these locomotives employed just two field shunts within their transmissions, the company installed a third along with higher traction motor gearing to mirror the existing K-class. BHP Port Kembla's non-activated D46 and the accident damaged D50 were scrapped for their parts, including engines, bogies and blower items, which were also forwarded to Western Australia.

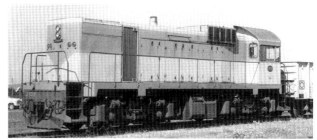

J102 working in Midland yard. (Peter Neve)

SPECIFICATIONS

	IMPERIAL (METRIC)
POWER UNIT:	ENGLISH ELECTRIC 12CSVT
TRACTION HORSEPOWER:	1795 (1339 KW)
STARTING TRACTIVE EFFORT:	67 000 LB (290 KN)
CONTINUOUS TRACTIVE EFFORT:	52 000 LB (231 KN)
TOTAL WEIGHT:	108.1 TONS (110 T)
	122 TONS (124 T) GOLDSWORTHY UNITS
GAUGE:	1435 MM
ROAD NUMBERS:	WAGR (ORIGINAL) 201–210
	GOLDSWORTHY LTD GML3–GML9. (EXCEPT FOR GML4, THESE BECAME BHP NOS D46, D47, D50, D48, D49 AND D51 RESPECTIVELY, ALTHOUGH D46 AND D48 WERE NEVER RESTORED OR TECHNICALLY RENUMBERED IN PORT KEMBLA OWNERSHIP.)

1966 WESTERN AUSTRALIAN GOVERNMENT RAILWAYS

J-class Bo-Bo

The WAGR adopted the basic Victorian Railway's Y-class Bo-Bo design of 1963 when it sought shunting power in 1965 for its 'under construction' standard gauge system.

The five units became that state's J-class and entered traffic over a three and half month period starting on 27 July 1966. Interestingly, their early deliveries shared the identical road numbering sequence of their Y-class brethren.

While powered with EMD's 567C 448 kW engine (as were the first 50 VR Y-class), these G6B units were carried on two Clyde Bo-Bo flexicoil bogies equipped with stronger 155 kW traction motors and were capable of speeds up to 62 km/h. Other design variations between the VR and WAGR units included a more tasteful body/cab and revised frame-skirting, and whereas the Y-class's 4546-litre fuel tanks were positioned immediately behind the cab, the J-class's 2730-litre tanks were located in the conventional place, underslung from the frame between the bogies.

On its introduction the J-class was used on Kwinana–Leighton standard gauge construction trains, but when regular services started was allocated to Avon, Leighton and Midland shunting yards.

With the gradual move to heavier unit trains over the next two decades, the need for light shunting locomotives waned and class-leader J101 was withdrawn at Midland Workshops in September 1986. Although operational when withdrawn, it became a source of spare parts for the 567C-engined main line A-class, its shell going to scrap in 1993.

The last unit in government service was J104, used for shunting at West Merredin until it and the remaining three sister units were delivered to the Melbourne-based Great Northern Rail Services in June 1995. After undergoing major rebuilds they saw some initial service under leased to the NRC for standard gauge shunting, transfer goods and ballasting duties.

Following the NRC's sale to Pacific National in February 2002, J104 and J105 were sold to FreightLink for shunting at Darwin and Alice Springs while J102 and J103 now belong to Specialized Container Transport.

A near-new 'third-series' X-class, X52, idles away its time in Wodonga depot on 11 May 1976, as it awaits its next rostered working, the *Southern Aurora* to Melbourne. (Leon Oberg)

SPECIFICATIONS

	IMPERIAL (METRIC)
POWER UNIT:	EMD 567C
TRACTION HORSEPOWER:	600 (447 KW)
STARTING TRACTIVE EFFORT:	35 800 LB (159 KN)
CONTINUOUS TRACTIVE EFFORT:	12 000 LB (53 KN)
TOTAL WEIGHT:	65.5 TONS (67 T)
GAUGE:	1435 MM
ROAD NUMBERS:	(VR) J101–105

1966 VICTORIAN RAILWAYS

X-class Co-Co

The amount of traffic generated by the standardisation of the Albury–Melbourne route early in 1962 was greater than anticipated. Victorian Railways' existing locomotive power found it increasingly difficult to cope with this traffic and the increase in freight haulage over the broad gauge Adelaide interstate route.

The last locomotive delivered representing the class's original nose/cab styling, 1491 kW-powered X44 rolls through Tottenham yard with a standard gauge train in September 1972. (John M. Wilson)

An order was therefore placed with the Clyde Engineering Co in Sydney for six 1342 kW Co-Co diesel-electric locomotives, two of them intended for standard gauge service. Up until then, the VR system had been standardised with Clyde/GM products and had 18 identically-powered streamlined S-class single-cab locomotives in heavy main line haulage. The contract for the new locomotives was thus a perpetuation of the S-class but in a hood car-body. The new locomotives became the X-class.

The hood design, with its low-profile nose section, made it possible to locate the driving controls on the right-hand side, favouring long-end leading. This gave VR a more useful locomotive in that it could be driven in both directions.

Class-leader X31 entered service on 16 August 1966 and by 15 November of that year all six were in operation.

In February 1969, two 1342 kW S-class streamliners were destroyed in the fatal *Southern Aurora* accident near Violet Town. This drain on locomotive power, coupled with steadily increasing traffic, led to the immediate ordering of another six (later increased to eight) X-class, but with a more modern and higher-powered 1491 kW diesel engine. The first of these was delivered in May 1970. (Two of them, X37 and X38, employed some parts salvaged from the two destroyed S-class.)

By the early 1970s, freight increases over both the Sydney–Melbourne and Melbourne–Adelaide corridors had risen to the point where VR was forced to hire three standard gauge GM-class cab units (similar to the existing S-class) from Commonwealth Railways. While this released VR standard gauge locomotives for broad gauge use elsewhere, the traffic

High-horsepower rebuild XR555 (originally X32), in mint condition at South Dynon workshops on 27 March 2005. (Stephen Molloy)

build-up continued and in mid-1974 an order for a further ten X-class was placed. Unlike all VR's EMD locomotives up to that point, which had been built in the manufacturer's Granville (Sydney) plant, these units became the first in Australia to be manufactured in Clyde's Rosewater (Adelaide) factory.

While boasting the 1491 kW prime mover, these locomotives were further up-graded with new AC alternators in lieu of the older DC generators. As well, following input from the VR crews' cab committee, they were equipped with airtight cabs and stylish angular noses. Because of these two changes, the controls were restored to the left-hand side of the cab, making the new units suitable only for traditional short-end running.

All had been delivered by 10 June 1976 and have proved to be one of Australia's more trouble-free locomotive types.

For a time during 1982–83, 'later-series' examples were employed on through Melbourne–Sydney express passenger services. The class became regulars on Melbourne–Adelaide interstate running until mid-1995, when the National Rail Corporation commissioned its new standard gauge operations between those two cities. After that time, the broad gauge examples could largely be found hauling Long Island steel and other metropolitan transfer goods services, in addition to Deniliquin and Wodonga superfreighter work. The few standard gauge units were working between Portland and Ararat.

The first cabless unit, XRB560, ran its trial trip to Wallan on 19 December 2005. It was pictured outside Dynon diesel shop shortly after that historic trip. (Peter Clark)

In April 1999, the entire class (except X35, which languished at Newport Workshops with a bent frame) was sold to private consortium Freight Victoria, which officially started running trains from 1 May 1999. By then, X47 and X49 had been converted to driver only, with lowered nose and larger windscreen area.

Further improvements were introduced, starting with X38, which was trialled to Seymour on 28 November 2001 equipped with an EMD 16-645E3B engine cascaded down from a company G-class. This effectively increased its traction output to 3000 hp (2237 kW). A new driver-only cab based on the 'later-series' units (with controls on the conventional left-hand side), an extra radiator on each of the two existing banks, an improved Wabtech QES3 control system (which reduced the number of electrical relays), wheel creep correction technology and an added rear hood section to accommodate a toilet, were also provided during the upgrade.

Six of a planned seven locos have already been randomly treated to spawn the XR-class and now bear the road numbers XR550–556. One of these was the forsaken X35, which came into the care of Seymour Rail Heritage Centre in 1998. In a fascinating deal aimed at speeding up the XR rebuild project, X35 was acquired on the understanding the originally-profiled class-leader, X31, would be made available on its eventual retirement, an arrangement that still stands under current Pacific National ownership. (Pacific National acquired Freight Australia on 1 September 2004.)

So successful was the programme that six more XRs have been built from the X-class, using new underframes, cabs and superstructure teamed with overhauled EMD 16-645E3C engines and associated electrics (sourced from North America). Other parts for the locomotives were largely supplied from existing spare parts inventories. Appearing from 2004, the first three, XR557 to XR559, were provided with cabs while, intriguingly, the final three were constructed as XRB-class cabless units. All had been commissioned by mid-May 2006, with XR555 and at least two of the XRBs seeing service across the Melbourne–Perth corridor by year's end.

All of the rebuilds were undertaken within the South Dynon workshops.

The abovementioned sale of Freight Australia saw X53 and X54 subsequently pass into the ownership (via an independent freight company) of QR National for Melbourne–Brisbane intermodal working.

SPECIFICATIONS

	X31–36 AS BUILT	X37–54 AS BUILT	XR550–559, XRB560–562
	IMPERIAL (METRIC)	IMPERIAL (METRIC)	IMPERIAL (METRIC)
POWER UNIT:	EMD 16-567C	EMD 16-645E	EMD 16-645 E3C
TRACTION HORSEPOWER:	1800 (1342 kW)	2000 (1491 kW)	3000 (2237 kW)
STARTING TRACTIVE EFFORT:	63 500 LB (282 kN)	72 500 LB (322 kN)	104 000 LB (465 kN)
CONTINUOUS TRACTIVE EFFORT:	53 500 LB (238 kN)	60 500 LB (269 kN)	76 200 LB (344.3 kN)
TOTAL WEIGHT:	114 TONS (116 T)	114 TONS (116 T)	120–122.5 TONS (122–124 T)
GAUGE:	1435 AND 1600 MM	1435 AND 1600 MM	1435 AND 1600 M
ROAD NUMBERS:	X31–36	X37–54	XR550–559 (THE INITIAL SEVEN REBUILT FROM X38, X35, X40, X33, X34, X32 AND X36 (YET TO BE REBUILT) RESPECTIVELY. CABLESS UNITS: XRB560–562

1966 QUEENSLAND RAILWAYS

1720-class Co-Co

This class of 56 lightweight but powerful Co-Co diesel-electric locomotives has become one of the most versatile types on the QR system.

The units, the first of which appeared in October 1966, were delivered under four separate contracts by the Clyde Engineering Co from the Salisbury (Brisbane) plant of subcontractor Comeng. The last unit in the class, 1775, appeared in May 1970.

Designated 1720-class, they were basically an improved version of QR's 1700-class of 1963. Whereas the earlier locomotives had been fitted with a 652 kW 8-cylinder 567C engine, the 1720-class received the new 8-cylinder 645E engine which increased the power available for traction to 745 kW.

Unlike the 1700s, which had been purchased for light branch line working, the heavier 1720s were principally acquired for Brisbane suburban passenger traffic. All were equipped with EMD's quick-start switch, which introduced a circuit giving modified

Class-leader 1720 at Toowoomba on 25 August 1985. (Peter Watts)

Locomotive 1753 at Charleville in January 2004, after receiving cab modifications under the maxi-cab project. Note the air-conditioner riding on top of the leading walkway. (Lyn Terrey)

excitation rates to the main generator field that provided faster acceleration for suburban trains.

Unit 1770 was suitably honoured in 1970 when it was named *James Cook* in commemoration of the bicentenary of Captain Cook's arrival in Botany Bay in 1770.

While ousted from suburban passenger working during the 1980s by metropolitan electrification, the survivors can be found today working across the state.

While all units were modified for driver-only operation (the last being 1724 in 1994), withdrawals started in June 1997 when 1765 was involved in a collision. Collisions continued, with 1726 and 1728 being destroyed in a fiery level crossing collision at Wanko on the Quilpie line on 25 June 2001.

The mid-1990s saw QR put considerable effort into its '90-tonne' main line fleet with the '60-tonne' units becoming rundown as a consequence. In 2000, locomotive 1764 was overhauled as a prototype for a possible general upgrade of the fleet to current standards. In 2001–02, Traveltrain sponsored the overhaul of 1734, 1771 and 1774 for its popular Cairns to Kuranda tourist service.

In 2003, Queensland Transport funded the overhaul of nine units for service in western Queensland. These overhauls differed from the Traveltrain overhauls with the fitting of a ZTR adhesion system allowing for a reduction in the electrical cabinet size and the consequent fitting of a scaled-down version of the maxi-cab as fitted to the earlier conversions.

As at 1 January 2010, of the original 56 units, 38 were listed as operational.

SPECIFICATIONS

	IMPERIAL (METRIC)
POWER UNIT:	EMD 8-645E
TRACTION HORSEPOWER:	1000 (745 kW)
STARTING TRACTIVE EFFORT:	39 650 LB (176 kN)
CONTINUOUS TRACTIVE EFFORT:	33 600 LB (149 kN)
TOTAL WEIGHT:	61 TONS (62 T)
GAUGE:	1067 MM
ROAD NUMBERS:	1720–1775

1967 WESTERN AUSTRALIAN GOVERNMENT RAILWAYS

L-class Co-Co

At the time it was introduced in October 1967, this locomotive type was by far the largest and heaviest diesel-electric in Australian government service.

Acquired from the Clyde Engineering Co for use over the newly-constructed 657 km Perth–Kalgoorlie standard gauge line, the L-class was based generally upon EMD's North American SD40 model, but reduced in height to suit the Australian loading gauge.

A total of 23 had been delivered to the WAGR by late April 1969 from the maker's Sydney plant, all running under their own power across NSWGR and VR's Sydney–Melbourne standard gauge system. From Dynon, they changed to broad gauge bogies for the haul to Port Pirie where they were restored to their original bogies for their under-power delivery via the Trans-Australian Railway. Interestingly, at least one L-class (No. 251) was hired by VR while passing through Victoria to run several regular freight trips between Dynon and Albury, due to a desperate locomotive shortage during the latter part of 1967.

Early assignments for the L-class in Western Australia included the haulage of the *Indian Pacific* express and Koolanyobbing iron ore trains. However, due to their high 137-tonne mass and 22.5-tonne axle loadings, they were removed from fast passenger traffic for fear of track damage.

The Western Mining Co of Western Australia financed an additional two L-class during August 1973 in connection with its giant nickel project at Mt Windarra (off the Kalgoorlie–Leonora line). Operated by government crews, the two were numbered onwards from the previous L-class deliveries.

The locomotives were powered with EMD's turbo-charged 16-645E3 series diesel engine, producing 2237

A fleet of ARG mixed-power EMD locomotives manhandling a contract Manildra grain train near Jerrawa in southern New South Wales on 20 March 2004, led by re-branded 3101, CLF3, 2201 and GM45. (Leon Oberg)

kW to the rail. In later years, examples could occasionally be seen in intersystem working over Australian National rails as far east as Port Augusta, and during the early 1980s, in another period of locomotive shortage on the VR brought about by a record grain harvest, several were leased for Melbourne–Albury goods haulage. Loco L252 even worked an evaluation trial to Sydney in May 1984.

Two copies were acquired by Comalco in March and June 1972 for bauxite haulage over its isolated 19.5 km standard gauge line between Andoom mine and Lorim Point at Weipa in far northern Queensland. Built by Clyde's Brisbane factory, they were specially ballasted to provide a mass of 148 tonnes for improved adhesion. The locomotives were rated to haul 6100-tonne train loads.

Comalco's class-leader, R1001, returned to Clyde for a complete rebuild and upgrade. In August 1994, when it was returned to service, its sister was sold

to Westrail where it joined the L-class prototypes carrying the number LW276. After some three years of stop-start service, principally between Kalgoorlie and Perth, it was withdrawn for its spare parts following engine failure.

The first to go was L269, which collided with a road train at Esperance on 30 May 1995 and was scrapped nine months later. Two years later, with the arrival of 19 locally-built 2862 kW Q-class EMD locomotives from July 1997, many L-class were stowed. But destiny prevailed and seven (251, 253, 254, 265, 270, 271 and LW276) were sold to Tranzrail in July 1998. After progressive overhauls and upgrades at National Railway Equipment's workshops in Whyalla beginning the following year, from June 2000 four were pressed into Australian Transport Network grain train operations out of western Victoria and southern New South Wales, taking their trains to Melbourne's new

Then recently overhauled L260, wearing the initial identity of the Australian Railroad Group, prepares to depart Forrestfield yard (Perth) on 7 December 2001. It has since been renumbered L3108. (Leon Oberg)

Appleton Dock grain export point and Port Kembla respectively. While retaining their road numbers, they collectively became the company's 250-class. The remaining three were stored at Rail Technical Services' Dynon servicing workshops. This company eventually negotiated a deal to buy outright the non-operable locomotives, along with the active L265. All subsequently passed into the ownership of what is now Queensland Rail National.

Meanwhile, 17 Westrail L-class survived to pass into the ownership of the Australian Railroad Group on 2 December 2000. Many were subsequently shopped, an initial four being branded 31-class for use on Alice Springs to Darwin railway construction trains and emerging in February and March 2002. The purchase of ARG by QRN continues to see rebuilds, with the units to receive numbers 3100–3122. Several are employed in contract NSW rural product haulage, mostly in the Gunnedah/Manildra to Nowra corridors.

Locomotive 1645 slumbering in Brisbane's Mayne locomotive depot yard on 18 October 1975. (Peter Watts)

SPECIFICATIONS

	IMPERIAL (METRIC)
POWER UNIT:	EMD 16-645E3
TRACTION HORSEPOWER:	3000 (2237 kW)
STARTING TRACTIVE EFFORT:	75 800 LB (337 kN)
CONTINUOUS TRACTIVE EFFORT:	66 900 LB (297.5 kN)
TOTAL WEIGHT:	134 TONS (137 T)
	PN's L251, L254, L271 NOW 129.5 TONS (132 T).
GAUGE:	1435 MM
ROAD NUMBERS:	(WAGR) L251–275 AND LW276
	(COMALCO) R1001, R1002 (LATTER UNIT TO WA AS LW276)
	(QRN-W UNITS) 3101–3122 (R1002/LW276 NOW RUNNING AS 3120)

1967 QUEENSLAND RAILWAYS

1620-class Co-Co

As explained earlier, QR ordered (in two contracts) 18 lightweight (62.5 tonne) Co-Co locomotives from English Electric's Rocklea plant for use over its far-flung, lightly laid branch lines west of Alpha and Roma. Of end-cab design, the first of these arrived in December 1962 as the 1600-class.

Looking to further dieselise its branch lines, QR had been impressed by the characteristics of five improved locomotives designed and built by EE for New Zealand Railways in 1966. Known in New Zealand as the DI-class and initially employed in the South Island between Christchurch and Picton, all were transferred to the North Island in 1969 for service in the Bay of Plenty area. The locomotive featured an American-style front hood nose which contained the electrical equipment.

Although less than a tonne heavier than the 1600-class, improvements to the 6-cylinder CSRKT engine's fuel intake and breathing were able to produce an extra 30 hp (22.3 kW). The first of QR's order appeared in January 1967 as the 1620-class. These more fashionable locomotives also differed from the 1600-class in that they were equipped with low weight transfer bogies and automatic couplers. By May 1969, the 1620-class had increased to 34 units and at that time could be found working in the Cairns, Rockhampton and Brisbane districts.

The 1620-class outlived all of QR's other EE locomotive types. While the first to be withdrawn was 1624 after a collision at Cloncurry on 1 November 1982, the last four in QR service were withdrawn in late December 1995.

Six were sold to John Holland Constructions, seeing initial service in the Philippines from September 1995, from where a recent report said examples were still working in Quezon Province. Some others were subsequently forwarded to Thailand and Malaysia.

Nos 1632, 1639 and 1649 are retained for preservation by the Mary Valley Heritage Railway at Gympie, class-leader 1620 is part of the QR Heritage Fleet, while 1650 is owned by the Queensland Division of the ARHS and presently stored at Redbank.

SPECIFICATIONS

	IMPERIAL (METRIC)
POWER UNIT:	EE 6CSRKT
TRACTION HORSEPOWER:	862 (641 kW)
STARTING TRACTIVE EFFORT:	41 500 LB (184.5 kN)
CONTINUOUS TRACTIVE EFFORT:	30 200 LB (135.5 kN)
TOTAL WEIGHT:	62 TONS (62.9 T)
GAUGE:	1067 MM
ROAD NUMBERS:	1620–1653

Former QR 1310 working in Tasmania as (ZC-class) 2141 at Devonport on the Goliath cement train from Railton on 25 February 1999 (Chris Walters)

1300-class Co-Co

This class of forty-five 1339 kW diesel-electrics locomotives, built by English Electric at Rocklea during 1967–72, was an upgraded version of Queensland Railways' 1270-class coal haul unit.

Designated 1300-class, these units boasted more powerful 1339 kW diesel engines in lieu of the 1270-class's 1145 kW engines, larger fuel tanks and sundry other engineering and electrical refinements.

All were acquired for the growing central Queensland export coal traffic, although some actually found their way south from time to time, ending up in Brisbane on coastal goods trains. When in Brisbane, it was not unusual for the husky mainliners to be rostered on metropolitan passenger services.

The poor reliability of the EE coal fleet resulted in their replacement with Clyde-built EMD units during the 1980s. Most of the 1300s then joined the general traffic pool. The cascading effect of diesels following Queensland coalfields electrification in 1987 saw the entire class become surplus, QR's preference at the time being for EMD products, the incompatible control systems (EMD's 72 volts versus EE's 110 volts) posing operational constraints.

QR 1300-class 1304 in original condition as pictured on 18 October 1975. (Peter Watts)

While Brazilian interests reportedly looked at acquiring the fleet, Australian National Railways considered life still remained in the locomotives and, since it was operating an EE fleet in Tasmania, cemented a deal with QR for the lot. The last 1300 to commercially operate in Queensland was 1329, which worked a Cooroy to Brisbane departmental work train on 9 November 1988.

All units were assembled in Gladstone and shipped to Tasmania's Bell Bay in three separate movements (15 locomotives at a time), beginning late in October 1988 with those in the best condition. All had been unloaded at Bell Bay by the last day of November. By then, some of the earlier arrivals had been shopped to make them compatible with AN Tasmanian Region operational standards and the first three were commissioned on 13 December 1988, officially reclassified as the ZC-class.

Initial clearance problems with the fuel tank saw their usage restricted to the higher-standard Bell Bay route. Thirty-three eventually entered service in Tasmania (most in their old QR livery), but not all could be counted actually operating at any given time. Some were later stored as a spare parts pool.

To some degree the ZCs proved to be a poor buy. Despite an initial period when the locomotives tended to dominate train working throughout the state, the number in actual service had dwindled to 13 by the end of 1995. Meanwhile, scrappings of some ZCs along with several original non-commissioned 1300s started in March 1993. Many more followed during the closing months of 1996 and with the acquisition of AN's Tasmanian rail interests in November 1997 by ATN, only six remained operational, these being re-classified into the 2140-class. The remaining operational locomotives were withdrawn in November 2004.

ATN sold 2142 and 2143 to CFCLA for a proposed Western Australian tourist project, both eventually passing into the ownership of a Senegal (West African) coal miner.

MKA-class

However, the story of these locomotives is not over. Railway engineering/manufacturing firm, Morrison Knudsen Australia, which established a plant at Whyalla early in the 1990s, bought eight surplus Tasmanian 1300/ZCs in April 1994 for 'remanufacturing' and two more for parts. Their design originally called for new raked cabs and the provision of metre gauge wheelsets for expected lease operation in South-East Asia. They were originally numbered on the factory floor as MKA1–4 and 13–16 (the latter four eventually being out-shopped as MKA5–8). The class-leader was tested in February 1995 over BHP's Iron Baron mineral line.

The first four eventually left Whyalla for Malaysia in early August 1995. By then, however, with work progressing on the remainder, the fifth and sixth units' rebuilds almost complete, Morrison Knudsen Australia was forced to cease trading due to complications with the parent company in the USA. A skeleton crew was allowed to remain on site to complete MKA7 and oversee remaining operations which from December 1996 included the lease of MKA5 and MKA6 to BHP Whyalla to overcome a

severe locomotive shortage caused by accidents. Staff remained on hand following the sale of the Whyalla plant to the National Railway Equipment Co-Alco in 1999. Work on the half-completed eighth unit (formerly ZC31 and ex-1330) continued under the new management and the unit was photographed by this author during February 2001 in a near-complete state carrying the road number MKA16 (becoming MKA8 upon its release into traffic).

In 2002, this company was able to negotiate the lease of MKA5 and MKA6 to Senegal (West Africa) for coal haulage in March 2001, while the four Malaysian units were returned to Whyalla for storage as they had been deemed unsuitable for work in that country. While several technical problems surfaced, the main gripe was the forward-facing control desk which made long-end leading operations difficult, with the locomotives needing to be turned at terminating stations.

Numbers MKA1–3 found further work from mid-2004 in their state of origin after Pacific National Queensland purchased them to train crews ahead of the company's move into Queensland. Experience with these saw Pacific National acquire MKA4, MKA7 and MKA8 for its Tasmanian operation in November 2004, where they were renumbered 2134, 2137 and 2138. Wired to work in tandem with US-derived types, 2134 was stored in May 2009 due to a rollover. All now belong to the Tasmanian Government after it (re)acquired the state's 726 km system on 30 November, 2009.

MKA7 and MKA8, renumbered 2137 and 2138 for Pacific National's Tasmanian operations, prepare to depart South Burnie around dusk in June 2006. (Tim Gray)

	IMPERIAL (METRIC)
POWER UNIT:	ENGLISH ELECTRIC 12CSVT
TRACTION HORSEPOWER:	1795 (1339 KW)
STARTING TRACTIVE EFFORT:	60 000 LB (267 KN)
CONTINUOUS TRACTIVE EFFORT:	48 500 LB (216 KN)
TOTAL WEIGHT:	88 TONS (89.5 T)
GAUGE:	1067 MM
ROAD NUMBERS:	(QR) 1300–1344.

(TASRAIL) ZC1–ZC45 (NOT ALL UNITS RENUMBERED) EXPORT LOCOS: MKA1 (EX-1320), MKA2 (1329), MKA3 (1321), MKA4 (1326), MKA5 (1325), MKA6 (1332), MKA7 (1330) AND MKA8 (1340). THOSE IN PACIFIC NATIONAL TASMANIA OWNERSHIP SO FAR HAVE BECOME: 2134 (EX MKA4), 2137 (EX MKA7) AND 2138 (EX MKA8)

1967 WESTERN AUSTRALIAN GOVERNMENT RAILWAYS

T-class 0-6-0 DE

Having already delivered locomotives to two private firms, and to the Tasmanian and Victorian Railways, Sydney-based heavy engineering company Tulloch Ltd's final locomotives were fifteen 0-6-0 shunting units for Western Australian Government Railways.

Unlike Tulloch's earlier creations, which employed hydraulic transmissions, these were diesel-electrics. The first appeared in July 1967 as the WAGR T-class and boasted a 490 kW Cummins V12 diesel engine. With a similar rating to the VR W-class of 1959, they were the product of a manufacturing agreement between Tulloch Ltd and the British firm, Brush Electrical Engineering Co Ltd.

Capable of a top speed of 65 km/h, the locomotives

TA-class 1814 as presently exhibited at Pine Creek in the Northern Territory. (Dick Holland)

were equipped with two 185 kW traction motors connected in parallel from a Brush 407 kW main generator.

After five were built, WAGR opted for an additional ten (in two contracts) but with 447 kW power packs. These became that railway's TA-class, the last one being delivered in 1970, shortly before Tulloch Ltd closed its works.

From December 1985 the locomotives were gradually retired, commencing with T1802, although it lingered on yielding parts until officially scrapped in March 1990. Three T-class and six TA-class were scrapped in March 1994 and the only one remaining in government hands today is TA1807, now working at the State Energy Commission's Bunbury powerhouse.

Those that survive include T1804, preserved at Geraldton; TA1807 at the Boyanup Transport Museum; TA1808 (the last one in Westrail service) is at Merredin Station Museum; TA1813 is used by locomotive-builder United Group Rail (formerly A. Goninan & Co) as its Bassendean works shunter, and TA1814 is on display at the Pine Creek Railway Museum in the Northern Territory.

	IMPERIAL (METRIC)
POWER UNIT:	CUMMINS VT-12-825
TRACTION HORSEPOWER:	650 (485 KW)
STARTING TRACTIVE EFFORT:	25 000 LB (111 KN)
CONTINUOUS TRACTIVE EFFORT:	15 460 LB (68.7 KN)
TOTAL WEIGHT:	36.75 TONS (37 T)
GAUGE:	1067 MM
ROAD NUMBERS:	T1801–1805/TA1806–1815

1968 WESTERN AUSTRALIAN GOVERNMENT RAILWAYS

R-class Co-Co

In Western Australia the 'lugging ability' and overall high performance of the standard gauge K-class led to WAGR's decision to acquire a 1067 mm gauge version, which became the system's R-class.

Employing the same engine and generator and updated traction motors, together with a lower gearing, the initial five units boasted a greater tractive effort at the rail head. In fact, except for their low-weight transfer bogies designed for better traction, the R-class was closely akin to the QR 1300-class, which at that time was being built beside them on

RA1908 in Forrestfield, Perth, on 15 July 1979. (Peter Watts)

English Electric's very same Rocklea (Queensland) factory floor.

Intended for burgeoning bauxite traffic, the R (unlike the K) was equipped with dynamic braking. These locomotives spawned an additional 13 slightly heavier and longer units for WAGR, again for mineral traffic. Since these did not have dynamic brakes, they became the RA-class, and all of them were operational by June 1972, a salt company financing the final two.

As a means of adding adhesion, R1903–1905 were given an extra 6 tonnes of ballast to increase their axle loadings from 15 to 16 tonnes.

After WAGR converted the Esperance line to standard gauge in 1974 due to the volume of nickel and salt traffic being carried, the last three RA-class units were converted to standard gauge and renumbered as KA-class 211 (ex RA1914), 212 (RA1917) and 213 (RA1918). These numbers ran on from the standard gauge K-class and the converted locomotives were run in conjunction with that type.

The arrival of the new GE P-class from 1989 marked the end for the hard-working R/RAs. All were withdrawn during 1990–91, the last one in traffic being R1902, used until September 1991 on Pemberton–Collie working while based at Picton. After nine years' preservation at the Cohuna Wildlife Park at Martin, this unit was leased to Hotham Valley Railway early in 2000 for subsequent tourist and heritage train operations, but today is used by Southern Silverton Rail, mainly on rail corridor work trains in West Australia.

KA212 remained in service into 1995, being regular power on Western Quarries' rock trains (between Cobblers Pool quarry and Kewdale) before also being acquired by Southern Silverton, which was using the unit as this book went to press. Sister unit KA211 was written off in March 1987 (and its cab and frame employed as a diesel engine test-bed at United Group Rail's Bassendean factory), while KA213 (ex RA1918) was converted back to its original RA form in 1985 and six years later donated to the ARHS for display in its Bassendean Rail Transport Museum. All other units were scrapped at Midland in September 1992.

SPECIFICATIONS

	R-CLASS	RA/KA-CLASSES
	IMPERIAL (METRIC)	IMPERIAL (METRIC)
POWER UNIT:	EE 12CSVT	EE 12CSVT
TRACTION HORSEPOWER:	1795 (1339 KW)	1795 (1339KW)
STARTING TRACTIVE EFFORT:	59 270 LB (264 KN)	67 000 LB (298 KN)
CONTINUOUS TRACTIVE EFFORT:	48 500 LB (216 KN)	50 500 LB (225 KN)
TOTAL WEIGHT:	88/95.5 TONS (90.5/97.5T)	92.5 TONS (94.5T)
GAUGE:	1067 MM	1067/1435MM
ROAD NUMBERS:	R1901–1905	RA1906–1918; KA211–213

1968 HAMERSLEY IRON

Alco C415 Bo-Bo

This all-American locomotive type marked a resurgence of interest in the original 1930s US centre-cab diesel-electric locomotive design. Alco unveiled the medium-powered Model C415 as its 'utility locomotive' in April 1966. Of the 26 built in the USA up until December 1968, thirteen were

KA212 as used by South Spur Rail Services at Forrestfield yard on 18 February 2005. (Andrew Rosenbauer)

The Alco C415, restored with its 1972 number, 1000, and pictured at the Pilbara Railway Historical Society's Dampier compound in March 2006. (Richard Montgomery)

equipped with medium-height cabs. A 2-year-old demonstrator unit was sold to Hamersley Iron Pty Ltd in May 1968 to haul ballast, work and supply trains following its US tour.

Initially numbered 008 in the Hamersley roster, the locomotive was renumbered 1000 four years later. It remained in service until 24 February 1982, when the ever-increasing weights of ore trains eventually became too much for it.

Since it was the only one of its type ever to leave North America, it was donated to the Pilbara Railway Historical Society in fully operational condition. After running numerous special picnic-type tours including trips with the British steam locomotive *Pendennis Castle* when it was in the society's care, the Alco exhibit was 'reacquired' by Hamersley Iron during September 1991. Renumbered 2000, it was then used to haul infrastructure (work and ballast) trains during the construction of the new 30 km

Marando line which branches off the company's main line at Rosella Siding.

SPECIFICATIONS

	IMPERIAL (METRIC)
POWER UNIT:	Alco 251C (8 CYLINDERS)
TRACTION HORSEPOWER:	1500 (1119 kW)
STARTING TRACTIVE EFFORT:	55 000 LB (244.8 kN)
CONTINUOUS TRACTIVE EFFORT:	41 600 LB (185.1 kN)
TOTAL WEIGHT:	107 TONS (109 T)
GAUGE:	1435 MM
ROAD NUMBER(S):	008, 1000 (IN 1972) AND 2000 (IN 1991).

1968 HAMERSLEY IRON PTY LTD, MT NEWMAN MINING AND CLIFFS, ROBE RIVER IRON ASSOCIATES

Alco 636 Co-Co

The easing of the embargo on iron ore exports in 1960 saw a flurry of activity in the Pilbara region of Western Australia and, as already mentioned, huge consortiums were soon releasing details of massive mining projects following the discoveries of seemingly endless mountains of iron ore.

After markets and mines had been established, one of the most essential needs was reliable transport, since some of the mining sites were hundreds of kilometres from planned sea ports. As a result, three first class railways were built in the torrid region, all to

Hamersley Iron C636 unit, 3011, at Dampier on 2 August 1979. (Peter Watts)

American Railroad Association's exacting standards. They were equal to anything in the world and became the catalyst for subsequent large-scale infrastructure upgrades on Australian government railways.

One of the first mining companies to go into production was the giant Hamersley Iron operation, which in 1965 imported five Alco model C628 2051 kW locomotives, firstly for construction service and then for mineral haulage.

At the same time, Hamersley Iron placed an order with Alco's Australian licence-holder, A.E. Goodwin Ltd of Sydney, for two larger model C636 units. This impressive 2685 kW type was to form the basis for heavy ore haulage throughout the Pilbara, with the Mt Newman Mining Company and Cliffs, Robe River Iron Associates also obtaining examples.

Hamersley soon increased its order for C636 units by ten, four of which were equipped experimentally with visual display speedometer equipment instead of the regular Hassler clock-face system.

The Mt Newman Mining Company, which had quietly been building a 427 km railway linking its mine at Mt Whaleback with Port Hedland, ordered five C636 locomotives from A.E. Goodwin.

The two Hamersley locomotives were the first to arrive in the Pilbara (during the first days of May 1968) and both were commissioned during mid-June, about the time Mt Newman was taking delivery of its first unit, 5452.

Within 12 years, Hamersley's 636 fleet had grown to 39 locomotives, while Mt Newman commissioned

54 up until December 1977. Due to spare capacity at Hamersley Iron at the time, their intended unit, 4045 (first) was acquired by Robe River during manufacture and went straight to that company on delivery, where it was repainted and numbered 1716 (later 9416).

During the construction period of these 94 Australian-built locomotives, several critical events occurred. One was the late 1969 collapse within the USA of Alco Products Ltd. Alco's catalogue was acquired by the Montreal Locomotive Works and thus, from March 1971, the C636 locomotive became the M636 model. Two years later, Australia's A.E. Goodwin failed. But that did not see the end of the rugged Alco locomotives either, for virtually right across the street from the collapsed company sat rival heavy engineering firm Commonwealth Engineering (Comeng), which had been building diesel locomotives on a small scale since 1950. Comeng immediately negotiated MLW's Australian franchise and continued to supply M636 locomotives to the mining companies, beginning with Mt Newman's 5485 in December 1973.

The last big mining company to set up in the Pilbara was Cliffs, Robe River Iron Associates (now Robe), which in 1972 opened a 162 km heavy-haul railway linking Mt Enid with Cape Lambert's port facilities. On placing an order with A.E. Goodwin for its initial two M636 units, Cliffs' construction authority acquired two former NSWGR 40-class locomotives to assist with materials haulage. The two Cliffs 636s were commissioned over a 4-month period starting in October 1971. Another four were acquired at intervals between March 1973 and February 1980.

Due to continuing locomotive shortages at Robe, the company was able to purchase one second-hand C636 from the Burlington North Railroad in the USA. Arriving in May 1981 and bearing the livery and the number (4369) of its previous owner, this locomotive was renumbered 9424 for its use in Australia. The big locomotive was originally built for the Spokane, Portland & Seattle Railroad in November 1968, carrying the number 343.

The operation of the C636 locomotive throughout the Pilbara was breathtaking. Very few places on earth offer such harsh conditions, with temperatures frequently soaring upwards to 52°C, coupled with regular dust storms (or the monsoon rains) which can reduce visibility to just a few metres. On the Hamersley system, during full Alco operations, non-stop full power was applied for three hours' duration on the 1 in 240 climb from Paraburdoo to Tom Price, with six locomotives to each train.

Maintenance cycles in those conditions had to be impeccable. The care actually provided to the locomotives was detailed at the time in figures published in Railways of Australia's *Network* magazine, which revealed how Hamersley's 636s were running 120 000 km each year, their diesel engines achieving 320 000 km between top overhauls and running a staggering 640 000 km between major overhauls. These figures were only 20 per cent lower than those achieved by other heavy mainline units working on mainstream government railways at the time which were actually hauling only a fraction of the loads in easier operating conditions.

By the early 1980s, the original Hamersley Alcos were in need of major overhauls and an initial six were forwarded to Comeng's Bassendean factory in Perth for an upgrade. Apart from electrical improvements, custom-designed accommodation for the enginemen was provided in the guise of a commodious, comfortable end-cab whose windscreens were angled downwards to reduce glare at night from yard lights.

The first modified locomotive, 3015, re-entered traffic in May 1981. A total of 24 were eventually rebuilt by Comeng in this way and the cab design became the basis for a host of C636/M636 General Electric Dash-7 and 8 rebuilds that followed for Robe and BHP until April 1996.

Robe even imported the usable remains of two US C636 Conrail locomotives (Nos 6781 and 6782) in 1986, and forwarded them to Comeng's plant for a 'Hamersley-style' rebuild. The first entered traffic as 9426 in November 1986 and the second as 9427 the following January.

At Mt Newman (now BHP Billiton), the collapse of Comeng in the mid-1980s meant that no locomotives were rebuilt as Alco/MLWs. A. Goninan & Co, holder of the General Electric licence in Australia, took over the rebuild work at Comeng's Bassendean factory. Goninan initially rebuilt eight Mt Newman C636 locomotives into GE Dash-7 units, the first re-entering service in January 1987 as Model CM36-7 carrying the new road number 5506. The others became 5507–5513 (see page 405).

By 1984, GE in the USA had improved on its Dash-7 by the provision of refined micro-processor technology and the GE Microsentry (computerised) adhesion system. This new Dash-8 model also boasted improved engine cooling and centrally located, simplified electronics. Goninan was able to incorporate this

Mt Newman Mining's (now BHP Billiton) M636 locomotive 5502 at Port Hedland on 8 August 1979. This unit eventually proved to be born under a lucky star for it is preserved today in running condition at the Pilbara Railway Museum. (Peter Watts)

technology into subsequent new locomotive orders and any further rebuilds.

After Goninan & Co won a contract from then BHP Iron Ore to construct four new Dash-8 units as Model CM39-8s between September and December 1988, Robe contracted Goninan from 1989 to progressively remanufacture 12 Alco/MLW units into CM40-8M locomotives, the last of which, 9410, was delivered in April 1996. Interestingly, that latter unit was erected on a former BHP M636 platform (thought to be loco 5500), one of three then stored at Goninan's Perth plant. This was done in a bid to speed up production to clear the factory floor for the upcoming construction of 60 NR-class locomotives for National Rail Corporation. When the rebuilt machine was delivered, it and then stored 'original' 9410 spent some time together before the latter's remains were forwarded in 1998 to the Pilbara Railway Museum, Dampier, for preservation.

Goninan went on to rebuild a further 34 Alcos into Dash-8s for BHP (as well as constructing new Dash-8s) for a fleet total of 40. While the rebuilt locomotives' former superstructures were scrapped, most of the discarded Alco 251F engines and their generators were at the time forwarded to South-East Asian countries for use as community power generators.

But as already seen, not all Robe rebuilds were undertaken on Australian-built 636 Alco frames, for they also included two C636s originally built by

Alco's Schenectady Works in 1968 for the Spokane, Portland & Seattle Railroad. Robe purchased both units from Chrome Crankshaft (Chicago), one late in 1980, the other in May 1989.

The remanufactured GE locomotives possessed 2980 kW engines (in place of the former 2685 kW Alco equipment), weighed 195 tonnes and boasted 18 600-litre fuel tanks. According to BHP Iron Ore, the maintenance bill for the rebuilt locomotives immediately fell by 80 per cent.

Following the commissioning of 29 new US-built Dash-9 GE locomotives at Hamersley from March 1995, for every two new units placed into service three 636s were removed. By then the company's surviving Alcos had been de-rated to about 2050 kW in a deliberate move to reduce stresses on their mechanical and electrical equipment.

Only one Hamersley 636 survives in Western Australia, loco 3017, which today graces the Pilbara Railway Museum. Others, 4033 and 4040 (the last to receive overhauls) were among ten acquired by Austrac (NSW) in August 1998 for a planned but non-eventuating rebuild programme. While these still remained in Perth in 2001, the balance were cut up on site by a Perth scrap firm over a 3-month period beginning with 4056 on 6 July 1998. As with the BHP 636 units, their engines and generators were sent to South-East Asia for deployment as village power generators. The traction motors went to the USA.

BHP's last Alco/MLW in general service was

Robe's 'originally configured' Alco 251-Plus locomotive 9416 at Dampier's Seven Mile yard in August 2003 was originally built for the BHP Newman railway as 4045 (first) but delivered direct to Robe River. (Richard Montgomery)

5495, withdrawn as a shunter in Hedland yard on 8 March 1995. Its chassis and bogies were briefly stored while a decision was finalised on whether to hold the materials for a future Dash-8 rebuild programme 'should an accident destroy an existing unit'. Three original configuration units have been preserved: 5497 at Port Hedland Machine Park; 5499 at the ARHS museum in Bassendean (Perth) and 5502 in running condition at the Pilbara Railway Museum (where 5495's cab also resides).

Thus the last Alco/MLWs in Pilbara commercial ore haulage were Robe's six. One (9412) in original condition, was retained throughout the late 1990s for standby service. The remainder, including the ex-Conrail units, were earlier equipped with Alco 251-Plus engines which increased their traction output to 4000 hp (2983 kW). These V16 engines were manufactured by GE, now the supplier of Alco spares. These rare engines, which had Alco stampings on their injector covers, boasted the GE motif as well.

However, there was more in store for some M636s for, following Robe's 27 March 2000 announcement that it was building a new 340 km line to its new $900 million West Angelas mining project, 'original cab' Alco 251-Plus units 9413 and 9416 were reactivated to shunt Cape Lambert and work construction trains. Meanwhile, contractors building a 250 km Anderson Point (Port Hedland) to Cloud Break Mine railway for new Pilbara iron ore player, Fortescue Metals, in 2006 acquired four ex-HI and two Robe C636R units for construction train duties. Owned by Coote Industrial, they were assigned the DR8401–DR8406 series using the ex-Robe 9426, HI 3007, HI 3013, Robe 9427 respectively. A further two HI units, 3011 and 3008 spawned DR8405 and DR8406 in 2008 as plans to increase mining intensified. The ex-HI units were among several dozen which had languished in UGR's Maddington (Perth) yard for many years. But the 2008/2009 global recession meant DR8406 was never completed.

SPECIFICATIONS

	IMPERIAL (METRIC)
POWER UNIT:	Alco 251F (16 CYLINDERS)
TRACTION HORSEPOWER:	3600 (2685 KW)
STARTING TRACTIVE EFFORT:	138 000 LB (614 KN)
CONTINUOUS TRACTIVE EFFORT:	90 600 LB (403 KN)
TOTAL WEIGHT:	188 TONS (191.5 T);
NEWMAN UNITS	179.5 TONS (183 T)
GAUGE:	1435 MM
ROAD NUMBERS:	HAMERSLEY IRON: 3006–3017, 4030–4056
	MT NEWMAN: 5452–5505
	ROBE RIVER: 9410–9416, 9421–9427
FORTESCUE METALS:	DR8401-DR8406 (* 8406 NOT AS YET COMPLETED) REACTIVATED FROM 9426, 3007, 3013, 9427, 3011 AND 3008 RESPECTIVELY.

D34 Co-Co

Although the Australian Iron & Steel Company (AI&S) had greatly modernised coal haulage from its Wongawilli and Mt Keira district collieries in 1950 with the introduction of diesel-electric motive power, continuing expansion of exports and domestic coal needs soon dictated greater production in the mines.

On the Wongawilli line, grades of 1 in 50 between old Brownsville and Unanderra were restricting train loads to 540 net tonnes for a single D1/D16-type Bo-Bo locomotive. With the emphasis on bigger trains, the AI&S motive power department was forced to roster two of these locomotives to each train, both of which had to be manned by individual crews due to a lack of multiple-unit control equipment.

With high-power Stan Lyons-designed EE Co-Co locomotives of 1339 kW output proliferating in Queensland and Western Australia by the late 1960s, AI&S ordered one customised version of the WAGR R-class early in 1968 specifically for coal haulage. EE's Rocklea designers provided a heavier frame and headstocks and an AI&S-pattern noseless end-cab which, because of the more generous loading gauge, was able to stand slightly higher.

Delivered from Brisbane under its own power but restricted in speed due to its weight of 132 tonnes, D34 entered coal service on 30 April 1969. Its worth to AI&S was quickly demonstrated during a test, being capable of hauling a 1500-tonne train up a gradient of 1 in 50, and able to handle the same load over a descending 1 in 40 grade while in dynamic-brake mode. However, its regular load was set at 1000 tonnes.

Maintained in pristine condition, the unique one-off D34 was fully overhauled in 1995 when it was provided with an external muffler system to meet increasingly stringent environmental protection standards to allow it to operate to Kemira and Elouera (Wongawilli) collieries.

But following National Rail Corporation's (now Pacific National) acquisition of rail haulage tasks at the now Bluescope steel plant, and the resultant use of conventional main line EMD and GE locomotives, D34, pictured on the following pages sans its external silencing equipment, is today restricted to internal works shunting and transfer service.

The sturdy steel and concrete Macquarie Rivulet bridge at Brownsville bears the substantial weight of locomotive D34 as it works an empty Wongawilli-bound coal train on 7 February 1983. (Leon Oberg)

SPECIFICATIONS

	IMPERIAL (METRIC)
POWER UNIT:	ENGLISH ELECTRIC 12CSVT
TRACTION HORSEPOWER:	1800 (1339 kW)
STARTING TRACTIVE EFFORT:	72 000 LB (321 kN)
CONTINUOUS TRACTIVE EFFORT:	57 000 LB (254 kN)
TOTAL WEIGHT:	129.5 TONS (132 T)
GAUGE:	1435 MM
ROAD NUMBER:	D34

1969 NEW SOUTH WALES GOVERNMENT RAILWAYS

422-class Co-Co

The 20 locomotives of this class, introduced in January 1969, were to change locomotive design trends throughout Australia. They also introduced EMD's newly-released 16-cylinder 645E diesel engine (a type better suited to turbo-blowing) to the NSWGR.

The 422-class was also the first diesel of Australian design to adopt non-streamlined box cabs at both ends of the locomotive, paving the way for a host of variations on the theme that are appearing from

manufacturers to this day. In addition, the class was equipped with improved high-adhesion bogies with unidirectional motor suspension.

Purchased by the NSWGR as a final stage in its dieselisation programme, all had been delivered by January 1970 and exclusively allocated to the Main Southern and Illawarra lines. The 422-class became the champions of such leading express services as the *Southern Aurora*, *Spirit of Progress* and *Intercapital Daylight*. They were also pressed into Sydney to Albury express freight services, being extended to Melbourne in 1983 after intersystem running was instigated.

All were built at the Clyde Engineering Co's Granville plant to a design by staff member Mervyn Hill, who felt a 'mansard' roofline would fit the available loading gauge better than a 'turtle-shaped' A-model. These 110-tonne locomotives exerted 1491 kW for traction purposes, and were equipped with a dynamic brake with a maximum capacity of 1497 kW. Trouble-free, fast and reasonable riders, true testimony to the design's soundness was poignantly illustrated in 1995 when all were retained after much younger Alco locomotives were purged from the system following the arrival of 89 new EMD locomotives.

With EMD's successful 1970s eight-year US testing of 'Super Series' technology (a then revolutionary means of controlling wheel slip through radar, electronics and computers), 42220 was forwarded to Clyde's Adelaide plant late in 1979 and returned on 28 July 1980 boasting the new equipment. Exhaustive trials soon backed EMD's claim that SS locomotives could pull up to 31 per cent greater loadings than conventionally powered locomotives. In September 1980, NSWSRA load tables allowed 42220 to haul 1450 tonnes over the predominantly 1 in 75 Cootamundra to Goulburn section, where the conventional 422 class was allowed only 970 tonnes.

The new technology led to the acquisition of eighty-four 81-class 2237 kW units from September 1982. Locomotive 42220 was also employed in the NSWSRA's high-speed main line trials throughout 1981–82 in preparation for its new Express Passenger Train programme, on several occasions reaching speeds of 140 km/h. And while 42220 and 42203 were retained (and air-conditioned) to work CountryLink's Griffith passenger operations, withdrawals of others started in May 1996 when 42202, in workshops for a general overhaul, was set-aside for its engine and key electrical parts. However sixteen units which during that decade saw several years' heavy freight service with the National Rail Corporation were sold to Genesee & Wyoming's South Australian-based Great Southern Railroad, their delivery effective from May 2000. While some saw instant service, four were rebuilt during 2001 at Port Augusta Workshops with air-conditioners and upgraded cabs, and reclassified 22-class for Darwin line construction. The first appeared in June that year as 2203 (ex-42214). Others have progressively been rebuilt, the units having since seen front line standard gauge service almost nation-wide.

However, the class was not destined to stay together for in the carve-up of locomotives following the sale of G & W's West Australian Australian Railroad Group business to QR in June 2006, saw eleven go with the sale where most became the DC-class. The restructured Genesee & Wyoming (Australia) retained 2207, 2210, 2212, 2214 and 2216.

The remaining NSW Government-owned units were also sold, 42202 and 42206 going to the Northern Rivers Railroad where both were rebuilt, passing into QR's Interail (now QR National) business from 31 May 2002. The two 'passenger units', 42203 and 42220, were sold to Chicago Freight Car Leasing (Australia) and registered as HL203 and FL220 respectively.

SPECIFICATIONS

	IMPERIAL (METRIC)
POWER UNIT:	EMD 16-645E
TRACTION HORSEPOWER:	2000 (1491 kW)
STARTING TRACTIVE EFFORT:	76 600 lb (323 kN)
CONTINUOUS TRACTIVE EFFORT:	60 927 lb (271 kN)
TOTAL WEIGHT:	108 tons (110 t)
GAUGE:	1435 mm
ROAD NUMBERS:	42201–42220

G & W Aust): 2207 (ex-42207); 2208 (42208); 2210 (42210); 2212 (42212); 2214 (42217); 2216 (42219)
(ARG): 2201 (ex 42205); 2202 (42213); 2203 (42214); 2204 (42216); 2205 (42201); 2206 (42204); 42209; 42211; 2213 (42215); 2215 (42218) and 2216 (42219)
CFCLA units: HL203 (ex 42203) and FL220 (42220)

The tenth member of the class, 42210 as running in August 1973. (Leon Oberg)

Brute strength in evidence. The collective muscle as Queensland Rail National EMDs, CLP11, CLF3, CLF1 and G534 exert some 15 800hp as they charge towards Yarra with a Brisbane to Melbourne intermodal train on 1 March 2009. Both the leading and trailing locomotives were wearing QRN's then newly-applied corporate livery. (Leon Oberg)

1970 COMMONWEALTH RAILWAYS

CL-class Co-Co

As a means of coping with projected traffic increases over the Trans-Australian line, Commonwealth Railways (later Australian National Rail Corporation) placed an order late in 1968 with the Clyde Engineering Co for five heavy 2237 kW Co-Co locomotives.

At that time work was well advanced on the East–West gauge standardisation project and the new locomotives, the most powerful then contemplated by CR, would allow for greater train handling economies over that system's portion of the route.

Built in Sydney, the class-leader emerged from the maker's plant in 16 January 1970 to run its initial load trial to Broadmeadow. Soon afterwards it began its lonely trek to Port Augusta, working via the just-completed standard gauge line through Broken Hill.

Mechanically and electrically, the CL-class was based on the WAGR L-class of 1967, but in terms of looks that package was now placed within a streamlined, trussed, pressurised car body which employed fibreglass panelling to limit the locomotive's total mass to 128.4 tonnes. The design also resurrected the famous streamlined nose/cab of the CR's popular GM-class which first appeared in 1951. It is interesting that the CL's streamlined styling was the last example of this 1930s US design built by any EMD licence holder in the world.

However, it almost did not happen, for when CR called tenders for the machines Clyde Engineering originally tendered a Do-Do locomotive with a US-style FP45 cab—which did not eventuate due to the difficulty constructing the underframe for such a lengthy locomotive.

The success of the first five locos, combined with

The stirring sight of triple-headed CLP-class locomotives CLP10, CLP9 and CLP14 at the head of a double-stack intermodal train nearing Port Augusta's Spencer Junction yard on 30 November 1997. (Leon Oberg)

better than expected traffic increases over the new line, saw the class increase to a total of 17 units, the last of which, CL17 *William McMahon*, was ceremoniously named during the October 1972 opening of the Whyalla line.

When fully commissioned, the CLs provided AN with a locomotive surplus and in October 1973 they started working the *Indian Pacific* express train beyond AN's borders. It was a move that would eventually pave the way for regular intersystem working of diesel locomotives on a grand scale. The CL-class soon found themselves running to Perth, and then in 1974 trials were held between Broken Hill and Lithgow (NSW). In March and April 1975, class-leader CL1 *John Gorton* returned to New South Wales for exhaustive haulage and fuel consumption trials between Sydney and Albury, working passenger services such as the crack overnight sleeper express, the *Southern Aurora*, and freight.

By 1993, more than 20 years after they first appeared, the CLs had become tired. Loco CL7, for example, had managed to clock up 5 482 000 kilometres. The question was whether to replace or overhaul them? By then, US locomotive rebuilding firm Morrison Knudsen had established a factory in Whyalla where they had been rebuilding locomotives for BHP, and negotiated a deal with AN to buy all 17 CLs, randomly upgrade them with improved EMD 16-645E3 engines, modern electrics/traction motors and lease them back to their former owner on a 12-year 'power by the hour' arrangement.

Since AN was planning to 'go it alone' and be solely responsible for operating the *Indian Pacific* (without operational input from State Rail and Westrail), the rail system's administration felt ten of the locomotives should be specially equipped to work that and other AN passenger trains. Accordingly, the builder came up with two locomotive classifications—seven CLF units for freight and coal service, and the other thirteen as CLPs for passenger service. The latter were equipped with higher gearing, allowing for a top service speed of 140 km/h (as against 125 km/h for the CLF). The CLPs have longer-range 11 360-litre fuel tanks and, as a means of powering train lighting, kitchens and air-conditioning, two 175 kVa head-end power Cummins/Onan diesel alternator sets in the passenger version's engine rooms. Because of this added weight, the CLP weighs 132 tonnes in fully fuelled working trim while the CLF officially tips the scales at 124.5 tonnes.

The first rebuild entered service on 29 June 1993, the last appeared in December of that year.

While CLP15 was destroyed in a multi-locomotive head-on collision at Mt Christie in February 1997, the remaining CLP/CLFs from 8 November 1997 came under the ownership of a consortium led by Genesee & Wyoming (becoming the Australian Railroad Group) and eventually found work throughout the mainland standard gauge network. When ARG sold its business to QRN-West on 1 June 2006, CLF1–4, CLF7 and CLP9–13 went to that buyer while the newly badged Genesee & Wyoming Australia retained the other six units for its domestic operations in South Australia.

The freight version (note clustered portholes) as exampled by CLF6 at Adelaide's suburban Dry Creek on 3 March 1995. (Leon Oberg)

SPECIFICATIONS
ORIGINAL CL-CLASS

	Imperial (Metric)
Power unit:	EMD 16-645E3
Traction horsepower:	3000 (2237 kW)
Starting tractive effort:	98 700 lb (439 kN)
Continuous tractive effort:	60 634 lb (270 kN)
Total weight:	126 tons (128.4 t)
Gauge:	1435 mm
Road numbers:	CL1–CL17

As rebuilt:	CLP-class	CLF-class
	Imperial (Metric)	Imperial (Metric)
Power unit:	EMD 16-645E3C	EMD 16-645E3C
Traction horsepower:	3200 (2460 kW)	3200 (2460 kW)
Starting tractive effort:	101 400 lb (434 kN)	104 000 lb (465 kN)
Continuous tractive effort:	66 850 lb (293 kN)	72 000 lb (315.6 kN
Total weight:	129.5 tons (132 t)	122 tons (124.5 t)
Gauge:	1435 mm	1435 mm
Road numbers:	CLP8–CLP17	CLF1–CLF7

1970 QUEENSLAND RAILWAYS

2100-class Co-Co

When Queensland Railways took delivery of the first of 12 heavy 2100-class locomotives from Clyde Engineering (Queensland) on 8 December 1970, few would have thought that the design would end up becoming the system's most prolific. No fewer than 209 units, of several classifications and power outputs but all sharing the basic theme, would be constructed over the following 13 years.

Their introduction ran parallel to the increasing fortunes of the Central Queensland coal mining industry, and as new mines were announced new railways and rolling stock followed, creating something of a boom for railways and their suppliers.

The first 12 were financed by the developers of the vast Goonyella open-cut coal mining consortium. Up until that time, QR's mainline diesel power had been restricted to 91.4 tonnes due to perway and bridge limitations. Because the new Goonyella line was built to a heavier standard, the 2100's permissible weight was increased to 97.5 tonnes fully laden. To allow the class to work over the 91.4-tonne sections of track, the designer shrewdly provided it with a 7273-litre fuel tank bearing two compartments. When working over lighter sections, the larger compartment could be left unfilled which, along with reduced sand capacity, made their use on such routes possible.

Locomotive 2122 rolls through Roma Street station (Brisbane) while undertaking commuter train duty on 30 July 1973. (Peter Watts)

The locomotives were also provided with two high-adhesion cast steel bogies. Their weight was transmitted to the bogies via a 3-point suspension which consisted of a centre plate carried in a socket and two rubber pack suspension units sliding on a stainless steel plate on the bogie frame. Each bogie was fitted with unidirectional mounted traction motors for minimum weight transfer.

Because the Goonyella coal line was not yet ready for use, early 2100-class deliveries were pressed into Brisbane area freight and suburban passenger service. As dynamic braking equipment had not yet arrived from the USA, the first five entered service without this feature.

They eventually entered coal service in November 1971, their immediate success leading to a follow-on order for 12 for the Peak Downs coal project. The last of these appeared in February 1973.

While the second order was being built, Clyde, and its American principals EMD, continued to refine their product. When tenders were called early in 1972 for eight main line locomotives for use over the $30 million Greenvale nickel line, Clyde offered the basic 2100-class type, but this time fitted with an AC alternator instead of the usual DC generator. Financed by the project's developers, these units became the 2200-class, delivered between May and December 1973 and normally confined to the 228.5 km Yabulu to Greenvale line. These eight locomotives were renumbered into the 2141–2148 series between May and October 1982 to make their original number series available for newer locomotives.

Meanwhile, another mining consortium had been developing an open-cut coal mine at Saraji, and between July 1974 and March 1975 financed the purchase of 11 additional AC alternator-equipped locomotives, which were to become the 2130-class. Of these, 2135–2140 were equipped with Locotrol command equipment. Locotrol, tested initially

Twin 2170s, locos 2185 and 2183, dropping down Black Mountain (above Yukon) with a coast-bound grain train on 18 March 1997. (Leon Oberg)

on unit 2111, was a means of operating a block of locomotives by remote control from the cab of the leading locomotive. With this facility, loads exceeding 10 000 tonnes, worked by three locomotives in the lead, and another three in the middle of the train, soon became regular—all of this on a 1067 mm gauge line.

The 2130-class also introduced a more flattened roofline to ensure adequate radio aerial clearance.

Mines continued to develop, and in connection with the big Norwich Park project, tenders closed on 5 July 1977 for 14 units. Again, Clyde won the day with its relatively trouble-free design and between December 1978 and August 1979 delivered the locomotives, further modified with the fitting of a Dash-2 modular control system for easier troubleshooting. In addition, since provision was being made to eventually air-condition the units, the normal nose and body mounted sandboxes were moved to the bogies. These locomotives became the 2150-class, the last three being provided with Locotrol command equipment and air-conditioning.

Continuing to further refine and improve the

locomotive type, Clyde's final model in the series became the improved GL26C-2, known to QR as the 2170-class. This type appeared on 3 March 1982 and was equipped with modified traction alternators and nose-mounted air-conditioning along with Clyde's 'clean-cab' feature, which minimised sharp edges within the cab for greater crew safety.

The first eleven were ordered for the German Creek coal project and the final orders, totalling 34, were received soon afterwards for the Oaky Creek, Riverside and Blair Athol coal projects. Twelve were equipped for Locotrol and were delivered by the end of February 1984, powered by EMD's strong 16-645E 1491 kW engine.

Electrification of much of the coalfields since then saw hosts of these locomotives issued to general traffic from the late 1980s, the last diesel-powered Locotrol operations taking place in 1989.

Driven by the urge to introduce driver-only locomotive operations, QR progressively lowered the noses of most to offer maximum forward visibility, and removed their second driving stations. In addition, all locomotives in this family, except for 2135–2140, 2150–2163 and 2202–2210, were lightened to 93 tonnes (which included a reduction in fuel capacity), just prior to driver-only modifications.

First casualty was 2175, scrapped following a multi-unit head-on collision at Mitakoodi on the Mt Isa line on 25 August 1989. No. 2187 was destroyed in a level crossing accident near Bowen in 1994. All others survived through the 1990s, but with conversions and extensive alterations well underway.

With the arrival of QR's AC4000-class EMD locomotives from October 1999, a number of the prolific 2100-class became surplus to requirements. On 19 September 2001, ten locomotives were shipped out to new owner Ferrocarril de Antofagasta

A member of the more refined 2170-class, 2198, after it received a modified driver-only cab/lowered nose job, pictured at Redbank workshops on 21 July 1991 upon release. (Leon Oberg)

a Bolivia in Chile, for service over its 948 km metre-gauge freight network based in Antofagasta. The $3.2 million deal saw QR mechanically and electrically repair the units, undercoat them and re-gauge their bogies. They had travelled between 2.4 and 2.8 million kilometres in their QR careers.

By 2004, it was clear Queensland coal mining outputs would continue to escalate. With rival freight companies clearly keen to acquire some of that business, QR formulated a plan to improve some of the most worn units from this hard-working family of locomotives to move that cargo. With 2142 (originally 2201) acting as the template, work got underway at QR's Redbank workshops in April 2004. The original 16-cylinder power plant was replaced by a turbocharged 12-cylinder version matched to an upgraded electrical system and higher rated traction motors with ZTR wheelslip control. Out-shopped as the 2250-class, the new locomotives are being equipped with a 'maxi cab' similar to those used in the upgrade of sixty of QR's 1550-type locomotives of 1972 into 2300-class.

Now tipping the scales at 110 tonnes, the first unit was released in January 2005, with at least 24 to be remanufactured. The remaining members of the 1119kW 1550-class are also being rebuilt to 2250-class specifications.

SPECIFICATIONS

	ORIGINAL IMPERIAL (METRIC)	AS REBUILT IMPERIAL (METRIC)
POWER UNIT:	EMD 16-645E	EMD 12-645E3C
TRACTION HORSEPOWER:	2000 (1492 kW)	2250 (1679 kW)
STARTING TRACTIVE EFFORT:	64 500 LB (287 kN)	70 589 LB (314 kN)
CONTINUOUS TRACTIVE EFFORT:	50 820 LB (226 kN)	58 450 LB (260 kN)
TOTAL WEIGHT:	96 TONS (97.5 T)	108.3 TONS (110.0 T)
GAUGE:	1067 MM	1067 MM
ROAD NUMBERS:	2100-CLASS: 2100–2123	2250-CLASS: 2251–2274
	2130-CLASS: 2130–2140	
	2150-CLASS: 2150–2163	
	2170-CLASS: 2170–2214	
	2200-CLASS: 2200–2207 (BECAME 2141–2148 FROM MAY 1982)	

1971 WESTERN AUSTRALIAN GOVERNMENT RAILWAYS

D-class Co-Co

When introduced to the WAGR system in February 1971, the D-class was the heaviest narrow gauge diesel locomotive in Australia.

Built by the Clyde Engineering Co in Sydney, the five units were ordered for the Jarrahdale–Kwinana bauxite traffic and in that service soon proved their worth. When in pairs, loads of up to 5710 tonnes were being hauled.

It is interesting to note that while the class was on the drawing board, developers of Queensland's vast Goonyella coal deposits had ordered ten units of similar power from Clyde, and the two types employed certain basic similarities of design, including power equipment. However, while the Queensland locomotives (which became the 2100-class) were built to certain weight limitations, including the

A survivor: D1562 had just been overhauled when pictured working at Forrestfield yard on 7 December 2001. (Leon Oberg)

The DA version: DA1571 working a South Bunbury-bound stone container train through Midland on 29 July 2004. (Peter Clark)

provision of lightweight specially-formulated high-yield steel underframes, the WAGR D-class was constructed on strengthened mild steel underframes. A more generous loading gauge allowed the hoods and cabs of the WAGR locos to be made roomier.

The D-class, with road numbers 1561–1565, was just as successful in Western Australia as the 2100-class in Queensland, and an order for another seven units soon followed. These new locomotives did not have dynamic brakes and were 12 tonnes lighter—they became the DA-class, road numbers 1571–1577, and were initially employed on the northern line to Geraldton. Loco 1577 had the distinction of being the last locomotive built in Clyde's Granville (Sydney) plant.

Westrail continued its association with this basic locomotive type by ordering, in two contracts, a further development of the model, with 13 delivered from March 1982 as the DB-class (see separate entry). These new units boasted full-width noses and rear-entry vestibules.

Prior to the arrival of narrow-gauge S-class EMD locomotives in 1998, the Ds could generally be found working ALCOA alumina, caustic and bauxite trains over the South-Western line. The DAs were based at Narngulu and Forrestfield and generally hauled wheat trains over the former Midland Railway route. But the S-class rendered the DAs surplus, and the first to go was D1563, shipped out to the metre-gauge Ferrocarril de Antofagasta a Bolivia in Chile in September 1998 to become their No. 2000.

This sale was followed by that of D1564

Formerly Westrail's D1565, Tasrail's 2020 was pictured at Railton on 31 December 2001, showing clearly its ATN-inspired cab/nose modifications carried out in New Zealand in 2000. The styling followed modifications to at least two of that country's DX-class GE locomotives. (Chris Walters)

(engineless) and D1565 to Tranz Rail, New Zealand, for reactivation in 2000 with modern design enhancements, including low-profile noses ahead of an updated, re-designed cab and traction control technology. Both were forwarded to the company-owned Tasrail (Tasmania) operation, where they entered service in August 2001 as 2021 and 2020 respectively, following the fitting of spare ZB-class English Electric-type EE548 traction motors. They were the largest and heaviest diesels seen in the state to that point and soon found work hauling the Burnie-Boyer-Burnie paper trains.

In Western Australia, D1561 and D1562 survived to pass into the ownership of the Australian Railroad Group on 2 December 2000, along with all DAs which, as they were being overhauled/upgraded, were progressively being renumbered into the 1900-class series. QRN-West acquired ARG's above-rail business from 1 June 2006 and all its locomotives except for DA1577 (renumbered 1907), which was sent to South Australia for a re-badged Genesee & Wyoming Australia.

SPECIFICATIONS

	IMPERIAL (METRIC)
POWER UNIT:	EMD 16-645E
TRACTION HORSEPOWER:	2000 (1491 kW)
STARTING TRACTIVE EFFORT:	72 500 LB (322 kN)
CONTINUOUS TRACTIVE EFFORT:	60 500 LB (269 kN)
TOTAL WEIGHT:	D-CLASS 111 TONS (109.5 T)
	DA-CLASS 97.6 TONS (96.1 T)
GAUGE:	1067 MM
ROAD NUMBERS:	D1561–1565
	DA1571–1577

D35-type Bo-Bo

The last vestiges of steam working within the AI&S plant at Port Kembla disappeared following the arrival of the eleven heavy-duty main line Bo-Bos in this class.

Commissioned in several batches between 5 November 1971 and 22 August 1975, their arrival, coupled with the introduction of air-tippling of slag vehicles, made it possible to shuffle locomotive rosters and come up with an all-diesel system. By that time, the plant was handling some 27.6 million tonnes of raw materials and finished product a year, a huge task for a private railway system of this type and a testament to the original design of the works site.

As with all earlier diesel locomotive types acquired by AI&S, these units were built by English Electric and came from its Rocklea (Brisbane) plant. Although in many respects their design followed the company's popular standard-purpose medium-powered Bo-Bo locomotives, they were equipped with EE's advanced 6-cylinder model CSRKT diesel engine instead of the earlier 8-cylinder SRKT type. They rode on advanced heavy-duty bogies that offered improved equalisation of the locomotive weight.

Despite having only six cylinders, the new units produced 692 kW instead of the 589 kW of the older units. In addition, they carried a cab and 'square-rigged' hood design personally prepared by then works traffic superintendent Mr J. Masters.

The new units were immediately pressed into some of the plant's heaviest internal service, including the haulage of coke and sinter trains. They also became the standard motive power over the Nebo and

Locomotive D41, wearing a revised AI&S livery, stands outside the merchant mill on 21 October 1986. (Leon Oberg)

Kemira colliery railways. For this service, all except locos 41, 42 and 43 were delivered with dynamic braking. Since those three were originally intended for steel mill traffic, it was decided they would not need this equipment, but provision was made for its installation (including the piping, connections and gauges) should the need arise.

A gradual downturn in steel production throughout the latter part of the 1970s produced something of a locomotive surplus at AI&S, and six of these new locomotives were leased to the NSW Public Transport Commission. While in government service they remained captive to the Illawarra line and generally worked ballast trains out of Bombo and Shellharbour quarries, coal trains from Bulli and some shunting services. Occasionally units would wander into Sydney on slow goods services and appear in Delec depot for 'bed and breakfast'.

The units were gradually returned to AI&S with two, D41 and D43, remaining in government service until 15 October 1982. All remained in traffic until a fatal head-on collision outside Central Loop (on the Kemira line) claimed D35 and D37 on 13 November 1993. Most remaining members have undergone refurbishment this decade, passing into the ownership of Pacific National which acquired all rail transport tasks for the company which since November 2003 has traded as Bluescope Steel.

SPECIFICATIONS

	Imperial (Metric)
Power unit:	English Electric 6CSRKT
Traction horsepower:	928 (692 kW)
Starting tractive effort:	59 000 lb (262 kN)
Continuous tractive effort:	40 000 lb (178 kN)
Total weight:	88 tons (90 t)
Gauge:	1435 mm
Road numbers:	D35–D45

1971 New South Wales Government Railways

442-class Co-Co

These units were the first 'second-generation' diesel-electrics in Australia and initially were planned as replacements for NSWGR's 20-strong 40-class A1A-A1As of 1951 vintage.

Because the 40s could not be economically rebuilt to suit modern conditions, the NSWGR awarded a contract to A.E. Goodwin Ltd for 20 large Co-Co units, with the stipulation that the 40-class be accepted as trade-ins. As a result, a limited number of 40-class parts were utilised in the construction of the new units.

While these were under construction, a further contract for 20 was placed with Goodwin, which allowed the whole main line system to be dieselised.

Although the class-leader was officially handed over at a builder's ceremony on 21 October 1970, the railway administration refused to accept delivery after rough riding traits were alleged during trials. A further five months passed before it was accepted, by which time an improved bogie had been fitted.

As deliveries continued, Goodwin Ltd collapsed as a locomotive builder, and production ceased for a period as rival firm Commonwealth Engineering finalised the details of taking over Alco's Australian franchise. Comeng technically completed the units from 44235 onwards. The Comeng units differed in that they were equipped with Mitsubishi AC alternators in lieu of the earlier DC generators. All 40 were running all main lines by 9 October 1973.

Two decades later, following NSWGR's block purchase in 1994 of new 82 and 90-class EMD locomotives, the days of the 442s were numbered. Nineteen were auctioned in December 1994.

Silverton Rail managed to acquire locos 44220, 44217, 44203 and 44202, and with the standardisation of the Adelaide–Melbourne line the four (now numbered 442s1–442s4 respectively) soon found heavy work with the National Rail Corporation, being leased for a year (from late 1995) to cover shortages while the rail operator was awaiting new locomotive power.

Austrac at Junee bought 44229 and 44233, equipped them with revised silencers and other upgraded features for extended lease to BHP Steel Port Kembla, principally for coal haulage. They remained there until June 2001.

Morrison Knudsen Australia obtained 12 and towed them to the company's Whyalla plant where, in February 1995, staff started stripping them for a planned rebuild. The first to undergo rebuild was 44227. With its frame extended 1.5 metres and an EMD 16-645F diesel engine partly fitted, this work well advanced, and most other units stripped, the Morrison Knudsen Corporation in the USA suffered trading problems and all work had ceased by mid-1995.

CFCLA-branded unit, 44208 in Goulburn yard on 31 March, 2004. (Leon Oberg)

Former Silverton 442s1 (ex-NSWGR 44220) in Coote Industrial livery at Tarago on 6 October 2009. (Leon Oberg)

Locomotive 700, carrying original SAR markings and pictured with vintage EE 905, at Mile End on 29 October 1978. (Peter Watts)

Two of the MK locomotives not stripped, 44223 and 44226, were sold to Silverton Rail during mid-1995 and forwarded to AN's Port Augusta Workshops for restoration to traffic as 442s-class. Initially trialled in that area late in 1997, they were delivered in May 1998 and, along with Silverton Rail's earlier four, found work in New South Wales. Two even found their way into BHP Steel Port Kembla's Wongawilli coal working from November 2000 to June 2001.

Silverton Rail acquired another two 442-class at auction on 22 January 1998 when it snapped up alternator units 44235 and 44237 for their parts; the remains were scrapped at Chullora workshops.

Of the remaining NSWSRA (FreightCorp) locomotives, some soldiered on in transfer goods service, the final two in government service, 44211 and 44212, being retired on 22 March 1998. No. 44211 was then deemed a heritage exhibit and placed in the hands of the NSWRTM as an operational locomotive.

But with the pending sale of FreightCorp, a major clean-up of surplus locomotive power saw fourteen 442-class sold to Victorian-based Great Northern Rail Services, all being delivered in June 2001. The first re-entered service following a contract overhaul as JL406 (formerly 44232) on 16 October 2001. But this and the return to traffic of several sisters was only a short-term measure, for about this time Chicago Freight Car Leasing Australia, which financed those locomotives' purchase, acquired 12 surplus General Electric C30-7A locomotives in the USA. Their overhauled diesel engines, alternators, exciters, auxiliary generators, traction motors, air-compressors and eddy current clutches were forwarded to Australia for a major 442-class rebuild programme. The first of CFCLA's planned twelve 132-tonne rebuilds appeared from United Goninan & Co's Broadmeadow (Newcastle) shops in January 2003 as the GL-class, boosted to 2240kW units and carrying road number GL101 of the class's allocated numbers GL101–GL112 (see page 432).

700-class

The SAR, which in 1971 had three 930-class World-Series Alco units on order from A.E. Goodwin Ltd, altered the contract and acquired copies of the 442-class (model DL500G) instead. These locomotives were delivered between June and September 1971 as the 700-class and placed on the broad gauge system based at Mile End depot. From here, their prime service was over the Adelaide–Serviceton route.

While these early 700s were being built, an additional contract for three units was awarded to cope with growing traffic over the new Broken Hill–Port Pirie standard gauge route. Two arrived in December 1971 and all were operating by March 1972.

The 700-class was fitted with normal generator plants but, as a means of reducing internal wear, the first three were delivered with steel-capped pistons.

The formation of Australian National Railways in 1978 and its subsequent takeover of all non-metropolitan railways in South Australia included the acquisition of the 700-class. All 700s were gradually transferred onto the standard gauge and based at Peterborough depot for *Indian Pacific* express and interstate goods haulage. Their electrical performance was improved under AN ownership with the acquisition of spare Alco C628 generators from Hamersley Iron.

Still under AN ownership, all were eventually phased into broad gauge running over the Adelaide–Melbourne corridor in the 1980s, where they remained until the new National Rail Corporation completed a new standard gauge link between those cities in 1995.

Loco 702, badly damaged in a fire on 26 September 1994, was stored for a time at Islington Workshops. With the NSWSRA selling off much of its fleet later that year, AN secured 44221, thinking it might blend this and the fire-damaged 702 into one operational unit. The project never eventuated and both were scrapped at Port Adelaide during the spring of 1997.

Five 700-class remain in traffic today under the ownership of Genesee & Wyoming Australia, based in Adelaide, where they work everything from Penrice broad gauge limestone trains to standard gauge grain hauls.

SPECIFICATIONS

	IMPERIAL (METRIC)
POWER UNIT:	Alco 251C
TRACTION HORSEPOWER:	2000 (1491 kW)
STARTING TRACTIVE EFFORT:	75 900 lb (338 kN)
CONTINUOUS TRACTIVE EFFORT:	52 000 lb (231 kN)
TOTAL WEIGHT:	113 tons (115 t)
GAUGE:	(NSW) 1435 mm
	(AN) 1435 and 1600 mm
ROAD NUMBERS:	NSWGR: 44201–44240
	SAR/AN: 700–705 (705 became 706), 44221 (acquired December 1994).

1971 Commonwealth Railways

NJ-class Co-Co

Due to the age and condition of diesel-electric locomotives working over the Central Australia Railway's very trying 1067 mm gauge Marree–Alice Springs route, CR administration turned to General Motors equipment when ordering six light replacement locomotives, late in 1969.

Until then, Sulzer-powered locomotives had been serving CR on the dieselised CAR and NAR routes, but the change to GM equipment was brought about through long experience with the reliability of similar power in main line service on the arid Trans-Australian Railway.

Built by the Clyde Engineering Co of Sydney, many of the locomotive's components were manufactured in that maker's new Bathurst plant. The class-leader NJ1 was named, rather appropriately, after former Australian Prime Minister Ben Chifley, who had been a locomotive driver at Bathurst before entering Federal Parliament.

Delivered between May and October 1971, the class served its masters very well indeed. Driver John Cornish once recalled to this author how crews would 'fight over getting an NJ because there was more room in the cab and engine room, the units were more reliable and comfortable'.

The locomotives' suspension was flexible enough to rock and roll over the poorly laid, narrow gauge Alice Springs (*Ghan*) route until a new standard gauge line was commissioned on 9 October 1980, linking Alice Springs with the Trans-Australian Railway at Tarcoola.

The new route rendered the NJ locomotives surplus but, because of their short, lightweight construction, it was not ideal to convert them to standard gauge despite their having been designed for this in principle. Since CR had become Australian National Railways in 1978, absorbing the railways of South Australia and Tasmania, all six NJs were transferred to the isolated Port Lincoln Division from January and October 1981. This move released Alco 830-class locomotives for transfer to Tasmania, where the decision had been made to use air-braked rolling stock.

Several teething problems arose with the NJs at Port Lincoln. Up until then the units had been ambling slowly along the old CAR line. When they began working over the excellently-maintained faster tracks of the Port Lincoln Division, all started to suffer from continuing ground relays (electrical shorts) once they attempted to change transition. Maintenance staff at Port Lincoln finally brought the problem under control and after that, except for the occasional level crossing accident resulting in fires and/or rollovers, the units were found to be equal to the task of working grain and gypsum traffic.

All NJs passed into the hands of the US-owned Genesee & Wyoming on 8 November 1997. Some were not destined to end their days on the Eyre Peninsula, however, for beginning February 2003,

NJ4, now renumbered 1604, and wearing the modifications of its current owner, pushing grain wagons toward Port Lincoln wharf on 21 July 2004. (Peter Clark)

NJ2 and NJ5 were forwarded to Western Australia for use on woodchip and caustic soda trains. Today they carry the numbers NJ1602 and NJ1605, and became the property of QR National-West in June 2006 on its purchase of ARG. The remainder (now renumbered 1601, 1603, 1604 and 1606) stayed with Genesee & Wyoming Australia for continued SA intrastate operations.

SPECIFICATIONS

IMPERIAL (METRIC)	
POWER UNIT:	EMD 12-645E
TRACTION HORSEPOWER:	1500 (1119 KW)
STARTING TRACTIVE EFFORT:	39 000 LB (173 KN)
CONTINUOUS TRACTIVE EFFORT:	35 664 LB (159 KN)
TOTAL WEIGHT:	65.7 TONS (67 T)
GAUGE:	1067 MM
ROAD NUMBERS:	(ORIGINAL) NJ1—NJ6 (THOSE REMAINING WITH G&WA) 1601, 1603, 1604, 1606

The Comsteel Bo locomotive pictured working at the Newcastle suburban plant on 1 May 2001, soon after receiving a facelift, at which time it also underwent a small nose profile change in a bid to eliminate radiator

1972 COMMONWEALTH STEEL CO

Goninan Bo

The Waratah (Newcastle) works of the Commonwealth Steel Co, which in 1972 operated a BHP subsidiary, was once a haven for small industrial locomotives. Until the arrival of Comsteel's first diesel-electric on 3 July 1972, these works had been using a selection of 0-4-0T steam locomotives.

Comsteel, which manufactures high-grade engineering and alloy steels including railway wheels and stainless steel plate for carriages, has been operating from the present plant for some seven decades. Allied to its business, the company until recently operated a sinuous labyrinth of standard gauge railway within its plant, linking up with the NSWSRA's network just north of Waratah station.

Weighing just 32.5 tonnes and built in Newcastle by A. Goninan & Co, the company's new diesel-electric locomotive was designed in association with BHP and closely followed the parent company's successful twin-engined centre-cab Bo-Bo units which first appeared from Goninan's plant in 1960.

In effect, the Comsteel unit was a full-width end-cab single-engined example of the BHP locomotives powered with a 201 kW supercharged 6-cylinder Cummins diesel engine. This was coupled to a General Electric-type GT558 generator. Although

of rigid frame, each axle was provided with a GE763 traction motor.

Originally appearing in a silvery blue colour scheme with white visibility stripes, the little locomotive received a complete facelift early in 1981, at which time it was out-shopped in BHP's new safety yellow.

The locomotive received another facelift in 2001 along with a small profile change. In a bid to eliminate radiator damage from airborne metal fibres, its conventional angled-back front radiator grille was covered with a vertical steel plate, fitted to allow space beneath the headlight for forced downdraft cooling.

The high cost of railway maintenance, including the need to re-lay much of the internal trackwork, eventually saw the plant's owner (since 1999), Smorgon Steel, close the system completely on 30 June 2002. The locomotive was returned to its manufacturer for an overhaul and in August 2003 delivered to the company's tube mills plant at Acacia Ridge (Brisbane) for internal shunting service, replacing a veteran US-built Plymouth diesel unit.

SPECIFICATIONS

IMPERIAL (METRIC)	
POWER UNIT:	CUMMINS NS743-B
TRACTION HORSEPOWER:	250 (186 KW)
STARTING TRACTIVE EFFORT:	22 000 LB (98 KN)
CONTINUOUS TRACTIVE EFFORT:	11 500 LB (51 KN)
TOTAL WEIGHT:	31.2 TONS (32.5 T)
GAUGE:	1435 MM

47-class Co-Co

The dawning of the 1970s saw the last remaining pocket of main line steam power operating in the Newcastle region of the NSWGR. Maintained there to work the area's coal traffic, the locomotives were starting to become a real thorn in the side of the administration, which was obliged to provide facilities for both steam and diesel traction.

Finally, to complete the dieselisation of its system, NSWGR signed a contract with Newcastle builder A. Goninan & Co in August 1971 for 20 medium-powered Co-Co diesel-electric units. To be introduced as the 47-class, the first locomotive was out-shopped just 12 months afterwards. All were running by May 1973.

Of hood configuration, the new locomotives were powered with a Caterpillar D399TA diesel engine which provided 746 kW for traction purposes. The general design work was done by the Japanese firm Hitachi, which also provided the electrical equipment.

Although intended for the Newcastle area, all were initially allocated to Bathurst depot for Western Main line and branch working. This move released older 48-class Alco units for coal line traffic. But teething troubles began to plague the new 47-class, particularly in respect to overheating, and for a time the class spent more time out of traffic than in. No. 4709 was withdrawn from service after just 16 months in stop-go service, following an electrical fire 12 kilometres west of Bathurst.

Sister unit 4710 was withdrawn in March 1977 after running into the rear of a train in the Parkes–Bogan Gate section. Both units were towed to Cardiff Workshops where their useable parts were removed and the remains scrapped—4709 on 2 May 1977 and 4710 on 15 July 1977.

The remaining units battled on but, partly due to their high maintenance needs, all were transferred (some towed) to Broadmeadow depot in January 1981 for coal traffic. Here they could be close to Cardiff Workshops. Following this move, all tended to operate exceedingly well and were pooled with that depot's 48-class.

During seasonal traffic downturns, the 47-class was usually the first to be withdrawn, only to be fired up again as conditions improved. But the steady upgrade of the coal lines to carry heavier locomotives and trains saw the need for the class disappear completely; the last two in service, 4705 and 4706, were finally withdrawn at Broadmeadow on 31 December 1990. In September 1989, loco 4719 had been converted into a test vehicle because of the class's super-strong underframe. This unit was totally gutted and equipped with dynamometer test equipment. A second cab, from 4715, was added at the rear end and the creation (numbered HTV2000) was for a time used throughout the state in locomotive performance testing.

While half the fleet was scrapped, enthusiast bodies did manage to acquire some. They include 4701, 4702, 4703, 4707, 4708 and 4716, some of which are commercially operational and technically based at the Lachlan Valley Railway, Cowra. HTV2000 is also there as a limited source of spare parts. In addition, commercial operator Independent Railways of Australia own and operate 4717.

Loco 4705 has been retained for static exhibition at Werris Creek while 4706 is housed at the Dorrigo Steam Railway and Museum.

One of the first of the class withdrawn, after just five years' service, was 4710, pictured at Bathurst on 7 February 1975. (Leon Oberg)

Loco 4705 has been retained for static exhibition at Werris Creek while 4706 is housed at the Dorrigo Steam Railway and Museum.

SPECIFICATIONS

	IMPERIAL (METRIC)
POWER UNIT:	CATERPILLAR D399TA
TRACTION HORSEPOWER:	1000 (746 kW)
STARTING TRACTIVE EFFORT:	53 800 lb (239 kN)
CONTINUOUS TRACTIVE EFFORT:	36 640 lb (163 kN)
TOTAL WEIGHT:	80 TONS (82 T)
GAUGE:	1435 MM
ROAD NUMBERS:	4701–4720

1972 E.M. BALDWIN & SONS

Bogie canefields locomotives B-B

Entry to the sugarcane and underground mining locomotive field by the Castle Hill (Sydney) firm of E.M. Baldwin & Sons was more by accident than design. Basically it came about through the persistence of an engineering staff member who was a longstanding railway enthusiast. And it was that man's creative thinking which eventually led to Baldwin's most successful product, the bogie cane locomotive.

Baldwin came into the cane and industrial locomotive scene rather late. Initially, the firm did not want to compete with well-established local manufacturers such as Clyde and Comeng. Rather, Baldwin accepted rebuilds of elderly products, including Tully Sugar Mill's 1937 Fowler diesel No. 8, and two 0-6-0 Ruston & Hornsby units last used in the Snowy Mountains Hydro-Electric scheme.

Mossman Sugar Mill's *Daintree* is typical of E.M. Baldwin's bogie cane locomotive type, pictured at Cassowary in far northern Queensland on 16 September 2002. (Chris Walters)

These were rebuilt for Gin Gin and Plane Creek sugar mills respectively.

The first Baldwin rebuilds were carried out in 1963; the product was well presented and offered excellent power for weight. Soon, Moreton Central Sugar Mill at Nambour sought a new 0-6-0 diesel-hydraulic. It entered service during July 1965, just in time for a new season start-up, named *Bli Bli*.

After thirteen 0-6-0s and twelve 0-4-0s had been built new or rebuilt, few of them alike, either in power plant or weight, Baldwin unveiled its revolutionary 8-wheel bogie cane locomotive designed for 610 mm gauge. Delivered in July 1972 to Kalamia Mill at Ayr, it was tested in association with the Sugar Research Institute. Named *Kilrie*, the unit immediately proved its worth—with increased power output, easier ride and faster operation. Today it works at nearby Inkerman Mill as *Iona*, a name previously applied to a now derelict Clyde 0-6-0DH.

By 1976, a total of 45 bogie locomotives had been delivered to cane tramways and for many years Baldwin's order book was seldom empty. The day of the rigid wheelbase cane locomotive had vanished with this model, and no rigid wheelbase deliveries have been made by any manufacturer since.

As with the early 0-6-0 and 0-4-0 Baldwin units, the bogie products varied according to the customer's needs, ranging from the 16-tonne 112 kW Moreton Central Mill's B-B *Coolum* to Farleigh Sugar Mill's 34-tonne 354 kW *Hampden* and *Foulden* of 1976 and 1977 respectively.

Because of the design variations, it is pointless to provide any further specifications, except to say that Caterpillar, General Motors and Ford V8 engines were among those mostly employed in Baldwin-built locomotives.

E.M. Baldwin & Sons also delivered numerous brakevans to the sugar industry based on locomotive chassis.

1972 QUEENSLAND RAILWAYS

1550-class Co-Co

The development of this family of 107 locomotives was directly paralleled by QR's larger and heavier 2100-class, which first appeared in December 1970.

Introduced as the 1550-class on 29 September

Representing the class's 'as-built' configuration, 2498 awaits duty in Mayne (Brisbane) passenger yard on 14 July 1991. (Leon Oberg)

Several state-owned railways and a private company observed Australia's bicentenary in 1988 by painting locomotives in special livery. One of the QR's candidates was 2401, pictured after receiving a chopped nose for driver-only operation, at Mayne (Brisbane) locomotive depot on 21 July 1991. Today it runs as 2331 following its maxi-overhaul earlier this decade. (Leon Oberg)

1972, and coming from Clyde Engineering's Eagle Farm (Brisbane) stable, this was a lighter, lower-powered version of the 2100-class and design-wise boasted similar cab, nose and styling but had an underframe modified at the centre to accommodate the different size engine and generator package.

Instead of being powered with EMD's 16-cylinder 645E diesel engine of 1492 kW capacity, the 1550-class appeared with the 12-cylinder 645E engine of 1119 kW traction. And unlike the 2100s, which tipped the scales at 97.54 tonnes, the 1550-class was restricted to QR's normal 91.4 tonnes to meet main line axle load limitations. The class's fuel tank, at 6364 litres capacity, was reduced in size from the 2100 class's 7273 litres.

Initially purchased for general traffic, 16 had been pressed into service by 28 April 1976, the last of which, 1565, was named *Alva G. Lee* in honour of a retiring QR Commissioner.

A further 11 units followed, financed by the Queensland Phosphate mining group. The last of the order, 1576, was equipped a year after delivery with

2470-class member 2497, with its chopped nose, prepares to depart Rockhampton on the evening of 19 March 1997. (Leon Oberg)

Maxi conversions 2310 (formerly class-leader 1550), with a goods train, and 2356 (ex-2451) on the *Inlander* at Charleville in January 2004. (Lyn Terrey)

a Clyde Kysor cab air-conditioning unit, becoming the first air-conditioned main line locomotive on an Australian government railway.

Continuing modernisation of the QR system, allied with steadily increasing traffic, saw the government place more orders for this basic design. Since its initial release, Clyde had been refining the model, including the incorporation of the modular Dash-2 control system into its electrical cabinet. Appearing from April 1977, this new version was originally to be numbered onwards from the last 1550-class (i.e. from 1577), but since the order had been increased several times while the locomotives

were under construction, its number series would have required the complete renumbering of earlier EE 1600-class branchliners. Being fitted with Dash-2 modules, the excuse presented itself to place the locomotives into a new group, and thus the 2400-class was born. By September 1978, no fewer than 24 had been built.

Clyde and EMD continued to refine the popular, relatively trouble-free type and later won a tender to supply 18 similarly styled locomotives for the Gregory coal project. These locomotives were further improved with the substitution of aluminium cabinet doors as a weight-saving measure. They were air-conditioned and came complete with windscreen washers, but with only one cab control stand, and became the 2450-class, delivered between May 1979 and June 1980. To enable larger trains to be more economically handled, eight came equipped with Locotrol command equipment.

Continued ordering by QR for coal projects since then has seen a total of 37 further improved units of the 2470-class acquired, in several contracts. Appearing from December 1980, these locomotives were gradually pressed into heavy coal hauls, including the feeding of Gladstone powerhouse. The final 11 were built for the Curragh project, the last appearing early in 1983.

Modifications to the 2470-class included the provision of a lighter AR6 alternator in lieu of the earlier AR10 type, and to increase crew safety all sharp edges inside their cabs were removed. As a further weight-saving measure, locos 2496 onwards were delivered without buffers and transition devices.

Although the 1550 and 2400 class units were designated 'general traffic', many saw use in Blackwater coal service in the early 1980s, working with their 2450 and 2470 class cousins. This occurred due to the retirement of increasingly unreliable English Electric units in an effort to improve tonnage flows.

As with the heavier 2100-class family, these locomotives also passed through Redbank and Rockhampton workshops for conversion to driver-only units in the late 1980s and early 1990s. However, 2410 to 2415 were retained initially in conventional form for Brisbane suburban passenger working.

Another conversion of note was unveiled on 3 November 1997, involving 1564. Its complete rebuild involved the fitting of a turbo-charger to the existing engine, upgraded radiators and traction motor blowers, the provision of a larger cab and other refinements as part of a maxi-overhaul programme. This project was designed to provide a more powerful (1679 kW) locomotive with improved crew comfort at less capital cost than a new locomotive. Nineteen 1550, eighteen 2400, seventeen 2450 and six 2470-class locomotives were eventually rebuilt and reclassified as the 2300-class, the last unit, 2389 (previously 2503) being out-shopped on 28 August 2002.

In addition to all these locomotives, Clyde delivered a one-off order to the Townsville Harbour Board on 14 December 1981. Numbered ST5 and painted in distinctive green and yellow, the unit spent a month under trial in the Brisbane area, identified with the temporary number 2499, before taking up duty at Townsville bulk sugar terminal during mid-January 1982. Fitted with a modular control system, it was similar to QR 2470-class units, except that no dynamic brake was fitted.

On 24 October 1988 this unit was absorbed into the QR fleet and numbered at the end of the 2470-class, becoming 2507. It was renumbered 2501 in October 2002 after the original 2501 had been converted under the abovementioned maxi-overhaul programme. At that time, it was also equipped with dynamic brakes.

Two original units, 1567 and 2467, have been scrapped following a head-on collision at Mitakoodi on the Mt Isa line on 25 August 1989 which also involved 1492 kW look-alike unit 2175. Loco 1562 was cut up after its involvement in a level crossing accident at Garbutt in Townsville on 1 December 1995.

The success of the maxi-overhaul rebuilding programme led to the remaining 1119 kW 1550-class units being slated for conversion to 1679 kW 2250-class locomotives—a project that has already started with the remanufacturing in QR's Redbank Workshops of several 2130/2140-class locomotives using EMD 12-645 turbocharged engines (see page 362). At the time of going to press, the 1550-class is set to follow the 2450-class into extinction, while six 2400-class and thirty-two 2470-class remain in service for QR's medium power requirements.

SPECIFICATIONS

	ORIGINAL	AS REBUILT
	IMPERIAL (METRIC)	IMPERIAL (METRIC)
POWER UNIT:	EMD 12-645E	EMD 12-645E3C
TRACTION HORSEPOWER:	1500 (1119 KW)	2250 (1679 KW)
STARTING TRACTIVE EFFORT:	60 500 LB (269 KN)	58 000 LB (258 KN)
CONTINUOUS TRACTIVE EFFORT:	50 820 LB (226 KN)	47 884 LB (213 KN)
TOTAL WEIGHT:	90 TONS (91.4 T)	93 TONS (94.5 T)
GAUGE:	1067 MM	1067 MM
ROAD NUMBERS:	1550-CLASS: 1550–1576 2320–2323,	2300-CLASS: 2301–2315,
	2400-CLASS: 2400–2423 2330–2339, 2346–2353, 2355–2366,	
	2450-CLASS: 2450–2467 2370–2374, 2387–2392	
	2470-CLASS: 2470–2507	
	TOWNSVILLE UNIT: ST5 (BECAME QR 2507 IN OCTOBER 1988 AND 2501D IN OCTOBER 2002)	

Z-class Co-Co

The advent of the export woodchip industry in Tasmania marked something of a watershed for the TGR. With much of the projected log input to be conveyed by rail, the TGR found itself building its first new branch line, from Launceston to Longreach and Bell Bay, in many years.

With train sizes projected to more than double, a programme of constructing new wagons and acquiring new locomotives began. Traditionally a user of English Electric locomotives on main line trains, the TGR contracted that company to supply four high-powered Co-Co diesel-electric locomotives from its Rocklea plant in Brisbane. Although EE was at the time developing a new high-powered design for QR, the need for quick delivery resulted in the adaptation of the WAGR R-class to Tasmanian requirements.

For all intents and purposes, the Z-class was a direct development of the WAGR R-class with ongoing technologically advanced engine and electrics. The design called for a low-profile nose and modified fuel tanks, but retained the prototype's low weight transfer bogies for added adhesion.

The locomotives were delivered to Tasmania in December 1972 and January 1973, in time for the opening of the line to Longreach. With 1380 kW available for traction and an all-up weight of 97.5 tonnes, these locomotives were huge when compared with the state's previous largest diesel locomotives (weighing only 58.4 tonnes). Not surprisingly, the new locomotives caused some problems with the track and the TGR was forced to embark on an upgrading program.

Before the start of woodchip traffic a decision was made to construct a second mill at Longreach, virtually doubling the projected log traffic. Further vehicles were constructed and another four locomotives ordered from English Electric (now General Electric Company of Australia). These more powerful locomotives, classified ZA, were to a new design being built for QR and were delivered from June 1973.

All ten new locomotives were employed across northern Tasmania on woodchip, coal and general goods trains, running as far west as Wiltshire Junction and as far south as Parattahand on the Fingal, Bell Bay and Mole Creek lines. Their area of operation was later extended to Hobart and Boyer.

The four Z-class locomotives were converted from vacuum to air brakes in 1984–85. In the mid-1990s, with the units more than 20 years old, various options for their future were explored, including the possibility of conversion to engineless slugs. However, the administration decided to give the locomotives heavy overhauls, accompanied by some modernisation, and the first rebuild was completed at the end of 1995.

Locomotive Z2 slumbers in Launceston locomotive depot on 17 October 1974. (Peter Watts)

All passed into the ownership of the Australian Transport Network (ATN), which included US operator Wisconsin Central and its NZ operational arm, Tranz Rail, on 14 November 1997 as a result of the sell-off of AN. The four locomotives were renumbered 2110–2113 in June/July 1998, and passed into the ownership of Pacific National from February 2004 and the Tasmanian Government in November 2009. All remain serviceable, having received driver-only cab modifications while in ATN custody.

SPECIFICATIONS

	IMPERIAL (METRIC)
POWER UNIT:	ENGLISH ELECTRIC 12CSVT MK 11
TRACTION HORSEPOWER:	1850 (1380 KW)
STARTING TRACTIVE EFFORT:	62 200 LB (277 KN)
CONTINUOUS TRACTIVE EFFORT:	53 956 LB (240 KN)
TOTAL WEIGHT:	96 TONS (97.5 T)
GAUGE:	1067 MM
ROAD NUMBERS:	Z1–Z4 (ATN RENUMBERED THEM 2110–2113 RESPECTIVELY IN JUNE/JULY 1998)

1973 QUEENSLAND RAILWAYS

2350-class Co-Co

A new era arrived in locomotive development for the QR in April 1973 when the first two of an order for 12 high-powered 1752 kW locomotives entered service.

Maintaining an all-up weight of 91.44 tonnes (the limit for general service units on this system), these locomotives were ordered for the central Queensland coal traffic between Blackwater, Moura and the port of Gladstone.

The class, built by the General Electric Co of Australia (formerly English Electric), was introduced with alternating equipment in lieu of a normal generation plant. Technical engine, traction and electrical developments had improved to such an extent in the 20 years which led up to this locomotive type's design that it was able to deliver twice the power, yet keep within axle loading limitations. In short, the development of the diesel engine had made it possible to pack 1752 kW into virtually the same engine dimensions as QR's 1953-introduced EE 1200-class, which was rated at 954 kW.

The first twelve were delivered with dual controls, but QR acquired an additional four units between

QR's 2361, 2358 and 1342 being prepared for a Callide-bound empty coal train at Gladstone on 3 August 1978. (Peter Watts)

March and December 1975 which were fitted with just one control stand. Also, due to complaints aimed at the square edges on the earlier deliveries, the manufacturer rounded the corners on the noses of the second batch, which became the 2370-class.

TGR ZA-class

Meanwhile, four basically identical locomotives to supplement their 1972 Z-class had been ordered from GEC by Tasmanian Government Railways to cater for the expanded woodchip log traffic in northern Tasmania. The TGR units became the ZA-class when delivered from June 1973. They were the most powerful locomotives yet seen in Tasmania. They differed from their Queensland counterparts in being fitted with low-weight transfer bogies for maximum adhesion, revised traction motors and cab layout (extra glass in cab front plate) and vacuum braking equipment.

The decision by a Tasmanian cement manufacturer to convert its energy needs from oil to coal led the TGR to acquire two more ZA-class locomotives in April and June 1976. These new units, like the second series QR locomotives, were provided with radiused edges where possible, and had the distinction of becoming the last locomotives built in Australia by that manufacturer. As a means of wresting more economical operation and load sharing, all 2350/2370 and ZA-class locomotives were de-rated to 1339 kW during the early 1980s.

The Tasmanian units were converted from vacuum to air braking between 1982 and 1984 under AN ownership. They continued to be heavily utilised, whereas in Queensland the sheer volume of more compatible EMD locomotives in coal working saw the 2350 and 2370 classes transferred to the general traffic pool in September 1982.

ZA6 at Conara Junction in Tasmania on 26 March 1982. (Peter Watts)

Electrification of the coal network, and its locomotive cascading effect, made the QR units redundant by 1987. All were sold to Tasrail and shipped to Tasmania two at a time between April 1987 and March 1988, where they became the ZB-class. There they initially suffered from reliability problems, particularly electrical, and ZB16 (QR 2373) actually saw just a couple of months' service before it was withdrawn in December 1988 with collision damage.

In 1995, fire-damaged ZB9 was sent to AN's Port Augusta Workshops for rebuilding. It was fitted with a raked cab similar to that seen on AN's mainland EL-class and eventually shipped back to Tasmania in April 1996. A further six months were to pass before it entered service as ZR1. By then, ZB6 had been selected for a rebuild in Tasmania and was fitted with a cab akin to a mainland AN DL-class, entering service as ZR2 in July 1997. During their rebuilds, both units were fitted with new microprocessor control systems which markedly improved their performance.

Following the acquisition of AN Tasmania by the Australian Transport Network on 14 November 1997, the ZA locos were renumbered 2114–2118 (excepting ZA4). The ten surviving ZB units became 2120–2129 (excluding ZB4) while the ZR-class units became 2100 and 2101 respectively. Earlier plans to rebuild more ZA/ZB locos were abandoned and four ZBs were sold to South Spur Rail Services in Western Australia in 2003, including 2124 (ex ZB8 and QR 2357) which was stripped for its parts at East Tamar.

Those ZBs activated, 2120, 2125 and 2129 saw some Western Australia infrastructure train service.

Meanwhile in Tasmania, four of the original 16 were operational into 2010, mainly on the Burnie–East Tamar paper traffic and Hobart intermodal trains.

SPECIFICATIONS

	IMPERIAL (METRIC)
POWER UNIT:	ENGLISH ELECTRIC 12CSVT MK III
TRACTION HORSEPOWER:	(ORIGINAL) 2350 (1752 KW)
STARTING TRACTIVE EFFORT:	78 000 LB (347 KN)
CONTINUOUS TRACTIVE EFFORT:	53 956 LB (240 KN)
TOTAL WEIGHT:	2350/2370/ZB-CLASSES 90 TONS (91.44 T)
	ZA-CLASS 96 TONS (97.5 T)
GAUGE:	1067 MM
ROAD NUMBERS:	(QR) 2350–2361, 2370–2373
	(TASRAIL) ZA1–ZA6, ZB1–ZB16 (EX 2350/2370 CLASSES)
	(ATN) 2100–2101; 2114–2118; 2120–2129

1973 TUBEMAKERS

Worimi 0-6-0DH

Apart from the wide variety of locomotives designed to operate on 610 mm gauge sugar railways, E.M. Baldwin & Sons of Sydney's Castle Hill also built one standard gauge machine for the Newcastle-based firm Tubemakers.

Known as *Worimi*, this unique 46-tonne rigid wheelbase 0-6-0DH locomotive, which was equipped

A fussily-maintained *Worimi* acting as GrainCorp's standby shunting locomotive at the Carrington wharf complex (Newcastle, NSW) on 1 May 2001. (Leon Oberg)

with a 370 kW V12 Cummins engine, was delivered in 1973 to shunt the company's 2 kilometres of sidings.

The fashionable end-cab unit was withdrawn from service during the late 1980s because its 'rigidity' allegedly caused derailments. In addition, since the firm employed a driver, a shunter and a spare hand for 'just one or two hours' work daily', Tubemakers believed it would be more cost efficient to contract associate company BHP, whose huge plant was located nearby (and whose rail system linked up with Tubemakers), for its subsequent shunting needs.

Worimi was last used by Tubemakers on day shift on 19 December 1986, and stored beneath a tarpaulin, virtually forgotten by all but a small band of informed enthusiasts until 1993, when it was acquired by GrainCorp as a standby shunter at the nearby Carrington wharf. (This operation introduced two West German-built Hermann Vollet remote-controlled 4-wheel diesel locomotives in 1981 to move bogie grain vehicles through its unloading area.)

Official receipt of GrainCorp's offer for *Worimi* was dated 15 September 1993 and the unit left Tubemakers' property 28 days later. Commissioned six weeks after that, *Worimi* continues to see service as needed, albeit limited.

SPECIFICATIONS

	IMPERIAL (METRIC)
POWER UNIT:	CUMMINS
TRACTION HORSEPOWER:	500 (373 kW)
TOTAL WEIGHT:	45.1 TONS (46T)
GAUGE:	1435 MM
NAME:	WORIMI

Alco C630 Co-Co

Increasing mining activity through the early 1970s by Western Australian iron ore miner Cliffs, Robe River Iron Associates (now Robe) necessitated the urgent purchase of additional motive power to meet the demand.

US railroad specialist Morrison Knudsen, which had earlier constructed the Robe River railway and other Pilbara mining company routes, was able to acquire four second-hand 2237 kW Alco C630s to meet the company's need. These locomotives had been manufactured in October 1967 at Alco's Schenectady plant for coal train haulage over the Chesapeake & Ohio Railroad (C&O) in the USA. They were numbered 2100–2103. Morrison Knudsen shipped the locomotives to Australia and they arrived at Cape Lambert in January 1975.

Basically similar in size and configuration as the five less powerful C628 units built for rival Pilbara iron ore miner Hamersley Iron, in 1965, the Model C630 was something of a stopgap type whose heavy role had been replaced on US, Canadian and Mexican railroads by the larger 636 model. While Hamersley's older C628 employed a DC generator, the C630 introduced the more reliable AC alternator.

All were overhauled in the USA prior to coming to Australia and upgraded to 3600 hp (2685 kW). The units were numbered 9417–9420 by Robe River and put to work side by side with seven Australian-built M636 locomotives hauling ore between Pannawonica and Cape Lambert. Restricted to 80 km/h, all were progressively air-conditioned and fitted with bigger radiators to cater for their up-rated power outputs and the hot Pilbara conditions. Soon afterwards, however, the locomotives were down-rated in power to 3250 hp (2390 kW).

The C630s' ranks started to thin in February 1979 when 9417 was extensively damaged and subsequently withdrawn from service due to a head-on collision involving six locomotives at Robe River's Siding 1.

Morrison Knudsen came to the company's aid once again, buying a used Alco C636 originally built in 1968 for the Spokane, Portland & Seattle Railroad (which later merged with other US railroads to form the Burlington Northern Railroad). This unit,

Cliffs, Robe River Iron Associates C630 No. 9419 leads two M636 units, 9421 and 9422, and a 94-vehicle coast-bound lumpy iron ore train on 3 August 1979. (Peter Watts)

maker's number 4366, was freighted to Perth where it was stripped of all useless parts and remanufactured by A. Goninan & Co, using a 2983 kW General Electric engine and GE Dash-8 electrics. It entered service as 9417 in its radically restyled (cab forward) guise at Robe in May 1989.

By March 1991, the remaining three C630s had been similarly remanufactured. Eight older M636 Alcos, three of which had been imported from the USA, were also rebuilt. All the imported locomotives could be identified by their standard pattern Hi-Ad bogies.

SPECIFICATIONS

	IMPERIAL (METRIC)
POWER UNIT:	ALCO 251E
TRACTION HORSEPOWER:	3250 (2390 kW) [FOLLOWING DERATION]
STARTING TRACTIVE EFFORT:	116 901 LB (520 KN)
CONTINUOUS TRACTIVE EFFORT:	94 420 LB (402 KN)
TOTAL WEIGHT:	171 TONS (174.5 T)
GAUGE:	1435 MM
ROAD NUMBERS:	9417–9420

1976 AUSTRALIAN NATIONAL RAILWAYS

AL-class Co-Co

This class of eight locomotives, introduced in October 1976, was based on Australian National's 1970 CL-class, having basically identical power and transmission equipment, bogies and fibreglass-sheathed truss construction. But instead of having a single streamlined cab, the AL-class was designed to feature flat-ended cabs at both ends, the inspiration coming from the NSWR's 422-class of 1969.

Acquired for use over the entire AN network, including the standard gauge Alice Springs link then under construction, the AL-class was fitted with EMD's improved Dash-2 control system. With this system, all electrical limits were preset on plug-in modules—in effect, printed circuit panels—which simplifies both manufacture and fault finding.

The AL-class initially tipped the scales at 133 tonnes and early deliveries were returned to the

AL20 was just a year old when pictured at the head of a steel products train in Whyalla yard on 9 February 1978. On its rebuilding by MKA in February 1994, this locomotive became ALF21. (Leon Oberg)

manufacturer for weight reduction. However, only 3 tonnes could be shed and thus the class was restricted to slower freight operations to minimise track pounding.

Powered with EMD's turbocharged 16-645E3 diesel engine producing 2237kW for traction purposes, three were loaned to the NSWSRA late in 1979 for design evaluation trials over both the Western and Southern lines, with the result that the SRA ordered 80 updated dual-cab units the following year as its 81-class.

Some minor modifications were carried out over the years, with AL19 becoming the first AN locomotive to receive a cab air-conditioner, a tremendous crew comfort considering the frequent 46°C summer temperatures on the Nullarbor.

As was the CL-class, the ALs were sold to US engineering firm Morrison Knudsen Australia and its banking partners in 1993 and rebuilt as single-ended locomotives (the rear cab was simply blanked off). They were randomly rebuilt in a similar manner to the CLF-class, with the first one emerging from MKA on 15 January 1994 as the ALF-class; the last was running on 6 April 1994. They have been used on everything from Broken Hill ore to Leigh Creek coal and Tailem Bend wheat trains. Some even started working into Melbourne from June 1996 at the head of intermodal freight trains.

On 8 November 1997, the ALFs were sold to Genesee & Wyoming, which on 2 December 2000 became the ARG. That business was sold to QR National-West on 1 June 2006 and while ALF25 passed to the new owner as ALZ25, the remainder stayed with the re-badged Genesee & Wyoming Australia for freight service in South Australia.

SPECIFICATIONS

	ORIGINAL	AS REBUILT
	IMPERIAL (METRIC)	IMPERIAL (METRIC)
POWER UNIT:	EMD 16-645E3	EMD 16-645E3C
TRACTION HORSEPOWER:	3000 (2237 kW)	3200 (2460 kW)
STARTING TRACTIVE EFFORT:	98 700 LB (439 kN)	104 000 LB (465 kN)
CONTINUOUS TRACTIVE EFFORT:	60 634 LB (270 kN)	72 000 LB (315.6 kN)
TOTAL WEIGHT:	127.5 TONS (130 T)	126 TONS (128.4 T)
GAUGE:	1435 MM	1435 MM
ROAD NUMBERS:	AL18–AL25	ALF18–ALF25 (QRN-W UNIT NOW ALZ25)

1977 Victorian Railways

C-class Co-Co

These ten rugged-looking diesel-electrics were a direct development of the WAGR's heavyweight L-class of 1967. Built by the Clyde Engineering Co at Rosewater in South Australia, the locomotives were acquired for heavy freight haulage over the Melbourne–Albury standard gauge and the Melbourne–Serviceton broad gauge routes.

Boasting 2237 kW traction horsepower, their introduction was reasoned to reduce double-heading of the steadily expanding freight task.

While basically an L-class copy, a union committee was involved in the cab design. Three distinct plans later, a low full-width nose of US styling was adopted to help reduce air resistance. This also provided an airtight cab, reducing draughts. Riding on four rubber mounts to remove frame-transmitted vibrations, the roomy accommodation also featured Clyde's 'clean cab' design, which eliminated sharp protrusions which could cause injury in the event of a collision.

Just days after entering Melbourne–Adelaide interstate working, C503 and former SAR (AN-liveried) Alco streamliner 953 prepare to depart Mile End (Adelaide) depot for Melbourne on 3 February 1982. (Leon Oberg)

The first arrived in May 1977 and was named *George Brown* at a special Spencer Street station ceremony, honouring a former VR board chairman. Despite brief industrial action which effectively banned the unit until certain cab modifications were completed, the husky locomotive was soon in service hauling 40 per cent greater payloads over the formidable 1 in 48 Ingliston bank and other equally impressive gradients.

All ten had been delivered by July 1978, by when the first four had been allocated to the standard gauge. From January 1982, the broad gauge locomotives started working through trains to Adelaide and their success soon saw the standard gauge units transferred to broad guage, their place being taken by GM-class locomotives leased from AN's Trans-Australian line.

Due to their weight in respect to the existing rail infrastructure, a lower maximum speed was imposed upon the class and thus they did not normally work passenger trains, except when no other suitable locomotives were available. However, representatives were noted working the *Overland* and *Southern Aurora* expresses on occasions.

In September 1988, some C-class returned to the standard gauge, this time to the through Melbourne–Sydney route. With the formation of the National Rail Corporation from 1992, all eventually passed into that authority's roster. However, due to their age and smaller load-hauling capability when compared to more modern units equipped with wheel-creep control, withdrawals started in April 1997 after C503 broke its crankshaft while working in South Australia. Following extended periods in store at both Junee and Adelaide, two were issued to shunting traffic in Melbourne during mid-1999 (where they remained for a further seven years).

All units came under the ownership of Pacific National with the sale of NRC and FreightCorp on 21 February 2002. Considered surplus, nine were offered for sale and on 20 February 2003 passed into the hands of Silverton Rail who progressively overhauled them at Broken Hill, initially randomly renumbering them in the Cs1–Cs9 series. As this work progressed, Silverton Rail became part of the Southern Shorthaul group which was acquired in 2007 by Coote Industrial who acquiredsix with the balance belonging to CFCLA. As they undergo rebuilds, all have been reverting back to their original road numbers and finding lease work in several states.

The class-leader C501 belongs to the Seymour Heritage Rail Centre and since its 2005 overhaul and repaint to original livery has seen extensive lease work too.

SPECIFICATIONS

	IMPERIAL (METRIC)
POWER UNIT:	EMD 16-645E3
TRACTION HORSEPOWER:	3000 (2237 kW)
STARTING TRACTIVE EFFORT:	74 190 LB (329 kN)
CONTINUOUS TRACTIVE EFFORT:	64 970 LB (276 kN)
TOTAL WEIGHT:	129.5 TONS (132 T)
GAUGE:	1435 MM TODAY
ROAD NUMBERS:	C501–C510
	SILVERTON: CS1–CS9 (SELECTED FROM THE FORMER V/LINE C502–510 SERIES)

1977 WESTERN AUSTRALIAN GOVERNMENT RAILWAYS

N-class Co-Co

This class of eleven 1790 kW diesel-electric locomotives was acquired to meet expanding aluminium, coal, woodchip and mineral sands traffic over Westrail's 1067 mm gauge network. Having acquired the Australian rights to manufacture Alco/MLW locomotives (following the collapse of A.E. Goodwin in 1973), Commonwealth Engineering tooled up its Bassendean (Perth) plant to build these units, the heaviest constructed at that location to that date.

NA1874 at Picton (WA) under South Spur Rail Services ownership, on 28 July 2004. (Peter Clark)

Known as the N-class, these locomotives were powered by Alco's 251CE 12-cylinder engine, which produced a beefy 1790 kW for traction purposes. The first one appeared on 1 August 1977. Initial trials found it to be rather light on its feet; thus, in an effort to improve adhesion, 12 tonnes of ballast was added to increase the locomotive's weight from 96 to 108 tonnes.

While the N-class remained the only Alco/MLW locomotive type of its power range seen in Australia, crews soon praised its riding ability and strength. But these units were also the butt of many jokes because of their unreliability, caused mainly by electrical and engine cooling failures. At one stage WAGR figures pointed out the class's availability was just 60 per cent.

Despite its young age, when N1875 suffered heavy engine damage in June 1991, Westrail management decided to cut its losses and wrote the unit off four months later to become a source of spare parts for its sisters, four of which had seen their vacuum-brake equipment replaced with the more universal Westinghouse air system. These converted units, 1871–1874, became the NA-class, the work having been carried out between July 1982 and June 1983.

By then the writing was well and truly on the wall for these Alcos. While it is believed Tasmania's Emu Bay Railway looked at acquiring some in 1993 for heavy ore traffic, Westrail cut up five for scrap during March/April 1994. At that stage five remained operational, being used between Forrestfield and nearby Kwinana and Leighton yards. A small reprieve seemed likely in January 1995 when, desperately in need of standard gauge locomotives, two of the Westinghouse-equipped units, NA1872 and NA1873, were fitted with second-hand standard gauge BHP Iron Ore Alco M636 locomotive bogies. Redesignated NB, they were intended for Perth metropolitan freight workings.

By March 1996, the only units operational were NA1874, based at Picton for use over the Worsley line, and NB1873 at Kwinana to work Alcoa trains to Pinjarra. However, the arrival of new Q-class EMD locomotives late in 1997 provided the excuse to withdraw them. Junee-based firm, Australian Traction Corp (Austrac), negotiated the purchase of the two NBs, which were delivered in February 1998. NB1873 made its initial commercial run to Sydney on 18 June 1998, re-registered as the 18-class. Both now belong to Patrick Port Link and see service between Port Adelaide and Bowmans in South Australia.

NA1874 became surplus and was finally on-sold to South Spur Rail Services in Western Australia in August 2001; after an overhaul, it now works on the standard gauge.

Specifications

	Imperial (Metric)
Power unit:	Alco 251CE (12 cylinders)
Traction horsepower:	2400 (1790 kW)
Starting tractive effort:	63 399 lb (282 kN)
Continuous tractive effort:	53 956 lb (240 kN)
Total weight:	106 tons (108 t)
Gauge:	1067/1435 mm
Road numbers:	N1871–N1881
	NA1871–1874
	NB1872, NB1873

1978 Hamersley Iron

50-class Co-Co

Until 1978, main line-type locomotives from the US General Electric stable had been ignored by Australian rail operators. although in the USA itself, following the collapse of the rival Alco company, it was a different story.

In 1978, however, Hamersley Iron, whose 497 km railway (like most in the Pilbara) had been established to the best US standards using high-capacity Alco/MLW locomotives, decided to trial GE mainliners in ore haulage. A. Goninan & Co, holder of the GE Australian licence, was contracted to build three 190-tonne 2685 kW monsters at its Newcastle plant. They were sea-freighted to the Pilbara, arriving in February 1978, and entered regular traffic between 2 May and 19 May that year.

These 50-class locomotives, known as the Dash-7 type (with the provision of high-tech modular card-mounted electronics), were the first of their type

All three 50-class locomotives, 5057, 5059 and 5058, leave Hamersley Iron's Seven Mile yard precinct on 11 August 1979 with an empty train. (Peter Watts)

built in the world. Being North American in design, the Hamersley units were provided with additional cooling to overcome perceived problems associated with the Pilbara's hot climate.

Initially, the 50-class was operated as a triple engine lash-up on ore trains but as time passed they were intermingled with Hamersley's potpourri of Alco and EMD motive power. With the introduction of 29 new GE Dash-9 locomotives early in 1995, the three 50-class saw their last main line ore hauls in September/October 1995. From then, until they were mothballed in March 1997, they were relegated to moving loaded and empty iron ore trains between Seven Mile yard, Parker Point and East Intercourse Island.

Tendered for sale in August 1998, all three were sold to US leasing firm National Railway Equipment, and shipped out four months later. They gradually saw service on the Northfolk & Southern Railroad but in June 2001 No. 5059 was sold outright to Minnesota Commercial Railroad. Repainted and renumbered 59, in 2006 it remained in traffic as 'backup unit'. The other two, 5057 and 5058, were stored at NRE's Silvis depot for many years but a late 2006 report to this author said both had been acquired by Brasil Ferrovias SA of Brazil, a holding company with investments relative to rail transport, and now carry the respective numbers 9380 and 9381.

While no more 50-class units were acquired by Hamersley Iron, they did pave the way for a contract with Mt Newman Mining (now BHP Billiton) for the rebuild of eight early Alco C/M 636 heavy-haul locomotives into Dash-7 units, the first re-entering service in January 1987 as Model CM36-7. Unlike the original 50-class, which was equipped with a low nose, the rebuilds were provided with more commodious end cabs (see page 405).

SPECIFICATIONS

	IMPERIAL (METRIC)
POWER UNIT:	GE FDL-16
TRACTION HORSEPOWER:	3600 (2685 KW)
STARTING TRACTIVE EFFORT:	130 000 LB (578 KN)
CONTINUOUS TRACTIVE EFFORT:	90 000 LB (400 KN)
TOTAL WEIGHT:	187 TONS (190.6 T)
GAUGE:	1435 MM
ROAD NUMBERS:	5057–5059

80-class Co-Co

Fortunately, the 1973 collapse of the Goodwin-Healing group (builders of Alco/MLW locomotives in Australia since 1955) did not see the end of Alco-powered motive power in Australia.

Waiting in the wings right across the road from A.E. Goodwin's Granville (Sydney) factory was Commonwealth Engineering, which had built many hundreds of passenger and freight cars for Australian and overseas railways, in addition to hosts of 610 mm gauge sugar industry and state government shunting locomotives.

Comeng immediately negotiated the Alco/MLW licence and the company's team of design engineers, augmented with key service and spare-parts staff from the collapsed Goodwin factory, set to work in a big way after it became known that the State Rail Authority of NSW wanted new locomotives in the 1491 kW power bracket. Comeng came up with a much improved 442-class by using a pioneering form of modular construction and fibreglass reinforced in plastic panel materials.

Initially 30 of these 80-class were ordered; this was later increased to 50 units. The fleet entered service between October 1978 and February 1983, the final delivery, 8050, having the honour of being the last Alco/MLW diesel locomotive built in Australia, because Comeng's Granville plant ceased trading from June 1989. The 80-class was the first in New South Wales to be equipped with cab air-conditioning equipment and an in-cab refrigerator, items which made them favoured power over the hot and dusty Parkes–Broken Hill route.

Equipped with the slightly faster-running and more efficient Alco 251CE engine and Mitsubishi electrical equipment (including traction motors),

The paint smelled fresh as brand-new 8039 prepared to enter general traffic in February 1982. (Leon Oberg)

the 80-class was initially pressed into service over all main line routes and heavy Hunter Valley coal traffic. For a time, some of the later deliveries were equipped for operation into South Australia (in a reciprocal through-locomotive working deal with AN). As recently as late 1993, seven were leased for a fortnight by AN to cover serious but temporary motive power shortages.

With the formation of the National Rail Corporation in 1992, most of the operational 80-class units were allocated to that operator from July 1995, working to Melbourne, Broken Hill and Brisbane. This was just a stopgap until NRC NR-class locomotives started working into New South Wales from December 1996. Those few not required for NRC yard shunting were returned and stored by 30 June 1997.

Very few Australian diesel locomotive classes have suffered more accidents than the 80-class. No. 8009 became a source of spare parts following a level crossing collision at Narromine on 15 July 1990. No. 8020, one of three 80-class involved in a level crossing smash at Condobolin, was withdrawn, as was 8043, which overturned after colliding with cattle at Kiacatoo early in 1996. Loco 8029, the victim of a serious four-loco collision at Delec depot on 13 July 1996, was also stowed, as was shunter 8002, seriously damaged in a collision in Acacia Ridge yard on 20 March 1997. On that occasion, a bogie and other essential equipment was shorn from beneath the unit. Seven months later—and in the same yard—class-leader 8001 was similarly retired following a violent collision with two driverless NR-class locomotives. (As an aside, parts from the Alco 251 CE diesel engines from 8001 and 8002 were subsequently sold to the Australian Navy as spares to help maintain two of its ships, HMAS *Kanimbla* and HMAS *Manoora*, which are fitted with Alco 16-cylinder 251 engines).

Meanwhile, a handful had been pressed into FreightCorp metropolitan shunting and yard transfer duties while 8015 and 8039 were used in several months of BHP Port Kembla coal haulage trials during late 1997. The future looked grim for the class until chassis cracks were found in most of the 86-class electric locomotives, causing their withdrawal from traffic, and large numbers of 80-class units were returned to general traffic as replacements from July 1998. With the sale of FreightCorp to Pacific National in 1999 some returned to South Australia, working superfreighters as far west as Port Augusta.

Despite the purging of 'older' locomotive types through the 1990s, the 80-class remained more or less intact and some continue to run into 2010. Twelve of these were operating with Pacific National as shunting and helper power while Coote Industrial regularly use several hauling infrastructure trains. Other PN and Coote-owned examples were stored at that time in depots awaiting possible reactivation.

SPECIFICATIONS

	IMPERIAL (METRIC)
POWER UNIT:	Alco 251 CE (12 cylinders)
TRACTION HORSEPOWER:	2000 (1491 kW)
STARTING TRACTIVE EFFORT:	80 000 lb (356 kN)
CONTINUOUS TRACTIVE EFFORT:	61 350 lb (273 kN)
TOTAL WEIGHT:	119.5 tons (122 t)
GAUGE:	1435 mm
ROAD NUMBERS:	8001–8050. Silverton units to date: 80s1 (ex 8026), 80s2 (8044). 80s3 (8021), 80s4 (8037)

1979 NEW SOUTH WALES STATE RAIL AUTHORITY

85-class Co-Co

On their introduction on 10 May 1979, this class of ten 2880 kW electric locomotives was theoretically considered the most powerful locomotive type in Australia.

Designed and built by Commonwealth Engineering at Granville, Sydney, these units were the first electric locomotives to be added to the NSW fleet since the British-built 46-class Co+Co type of 1956.

Known as the 85-class, the new locomotives were acquired for heavy coal haulage over the 1500V DC Lithgow (Western) line. Although standing on larger, 125 cm wheels, their styling somewhat mirrored the 80-class diesel-electric type which was also under construction in the Granville factory. The diesel and

The last of the class, 8510, stands at Delec depot on 6 August 1983 (Leon Oberg)

85-class cabs possessed a similar internal layout.

Held in high regard by their crews, the 85-class became the unheralded 'maids of all work' in State Rail's coal haulage which, following electrification to Wollongong and the nearby Port Kembla coal loader in 1985, considerably expanded their sphere of operation.

While no more were ordered or built, these locomotives paved the way for State Rail's 1982 acquisition of fifty 3328 kW Comeng-built 86-class electric locomotives.

Despite a series of early accidents, all continued in service until 6 January 1998, when 8503 and 8505 were involved in an accident in Enfield yard. With coal mine closures in western New South Wales and State Rail's lesser reliance on electric locomotives following the formation of National Rail Corporation, along with the perceived high cost of electrical energy, these two locomotives were immediately stored.

The remaining class members, although mostly operational, were considered surplus to requirements and stored, the last to be officially withdrawn being 8501 and 8508 on 29 April 1998.

Technically passing into the ownership of Pacific National with the sale of FreightCorp/National Rail on 21 February 2002, all ten 85-class were sold inoperable to Silverton Rail on 20 February 2003 and hauled to Broken Hill for dry climate storage. Passing into ownership of Allco Finance, 8501 was in late 2006 acquired by the Sydney Electric Train Society and 8507 by the Dorrigo Steam Railway and Museum. The remainder were sold to Smorgon Steel, with scrappings starting in December 2006.

SPECIFICATIONS

	IMPERIAL (METRIC)
ELECTRICAL EQUIPMENT:	MITSUBISHI 1500V DC
MAXIMUM HORSEPOWER:	3859 (2880 kW)
STARTING TRACTIVE EFFORT:	81 355 lb (362 kN)
TOTAL WEIGHT:	120.6 TONS (123 T)
GAUGE:	1435 MM
ROAD NUMBERS:	8501–8510

1981 NEW SOUTH WALES STATE RAIL AUTHORITY

XP-class Bo-Bo

The unveiling of the Express Passenger Train (XPT) at Commonwealth Engineering's Sydney plant in August 1981 heralded the dawn of a new era for both Australian passenger train concepts and locomotive technology.

The train came about following many years' procrastination over what kind of conveyance would best serve country New South Wales train travellers. Some manufacturers tendered conventional locomotive-hauled train sets while others presented developments of railmotors.

Comeng successfully tendered an Australianised version of the tried and proven British Intercity 125 High Speed Train (HST) concept, which provided locomotives at both ends of the train—one pulling and one pushing. The firm won the day and, in a contract worth $39 million, State Rail initially ordered ten locomotives (to be officially known as 'power cars') and 20 matched coaching vehicles.

Because Australian operating conditions were vastly different to those experienced in Britain, the Australian XPT was virtually re-designed from the bogies up. Australia's more generous loading gauge allowed for longer, wider and higher passenger cars; also, while the British HST was constructed of welded steel, the Comeng version used the stainless variety.

The XPT locomotives, which became the XP-class, introduced a new-look modular construction technique to Australia. Each locomotive was equipped with the same Paxman Valenta 12-cylinder RP200L 4-stroke turbocharged engine as employed in the British HST, but de-rated to 1491 kW to suit Australia's hotter ambient temperature. The traction gear ratio was reduced slightly to provide a 1000 lb (4.1 kW) greater maximum tractive effort to enable the train to negotiate lengthy steep gradients (such as the 1 in 33 gradients experienced on the Blue Mountains route). With bogie frame-mounted traction motors (to reduce track-pounding unsprung weight) and flexible drive, the XPT's top speed was set nominally at 160 km/h, some 40 km/h slower than the HST.

The train became so popular with the public that more were gradually acquired and today 19 locomotives can be seen working trains over the

Still in brand-new condition, locomotive XP2001 was pictured pausing at Towrang while undergoing extensive high-speed train braking trials on 21 January 1982. (Leon Oberg)

On Thursday 19 August 2006, a complete train set wearing CountryLink's latest livery was assembled for publicity photography as it worked over the NSW North Coast route. Locomotives XP2001 (nearest camera) and XP2000 were employed on that movement. (Leon Oberg)

Sydney to Dubbo, Albury, Melbourne, Grafton and Brisbane routes every day of the week. The final four locomotives (and their cars) which were delivered during 1992–93, were built in Victoria by ASEA Brown Boveri under licence, because Comeng had by then ceased to be a rolling-stock builder. Two of the locomotives were financed by the Victorian government.

When testing the first locomotive of this final order, XP2015, State Rail decided to titillate the public and establish yet another rail speed record. After several fast passes between Culcairn and Gerogery on 18 September 1992, a record speed of 193 km/h was sustained over a 2 km length of track.

Over the years, the XPT locomotives (and carriages) have undergone tremendous change to better equip them for their constant task. According to former XPT Maintenance Centre head John Shields, almost 150 detail changes were carried out

on the locomotives' engines and traction equipment during his tenure, and many of the improvements were exported back to England. They included modified load regulation characteristics in respect of alternators and traction motors to increase the allowable current to those motors for starting and low speed operations. He said this became necessary when the trains were increased from the original five cars to seven in 1986.

In February 1995, the NSW Government imported three tilt carriages for a 4-month evaluation and two XP-class locomotives, XP2000 and XP2009, were modified to work the train. Although these units did not tilt, they were equipped with head-end power sets to provide electricity to drive the train's tilt computer in addition to the on-board lighting, air-conditioning and kitchen equipment. The head-end power sets increased the two locomotives' weight at their rear ends by some 2.2 tonnes. Heavier springs then became necessary.

A number of national occasions have warranted one-off livery changes. Unit XP2000 was adorned in a special Olympics 2000 paint job from September 1996, while XP2001 was bedecked in dazzling orange and white colours to promote the 2001 Centenary of Federation.

By then, the old 12RPL200L engines had run their course and moves to upgrade the locomotives finally came to fruition in June 2000 with the fitting of a new Paxman 12VP185 to XP2016—a more efficient design employing two high-pressure and four low-pressure turbochargers in lieu of the former engine's one. The latest in remote engine monitoring equipment was also provided. CountryLink support engineer Bill Mair told this author that while the new engine was technically capable of exerting 2050 kW (2750 hp), the original engines' outputs and traction curves were maintained due to the limitation of the existing electrical package, which was not replaced. The rest of the fleet was similarly treated by December 2001 at a cost of $22 million.

The locomotives have just passed through the workshops for upgrades and we can report that, as at 1 January 2010, locomotive XP2001 had already clocked up an amazing 9.291 million kilometers of hard, fast service.

SPECIFICATIONS

	Imperial (Metric)
Power unit:	Paxman 'Valenta' 12RPL200L upgraded from 6/2000 with 12VP185
Traction horsepower:	2000 (1491 kW)
Starting tractive effort:	18 994 lb (84 kN)
Continuous tractive effort:	17 311 lb (77 kN)
Total weight:	72.5 tons (74 t)
Gauge:	1435 mm
Road numbers:	XP2000–2018

1981 NSW Grain Elevators Board

Hermann Vollert 4wBE

NSW Government-operated specialist business, the (NSW) Grain Elevators Board, in 1981 quietly introduced two of the most unusual standard gauge locomotives ever to hit Australian shores.

Built by Hermann Vollert of Maschine Fabrik Weinsberg, West Germany, the remote-controlled 4-wheel battery-electric locomotives, model 11EL, were acquired to move bogie grain vehicles through the Board's Port Waratah (Carrington) unloading/wharf area.

Due to the nature of the work, these locomotives, known as 'shunting robots,' go unseen by virtually all but the most intrepid enthusiasts because they are tucked away on the out-of-bounds wharf side of the terminal. That said, the lightweight units have become an institution at the plant, now operated by GrainCorp. They carry no local identification road numbers, and are simply distinguished as the *Red Vollert* and the *Blue Vollert*.

Actually built in 1980 and going into traffic early in 1981, the two locomotives quaintly bear identical builder's numbers—80/009.

Circa 2000, both locomotives were rebuilt as diesel-hydraulics and have been described as 'generally trouble free'. They are driven by radio signal from a control room located within the grain unloading area and when a unit is out of service for maintenance, the 45-tonne 373kW diesel hydraulic locomotive known as *Worimi* stands by (see page 379).

The specialist West German firm prides itself on being able to build an individual diesel or straight electric locomotive product to meet any customer's specification. Their suspension system, sanding gear, radio remote-control type, bogie design and even an anti-stick slip device can be incorporated to meet the specific need.

Those employing electric drive can have their energy supplied by means of a cable drum, trailing cable, contact line, battery or current aggregate. The company advertises locomotives that can exert traction forces up to 480 kN (107 000 lb).

Remote-controlled *Red Vollert* pictured shunting bogie grain wagons at GrainCorp's large Newcastle (NSW) Carrington wharf export terminal on 1 May 2001. It is one of two in constant side-by-side service at that busy location. (Leon Oberg)

DB1591 and DB1585 await their next call to duty outside Forrestfield Workshops compound on 7 December 2001. (Leon Oberg)

1982 WESTERN AUSTRALIAN GOVERNMENT RAILWAYS

DB-class Co-Co

This class of 13 Co-Co locomotives represented a radical departure from established diesel-electric locomotive practice in Australia, particularly in respect to cab design.

Built at the Clyde Engineering's Rosewater (Adelaide) factory, the DB (which was an updated version of the D/DA-classes) employed a vestibule entry to the cab, a feature teamed with an airtight low-profile nose which was attached to the cab. This nose/cab unit was designed to ride on heavy-duty rubber mountings. The thinking behind this design was the all-sealed nose would eliminate dust, the rubber mounts would reduce noise and vibration, and the vestibule entry would isolate the cab from further noise from the engine room.

The whole body was pressurised in an effort to reduce dust in the engine-room area, and the class was further improved with the provision of dual air and vacuum braking systems.

Ten units were ordered initially for heavy bauxite haulage over WAGR's 1067 mm gauge South-West line, with three more ordered prior to the delivery of the first unit in March 1982. All were running by April 1983. Because of the intended association with the south-west routes, all units were named after cities and shires encountered along the way.

Until the arrival of the Clyde-built S-class in 1998, the DB-class was mainly used on Bunbury to Lambert woodchip trains and, in season, the heaviest grain trains to the port of Albany. Early 1999 saw them transferred to Albany for use on the Great Southern and Lakes area lines, often running in combination with the GE P-class.

All 13 locomotives passed into the ownership of the ARG on 2 December 2000 and, until they were sold to QR National-West on 1 June 2006, were being shopped and renumbered into the 23-series, the first example treated being 1593 (renumbered 2313). The DBs today generally work over the Great Southern line, from Wagin to Albany and the Lakes area.

SPECIFICATIONS

	IMPERIAL (METRIC)
POWER UNIT:	EMD 16-645E
TRACTION HORSEPOWER:	2000 (1491 kW)
STARTING TRACTIVE EFFORT:	72 500 LB (322 kN)
CONTINUOUS TRACTIVE EFFORT:	60 500 LB (269 kN)
TOTAL WEIGHT:	106 TONS (108 T)
GAUGE:	1067 MM
ROAD NUMBERS:	1581–1593 (BECOMING 2301–2313

1982 HAMERSLEY IRON

60-class Co-Co

Giant Western Australian mining company, Hamersley Iron Pty Ltd, has always been an

Brand-new class-leader 6060 stands in Paraburdoo yard for crew training purposes on 15 July 1982. (John Orr)

innovator—one eager to try sound new equipment. When needing replacements for its five ageing C628 Alco locomotives in the early 1980s, the company placed an order with the Clyde Engineering Co for five EMD heavy-haul 'almost off-the-shelf' US Model SD50S Co-Co locomotives.

Built at Clyde's Rosewater (Adelaide) plant, the first of these 190-tonne Super-Series 16-cylinder 645F3-powered machines was delivered in July 1982. They were the first EMD locomotives in Australia to employ that designer's 'F' 950-rpm crankcase and this, when teamed with the higher-rated turbocharger, gave the units 2610 kW of traction output.

Capable of a 105 km/h top speed, standing 4668 mm tall and possessing huge 15 140-litre fuel tanks, these locomotives were North American in every way—right down to their warning bells. However, they were provided with some custom features, such as two different size radiator-intake grilles, double-sheathed roofs and air-conditioners to better equip them for the high ambient temperatures experienced in the Pilbara.

Despite some early teething troubles, largely traction motor suspension bearing failures, the classic units spent more than a decade storming the Hamersley railway. On some stirring occasions, triple 60-class units were used as bankers on ore trains over the steeply-graded Paraburdoo to Tom Price section.

With the commissioning of twenty-nine GE Dash-9 locomotives during 1995, all five EMDs were withdrawn from mainline ore haulage, the last in service being 6062, lingering on in railway construction and fuel train service until withdrawn in November of that year.

Tendered for sale in August 1998, the locomotives were shipped out to the Northfolk & Southern Railroad in the USA four months later and given

overhauls, initially entering service there under lease from National Railway Equipment and still wearing Hamersley Iron colours and numbering. While the units were generally kept in the east, one was noted by US rail historian Andy Inserra temporarily working for the Indiana Rail Road during the 2001 autumn. Soon afterwards, all were purchased by the Utah Railroad and repainted in that company's grey body/red band livery while retaining their original road numbers. They remain in service with Utah to this day, bound principally to coal haulage.

SPECIFICATIONS

	IMPERIAL (METRIC)
POWER UNIT:	EMD 16-645F3
TRACTION HORSEPOWER:	3500 (2610 kW)
STARTING TRACTIVE EFFORT:	140 000 lb (623 kN)
CONTINUOUS TRACTIVE EFFORT:	93 075 lb (414 kN)
TOTAL WEIGHT:	187 tons (190 t)
GAUGE:	1435 mm
ROAD NUMBERS:	6060–6064

1982 NEW SOUTH WALES STATE RAIL AUTHORITY

81-class Co-Co

The NSW State Rail Authority's order for 80 diesel-electric locomotives, placed with the Clyde Engineering Co in October 1980, represented not only the largest single order for motive power ever placed in Australia at the time but also the biggest placed with a GM licence-holder anywhere in the world.

Ongoing technical developments carried out in the USA by General Motors had led to the testing in 1972 of what later became Super Series wheel-creep correction technology. An EMD engineering and scientific team's research into the fundamental mechanics of the grip between powered railway wheels and the rails revealed the previously unknown fact that a steel wheel exerting a high tractive effort on a rail creeps (skids) a significant amount. So they set about designing an electrical control system to take advantage of this knowledge.

Thus Super Series locomotives were equipped with ground speed radar and programmed traction motor characteristics, along with the dynamic parameter of traction motor electrical current to set constantly changing voltage output limits. This in

The last locomotive of the original contract, 8180, as running on 20 December, 1987. (Leon Oberg)

turn controlled the allowable wheel slip within the horsepower setting of the locomotive.

In short, should a locomotive fitted with Super Series technology run over a wet and/or oily patch of rail, the computer-linked radar which is reading forward ground speed will sense a particular traction motor is revolving faster than it should, and voltage to that axle will automatically be reduced to maintain optimum wheel speed and tractive efforts for the conditions.

EMD claimed a locomotive fitted with this technology was able to haul 31 per cent greater loads than a similarly-powered locomotive without the equipment. The exhaustive trials were carried out in 23 prototype locomotives which were employed on all class one US railroads over an 8-year period before the technology was released to the world. (Clyde unveiled this technology in Australia in July 1980, when it voluntarily rebuilt NSW State Rail's 1491 kW 422-class unit 42220.)

Built at Clyde's Bathurst plant, the 81-class certainly lived up to expectations for, during trials over the largely 1 in 75 Cootamundra to Goulburn portion of the Main Southern line in October 1982, a test locomotive managed a controlled load of 2200 tonnes. Fitted with a modular control system and Clyde's 'clean cab' approach to crew safety, its girder underframe (in lieu of a trussed car body) and removable engine-room covers made it unlike any other full-width bodied locomotive then seen in Australia.

As additional units were received, coal haulage in the state's Hunter Valley was completely revolutionised. For a time, 81-class units were worked in quad engine lash-ups with 8400-tonne coal trains trailing along behind.

Geared for 125 kph, the class was phased into superfreighter working between Sydney and Albury (and eventually onwards to Melbourne) from August 1983, with spectacular results. These units allowed the complete revamp of the Southern Region's wheat haulage.

An investigation of State Rail's stores inventory

at the time by chief executive Ross Sayers led to the construction (on new underframes) of an additional four 81-class from 'spare parts on hand'. The original maker was given the job to assemble the new locomotives, which entered traffic between July and September 1991.

The introduction of 2862 kW 90-class locomotives from July 1994 led to the replacement of all Hunter Valley coal road 81-class, which were then substituted for life-expired Alco mainliners throughout the state. This saw the 81-class's route availability extended to Brisbane and Broken Hill.

With the establishment of the National Rail Corporation in September 1991, thirteen 81-class were acquired by that body and used system-wide (from Brisbane, Melbourne, Adelaide and Perth), some in shunting roles. Other examples were dedicated to Bluescope Steel coal working following the initial trialling of 8124 to Wongawilli on 2 March 2001 after NRC acquired the haulage contract.

The privatisation of FreightCorp and NRC in February 2002, which saw the formation of Pacific National, saw all 81-class 'brought back into the fold'. Their route availability today includes the entire mainland standard gauge eastern seaboard (including a return to Hunter Valley coal) with regular forays into South Australia and Western Australia.

Beginning with 8113 in 2004, the class is now being cycled through EDI plants for its second round of overhauls, except for 8147, which was burnt out due to a 17 March 2007 level-crossing collision near Forbes.

SPECIFICATIONS

	Imperial (Metric)
Power unit:	EMD 16-645E3B
Traction horsepower:	3000 (2237 kW)
Starting tractive effort:	104 000 lb (465 kN)
Continuous tractive effort:	75 730 lb (330 kN)
Total weight:	126 tons (129 t)
Gauge:	1435 mm
Road numbers:	8101–8184

Locomotive 8604 awaiting its next call while standing in Delec depot on 6 August 1983. (Leon Oberg)

1983 NEW SOUTH WALES STATE RAIL AUTHORITY

86-class Co-Co

Following on from Commonwealth Engineering's ten 85-class 2880 kW electric locomotives delivered to the NSWSRA in 1979, the builder obtained a follow-up contract to supply fifty 3328 kW 86-class units.

Initially commissioned 15 March 1983, these locomotives, recognised as theoretically the most powerful of any steam, diesel or electric yet seen in Australia, were heavily employed in coal haulage between Lithgow and Port Kembla, and also spent many years working heavy goods trains over the electrified Sydney to Broadmeadow route. Lacking the sophisticated wheel-creep control equipment of modern locomotives, the 86-class tended to be a little light on their feet and, because they collected their power from an ages-old 1500 volt DC system, particularly when working in multiple on heavy coal trains they tended to 'drag the power' from the overhead resulting in a greatly reduced supply to each locomotive.

During the latter part of the 86-class's short construction period, Comeng approached State Rail for permission to redesign the last unit of the order, 8650, as a Bo-Bo-Bo (TriBo) locomotive. Comeng and State Rail both believed 8650 would become a useful test-bed for possible future TriBo designs. Unlike the conventional 3-axle 2-bogie Co-Co design, the TriBo configuration employed three 4-wheel bogies placed evenly beneath the locomotive chassis. While the two outer-end bogies were pivoted as normal, the centre bogie was allowed to move laterally by means of a Flexicoil spring and thus enabled the locomotive to pass through curves.

According to its designers, such a system would improve wheel life, because 4-wheel bogies tended to steer better than 6-wheel ones, reduce track forces and maintenance, and enhance the ride. Developed under the auspices of an Australian Industrial and Research Development Incentives Board grant, 8650 began an extensive series of in-service tests in January 1986.

Although experiencing early teething problems, mainly due to the lateral stiffness of its centre bogie, it eventually settled into the regular roster patterns. While no other units of this configuration were added to the NSW fleet, the lessons learned helped Comeng when constructing some 76 TriBo 3100/3200-class electric locomotives for Queensland Railways' coal haulage the following year.

With the formation of the National Rail Corporation, and lessening reliance on electric traction following the closure of some western coal mines, no fewer than 19 locomotives of the 86-class, exhibiting frame fractures, had been stored 'surplus to requirements' by January 1998. In 2002, with their leases expiring, all units were stopped just prior to 8646 operating a farewell rail enthusiast excursion on 7 September 2002 which saw a class member visit Kiama on the South Coast for the first time.

On 20 February 2003 all 50 were officially disposed of, 48 units to Silverton Rail, No. 8606 to the Sydney Electric Train Society and 8646 in operational condition to the NSWRTM. Most of the Silverton Rail locomotives were stored at Broken Hill and while four (including the class-leader) were reactivated late in 2004 for the haulage of work trains in the Sydney area, scrappings started in Broken Hill with 8604 in May 2005.

Loco 8619 was sold to Specialized Container Transport in February 2006 and forwarded to Adelaide for a planned (but subsequently abandoned) scheme for conversion into a non-powered crew car with full driving station. Negotiations were finalised late in 2006 with the Dorrigo Steam Railway and Museum to preserve TriBo 8650, along with 8601. Scrappings of the balance started at that time.

SPECIFICATIONS

	IMPERIAL (METRIC)
ELECTRICAL EQUIPMENT:	MITSUBISHI 1500V (DC)
MAXIMUM HORSEPOWER:	4460 (3328 kW)
CONTINUOUS HORSEPOWER:	4198 (3132 kW)
STARTING TRACTIVE EFFORT:	94 900 LB (420 kN)
TOTAL WEIGHT:	115.7 TONS (118 T)
GAUGE:	1435 MM
ROAD NUMBERS:	8601–8650

Locomotive 2612 as rebuilt, and pictured with 1491 kW EMD 2158 at Mackay on 8 June 2006. (Tony Wells)

1983 Queensland Railways

2600-class Co-Co

The 1067 mm gauge Queensland Railways made a 'trial' purchase of 13 GE-powered Goninan-designed mainliners between 29 November 1983 and 17 July 1984. These locomotives became the railway's 2600-class, a type based upon GE's US U22C model.

An off-the-shelf design would have been much too heavy for Queensland's lighter axle-load limitations so the entire locomotive, including the mechanical and structural components, had to be redesigned to meet stringent load limits. The builder even had to provide an Australian bogie to meet QR's narrow gauge requirements.

To meet the Queensland government's 'local built' requirement, Goninan & Co constructed a plant in Townsville especially to build the locomotives. Despite the weight-saving initiatives, the locomotives tipped the scales at a rather heavy 97.6 tonnes.

At the time, these locomotives were the most powerful working on the QR and when pressed into service over the McNaughton and Newlands route in central Queensland, four were able to haul 82-wagon trains (5986 tonnes) of coal over a ruling gradient of 1 in 80.

While the bulk of their lives was spent at Pring depot (near Bowen) for Collinsville coal service, moves to replace them with new EDI 4000-class units saw the 2600-class progressively rebuilt by their original builder and ballasted to 109.3 tonnes between July 2000 and May 2001. All were equipped with cab extensions at this time. After this they commenced a new career on the Mt Isa line.

Generally they are used on heavy freight and mineral workings, often as second units, but 2601 was noted working the *Inlander* passenger train out of Mt Isa in February 2002.

Two original cabs were salvaged for preservation by the ARHS and at last report were stored in Townsville.

Specifications

	Imperial (Metric)
Power unit:	GE FDL12
Traction horsepower:	2200 (1640 kW)
Starting tractive effort:	66 910 lb (299 kN)
Continuous tractive effort:	56 876 lb (253 kN at 17 km/h)
Total weight:	96 tons (97.6 t) Units ballasted to 109.3 tonnes in 2000–01.
Gauge:	1067 mm
Road numbers:	2600–2612

1983 Australian National

BL-class Co-Co

With a record eighty 2237 kW 81-class Super Series locomotives on order to the State Rail Authority of NSW, Australian National's administration started to take a keen interest in this model's attributes. Needing additional motive power to replace an ageing standard gauge fleet, AN ordered ten similarly-powered units in 1982, on theoretical reputation alone. These locomotives were designated the BL-class.

Their styling differed in that the BL was provided with a trussed car body, conventional framing and flat-topped cabs in lieu of the 81-class's full-strength deep girder underframe and intermediate, removable full-width engine-room hoods flanked by cabs with downward sloping ends of AN's AL-class parentage.

A spick and span BL32 powers an Adelaide-bound broad gauge interstate freight train between Parwan and Bacchus Marsh on 8 February 1985. (Leon Oberg)

The BL-class was a product of Clyde Engineering's Rosewater (Adelaide) factory. The first one entered service on 1 September 1983. Although ordered for the standard gauge, the latter half of the order was assigned to the broad gauge system where their high power and Super Series wheel-creep feature quickly became legend in the torrid Adelaide Hills (over the interstate Melbourne route), where continuous grades of 1 in 45 face trains in both directions on the Tailem Bend section.

While the BL fleet was under construction, neighbouring operator V/Line, which desperately needed new locomotives to streamline its wheat haulage into Portland, managed to complete a deal with Clyde and AN to obtain, at really short notice, five units which were actually on option to AN. These appeared as the G-class on the Victorian broad gauge between November 1984 and January 1985 (see separate story).

Working everything from Broken Hill ore to Leigh Creek coal, all BL-class locomotives were at one stage placed on broad gauge interstate operation between Adelaide and Melbourne for reciprocal interstate operating agreements between V/Line and AN.

With gauge standardisation of the Melbourne–Adelaide route completed in May 1995, all members of the BL-class passed into captive NRC ownership and from early 1999, for a time some received a taste of unexpected glory when they were regularly rostered to work Great Southern Railway's *The Overland* (and later) *The Ghan* passenger services between Melbourne and Adelaide under a 'hook and pull' arrangement with the trains' owner, Great Southern Railway.

In addition to this, the BLs' route availability was being extended to include the haulage of NRC steel trains to Port Kembla and Newcastle in New South

Wales as a prelude to basing several in Newcastle from October 2000. Here their large 10 230-litre fuel tanks made them favoured power on ore concentrate haulage from western New South Wales mines, including Parkes. By then, the BL-class's ranks had diminished with the storage of BL28 and BL35 at Islington workshops from 1997 to provide spare parts. But this was only academic, for all locomotives passed into the ownership of Pacific National on 21 February 2002 and the stowed BLs were fully overhauled in 2004 to satisfy a burgeoning freight haulage task. Today the BL-class can also be seen working intermodal traffic in the Brisbane, Sydney, Melbourne and Adelaide corridor.

SPECIFICATIONS

	Imperial (Metric)
Power unit:	EMD 16-645E3B
Traction horsepower:	3000 (2237 kW)
Starting tractive effort:	104 000 lb (465 kN)
Continuous tractive effort:	75 764 lb (337 kN)
Total weight:	130 tons (132 t)
Gauge:	1435 mm and 1600 mm
Road numbers:	BL26–BL35

1983 V/Line

A-class Co-Co

In the early 1980s V/Line made a decision to upgrade its long-distance country express passenger services. While part of this plan was the construction of comfortable new carriages, a battery of fast express locomotives capable of withstanding the daily rigours of constant high-speed travel was another consideration.

The first of the 1952 B-class to appear in rebuilt form as the new A-class was A73 on 21 December 1983. It is shown nearing Wandong with the Melbourne-bound *Goulburn Valley Limited* from Shepparton on 27 October 1988. (Leon Oberg)

New locomotives were expensive. The solution seemed to lie in Clyde Engineering's 26 pioneer B-class 1119 kW streamlined double-end locomotives of 1952 vintage, all of which were in need of complete rebuilds. By then, most had travelled almost 6 million kilometres. Because the locomotives seemed to possess sound underframes, Clyde came up with a perceived cost-effective scheme to 'remanufacture and re-power' them for the new express duties. Although their stylish noses and cabs were retained, along with chassis and bogies, the original 16-567B engines, generators, cooling systems and traction equipment were discarded and replaced with modern turbo-blown 12-645E3B engines (which could provide 1678 kW for traction) and improved alternator packages.

An upgraded driving position, a safer cab/control design and air-conditioning improved conditions for crews while modern inertial filters were fitted to reduce maintenance costs and the electrical cabinet, which employed the latest Dash-2 modular plug-in electrics, was pressurised with filtered air to ensure the trouble-free operation of relay controls.

The first unit treated was B73, which had suffered a serious electrical fire. It arrived in Clyde's Rosewater (Adelaide) plant early in 1982, emerging in its new form in December 1983 as an A-class. Although re-classified, it and subsequent rebuilds mostly retained their original road numbering.

But it was not an easy task to convert these old war horses. Clyde's then engineering manager David Butters said the first problem that had to be overcome was the short distance between the cabs:

'The adoption of the modern 12-cylinder turbo-charged engine gave us a lighter, 50 per cent more powerful locomotive along with the additional space. We also adopted an old EMD [USA] practice of mounting the cooling system above the engine and the inertial filter/traction motor cooling [blower] assembly was able to be hung from the roof, a special L-shaped electrical cabinet having been designed to allow for its position.'

Despite the rebuild's technical success, the Victorian Government abandoned the programme after the eleventh unit (A81) was completed in August 1985. Given the amount of stripping, cleaning and repair work necessary—along with the substantial amount of new power and control equipment being provided—the cost savings compared to brand-new locomotives was seen to be too small. In addition, space limitations within the now-cramped engine room made it difficult for maintenance fitters to exchange parts, particularly the turbo-charger clutch drives which tended to burn out prematurely due to the stop-start variations in engine loadings in passenger service.

As compensation for the forsaken A-class rebuilds, the maker received a contract to build new express locomotives using the same basic engine/electrical package. Thus was born V/Line's N-class, of which no fewer than 25 were built between August 1985 and July 1987 (see page 399).

The gradual scaling down of long-distance loco-hauled passenger services in Victoria from the early 1990s saw most A-class locomotives (which lacked head-end power equipment) permanently transferred

Locomotive P16 (formerly T332) awaits its next duty cycle at Bacchus Marsh on 14 February 1986. (Leon Oberg)

to V/Line's freight division. Only four were dedicated to passenger working, being used principally on Seymour and Bacchus Marsh commuter services, a role some continued to play into 2006. The remaining seven units, A71, A73, A77–79, A81 and A85, were sold to Freight Victoria in February 1999 as a result of the Victorian state government's privatisation of its rail business. By 2002 these locomotives had been progressively improved by the fitting of QTRAC 1000 adhesion-control systems, which increased their continuous tractive effort to about 60 150 lb (267 kN), and today belong to Pacific National.

SPECIFICATIONS

	IMPERIAL (METRIC)
POWER UNIT:	EMD 12-645E3B
TRACTION HORSEPOWER:	2400 (1790 kW)
STARTING TRACTIVE EFFORT:	65 000 lb (297 kN)
CONTINUOUS TRACTIVE EFFORT:	48 505 lb (212 kN)
TOTAL WEIGHT:	119.3 tons (121.2 t)
GAUGE:	1600 mm
ROAD NUMBERS:	A60, A62, A66, A70, A71, A73, A77–A79, A81, A85

1984 V/Line

P-Class Bo-Bo

In company with V/Line's early 1980s drive to improve the accommodation and speed on long-distance country expresses, the needs of commuters living on the rural outskirts of Melbourne were also addressed. V/Line embarked on a programme of rebuilding surplus Harris suburban electric carriages. Marshalled into 3-car sets, these considerably updated trains (which were equipped with air-conditioning) were seen as replacements for ageing railmotors, some of which had been around for about 50 years.

V/Line did not have the money to buy new medium-power locomotives to haul the trains, and hit on the idea of rebuilding thirteen 27-year-old T-class Bo-Bo units that had reached the end of their economic lives. As the locomotives still possessed sound underframes, bogies and bodies, V/Line contracted their original maker, Clyde Engineering, to 'remanufacture, restyle and update' them as the P-class.

The locomotive (and carriage) project was given to the manufacturer's Martin & King factory at Somerton, Melbourne. This plant came into being way back in 1894 to build road vehicle bodies (they assembled Australia's first Rolls Royce). Clyde Industries acquired the company in 1954, just in time to assemble Volkswagen cars.

The P-class rebuilds incorporated a 746 kW EMD 8-645E engine in place of the original 653 kW EMD 8-567C. The original low-level cab was replaced by a comfortable, air-conditioned high-level one which provided improved vision. It was fully isolated from the mainframe to reduce vibrations and further reduce noise. Improved traction motor blowing and radiator fan systems were incorporated into the design, as was a vastly improved driver's control system.

Because the locomotives were specially designed to haul a fixed rake of carriages, the P-class was equipped with a separate 105 kW Detroit Diesel-powered alternator to provide head-end power to drive the train's lighting and air-conditioning needs. Entering service from 11 May 1984, these beautifully proportioned locomotives became an instant success story. All were delivered within four months.

A decade later, some had covered 700 000 kilometres in constant stop-start service which included daily haulage of trains to Bacchus Marsh, Leongatha, Seymour and Kyneton. When the delivery of Sprinter railcars during 1994–95, and the closure of several routes, reduced the call on locomotive-hauled commuter trains, several P-class were phased into intrastate freight service, their head-end power being valuable in powering perishable trains' refrigeration units. Five (P19–23) were accordingly sold to Freight Victoria in February 1999 (which became part of Pacific National in September 2004). The remaining units passed into the control of National Express Group PLC five months later following the privatisation of Victorian passenger interests. However, that company went into receivership in January 2003 and the business and locomotives returned to Victorian government ownership.

It is interesting that the Public Transport Corporation, Victoria, pioneered a push-pull configuration for some of its larger commuter trains utilising P-class units.

Wearing the livery of its most recent owner, Pacific National, G527 is pictured with a stone train in the Hanson quarry siding at Kilmore East on 3 November 2005. (Leon Oberg)

SPECIFICATIONS

	IMPERIAL (METRIC)
POWER UNIT:	EMD 8-645E
TRACTION HORSEPOWER:	1000 (746 kW)
STARTING TRACTIVE EFFORT:	42 500 lb (189 kN)
CONTINUOUS TRACTIVE EFFORT:	34 200 lb (149 kN)
TOTAL WEIGHT:	75.1 TONS (77 T)
GAUGE:	1600 MM
ROAD NUMBERS:	P11–P23 (PREVIOUSLY T's 336, 329, 340, 330, 344, 332, 327, 339, 331, 337, 338, 328 AND 326 RESPECTIVELY)

1984 V/LINE

G-class Co-Co

While Australian National Rail's ten BL-class locomotives of 1983 were being built, neighbouring operator V/Line, which desperately needed new broad gauge locomotives for grain haulage into Portland, managed to complete a deal with builder, the Clyde Engineering Co, and AN to obtain at really short notice five BL-class units which were actually on option to AN.

Assembled at the builder's Rosewater (Adelaide) factory, these locomotives appeared between November 1984 and January 1985 as the G-class. With their advanced features, including trademark Super Series wheel-creep control capabilities, they were an instant success—so much so that subsequent ordering saw the class swell to 33. All deliveries after the initial five were progressively customised to better suit V/Line's individual requirements, being equipped, for instance, with smaller 9600 litre fuel tanks against the prototype BL/G's 10 230 litre versions. Body styling varied slightly as orders progressed too, a move aimed at improving access for fitters.

The final 18, which were built in Victoria at the builder's Martin & King plant, received 6-cylinder air-compressors in lieu of the initial 2-cylinder variety while the last locomotive in the series, G543, delivered on 30 November 1989, boasted new generation desk controls with WABCO braking, and minor electrical improvements.

One significant variation saw the initial BL/G design's AR16 main alternator (similar to NSW State Rail's 81-class) replaced with the AR11 type from locomotive G516 onwards. The AR16 type boasted high field characteristics operating in full parallel, which for the crew meant that no noticeable transition changes were felt. The AR11 alternators possessed the more conventional, noticeable and sometimes fierce field-shunt progressions.

In pre-NRC days, 12 G-class were at some stage issued to the standard gauge Sydney route, and with similar reciprocal interstate operation agreements in place between V/Line and AN, G and (first-run) BL-class locomotives were pooled on the interstate Melbourne–Adelaide broad gauge line as well.

While some enjoyed stints working with NRC with one unexpectedly visiting Brisbane on 15 March 1998, domestically the G-class was shared between standard and broad gauge assignments hauling intrastate superfreighter and wheat trains, all having been acquired by Freight Victoria following the sell-off of V/Line Freight's assets in February 1999. But their ranks thinned on 26 November 1999 when locos 517 and 518 collided at Ararat. Both were scrapped for their re-usable parts.

From October 2000, the company started re-powering G-class with 16-645F3B 3800 hp (gross) engines after winning a contract to haul a customer's freight across the nation. The first of eight transformed was G523, which now exerted a more useful 2685 traction kW. From September 2004, Freight Australia (and the surviving G-class) became part of Pacific National, but under a deal struck earlier with an independent freight company, G516 and G534 were on-sold to QR National on 26 November for Melbourne–Brisbane intermodal working. Soon afterwards, Specialized Container Transport acquired nine which, during late 2009, were disposed of, CFCLA gaining Gs 511, 512 and 515; SSR G513 and G514 and AWB Gs 521, 532, 533 and 535.

SPECIFICATIONS

	ORIGINAL	AS REBUILT
	IMPERIAL (METRIC)	IMPERIAL (METRIC)
POWER UNIT:	EMD 16-645E3B	EMD 16-645F3B
TRACTION HORSEPOWER:	3000 (2237 KW)	3500 HP (2610 KW)
STARTING TRACTIVE EFFORT:	104 000 LB (465 KN)	140 000 LB (623 KN)
CONTINUOUS TRACTIVE EFFORT:	75 764 LB (337 KN)	93 100 LB (415 KN)
TOTAL WEIGHT	(G511–515): 130 TONS (132 T)	
	(G516–543):125.8 TONS (128 T)	125.6 TONS (127.2 T)
GAUGE:	1435 MM AND 1600 MM	1435MM
ROAD NUMBERS:	G511–G543	G523, G526, G529, G530, G531, G536, G541, G543

1985 V/LINE

N-class Co-Co

In December 1983, Victoria's long-distance train travellers were introduced to the A-class, a re-manufactured version of that rail system's 1952-era dual-cab B-class.

At the time, the Victorian Government had contracted the B-class's original maker, Clyde Engineering, to upgrade all 26 locomotives in the class to make them suitable for high-speed long-distance intercity express service. After the eleventh unit had been completed, the programme was truncated because the cost margin below brand-new locomotives was seen to be too small.

As compensation for the abandoned rebuild programme, Clyde received a contract to build 25 new express locomotives using the same basic engine/electrical package as the A-class. These locomotives became the N-class and were delivered between August 1985 and July 1987.

The new locomotives were fitted with a separate 240 kW diesel-driven alternator package to provide head-end power for passenger train air-conditioning, lighting and kitchens.

Wearing V/Line's distinctive red and blue passenger livery, N471 *City of Wangaratta* stands in Geelong locomotive servicing area on 1 November 2005. (Leon Oberg)

The N-class was based on a platform-type underframe and it introduced to Australia yet another design style, the 'dog bone' look. A full-width G-class type cab was positioned at each end of the locomotive's frame but the engine-room covers, instead of being full width, were built to a narrow hood design with external walkways down each side.

Minor nuisance teething faults, including 'computer software interference problems and wiring errors', surfaced with the initial deliveries and were gradually corrected. This meant that the first unit did not enter revenue service until 22 January 1986.

Since then, the class has suffered from high turbo-charger clutch-drive failure rates which senior Dynon Workshops fitters say are caused by the stop-start nature of their passenger work. This is due in many respects to the light passenger train weights and the undulating nature of many routes. When these factors are combined with the fast timetables, drivers need to constantly vary locomotive throttle settings with the result that the locomotives' turbo-clutches are being ridden abnormally, burning them out. Because they are mounted internally, in a bid to reduce the four days' work required to change the equipment, fitters modified the engine-room side doors to allow the components to be removed more easily.

Despite these problems, N453 (the first unit to actually enter revenue service) had covered a staggering 1.4 million kilometres in its first eight years.

While the N-class is 'thick on the ground' working Melbourne–Geelong passenger services (taking full advantage of their driver-only status) and several other regional broad gauge passenger services in Victoria, some at times ventured into freight service.

Following a rationalisation of Victorian rail businesses in 1997, however, all were officially declared captive to passenger working. About this time their original D43 traction motors (provided to reduce their unsprung mass for high-speed running) were progressively changed out for the robust D78 type, in line with the A-class.

Carrying the names of Victorian cities, all units remain in Victorian government service, with N453, N469 and N470 allocated to standard gauge for the Seymour to Albury ex-broad gauge line's 26 June 2011 commissioning.

SPECIFICATIONS

IMPERIAL (METRIC)

POWER UNIT:	EMD 12-645E3C (N451–N460) AND 12-645E3B (N461–N475)
TRACTION HORSEPOWER:	2400 (1790 KW)
STARTING TRACTIVE EFFORT:	68 610 LB (304 KN)
CONTINUOUS TRACTIVE EFFORT:	60 350 LB (253 KN)
TOTAL WEIGHT:	115.7 TONS (118 T)
GAUGE:	1600 MM
ROAD NUMBERS:	N451 TO N475

1986 HYDRO-ELECTRIC COMMISSION OF TASMANIA

Hydrostatic 0-4-0DH

Western Australian engineering company George Moss Ltd was awarded a $1 million contract in 1985 to supply the Hydro-Electric Commission of Tasmania with five special-purpose diesel tunnel locomotives to haul spoil.

These locomotives, delivered from the firm's Osborne Park factory between May and September 1986, were the first hydrostatic diesel-hydraulic units produced for mining use in Australia.

The Commission's Senior Design Engineer (Tunnels), Mr A.J. Bowling, said the units were ordered for use in the construction of the King River power development. This work included the excavation of a 7 km headrace tunnel under the West Coast Range to the John Butters Power Station, in which the locomotives were employed hauling rail-mounted excavation equipment and spoil trains.

Under the hydrostatic system, the locomotives' engine power variable displacement hydraulic pumps provide high-pressure oil to variable displacement drive motors on axle-hung transmission units, described as a 'foolproof' design. The driver has just two controls, a forward/reverse selector and engine throttle lever. He need only select the required engine speed and the hydraulic system itself selects the speed ratios for the transmission, based upon the prevailing load and gradient.

Another unusual feature was the automatically applied engine-braking system incorporated into the throttle control, a feature up until then not available through hydrodynamic transmission systems.

All five were fitted with stainless steel exhaust water scrubbers, which were combined with a

Energy Brix Australia's 2, 5 and 1 approaching the Morwell ditch bunker with a loaded train on 4 July 1999. (Darren Hodges)

pre-combustion system to ensure that all exhaust emissions were well below those prescribed by the Mines Department. The locomotives' cabs, which were insulated against noise and cold, were equipped with high quality ergonomic seating.

When work on the King River development was completed in 1989, the locomotives and other rail-mounted equipment were transferred to the Anthony Power development north of Queenstown and used in the excavation of a 4.5 km section of this development's headrace tunnel. At the completion of this project in 1991, the five locomotives and allied rail equipment were advertised for sale. After spending a large part of the decade in storage, the units were eventually sold to the National Logistics Coordinators Group (NLC), the accredited rail operator of brown coal trains over the 16.5 km link between Victoria's Yallourn open cut to Energy Brix Australia Corporation's ditch bunker at Morwell. Each unit was rated to haul eight 50-tonne loaded wagons; in 2000, the railway was rated to haul 1 million tonnes a year with up to three locomotives working the trains.

From late 1999, NLC started upgrading the units' hydraulic drives which, according to operations and maintenance general manager Noel Hutchinson, was 'to align them for long distance haulage'. But with the development of a new brown coal field encroaching on the railway, combined with the need to upgrade the permanent way, a decision was made to change over to road transport. The last train, hauled by two 0-4-0DH locomotives, ran between Yallourn and Morwell in October 2000.

After a short period in open storage, all five (now numbered 1–5), along with two ex Queensland DH-class locomotives, were auctioned in November 2001. While two 0-4-0DHs found new homes at Trafalgar, the remaining somewhat derelict units were held at Yallourn until offered at a public liquidation auction in Morwell on 3 December 2002. Some were

noted being scrapped at Trafalgar during the 2006 autumn.

SPECIFICATIONS

	IMPERIAL (METRIC)
POWER UNIT:	CATERPILLAR 3306 PCT
TRACTION HORSEPOWER:	300 (149 kW 2000 RPM)
MAXIMUM TRACTIVE EFFORT:	8900 LB (40 kN)
TOTAL WEIGHT:	26.5 TONS (27 T)
GAUGE:	1067 MM
ROAD NUMBERS:	P311–P315 (RENUMBERED 1–5 BY NLC)

1986 QUEENSLAND RAILWAYS

3100/3200-class Bo-Bo-Bo

Believing massive cost benefits could be had by electrifying the central Queensland (Bowen Basin) coal railways, Queensland Railways let contracts in the winter of 1984 for record numbers of 25 kV AC electric locomotives.

Joint venturers Comeng/Hitachi subsequently received a $97.9 million contract to build seventy-six 2900 kW units. In a break with Australian tradition, all these 110-tonne locomotives were of the Bo-Bo-Bo (triple powered bogie) configuration, a move initiated to help reduce wheel and rail wear through curves and turnouts and to improve the spread of each unit's all-up weight over bridge spans.

While the two outside bogies rotated on curves in the normal way, the intermediate bogie was provided with 'built in flexibility' to allow it to move transversely (as much as 200 mm) either side of centre but in so doing remain parallel to the body. To further reduce track forces, rubber springs were used on the locomotives' primary suspension. To provide optimum transmission of traction and braking forces,

Locomotive 3286 (with 3160) poses outside Jilalan depot on 17 March 1997. (Leon Oberg)

3700-class locomotive 3702 between Braeside and Mindi during a test run on 22 June 2006. Note the blanked-off No. 2 end cab. Three EMD diesels accompanied the locomotive to provide variable drawbar forces. (Tony Wells)

traction rods were specified to provide minimum weight transfer for the highest possible adhesion.

The Comeng/Hitachi class-leader 3101 was unveiled on 26 May 1986, and the first five soon started hauling 10 500 (gross)-tonne coal trains from Peak Downs mine to Hay Point, a route on which grades of 1 in 100 are encountered. Early teething problems arose with the class's traction motor blower fans which, due to their high operational speed, tended to shed blades.

As with the diesel coal locomotives before them, several units were equipped with the microprocessor-based Locotrol 2 system (a means of placing unmanned locomotives midway through a train and operating them by radio signal from the cab of the train's leading locomotive). Twenty of the Comeng/Hitachi remote-control command units became the 3100-class while the units capable of receiving their command were numbered within the 3200-class.

As the electrified network continued to grow,

QR contracted Comeng/Hitachi to construct an additional ten units. All 86 locomotives were delivered by 14 December 1989 and are principally based at Jilalan depot (near Sarina).

With the classes operating mainly over the Goonyella–Hay Point system, an extra 10 tonnes weight was added to four original locomotives from early 1997 to improve adhesion characteristics.

Non-command units 3267, 3279 and 3282 were badly damaged as a result of a huge coal train high-speed derailment (which involved four locomotives) at Black Mountain on 17 November 1994. The three were officially written off at Rockhampton workshops three years afterwards, 3267 and 3282 being cut up in December 2000. It is understood the third unit of the trio was deliberately retained for possible rebuild.

Seven years passed and another accident at the same location saw the destruction of 3255 and more modern unit 3410, on 1 July 2001. A subsequent investigation determined the $20.6 million accident was initially caused by a Locotrol signal failure and an O-ring malfunction within a brake pipe control valve. Loco 3255's remains were disposed of, following stripping of useful parts, in September 2002.

On 5 November 2002, mid-train units 3226 and Clyde-built 3413 rolled over in a violent derailment in Waitara loop while working an empty Jilalan to German Creek coal train. Both locomotives were eventually returned to service, 3413 after lengthy repairs at Redbank, and 3226 after its rebuilding to AC traction prototype 3701, emerging late in 2005.

The 3700-class came about in response to pressures to move even more coal. In 1997 QR electrical engineers came up with a means of overcoming the need for command units to send radio signals to remote (ELRC) vehicles attached to the central bank of locomotives in coal trains, reasoning that an extra wagon of coal could be hauled if the ELRC was eliminated. A trial conversion of 3116, 3272 and 3276 to 'improved' 3100-class was started and in July that year the three units were phased into test workings, also equipped with electrical brake controls in lieu of their air-operated equipment.

Their No. 2 end cabs were isolated during this work to provide spare parts for the conversion, which also required the energy signal between the drivable and remote units to be altered from electrical to radio. Additional solenoid valves were added to the converted locomotives' brake racks.

Experience gained with these locomotives eventually led to a contract being signed with United-Goninan in 2003 for the conversion in Townsville of units 3226, 3213 and 3217 to prototypes of what became the 3700-class. Emerging from November 2005, this project included the provision of AC traction equipment boosting the units' at-rail output to 4000 kW (5360 hp). Electronic control equipment replaced the original electro-pneumatic in the revised, now single-cab units, whose total weight was boosted to 126 tonnes. Another 60 are expected to be similarly converted, for the purpose of three replacing five unmodified DC units per train.

These locomotives have spawned the 3800-class, a fleet of 45 identically powered locomotives delivered out of Siemens' Munich (Germany) factory with first deliveries arriving on 23 June 2008. The 132-tonne units have seamlessly integrated with the 3700-class. PNQ has since acquired 23 copies (see pages 442–43).

SPECIFICATIONS

	ORIGINAL IMPERIAL (METRIC)	AS REBUILT IMPERIAL (METRIC)
ELECTRICAL EQUIPMENT:	HITACHI/GEC 25 kV	SIEMENS 25 kV
MAXIMUM HORSEPOWER:	3890 HP (2900 kW)	5360 HP (4000 kW)
STARTING TRACTIVE EFFORT:	84 303 LB (375 kN)	113,995 LB (500 kN)
CONTINUOUS TRACTIVE EFFORT:	60 698 LB (270 kN AT 40 KM/H)	96,629 LB (430 kN
TOTAL WEIGHT:	108.1 TONS (109.8 T)	124 TONS (126 T)
GAUGE:	1067 MM	1067 MM
ROAD NUMBERS:	(COMMAND UNITS) 3101–3104, 3108, 3112, 3116, 3120, 3124, 3128, 3132, 3136, 3140, 3144, 3148, 3152, 3156, 3160, 3164, 3168.	
	(NON-COMMAND UNITS): 3205–3207, 3209–3211, 3213–3215, 3217–3219, 3221–3223, 3225–3227, 3229–3231, 3233–3235, 3237–3239, 3241–3243, 3245–3247, 3249–3251, 3253–3255, 3257–3259, 3261–3263, 3265–3267, 3269–3286.	
	(AS REBUILT) 3701-3763 (SOME STILL BEING CONVERTED)	

1986 QUEENSLAND RAILWAYS
3500/3600/3900-class Bo-Bo-Bo

Another successful tenderer for motive power under Queensland Railways' decision to electrify its lucrative central Queensland coal lines was the long-standing Queensland rolling-stock builder Walkers Ltd, which stitched up a joint partnership with veteran Swedish electric traction specialist ASEA (Brown Boveri) and the Australian builder Clyde Engineering Co. This partnership was awarded a $90.9 million contract to build seventy 2900 kW electric units.

Known as the 3500/3600-class, these locomotives, while equal in power output to the above-mentioned Comeng/Hitachi 3100/3200-class, were quite different in appearance and design. The Walkers units used a fluted stainless-steel car body structure, the first such use of this material on a locomotive in Australia. However, several items of equipment were interchangeable between the two types, such as air-conditioners, pantographs, brake equipment and traction control.

The two manufacturers unveiled their first units within days of each other, the first Clyde/ASEA-Walkers example (3502) entering service on 28 October 1986. The first Walkers locomotives were used (four to an 8750-tonne train) hauling coal from the Curragh mine (near Blackwater) to the port of Gladstone.

A mixed brace of electric power, including 3500/3600-class units 3504 (leading) and 3622 (trailing) assisted by newer Clyde locomotive, 3411, leaving Mt Larcom with a loaded train on 21 March 1997. (Leon Oberg)

Nineteen Walkers locomotives were equipped with microprocessor-based Locotrol-2 command equipment, becoming the 3500-class. The balance became the 3600-class.

As construction advanced, so too did Queensland electrification. By now, work on upgrading the 630 km Brisbane–Rockhampton north coast main line was well underway. Several hilly sections of line were bypassed altogether, including the testing Blackall Range in the Eumundi district, by expensive high-speed deviations.

As the work advanced it became obvious that more electric locomotives would be required, and each manufacturer was awarded contracts to build an additional ten units. While the Comeng/Hitachi locomotives were built to the same specifications as before, Walkers and partners agreed to alter the final 20 of their original contract and merge those with their new order for ten to come up with a new class of thirty 100 km/h locomotives specifically for the north coast railway.

When introduced from 5 September 1988, these locomotives became the 3900-class. Visually, parts of their bodies were slightly trimmed back to allow them to negotiate the Brisbane area's tight-clearance tunnels. Their traction motors and gear cases were attached to

the bogie frames rather than simply hung unsprung on the wheel-sets' axles, as was the case with the earlier units. This revised mounting enabled the 3900-class to operate at higher speeds (through a reduction in dynamic forces) on the lighter north coast rail.

The last 'coal' unit delivered was 3641 on 13 September 1988 and the last north coast locomotive, 3930, appeared on 16 February 1990. While early trials were undertaken using 3900-class in central Queensland coal traffic (where these units could be used as trailing power in remote control working), they were generally dedicated to the main Rockhampton–Brisbane and Rockhampton–Emerald routes until June 2001, when four were placed into coal haulage out of Callemondah depot at Gladstone in company with the 3500/3600s.

As with the 3100/3200 classes described in the previous article, pressures to move even more coal led electrical engineers to devise a means of overcoming the need for command units to send radio signals to a remote (ELRC) vehicle attached in coal trains. A trial conversion of 3508, 3633 and 3643 to 'improved' 3500-class was inaugurated, and by July 1997 these units were phased into test workings, having been equipped with electrical brake controls in lieu of their air-operated equipment. Their No. 2 end cabs were isolated during

3900-class 3908 dashes through Eumundi with a Rockhampton-bound intermodal train on 10 October 1989. (Leon Oberg)

this work to provide spare parts for the conversion, which also required the energy signal between the drivable and remote units to be altered from electrical to radio. Additional solenoid valves were added to the converted locomotives' brake racks.

The only locomotive in this family to be withdrawn to date, 3902, was involved in a head-on collision with class-leader 3901 at Beerburrum on 28 July 1994 and became a source of spares at Rockhampton Workshops until its remains were disposed of in October 2000. No. 3901 was returned to service on 15 April 1997. Loco 3548 overturned at a line washaway at Taurus Creek while leading a loaded coal train towards Blackwater on 23 April 1998, but was subsequently returned to service.

With coal tonnages increasing steadily, a decision was made to gradually allocate all 3900-class to coal haulage; for this service their traction motors are being fitted to the wheel sets in the same way as in the 3500/3600-class, reducing their speed limit to 80 kph. An extra step was added to the coal locomotives' sides, making them out of gauge for general service. The ten units (including the class-leader) allocated to this traffic by mid-2002 were re-registered as 3900C-class. This move paved the way for a decision to fully overhaul and upgrade nineteen 3900s (3901–3919, except for scrapped 3902) for coal use, the work to be done in the QR Rockhampton workshops.

The first unit treated, 3906, emerged for trials in January 2003, renumbered 3556. This work put QR in a healthy position to help it win a contract in March 2003 to build a $200 million rail line from Blackwater to Rolleston to service MIM's new central Queensland open-cut thermal coal mine. The 100 km rail line to the new mine was designed to carry 8 million tonnes of export coal annually to Gladstone. Pressure from the coal sector saw all 3900-class allocated to that traffic by late May 2005. While all were to have been rebuilt to 3551-class specifications by EDI's Maryborough plant, the introduction of new locomotives halted that project after eighteen were treated. The remainder were overhauled to existing specifications.

SPECIFICATIONS

	3500/3551/3600-CLASS	3900-CLASS
	IMPERIAL (METRIC)	IMPERIAL (METRIC)
ELECTRICAL EQUIPMENT:	ASEA/CLYDE 25 KV	ASEA/CLYDE 25 KV
MAXIMUM HORSEPOWER:	3890 (2900 KW)	3890 (2900 KW)
STARTING TRACTIVE EFFORT:	84 303 LB (375 KN)	67 442 LB (300 KN)
CONTINUOUS TRACTIVE EFFORT:	60 698 LB (270 KN AT 40 KM/H)	48 334 LB (215 KN AT 40 KM/H)
TOTAL WEIGHT:	108.1 TONS (109.8 T)	108.1 TONS (109.8 T)
GAUGE:	1067 MM	1067 MM
ROAD NUMBERS:	COMMAND UNITS: 3501–3504, 3508, 3512, 3516, 3520, 3524, 3528, 3532, 3536, 3540, 3544, 3546–3550. NON-COMMAND UNITS: 3605–3607, 3609–3611, 3613–3615, 3617–3619, 3621–3623, 3625–3627, 3629–3631, 3633–3635, 3637–3639, 3641–3643, 3645. MAINLINE LOCOMOTIVES: 3901–3930 (BEING CONVERTED TO 3551-CLASS: 3551, 3553-3567, 3569 AND 3573.)	

1987 Mt Newman Mining Co

GE Dash-7 Co-Co

A. Goninan & Co received a contract from Mt Newman Mining (now BHP Billiton Iron Ore) for the rebuild of eight early Alco C/M 636 heavy-haul locomotives into Dash-7 units, Model CM36-7, the

Wearing striking Pilbara Rail livery, rejuvenated Dash-7 locomotives 5052 and 5051 (ex BHP Iron Ore 5507 and 5508) approach the company's Seven Mile yard with empties from East Intercourse Island on 11 January 2005. (Richard Montgomery)

first re-entering service in this form during January 1987. They carried the road numbers 5506–5513.

Ongoing technical improvements provided an extra 31 kN continuous tractive effort boost in the rebuilt version; 5510 was further improved in June 1993 when it received Dash-8 radiators following a collision with a loading chute. (Dash-7 radiator spares were no longer available.)

For Goldsworthy operations, all Dash-7s were equipped with higher capacity air-compressors to cater for the bottom air discharge vehicles and fitted with a 'gentler air brake', cab mirrors and an assortment of electrical modifications.

With the ordering of eight AC6000-class 4474 kW locomotives direct from GE (USA) early in 1998, the writing was on the wall for these locomotives and when 5511 snapped a crankshaft in March of that year, it was condemned. The remainder were progressively withdrawn during April–August 1999 with the arrival of the new locomotives. While some were temporarily maintained as standby power, all were eventually offered for sale. As no buyers were forthcoming, ownership officially passed to the builder who in May 2002 started dismantling the units, beginning with 5507, for conveyance to its Perth factory compound.

But in a surprise rejuvenation brought about by severe locomotive shortages on the Pilbara Rail network (originally the Hamersley Iron railway), two of the long-stored BHP Dash-7 GE locomotives, 5507 and 5508, were given cab, bogie and engine overhauls at United-Goninan, Perth, and in early 2003 leased to Pilbara Rail. They carry the numbers 5051 and 5052 respectively.

Because they were not provided with modern on-board signalling equipment, both units were initially put in work as trailing power and, more recently, dedicated as a coupled set in port unloading duties. Nicknamed *Bill* and *Ben* by crews, both were stored in 2009 at the company's Six Mile yard, Dampier. In another surprise move, 5509 has been transported to United-Group Rail's (the company's new trading name) Landsdowne plant (outside Taree, NSW) as an engine test-bed unit.

SPECIFICATIONS

	Imperial (Metric)
Power unit:	GE FDL-16
Traction horsepower:	3600 (2685 kW)
Starting tractive effort:	130 000 lb (578 kN)
Continuous tractive effort:	90 010 lb (400 kN)
Total weight:	187 tons (190.6 t)
Gauge:	1435 mm
Road numbers:	5506–5513 (5507 and 5508 renumbered 5051, 5052 in 2003 for use by Pilbara Rail, formerly Hamersley Iron)

1988 BHP Iron Ore

GE Dash-8 Co-Co

Although Hamersley Iron had introduced a trial acquisition of three Dash-7 General Electric locomotives onto its Pilbara railroad in 1978, the heavy-haul iron ore miners continued their love affair with Alco equipment. This was due mainly to their great number, availability of spares and maintenance staff know-how.

But locomotives eventually wear out. Alco/MLW's Australian manufacturing company, Comeng, which had been rebuilding some of the older Alco C636 units at its Bassendean (Perth) plant, collapsed. The work was promptly taken over by A. Goninan & Co, the holders of the US-based General Electric Corporation licence.

After rebuilding eight Alco 636 units for Mt Newman Mining (now BHP Iron Ore) as GE Dash-7 units in 1987 (see previous entry), the firm was able to offer Australian railways an improved GE-powered Dash-8 locomotive type.

This included refined microprocessor technology and the company's Microsentry (computerised) Adhesion System, which is integrated with the locomotive's control system to detect and rapidly control any wheelslip. GE claimed that this feature improved the continuous tractive effort by 12.1 per cent and increased adhesion by 7.7 per cent With its greater motor ratings and higher capacity dynamic brake grid package, a 28.4 per cent improvement in the overall braking capacity with less resultant rail and wheel wear was provided.

Improved engine cooling, centrally located and more simplified electronics and a host of allied refinements made up the new-look locomotive design.

Interest in the product was swift and the manufacturer received a contract from Mt Newman Mining (now BHP Billiton) to construct four new Dash-8 units for its 426 km Mt Newman railway. Manufactured at Goninan's old Welshpool (Western Australia) plant, they were delivered with Rockwell bogies between September and December

Locomotive 5665 *Rotterdam* was the last of the three cabless units in operation and this is perhaps the very last photograph taken of it in that form while awaiting conversion. It was returned to service as a cab unit on 20 June 1997. (Les Standen)

Originally built as a cabless unit, 5663 *Newcastle* (built on Alco 5476's chassis) leads sister locomotive 5640 *Ether Creek* (ex 5479) and an ore train in 2004. (Richard Montgomery)

Two Robe units, 9417 and 9420, which were rebuilt as GE CM40-8M locomotives by Goninan & Co in Perth. The lead loco had been built as an Alco C636 in 1968 for the Spokane, Portland & Seattle Railroad and was acquired for Robe after the original 9417 (a C630 model) was extensively damaged in a collision. It entered service as 9417 (2nd) in its radically restyled (cab-forward) guise at Robe in May 1989. Loco 9420 was one of three Robe C630s rebuilt under the upgrade programme and the two are pictured at Cape Lambert on 14 October 2004. (Richard Montgomery)

1988 as the GE Model CM39-8. These 2908 kW locomotives were bestowed the 5630–5633 road number sequence.

Robe River, operator of a nearby 201 km heavy-haul line, then contracted A. Goninan & Co in 1989 to remanufacture three Alco units (progressively extended to 12 with the last delivery, No. 9410 having been completed as recently as 8 April 1996).

More locomotives followed for BHP from July 1991, this time using Alco underframes and their salvaged 'Hi Ad' bogies. During this time, another two units, 5646 and 5647, were built from all new parts and delivered in November 1992 and January 1993 respectively, emerging from Goninan's newer Bassendean plant. By 1992, ongoing developments had seen the manufacturer's engines improved to provide 2983 kW, thus producing a model CM40-8.

As the rebuild programme continued, a variation to the now tried and proven theme was unveiled during the closing days of August 1994. In company with Goninan, BHP Iron Ore did some sums and found individual locomotive savings of up to $400 000 could be obtained if a locomotive was rebuilt minus its cab. As a result, BHP altered the contract early in 1994 to remanufacture eight (later reduced to three) old Alcos as cabless Dash-8 units. The first of those was Goodwin-built M636, No. 5476, which when returned to the Pilbara carried road number 5663. After all rebuilt locomotives had been delivered by 7 June 1995, BHP was operating no fewer than 40 Dash-8 locomotives over its present 770 km railway (which today includes the former 208 km Goldsworthy Mining line to Yarri).

As these locomotives were being manufactured, the GE parent had further improved the technology and in the USA was producing Dash-9 locomotives. Goninan & Co was able to integrate some of the upgraded features such as engine split cooling (which makes intake air for combustion purposes more dense) and electronic fuel injection and software (the first units in Australia to be so fitted) into the final four deliveries.

From locomotive 5648 onwards, the Integrated Function Control (IFC) monitoring system was fitted to all locomotives bearing cabs. This Australian first consisted of two screens that replaced all the conventional indicators and gauges, providing essential data such as operational speed, train line air-pressure, alerter, end of train security and clock readings. In addition it displayed the status of various warning systems. It also provided fault diagnostic information.

All these remanufactured locomotives (including the final four with some Dash-9 features) possess 2983 kW engines in place of the former 2685 kW Alco equipment, boast 18 600–19 000 litre fuel tanks and can travel up to 112 km/h. According to BHP Billiton, the maintenance bill for the rebuilt locomotives fell 80 per cent when compared to the older Alcos.

Despite the cabless locomotive construction programme's good intentions, these units at times were found to be difficult to roster, particularly with new mines coming on stream, and the manufacturer was contracted during mid-1996 to construct and fit cabs to the three. Loco 5663 was the first out-shopped in its new form on 6 December 1996. The work was undertaken under a $9 million upgrade of early Dash-8 units which included their promotion to Model CM40-8 specification in addition to the provision of IFC screens, Epic brakes, Locotrol 111 equipment, 350-watt headlights and a host of internal cab refinements.

The last to receive a cab, 5665, was returned to service on June 20 1997.

While 240 cars for 33 500 tonnes had been for years the normal load over the BHP system, the company introduced some 42 000-tonne 300-car trains from its Yandi mine to Nelson Point load-out following a test on 10 March 1994. Powered with five Dash-8 locomotives on the front with two more mid-train, the then Australian record train was run to select an optimum configuration for railing ore from that relatively new mine.

Not wanting to be left out of the record books, Robe River operated an even larger 44 100-tonne 350-car train between its J Mesa mine and Cape Lambert, a distance of 200 kilometres, in March 1995. The company had just introduced Locotrol 111 and this was a grand opportunity to trial the system. Nine Dash-8 locomotives were used in various blocks throughout the train—which represented 42 per cent of the company's entire locomotive/rolling-stock fleet.

Both those records paled into insignificance on 28 May 1996 when BHP decided to operate a 540-car train which employed 10 Dash-8 locomotives for a then world record 70 381-tonne load. This monster 5892 metre-long movement, which was restricted to 75 km/h, was also operated to test BHP's Locotrol 111 equipment.

Meanwhile, the last Pilbara Dash-8 built in

Wearing the latest BHP Billiton corporate livery, 5632 *Poseidon* was one of an initial three constructed from new materials and employing Rockwell bogies late in 1988 as the GE Model CM39-8. Many subsequent deliveries, mostly constructed on salvaged Alco underframes, benefited from ongoing traction developments thus producing Model CM40-8. Earlier units were retrofitted with the improved technology. The train is approaching Boodarie yard on 2 August 2004. (Richard Montgomery)

Australia was a locomotive delivered to Robe as 9410 on 8 April 1996 and believed to have been constructed on the chassis of former BHP unit 5500, one of two earlier sent to Goninan & Co Bassendean for parts. Robe's Railroad Superintendent Eric Girdler told the author at the time that 'in a bid to speed up construction to clear the factory floor for wholesale assembly of NR-class for the National Rail Corporation, it was agreed to use the BHP unit as a platform'. Until details of the original 9410's disposal could be worked out, two 9410s existed at Robe and, uniquely, were photographed side by side at Cape Lambert when the newly-rebuilt unit was delivered.

Unlike the final four BHP Dash-8 locomotives which boasted some Dash-9 features, Robe's 9410 was built to conventional specifications.

Footnotes
1. A further three Alco/MLW 636 units, 5503–5505, had been forwarded to Bassendean after they were sold in 1994 to Hamersley Iron to begin a planned Dash-8 rebuild programme for that company. The programme was shelved when that company decided to acquire new Dash-9 locomotives from the USA. The three M636s were scrapped in 1995.
2. Sharp-eyed readers may have picked up what appears to be an inconsistency in the final deliveries of BHP's Dash-8 locomotives. As mentioned, the final eight (from 5663) were to have been built less cabs, which would have taken the number sequence to 5670. However BHP, while altering the contract to just three cabless units (5663–5665), also cancelled the order for the last locomotive. A maker's number (8412-03/95-161) and the cabside nameplate *Shanghia* had already been allocated when the contract was changed.

SPECIFICATIONS

	IMPERIAL (METRIC)
POWER UNIT:	GE 7FDL-16
TRACTION HORSEPOWER:	3900 (2908 kW) ORIGINAL FOUR BHP UNITS. THESE WERE LATER UPGRADED. 4000 (2983 kW)
STARTING TRACTIVE EFFORT:	136 150 LB (628 kN)
CONTINUOUS TRACTIVE EFFORT:	108 210 LB (485 kN)
TOTAL WEIGHT:	191.4 TONS (195 T)
GAUGE:	1435 MM
ROAD NUMBERS:	(BHP IRON ORE) 5630–5669 (5663–5665 BUILT CABLESS) NOS. 5650–5658 FITTED WITH LOCOTROL COMMAND. (ROBE RIVER) 9410 (2ND), 9411, 9414, 9417–9425.

1988 AUSTRALIAN NATIONAL RAILWAYS

DL-class Co-Co

EMD in the USA was continuing its research and development and by the mid-1980s had virtually ceased production of its tried and proven 645-type engine, which had an individual cylinder displacement of 10.57 litres, in favour of a 710-series engine which provided a 10 per cent increase in cylinder displacement (11.6 litres) obtained with a slightly longer piston stroke. The new engine possessed a larger diameter crankshaft, larger diameter plunger fuel injectors and greatly improved breathing, which allowed a plant of 12 cylinders (turbo-blown) to exert the same output as a turbo-blown 16-cylinder 645E3B.

Extensively road tested in North America before its commercial release in 1985, experience found a reduction from 0.365 pounds per brake horsepower

DL47, wearing National Rail Corporation livery, in Dry Creek (Adelaide) yard on 12 March 1999. (Leon Oberg)

hour to just 0.32 lb/BHP hour between the 710 engine and the older but faithful 645 plant. An annual fuel saving of around 28 per cent was possible in comparable work.

The first Australian railway to sample the new technology was Australian National, which needed replacements for its ageing GM-class locomotives. Twelve DL-class units were ordered from the Clyde Engineering's Bathurst (NSW) plant in October 1986, later increased to 15. Equipped with the 12-cylinder 710G engine package, which exerted 2260 kW for traction, the DL also employed more advanced traction motors and electronic control system monitors and an on-board computer to theoretically diagnose and sometimes remedy faults.

The DL was equipped with an isolated custom-designed low-profile full-width cab blended into a full-width pressurised car body. The first of these 121.5-tonne units was officially roadtested between Port Augusta and Whyalla on 11 March 1988. Not long afterwards it began working 80-vehicle Leigh Creek coal trains. When sufficient sister machines were available, DLs could be found heading most of the railway's *Westliner/Eastliner* freight services between Adelaide and Kalgoorlie.

But enginemen started complaining of vibrations coming from the class's diesel engines. Initially EMD suggested altering the firing order, which would involve installing a new camshaft at AN's expense. The railway operator refused. The engine's crankshaft balance beams were subsequently improved.

The entire class was transferred to the National Rail Corporation in 1995. Loco DL41 had the distinction of becoming the first locomotive in Australia painted in NRC colours, a month ahead of the official opening of the Melbourne–Adelaide standard gauge line by Prime Minister Paul Keating on 3 June 1995.

Ranks of the DL-class began to shrink on 14 January 1996 when DL37 was totally destroyed in a horrific fatal collision with a loaded Westrail fuel train at Hines Hill crossing loop (near Merredin). Nothing was salvageable and after sitting for some months in a Coroner's quarantine compound beside Port Augusta Workshops, the loco's mauled remains were quietly disposed of in October 1997. At the time DL36 was sitting outside the same workshop with a damaged engine.

Their route availability was increased in March 1999 when two were forwarded to New South Wales for ballast stone haulage between Dunmore and Sydney. Units have since gravitated into other general freight service throughout that state.

With the joint sale of NRC/FreightCorp in February 2002, fourteen DLs passed into the ownership of Pacific National.

SPECIFICATIONS

	IMPERIAL (METRIC)
POWER UNIT:	EMD 12-710G3A
TRACTION HORSEPOWER:	3010 (2260 KW)
STARTING TRACTIVE EFFORT:	138 800 LB (600 KN)
CONTINUOUS TRACTIVE EFFORT:	92 500 LB (413 KN)
TOTAL WEIGHT:	119.3 TONS (121.5 T)
GAUGE:	1435 MM
ROAD NUMBERS:	DL36–DL50

1990 Goldsworthy Mining Co

GML10 Co-Co

Goldsworthy Mining Ltd, operating in Western Australia's Pilbara region, had been relying on aged 1339 kW English-Electrics when it turned to the Clyde Engineering Co and its new 710G-powered EMD locomotive package on ordering replacement motive power in 1989.

Utilising a design that perpetuated the 'dog bone' configuration of V/Line's N-class of 1985, the 129.5-tonne one-off locomotive became known as GML10 when delivered to its new owner in May 1990. The unit received the 12-cylinder engine package similar to the N-class which provided a useful 2260 kW of power at the wheels. (This purposeful locomotive was even delivered from Clyde's Bathurst Workshops in the standard V/Line paint scheme.) It entered Goldsworthy Mining service from 20 May 1990.

Built specifically for heavy haul, the locomotive's 70:17 traction motor gearing ratio restricted it to 113 kph.

On 1 March 1991, BHP Iron Ore assumed ownership of Goldsworthy Mining and, following a complete upgrade of the Goldsworthy rail system to US heavy-haul standards, introduced its existing 2685 kW General Electric Dash-7 locomotives to the route.

In mid-1992, GML10 was renumbered GML20 to eliminate computer confusion between it and an existing BHP ore locomotive which at the time also carried a '10' in its number. However, despite its youth, the 'non-standard' locomotive became spare to requirements. Initially offered to V/Line and to BHP Steel's Port Kembla plant for coal train haulage, it eventually found a home at Weipa in far northern Queensland, taking up bauxite train haulage over Comalco Aluminium Ltd's

Locomotive GML10 in Mt Goldsworthy service in June 1990, less than two weeks after entering service. Initially painted in V/Line colours, the locomotive was later repainted in BHP's predominantly blue markings and renumbered GML20 to meet administrative computer tracking needs. (Author's collection)

19.5 km railway in August 1994. Its last run on the Goldsworthy system was on 1 July 1994.

Comalco renumbered the unit R1104 which handled 4125-tonne trains between Andoon bauxite mine and Lorim Point dumping facility until replaced by two new JT-42C Co-Co locomotives in August 2009. The company, now Rio Tinto Aluminium, acquired the new units in connection with its upgraded port facilities. While retaining similar 'dog-bone' styling, they were virtual standard-gauge copies of the Western Australian S-class of 1997. R1004 was sold in 2009 and today belongs to POTA, entering Melbourne-Adelaide service in July 2011.

Specifications

	Imperial (Metric)
Power unit:	EMD 12-710G3A
Traction horsepower:	3010 (2260 kW)
Starting tractive effort:	138 800 lb (600 kN)
Continuous tractive effort:	92 500 lb (413 kN)
Total weight:	127 tons (129.5 t)
Gauge:	1435 mm
Road number:	Built as GML10 (later GML20). Now Comalco's R1004.

1990 Australian National Railways

EL-class Co-Co

Australian National Railways and its predecessor, Commonwealth Railways, a customer of Clyde/EMD since 1951, turned to Goninan/GE when seeking new motive power in 1989. The 14-member EL-class, introduced in July 1990, was acquired for system-wide fast freight and passenger service.

These CM30-8 locomotives introduced a new configuration to the Australian general-purpose locomotive scene—a raked aerodynamic cab not unlike that of the NSW State Rail Authority's distinctive 160 km/h XPT locomotives.

A. Goninan & Co had to customise GE's Dash-8 electrics to suit AN's tender requirements, which called for a locomotive type suitable for high-speed 140 km/h operation. Equipped with a 12-cylinder turbo-blown GE engine capable of providing 2380 hp (1880 kW) for traction and weighing a surprisingly light 114 tonnes, all 14 were built at the manufacturer's Newcastle plant and delivered to AN under their own power by October 1991. They were quickly absorbed into exacting *Indian Pacific* and *The*

Fish River railway bridge feels the weight of EL63, EL51 and GL104 while working an Interail (QRN) Melbourne–Brisbane train on 28 August, 2004. All locomotives carry the CFCLA ownership markings. (Leon Oberg)

Ghan passenger working in addition to super fast *Westliner/Eastliner* and *TrailerRail* freight services.

Their ranks started to thin from 22 February 1997, when EL59 was wrecked in a fiery head-on collision at the remote Nullarbor Plains siding, Mt Christie. By that time the class had come under the control (but not the ownership) of the National Rail Corporation, which actually handed them back to the Commonwealth Government by October 1997 after receiving sufficient new NR-class GE locomotives. Because they were not part of AN's intrastate operations at the time of Australia Southern Railroad's (ASR) asset acquisition, the remaining operational units were stored at Islington, about five being leased to ASR during December 1997–January 1998 to overcome a serious seasonal locomotive shortage. All were in need of general overhauls at the time of storage.

On 13 November 1998, all except for the accident-damaged EL59 were sold to the US-based Chicago Freight Car Leasing Co and progressively rebuilt/upgraded and re-geared for traction rather than speed at A. Goninan & Co's Bassendean works. This revision, which saw their original 90:22 traction motor gearing reworked to 93:19, increased their tractive effort by almost 20 per cent.

Beginning with EL57, the units were provided with new blue and silver liveries and named after iconic Australian racehorses. The first lease agreement was signed in September 1999 with ASR (later ARG) for an initial two units to assist with grain haulage. Within months others were running in Victoria and New South Wales, hauling everything from wheat to

ballast, logs to shipping containers, the last of the 13 re-entering service in May 2000.

All units retained their original road numbering and today are generally found working grain and intermodal trains throughout NSW.

SPECIFICATIONS

	As built	CFCLA as regeared
	Imperial (Metric)	Imperial (Metric)
Power unit:	GE 7FDL-12	GE 7FDL-12
Traction horsepower:	2450 (1880 kW)	2450 (1880 kW)
Starting tractive effort:	69 600 lb (308 kN)	83 710 lb (369kN)
Continuous tractive effort:	44 240 lb (197 kN 34 km/h)	54 350 lb (232kN at 28 km/h)
Total weight:	112.1 tons (114 t)	112.1 tons (114 t)
Gauge:	1435 mm	1435 mm
Road numbers:	EL51–EL64	EL51–EL58, EL60–EL64

1990 Fairymead Sugar Mill

Eimco B-B

The Alexandria (Sydney) engineering firm, Eimco, entered the cane locomotive manufacturing field in 1990 with an order to build a 32-tonne bogie diesel-hydraulic locomotive for Queensland's Fairymead sugar mill.

Equipped with a 2-stroke Detroit Diesel model 12V-92TA 12-cylinder Vee formation (turbo-charged) engine rated at 537 kW, the locomotive was fitted with the Detroit Diesel Electronic Control microprocessor system to manage engine functions.

Loco No. 20 *Boonganna* near Marian Sugar Mill on 20 August, 2009. (Chris Walters)

This equipment was capable of programming a maximum 300 kW of traction energy when starting, with the entire 537 kW available from 7 kph. The advantage of this programme was a reduction in the incidence of broken sugar bin couplings when starting heavy trains.

Provided with a Voith L3r2V2 hydraulic gearbox coupled by cardan shafts to the diesel engine and the Eimco-designed bogie-mounted final drives, the locomotive boasted European hood-unit styling for maximum operator vision.

Delivered in October 1990, the locomotive was soon found to be too heavy for the customer and was on-sold to Mackay Sugar for use at Farleigh Sugar Mill and identified as No. 36 *Farleigh*.

Eimco had in 1989 received an order from Mackay Sugar to build three similar locomotives. With the planned connection of its Marian and Cattle Creek sugar mills, coupled with the difficulty encountered by Marian Mill's existing lightweight locomotive power in shifting the increasing cut cane tonnages, Mackay Sugar realised heavier, more powerful B-B diesel-hydraulic locomotives would be the answer. The first of the trio, delivered at monthly intervals, arrived on 5 October 1990, the last on 1 December 1990.

These four Eimco locomotives, given both road numbers and names, marked the start of a 1990s motive-power revolution in the Queensland cane fields, which saw the construction of several new powerful types in addition to the wholesale upgrade of large numbers of used ex-Government diesel-hydraulics to sugar railway specifications.

All four were operating out of Marian Mill as at the 2010 harvest.

SPECIFICATIONS

	IMPERIAL (METRIC)
POWER UNIT:	DETROIT DIESEL 12V-92TA
TRACTION HORSEPOWER:	720 (537 KW)
MAXIMUM TRACTIVE EFFORT:	24 610 LB (110 KN)
TOTAL WEIGHT:	36.5 TONS (38 T)
GAUGE:	610 MM
ROAD NUMBERS/NAMES:	36 FARLEIGH, 18 GARGETT, 19 NARPI, 20 BOONGANNA

1991 WESTRAIL

P-class Co-Co

Seventeen P-class Co-Co units were acquired by Westrail in 1988, principally for bulk grain and general goods traffic. Built at A. Goninan & Co's Bassendean factory, the first of these 1830 kW locomotives was trialled to Forrestfield on 9 November 1989.

When placed into service from 8 December 1989, the locomotives enabled a 30 per cent improvement in tractive effort and a 15 per cent reduction in operating expenses when compared to the locomotives they replaced. All 17 were running by April 1991, and effectively allowed for the retirement of two A-class EMDs, all three C-class, 11 RA-class and five R-class English Electrics (21 locos in all). The seventeenth unit, financed by the then Allied Minerals Company for use over the Eneabba line, has generally been based at Geraldton and carried cab-side AMC lettering.

P-class locomotives, known as GE's CM25-8 model, initially could be seen working all lines except those east of Merredin and south of Picton. Due to their impressive strength (loads up to 3725 tonnes

Locomotives P2004 and P2012 load their grain train at Mingenew (on the old Midland line) for export through Geraldton, on 19 August 2004. (Peter Clark)

can be hauled up a 1 in 100 gradient), they became the favoured power on most mineral sands and wheat trains on the Midland Railway and down the south-west route.

In creating the P-class, Goninan was forced to customise the US Dash-8 design in various ways to suit the customer's needs. It became the first locomotive type in the world to utilise this technology on a narrow 1067 mm gauge.

All were named after Western Australian cities and shires.

The P-class passed into the ownership of the Australian Railroad Group on 2 December 2000. This consortium included local icon Wesfarmers and US firm Genesee & Wyoming.

ARG started overhauling the units, beginning with accident-damaged locomotive 2005, which emerged bearing the new road number 2505. Others were being renumbered accordingly when, on 1 June 2006, ARG and the P-class were sold to QRN-West, at which time the class was principally running over the north-east wheat belt country and Mullewa to Geraldton ore haulage.

SPECIFICATIONS

	Imperial (Metric)
Power unit:	GE 7FDL-12
Traction horsepower:	2450 hp (1830 kW)
Starting tractive effort:	84 100 lb (375 kN)
Continuous tractive effort:	54 500 lb (286 kN 19 km/h)
Total weight:	96.1 tons (98.5 t)
Gauge:	1067 mm
Road numbers:	2001–2017 (being renumbered 2501–2517)

1991 Fairymead Sugar Mill

Bundaberg/ Hunslet B-B

Thirty-seven years after the last narrow gauge Queensland sugar industry steam locomotive was out-shopped, in 1990 Bundaberg Foundry Engineers Ltd signed an agreement with the veteran British builder Hunslet GMT, Leeds, to produce diesel-hydraulic motive power in Australia.

Bundaberg Sugar, which at the time owned six productive sugar mills along the east coast of Queensland, believed the time was right to design a modern locomotive type to replace the hundreds of first generation diesel-mechanical and diesel-hydraulic locomotives at work in the sugar industry. Some of them dated back to the mid-1950s.

Two of the mills, Fairymead (at Bundaberg) and Babinda (at Babinda), were expressing a need for new higher-capacity locomotives. With Hunslet GMT supplying a conceptual design, equipment and parts, Bundaberg Foundry took the trouble to bring locomotive drivers and mill maintenance staff in on the subsequent locomotive's design. The mills ordered one unit each and thus a new locomotive type was born, one which subsequently brought a further touch of European styling to the cane fields.

Powered by Detroit Diesel's 12V92-TA 18.1-litre diesel engines, the locomotives' engine management system employs a microprocessor system that can, if required, be programmed to reduce power on starting a train, thus eliminating surges.

Fairymead Mill's unit, named *Bundaberg*, was the first of the two to enter service (in August 1991),

The first of the two Hunslets, which then carried the name *Bundaberg*, nears the Fairymead Mill where it was initially employed, in July 1995. (Barry Blair)

Invicta Sugar Mill's husky B-B, *Strathalbyn*, stands in the mill yard in October 1991, just one month after it entered regular service. (Tony Wells)

followed by Babinda's locomotive, named after its mill, the following month.

Known for their 'rollicking' ride, both were rated to haul 800-tonne trains on level track.

Since entering service *Bundaberg* has been re-named *Booyan*, and *Babinda* was transferred south to Millaquin Mill in 1999 as *Elliott*. They continue to haul seasonal Bundaberg-district cane to this day.

SPECIFICATIONS

	IMPERIAL (METRIC)
POWER UNIT:	DETROIT DIESEL 12V-92TA
TRACTION HORSEPOWER:	625 (466 kW)
MAXIMUM TRACTIVE EFFORT:	23 400 LB (103 kN)
TOTAL WEIGHT:	31.5 TONS (32 T)
GAUGE:	610 MM
ROAD NAMES:	(FAIRYMEAD MILL) BUNDABERG (NOW BOOYAN)
	(BABINDA MILL) BABINDA (NOW ELLIOTT)

1991 INVICTA SUGAR MILL

Westfalia B-B

On 20 August 1991, leading international underground mining locomotive builder Westfalia Becorit delivered a new 32-tonne B-B diesel hydraulic unit to Invicta Mill at Giru in far northern Queensland. Commissioned the following month, the new locomotive represented a total re-design of the 1972 E.M. Baldwin B-B bogie cane locomotive, Westfalia Becorit having acquired Baldwin's locomotive catalogue in mid-1989.

Built at Westfalia's Rooty Hill (Sydney) plant, the locomotive, known as *Strathalbyn*, became the most powerful cane field machine yet produced, being

able to manage 850-tonne cane trains during early testing.

Among the improvements to the earlier design was the provision of 840 mm wheels in a 1650 mm bogie wheelbase in lieu of the Baldwin standard 724 mm wheels in a 1320 mm wheelbase. With disc brakes and a bigger axle drive, the new bogie delivered considerably more power to the rail.

The new locomotive was powered by a 537 kW 12-cylinder Vee Detroit diesel driving through an ultra-smooth Voith transmission.

Crews were not forgotten either. While an air-conditioner was provided, seating for both driver and shunter was designed for equal comfort with a minimum of adjustment, irrespective of whether the locomotive was operating forwards or backwards.

SPECIFICATIONS

	IMPERIAL (METRIC)
POWER UNIT:	DETROIT DIESEL 12V-92TA
TRACTION HORSEPOWER:	720 (537 kW)
MAXIMUM TRACTIVE EFFORT:	23 400 LB (103 kN)
TOTAL WEIGHT:	31.5 TONS (32 T)
GAUGE:	610 MM
ROAD NAME:	STRATHALBYN

1992 AUSTRALIAN NATIONAL RAILWAYS

AN-class Co-Co

Australian National's continuing desire to purge itself of first generation life-expired locomotives, many of which had exceeded 6 million kilometres of service, led to an order being placed with Clyde Engineering in 1991 for eleven state-of-the-art 2862 kW locomotives.

The raked cab and full-width car body configuration of the AN-class is evident here as AN8 rolls into Port Augusta's Spencer Junction yard on 26 November 1996 with an east-bound freight train. (Leon Oberg)

Known as the AN-class, this new machine employed EMD's 16-cylinder 710G3A engine for a traction output of 2862 kW. The class's body styling was a radical departure from Clyde Engineering's usual designs, the cab being raked back at a considerable angle, much like AN's GE Goninan-built 2350 kW EL-class locomotives of 1990.

All were built at Clyde's Somerton (Martin & King) Victorian plant and were delivered to Adelaide via New South Wales between October 1992 and March 1994. Following crew and maintenance staff training, the husky locomotives were quickly absorbed into fast freight train operations between Adelaide and Kalgoorlie, and also progressively pressed into heavy freight service on the general Alice Springs and Whyalla lines. For a short period early in their careers, some even gravitated into coal haulage between Leigh Creek mine and Port Augusta's high-volume Northern Power Station.

Early teething troubles included engine vibrations so that from AN6 onwards 1.5 kg of extra metal was added to their crankshafts to better balance them.

By far the most powerful locomotive on the Australian National system, a single AN-class unit in heavy goods working was allowed 2100 tonnes over the heavy Port Pirie to Broken Hill route, compared with 960 tonnes for a 1342 kW GM12 type, 1400 tonnes for an EL-class and 1750 tonnes for the AN 2237 kW fleet. The AN units were provided with 10 800 litre fuel tanks.

Although never operated at such speed, the AN-class has a top speed of 152 km/h.

All these locomotives passed into National Rail Corporation control in mid-1995. However, their number was reduced by one when AN10 was totally destroyed in a fiery fatal collision at Hines Hill crossing loop (near Merredin) on 14 January 1996. After a lengthy period quarantined in a special Coroner's compound beside the Port Augusta Workshops, its rusty remains were quietly disposed

of as scrap in October 1997. Meanwhile, sisters AN2 and AN5 became victims of yet another fiery collision, this time at Mt Christie, on 22 February 1997. Both were repaired, AN2 being the last to re-enter service (in National Rail livery) in March 1999.

By then, the class's route availability had been extended to take in Melbourne. But, with an average 1.6 million kilometres already on their clocks, unreliability problems were beginning to surface, and all remaining units except for the Mt Christie rebuilds were placed in temporary store on 1 July 2000.

The remaining ten passed into the ownership of Pacific National on 21 February 2002 following the joint sale of National Rail and FreightCorp. Overhauls followed, with loco AN3 being painted red in July 2004 to work the luxury Great Southern Railway's *The Ghan* between Adelaide and Darwin.

SPECIFICATIONS

	IMPERIAL (METRIC)
POWER UNIT:	EMD 16-710G3A
TRACTION HORSEPOWER:	4000 (2862 kW)
STARTING TRACTIVE EFFORT:	105 120 lb (470 kN)
CONTINUOUS TRACTIVE EFFORT:	72 500 lb (323 kN)
TOTAL WEIGHT:	127.5 TONS (130 T)
GAUGE:	1435 MM
ROAD NUMBERS:	AN1–11

1994 NEW SOUTH WALES STATE RAIL AUTHORITY

90-class Co-Co

With some of its first generation Alco fleet nudging 32 years of age as the 1980s were drawing to a close, NSW State Rail's maintenance bill was understandably very high. Added to the fuel inefficiency of the older units and a general lack of acceptable haulage capability, it was not surprising that almost every conversation within the traffic department's hallowed halls of power centred on potential replacements.

All agreed that this would be expensive, and NSW Treasury simply did not have the money to spend on large numbers of new locomotives. Following considerable soul-searching, chest-pounding rhetoric, which included calls for 'expressions of interest', and protracted discussions with several locomotive

EDI Cardiff-built, 9034 branded in Pacific National livery nears Belford in September 2007. (Leon Oberg)

manufacturing companies, State Rail's then Freight Rail division eventually called tenders for two types of freight locomotive under the US 'power by the hour' ('Ready Power') philosophy.

The Clyde Engineering Co, supported by its licensee, EMD, and a banking partner, eventually won the contract to supply 29 single-cab 2862 kW locomotives and 55 dual-cab 2259 kW locomotives. Weighing 165 tonnes, the single-cab 90-class locomotives were designed for heavy duty Hunter Valley coal haulage while the dual-cab 82-class machines were intended for general purpose mainline work, weighing a 'conventional' 132 tonnes.

Because the locomotives were needed urgently, the construction of the 29 single-cab units was outsourced to General Motors Diesels' Ontario (Canada) plant. Due to a 'Ready Power' clause insisting upon 100 per cent locomotive availability, an extra two locomotives were built by the manufacturer as back-ups. All 31, equipped with EMD's 16-cylinder 710G3A turbo-blown diesel engine capable of exerting 2862 kW at the rail, were shipped to Newcastle in three boat-loads, the first six arriving in April 1994.

Following exhaustive testing they were issued to Saxonvale and Mt Thorley coal trains on 30 May 1994. All 31 were operating by October 1994.

The trouble-free introduction of the 90-class allowed the mass transfer of forty 2237 kW 81-class locomotives which for more than a decade had largely been dedicated to coal haulage. These in turn replaced older Alcos in other duties including superfreighter services over the North Coast line to Brisbane.

Under the initial 'Ready Power' agreement, the 90-class was maintained by the manufacturer and its partners at the Motive Power Company Pty Ltd's Kooragang Island (Newcastle) servicing facility. All were acquired by Pacific National on 21 February 2002 as part of the joint sale of FreightCorp and National Rail. In early 2005 Pacific National ordered an additional four units for expanding coal haulage. These were built locally at EDI Rail's Cardiff plant, appearing in November 2005.

SPECIFICATIONS

	IMPERIAL (METRIC)
POWER UNIT:	EMD 16-710G3A
TRACTION HORSEPOWER:	4000 (2862 kW)
STARTING TRACTIVE EFFORT:	139 200 (616 kN)
CONTINUOUS TRACTIVE EFFORT:	102 050 lb (437 kN)
TOTAL WEIGHT:	162 tons (165 t)
GAUGE:	1435 mm
ROAD NUMBERS:	9001–9035

1994 NEW SOUTH WALES STATE RAIL AUTHORITY

82-class Co-Co

In company with the Canadian-built 90-class heavy coal locomotives described above, the NSW State Rail Authority's Freight Rail needed a large number of general-purpose main line locomotives to replace an extensive collection of ageing machines then working over the state's main line corridors.

The Clyde Engineering Co, supported by its US licensee EMD and a banking partner, eventually won a contract to supply 55 dual-cab 3010 hp (2260 kW) locomotives designated the 82-class. Unlike the heavier single-cab 90-class order, these were built locally at leased premises in the Southern Highlands village of Braemar. While the official handover of the first four occurred on 23 March 1994, no examples entered service until 1 June 1994.

Class-leader 8201 exhibits its unique chunky styling in this photograph taken at South Australia's Northern Power Station on 8 December 2002. Pacific National bases three 82-class at that location to work Leigh Creek coal trains. (Leon Oberg)

While the 82-class employed the 'dog bone' styling introduced with Victoria's V/Line N-class a decade earlier, the cab configuration was altered to provide an inwardly-sloping windscreen to reduce night-time glare. After three months spent hauling Hunter Valley coal trains, the 82-class was released for state-wide general freight duties, quickly taking over grain, limestone, fuel oil, ballast and superfreighter workings. Throughout 1996 and much of 1997, up to 25 were 'side leased' to the National Rail Corporation, principally for service over the NSW North Coast and Broken Hill routes.

Although the numerically last class-member, 8258, was out-shopped on 5 May 1995, unit 8255 remained at the plant due to a protracted rail union dispute allegedly involving equipment and comfort levels. It was eventually released on 22 May and entered traffic nine days later.

Like the 90-class, the 82-class's maintenance was entrusted to the Motive Power Company Pty Ltd's Kooragang Island servicing facility. But life has not been kind to the 82s—apart from early software problems, crews soon complained of nuisance vibrations within the cabs and soon afterwards the locomotives started experiencing crankshaft balance-weight failures. This necessitated blanket warranty correction in North America.

The class made an accident-prone name for itself too. Apart from 8244, which was seriously 'concussed' (but later repaired) in a violent collision at Delec in July 1996, engines 8219, 8246 and 8247 were subsequently written off following a spectacular coal train crash at Beresfield on 23 October 1997. While 8219 was scrapped outright, the other two were taken to Clyde's Bathurst shops in June 1998 for evaluation. They were deemed to be beyond economic repair and in time yielded operational parts for their sisters.

Locos 8212 and 8256 also disgraced themselves when they rolled over at Saxonvale Junction on 24 August 2000 while working a coal train. Both were repaired.

The 55 operational units passed into the ownership of Pacific National on 21 February 2002 following the joint sale of FreightCorp and National Rail, and three are generally captive to Leigh Creek coal trains in South Australia.

SPECIFICATIONS

	IMPERIAL (METRIC)
POWER UNIT:	EMD 12-710G3A
TRACTION HORSEPOWER:	3010 (2260 kW)
STARTING TRACTIVE EFFORT:	138 800 lb (600 kN)
CONTINUOUS TRACTIVE EFFORT:	92 500 lb (413 kN)
TOTAL WEIGHT:	129.5 TONS (132 T)
GAUGE:	1435 MM
ROAD NUMBERS:	8201–8258

1994 QUEENSLAND RAILWAYS

3300/3400-class Bo-Bo-Bo

With increasing coal tonnages from Blair Athol mine (on the Goonyella system) coinciding with the planned opening of the Ensham mine near Blackwater, Queensland Railways signed a contract with the Clyde Engineering Co for 13 (later expanded to 22) new Bo-Bo-Bo locomotives.

By and large, the design was meant to be an improved version of the 3100/3200-class Comeng/ Hitachi units of 1986. Although QR's earlier electric

The class-leader, 3301, pilots earlier Walkers product 3629 towards Mt Larcom with an empty train on 21 March 1997. (Leon Oberg)

classes were built in Queensland, the 3300/3400s, both command and non-command types, were to be assembled at Clyde's Bathurst (NSW) plant. Originally scheduled for introduction in mid-1992, delays tended to dog their manufacture, caused in part by ongoing body design changes and a range of 'technical problems'.

The class-leader, 3301, eventually reached Callemondah electric depot on 21 February 1994. This class was slightly longer than the 3100/3200-class prototype and, because of early failures with the Comeng units' high-speed traction motor cooling fan (blower) blades, the new locomotives were equipped with slower blowers. In a bid to provide an identical volume of air, these were of larger diameter, which had necessitated alterations to the internal layout.

The 3300/3400-class also featured Clyde-design bogies which were radically different to all QR's preceding electric locomotives. These bogies were provided with heavier traction rods, an improved traction transfer system and a suspension system aimed at giving greater ride control.

Clyde/GM diesel-type porthole windows were substituted down the body sides for the square windows of the 3100/3200-class.

During preliminary pre-service manufacturer's trials, a Clyde spokesperson revealed to this author, the fans were found to be working 'flat out' due to the limited space available. This left no room for abnormal conditions and expensive failures of the equipment were predicted. Internal ducting in body shells awaiting manufacture into locomotives was thus re-engineered at the factory and alterations carried out to the many units which had already been assembled.

As a means of freeing up this work, some body shells were forwarded to Clyde's leased Braemar (NSW) factory while a decision was made to complete the final seven locomotives (less bogies)

at Clyde's Somerton (Victoria) plant. The earliest deliveries lay in storage in Clyde's Callemondah locomotive depot compound until October 1994, when the first two entered revenue service, initially as trailing units in multiple locomotive lash-ups.

All 22 were eventually delivered to Callemondah depot by August 1995, where the last to be commissioned was 3419 on 15 December 1995.

The dramas continued when locomotive 3409 was damaged in an accident at Wycarbah on 12 June 1996. It was forwarded to Clyde's Bathurst shops for rebuild, this work being completed in April 1997. A year later it featured in a serious derailment while crossing flooded Taurus Creek (near Blackwater) on 23 April 1998.

After about five years captive to the Blackwater coal system, running in company with 3500/3600 classes, the whole fleet was progressively transferred to Jilalan depot from early 1999 to help deal with rising tonnages and replace accident victims, running randomly in tandem with the Comeng 3100/3200 classes. It was while working mid-train with Comeng unit 3255 on 1 July 2001 that 3410 met its end in a horrific derailment involving a 13 000-tonne, 120-wagon loaded coal train from Norwich Park, which was descending the 1 in 50 Connors Range above Yukan. Seventy-five wagons derailed and 3410 was flung 35 metres into adjacent rainforest. A subsequent investigation determined the $20.6 million accident was initially caused by a Locotrol signal failure and an O-ring defect in a brake pipe control valve. No. 3410's remains were disposed of following stripping of useful parts in September 2002.

On 5 November 2002, mid-train unit 3413 and Comeng loco 3226 rolled over in a violent derailment in Waitara loop while working an empty Jilalan to German Creek coal train. Loco 3413 was subsequently repaired at Redbank Workshops, emerging in October 2004.

SPECIFICATIONS

	IMPERIAL (METRIC)
ELECTRICAL EQUIPMENT:	HITACHI/CLYDE 25 kV
TRACTION HORSEPOWER:	3886 (2970 kW)
STARTING TRACTIVE EFFORT:	84 100 LB (375 kN)
CONTINUOUS TRACTIVE EFFORT:	58 940 LB (260 kN AT 40 KM/H)
TOTAL WEIGHT:	111 TONS (112.8 T)
GAUGE:	1067 MM
ROAD NUMBERS:	(COMMAND UNITS) 3301–3304, 3316–3318
	(NON-COMMAND UNITS): 3405–3415, 3419–3422

A more recent Pilbara Rail delivery, 9404, leads original Hamersley Iron unit 7076 as they depart Seven Mile for Parker Point with a loaded ore train on 14 October 2004. (Richard Montgomery)

1995 Hamersley Iron

70-class Co-Co

In February 1995 Hamersley Iron, which then operated a 497 km railway through the scorching, rugged Pilbara region of Western Australia, introduced yet another locomotive design to the Australian railway scene.

Needing replacements for its elderly Alco 636 fleet (many of which had been de-rated from their original 2685 kW to 2050 kW to reduce the stresses upon them), the company ordered 29 tasteful General Electric Dash-9 3340 kW Co-Co units from the maker's Erie (USA) plant late in 1993. All were delivered in one shipment in February 1995, with GE's Australian licence-holder, A. Goninan & Co, responsible for their commissioning.

Not only were these the most powerful locomotives in Australia, they became the first Hamersley Iron locomotives to wear the company's striking new grey/silver/red/blue/yellow/black livery.

Becoming the railway's 70-class, the hood-type locomotive, known by GE as Model C44-9W, was identical to 115 examples supplied earlier to the Chicago & North Western Railroad in the USA.

The Hamersley units featured electronic fuel injection, Wabco electronic EPIC brake valves and GE's optional Integrated Function Control monitoring system. The latter consisted of two screens that replaced all conventional indicators and gauges, the associated equipment providing constant on-screen speed, air pressure, alerter, end of train and clock readings in addition to the status of various warning systems, and also providing fault diagnostic information.

The full-width cabs were specially equipped with CD players, microwave ovens and refrigerators, along with double-glazed windows. Outside, illuminated digitised external tank fuel gauges were provided to help crews quickly read fuel levels at night. All in all, the 70-class was more fully optioned than any US domestic locomotive type, and American railroaders who inspected the units before delivery to Australia nicknamed them 'the Cadillacs'.

But there was a downside too. Thirteen of the fleet were shipped to Australia as deck cargo and close inspection of their undersides revealed that corrosion, caused by sea spray, had set in. All affected metal faces had to be cleaned back to bare metal and repainted.

Meanwhile, the first train hauled by 70-class left Dampier for Mt Tom Price with three lashed-up units on 17 March 1995. Hamersley Iron subsequently was able to replace three Alco M636 units with two Dash-9s for a trailing load of two hundred and ten 120-tonne (gross) ore cars. All 29 units were running by 17 June 1995.

By mid-1996, Hamersley Iron's planned 148 km spur into a new mine development at Yandicoogina had led to a decision to acquire another three 70-class locomotives, which became operational out of Dampier in February 2002. Revised operational conditions had by then seen a merger with Robe, thus forming the Pilbara Rail Company, which today is responsible for some 1184 km of heavy-haul railway (including yards). Those locomotives were issued to traffic numbered in the Robe series 9470–9472 (now 9401–9403). Another four were added to the respective fleets in October 2004, and exploding mining contracts resulted in the acquisition of a further six late in 2005. The ten most recent, 7043–

7050, 9435 and 9436, arrived in December 2006. All 72 locomotives in the class have now been fitted with an in-cab signalling system that displays data connected with the track conditions facing drivers.

The first major hiccup to the fleet occurred on 6 January 2007 when two trains collided head-on outside Cape Lambert. The future of the most damaged units, 9406, which rolled down an embankment, and 7079, was not known when this book went to press.

Footnote: In 2006, emerging Pilbara mining company, the Fortescue Metals Group, ordered 15 similar locomotives for its $3.7 billion Christmas Creek and Cloud Break Pilbara project, for expected delivery in mid-2007.

SPECIFICATIONS

	IMPERIAL (METRIC)
POWER UNIT:	GE 7FDL16
TRACTION HORSEPOWER:	4380 (3266 kW)
STARTING TRACTIVE EFFORT:	158 500 lbs (705 kN)
CONTINUOUS TRACTIVE EFFORT:	117 900 lbs (525 kN)
TOTAL WEIGHT:	193.7 tons (196.9 t)
GAUGE:	1435 mm
ROAD NUMBERS:	7043–7050, 7053–7098; 9401–9409; 9428–9436

1995 QUEENSLAND RAILWAYS

2800-class Co-Co

With Queensland Railways placing its faith in electrification projects through much of the 1980s, no new diesels were delivered from March 1984 until 1993, when A. Goninan & Co successfully tendered to build 40 double-cab 2240 kW main line diesel-electric locomotives for use over the non-electrified Townsville–Mt Isa and Rockhampton–Cairns routes.

These 'dog bone' 2800-class locomotives rode on Goninan-fabricated Co-Co bogies and were the first diesels in Queensland to be given cabs at both ends, eliminating the need for turning at terminating stations.

Although the first one emerged from the maker's Townsville factory for testing on the Greenvale line on July 1995, none entered actual revenue service until 15 September 1995. By then four had been built.

In June 1996, with just over half the fleet delivered, QR signed a contract with the manufacturer for an additional ten. All 50 were running by August 1998. Designated Model CM30-8, they were the most powerful diesels operated by QR up to that point.

In many respects, the 2800-class's technical prototype in Australia was the Westrail P-class which, when introduced from December 1989, became the first narrow (1067 mm) gauge railway in the world to utilise GE's Dash-8 technology.

The 2800-class was originally built with 920 mm diameter wheels, which were changed to 950 mm units from about the seventh delivery. The larger wheels were provided to enable two flange turnings during their lifetime, rather than one. The bigger wheels placed the draft gear higher, which thus had to be reworked to bring it into line with the vehicle couplings. Earlier deliveries were subsequently

Locomotive 2834 at Mt Isa on 26 April 2008. (Leon Oberg)

retrofitted with the revised equipment.

Because the 2800-class's bogies are tri-mounted on rubber, early problems surfaced due to the tight curvatures in some QR yards distorting the rubbers. By far the biggest problem encountered, though, was lateral movement of the loco body on the bogies. With the class built to the absolute limits of the QR loading gauge, random fouling was common. Various modifications were undertaken to limit movement, which subsequently enabled the class to be used on the Brisbane to Rockhampton corridor, with its tighter clearances (especially in the Brisbane suburbs). The class commenced regular use to and from the Queensland capital in early 2001.

Of interest was the return of 2808 to the manufacturer following serious damage sustained as a result of a washaway derailment and subsequent rollover at Bungalien on the Mount Isa line on 1 October 1996. An entirely new frame had to be manufactured along with many body components. The 'rebuilt' machine was recommissioned on 4 July 1997.

The class's route availability was extended from February 2006 when loco 2819 emerged with standard gauge bogies for use on QR National's NSW and Victorian intermodal contracts. Never a success, it was hauled to Forrestfield (WA) in August 2009 for restoration to narrow gauge for planned ARG mineral service as the PA-class.

SPECIFICATIONS

	Imperial (Metric)
Power unit:	GE 7FDL12
Traction horsepower:	3000 hp (2240 kW)
Starting tractive effort:	69 690 lb (310 kN)
Continuous tractive effort:	59 799 lb (266 kN at 18 km/h)
Total weight:	114.9 tons (116.7 t)
Gauge:	1067 mm
Road numbers:	2801–2850

1996 National Rail Corporation

NR-class Co-Co

Until the National Rail Corporation Ltd came into being in 1992, each State and Commonwealth government-owned rail system was responsible for train operations and financial accounting within its own borders.

Freight customers, used to running financially lean and sophisticated national and international operations, correctly saw Australia's rail network as hamstrung by decades-old manning practices, unyielding network bureaucrats and non-competitive train operations.

This situation had certainly led to higher than necessary freight haulage charges, with more and more haulage tasks having fallen to road transport. Eventually governments came to realise the true value of rail transport and finally the National Rail Corporation was born. This limited company (with the federal government and two states as shareholders) began running its first company-crewed trains in the Melbourne to Adelaide corridor in November 1993. Other interstate routes gradually followed.

Initially, the NRC used diesel locomotives from the three existing railway shareholding systems. But while many of these, such as AN's AN and DL classes were near new, others, including V/Line's C-class and State Rail's 422-class, were two decades old. Clearly, a number of new locomotives would be required to maintain the NRC's faster scheduling and to cover anticipated growth.

After detailed assessment of its needs, the NRC announced on 31 May 1995 that the Newcastle-based GE licensee A. Goninan & Co was to receive the contract to build 80 (increased to 120 the following February) 2862 kW Dash-9 locomotives. The date of the announcement was selected to coincide with the opening of NRC's Melbourne–Adelaide standard gauge railway, three days later.

Locomotives numbered NR1–60 were manufactured in Goninan's Newcastle (NSW) plant, those numbered NR61–120 emerged from the maker's Bassendean (WA) factory. Although the first unit, NR1, ran its trial between Broadmeadow and Maitland on 31 August 1996, the first example to enter actual revenue service was a Bassendean unit which worked a Kewdale (Perth) to Kalgoorlie train on 26 October 1996.

As more locos emerged, their sphere of operation was gradually extended. By early December some were working into Melbourne while on 20 December 1996 the class was phased into the Broken Hill to Sydney corridor. When NR60 was delivered from the Newcastle plant on 19 December 1997, all 120 were in traffic.

Although of single-cab configuration, dual controls were fitted to enable bi-directional operation. The units are controlled by three computers and boast GE's Integrated Function Control, whereby

Locomotives NR18 and NR52 (wearing an Indigenous livery) sandwich EMD helper, DL45, as they roll away from Moorabool (above Geelong, Victoria) with a Perth–Melbourne intermodal on 1 November 2005. (Leon Oberg)

For the opening of the Alice Springs to Darwin railway, three NR-class locomotives were specially painted red and white to haul Great Southern Railway's *The Ghan*. The first locomotive treated was NR75, which for a time carried the name and photograph of one of the nation's favourite characters, the late Steve Irwin, who was known internationally as 'The Crocodile Hunter'. (Leon Oberg)

all relevant train running information is displayed before the driver on computer screens. A refreshingly new inclusion has been the provision of a 'variable horsepower' feature enabling the full 3000 kW to be used, 2655 kW or 2162 kW, depending on the application in hand. This was provided as a fuel-saving measure and to help reduce unnecessary exhaust emissions.

The locomotives' 13 500 litre fuel tanks, which are part of the mainframe structure, give sufficient range to run the 1930 km from Brisbane to Melbourne.

The 120 locomotives, collectively worth $395 million, were equipped from new with local, satellite, cellular and global positioning communications equipment. Their computers are linked to the locomotive maintenance centre at Spotswood, Melbourne, where technical staff are able to correct most on-board faults from their computer terminals.

Their extremely roomy cabs are fitted with CD/tape/radio equipment for the comfort of the crews and the units are gradually being named after the cities, towns and shires they pass in traffic. Additionally, 15 have been adorned in special liveries characteristic of some of the NRC's regular business, including Trailerail, SeaTrain, SteelLink and express passenger workings. Most notable are *The Ghan*, for which NR74, NR75 and NR109 were painted red, while NR25 and NR28 were adorned in blue for *Indian Pacific* operations. Units NR30 and NR52 received Indigenous designs.

Several have been involved in serious accidents, the worst to date being a level crossing accident near Lismore (Victoria) on 25 May 2006 which totally destroyed NR33, and an earlier pre-dawn catastrophe near Robertson (NSW) on 19 May 1998, which sadly claimed the lives of two enginemen and badly damaged NR3. The latter locomotive was eventually repaired and re-issued to traffic on 16 April 2000 as NR121.

The NR-class passed into the ownership of Pacific National on 21 February 2002, as a result of the joint sale of the National Rail Corporation and the NSW State-owned FreightCorp. With refits underway, the most travelled unit, NR20, had already travelled 3,536,900 km as at 14 March 2010!

SPECIFICATIONS

	Imperial (Metric)
Power unit:	General Electric GE7FDL16
Traction horsepower:	4023 (3000 kW) maximum (variable)
Starting tractive effort:	117 875 lb (521 kN)
Continuous tractive effort:	84 250 lb (388 kN)
Total weight:	129.5 tons (132 t)
Gauge:	1435 m
Road numbers:	NR1–121 (NR121 was formerly NR3)

1997 WESTRAIL
Q-class Co-Co

Westrail's husky standard gauge Q-class technical prototype, which emerged for trials on 14 July 1997, was to some extent a lighter, improved version of the NSW Ready Power 90-class coal locomotives. Manufactured in Perth by the Clyde Engineering Co from parts supplied by its Camperfield (Victoria) and Bathurst (NSW) plants, the Q-class followed a design prepared early in 1995 for the National Rail Corporation tendering process.

Fifteen were initially ordered but within months of signing the contract this was increased to 19 units. Following extensive trials, the first to actually enter revenue service were Q301 and Q303, on 6 September 1997. The final batch came on line in May and June 1998.

The Q-class was intended to become a replacement for the hard-working Clyde-built L-class of 1967 vintage (built for WAGR) in hauling trains such as interstate contract freight, Kalgoorlie oil and mineral movements. With Westrail at the time planning to tender for coal haulage in the NSW Hunter Valley, it made sense to have locomotives of basically equal theoretical output (without the adhesive weight) as the lusty 90-class already working in that role.

All were fitted with the maker's new radial steer (to improve higher adhesion and reduced wheel/rail wear) fabricated steel bogies, extra heavy duty couplers and draft gear. The single cabs were fitted with EMD/Rockwell Integrated Cab Electronics with fully computerised driver information displays. Capable of 115 kph, each locomotive was equipped with long-range 12 000 litre fuel tanks.

All 19 Q-class units passed into the ownership of the Australian Railroad Group (ARG) on 2 December 2000.

In 2002, a bad year was had by four class members, starting with Q305 and Q306 which were seriously damaged in a head-on depot collision at Kalgoorlie on 12 February. Twenty-two days later, Q309 and Q311, working an empty Koolyanobbing ore train

Westrail's Q314 at Midland with a freight train from Malcolm in June 2006. (Richard Montgomery)

FreightLink's FQ04, which came out of the same mould as the original Westrail Q-class and FA V-class, pictured in Port Augusta's Spencer Junction yard on 7 January 2006 with a Darwin-bound train. (Richard Montgomery)

out of Esperance, collided with a road train on a level crossing. While one was repaired in Perth, the three worst damaged units were road freighted to the railway's partner's Port Augusta EDI workshops, where they were gradually brought back to life during 2003 with at least one receiving a brand-new frame.

Overhauls of the class after November 2004 were seeing the rebuilds issued to traffic numbered in the 4000 series. All are today owned by QRN-West following that operator's June 2006 acquisition of ARG.

FQ-class

Meanwhile, the completion of the 1420 km Alice Springs to Darwin railway in January 2004 provided additional opportunities for an ARG parent company, Genesee & Wyoming (Australia), who joined the Asia Pacific Transport's FreightLink consortium as the new route's technical operator. Accordingly, four new Q-class were built at EDI's (formerly AN) Port Augusta Workshops.

Delivered between September and November 2003 as the FQ-class, the initial two were provided with liveries of Indigenous design, and worked the first official freight service over the line on 16–17 January, 2004. These four locomotives differ from the prototype in that they have just one control stand whereas the Q-class was equipped with two.

Footnote: Freight Australia acquired one similar locomotive as a replacement for two G-class destroyed at Ararat on 26 November 1999. Assembled at EDI's Cardiff (Newcastle) plant, V544 was delivered to Melbourne on 10 May 2002 (see page 430).

SPECIFICATIONS

	IMPERIAL (METRIC)
POWER UNIT:	EMD 16-710GB-ES
TRACTION HORSEPOWER:	4000 (2862 kW)
STARTING TRACTIVE EFFORT:	139 200 lb (616 kN)
CONTINUOUS TRACTIVE EFFORT:	92 400 lb (408 kN)
TOTAL WEIGHT:	130 tons (133.5 t)

Penultimate delivery S-class 2110, with a loaded bauxite train at Mundijong Junction in June 2006. (Richard Montgomery)

GAUGE:	1435 MM
ROAD NUMBERS:	ORIGINAL WESTRAIL: Q301–Q319 (TO BECOME Q4001–4019)
	FREIGHTLINK: FQ01–04

1997 WESTRAIL

S-class Co-Co

These dual-cab locomotives were ordered in 1996 by Westrail for intrastate 1067 mm gauge freight haulage. Nine were initially ordered as the system's S-class but within months of the Clyde Engineering Co receiving the contract, an additional two were requested.

Technically, these units were an improved NSW Ready Power 82-class equipped with an upgraded 12-710G-ES which boasted a 'new firing order' cam. The engine revision came about following vibration complaints with 12-710G engines delivered in locomotives in both Australia and England before this order was received.

The new locomotives, which were manufactured in Perth from parts supplied by Clyde Engineering's Camperfield (Victoria) and Bathurst (NSW) plants, were also fitted with the maker's radial steer, fabricated steel bogies—a system designed to reduce wheel and rail wear while at the same time improve adhesion on curves. Extra heavy duty couplers and draft gear was also supplied.

The two cabs were fitted with Rockwell Integrated Cab electronics with fully computerised driver information displays. Other special cab features include a safety device for driver-only operation, a microwave oven, refrigerator and CD/tape/radio. Crew seating boasts headrests, lumbar supports, armrests and a variety of adjustment configurations.

Capable of a maximum 90 kph speed limit, the first locomotive emerged for trials on 6 March 1998. All had been delivered to Westrail by August that year and engaged in the haulage of South-West Region ore and mineral traffic. This resulted in the transfer of the DB-class locomotives for use in the Great Southern and Lakes areas.

The locomotives passed into the ownership of the Australian Railroad Group on 2 December 2000 as part of Western Australia's railway privatisation policy. The business was on-sold to QRN-West in June 2006. At that time class members were being renumbered into the 3300 series and were generally captive to the South-West main Kwinana to Bunbury line and up to Collie (and the alumina refineries between).

Footnote: These were the last locomotives ordered from the traditional Clyde Engineering Co, for during the S-class's preliminary construction in 1997, the company was acquired by Evans Deakin Industries.

SPECIFICATIONS

	IMPERIAL (METRIC)
POWER UNIT:	EMD 12N-710GB-ES
TRACTION HORSEPOWER:	3010 (2260 kW)
STARTING TRACTIVE EFFORT:	108 220 LB (486 kN)
CONTINUOUS TRACTIVE EFFORT:	74 440 LB (334 kN)
TOTAL WEIGHT:	116 TONS (118.5 T)
GAUGE:	1067 MM
ROAD NUMBERS:	S2101–2111 (3301–3311)

Wearing a fresh coat of 'bubble' livery, BHP Billiton AC6000 4474 kW unit 6076 pilots SD40-2 3091 through Goldsworthy Junction with a Yandi-bound empty train in 2004. (Richard Montgomery)

1998 BHP Iron Ore

60-class AC6000 Co-Co

This class of eight locomotives, the first four of which arrived in the West Australian Pilbara in December 1998 aboard the *Titan Scan*, was the first locomotive type in Australia equipped with an AC electrical power system. Built by General Electric at its Erie, Pennsylvania plant in the USA, these state-of-the-art Model AC6000 locomotives featured the streamlined cab first used in Australia on Hamersley Iron's GE Dash-9 70-class in 1995. That was where the similarity stopped, however, for being an AC locomotive the hooded engine room was totally re-arranged.

Unlike Model AC6000 locomotives already working on class one US railroads which were provided with desk-top control stands, the BHP locomotives were custom equipped with conventional control stands at the insistence of BHP cab committee members. Their concerns were that desk-top controlled locomotives were 'hard on drivers' backs, some of whom were working up to 11 hours on the locomotives at single stretches'. This requirement delayed delivery, the last four not arriving until April 1999.

Although already tested over 2000 miles (3200 km) in the USA by the makers before delivery, exhaustive evaluation was also carried out by BHP, with the first unit to be attached to a train in the Pilbara being 6071, tested with BHP standard Dash-8 units on a Yandi train on 9 May 1999. The first all 60-class commercial operation took place on 14 June 1999 when three locomotives worked a Yandi service.

All eight were running the following week and their commissioning enabled the immediate withdrawal of the company's Dash-7 rebuilds, the new locomotives taking the cabside local feature nameplates from those latter units.

During US testing, the 60-class's cabs become the envy of every railroader, GE later telling BHP enginemen that the new locomotives exceeded every imaginable GE comfort level in the world.

Their introduction was not without its moments, however, with turbo problems (each locomotive possesses two) surfacing. This was so acute that GE avionics experts from the USA were flown to the Pilbara in March 2000 to solve the ills. And in January 2002, all units were relegated to second engine status while engineers overcame an independent brake fault. At least one, 6077, was de-rated for a short time to 2862 kW (4000 hp) in December 2002 when engine vibration beset several units.

Meanwhile, history was made on 21 June 2001 when all eight 60-class were used to work a world record 84 000 tonne, 7.4 km long train from the company's 275 km point (where the Yandi branch meets the Newman line) to Port Hedland. The locomotives were used in pairs at conventional train lengths throughout the movement. In establishing a world record, the train's operation coincided with the filming of a special US documentary.

Withdrawals started on 28 May 2011 when mid train units 6070 (with SD70Ace 4301) were wrecked in a derailment at the 120km. The GE suffered a bent frame.

SPECIFICATIONS

	Imperial (Metric)
Power unit:	General Electric GE 7HDL16
Traction horsepower:	6000 (4474kW) maximum (variable)
Starting tractive effort:	201 060 lb (890 kN)
Continuous tractive effort:	168 220 lb (753 kN at 19km/h)
Total weight:	196.5 tons (199.6t)
Gauge:	1435 mm
Road numbers:	6070–6077

QR's 4017 leads sister unit 4004 past Callemondah (Gladstone) depot and yard on 12 December 2001. (Chris Walters)

4000-class AC Co-Co

These 49 heavy-haul Queensland Rail locomotives were the first narrow gauge units in the world to employ the high-adhesion AC traction system. Classified 4000-class, costing $132 million and built by Evans Deakin Industries Ltd subsidiary, Walkers, they were also the heaviest diesel-electrics on the Queensland Railways (120 tonnes) when the first was delivered for trials on 23 October 1999. (EDI had acquired the Clyde Engineering Co and its EMD manufacturing licence in 1997.)

The class was acquired principally for heavy coal haulage, particularly out of Gladstone where their AC traction rating of 37 per cent made it possible to replace four existing 1491 kW locomotives in Moura traffic with two 4000-class. All are equipped with 12-cylinder 710G3B-ES engines which had been considerably modified by the manufacturer through the provision of revised firing order and electronic fuel injection. This improvement allowed this type of engine to run much more smoothly than 12-710G engines fitted to many earlier locomotives in Australia.

In a departure from all previous Clyde-GM mainline locomotives, which had utilised EMD traction motors, the 4000-class was designed to operate with Siemens ITB2622 AC traction motors. Rockwell Integrated Cab Electronics screen-based instrumentation was provided inside the single cab, based on Rockwell's considerable aerospace technology.

As with the Westrail Q and S classes from the EDI/Clyde-GM stable, the 4000-class was equipped with radial steer bogies, reducing wheel flange and rail wear and improving ride and adhesion characteristics through curves. The locomotives, whose single cabs are equipped with dual controls, can operate at up to 100 kph.

Following months of trials and crew training, the first four were handed over for general coal service out of Callemondah (Gladstone) depot on 19 May 2000. Each unit was rated to haul 3034 tonnes over the Moura Short Line. In comparison, the previously used 2150-class managed just 1500 tonnes per unit.

Burgeoning coal haulage saw the initial order for 38 increased by 11 in March 2003, a further 15 in 2006. Most have since been ordered. Because the latter batch is equipped with Mitsubishi traction motors in lieu of the original locomotives' Siemens product, the last 40 units became the 4100-class and numbered (when contracts are fulfilled) in the 4101–4175 series. Examples to date are working on Moura, Blackwater and Newlands line coal trains.

The basic 4000AC design was perpetuated by

The first of Pacific National Queensland's new locomotives, PN01, pauses in Rockhampton close to midnight on 21 January 2005 while en route to Townsville for crew training. (Bruce Russell)

Lone 24-class locomotive 0401/3620 with a test train in Jungara as it prepares to tackle the climb up the Kuranda Range from Redlynch on 4 July 2002. The carriages are former Brisbane commuter SX-class stainless steel vehicles. (Bruce Russell)

Pacific National Queensland (PNQ) after it took over containerised freight haulage for related freight-forwarding companies between Brisbane and North Queensland centres in March 2005. The firm ordered 13 copies from EDI Rail's Maryborough workshops in November 2003. Registered as the PN-class, the first underwent initial trials from Maryborough West to Gympie North on 20 December 2004. All had been delivered by the end of August 2005.

SPECIFICATIONS

	Imperial (Metric)
POWER UNIT:	EMD 12N-710G3B-ES
TRACTION HORSEPOWER:	3029 (2260 kW)
STARTING TRACTIVE EFFORT:	121 396 lb (540 kN)
CONTINUOUS TRACTIVE EFFORT:	103 411 lb (460 kN at 14.4 km/h)
TOTAL WEIGHT:	118 tons (120 t)
GAUGE:	1067 mm
ROAD NUMBERS:	(QR) 4001–4049; 4101–4175
	(PNQ) 001–013

2002 CAIRNS KURANDA STEAM TRAINS

24-class 2-8-4

Created for use in South Africa and only finding its way to Australia in its twilight years, this hefty 130-tonne 2-8-4 Berkshire locomotive was imported specifically to work tourist trains.

Built by the North British Locomotive Co, it is one of 100 placed into service during 1948 and 1949 for use on branch lines with track as light as 40lb/yard, and originally intended for service on the South-West Africa system. They also saw service in the Cape, the Transvaal and a few in Orange Free State. The only 2-8-4s on the system, they were popular in many workings including the haulage of 6-car suburban traffic between Springs and Nigel, where their exceptional acceleration is reported to have made them a match for the multiple-unit electric sets which replaced them in 1976.

The 24-class was provided with a one-piece steel mainframe cast integrally with the cylinders, the first time this technique was used on a South African Railways locomotive. Vanderbilt tenders riding on 6-wheel Buckeye bogies were also used.

Loco 3620 was bought by Cairns Kurunda Steam Trains Limited Partnership for steam-hauled passenger work in Queensland's far north. Using rebuilt former Queensland Rail Brisbane suburban stainless steel carriages, the train was put together to cater for tourists travelling between Cairns and the pretty rainforest village of Kuranda, negotiating the World Heritage listed rainforest and treading the Barron River gorge.

The locomotive was initially forwarded to Auckland, New Zealand, for conversion from coal to oil firing, the fitting of a Westinghouse brake system and loading gauge reduction work. It arrived in Australia in February 2002 and between May and July that year underwent a series of compliance tests.

Following a general overhaul of the engine's running gear, a series of trials was conducted, including tests double-heading with the company's former Emu Bay Railway Walkers-built diesel-hydraulic 1101. The first revenue tourist train trip to Kuranda (and formal launch of the service) was made on 3 March 2004. By April 2004 it was working between Freshwater and Kuranda five days a week.

Because Queensland Rail had an electric locomotive registered to carry the road number 3620, the 2-8-4 officially became 0401. However, its original number plates were retained for historical purposes.

After seven months working regular tourist operations, the company decided to suspend its full-time steam service due to spiralling costs, storing the engine for charter and special trip workings.

SPECIFICATIONS

	IMPERIAL (METRIC)
CYLINDERS:	(2) 19 x 26 IN (48 x 66 CM)
BOILER PRESSURE:	200 PSI (1378 KPA)
COUPLED WHEELS:	4 FT X 3½ IN (130 CM)
TRACTIVE EFFORT:	31 000 LB (138 KN)
GRATE AREA:	36 SQ FT (3.345 M²)
TOTAL WEIGHT:	126.8 TONS (130 T)
GAUGE:	1067 MM
ROAD NUMBER:	0401 (3620)

V-class Co-Co

The Victorian-based firm, Freight Australia, ordered one 2862 kW locomotive as a replacement for two 2240 kW G-class EMDs of 1980s manufacture destroyed at Ararat on 26 November 1999. Assembled at EDI's Cardiff (Newcastle) plant to the same basic plans as Westrail's Q-class (see page 424), the locomotive, numbered V544, arrived in Dynon on delivery on 10 May 2002.

As was its prototype, the V-class was equipped with radial steer bogies, a device aimed at reducing wheel flange and rail wear and improving ride and adhesion characteristics through curves. But when compared to its Q-class prototype, V544 differed through the provision of just one control stand (the prototype boasted two).

Following a series of exhaustive trials both in Victoria and out of Adelaide, V544 underwent a prolonged period working out of Adelaide banking company-operated freight trains through the Adelaide Hills as far as Tailem Bend. During this time, the builders were correcting an alleged rough riding trait.

The husky locomotive was finally cleared for full unrestricted service in November 2002, making its first trip assisting two G-class on a Perth-bound

Locomotive V544 between Port Augusta and Tent Hill with a Perth-bound SCT freight train on 9 December 2002 (Leon Oberg)

SCT train soon afterwards.

Freight Australia engineers had earlier devised an automatic continuous locomotive refuelling system, in the shape of purpose-built 60 000-litre rail tankers, for the company's G-class operations between Adelaide and Perth. They provided the necessary through piping on V544 to support this system and facilitate the loco's uninterrupted use on across-nation freight trains. The refuelling tankers, specially equipped with strengthened frames, headstocks and couplings to withstand the stresses of huge trailing loads, are marshalled immediately behind the locomotive, and through a series of plug-in fuel lines ensure a constant supply of diesel fuel. A pump initially establishes a fuel flow to the locomotive's fuel tank, from which point gravity takes over.

Loco V544 passed into the ownership of Pacific National on 1 September 2004 when it acquired Freight Australia, its rolling stock and business interests. In company with two other EMD locomotives, V544 is today captive to the 16 500 tonne Flinders Power contract coal train which runs daily between Leigh Creek and Port Augusta (SA).

SPECIFICATIONS

	IMPERIAL (METRIC)
POWER UNIT:	EMD 16-710GB-ES
TRACTION HORSEPOWER:	4000 (2862 kW)
STARTING TRACTIVE EFFORT:	139 200 LB (616 kN)
CONTINUOUS TRACTIVE EFFORT:	92 400 LB (408 kN)
TOTAL WEIGHT:	130.5 TONS (133.5 T)
GAUGE:	1435 MM
ROAD NUMBER:	V544

423-class Co-Co

Back in 1967 Queensland Railways' venerable 1119kW EMD-powered 1502-class had appeared, a fleet of 29 Co-Co locomotives that were a direct development of the look-alike 977 kW 1460-class of 1964.

Despite the proliferation of more modern and powerful locomotive types encroaching on their well-worn territory, sixteen 1502-class members soldiered on for three decades until being withdrawn en masse on 9 December 1999 and stored operational at Redbank Workshops. They had been made surplus by the cascading effect following the entry to service of new 2260 kW EDI-Walkers AC4000-class 'super power' EMD locomotives.

However, life in a new form emerged for some when they were selected for employment on QR's standard gauge arm, Interail, which was officially launched in Casino (NSW) on 31 May 2002. The converted locomotives became the 423-class and six had been commissioned by 31 March 2005.

Rebuilt at QR's Redbank Workshops, the largest bodywork change was the fitting of a QR standard maxi-cab and low nose assembly. The first two locos were set up in Queensland configuration (driver on the right hand side), the remainder with 'reversed' cabs and the controls on the 'interstate side'. The standard range of safety and crew accommodation improvements (as per current QR overhauls) was undertaken, including air-conditioning, headstock

Loco 42304 and class-leader 42301 *Lismore* with a railway infrastructure train at Taree on 12 March 2005. (Andrew Rosenbauer)

visibility lights, twin tower air filter and Fischer Electronic Vigilance system. Only one control stand was retained, with B7EL brake valves as original. Everything else behind the cab was unchanged.

The rebuilt locomotives rode on Co-Co bogies 'donated' by a small fleet of former NSWGR 49-class EMDs already in Interail's hands as a result of purchasing the Casino-based operator, Northern Rivers Railroad Pty Ltd.

Although not the prettiest locomotive type in respect to aesthetics, the 423-class has nevertheless been described as a 'great performer' and all units regularly see service in Hunter Valley coal traffic, specifically in the Stratford–Craven area, and on contract infrastructure trains.

SPECIFICATIONS

IMPERIAL (METRIC)

POWER UNIT:	EMD 12-645E
TRACTION HORSEPOWER:	1500 (1119 kW)
STARTING TRACTIVE EFFORT:	64 520 lb (287 kN)
CONTINUOUS TRACTIVE EFFORT:	50 820 lb (226 kN at 14.2 km/h)
TOTAL WEIGHT:	93.6 tons (95.1 t)
GAUGE:	1435 mm
ROAD NUMBERS:	42301–42306 (formerly 1504, 1507, 1518, 1524, 1526 and 1520 respectively).

GL-class Co-Co

Launched at Sydney's Powerhouse Museum on 28 January 2003, class-leader GL101 marked a milestone in the fortunes of Chicago Freight Car Leasing (Australia's) operations. The locomotive, the first of 12 of this type,, had been heavily re-manufactured from discarded life-expired 115 tonne 1491kW 442-class Alco locomotives delivered to the NSW Government-owned railway system between 1971 and 1973.

The original locomotives were forwarded to United-Goninan's Broadmeadow plant where they were completely stripped to the bare chassis and re-manufactured from the ground upwards, virtually the only equipment retained being the bogies and main frames with internal fuel tanks.

The original 12-cylinder Alco 251C engines and AEI main generators were discarded, replaced with imported fully overhauled GE 7FDL-12 2862 (gross) kW diesel engines and associated alternators. In this form the GL-class's traction output became 2237kW.

All-new cabs (with desk-top controls and improved collision protection) and car bodies that

Locomotives GL102 and GL101 power through the Cullerin Ranges of New South Wales with their very first loaded GrainCorp movement, bound for Port Kembla export grain terminal, on Sunday 11 January 2004. CFCLA unit EL64 'went along for the ride'. (Leon Oberg)

retained a dual-cab configuration were provided while GE Bright Star microprocessor control systems were also employed, increasing the traction output by about one third (from 231 kN to 347 kN continuous).

Although the class-leader's handover took place in January 2003, extensive trials on the NSW Main Northern line did not start for several more weeks. As was the EL-class before them, each GL locomotive was pressed into lease service, starting with Lachlan Valley Rail Freight on its regular Sandgate (Newcastle) to Sydney haul, on 10 June 2003.

GrainCorp leased several units from late 2003 to November 2006 to haul its unit trains over the NSW southern grain belt, and others were absorbed into Freight Australia and Pacific National workings by March 2004 (including coal haulage centred on Port Kembla). Examples are also used in the Melbourne to Adelaide corridor.

All 12 had been delivered by 22 October 2004 in a programme reported to have cost $30 million for their manufacture and ongoing maintenance. As with the EL-class, all carry the names of famous racehorses, including *Think Big* and *Let's Elope*.

SPECIFICATIONS

	IMPERIAL (METRIC)
POWER UNIT:	GE 7FDL-12
TRACTION HORSEPOWER:	3000 (2237 kW)
STARTING TRACTIVE EFFORT:	110 020 lb (490 kN)
CONTINUOUS TRACTIVE EFFORT:	76 500 lb (347 kN)
TOTAL WEIGHT:	130 tons (132.5 t)
GAUGE:	1435 mm
ROAD NUMBERS:	GL101–GL112 (PLATFORMS USED IN REBUILDS WERE FORMERLY NSWGR 44207, 44216, 44228, 44230, 44201, 44218, 44233, 44222, 44229, 44215, 44232 AND 44212 RESPECTIVELY)

2003 BHP BILLITON IRON ORE

SD40-2 type Co-Co

Burgeoning orders for iron ore throughout 2003 as the world emerged from recession also saw China cement itself as a strong customer as it aggressively entered the energy and development race. The Western Australian Pilbara region was quick to feel the surge, with BHP Billiton preparing for the upswing by opening what was locally known as

Wearing fresh BHP Billiton bubble livery, locomotive 3086 (formerly US Southern Pacific 7354) stands at BHP's Nelson Point yard moments after arrival in June 2004. (Richard Montgomery)

Mining Area C (or MAC) off its Yandi 1 line.

This created an urgent need for stopgap locomotive power on the company's already significant railway system. Accordingly, nine EMD domestic US model SD40U and twelve SD40-2 Co-Co locomotives were sourced from GETS San Luis Potosi, Mexico. The units had principally worked on the US Union Pacific and Southern Pacific railroads, the oldest being 3078 with a 1966 delivery.

The first three locomotives, including 8335, a former SP tunnel motor unit specifically acquired to yield spare parts, departed the USA aboard the heavy lift ship *BBC Frisia*, arriving at Port Hedland wharf on 9 November 2003. More units arrived in three batches of six over following months. Because these locomotives all lacked the on-board facilities required in the exacting Pilbara operations, such as cab air-conditioning and microwave ovens, they were relegated to 'trailing or mid train status' once activated.

All 21 locomotives had been delivered by 8 August 2004. Some 500 ore wagons had also been procured to satisfy ore contracts.

Some of the early arrivals retained their most recent North American road numbers and paint schemes in Pilbara service, while later deliveries, starting with 3086 (ex-SP 7354) were decked out in BHP Billiton's latest bubble livery. The purchase of these locomotives, albeit second-hand, was believed to have been in the nature of a test to gauge the performance of EMD locomotives on what since its inception in 1968 had been a strictly Alco/GE system. The new locomotives bedded in quickly once some teething problems were sorted out. For instance, former GECX 6415 (now BHP Billiton 3079), delivered on 7 November 2003, was found to have a seized engine when an attempt to start it was made.

Fleet numbers 3078–3080, delivered in the blue and yellow livery of Iowa, Chicago & Eastern

equipped these three for driver-only operation in yard pilot work. Locomotives 3081–3085, while rebuilt prior to arrival, were painted in grey primer. Units 3086–3097 arrived in the new bubble paint scheme and had undergone rebuilds. These two groups, which possess longer chassis, regularly run the main line, but as trailing units.

Although having a planned BHP Billiton service life of eight years, given the growth of mining to satisfy iron ore orders and resultant mine development, observers insist some SD40-2s will be operating well beyond that time. To strengthen that argument, eight received in-cab modifications from early 2005, allowing them to operate as lead units for planned feeder train service between selected mines and the main line. That said, most were in store as this edition closed for press.

SPECIFICATIONS

IMPERIAL (METRIC)

POWER UNIT:	EMD 16-645E3B
TRACTION HORSEPOWER:	3000 (2237 kW)
CONTINUOUS TRACTIVE EFFORT:	83 160 LB (370 kN)
TOTAL WEIGHT:	163.6 TONS (167 T)
GAUGE:	1435 MM
ROAD NUMBERS:	3078–3097, 8335

5000-class Co-Co

This class of 12 locomotives is something of a heavy-haul development of the NR-class locomotives built for National Rail Corporation main line use from 1996. Even their general appearance and most of their above-chassis power equipment, such as diesel engine, cooling system and traction motor blowing, is similar.

However, since the 5000-class was acquired to satisfy a huge Queensland National coal haulage contract out of Mt Arthur (near Muswellbrook) along with additional expected coal agreements, the locomotives were ballasted to 180 tonnes, equipped with AC drive and provided with GE's own pattern high-adhesion bolster-less cast frame bogies in a bid to get super power to the rail.

Known as Model C40aci, and manufactured at United Group Rail's Broadmeadow plant, the initial two appeared for Ulan line trials on 6 May 2005. Placed in regular service from June 2005, two locomotives have been rated to haul seventy-four 120-tonne (loaded) coal wagons from Mt Arthur to Newcastle harbour, which represents a total gross trailing load of 8880 tonnes.

While AC traction was not new in Australia, with examples having worked in the Western

The 5000-class locomotive 5004 climbs Minimbah bank with a port-bound coal train on 17 January 2006. (Peter Watts)

BHP Billiton's 4309 profiles the chunky lines of the EMD model SD70ACe as it leads an ore train into Pring Siding on 25 February 2006. (Richard Montgomery)

Australian Pilbara and on Queensland Rail since 1999, AC technology enables locomotives' traction control systems to react faster to changes in friction between the driving wheels and the rails than the more conventional DC locomotives. Writing in *Motive Power* magazine in September 2005, soon after these AC4400 locomotives entered full-time service, engineer Graham Haywood pointed out additional tractive effort could be applied to the rail through the combined use of modern wheel-creep technology and AC traction.

Due to their great weight, which approaches Pilbara heavy-haul railway standards, the 5000-class is restricted to 80 km/h to limit the dynamic forces of the heavy axle-mounted GE 5GEB13 traction motors which are capable of exerting about 750 kW (1000 hp). This means the locomotives are strictly captive to the Hunter Valley's class 1 trackage.

All had arrived by April 2007. Further coal contracts saw QRN order 17 more late in 2009 boasting updated features of the 6000-class (page 444). Numbered 5021-5039 and mostly built at Chullora, Hunter Valley trials started on 11 November, 2010.

SPECIFICATIONS

	IMPERIAL (METRIC)
POWER UNIT:	GENERAL ELECTRIC GE7FDL16
TRACTION HORSEPOWER:	4000 (2862 KW) MAXIMUM (VARIABLE)
STARTING TRACTIVE EFFORT:	168 050 LB (760 KN)
CONTINUOUS TRACTIVE EFFORT:	128 660 LB (585.6 KN)
TOTAL WEIGHT:	176 TONS (180 T)
GAUGE:	1435 MM
ROAD NUMBERS:	5001–5012

2005 BHP BILLITON IRON ORE

43-class SD70ACe Co-Co

Since the 1960s inception of heavy-haul railways in the Western Australian Pilbara region, 4-stroke locomotives have virtually reigned supreme, with class after class of North American standard Alco and GE locos bearing the brunt of the line haul. In what was seen to be a major shift in locomotive policy, BHP Billiton turned to EMD when ordering thirteen 185-tonne 3200 kW locomotives in December 2004 as its new generation main line power.

With the expected life span of BHP Billiton's trusty, hard-working Dash-8s drawing to a close, together with continuing hefty increases in iron ore exports due to booming Asian markets, the mining company sought locomotives that would offer improved reliability and serviceability. They settled on the relatively new US domestic model SD70ACe type which promised 184-day maintenance cycles and improved fuel efficiencies. This type first appeared in the USA during 2003, built to meet strict new regulatory environmental standards in that country.

Uniquely, a fourteenth complete unit was to be supplied with the order as a 'source of spare parts/ spare power in the event one of its 13 sisters suffered a major failure'. That locomotive, oddly, was class-leader 4300, which was the last of the initial order to be unloaded on 26 February 2006.

This author was told it was 'cheaper to do it this way than ship in a whole locomotive inventory of spare parts'. Despite having undertaken a local trial run, 4300 was dismantled for parts, including traction motors, within weeks of arrival. By June 2006, it had been completely dissected and its gleaming new body hulk stowed in the yard.

Built in London, Ontario (Canada) on behalf of the company's Australian EMD representatives, EDI Rail, the first five locomotives arrived at Port Hedland aboard the *Jumbo Vision* on 21 October 2005. As the first examples started operating from December 2005, a contract was signed by BHP/EDI Rail for the supply of an additional ten units with deliveries from January 2006. Unlike the original deliveries, whose cabs were hard-fixed on the frame, creating harshness and cab noise, the latter ten boasted the US-optioned isolated 'whisper cab'. They were contracted for commissioning by May 2007.

The first to run in a train was 4301 on 19 November 2005. Orders continued with rising tonnage demands seeing the miner cement a deal at short notice for ten US D70ACe's then under construction for USA railroad BNSF which arrived in that Road's orange body livery, with roof-mounted number boxes and lights in their noses. Orders continued with 90 expected on hand by March 2012 with another 92 scheduled by 2015 with Nos 4301-4313 to be offered as trade-ins.

SPECIFICATIONS

	IMPERIAL (METRIC)
POWER UNIT:	EMD 16-710G3C-T2
TRACTION HORSEPOWER:	4300 (3200 KW)
STARTING TRACTIVE EFFORT:	205 000 LB (866 KN)
CONTINUOUS TRACTIVE EFFORT:	160 000 LB (712 KN)
TOTAL WEIGHT:	181 TONS (185 T)
GAUGE:	1435 MM
ROAD NUMBERS:	ROAD NUMBERS: 4300-4390 (4300 DISMANTLED FOR PARTS UPON DELIVERY)

2005 CHICAGO FREIGHT CAR LEASING (AUSTRALIA)

RL-class Co-Co

The first unit in this fascinating class appeared in December 2005 for Adelaide-district trials— wearing nothing but its undercoat.

Manufactured by NREC Alco Locomotive Pty Ltd at Adelaide's Islington workshops, the planned ten units in this class were more than a decade in the making. The concept was initiated back in 1994 when Whyalla-based locomotive remanufacturing firm Morrison Knudsen Australia (MKA) acquired ten life-expired NSWGR 442-class Alco-MLWs. This company's plan was to use their underframes and bogies to produce a fleet of heavy-haul locomotives powered with overhauled EMD 16-645F3B engines and alternator assemblies.

Work on one locomotive using the chassis of 44227 commenced in 1994. Due to the extra platform length required to accommodate the revised power assembly, the chassis had to be cut in two and an extra 1.5-m centre section added.

The locomotive, to be numbered MKA5, could not be completed before the company failed, its assets and the manufacturing plant eventually being taken over by NREC Alco Locomotive Pty Ltd. Although the latter company revisited the project, it was not until it moved operations and the remaining 442-class platforms (including six modified ones) to Islington that work was again started, this time initially on behalf of Chicago Freight Car Leasing (Australia).

In the end, following subsequent 'finite element analysis' by NREC, it was decided to use new platform ends as well in a bid to extend the service lives of the underframes. CFCLA motive power

Wearing Coote Industrial livery, RL306 works with Alco MLW, 80s1 on 5 September 2009. (Leon Oberg)

manager Jason Ferguson told this author that the only components from the 442s now used in the RL project were the Dofasco bogies (modified to accommodate the extra locomotive mass) and the air-compressors. Further to that, since there were only 16 bogies available from the 442s, the final two units were to be equipped with new cast-steel ones.

Externally, a whole new body and cab styled to somewhat resemble CFCLA's existing EL-class and Pacific National's AN-class was provided. All major components used, including the engine, alternator, traction motors and electrics, were reconditioned items supplied by NREC out of the USA. For added usefulness, the locomotives have been equipped with modern computer-controlled QES3 wheel-creep control technology suitably calibrated for very low speed operations should units be employed in grain or coal loading/unloading roles.

Originally intended to be released as the SL-class, the class-leader RL301 ran its load trial to Whyalla on 12 December 2005. Their first taste of commercial activity saw the initial two hired by the manufacturer to South Spur Rail Services from mid-May 2006. Although initially under the technical ownership of Allco/CFCLA Joint Venture Rail Fund, all (including four then to be completed units) were sold to WA-based operator Coote Industrial during the 2008 winter, where their route availability quickly saw examples running in several states with the numerically last unit, RL310, delivered in October 2010. All now belong to Cube Rail, who acquired Coote/South Spur earlier that year. RL308 is yet to be completed due to a damaged frame.

SPECIFICATIONS

	IMPERIAL (METRIC)
POWER UNIT:	EMD 16-645F3B
TRACTION HORSEPOWER:	3500 (2610 kW)
CONTINUOUS TRACTIVE EFFORT:	69 600 LB (313 kN)
TOTAL WEIGHT:	129.5 TONS (132 T)
GAUGE:	1435 MM
ROAD NUMBERS:	RL301–310

14-class Co-Co

In perhaps the most intriguing locomotive acquisition this country has yet witnessed, Lachlan Valley Rail Freight, trading since August 2006 as Independent Railways of Australia, is importing a fleet of surplus turbo-charged 20-cylinder 645-E3 2685 kW (3550 hp) locomotives from Denmark State Railways (DSB).

The first five units were loaded aboard the MV *Egmondgracht* at Copenhagen Free Port on 15 February 2006, arrived in Newcastle harbour (NSW) on 4 April that year and were immediately forwarded to Bradken Rail, Braemar, for commissioning.

Originally built by NoHAB (Nydqvist & Holm AB), Trollhättan, Sweden in 1972–74 as that railway's MZ3-class, the locomotives were based on a 16-cylinder Co-Co design known as the MZI which debuted in Denmark during 1967. Ten of these were delivered by 1969, carrying the numbers 1401–1410, An identical second batch, recorded as the MZ2, followed in 1970, and were numbered 1411 through to 1426. Both batches were catalogued as EMD model SD40 units.

Further orders were placed with NoHAB but due to the need to provide extra power for passenger-train heating, subsequent batches were provided with a rather intimidating V20 version of the lusty 645E engine. Twenty of these powerful 21-metre long locomotives (fractionally shorter than a BHP Billiton Dash-8), boasting enhanced exhaust silencers, appeared as the MZ3 during 1972–74 and were numbered 1427–1446. This third batch proved a little troublesome in service, and a slightly altered and improved version materialised as the MZ4 during 1977–78, numbered 1447–1461, both sub-classes falling into EMD's SD45-2 model grouping.

The four groups were used for both passenger and freight in their homeland, although they became better known for goods haulage as the years progressed and newer locomotive and train-set designs appeared.

Class-leader MZ1401 is preserved in the DSB Museumstog (Denmark State Railways' museum), and some of the Mk 2 and 4 units now work for private freight hauler Railon. All the Mk 3 units were stored by DSB between 1997 and 1999, and none from this batch are now in operation in Denmark. It was locomotives from this MZ3 group that attracted

The first to enter NSW service was 1437. Resplendent in Independent Railways of Australia silver livery, it is seen at Blayney in January 2009. (Leon Oberg)

the LVRF's eye and 16 had arrived in several batches, 14 of them entering service between 11 October 2006 and August 2009 regeared prior to arrival from 160 to 105m/h operation. (Nos 1441 and 1444 were damaged beyond repair at sea when their ship, the MV *Emmagracht*, hit rough seas in the Bermuda region. (A decision is pending whether 1441 can be reactivated). Examples, known as an EMD J30C-2 model, are working IRA trains within the Sydney metropolitan area, New England and Western NSW, two boasting an LPG-injection system. All retain their DSB numbers.

SPECIFICATIONS

	IMPERIAL (METRIC)
POWER UNIT:	EMD 20-645E
TRACTION HORSEPOWER:	3550 (2685 kW)
STARTING TRACTIVE EFFORT:	91 700 LB (410 kN)
CONTINUOUS TRACTIVE EFFORT:	82 280 LB (366 kN AT 18 km/h)
TOTAL WEIGHT:	123 TONS (125 T)
GAUGE:	1435 MM
ROAD NUMBERS:	1427–1429, 1431–1435, 1437, 1438, 1440, 1441, 1443–1446 (1441 AND 1444 ACCIDENT DAMAGED)

2007 CHICAGO FREIGHT CAR LEASING (AUSTRALIA)

VL-class Co-Co

With the appetite for locomotive power around Australia failing to wane as rail privatisation offered opportunities for a multitude of players on a much grander scale, the nation's biggest equipment charter firm, Chicago Freight Car Leasing (Australia), contracted Melbourne-based Avteq Pty Ltd late in 2005 to build twelve EMD-powered main line locomotives.

The company, which had previous aircraft industry consultancy, design and manufacturing skills, was launched as a locomotive builder and maintenance provider in January 2005 after accepting the VL-class contract. Before the first unit appeared for trials in February 2007, CFCLA was fielding expressions of interest from at least three major railway operators for examples. Based on a traditional US SD40 design with a modified, flatter Victorian Railway's C-class nose profile, the class is equipped with the modern Wabtech QES3 control system (which reduces the number of electrical relays) including its associated wheel-creep correction technology.

The locomotives are geared for 115 km/h and boast a fuel capacity of approximately 9200 litres. The last unit was commissioned on 11 March 2009 and most are today captive to FreightLink's Adelaide to Darwin route hauling intermodal and expanding minerals traffic. Others have been seen hauling grain and intermodal traffic in several states. All bear the names of famous Australian racehorses.

SPECIFICATIONS

	IMPERIAL (METRIC)
POWER UNIT:	EMD 16-645E3B AND 16-645E3C
TRACTION HORSEPOWER:	3000 (2237 kW)
STARTING TRACTIVE EFFORT:	104 000 LB (465 kN)

VL351 Dane Hill, showing its rather chunky styling to full advantage. (Leon Oberg)

CONTINUOUS TRACTIVE EFFORT: 76 200 LB (344.3 KN)
TOTAL WEIGHT: 129.5 TONS (132 T)
GAUGE: 1435 MM
ROAD NUMBERS: VL351–362

2007 SOUTH SPUR RAIL SERVICES

GE Model UM20C Co-Co

This 90-tonne 1491 kW GE-powered locomotive is one of the more unique diesel-electrics yet to grace Australia's shore. It was built in March 1997 by PT Lokindo (Indonesia) for the International Container Terminal Services (ICTS) in the Philippines to haul container trains over Philippine National Railways' trackage between the Port of Manila and the company's inland intermodal container facility at Santa Rosa/Calamba to the south.

It boasted a raked cab which was supplied by Australia's GE supplier, A. Goninan and Co's Lansdowne Engineering workshop outside Taree, NSW and styled on the EL-class cab earlier built by that company for AN.

ICTS ceased using its rail base in 2001 and the loco and her wagons were stored at the company's Calamba facility. The equipment's existence was quietly mentioned to Wilson Brothers, the then owners of South Spur Rail Services (later a division of Coote Industrial and since April 2010 part of P&O Trans Australia) in 2007 by a Perth port official. The brothers were seeking motive power ahead of possible 1067mm gauge ore haulage contract into Geraldton (WA).

A subsequent visit resulted in the locomotive (complete with cab-side bullet holes) and the flat-top wagons being shipped to Fremantle, arriving May 2007. The locomotive was serviced, re-wired

The newly repainted and renumbered U201 in South Spur Rail Services Bellevue (Midland) compound in June 2009. (Leon Oberg)

and modified for Australian conditions, its present address being the company's Bellevue (Midland) servicing complex where it is the only GE product in a generous roster of narrow and standard gauge EE locomotives mainly used on infrastructure trains throughout Western Australia.

During an early 2009 repaint, the orphan (known as ICTSI-1) was given a new Coote identity and road number U201. Its only recorded work to date has been a shunting turn in Gemco/Coote's Bellevue yard on 17 February 2009.

While this was the only unit sporting the raked cab, eighteen 1600 kW U20C locomotives were built by PT Lokindo for use, principally on passenger trains, in Indonesia. These employed conventional 'snub noses and cabs'.

SPECIFICATIONS

	IMPERIAL (METRIC)
POWER UNIT:	GE 7FDL-12
TRACTION HORSEPOWER:	2000 (1491 kW)
STARTING TRACTIVE EFFORT:	59 300 lb (265 kN)
CONTINUOUS TRACTIVE EFFORT:	58 300 lb (259.5 kN) AT 19.9 km/hr
TOTAL WEIGHT:	87.2 TONS (88.9 T)
GAUGE:	067 mm
ROAD NUMBERS:	U 201

2007 SPECIALIZED CONTAINER TRANSPORT

SCT-class Co-Co

When Specialized Container Transport (SCT) ordered 11 (soon afterwards extended to 15 and further increased in 2010 by a further nine), EMD GT46Ce AC diesel electric locomotives for use across the nation, it said the builder EDI Rail was offering a 'technologically advanced locomotive capable of providing more tractive power than any other locomotive in Australian mainline operation'.

Emerging from the maker's Cardiff (Newcastle) plant for its trial to nearby Maitland in October 2007, the first two were delivered to SCT'S Melbourne complex on 22 December that year. Boasting six traction motors capable of providing 500 kN of continuous tractive effort each, the locomotive type has been equipped with solid state inverters controlled by EMD's EM2000 microprocessor control system that ensure the highest possible adhesion levels as well as full diagnostics capability. The class has been equipped with an EDI Rail-designed semi-steer bogie boasting a lightweight fabricated frame. The builder says the bogie aims to contribute to higher adhesion by reducing friction between wheel flange and rail and also helps to increase wheel life.

All 15 were delivered by 21 August 2008 resulting in a locomotive surplus and the company temporarily leased two to QR company, ARG in Western Australia, along with some of its G-class, both types finding work in 2009 assisting Q-class rosters mainly in the Forrestfield–Kalgoorlie–Esperance corridor on heavy freight, ore and/or wheat traffic.

LDP-class

EDI Rail was so confident with its product that by then it was building additional copies for an in-house locomotive leasing programme launched as

Two gleaming SCT-class locomotives, Nos 006 and 008, roll past 'old' Kalgoorlie locomotive depot while hauling train No. 2PM9 on 16 June 2009. (Leon Oberg)

Locomotives 8147, 8124 and 8107 forge their way upgrade toward Tom Price on 19 August 2009. (Jim Bidsee)

Locomotive Demand Power P/L. The first one emerged as the LDP-class in mid December 2008 and found work two months later with Queensland Rail National (QRN) hauling intermodal traffic between Brisbane and Melbourne. To reinforce the maker's confidence, a formal wet rail test up the 1 in 40 Cowan Bank in NSW in September 2009 saw three LDPs haul a 4250 tonne coal train, running the 11 km section two minutes faster than the specified freight train section time. (This performance was unofficially mirrored in December 2009 after SCT003 was removed from a 77 vehicle, 5556 tonne, 1790 metre-long Perth-bound SCT service at Stewart (WA), some 500 km short of its destination. Loco SCT006 then set off alone, accelerating to 19 km/h from a standing start on the siding's 1 in 90 rising gradient, reportedly 'without wheel slip').

QRN lease nine under a $45 million five year (extendable) lease deal while another twelve are in use by PN as its TT-class, the first three entering traffic by working a Port Waratah to Bloomfield Colliery train on 7 January 2010 following initial trials by a class member to Wyong on 25 November 2009. The first six TTs carry 2.5 tonnes of lead ballast under their front and rear draw gears for heavy-haul NSW Hunter Valley Coal work. The final six are being delivered as originally designed, as have three more which have been bought by Whitehaven Coal for Upper Hunter service.

SPECIFICATIONS

	IMPERIAL (METRIC)
POWER UNIT:	EMD 16-710G3C-ES2
TRACTION HORSEPOWER:	4300 (3207 KW)
TARTING TRACTIVE EFFORT:	138 800 LB (600 KN)
CONTINUOUS TRACTIVE EFFORT:	112 000 LB (500 KN) AT 19.9 KM/HR. TT-CLASS 520 KN AT 19.6 KM/H
TOTAL WEIGHT:	131 TONS (134 T). FIRST SIX TTS BALLASTED TO 139 T
GAUGE:	1435 MM
ROAD NUMBERS:	SCT: SCT001-015
	PN: TT01-06; TT101-119
	WHITEHAVEN COAL: WH001-003
	GWA: GWA001-006

2008 PILBARA RAIL

General Electric ES44DCi

The ahead-of-schedule start-up of mining at the Hope Downs mine (a joint venture between Rio Tinto and Gina Rinehart's Hancock Prospecting), in November 2007 placed considerable pressure on the Pilbara (Hamersley Iron) Rail operations, battling to satisfy its own burgeoning mining contracts.

Fifty-one heavy-haul new generation 4400 hp locomotives were ordered in two batches from GE's Erie Pennsylvania USA plant, to satisfy Hope Downs (located 75 km north-west of Newman) and update the company's traditional needs. The first ten were sea freighted into Dampier on 10 February 2008 and commissioning followed equipping them for local conditions.

Trademarked as GE's Evolution Series and known as the ES44DCi model, the locomotives were championed as being 'leaner and cleaner' than all that had gone before, producing 40 per cent less emissions, improved fuel efficiency from their GE VO turbo-charged V12 prime movers offering extended ten-year overhaul intervals to boot.

Advances in USA locomotive technology saw the Evolution Series equipped with an improved microprocessor slip/slide system along with a single inverter per traction motor 'to optimise bogie adhesion under every possible rail conditions'. Another modification included improved engine cooling to offset the high temperature Pilbara climate which can reach 55 degrees Centigrade.

The arrival of these locomotives also coincided with Rio Tinto's $A1.6 billion Dampier Port upgrade increasing its capacity by 90 per cent, from 74 million tonnes a year four years earlier to 140 million tonnes.

Further orders have seen the class swell to sixty-six units, the most recent deliveries having arrived in mid 2011, having EPC (electronic) braking capacity.

SPECIFICATIONS

	IMPERIAL (METRIC)
POWER UNIT:	GEVO V12
TRACTION HORSEPOWER:	4380 (3266 KW)
STARTING TRACTIVE EFFORT:	158 500 LB (705 KN)
CONTINUOUS TRACTIVE EFFORT:	117 900 LB (525 KN)
TOTAL WEIGHT:	193.8 TONS (197 T)
GAUGE:	1435 MM
ROAD NUMBERS:	8100–8165

3800-class Bo-Bo-Bo

When 3200-class QR electric locomotive 3226 rolled over in a violent derailment in Waitara loop while working an empty Jilalan to German Creek coal train on 5 November 2002, little did anyone think at the time that it would eventually offer an incentive to establish two new locomotive classes.

With pressures already on QR to move greater payloads, engineers had already planed ways of overcoming the need for 'command' units to send radio signals to remote (ELRC) vehicles attached to the central banks of locomotives in coal trains. As enunciated on page 403, the trial conversion of 3116, 3272 and 3276 to 'improved' 3100-class was started and by July 2001, the trio had been phased into test workings, having been equipped with electrical brake controls in lieu of their air-operated equipment.

Experience learned with those locomotives led to further conversions and Siemens' Munich (Germany) factory winning a contract to build a new fleet of 20 (later extended to 45) identically powered locomotives to be known as the 3800-class. The first two 132-tonne units designed to 'seamlessly' work with the 3700-class on the Goonyella system and carry road-numbers in the 3801–3845 fleet series, were unloaded at Brisbane on Monday, 23 June 2008. Following formal registration, each was forwarded

PN's 7101 basks in the late afternoon sun at the Port of Brisbane on Sunday, 26 April 2009, after arriving on the ship *Taronga* three days earlier. (Michael James)

Near-new 9207 and 9209 near Mt Thorley (Singleton) in December 2008. (Leon Oberg)

north to Jilalan depot for testing.

In early trials QRNational engineers quickly noted the design's performance slightly exceeded the 3700-class, guaranteeing the expected "three-for-five" locomotive replacement programme on typical 120 x 106 tonne coal trains used in the Goonyella System.

71-class

But the 3800-class story was just beginning. Aggressive marketing by Pacific National Queensland also resulted in contracts to haul coal from Goonyella System.

Accordingly, PNQ ordered twenty-three 3800-class copies from Siemens during the winter of 2008. Known as the 71-class, the class leader docked in Brisbane on 23 April 2009. Following extensive trials PNQ's first fully loaded electric train ran from Moranbah North to Darymple Bay Coal Terminal on 17 July 2008 employing locos 7101, 7102, 7103. The 120 wagon train weighed 12720 tonnes for a 9879 payload. A further nine have since arrived.

SPECIFICATIONS

	IMPERIAL (METRIC)
ELECTRICAL EQUIPMENT:	SIEMENS 25 kV
MAXIMUM HORSEPOWER:	5360 HP (4000 kW)
STARTING TRACTIVE EFFORT:	116 200 LB (525 kN)
CONTINUOUS TRACTIVE EFFORT:	101 000 LB (450 kN)
TOTAL WEIGHT:	129.5 TONS (132 T)
GAUGE:	1067 MM
ROAD NUMBERS:	QRN: 3801–3845
	PNQ: 7101–7132

92-class Co-Co

Expanding Pacific National coal and intermodal operations had by the late 2000s seen the need for a locomotive type that would meet both tasks. United Group Rail had already prepared specifications for a 4500hp (gross) AC traction locomotive which was based on QRN's successful 5000-class (see page 434). The design offered the haulage capability of PN's existing heavy axle-load 90-class EMD coal locomotives and the flexibility to operate on the interstate main lines, something so far unseen. PN ordered 15, the first emerging from the maker's Broadmeadow plant for north-west NSW trials on 15 August 2008 as the 92-class.

The key to the units' availability to work heavy-haul coal on high axle load routes or general traffic over lighter lines, is the provision of variable level fuel tanks. When fully fuelled with 13 500 litres, the all-up weight for maximum adhesion is 139 tonnes while in intermodal work with 7300 litres, the total working weight is 134 tonnes A medium 10 000 litres setting provides a 136 tonnes mass.

Because 7300 litres restricted long-distance intermodal work, designers provided for in-line fuelling from tankers attached to the locomotives. But a decision during construction to exclusively locate the units in coal, only a handful were fully equipped with provision to retrofit the balance on a needs basis.

Another feature incorporated into the design was 'remote control secondary position' equipment to allow drivers to remove the driving controls and operate units from outside the cab at loading and unloading points or yards should it be necessary. Another feature is closed circuit TV for forward event video and external audio recording, to assist in incident investigations.

The first three were officially handed over at a Port Waratah (Newcastle) ceremony on 26 September 2008, and on 4 October entered regular traffic working a heavy coal diagram to Ulan mine and return. All were running by April 2009.

Others acquire copies

By then Queensland Rail's bulk freight subsidiary, the Australian Railroad Group in Western Australia, faced with additional Koolyanobbing -–Esperance iron ore traffic, has fourteen AC-class, commissioning the class-leader on 29 August 2009. The parent company QR, flushed with the success of its expanding QRN-branded Brisbane–Melbourne–Adelaide–Perth intermodal traffic, exercised its original intention by ordering 12, taking delivery between September and December 2009. They became the 6000-class. Another four were ordered in April 2010.

Newcomer Xstrata Rail is commissioning twenty, three being unveiled at Mt Owen mine on 21 September 2010. Four copies have also been ordered by CFCLA while Centennial Coal will receive seven in 2012 and GWA nine for ore haulage. Although similar, the classes boast individual features such as engine output, brake system/software variations, forward-looking video/audio recording gear but the remote control feature is so far limited in theory to the 92-class.

SPECIFICATIONS

	Imperial (Metric)
Power unit:	General Electric GE7FDL16
Traction horsepower:	4270 (3185 kW) maximum (variable)
Starting tractive effort:	168 050 lb (760 kN)
Continuous tractive effort:	128 660 lb (585.6 kN)
Total weight:	137 tons (139 t)
Gauge:	1435 mm
Road numbers:	(PN) 9201–9215
	ARG: AC4301-4308; AC4401-4406
	QRN: 6001-6012
	Xstrata Rail: XRN001-020
	CFCLA: CF4401-4404
	Centennial Coal: CEY001-007
	GWA: nine units

83-class Co-Co

Following on from Pacific National Queensland's (PNQ) 2004 launch of its Brisbane/Mackay/Townsville/Cairns intermodal services, the company established a PN Queensland coal division to operate export coal trains along the Blackwater (serving the port at Gladstone) and Goonyella (exporting at Hay Point/Dalrymple Bay) networks. A feature of this investment was not only the procurement of twenty-three 71-class Bo-Bo-Bo electric locomotives (see page 443), but of thirteen 83-class diesel-electrics from Downer EDI Rail at Maryborough (Q).

Testing of the 83-class started in January 2009 between Maryborough West and Meadowvale (outside Bundaberg) and on 8 April four units were assembled for a special test run to Oaky Creek as train No. 96T2 and led by locos 8304 and 8305 with 8303 and 8301 placed remotely within that special 100 wagon consist.

The 83-class was a further development of EMD's 'GT42CU' family of locomotives previously delivered as the 4000/4100-class (for QRN) and perpetuated as the PN-class (for PNQ). As such, these 120 tonne AC-traction locomotives are rated at 2260 kW and boasting lower gearing are primarily used today on the Blackwater coal system (working normally in pairs). They have also seen service on the Goonyella system further north—initially to cover insufficient 71-class electric unit numbers due to ongoing deliveries.

Unlike their prototype, the 83-class is equipped (like the company's 71-class) with electronically controlled pneumatic braking for use with the existing coal wagon fleet. Pacific National claims this braking system allows their 12 720-tonne, 80 km/h coal trains to be brought to a standing stop within 650 metres of application!

With new traffic including Mt Isa line magnetite haulage, this class now totals 33 units.

SPECIFICATIONS

	Imperial (Metric)
Power unit:	EMD 12-710G3B-ES
Traction horsepower:	3029 (2260 kW)
Starting tractive effort:	21 396 lb (540 kN)
Continuous tractive effort:	103 411 lb (460 kN)
Total weight:	118 tons (120 t)
Gauge:	1067 mm
Road numbers:	8301–8333

Loco 8310 stabled at Gladstone on 9 December 2009. (Peter Clark)

INDEX TO LOCOMOTIVES
GOVERNMENT ORIGIN

79-class Bo-Bo **228**
80-class Co-Co **385**
81-class Co-Co **391**
82-class Co-Co **417**
85-class Co-Co **386**
86-class Co-Co **393**
90-class Co-Co **416**
XP-class Bo-Bo **387**

QUEENSLAND RAILWAYS

Steam
AY/BY-classes 2-6-0 **71**
AC16-class 2-8-2 **224**
B (A10)-class 0-4-2 **26**
B15-class 4-6-0 **86**
B18¼-class 4-6-2 196
BB18¼-class 4-6-2 243
C16-class 4-8-0 **123**
C17-class 4-8-0 **172**
C19-class 4-8-0 **176**
DD17-class 4-6-4T **233**
Double Fairlies 0-4-4-0/0-6-6-0 **31**
F(B13)-class 4-6-0 **58**
Garratt-type 4-8-2+2-8-4 **239**
PB15-class 4-6-0 **106**
6D9½-class 4-6-0T 175

Non-steam
1200-class Co-Co **268**
1210/1300/1150-class Co-Co **265**
1230/1400-class A1A-A1A **288**
1250-class Co-Co **306**
1270-class Co-Co **332**
1300-class Co-Co **349**
1460/1502/423-class Co-Co **333-335**
1550-class Co-Co **373**
1600-class Co-Co **325**
1620-class Co-Co **348**
1700-class Co-Co **326**
1720-class Co-Co **345**
2100-class Co-Co **362**
2130-class Co-Co **362**
2150-class Co-Co **363**
2170-class Co-Co **363**
2200-class Co-Co **362**
2350/2370-class Co-Co **378**
2400-class Co-Co **375**
2450-class Co-Co **376**
2470-class Co-Co **376**
2600-class Co-Co **394**
2800-class Co-Co **421**
3100/3200/3700-classes Bo-Bo-Bo **401-403**
3300/3400-class Bo-Bo-Bo **418, 419**
3500/3551/3600/3900-classes Bo-Bo-Bo **403-405**
3800-class 442
4000-class Co-Co **428**
423-class Co-Co **431**
5000-class Co-Co **434**
5020-class 435
6000-class 444
DH-class B-B **327**
DL-class 2-6-0DM **216**

SOUTH AUSTRALIAN RAILWAYS

Steam
2-4-0WT **18**
300-class 4-8-2+2-8-4 **226**
400-class 4-8-2+2-8-4 **271**
500-class 4-8-2 **193**
520-class 4-8-4 **229**
600-class 4-6-2 **194**
620-class 4-6-2 **214**
700-class 2-8-2 **195**

720-class 2-8-4 **210**
B-class 2-4-0 **19**
D-class 4-4-0 **22**
F-class 4-6-2T **122**
J-class 0-6-0 **39**
P-class 2-4-0T **64**
R/Rx-classes 4-6-0 **74**
S-class 4-4-0 **97**
T/Tx-classes 4-8-0 **124, 125**
W-class 2-6-0 **46**
Wx-class 2-6-0 **47**
X-class 2-6-0 **52**
Y/Yx-class 2-6-0 **65, 66**

Non-steam
350-class Bo-Bo **236**
500-class Bo-Bo **335**
600-class Co-Co **324**
700-class Co-Co **369**
800-class Bo-Bo **304**
830-class Co-Co **308**
900-class A1A-A1A **253**
930-class Co-Co **297**

TASMANIAN GOVERNMENT RAILWAYS

Steam
A-class 4-4-0 **95**
B-class 4-4-0 **72**
C/CC/CCS-classes 2-6-0 **65**
Ds-class 2-6-4T **217**
F-class 2-6-0 **66**
G-class 0-4-2T **103**
H-class 4-8-2 **248**
J-class 2-6-4-0 **111**
K-class 0-4-0+0-4-0 **143**
L-class 2-6-2+2-6-2 **153**
M-class 4-4-2+2-4-4 **152**
M-class 4-6-2 **257**
Q-class 4-8-2 **178**
R-class 4-6-2 **180**

Non-steam
V/VA-classes 0-6-0DM **235**
X/XA-classes Bo-Bo **242**
Y-class Bo-Bo **319**
Z-class Co-Co **377**
ZA/ZB-classes Co-Co **378, 379**
ZC-class Co-Co **349**
ZR-class Co-Co **379**

VICTORIAN RAILWAYS

Steam
No. 1 2-2-2 **21**
No. 100 2-4-0 **35**
A-class 4-4-0 **62**
(New) A/AA-classes 4-4-0 **83, 84**
A2-class 4-6-0 **136**
B-class 2-4-0 **24**
C-class 2-8-0 **168**
D3-class 4-6-0 **118**
DD-class 4-6-0 **117**
DDe-class 4-6-2T **141**
E-class 2-4-2T **85**
EE-class 0-6-2T **85**
G-class 2-6-0+0-6-2 **190**
H-class 4-4-0 **42**
H-class 4-8-4 **218**
J-class 2-8-0 **273**
K-class 2-8-0 **177**
L-class 2-4-0ST **23**

N-class 2-8-2 **186**
Na-class 2-6-2T **105**
O-class 0-6-0 **25**
Q-class 0-6-0 **36**
R-class 0-6-0 **49**
(New) R/Ry-classes 0-6-0 **87, 88**
R-class 4-6-4 **247**
S-class 4-6-0 **43**
S-class 4-6-2 **200**
T-class 0-6-0 **36**
V-class 2-8-0 **109**
X-class 0-6-0 **76**
X-class 2-8-2 **206**
Y-class 0-6-0 **82**

Non-steam
1100-class Bo-Bo **181**
A-class Co-Co **395**
B-class Co-Co **264**
C-class Co-Co **382**
F-class 0-6-0DE **254**
G-class Co-Co **398**
H-class Bo-Bo **292**
L-class Co-Co **270**
N-class Co-Co **399**
P-class Bo-Bo **397**
S-class Co-Co **286**
T-class Bo-Bo **292**
V-class Co-Co **430**
W-class 0-6-0DH **312**
X/XR/XRB-classes Co-Co **343-345**
Y-class Bo-Bo **331**

WESTERN AUSTRALIAN GOVERNMENT RAILWAYS

Steam
A-class 2-6-0 **46**
D-class 4-6-4T **153**
Dm/Dd-classes 4-6-4T **230**
E-class 2-4-4-2 Fairlie **48**
E-class 4-6-2 **119**
Ec-class 4-6-2 **112**
F-class 4-8-0 **120**
G-class 2-6-0/4-6-0 **66, 70**
K-class 2-8-4T **96**
Msa-class 2-6-0+0-6-2 **208**
N-class 4-4-4T **98**
Pm/Pmr-classes 4-6-2 **237**
R/Ra-classes 4-4-0 **104**
S-class 4-8-2 **223**
U-class 4-6-2 **232**
Ut-class 4-6-4T **233**
V-class 2-8-2 **281**
W-class 4-8-2 **245**

Non-steam
A/AA/AB-classes Co-Co **312, 313**
B-class 0-6-0DH **321**
C-class Co-Co **325**
D/DA-classes Co-Co **364, 365**
DB-class Co-Co **390**
F-class A1A-A1A **306**
G-class Co-Co **306**
H-class Bo-Bo **336**
J-class Bo-Bo **342**
K-class Co-Co **340**
Ka-class Co-Co **352**
L-class Co-Co **346**
M/MA-classes B-B **330**
N/NA/NB-classes Co-Co **383, 384**
P-class Co-Co **413**
Q-class Co-Co **425**
R/RA-classes Co-Co **351, 352**
S-class Co-Co **426**
T/TA-classes 0-6-0DE **351**
X-class 2-Do-2 **274**

OTHER OPERATORS

ARG (QRN subsidiary)
AC-class Co-Co **444**

Australian Iron & Steel
B-class 0-6-0ST **207**
D1/16-type Bo-Bo **240**
D9-type B-B **304**
D34 Co-Co **357**
D35-type Bo-Bo **366**
D46-type Co-Co **341**

Australian Kerosene Oil & Mineral Co
Barclay 0-4-0T/0-6-0ST **50**

Australia Paper Manufacturers
Whitcomb B-B **234**

AWB
G-class Co-Co **399**

Bellambi Coal Co
Avonside 0-6-0ST **121**

Broken Hill Proprietary Co
Baldwin 4-6-0 **167**
Baldwin 2-8-2 **174**
Davenport Bo-Bo **202**
Cooper-Bessemer Bo-Bo **278**
DE-class Bo-Bo **295**
E-class Bo-Bo **189**
GE-type Bo-Bo **314**
DH-class B-B **320**
Steam (general) **156-163**

Cairns Kuranda Steam Trains
24-class 2-8-4 **429**

Chicago Freight Car Leasing (Aust)
GL-class Co-Co **432**
RL-class Co-Co **436**
TL-class Bo-B0 **291**
VL-class Co-Co **438**

Cliffs, Robe River Iron Associates
Alco RSC3 Bo-Bo **256**
Alco C630 Co-Co **380**
Alco M363 **355**
GE Dash-8 Co-Co **408**

Commonwealth Portland Cement
Barclay 0-4-0T/0-6-0T **144**

Colonial Sugar Refinery
Drewry 0-6-0DM **267**
Hudswell Clarke 0-6-0 **163**
Walkers B-B **330**

Commonwealth Land Transport Board
ASG-type Garratt 4-8-2+2-8-4 **225**

Commonwealth Department of Munitions
79-class Bo-Bo **228**

Corrimal Coal Co
Burra 0-4-0ST **182**

Clyde Engineering
Sugar and industrial locomotives 0-6-0DH **275**

Commonwealth Engineering
Sugar and industrial locomotives 0-4-0/0-6-0/B-B **279**

Commonwealth Steel Co
Goninan Bo **371**

East Greta Railway Co
10-class 2-8-2T **151**

13-class 0-8-2T **139**
15-class 4-6-4T **130**

Emu Bay Railway Co
10-class B-B **327**
11-class B-B **330**
ASG type 4-8-2+2-8-4 **226**
Beyer-Garratt 4-8-2+2-8-4 **209**
Dubs 4-8-0 **109**
PVH1 0-8-0DH **269**

Fairymead Sugar Mill
Bundaberg/Hunslet B-B **414**
Eimco B-B **412**

FreightLink
FQ-class Co-Co **425**

G & C Hoskins Ltd
B-class 0-6-0ST **207**
Iron Duke 4-6-4T **171**
Various **131**

Goldsworthy Mining Co
EE Bo-Bo **336**
EE Co-Co **340**
GML10 Co-Co **411**

GrainCorp (NSW)
Vollert 4wBE **389**
E.M. Baldwin 0-6-0DH *Worimi* **379**

Hamersley Iron/Pilbara Rail
Alco C415 Bo-Bo **352**
Alco C828 Co-Co **337**
Alco/MLW 636 Co-Co **354**
50-class Co-Co **384**
60-class Co-Co **390**
70/94-class Co-Co **420**
GE ES44DCi **xxx**

Hydro-Electric Commission, Tasmania
Hydrostatic 0-6-0DH **400**

Hebburn Colliery
Stephenson 2-6-2T **282**

Independent Railways of Australia
MZ3-type Co-Co **437**

Invicta Sugar Mill
Westfalia B-B **415**

Industrial/Sugar
Bogie sugar locos **373**
Krauss 0-4-0/0-6-0/0-6-2T and WT **77**
Perry 0-4-2/0-6-2T **211**
Ruston & Hornsby 0-4-0/0-6-0 **212**
Shay locomotives **114**
William Sanford/G & C Hoskins **131**

John Lysaghts
Goninan B-B **301**
Goninan Bo-Bo **316**
Locomotive Demand Power
LDP-class Co-Co **440**

Melbourne & Hobsons Bay Railway
2-2-2WT **14**
2-4-0WT **14**
4-4-0WT **33**
Pier Donkeys 0-4-0WT **20**

Midland Railway Co
C-class 4-6-2 **154**
F-class A1A-A1A **306**
G-class Co-Co **306**

Mt Isa Mining Co
Walkers B-B **330**

Mt Lyell Mining & Railway Co
Abt type 0-4-2T **102**

Mt Magnet Mining Co
Mallet 0-4-4-0T **111**

Mt Newman Mining Co
Aka BHP Billiton (Iron Ore)
Alco/MLW 636 Co-Co **354**
GE Dash-7 Co-Co **405**
GE Dash-8 Co-Co **406**
SD40-2 Co-Co **433**
60-class AC6000 Co-Co **427**
43-class (SD70Ace) Co-Co **435**

Mourilyn Sugar Mill
Fowler 0-4-2T **57**

Mulgrave Sugar Mill
Bundaberg Fowler 0-6-2T **258**

North Farrell Mining Co
Wee Georgie Wood 0-4-0T **184**

Newell & Co
Baldwin 0-6-0ST **60**

Pacific National
92-class Co-Co **443**
TT-class Co-Co **441**

Pacific National Queensland
PN-class Co-Co **428**
71-class Bo-Bo-Bo **xx**
83-class Co-Co **xx**

Public Works Dpt (WA)
Barclay 4-6-0 **200**

Richmond Vale Railway
Beyer, Peacock 0-6-4T **135**
Kitson 2-8-2T **138**
Robinson 2-8-0 **191**

Rhodes Timber Co
The Final Flutter **181**

Silverton Tramway, The
A-class 4-6-0 **145**
Alco DL-531 Co-Co **308**
W-class 4-8-2 **251**
Y-class 2-6-0 **65**

South Spur Rail Services (now P&O Trans Australia)
GE model UM20C Co-Co **439**

Southern Portland Cement
GE Bo-Bo **316**

Specialized Container Transport
SCT-class Co-Co **440**

Sulphide Corp, The
GE Bo-Bo **316**
Sydney Railway Co, The
1-class 0-4-2 **15**

Sydney Water Board
Vulcan 0-4-0ST **146**

State Electricity Commission (Victoria)
Electric Bo-Bo **197**

F-class 0-6-0DE **254**

State Electricity Commission (WA)
Electric Bo-Bo **185**

Southern Coal Co
Yorkshire 0-6-0T **80**

Tubemakers
Worimi 0-6-0DH **379**

Tasmanian Main Line Co
Hunslet 4-6-0T **37**

Tyers Valley Tramway
Climax Bo-Bo **203**

Watt, J.B.
Kitson 0-6-0ST **32**

Western Australia Timber Co, The
Ballaarat 0-4-0WT **34**

Whitehaven Coal
WH-class Co-Co **441**

Xstrata Rail (Freightliner)
XRN-class Co-Co **444**

INDEX TO LOCOMOTIVE BUILDERS

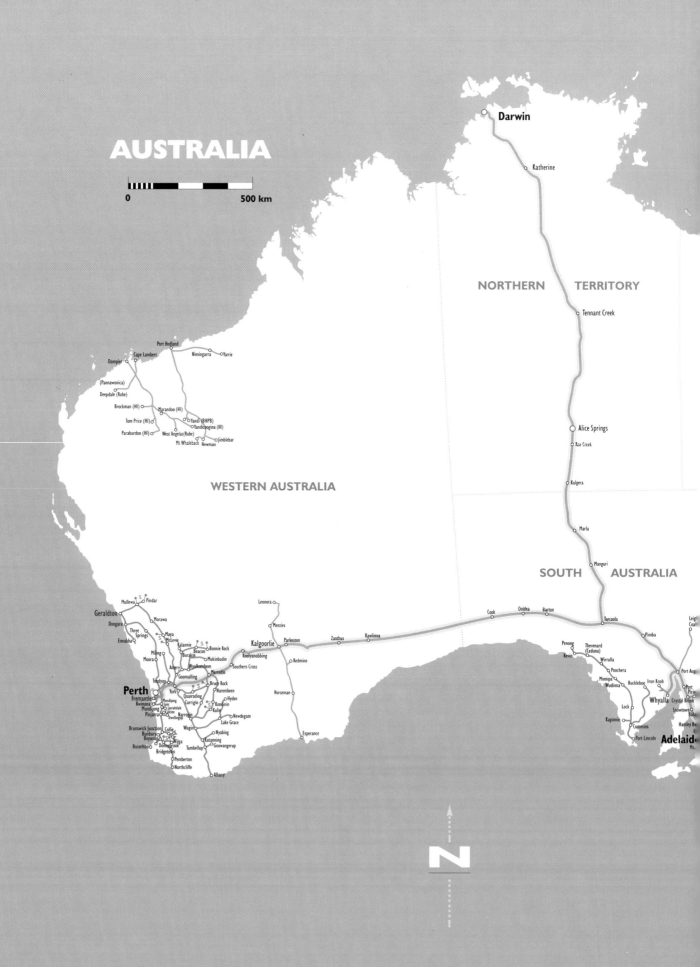

AUSTRALIA

0   500 km

Darwin
Katherine

NORTHERN   TERRITORY

Tennant Creek

Port Hedland
Dampier Cape Lambert   Nimingarra Yarrie

(Pannawonica)
Deepdale (Robe)
Brockman (HI)   Marandoo (HI)
Tom Price (HI)   Yandi (BHPB)
Paraburdoo (HI)   Tandicnogina (HI)
West Angelas (Robe)   Jimblebar
Mt Whaleback   Newman

Alice Springs
Roe Creek

WESTERN AUSTRALIA

Kulgera

Marla

Manguri

SOUTH   AUSTRALIA

Leonora
Menzies   Cook   Ooldea   Barton
Tarcoola
Leigh
Coal
Mullewa Pindar   Parkeston Zanthus Rawlinna   Pimba
Geraldton   Morawa   Kalgoorlie   Penong Thevenard
Dongara   Three   Maya   Koolyanobbing   (Ceduna)
Eneabba   Springs   McLevie   Southern Cross   Kevin   Wirrulla
Miling   Kalannie   Redmine   Minnipa Poochera
Moora   Burakin Bonnie Rock   Wudinna Buckleboo Iron Knob
Amery Wyalkatchem   Mukinbudin   Port
Tockyan Goomalling Merredin   Lock   Whyalla Crystal Brook
Perth   York   Narembeen   Snowtown
Fremantle   Quairading   Bruce Rock   Kapinnie Cummins   Hamley Be
Kwinana Hyden   Norseman   Port Lincoln
Mundijong Jarrahdale Corrigin Kondinin   **Adelaid**
Pinjarra   Kulin   Mt
Dwellingup Narrogin Newdegate
Brunswick Junction   Wagin Lake Grace
Bunbury Collie   Nyabing
Boyanup   Wagin
Bridgetown   Katanning Gnowangerup
Busselton   Tambellup
Pemberton   Esperance
Northcliffe   Albany

N